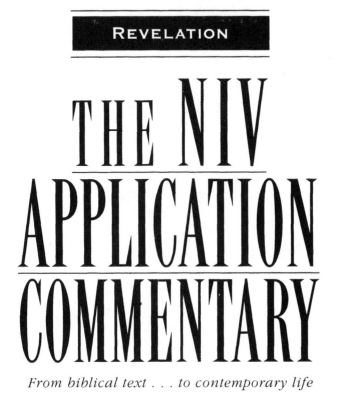

REVELATION

THE NIV
APPLICATION
COMMENTARY

From biblical text . . . to contemporary life

THE NIV APPLICATION COMMENTARY SERIES

EDITORIAL BOARD

General Editor
Terry Muck

Consulting Editors
New Testament

Eugene Peterson　　　　　　　*Scot McKnight*
Marianne Meye Thompson　　　*Klyne Snodgrass*

Zondervan Editorial Advisors

Stanley N. Gundry
Vice President and Editor-in-Chief

Jack Kuhatschek　　　　　　　*Verlyn Verbrugge*
Senior Acquisitions Editor　　　Senior Editor

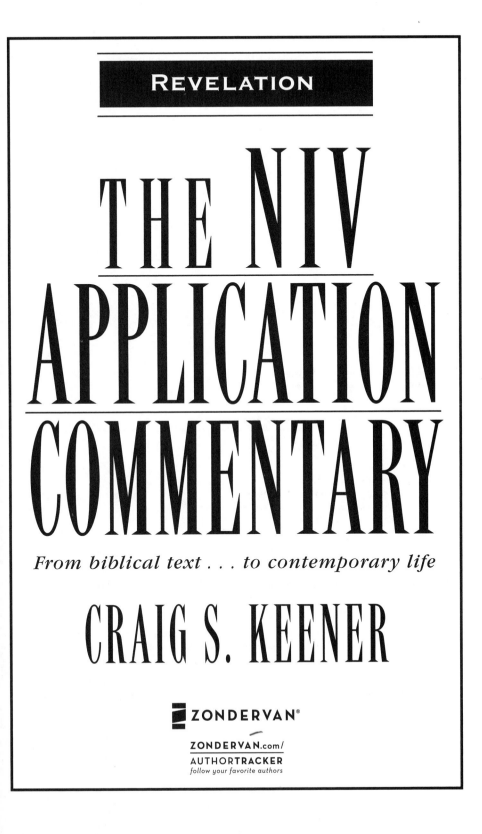

REVELATION

THE NIV APPLICATION COMMENTARY

From biblical text . . . to contemporary life

CRAIG S. KEENER

ZONDERVAN®

ZONDERVAN.com/
AUTHORTRACKER
follow your favorite authors

We want to hear from you. Please send your comments about this
book to us in care of zreview@zondervan.com. Thank you.

ZONDERVAN

The NIV Application Commentary: Revelation
Copyright © 2000 by Craig Keener

Requests for information should be addressed to:
Zondervan, *Grand Rapids, Michigan 49530*

Library of Congress Cataloging-in-Publication Data

Keener, Craig S., 1960-
    Revelation / Craig S. Keener.
        p. cm.—(NIV application commentary)
    Includes bibliographical references and index.
    ISBN 978-0-310-23192-9
    1. Bible. N.T. Revelation Commentaries. I. Title. II. Series.
BS2825.3.K43 1999
238'.077—dc21   99-26622

All Scripture quotations, unless otherwise indicated, are taken from the Holy Bible, *New International Version*®, *NIV*®. Copyright © 1973, 1978, 1984 by Biblica, Inc.™ Used by permission of Zondervan. All rights reserved worldwide.

Any Internet addresses (websites, blogs, etc.) and telephone numbers printed in this book are offered as a resource. They are not intended in any way to be or imply an endorsement by Zondervan, nor does Zondervan vouch for the content of these sites and numbers for the life of this book.

All rights reserved. No part of this publication may be reproduced, stored in a retrieval system, or transmitted in any form or by any means—electronic, mechanical, photocopy, recording, or any other— except for brief quotations in printed reviews, without the prior permission of the publisher.

Printed in the United States of America

09 10 11 12 13 15 16 • 31 30 29 28 27 26 25 24 23 22 21 20 19 18 17 16 15 14 13

To Dr. Danny McCain
of the International Institute of Christian Studies,
and all the precious students he gave me the opportunity
to teach in northern Nigeria
in the summers of 1998 and 1999

Contents

The NIV Application Commentary Series

When complete, the NIV Application Commentary
will include the following volumes:

Old Testament Volumes

Genesis, John H. Walton
Exodus, Peter Enns
Leviticus/Numbers, Roy Gane
Deuteronomy, Daniel I. Block
Joshua, Robert L. Hubbard Jr.
Judges/Ruth, K. Lawson Younger
1-2 Samuel, Bill T. Arnold
1-2 Kings, Gus Konkel
1-2 Chronicles, Andrew E. Hill
Ezra/Nehemiah, Douglas J. Green
Esther, Karen H. Jobes
Job, Dennis R. Magary
Psalms Volume 1, Gerald H. Wilson
Psalms Volume 2, Jamie Grant
Proverbs, Paul Koptak
Ecclesiastes/Song of Songs, Iain Provan
Isaiah, John N. Oswalt
Jeremiah/Lamentations, J. Andrew Dearman
Ezekiel, Iain M. Duguid
Daniel, Tremper Longman III
Hosea/Amos/Micah, Gary V. Smith
Jonah/Nahum/Habakkuk/Zephaniah
   James Bruckner
Joel/Obadiah/Malachi, David W. Baker
Haggai/Zechariah, Mark J. Boda

New Testament Volumes

Matthew, Michael J. Wilkins
Mark, David E. Garland
Luke, Darrell L. Bock
John, Gary M. Burge
Acts, Ajith Fernando
Romans, Douglas J. Moo
1 Corinthians, Craig Blomberg
2 Corinthians, Scott Hafemann
Galatians, Scot McKnight
Ephesians, Klyne Snodgrass
Philippians, Frank Thielman
Colossians/Philemon, David E. Garland
1-2 Thessalonians, Michael W. Holmes
1-2 Timothy/Titus, Walter L. Liefeld
Hebrews, George H. Guthrie
James, David P. Nystrom
1 Peter, Scot McKnight
2 Peter/Jude, Douglas J. Moo
Letters of John, Gary M. Burge
Revelation, Craig S. Keener

To see which titles are available,
visit our web site at http://www.zondervan.com

NIV Application Commentary
Series Introduction

THE NIV APPLICATION COMMENTARY SERIES is unique. Most commentaries help us make the journey from our world back to the world of the Bible. They enable us to cross the barriers of time, culture, language, and geography that separate us from the biblical world. Yet they only offer a one-way ticket to the past and assume that we can somehow make the return journey on our own. Once they have explained the *original meaning* of a book or passage, these commentaries give us little or no help in exploring its *contemporary significance*. The information they offer is valuable, but the job is only half done.

Recently, a few commentaries have included some contemporary application as *one* of their goals. Yet that application is often sketchy or moralistic, and some volumes sound more like printed sermons than commentaries.

The primary goal of the NIV Application Commentary Series is to help you with the difficult but vital task of bringing an ancient message into a modern context. The series not only focuses on application as a finished product but also helps you think through the *process* of moving from the original meaning of a passage to its contemporary significance. These are commentaries, not popular expositions. They are works of reference, not devotional literature.

The format of the series is designed to achieve the goals of the series. Each passage is treated in three sections: *Original Meaning, Bridging Contexts,* and *Contemporary Significance.*

THIS SECTION HELPS you understand the meaning of the biblical text in its original context. All of the elements of traditional exegesis—in concise form—are discussed here. These include the historical, literary, and cultural context of the passage. The authors discuss matters related to grammar and syntax and the meaning of biblical words.[1] They also seek to explore the main ideas of the passage and how the biblical author develops those ideas.

---

1. Please note that in general, when the authors discuss words in the original biblical languages, the series uses a general rather than a scholarly method of transliteration.

After reading this section, you will understand the problems, questions, and concerns of the *original audience* and how the biblical author addressed those issues. This understanding is foundational to any legitimate application of the text today.

THIS SECTION BUILDS a bridge between the world of the Bible and the world of today, between the original context and the contemporary context, by focusing on both the timely and timeless aspects of the text.

God's Word is *timely*. The authors of Scripture spoke to specific situations, problems, and questions. The author of Joshua encouraged the faith of his original readers by narrating the destruction of Jericho, a seemingly impregnable city, at the hands of an angry warrior God (Josh. 6). Paul warned the Galatians about the consequences of circumcision and the dangers of trying to be justified by law (Gal. 5:2–5). The author of Hebrews tried to convince his readers that Christ is superior to Moses, the Aaronic priests, and the Old Testament sacrifices. John urged his readers to "test the spirits" of those who taught a form of incipient Gnosticism (1 John 4:1–6). In each of these cases, the timely nature of Scripture enables us to hear God's Word in situations that were *concrete* rather than abstract.

Yet the timely nature of Scripture also creates problems. Our situations, difficulties, and questions are not always directly related to those faced by the people in the Bible. Therefore, God's word to them does not always seem relevant to us. For example, when was the last time someone urged you to be circumcised, claiming that it was a necessary part of justification? How many people today care whether Christ is superior to the Aaronic priests? And how can a "test" designed to expose incipient Gnosticism be of any value in a modern culture?

Fortunately, Scripture is not only timely but *timeless*. Just as God spoke to the original audience, so he still speaks to us through the pages of Scripture. Because we share a common humanity with the people of the Bible, we discover a *universal dimension* in the problems they faced and the solutions God gave them. The timeless nature of Scripture enables it to speak with power in every time and in every culture.

Those who fail to recognize that Scripture is both timely and timeless run into a host of problems. For example, those who are intimidated by timely books such as Hebrews, Galatians, or Deuteronomy might avoid reading them because they seem meaningless today. At the other extreme, those who are convinced of the timeless nature of Scripture, but who fail to discern its timely element, may "wax eloquent" about the Melchizedekian priest-hood to a sleeping congregation, or worse still, try to apply the holy wars of the Old Testament in a physical way to God's enemies today.

The purpose of this section, therefore, is to help you discern what is time-less in the timely pages of the Bible—and what is not. For example, how do the holy wars of the Old Testament relate to the spiritual warfare of the New? If Paul's primary concern is not circumcision (as he tells us in Gal. 5:6), what *is* he concerned about? If discussions about the Aaronic priesthood or Melchizedek seem irrelevant today, what is of abiding value in these passages? If people try to "test the spirits" today with a test designed for a specific first-century heresy, what other biblical test might be more appropriate?

Yet this section does not merely uncover that which is timeless in a passage but also helps you to see *how* it is uncovered. The authors of the commentaries seek to take what is implicit in the text and make it explicit, to take a process that normally is intuitive and explain it in a logical, orderly fashion. How do we know that circumcision is not Paul's primary concern? What clues in the text or its context help us realize that Paul's real concern is at a deeper level?

Of course, those passages in which the historical distance between us and the original readers is greatest require a longer treatment. Conversely, those passages in which the historical distance is smaller or seemingly non-existent require less attention.

One final clarification. Because this section prepares the way for dis-cussing the contemporary significance of the passage, there is not always a sharp distinction or a clear break between this section and the one that fol-lows. Yet when both sections are read together, you should have a strong sense of moving from the world of the Bible to the world of today.

THIS SECTION ALLOWS the biblical message to speak with as much power today as it did when it was first written. How can you apply what you learned about Jerusalem, Ephesus, or Corinth to our present-day needs in Chicago, Los Angeles, or London? How can you take a message originally spoken in Greek, Hebrew, and Aramaic and com-municate it clearly in our own language? How can you take the eternal truths originally spoken in a different time and culture and apply them to the similar-yet-different needs of our culture?

In order to achieve these goals, this section gives you help in several key areas.

(1) It helps you identify contemporary situations, problems, or questions that are truly comparable to those faced by the original audience. Because

contemporary situations are seldom identical to those faced by the original audience, you must seek situations that are analogous if your applications are to be relevant.

(2) This section explores a variety of contexts in which the passage might be applied today. You will look at personal applications, but you will also be encouraged to think beyond private concerns to the society and culture at large.

(3) This section will alert you to any problems or difficulties you might encounter in seeking to apply the passage. And if there are several legitimate ways to apply a passage (areas in which Christians disagree), the author will bring these to your attention and help you think through the issues involved.

In seeking to achieve these goals, the contributors to this series attempt to avoid two extremes. They avoid making such specific applications that the commentary might quickly become dated. They also avoid discussing the significance of the passage in such a general way that it fails to engage contemporary life and culture.

Above all, contributors to this series have made a diligent effort not to sound moralistic or preachy. The NIV Application Commentary Series does not seek to provide ready-made sermon materials but rather tools, ideas, and insights that will help you communicate God's Word with power. If we help you to achieve that goal, then we have fulfilled the purpose for this series.

The Editors

General Editor's Preface

No BOOK IN THE BIBLE has been interpreted as variously as Revelation. Students of prophecy and mystics especially have found in the visions of Revelation fertile ground for speculation and spiritualization. It seems as if every new commentary on Revelation reveals a new approach.

Craig Keener, the author of this volume on Revelation, offers a "new" approach by focusing on the "old." In order to understand this fascinating book, he says, we must focus on its "ancient rather than modern" background: "If today's newspapers are a necessary key to interpreting the book, then no generation until our own could have understood and obeyed the book."

In focusing on Revelation's message to its original audience, Keener is not denying the genre of the book (apocalyptic), its purpose (prophecy), its method (use of symbols), or its message for readers today (God's awesome majesty and control). On the contrary, Keener reaffirms the value of all previous approaches—idealistic, historical, preterist, futurist—in understanding the message of this book, or at least certain aspects of it.

His main point, however, is that focusing totally on present-day application may sell millions of books and pay lip service to the authority of Scripture over all aspects of modern life, but such an approach only *seems* to do that. In reality, what it does is call into question or make problematic two fundamental bedrocks of Christian faith.

(1) It questions the universal and timeless nature of God's truth. When the great visions of Revelation are interpreted as dependent on the great evil empires of the twentieth century—Germany, Japan, the Soviet Union, China, the Islamic world—then every shift of modern political fortune changes our understanding of the book. As Professor Keener so ably shows, the great symbols of Revelation were aimed at early Christian ears, not twentieth-century ones. We learn what they mean by understanding what they meant.

(2) We are tempted to forget that God has acted and continues to act in all political contexts. We have no monopoly on God's attention. The great prophecies of Revelation meant as much to Augustine, Aquinas, Luther, Calvin, Wesley, Edwards, and Barth as they mean to us today. Just as the visions of Revelation make up parallel rather than serial understandings of God's mighty deeds, so every Christian age develops an understanding of what Revelation means that is parallel to all other ages, not a chronological series of events.

General Editor's Preface

Indeed, one of the great marvels of God's gracious activity toward us is that it occurs in real time without being prejudiced in favor of any particular age. Just because we are the latest does not mean we are the best. The effects of sin prevent any age—including ours—from being "golden," at least in the spiritual sense. Every Christian generation learns equally the lessons of Revelation—that God is in control, that the powers of the world are minuscule when compared with God, that God is as likely to work through apparent weakness and failure as through strength and success, and that in the end God's people will prevail.

Revelation is the last book of the Bible. It reveals important truths about the end times. But it is also last in another important sense—it calls on all the hermeneutical courage, wisdom, and maturity one can muster in order to be understood properly. In many ways it serves as a graduation exercise for the NIV Application Commentary Series, an opportunity to fully apply the many lessons we have learned in the Bridging Contexts sections of previous volumes.

God's time is his, not ours. The story of God's gracious activity on our behalf will be fulfilled in a great and glorious conclusion. But all Christians, everywhere and at all times, have equal access to the time. That access has been and is made possible by God's message in the book of Revelation.

Terry C. Muck

Author's Preface

As a new Christian recently converted from atheism, I eagerly hurried through Paul's letters, reaching Revelation as soon as possible. Once I reached it, however, I could hardly understand a word of it. I listened attentively to the first few "prophecy teachers" I heard, but even if they had not contradicted one another, over the years I watched as most of their detailed predictions failed to materialize.

Perhaps six years after my conversion, as I began to read Revelation in Greek for the first time, the book came alive to me. Because I was now moving through the text more carefully, I noticed the transitions and the structure, and I realized it was probably addressing something much different from what I had first supposed. At the same time, I catalogued parallels I found between Revelation and biblical prophets like Daniel, Ezekiel, and Zechariah. I also began reading an apocalypse contemporary with Revelation, 4 Ezra (2 Esdras in the Apocrypha), to learn more about the way Revelation's original, first-century audience may have heard its claims.

Yet even in my first two years as a Christian, Revelation and other end-time passages proved a turning point for me. As a young Christian, I was immediately schooled in a particular, popular end-time view, which I respectfully swallowed (the particular view is not of consequence to the point of this story). But as I kept reading the Bible in context, I found myself increasingly uncertain of what I had been taught. A visiting evangelist, recognizing my dilemma, patiently set aside an afternoon in 1976 and took me through every argument he had for the popular view. But at each point I examined the context and showed that his view did not fit the text on which he based it. Finally, exasperated, he exclaimed, "Who do you think you are to disagree with this view? All men of God hold this view—Jim Bakker, Jimmy Swaggart, and all the others! You've been a Christian less than two years!" I realized that he was right; who was I to question all these men of God, no matter what I thought I saw in the text?

A couple months later, I visited a church where the pastor began teaching about the end times. He began articulating the very view I thought I had found in the text myself, and noted that it was the dominant view through all of church history: the view of the early church fathers, Augustine, Luther, Calvin, Wesley, and others. He also named some prominent men and women of God in our time who held this view. Meanwhile, the view that others had insisted I believe had been discerned in Scripture by no one until a century and a half before. That day I decided I would never believe anything anyone told me the Bible said without checking it out for myself. I decided I would study and research every matter before teaching it to anyone else. It was in a sense at that time, around age sixteen, that I started on the quest that led me toward biblical scholarship—not because I was interested in simply knowing all the views held by various scholars, but because I wanted the best tools for understanding the Bible's own message.

Over the years, that one issue became less a matter of controversy for me as I recognized more and more of Revelation's message that today's church needed to hear. God wanted to wake up his church to his agendas, to care about the things that mattered to him (like evangelizing the world or meeting human need) rather than the things that mattered to most of us (like making ourselves as comfortable in this world as possible). I continued to save my research on Revelation and to preach and teach from the book.

After I had finished a Matthew commentary and was in the midst of a commentary on John, I felt as if the Lord wanted me to contact Zondervan and suggest to them writing a practical, pastoral application of the principles contained in Revelation. Being so busy with John, however, I decided to wait until later in the year to contact them. But before that time came, Jack Kuhatschek from Zondervan called and asked if I could work on a New Testament commentary for them in the NIV Application Series.

"I am pretty far behind on the John commentary I am writing right now," I noted hesitantly, though I would have counted it an honor to write for that series. "What book of the New Testament is it on?"

"Revelation," he replied. I immediately recognized the Lord's providence in the invitation from Zondervan. I pray that this commentary will prove in some way worthy of such an important assignment.

I appreciate my editors at Zondervan who have invested a great deal of time into this volume, especially Jack Kuhatschek, Terry Muck, Scot McKnight, and Verlyn Verbrugge. I am grateful to my classes that allowed me to "test out" this material on them: my class on Revelation for the Center for Urban Theological Studies (CUTS) in Philadelphia, my classes on apocalyptic literature and Johannine literature at Hood Theological Seminary in North Carolina, and my International Institute of Christian Studies (IICS) students from various institutions in and near Jos, Nigeria, who allowed me to teach them the "Bible backgrounds" part. I am also grateful to Emmanuel Itapson, my assistant and dear friend, who graded the Revelation class at CUTS.

Due to space constraints, I had to omit some of my material and much of my documentation, but I hope the present commentary will nevertheless prove useful. In the application sections most of my secular citations come from one or two news magazines; I should note that this is not intended to endorse these over others but to admit that, for economic reasons, I have only been reading one regularly in the past decade and chose to cite the one whose information was already in my files.

Craig S. Keener
Easter, 1999

Abbreviations

Note: In addition to the abbreviations listed here, this commentary uses standard abbreviations for ancient classical sources, the Dead Sea Scrolls, the Pseudepigrapha, rabbinic literature, and the church fathers.

AB	Anchor Bible
ABD	*Anchor Bible Dictionary*
AGJU	Arbeiten zur Geschichte des Judentums und Urchristentums
ANET	*Ancient Near-Eastern Texts Relating to the Old Testament*, ed., J. Pritchard.
ANRW	*Aufstieg und Niedergang der römischen Welt*
AUSS	*Andrews University Seminary Studies*
BA	*Biblical Archaeologist*
BAR	*Biblical Archaeology Review*
BASOR	*Bulletin of the American School of Oriental Research*
BibNot	*Biblische Notizen*
BibSac	*Bibliotheca Sacra*
BibTrans	*The Bible Translator*
BJRL	*Bulletin of the John Rylands Library*
BTB	*Biblical Theology Bulletin*
BZ	*Biblische Zeitschrift*
CIG	*Corpus inscriptionum graecarum*
CIJ	*Corpus inscriptionum judaicarum*
CIL	*Corpus inscriptionum latinarum*
CPJ	*Corpus papyrorum judaicarum*
CT	*Christianity Today*
ÉPROER	Études préliminaires aux religions orientales dans l'empire romain
ETL	*Ephemerides theologicae lovanienses*
EvQ	*Evangelical Quarterly*
HTR	*Harvard Theological Review*
IEJ	*Israel Exploration Journal*
Interp	*Interpretation*
ITQ	*Irish Theological Quarterly*
JBL	*Journal of Biblical Literature*

JBLMS	Journal of Biblical Literature Monograph Series
JHS	*Journal of Hellenic Studies*
JJS	*Journal of Jewish Studies*
JPFC	*The Jewish People in the First Century* (2 vols., ed. S. Safrai, M. Stern, D. Flusser, and W. C. van Unnik)
JQR	*Jewish Quarterly Review*
JRS	*Journal of Roman Studies*
JSJ	*Journal of Study of Judaism*
JSNT	*Journal for the Study of the New Testament*
JSNTSup	Journal for the Study of the New Testament Supplements
JSP	*Journal for the Study of the Pseudepigrapha*
JSS	*Journal of Semitic Studies*
JTS	*Journal of Theological Studies*
LCL	Loeb Classical Library
LEC	Library of Early Christianity
MM	*Mountain Movers*
MNTC	Moffatt New Testament Commentary
Neot	*Neotestamentica*
NICNT	New International Commentary on the New Testament
NIV	New International Version
NovT	*Novum Testamentum*
NovTSup	Supplements to *Novum Testamentum*
NTA	*New Testament Abstracts*
NTS	*New Testament Studies*
NW	*Newsweek*
OTP	*The Old Testament Pseudepigrapha* (2 vols., ed. by James H. Charlesworth)
PGM	*Papyri graecae magicae*
POTTS	Pittsburgh Original Texts and Translation Series
RB	*Revue biblique*
RevExp	*Review and Expositor*
RevQ	*Revue de Qumran*
RHPR	*Revue d'histoire et de philosophie religieuses*
RSR	*Recherches de science religieuse*
SBLBMI	Society of Biblical Literature, the Bible and Its Modern Interpreters
SBLDS	Society of Biblical Literature Dissertation Series
SBS	Sources for Biblical Study
SCP	*Spiritual Counterfeit Project*
SEG	*Supplementum Epigraphicum Graecum*

Abbreviations

SJT	*Scottish Journal of Theology*
SNTSM	Society for New Testament Studies Monographs
SNTU	Studien zum Neuen Testament und seiner Umwelt
ST	*Studia Theologica*
TDGR	Translated Documents of Greece and Rome
TDNT	*Theological Dictionary of the New Testament,* ed. G. Kittel
TNHL	*The Nag Hammadi Library*
TrinJ	*Trinity Journal*
TynBul	*Tyndale Bulletin*
UNDCSJCA	University of Notre Dame Center for the Study of Judaism and Christianity in Antiquity
USNWR	*U.S. News and World Report*
WPR	*World Press Review*
ZAW	*Zeitschrift für die alttestamentliche Wissenschaft*
ZNW	*Zeitschrift für die neutestamentliche Wissenschaft*

Introduction

ALTHOUGH MANY DETAILS in Revelation (and in this commentary) are debatable, the basic thrust is not. The true and living God summons us from our preoccupation with the world to recognize, in light of his ultimate plan for history, what really matters and what really does not. God first gave Revelation to a culture where people would hear the words of the book and imagine the stark and terrifying images; to be struck by the full force of the book, we must likewise use our imaginations to grasp the images of terror. Revelation is not meant for casual or "lite" reading; to genuinely hear it summons us to grapple with God's judgment on a world in rebellion against him.

The Key to Interpretation?

SOME READERS BELIEVE that current events unlock the meaning of the biblical prophecies. Thus, for example, one writer opines that even Luther and Calvin "knew little about prophecy," but that study-Bible editor C. I. Scofield rightly pointed out that Revelation was written to allow end-time interpreters to unlock its meaning.[1]

Yet this approach seems to me wrongheaded—I believe that it runs up against the evidence of Revelation itself. John writes to seven literal churches in literal Asia Minor, following the same sequence in which a messenger traveling Roman roads would deliver the book (see the more detailed comment in the Bridging Contexts section on 1:4–8). If we take seriously what the book itself *claims*, then it was a book that must have made good sense to its first hearers, who in fact were "blessed" for obeying it (1:3). That John wrote the book in Greek probably suggests that he also used figures of speech and symbols that were part of his culture more than ours. That the book was to remain "unsealed" even in his generation also indicates that it was meant to be understood from that time forward (22:10; contrast Dan. 12:9–10).

Perhaps an even more compelling reason exists to argue for focusing on ancient rather than modern background for understanding the book of Revelation. If today's newspapers are a necessary key to interpreting the book, then no generation until our own could have understood and obeyed the book (contrary to the assumption in 1:3). They could not have read the book as Scripture profitable for teaching and correction—an approach that

---

1. Lindsey, *New World Coming*, 21.

does not fit a high view of biblical authority (cf. 2 Tim. 3:16–17). If, however, the book was understandable for the first generation, subsequent generations can profit from the book simply by learning some history. Some popular prophecy teachers have ignored much of the history that is available, preferring to interpret the book in light of current newspaper headings. That is probably why most of them have to revise their predictions every few years as the headlines change.

Another matter of interpretation is that some want to take everything in Revelation literally. Whether one should attempt this approach depends in a sense on what one means by the term *literally*. When Reformers like Luther talked about interpreting the Bible "literally," they were using a technical designation (*sensus literalis*) that meant taking each part of Scripture according to its "literary sense," hence including attention to genre or literary type. But they did not mean that we should downplay figures of speech or symbols. We should take literally historical narrative in the Bible, but Revelation belongs to a different genre, a mixture of prophetic and "apocalyptic" genres, both of which are full of symbols. The Reformers did not demand that we interpret symbols as if they were not symbols, and this kind of literalism is actually at odds with what they meant.[2]

In fact, to take every symbol in Revelation nonsymbolically is so difficult that no one ever really attempts it. No one takes Babylon the Great as a literal prostitute or mother of prostitutes (17:5), no one takes new Jerusalem as a literal individual who is a bride, and few Protestants take the mother in chapter 12 as a literal mother (certainly not one literally clothed with the sun). "Take literally as much as *possible*," comes the response. But the amount that is "possible" is usually determined by one's presuppositions. Are literal monsters like those in chapter 9 possible? God could certainly create them, but they do bear many striking resemblances to creatures that simply represent locusts in the book of Joel. Is it not more important to be consistent with how the rest of Revelation and prophetic literature invites us to interpret them (much of which is plainly symbolic) than to try to take all its language literally? Is it not more respectful to Revelation to hear it on its own terms (symbols included) than to read into it a system of interpretation the book

---

2. Sproul, *Last Days*, 65–66; Robert B. Strimple, "An Amillennial Response to Craig A. Blaising," 256–76 in *Three Views of the Millennium*, ed. Bock, 262. John Chrysostom and his "Antiochene" followers more often followed this "literal" sense, as opposed to Gnostics and often the Alexandrians (Carl A. Volz, "The Genius of Chrysostom's Preaching," *Christian History* 44 [1994]: 24–26 [p. 24]); Stephen M. Miller, "Malcontents for Christ," *Christian History* 51 [1996]: 32–34 [p. 32]). Some Americans used what they regarded as "literalism" to justify slavery, whereas others responded from biblical principles ("Broken Churches, Broken Nation," *Christian History* 33 [1992]: 26–27 [p. 27]).

itself nowhere claims? That Revelation clearly includes symbols and some-times tells us what they mean (e.g., 1:20) should lead us to suspect any inter-pretive method that ignores the intense symbolism of the rest of the book.

Revelation begins by telling us that God "signified" the book to John (1:1; NIV, "made it known"), a word that is related to the one John occa-sionally uses for "sign" or "symbol" (12:1, 3; 15:1). This suggests that the opening verses forthrightly announce a book communicated by symbols.[3] Revelation's Jewish contemporaries were accustomed to the sorts of symbols the book employs. Thus one reads in a first-century addition to the early Jew-ish apocalypse 1 Enoch, for example, of mysterious animals (1 Enoch 85:3) impregnated by stars (ch. 86), a vision clearly not intended literally in the context. Likewise, John's "locusts" (Rev. 9:3–11) have much in common with Joel's; we who rightly recognize that we should not interpret literally all the graphic language about a locust army in Joel 1–2 (1:4; 2:11, 20, 25) should interpret Revelation the same way. As many evangelical and other com-mentators note, the visions are primarily to confront us with God's demands and promises, not to satisfy our curiosity about minute end-time details. Rev-elation shares no common ground with unbiblical prognosticators like Jeanne Dixon, Edgar Caycee, or tabloid horoscopes.

Prophetic Failures

THE MASSIVE LOSS of life among David Koresh's followers in Waco, Texas, involved a misreading of the book of Revelation.[4] Prophetic speculation is not, however, a new phenomenon. Jewish works sometimes guessed numbers and times still future—and history proved them wrong (e.g., Sib. Or. 11.265–67; Test. Moses 2:3). Early church fathers also indulged in some specula-tions that never materialized, such as Hippolytus's view that the world would end in A.D. 500. Unfortunately, many modern prophecy teachers have not scored much better.[5]

Jerome studied in biblical lands to better understand the literary forms and contexts of the Bible, including Revelation. Many interpreters, however, have failed to learn the original setting of the book and have in effect "added

---

3. See Beale, *Revelation*, 50–51, who finds background for this language in Daniel's use for dream-visions (Dan. 2:28–30, 45 LXX). Prophecy could include *mashal* (Num. 23:7, 18), a literary type that includes "parables."

4. Craig L. Nessan, "When Faith Turns Fatal: David Koresh and Tragic Misreadings of Revelation," *Currents in Theology and Mission* 22 (June 1995): 191–99.

5. On Hippolytus, see Lewis, *Questions*, 16. For modern prophecy teachers, see Dwight Wilson, *Armageddon Now! The Premillenarian Response to Russia and Israel Since 1917* (Grand Rapids: Baker, 1977).

to" it, despite its warning (22:18), by reading into it theological systems not justified by the text itself.[6] Of course, Jehovah's Witnesses are known for such activities. Whereas most groups that have set dates gave up after they missed once or twice, "Jehovah's Witnesses won't quit. Their leaders have earmarked the years 1874, 1878, 1881, 1910, 1914, 1918, 1925, 1975, and 1984 as times of eschatological significance."[7] Religion scholars have noted how various sects like Mormons, Jehovah's Witnesses, and Christian Science adherents have used Revelation arbitrarily to support the views they already held.[8] Because Jehovah's Witnesses are the best-known purveyors of prophetic pessimism that never panned out, and also because readers of this commentary will be fairly unanimous that the Witnesses are in error, I often use them in this commentary to illustrate obvious errors in interpretive method.

But unfortunately, while Jehovah's Witnesses are the best-known transgressors, history is littered with such failed predictions from all segments of Christendom, perhaps most obviously in the twentieth century from popular evangelicalism. In the 1920s, some dispensational prophecy teachers viewed *The Protocols of the Elders of Zion*—now recognized as a forgery promoted by the Nazis—as confirming their prophetic ideas. (Some later repudiated the *Protocols*, but others never did.)[9] To their credit, this stream of prophetic interpretation proved strikingly right about Israel's becoming a nation, a significant matter (although it is also true that they were not the only group to expect it).[10] The parts of the body of Christ involved in this stream of interpretation also often demonstrated a commendable commitment to missions and world evangelism second to none. But when speculating on details, many popular prognosticators proved wrong on the identity of the Antichrist and other matters. "Nobody anticipated the demise of the Soviet empire or most aspects of the Gulf War. When history takes unexpected turns, the experts have to make adjustments, redraw their maps, and come out with new editions."[11]

Lest we think that evangelicals on the whole learned humility from early mistakes, plenty of examples provide warnings to the contrary. In 1979 Colin

---

6. See the observation by John Randall, *The Book of Revelation: What Does It Really Say?* (Locust Valley, N.Y.: Living Flame, 1976), 11.

7. Kyle, *The Last Days*, 93.

8. See W. Thiede, "Ein süsses und doch schwerverdauliches Büchlein: Zur Auslegung der Johannes-Offenbarung in christlichen Sondergemeinschaften," *Kerygma und Dogma* 41 (1995): 213–42.

9. Timothy P. Weber, "How Evangelicals Became Israel's Best Friend," *CT* (Oct. 5, 1998), 38–49 (p. 43).

10. Many outside this tradition expected at least an end-time conversion of Jewish people before the Second Coming, such as nineteenth-century premillennialist Lord Shaftesbury (John Wolffe, "Dismantling Discrimination," *Christian History* 53 [1997]: 37–39 [38]).

11. Weber, "Israel's Best Friend," 49.

Deal's book showing why Christ would return by 1988 circulated information about a computer in Belgium known as "the beast," claiming that this was the Antichrist.[12] His source seemed "unaware that the computer was only a fictional creation from a novel."[13] That the devil could lure modern interpreters into such errors is not surprising; Saint Martin of Tours, who died in 397, alleged that "there is no doubt that the Antichrist has already been born." (If Martin is right, the Antichrist displays remarkable longevity.) Others predicted his coming for the years 1000, 1184, 1186, 1229, 1345, 1385, etc.[14]

Every end-time view can seem reasonable if one has never sympathetically studied other views. Thus I wish that all those committed to particular end-time scenarios would survey Richard Kyle's *The Last Days Are Here Again* (Grand Rapids: Baker, 1998), Dwight Wilson's *Armageddon Now! The Premillenarian Response to Russia and Israel Since 1917* (Grand Rapids: Baker, 1977), Gary DeMar's *Last Days Madness: The Folly of Trying to Predict When Christ Will Return* (Brentwood, Tenn.: Wolgemuth & Hyatt, 1991), or other works like these. By reviewing the history of end-times speculation littered with failed predictions and even the varied views on major end-times issues by respected Christian leaders, they help us put our own views in perspective.

One may take as an example of diverse end-time views among Christians the Millennium, or the thousand-year reign of Christ in Revelation 20. Does Jesus return before the future Millennium (the premillennial view, the most common among North American evangelicals today) or after it (the postmillennial view), or is this period merely a symbol for the present era (the amillennial view)? Many readers may be surprised to learn that most Christian leaders in history were amillennial (like Augustine, Luther, and Calvin), many leaders in North American revivals were postmillennial (like Jonathan Edwards and Charles Finney), and most of the early church fathers were premillennial (but posttribulational).

If Calvin, Wesley, Finney, Moody, and most Christians today each have held different views, is it possible that God's blessing may not rest solely on those who hold a particular end-time view?[15] If different views strongly dominated different eras of history (e.g., amillennialism during the Reformation;

---

12. Colin Deal, *Christ Returns by 1988—101 Reasons Why* (Rutherford College, N.C.: Colin Deal, 1979), 86, as cited in Richard Abanes, *American Militias* (Downers Grove, Ill.: InterVarsity, 1996), 91.

13. Abanes, *American Militias*, 91.

14. Ibid., 90.

15. D. L. Moody was the first prominent North American evangelist who was premillennial, but he does not appear to have been committed to dispensational details like pretribulationalism (Stanley N. Gundry, "Questions About Moody's Theology," *Christian History* 25 [1990]: 19), at least not publicly.

postmillennialism during the U.S. Great Awakenings; premillennialism today), is it possible that our own views are more historically shaped than we care to admit? Studying various views better equips us to read Revelation more objectively on its own terms.

The Turkish Ottoman Empire once constituted a great threat to the Western world from the East, but after its fall the World War II generation naturally read the "kings from the East" (16:12) as a reference to Japan (the seven churches of Asia were clearly not thinking of Turkey). After Japan's collapse and communism's rise in China, the title was transferred accordingly. Most prophecies have been reapplied as newspaper headlines have changed, so that modern prophecy teaching is rarely relevant for more than a decade. As one historian mourns, "end-time thinking has been incredibly elastic"; elements of the "prophetic jigsaw puzzle" have achieved "a chameleon-like character—it has been regularly adjusted to suit the changes in current events."[16] As we will see, the "revelation of Jesus Christ" to John (1:1) uses not only the Greek language but images and symbols that made sense in his generation, and modern prophecy teachers have often tried to jump to what it "means" without first understanding what it "meant."

In one sense, however, Revelation and other end-time texts in the Bible lend themselves to more moderate comparisons with current events. Who would doubt that the return of Israel to the land (accepted by many teachers of different end-time persuasions through history) has some significance in God's plan, even if we debate about which texts might imply this? The recognition of antichrists and other signs that make us yearn more fervently for Christ's coming is natural when we recognize that each generation could be the last one. (After all, if Jesus said no one knows the hour of his return, that includes the devil, who thus must have antichrists in waiting for each generation.) But we need the humility to leave "could be the last generation" as is and not upgrade "could" prematurely to "is."

Although John probably did not expect a delay of the Lord's return for the many generations between his and our own, he might have had some sympathy with those who wish to reapply the images of Revelation to their own generation, just as they made sense to his generation.[17] Any generation is potentially the final one, and John was probably familiar with *pesher* interpreters among his contemporaries who reapplied biblical prophecies to their

---

16. Kyle, *The Last Days*, 187, 99.

17. On John's symbolism as "tensive, evocative, and polyvalent," see esp. Boring, *Revelation*, 55; the book's graphic word pictures are meant to provoke reflection, not harmonization (ibid., 57; cf. Michaels, *Interpreting Revelation*, 16–17; for an example of deliberate polyvalence, see 17:9–10; Michaels, ibid., 106).

own time.[18] The danger in pursuing this approach is that too many of us assume, like the *pesher* interpreters of Qumran, that we must be the final generation—usually based on a misinterpretation of Mark 13:28—and that these prophecies apply literally and only to our own generation.[19] This assumption has so far been proved wrong among every generation that has held it, though it is ultimately liable to be vindicated in some generation—by the sheer fact that someday the Lord will return!

Approaches

HISTORY HAS PRODUCED various approaches to the book of Revelation, many of which have some elements that commend them, provided we do not press too far their denials of elements in other positions.

The Idealist Approach

THE IDEALIST APPROACH finds timeless principles in Revelation. Everyone who preaches from the book will affirm this general conviction, but in the view's most extreme form it simultaneously denies any specific historical or future meaning for the book. As Tenney observes, to its principles "almost any interpreter of Revelation could give assent regardless of the school to which he belongs. The idealist view does contain much that is true. Its flaw is not so much in what it affirms as in what it denies."[20] Was Revelation teaching merely timeless general principles, with no concern for pressing issues at hand in the seven churches?

The Historicist Approach

SOME HAVE ARGUED, from at least the time of the fourteenth-century writer Nicolas of Lyra, that Revelation provides a detailed map of history from its own day until Jesus' future return. This historicist view of Revelation as church history dominated views about the book through the seventeenth and eighteenth centuries. It is rarely advanced today; the links between Revelation's contents and history's events always have proved forced.

---

18. On *pesher* interpreters, see, e.g., Devorah Dimant, "Pesharim, Qumran," *ABD*, 5:244–51; J. G. Harris, "Early Trends in Biblical Commentaries as Reflected in Some Qumran Texts," *EvQ* 36 (1964): 100–105.

19. The "generation" in Mark 13:30 and parallel texts means what the term nearly always means in the Gospels: Jesus' generation, when the temple's destruction was fulfilled (although Jesus' return was not necessarily meant to be; see, e.g., Craig Keener, *Matthew* [Downers Grove, Ill.: InterVarsity, 1997], 343, 348–49, 353; for the different idea that even the return is symbolic and was fulfilled, see, e.g., Sproul, *Last Days*, 51–68).

20. Tenney, *Revelation*, 143.

The Preterist Approach

PRETERISTS READ THE book of Revelation the way they believe John's original audience in the seven churches would have. In other words, they seek to
apply to Revelation the same interpretive method we apply to every other
book of the Bible, namely, that we should read it in its historical context.
Because the most radical preterists insist, however, that the events of Revelation were entirely fulfilled in the first century, they read it in a manner that
John's original audience probably would not have. Whatever else may already
have been fulfilled (and Revelation, like most apocalypses, includes at least
some rehearsal of the past; see 12:1–5), most early Christians would not
have recognized in any first-century events the fulfillment of the great white
throne judgment (20:11–15) or the arrival of the holy city (21:1–22:5). Thus
more moderate preterists do not insist that every event of Revelation was fulfilled in the first century. Even most commentators today who are not completely preterist accept the preterist contention that the Revelation must
have made sense to its first hearers (22:10).

The Futurist Approach

FUTURISTS ARE CERTAINLY right to claim that some events in the book await
fulfillment, such as God's unchallenged eternal city supplanting the kingdoms of this world (21:1–22:5). But the futurist position, like the other ones,
can be pressed too far; in its radical form, it "implies that the book had nothing to say to the many generations between John of Patmos and the interpreter."[21] Further, some pivotal clues in the book (see comment on 12:5–6)
may suggest that the time frame much of the book reports is not merely a
future tribulation, but also a present one.

Although the dominant popular approach today, futurism was not popular in many periods in church history. A number of evangelical scholars
hold this view, usually either in the traditional dispensational form or more
commonly the historical premillennial view. The former requires a seven-year
tribulation, or sometimes half that period; the latter typically does not differentiate the future tribulation from the past or present as sharply, though
many maintain a future tribulation followed by Christ's return.

An Eclectic Approach

OTHERS PREFER SOME mixture of historical or preterist approaches with a
futurist approach. Some interpreters from at least the time of the late

---

21. González, *Revelation*, 9. Many interpreters have neglected Revelation's significance
for its first audience (see Guthrie, *Relevance*, 12–17).

sixteenth-century Spanish Jesuit Ribeira have suggested that Revelation portrays events about to occur in John's day as well as immediately preceding Jesus' return, with not much in between. Alcasar, another Spanish Jesuit (d. 1614), suggested that Revelation 4–19 were fulfilled in the conflicts of John's era but chapters 20–22 represent the church's triumph after Constantine.[22]

But other eclectic (mixed) approaches also exist. Most commentators who seek to apply Revelation will opt for some eclectic approach, usually combining some futurist, preterist, and idealist elements. Some elements in the book are clearly future (the second coming and resurrection of the saints, if nothing else!); some are past; some probably typify characteristic judgments in the present age.[23] On most of these differences of opinion there is room for charitable differences of opinion. But on any interpretation, all elements warn us to contemplate God's ways and to live accordingly.[24]

Once we understand what God was saying to the churches of Asia through John, we can begin to draw analogies for how the same message is relevant to our churches today. Thinking concretely how to bridge the gap between Scripture's words in the past and our culture today is important; the very reasons biblical writers said what they did in one setting caused biblical writers to say different things for different settings, and we need to hear them clearly before we reapply their words to our setting. Sometimes we and our historical predecessors have simply passed on traditions, adding a few new ones along the way for future generations. Many leaders through church history, however, like the Reformers or many missionaries or leaders in great revivals, have sought to recontextualize the biblical message for their generation and culture, just as the biblical writers contextualized their revelations for their generations and cultures. We must do the same, but before we can do so, we must make sure we understand the Bible properly.

---

22. For this summary, see Mounce, *Revelation*, 40–41; see also the summary in Johnson, *Revelation*, 12–15. For a full survey of views, see Isbon T. Beckwith, *The Apocalypse of John* (New York: Macmillan, 1922), 318–34; Craig R. Koester, "On the Verge of the Millennium: A History of the Interpretation of Revelation," *Word & World* 15 (1995): 128–36; and Inter-Varsity's commentary on Revelation from the writings of the early church fathers (at the time of this writing, the Revelation volume remains forthcoming).

23. A basic problem is distinguishing which elements belong to which categories. This commentary will suggest that much of the book provides principles for the end-time church living in the present era between the first and second comings, and argue that chapters 19–22 are completely future.

24. See Gordon D. Fee, *New Testament Exegesis: A Handbook for Students and Pastors* (Philadelphia: Westminster, 1983), 42–43, who follows a partial apocalyptic approach; also the eclectic approach in Beale, *Revelation*, 44–49.

Symbolism

AS NOTED ABOVE, on any view, Revelation employs much symbolism. Although one should read most narratives in the Bible literally, prophetic and apocalyptic texts (see next sec. on Genre) are different, as anyone who has spent much time with them will recognize. They contain considerable symbolism, and often were fulfilled in unexpected ways. Various texts both in the Old Testament (e.g., Judg. 5:4; Ps. 18:4–19) and among John's contemporaries (e.g., Sib. Oracles 3.286–92; 4.57–60) could employ the language of cosmic catastrophe to describe events taking place in their own or recent times. Many such texts review history (such as 1 Enoch's "dream-visions"), and some such texts even blend clearly past events with images of the end time (Sib. Oracles 5.336).

Revelation's symbols may appear obscure to us, but they were mostly fathomable (or at least evocative) to the believers in the seven churches, at least after some reflection. One commentator notes that "John used symbols in order to communicate that which cannot be expressed in any other way, not to conceal something that could be said more straightforwardly."[25]

The symbolic use of numbers characterizes Revelation, as it does many other apocalypses.[26] This is not surprising, given how common symbolic use of numbers was throughout the ancient Mediterranean world, especially through the influence of a Greek philosophical sect called the Pythagoreans.[27] Richard Bauckham provides a thorough list of detailed numerical patterns in Revelation, especially sevens, such as the "Lamb" being mentioned twenty-eight times (exactly seven of which are alongside God).[28] Some designations of time, such as "one hour" in 17:12, are plainly not literal; an interpreter is therefore not obligated to take other time designations literally without compelling reason. Among John's contemporaries, numbers like seven and twelve often functioned symbolically.[29] In Jewish texts, twelve most often

---

25. Boring, *Revelation*, 55.

26. E.g., the sevens in T. Moses 3:14. On numerical symbolism, see Adela Yarbro Collins, "Numerical Symbolism in Jewish and Early Christian Apocalyptic Literature," *ANRW* 2.21.2, 1221–87.

27. See Plut. *E at Delphi* 8, *Mor.* 388C; *Gen. of Soul* 18, *Mor.* 1018C; R. A. Laroche, "Popular Symbolic/Mystical Numbers in Antiquity," *Latomus* 54 (1995): 568–76; M. J. J. Menken, *Numerical Literary Techniques in John: The Fourth Evangelist's Use of Numbers of Words and Syllables*, NovTSup 55 (Leiden: E. J. Brill, 1985), 27–29. Many cultures use symbolic numbers in relation to divine matters (e.g., John S. Mbiti, *African Religions and Philosophies* [Garden City, N.Y.: Doubleday, 1970], 73).

28. Bauckham, *Climax of Prophecy*, 22–37.

29. For seven, see, e.g., Aulus Gellius, 3.10; Apuleius, *Metam.* 11.1; Jos. & Asen. 2:6/10–11; Philo, *Abraham* 28; *Creation*, 99–100, 111–16; *Spec.* 2.56–62.

---

stood for the tribes of Israel, but also functioned in various other ways.[30] In Revelation, where twelve and multiples of twelve appear around sixty times, the number most often points to Israel.[31]

Genre

ALTHOUGH SCHOLARS DEBATE the specific type of literature into which Revelation falls, most agree that it fits at least in part what modern scholars call "apocalypses."[32] Some have used the term *apocalypse* to refer loosely to any Jewish end-time thought, others more specifically for visionary literature, often including heavenly ascents and revelations. The apocalyptic genre flourished in early Judaism, and most scholars include Revelation in this category.[33] In this sort of text in the most specific sense, the seer has visions and revelations—"apocalypse" literally means "revelation"—often including cosmological speculation (e.g., 1 Enoch 72–82). Revelation includes little cosmological speculation and lacks journeys (1 Enoch 17–18); unlike some of its modern interpreters, Revelation does not sidetrack from its agenda to pursue matters of curiosity.

But more commonly modern scholars apply the term *apocalyptic* to most early Jewish texts that focus on revelations of some sort relevant to the end time.[34] Like most apocalypses, John follows the Semitic language and visionary figures of speech found in biblical prophetic books (e.g., "I looked, and there before me was . . . ," Rev. 4:1; 6:2, 5, 8); this accounts for many of the language differences between Revelation and other New Testament books.

Just as Jewish teachers used riddles, so Jewish prophetic writers used enigmatic predictions or riddles, often to provoke thought (e.g., Sib. Oracles 5.14–42). Some have even regarded Revelation as using code-language to avoid persecution; Roman readers would, however, immediately recognize

30. For other functions in ancient texts, see T. Abram. 2:5A; Jos. & Asen. 3:2/3; *p. Meg.* 1:9, §12; Arrian, *Alex.* 5.29.1; *PGM*, 36.19.

31. See A. Geyser, "The Twelve Tribes in Revelation: Judean and Judeo-Christian Apocalypticism," *NTS* 28 (July 1982): 388–99 (p. 388).

32. Some view it in other ways, such as a drama (Bowman, *First Christian Drama*, 9; J. L. Blevins, "The Genre of Revelation," *RevExp* 77 [1980]: 393–408).

33. In fact the title for the genre, "apocalyptic," comes from the Greek title of Revelation, *Apocalypsis*. On the genre, see, e.g., James H. Charlesworth, *The Old Testament Pseudepigrapha and the New Testament: Prolegomena for the Study of Christian Origins*, SNTSM 54 (Cambridge: Cambridge Univ. Press, 1985), 87; F. F. Bruce, *The New Testament Documents: Are They Reliable?* (5th rev. ed.; Grand Rapids: Eerdmans, 1981), 11; Hugh Anderson, "A Future for Apocalyptic?" 56–71 in *Biblical Studies: Essays in Honor of William Barclay*, ed. J. R. McKay and J. F. Miller (Philadelphia: Westminster, 1976), 68.

34. Others used such language; see similar images of a future golden age in Virgil, *Ecl.* 4.4–25; Roman portents of doom (e.g., Herodian, 1.14.1); even visions of the afterlife (Plutarch, *Divine Vengeance, Mor.* 548A–568A) and visions of the spirit world (*PGM*, 4.662–64).

the anti-Roman portrait of the ruling city on seven mountains (17:9).[35] Revelation's riddles are to provoke thought, not to conceal most of its meaning.

Noting differences between Revelation and many apocalypses mentioned above, as well as how much of Revelation is rooted in biblical prophecy, some scholars have argued that Revelation is prophecy rather than apocalypse.[36] Among apocalypses, John's Revelation is certainly closer to the biblical prophets than his contemporaries.[37] A forced choice between "apocalyptic" and "prophetic" genres, however, is pointless. To be sure, nearly everything in Revelation can be paralleled in the Old Testament prophets, but the specific features that predominate are also those most common among Revelation's early Jewish contemporaries. A line of demarcation is arbitrary; preexilic biblical prophets like Isaiah and Joel, and especially exilic and postexilic prophets like Ezekiel, Daniel, and Zechariah, use the sorts of images from which later apocalyptic texts draw. John also has every reason to articulate his revelation in terms intelligible to his contemporaries, as God had been doing throughout history!

Later apocalypses could also consider themselves "prophecy" (e.g., 4 Ezra 12:42), so it is not surprising that Revelation does the same (1:3; 22:7, 10, 18–19).[38] Whether apocalyptic writers used visions merely as literary devices or also believed they had experienced them is debated.[39] It seems likely, however, that at least John reports authentic visions that determined the genre in which he would write, even if John then exercises the freedom to report them in a dramatic literary manner.[40]

Western Asia Minor (where the seven churches were located) boasted various oracular centers, so we know that even new Gentile converts in the seven churches were familiar with the idea of prophecy.[41] Further, these oracles could prove political in nature, and in an earlier period had sometimes

---

35. See Caird, *Commentary on Revelation*, 216–17. Slaves likewise used fables to depict reality without punishment (Phaedrus 3, prologue 33–44).

36. See James Kallas, "The Apocalypse—An Apocalyptic Book?" *JBL* 86 (March 1967): 69–80; cf. Ellul, *Apocalypse*, 20–35; Fiorenza, *Revelation*, 170.

37. See the judgment of Bowman, *First Christian Drama*, 11.

38. See Talbert, *Apocalypse*, 4; on blending of elements, see also Aune, *Prophecy in Early Christianity*, 274; Beasley-Murray, *Revelation*, 19. Many writers regard its genre as composite (Feuillet, *Apocalypse*, 8; Corsini, *Apocalypse*, 24–34; Roloff, *Revelation*, 8; Hill, *New Testament Prophecy*, 71–75; Beale, *Revelation*, 37–43; Aune, *Revelation*, 1:lxx-xc).

39. M. E. Stone, "Apocalyptic—Vision or Hallucination," *Milla wa-Milla* 14 (1974): 47–56 (*NTA*, 20:91), argues that the authors believed themselves genuinely inspired.

40. See Rissi, *Time and History*, 20–21; Richard J. Bauckham, "The Role of the Spirit in the Apocalypse," *EvQ* 52 (1980): 66–83. Aune, *Prophecy in Early Christianity*, 274–75, argues for "a combination of prophetic experience and literary artifice."

41. T. L. Robinson, "Oracles and Their Society: Social Realities as Reflected in the Oracles of Claros and Didyma," *Semeia* 56 (1991): 59–77.

extended to denunciations of Rome.[42] But the clear and primary background against which to read the book's prophecies, a background shared with other Jewish apocalyptic works, is the Old Testament.

Revelation, like the Fourth Gospel, is full of implicit allusions to the Old Testament; indeed, it contains more biblical allusions than any other early Christian work, which some estimate appear in nearly 70 percent of Revelation's verses. But unlike John's Gospel it includes no extended quotations of the Old Testament. Many of the allusions recall also the context of their biblical source; many, however, blend various biblical allusions, and Revelation regularly recycles its images to apply them in a fresh way. (Everyone agrees, for example, that Revelation's plagues of hail mixed with fire, water turned to blood, and so forth recall the plagues of Moses' day, but also that Revelation is not simply referring to past biblical events.) Other Jewish texts could draw end-time imagery from biblical prophets (Sib. Oracles 3.788–95); some other works, like Qumran's Manual of Discipline, might include few biblical quotations (e.g., 1QS 5.15; 8.15) but many allusions. Like other early Jewish interpreters, Revelation also blended end-time images in eclectic ways and recycled the images of earlier prophecies—even fulfilled ones—in new ways.[43]

Structure

USING AN EARLY scissors-and-paste approach to criticism, some commentators like R. H. Charles rearranged Revelation into an order more to their liking, considering the work's original editor incompetent.[44] The consensus

---

42. John J. Collins, *The Sibylline Oracles of Egyptian Judaism*, SBLDS 13 (Missoula, Mont.: Society of Biblical Literature, 1972), 4–5, 117; G. W. Bowersock, *Augustus and the Greek World* (Oxford: Clarendon, 1965), 110; in Judaism, Sib. Oracles 3.350–80. In this period, however, many embraced Rome's propaganda (A. Erskine, "The Romans as Common Benefactors," *Historia* 43 [1994]: 70–87); prophets had long been used to legitimate rulers (see, e.g., J. N. Bremmer, "Prophets, Seers, and Politics in Greece, Israel, and Early Modern Europe," *Numen* 40 [1993]: 150–83).

43. For diverse end-time views in the Dead Sea Scrolls, see S. L. Mattila, "Two Contrasting Eschatologies at Qumran (4Q246 vs 1QM)," *Biblica* 75 (1994): 518–38; for reuse of prophetic language, see, e.g., H. W. Parke, *Sibyls and Sibylline Prophecy in Classical Antiquity*, ed. B. C. McGing (New York: Routledge, 1988), 15. For a thorough examination of Revelation's use of the Old Testament (with recognition of the value of the Old Testament contexts), see Beale, *Revelation*, 76–99.

44. Today usually the furthest commentators go is to suggest an arrangement of heterogeneous traditions collected by a single author (Elisabeth Schüssler Fiorenza, "The Revelation to John," 99–120 in *Hebrews-Revelation*, ed. G. Krodel [Philadelphia: Fortress, 1977], 100–101), though Ford thinks it was a Jewish apocalypse (with material from John the Baptist) later edited by Christians (*Revelation*, 4–7, 22–26). Aune's thorough commentary, however, is exceptional in its revival of source criticism (Aune, *Revelation*, 1:cxviii-cxxxiv, in my view not taking sufficient account of the different genre of Rev. 2–3 here).

today, however, is that Revelation represents a unified work.[45] It is, in fact, an exquisite product of literary design, despite the basic apocalyptic syntax of much of its language.[46]

At points the specific structure is debated, but what is clear is the general outline.[47] Between the letters to the seven churches and the promised future lie, in addition to scenes of heavenly worship and periodic interludes, three series of seven judgments, each ending (usually in the sixth element) with an end-of-the-age cataclysm then resolved in the seventh element (6:12–17; 8:1; 9:13–21; 11:15–19; 16:12–21). Such cataclysmic, cosmic imagery occasionally refers to events within history, but in most cases appears in early Jewish literature for the end of the age; it is therefore most natural to take these images in the same way in Revelation.

Some writers have tried to make Revelation a continuous chronological account from beginning to ending, but this view is not widely held today. The dominant view, proposed by Victorinus in the late third century, is that the various series of judgments parallel one another rather than following successively.[48] Since each of these series of judgments seem to conclude with the end of the age (as noted above), this line of interpretation is almost certainly correct. The sort of events closing the seals, trumpets, and bowls cannot repeat unless the world as we know it can come to an end several times (these three references plus 19:11–21)!

But what is the primary period depicted in Revelation? It seems to end with the end of the age, but what is less clear is when it begins. The seals seem to fit the present age (see comment on 6:1–8), but the clearest clue comes in 12:5–6: The period of tribulation seems to begin with Jesus' exaltation nearly two millennia ago. If this is in fact the point in that passage, then Revelation radically reapplies Daniel's picture of end-time tribulation in a different way. (This is not to claim that he disagrees with Daniel's meaning,

---

45. E.g., Feuillet, *Apocalypse*, 23–36; Rissi, *Time and History*, 17–18; Fiorenza, *Revelation*, 163; Charlesworth, *The Old Testament Pseudepigrapha and the New Testament*, 87.

46. Many irregularities in the grammar occur in Old Testament allusions, reflecting especially LXX language (Beale, *Revelation*, 100–105); on Revelation's syntax, see further Aune, *Revelation*, 1:clxii–ccvii.

47. For different outlines of specific points, see, e.g., Tenney, *Revelation*, 32–35; Bowman, *First Christian Drama*, 13; Caird, *Commentary on Revelation*, 105; Ford, *Revelation*, 46–50; Talbert, *Apocalypse*, 12. Most interesting—but unlikely—is the linking of Revelation with a lectionary calendar (M. D. Goulder, "The Apocalypse as an Annual Cycle of Prophecies," *NTS* 27 [April 1981]: 342–67; cf. the paschal liturgy in Shepherd, *Paschal Liturgy*, 77–84).

48. Mounce, *Revelation*, 39, 45; Beale, *Revelation*, 108–51 (though Aune, *Revelation*, 1.xci-xciii, is skeptical). Talbert, *Apocalypse*, 7, provides parallels in apocalyptic texts and explication from a rhetorical handbook.

only to argue that he recycles the same image to make an additional point.) Other clues in that passage and Revelation's regular reapplication of earlier symbols may support this view, held by many scholars.

The 1260 days may refer to the period between the first and second comings of Jesus, characterizing the entire church age as a period of tribulation in some sense. This would not rule out a final intensification of suffering toward the end of this period, which would be consonant with the period's eschatological character; but that is probably not the primary point in Revelation. In this case, Revelation would not directly even address the sort of future "tribulation" often discussed in modern "prophecy teaching." This is not to comment on whether other biblical passages might not address it, but to suggest that Revelation is more practically focused on the state of believers in this age, and that it is therefore a good resource for encouraging believers in this age; Christians must always be prepared to suffer for Christ.

That Revelation's "tribulation" is longer than a literal 1260 days seems the point of the text but is not, however, beyond debate. One could argue for a gap between Christ's exaltation and the beginning of the days— although no such gap is stated and resymbolization, including of numbers, is pervasively characteristic of the book. Yet on the level of application, the point would still be the same even if the period of time were a literal 1260 days: We may learn from the model of future "tribulation saints" just as we may learn from reading the Old Testament or the Gospels. Thus interpreters from various theological backgrounds can often preach and apply the text in similar ways.

Date and Setting

SINCE WE AFFIRM that Revelation is inspired by God, some readers may wonder what difference its date and setting make. Is its message not timeless? But the message of Romans and Philippians and 1 Peter is also timeless, yet we recognize that God inspired apostles to write these letters to real people who are explicitly identified as their audiences. Just like those letters, Revelation informs us of its intended audience (1:4, 11). Knowing the background that the Bible's first readers could take for granted helps us understand the issues the writer was inspired to address first and foremost. We can apply the Bible's principles much more concretely if we understand the concrete needs they originally addressed.

Early church fathers suggested that Revelation stems from the time of the evil emperor Domitian at the end of the first century, and that John returned from Patmos only after Domitian's death (e.g., Irenaeus, *Her.* 5.30.3;

Eusebius, *H.E.* 3.18.1–3; 3.20.9; 3.23.1).[49] Some have proposed a date under an earlier evil emperor named Nero, which does fit what we know of persecution in Rome (Tacitus, *Ann.* 15.44; 2 Tim. 4:16–18).[50] Some of the less explicit external evidence could also be read this way, though not the more explicit testimony of Irenaeus.[51] But Nero's persecution seems largely restricted to Rome (though authors in Rome could expect persecution to spread further, 1 Peter 1:1; 4:12; 5:9, 13), and Jesus' prophecy to Ephesus in 2:1–7, which suggests that the church guarded itself well against error, does not fit Nero's day (Acts 20:29–30; 1 Tim. 1:3–7; 2 Tim. 2:17–18).

Moreover, Revelation seems to portray a return of the wicked ruler Nero (Rev. 17:11)—not a likely subject of attention before Nero's demise in A.D. 68. By contrast, Domitian so persecuted the church that their tradition explicitly viewed him as Nero's successor (Eusebius, *H.E.* 3.17, 20). Others prefer for a date the period of turmoil immediately following Nero's death or the time of Vespasian, but explicit evidence is scanty.[52] The earlier dates allow some interpreters to understand Christ's coming in Revelation as his impending destruction of Jerusalem, but this is hardly the most natural sense of images such as the removal of mountains and islands (6:14; 16:20) or the resurrection of the righteous dead (20:4–5).[53] The church tradition that dates Revelation to the time of Domitian in the late first century is thus likely; while less than certain, it is better supported than the alternatives. Domitian's claims to deity and the centrality of his cult in Asia fit especially the later part of his reign, around the mid-90s.[54]

---

49. See Mounce, *Revelation*, 32, for other references; see more fully Beale, *Revelation*, 4–27. Clement of Alexandria, *Who Is the Rich Man That Shall be Saved?* 42, places this less explicitly under the "tyrant." This remained the majority view at least through the late twentieth century (Hemer, *Letters to the Seven Churches*, 3; H. Koester, *Introduction to New Testament* (Philadelphia: Fortress, 1982), 2:250; A. C. Isbell, "The Dating of Revelation," *Restoration Quarterly* 9 [1966]: 107–17; Charlesworth, *Old Testament Pseudepigrapha and New Testament*, 87).

50. See Sproul, *Last Days*, 141–45, following Kenneth L. Gentry Jr., *Before Jerusalem Fell: Dating the Book of Revelation* (Tyler, Tex.: Institute for Christian Economics, 1989).

51. Against contrary arguments, when Irenaeus speaks of something "seen" in Domitian's time, he undoubtedly refers to the vision he just noted that John "saw."

52. For dates from A.D. 68–70, see John A. T. Robinson, *Redating the New Testament* (Philadelphia: Westminster, 1976), 221–53; E. Lipinski, "L'apocalypse et le martyre de Jean à Jérusalem," *NovT* 11 (1969): 225–32; Albert A. Bell, Jr., "The Date of John's Apocalypse: The Evidence of Some Roman Historians Reconsidered," *NTS* 25 (Oct. 1978): 93–102. Others suggest that he wrote in Domitian's time, but like other writers of apocalypses antedated his work (to Vespasian's; Feuillet, *Apocalypse*, 93).

53. For the imminent destruction of Jerusalem here, see, e.g., Brooke Foss Westcott, *The Gospel According to St. John: The Authorized Version with Introduction and Notes* (Grand Rapids: Eerdmans, 1950, reprint of 1881 ed.), p. lxxxvii.

54. Aune, *Revelation*, 1:lvii-lxx, dates the traditions in the 60s or earlier, but the final edition late in Domitian's or early in Trajan's reign. Claims that Revelation also opposes a

One issue that would have been central in the latter part of Domitian's reign was worship of the emperor. Greeks had long drawn the lines between humans and deities rather thinly.[55] Thus it is not surprising that when Alexander the Great conquered most of the Middle East, he readily adopted the common idea that rulers were gods and accepted the worship of those subjects inclined to grant it.[56] When Rome gained control of the eastern Mediterranean world, they allowed the eastern part of the empire, including the prosperous cities of Asia Minor, to show loyalty to the Roman state by worshiping the emperor.[57] Ancient sanctuaries used for the worship of other deities often honored the emperor as well.[58]

Most Romans themselves were far more restrained; they recognized that the emperor was a mortal and could be made a god only after death (an act that required senate approval).[59] To claim deity while still alive in Rome itself was considered an act of hubris, of supreme arrogance, and usually resulted in the cursing of the emperor's name after death. Gaius Caligula, Nero, and Domitian were the only emperors in the first century to demand worship while alive; consequently, they were the only emperors who reigned more than a few months to whom the state denied the privilege of being called a god after death.[60]

In the eastern Mediterranean, however, most peoples showed their loyalty to Rome by worshiping not only the goddess Roma (Rome) but also the emperor. Different Asian cities had competed for the honor of hosting emperor temples, with Ephesus and then Smyrna as the principal sites of such cults. All seven cities of Asia Minor whose churches are directly

---

proto-Gnosticism by reinvigorating eschatology (Elisabeth Schüssler Fiorenza, "Apocalyptic and Gnosis in the Book of Revelation," *JBL* 92 [Dec. 1973]: 565–81 [p. 581]) are possible but lack much evidence.

55. Cf., e.g., Homer, *Iliad* 2.407; 7.47; *Od.* 3.110; 17.3, 54, 391; Sophocles, *Oed. Rex.* 298; Euripides, *Andromache* 1253–58.

56. E.g., Arrian, *Alex.* 4.10.5–7; 7.29.3; for his successors, e.g., *P. Petr.* 3.43, col. 3.11–12.

57. People even swore by the emperor (*CIL*, 2.1963; Apuleius, *Metam.* 9.42; by a Jew in *CPJ* 2:213–14, §427); oaths of loyalty to the emperor were common (e.g., *CIG*, 3.137; *CIL*, 2.172) but resisted by Christians (see B. F. Harris, "Oaths of Allegiance to Caesar," *Prudentia* 14 [1982]: 109–22). On divine honors for the emperor, see sources in Jane F. Gardner, *Leadership and the Cult of Personality* (London: J. M. Dent, 1974), 117–24.

58. Cf. Pausanius, 1.40.1; 3.11.5.

59. E.g., Herodian, 4.2.1, 11. On the Roman ideal in theory limiting imperial claims, cf. A. Wallace-Hadrill, "Civilis Princeps: Between Citizen and King," *JRS* 72 (1982): 32–48; for Greek limitations, see S. R. F. Price, "Gods and Emperors: The Greek Language of the Roman Imperial Cult," *JHS* 104 (1984): 79–95.

60. On avoidance of this act of *hubris* in the west, see *P. Lond.* 1912.48–51; Tacitus, *Ann.* 4.38; for similar attitudes even among Greeks, see Sophocles, *Ajax* 758–79; Arrian, *Alex.* 4.11.1–9; 4.12.1. For posthumous execration, see Dio Cassius, 60.4.5–6; Herodian, 1.15.1.

addressed in Revelation were exposed to the imperial cult.[61] Increasingly as Domitian's reign went on, people were calling Domitian "master" and "god" (Dio Cassius, 67.13.4).[62] Domitian also became a tyrant who repressed a number of minority groups he saw as potentially threatening, including Roman Jews, philosophers, and astrologers.[63]

Everyone in Asia understood that Jews were exempt from explicitly worshiping the emperor because they worshiped only one God.[64] This unofficial exemption probably protected some Jewish Christians from being invited to participate in popular pagan religion. In Roman Asia, however, many Jews had become upwardly mobile and more accepted into mainstream society than elsewhere; they were welcomed more than in Alexandria and even Rome. They knew that they had much to lose from prophetic movements claiming to follow another king than Caesar; like Jews throughout the empire, they had to pay a special tax because of the revolt of Judean Jews in A.D. 66.[65]

Furthermore, after the destruction of Jerusalem in A.D. 70, many Palestinian Jews who mistrusted Jewish Christianity undoubtedly settled in Asia Minor, exacerbating tensions that already existed there (Acts 19:9, 33–34; 21:27–29).[66] Probably for these and other reasons, Jewish Christians became unwelcome in some prominent synagogue communities of Asia Minor at the end of the first century (2:9; 3:9).[67] Christians claimed to be religiously Jewish, representing the true faith of ancient Israel; thus they should profit

---

61. See Yamauchi, *The Archaeology of New Testament Cities*, 57, 66, 83–85; Ramsay, *Letters to the Seven Churches*, 231–32, 283, 366–67, 410; Aune, *Revelation*, 2:775–79. For Ephesus in particular, see Sjef van Tilborg, *Reading John in Ephesus*, NovTSup 83 (Leiden: Brill, 1996), 40–47, 174–212; R. Oster, "Christianity and Emperor Veneration in Ephesus: Iconography of a Conflict," *Restoration Quarterly* 25 (1982): 143–49.

62. The title "lord" also applied to earlier emperors, including Augustus and Nero; see G. Adolf Deissmann, *Light From the Ancient Past* (Grand Rapids: Eerdmans, repr. 1978), 351–55 (against Arthur Darby Nock, *Early Gentile Christianity and Its Hellenistic Background* [New York: Harper & Row, 1964], 34; Dio Cassius shows that this is not simply an Egyptian custom). This contrasts starkly with the title applied to Christ (Oscar Cullmann, *The Christology of the New Testament* [Philadelphia: Westminster, 1959], 228).

63. E.g., Suetonius, *Dom.* 12; Aulus Gellius, 15.11.3–5; Philostratus, *V.A.* 7–8; cf. M. H. Williams, "Domitian, the Jews and the 'Judaizers'—A Simple Matter of Cupiditas and Maiestas?" *Historia* 39 (1990): 196–211; *Sifre Deut.* 344.3.2; Sib. Oracles 5.39–46.

64. Rome required of them other forms of respect; see Alfredo Mordechai Rabello, "The Legal Condition of the Jews in the Roman Empire," *ANRW* (1980) 10.13.662–762 (pp. 703–4).

65. E.g., *CPJ*, 2:125–28, §§183–93.

66. Other evidence, such as a Smyrnean inscription, demonstrate that Judean immigration to Asia continued in the second century A.D. (*IGR* 4.1431.29 in Aune, *Revelation*, 1:164).

67. For conflict in second century and later sources, see, e.g., R. T. Herford, *Christianity in Talmud and Midrash* (Clifton, N.J.: Reference Book, 1966), 221–26, 282–85.

---

from the toleration Rome accorded local Jewish communities. Once Christians proved unable to persuade the authorities that they were Jewish, however—once the synagogues expelled them—they risked suppression and even death at the hands of the authorities.[68]

In the early second century, when Trajan was emperor, a relatively new governor of Bithynia in Asia found pagan temples being forsaken because of massive conversions to faith in Christ. This governor tortured Christians for information and offered to release them if they would simply worship Caesar's image; but finding them too "arrogant" to worship Caesar, he ordered them executed (Pliny, *Ep*. 10.96). From his correspondence with Trajan we gather that the practice of arresting Christians outside Rome did not start with Trajan; more than likely it started some time earlier, probably during the reign of Domitian.[69] In the early second century, the state demanded that Christians call Caesar "Lord" and offer sacrifice if they wished to be released (Mart. Poly. 8). Thus the Christians faced a crisis that recalled crises faced by Jews in the times of Daniel and Antiochus IV Epiphanes: One dare not render to Caesar what was God's alone.[70]

Traditionally scholars have viewed Revelation as addressing oppressed Christians facing persecution from the mighty Roman state. Today many emphasize instead that the book addressed "complacent, spiritually anemic Christians."[71] In fact, when one examines the letters to the seven churches one finds both situations coexisting in different places. Revelation speaks to churches both alive and dead, but more of the churches are in danger of compromising with the world than of dying from it. This makes the book relevant to North American Christianity today.

---

68. For potential troubles created by the clash of the church and imperial cult in this period, see, e.g., F. C. J. D. Cuss, *Imperial Cult and Honorary Terms in the New Testament* (Fribourg: Fribourg Univ. Press, 1974); S. R. F. Price, "Between Man and God: Sacrifice in the Roman Imperial Cult," *JRS* 70 (1980): 28–43.

69. See Tertullian, *Apol*. 5.4. For Domitian's claims to deity, see, e.g., Suetonius, *Dom*. 12; Dio Cassius, 67.13.4. For genuine persecution (whether official or unofficial) under Domitian, see Hemer, *Letters to the Seven Churches*, 7–11; W. M. Ramsay, *The Church in the Roman Empire Before A.D. 170* (New York: G. P. Putnam, 1893), 196–213; rabbinic texts also suggest Roman persecution of Christians. Others think that it reflects merely sporadic persecution (Adela Yarbro Collins, "Dating the Apocalypse of John," *Biblical Research* 26 [1981]: 33–45); in any case, Revelation reflects some suffering (e.g., 2:13) and expectation of more.

70. For the motif of challenge from an empire's suppression of local religions, see, e.g., Dan. 3:1–18; Judith 3:8; 2 Macc. 11:23. Eastern rulers also demanded reverence (Philostratus, *V.A.* 1.27–28).

71. Talbert, *Apocalypse*, 25. Beale, *Revelation*, 28–33, allows both, but sees compromise as the primary threat.

Message of Revelation

APPLICATION, BY ITS very nature, is most often contextual—adapted for a specific culture, church (in preaching), or individual (often in personal devotions). For that reason, most applications in this commentary are samples of the sorts of applications we can draw. While I have tried to draw examples from a range of cultures that would remain relevant for the majority of the commentary's likely audience, my own background in some parts of North American evangelicalism, African-American churches, messianic Jewish circles, and elsewhere does not cover every conceivable base for application. I do trust, however, that readers will find useful models for drawing analogies between issues the biblical text addresses and today's issues.

At the same time, however, Revelation addresses many issues that have not changed because human nature and God's character have remained constant. It is these themes on which we focus in this section. Happily, these themes arise repeatedly throughout Revelation. Because the book was delivered as an entire book and, apart from the letters to the seven churches in some sense, not intended to be read or preached piecemeal, it is important that every time we read, teach, or preach any passage in Revelation, we do so in light of the themes of the entire book the passage reflects.

I have done my best to honor the text and develop my views on the basis of the text rather than the reverse; my current views differ considerably from what I was originally taught. At the same time, I want to emphasize that when I cite other scholarly positions, it is out of respect and a desire to dialogue with them. I doubt, for example, that most readers would classify me as a dispensationalist (though one of my progressive dispensationalist friends has drawn dispensational boundaries so widely that he tells me I might qualify as an honorary dispensationalist!). But it would be unfair to any evangelical position to simply ignore their views, so I cite them both when I disagree and when I can learn from them. But despite different views among various scholars on fine points of end-times events, all readers can agree on the most important issues in Revelation. Scholars of various persuasions will also share many of my exegetical convictions on various passages.

When we think of Revelation today, many of us think of debates on fine points of end-times events, but these details are hardly the primary message of Revelation. In fact, on some matters of detail, it is possible that most of us will be surprised. After showing how God regularly surprised his people by the way he fulfilled both Old and New Testament prophecies, one writer inquires, "Is it not possible that God could fulfil some of his predictions in ways that humans have not yet conceived?"[72]

---

72. Lewis, *Questions*, 133; see also 89.

A few of John's revelations were not even meant to be understood in our time (10:4), though most of them were so intended on the points that matter most (22:10). Neither in the New Testament nor among early Christian confessions of faith do end-time details appear as part of a confession of faith; detailed end-time views do not constitute a test of Christian orthodoxy. The only "consensus among conservative Christians [is] that the personal, literal and visible second coming of Jesus belongs in the essential core of doctrine, but beyond that the consensus breaks down."[73]

But as Billy Graham points out, rather than getting lost in the smaller brushstrokes, debating all the details, we need to step back and catch the majesty of the book's "grand design."[74] We can acknowledge ambiguities and uncertainties and even differ from other Christians on some larger end-time scenarios, such as the nature of the Millennium; but the most important applications to our lives today are usually clear. In discussing New Testament teaching about Jesus' return, can we miss the summons to holiness in readiness for Christ's return, one of the most pervasive Second-Coming themes in the New Testament (Mark 13:33–37; 1 Thess. 3:13; 5:6–7, 23; Titus 2:12–13; 1 Peter 1:7; 2 Peter 3:14; 1 John 2:28–3:3)?

What then is Revelation's message? We mention several points below, though we develop most of them later in the commentary on specific passages.

- That God is awesomely majestic, as well as sovereign in our troubles
- That Jesus' sacrifice as the Lamb ultimately brings complete deliverance for those who trust him
- That God's judgments on the world are often to serve notice on the world that God will avenge his people
- That regardless of how things appear in the short run, "sin does not go unpunished," and God will judge[75]
- That God can accomplish his purposes through a small and persecuted remnant; he is not dependent on what the world values as power
- That worship leads us from grief over our sufferings to God's eternal purposes seen from a heavenly perspective
- That proclaiming Christ invites persecution, the normal state of committed believers in this age
- That Christ is worth dying for
- That a radical contrast exists between God's kingdom (exemplified in the bride, the new Jerusalem) and the world's values (exemplified in the prostitute, Babylon)

---

73. Ibid., 129–30.
74. Graham, *Approaching Hoofbeats*, 19–20.
75. As noted in ibid., 23.

- That the hope God has prepared for us far exceeds our present sufferings
- That God's plan and church ultimately include representatives of all peoples

Revelation also proclaims Christ's Lordship more explicitly and frequently than some parts of the New Testament; under normal circumstances we confront opposition not by softening our witness for Christ but by testifying more boldly. Certainly Revelation, while distinguishing the Father from the Lamb, attributes to Jesus full deity—language common shortly after its writing (Pliny, *Ep.* 10.96; Ignatius, *Rom.* 3; Justin, *First Apol.* 67; *Second Apol.* 13). Revelation repeatedly invokes Old Testament passages about God and applies them to Jesus (Dan. 7:9 in 1:14; Isa. 2:19 and Hos. 10:8 in 6:15–17; Isa. 49:10 in 7:17; Deut. 10:17 in 17:14 and 19:16; Isa. 63:2 in 19:13; Isa. 60:19–20 in 21:23).

Other titles or expressions applied to Jesus were applied to deity in surrounding cultures (e.g., 2:18), and titles of God in Judaism, such as "Living One," apply to Jesus (1:18). Jesus performs divine functions; whereas in the Old Testament "This is what the LORD says" often introduces prophecies, in Revelation it is Jesus who inspires prophecy by the Spirit (2:1, 8, 12, 18; 3:1, 7, 14). John's Jewish contemporaries attributed the keys of the realm of the dead to God alone (Wisd. Sol. 16:13); Revelation attributes them to Jesus (Rev. 1:18). In contrast to contemporary Jewish expectations, Jesus receives doxologies (1:5–6) and full worship (5:8–14) and is invoked in blessings on readers (1:4–5).

Revelation's application of divine titles to Jesus may be most explicit when it calls Jesus "the First and the Last" (1:17; 2:8; 22:12–13), a title applicable only to God according to Isaiah (Isa. 41:4; 44:6; 48:12), and exactly equivalent in sense to "the Alpha and the Omega," which is applied to the Father in Revelation (1:8; 21:5–7; Jesus in 22:13). For his audience, John's Christology was also eminently practical: Revelation was written to assure pressed believers that "their victory was not in doubt; Jesus, not Caesar, had been invested by the Almighty with the sovereignty of the world."[76]

But Revelation's most distinctive contribution to the New Testament is one that many of us find uncomfortable, especially when we find full satisfaction in this world. Revelation provides a better hope for a church enamored with this age or despairing of the next: "It is only in that interval of the already and the not yet that hope is situated, in what can be experienced as the silence

---

76. Bruce, *New Testament Documents*, 11; cf. idem, *The Message of the New Testament* (Grand Rapids: Eerdmans, 1981), 86–87; Vincent Taylor, *The Atonement in New Testament Teaching* (London: Epworth, 1945), 34.

of God, or dryness, when it seems difficult to continue to believe."[77] Revelation reminds us that we do not belong to this world and must not be seduced by what it values. John's Revelation calls for persecuted churches to remain vigilant (2:10; 3:11) and other churches to resist compromise with the spirit of their age (2:16, 25; 3:3, 18–20).[78]

---

77. Ellul, *Apocalypse*, 58.
78. Many scholars have sought to understand and articulate Revelation's relevance; see examples in Wainwright, *Mysterious Apocalypse*, 161–222.

Outline

I. **Introduction** (1:1–3:22)
   A. Title and Blessing (1:1–3)
   B. Epistolary Introduction (1:4–8)
   C. Narrative Introduction (1:9–20)
      1. Setting (1:9–11)
      2. Vision of the Son of Man (1:12–16)
      3. Jesus' Message (1:17–20)
   D. Letters to the Seven Churches (2:1–3:22)
      1. Ephesus: Lost Love (2:1–7)
      2. Smyrna: Suffering Saints (2:8–11)
      3. Pergamum: Fornicating Faction (2:12–17)
      4. Thyatira: Compromising Christians (2:18–27)
      5. Sardis: Sinful Slumber (3:1–6)
      6. Philadelphia: Persevering Pillars (3:7–13)
      7. Laodicea: Prosperous Paupers (3:14–22)

II. **Visions of the Heavenly Temple** (4:1–5:14)
   A. Worship in Heaven (4:1–11)
   B. Worthy to Open the Book (5:1–7)
   C. In Praise of the Lamb (5:8–14)

III. **The Seals** (6:1–8:1)
   A. The Horse Riders (6:1–8)
      1. Conquest (6:1–2)
      2. War (6:3–4)
      3. Famine (6:5–6)
      4. Death by Various Means (6:7–8)
   B. Martyrdom and Doomsday (6:9–17)
      1. Martyred for Their Good News (6:9–11)
      2. Cosmic Dissolution (6:12–17)
   C. Interlude: Saints on Earth and in Heaven (7:1–17)
      1. God's End-Time Army (7:1–8)
      2. The Multicultural Multitude of Martyrs (7:9–17)
   D. The Seventh Seal (8:1)

IV. **The Trumpets** (8:2–11:19)
   A. Prayers as the Preface of Judgment (8:2–6)
   B. First Four Plagues (8:7–13)

Annotated Bibliography

Commentaries

Aune, David E. *Revelation.* 3 vols. Word Biblical Commentary 52a–c. Dallas: Word, 1997–1998. The most thorough examination of Greco-Roman parallels to images and concepts in Revelation, and, with Beale, the most up-to-date and thorough Revelation commentary.

Beale, Gregory K. *The Book of Revelation: A Commentary on the Greek Text.* Grand Rapids: Eerdmans, 1999. Including a massive amount of information in a single volume, this will prove the most useful Revelation commentary for many readers; with Aune, this is the most up-to-date and thorough Revelation commentary to date (though released too recently for discussion in this commentary as fully as it merits).

Beasley-Murray, G. R. *The Book of Revelation.* The New Century Bible. Greenwood, S.C.: Attic; London: Marshall, Morgan & Scott, 1974. One of the most thorough and useful commentaries on Revelation, providing detailed discussion of the background and various views on each passage.

Boring, M. Eugene. *Revelation.* Interpretation. Louisville: John Knox, 1989. This work is thorough and nuanced in explaining interpretive methods, as well as concerned with application from a mainline Protestant perspective.

Bowman, John Wick. *The First Christian Drama: The Book of Revelation.* Philadelphia: Westminster, 1968. This is a popular-level, readable, conservative, amillennial work, which views the Tribulation as the entire course of history from the first to the second coming.

Caird, G. B. *A Commentary on the Revelation of Saint John the Divine.* Harper's New Testament Commentaries. New York: Harper & Row, 1966. Like Beasley-Murray above, one of the most thorough and useful commentaries on Revelation, providing detailed discussion of the background and various views on each passage.

Corsini, Eugenio. *The Apocalypse: The Perennial Revelation of Jesus Christ.* Translated and edited by Francis J. Moloney. Good News Studies 5. Wilmington, Del.: Michael Glazier, 1983. Despite some good insights, this work forces Revelation's images into a salvation-historical interpretation they cannot naturally fit.

Ellul, Jacques. *Apocalypse: The Book of Revelation.* Translated by George W. Schreiner. New York: Seabury, 1977.

Feuillet, André. *The Apocalypse.* Staten Island, N.Y.: Alba House, 1965. This book is especially helpful for its breadth of bibliographic work up to its time.

Fiorenza, Elisabeth Schüssler. *The Book of Revelation: Justice and Judgment.* Philadelphia: Fortress, 1985. This work provides numerous exegetical insights and is concerned with some liberationist themes and applications in the book.

Ford, J. Massyngberde. *Revelation.* Anchor Bible 38. Garden City, N.Y.: Doubleday, 1975. Despite some eccentricities (especially her view that much of the work stems from prophecies of John the Baptist), this work provides much helpful background, especially from Jewish sources.

González, Catherine Gunsalus, and Justo L. González. *Revelation.* Westminster Bible Companion. Louisville, K.Y.: Westminster/John Knox, 1997.

Johnson, Alan F. *Revelation.* The Expositor's Bible Commentary. Grand Rapids: Zondervan, 1996. Evangelical, premillennial.

Lindsey, Hal. *There's a New World Coming: A Prophetic Odyssey.* Santa Ana, Calif.: Vision House, 1973. A popular-level reading of Revelation's symbols in the light of modern events, from a dispensational perspective. Lindsey has since revised some of his assessments (such as the suspicion that Christ would come within 40 years of 1948), but many progressive dispensationalists view his work as eccentric and not mainstream dispensationalism.

Metzger, Bruce M. *Breaking the Code: Understanding the Book of Revelation.* Nashville: Abingdon, 1993. A useful, readable work by a top biblical scholar; much less documented than Talbert.

Michaels, J. Ramsey. *Revelation.* The IVP New Testament Commentary Series. Downers Grove, Ill.: InterVarsity, 1997. An popular-level, application-oriented commentary by a senior evangelical New Testament scholar.

Moffatt, James. "Revelation." Pages 281–494 in vol. 5, *The Expositor's Greek Testament.* Edited W. Robertson Nicoll. Reprint ed.: Grand Rapids: Eerdmans, 1979. Although written early in the twentieth century, this commentary remains a valuable resource because of Moffatt's excellent command of the historical sources and critical evaluation of scholarly options available in his day.

Mounce, Robert H. *The Book of Revelation.* The New International Commentary on the New Testament. Grand Rapids: Eerdmans, 1977. A thoughtful, well-researched and well-documented commentary on Revelation, among the most useful.

Richard, Pablo. *Apocalypse: A People's Commentary on the Book of Revelation.* The Bible & Liberation Series. Maryknoll, N.Y.: Orbis, 1995.

Roloff, Jürgen. *The Revelation of John: A Continental Commentary.* Translated John E. Alsup. Minneapolis: Fortress, 1993.

Ryrie, Charles Caldwell. *Revelation.* Chicago: Moody, 1968. A popular-level commentary from a traditional dispensational perspective.

Talbert, Charles H. *The Apocalypse: A Reading of the Revelation of John.* Louisville, Ky.: Westminster/John Knox, 1994. A literary reading of Revelation concerned with contemporary praxis as well as exegesis. One of the most useful works on a fairly popular level, it is written by a scholar conversant with the book's background. In contrast to many commentaries (which often recycle earlier discussions), Talbert also offers a fresh reading of primary sources.

Tenney, Merrill C. *Interpreting Revelation.* Grand Rapids: Eerdmans, 1957.

Walvoord, John F. *The Revelation of Jesus Christ: A Commentary.* Chicago: Moody, 1966. One of the more thorough commentaries from the older dispensational perspective.

Wesley, John. *Commentary on the Bible: A One-Volume Condensation of His Explanatory Notes.* Edited G. Roger Schoenhals. Grand Rapids: Zondervan, 1990.

Special Studies

Aune, David Edward. *The New Testament in Its Literary Environment.* Library of Early Christianity 8. Philadelphia: Westminster, 1987. This work (which covers each genre in the New Testament) is important for explaining the kind of work Revelation is, hence how to interpret it.

_____. *Prophecy in Early Christianity and the Ancient Mediterranean World.* Grand Rapids: Eerdmans, 1983. This work provides insight into how ancient Mediterranean peoples understood prophecies. Aune's (apparently forthcoming) work on Revelation will also prove invaluable.

Bauckham, Richard. *The Climax of Prophecy: Studies on the Book of Revelation.* Edinburgh: T. & T. Clark, 1993. One of the most thorough and insightful resources on Revelation available for academic study. As far as providing fresh insights, it constitutes one of the most useful resources of the 1990s.

Beale, G. K. "The Use of Daniel in the Synoptic Eschatological Discourse and in the Book of Revelation." Pages 129–53 in vol. 5, *Gospel Perspectives.* Edited by R. T. France, David Wenham, and Craig Blomberg. Sheffield: JSOT, 1980–1986. (Vol. 5: *The Jesus Tradition Outside the Gospels.* Edited by David Wenham. Sheffield: JSOT, 1984.)

Bock, Darrell L., editor. *Three Views on the Millennium and Beyond.* Grand Rapids: Zondervan, 1999.

Bruce, F. F. "The Spirit in the Apocalypse." Pages 333–44 in *Christ and Spirit in the New Testament: Studies in Honour of C. F. D. Moule.* Edited by Barnabas Lindars and Stephen S. Smalley. Cambridge: Cambridge Univ. Press, 1973.

Charlesworth, James H., editor. *The Old Testament Pseudepigrapha.* 2 vols. Garden City, N.Y.: Doubleday, 1983–1985. After the Old Testament itself and along with the Dead Sea Scrolls, this is probably the most important source for understanding Revelation's images; of greatest value (roughly in order of significance) are 1 Enoch; 4 Ezra; 2 Baruch; Sibylline Oracles.

Collins, Adela Yarbro. *Crisis and Catharsis: The Power of the Apocalypse.* Philadelphia: Westminster, 1984. A literary critical discussion of the function of some of the apocalyptic language of Revelation.

Fekkes, Jan. *Isaiah and Prophetic Traditions in the Book of Revelation: Visionary Antecedents and Their Development.* JSNTSup 93. Sheffield: Sheffield Academic, 1994.

George, David C., ed. *Revelation: Three Viewpoints.* Nashville: Broadman, 1977. This work provides some different views and insights on Revelation from Southern Baptist scholars.

Graham, Billy. *Approaching Hoofbeats: The Four Horsemen of the Apocalypse.* Waco, Tex.: Word, 1983. Avoiding the more controversial eschatological issues, this work focuses on the contemporary application of Revelation's dramatic images.

Guthrie, Donald. *The Relevance of John's Apocalypse.* Grand Rapids: Eerdmans, 1987.

Hanfmann, George M. A., editor. *Sardis From Prehistoric to Roman Times: Results of the Archaeological Exploration of Sardis 1958–1975.* Assisted by William E. Mierse. Cambridge, Mass.: Harvard Univ. Press, 1983.

Hemer, Colin J. *The Letters to the Seven Churches of Asia in Their Local Setting.* JSNTSup 11. Sheffield: University of Sheffield, 1986. Updating (though often following the same contours as) Ramsay's work, this work includes a heavy use of inscriptions and numismatic evidence.

Hill, David. *New Testament Prophecy.* New Foundations Theological Library. Atlanta: John Knox, 1979.

Keener, Craig S. *The IVP Bible Background Commentary: New Testament.* Downers Grove, Ill.: InterVarsity, 1993. The Revelation section of this work focuses almost exclusively on cultural and historical details relevant for interpreting Revelation; written on a popular level.

Kraabel, Alf Thomas. "Judaism in Western Asia Minor Under the Roman Empire, With a Preliminary Study of the Jewish Community at Sardis, Lydia." Th.D. diss.; Cambridge, Mass.: Harvard Divinity School, 1968.

Kraybill, J. Nelson. *Imperial Cult and Commerce in John's Apocalypse.* JSNTSup 132. Sheffield: Sheffield Academic, 1996. This is a thoroughly researched work, well-documented, up-to-date on the latest archaeological and epigraphic sources and providing a genuinely fresh perspective. This work is indispensable for Revelation scholarship.

Kyle, Richard. *The Last Days Are Here Again: A History of the End Times.* Grand Rapids: Baker, 1998. Details the intriguing history of end-time speculation, including failed predictions from the second century through the end of the twentieth century. Both readable and accessible; of several good books related to this subject, this is the most recent and one of the broadest in its scope.

Ladd, George Eldon. *The Last Things*. Grand Rapids: Eerdmans, 1978. A respected evangelical scholar provides many insights about the end times and the interim state from a historic premillennial perspective.

Lewis, Daniel J. *3 Crucial Questions About the Last Days*. Grand Rapids: Baker, 1998. This work measures the various theological frameworks for interpreting Revelation against their Old Testament context.

Michaels, J. Ramsey. *Interpreting the Book of Revelation*. Grand Rapids: Baker, 1992. This work provides and concretely illustrates some basic principles for interpreting the book.

Morrice, W. G. "John the Seer: Narrative Exegesis of the Book of Revelation." *Expository Times* 97 (Nov. 1985): 43–46. Written in the first-person as if by John the seer, this article communicates the major features of Revelation in a lively manner and provides an extremely useful resource for teaching the book to students or laypersons.

Moyise, Steve. *The Old Testament in the Book of Revelation*. JSNTSup 115. Sheffield: Sheffield Academic, 1995.

Newton, Sir Isaac. *Observations Upon the Prophecies of Daniel and the Apocalypse of St. John. In Two Parts*. London: J. Darby and T. Browne, 1733. Helpful for providing historical perspective on an early historicist premillennial view.

Osei-Mensah, Gottfried. *God's Message to the Churches: An Exposition of Revelation 1–3*. Achimota, Ghana: Africa Christian, 1985. An application-oriented exposition of Revelation 1–3 from an African perspective.

Petersen, Rodney L. *Preaching in the Last Days: The Theme of "Two Witnesses" in the Sixteenth and Seventeenth Centuries*. New York: Oxford Univ. Press, 1993.

Peterson, Eugene H. *Reversed Thunder: The Revelation of John and the Praying Imagination*. San Francisco: Harper & Row, 1988. Often poetic application of Revelation's content in the author's well-known, engaging literary style.

Ramsay, William M. *The Letters to the Seven Churches of Asia*. London: Hodder & Stoughton, 1904; reprint: Grand Rapids: Baker, 1979.

Revelation: Its Grand Climax At Hand! New York: Watch Tower Bible & Tract Society, 1988. Circulated by Jehovah's Witnesses; with 19.5 million copies in print in 65 languages, it has been more widely read than any other work in this bibliography. We include it in our discussion as one of several examples of serious misinterpretation of Revelation.

Rissi, Mathias. *The Future of the World: An Exegetical Study of Revelation 19.11–22.15*. Studies in Biblical Theology, 2d ser., 23. Naperville, Ill.: Alec R. Allenson, n.d.; from 1966 German edition.

_____. *Time and History: A Study on the Revelation.* Translated by Gordon C. Winsor. Richmond, Va.: John Knox, 1966.

Shepherd, Massey H., Jr. *The Paschal Liturgy and the Apocalypse.* Ecumenical Studies in Worship 6. Richmond, Va.: John Knox, 1960.

Sproul, R. C. *The Last Days According to Jesus.* Grand Rapids: Baker, 1998. Defending what he terms a moderate preterist approach, Sproul allows for future events such a resurrection of the righteous, but regards much of the New Testament's futuristic prophecy as fulfilled in A.D. 70. (He finds a pre-70 date for Revelation attractive.)

Wainwright, Arthur W. *Mysterious Apocalypse: Interpreting the Book of Revelation.* Nashville: Abingdon, 1993. This work provides historical perspective on the variety of interpretations of Revelation.

Walvoord, John F. *The Prophecy Knowledge Handbook.* Wheaton: Victor, 1990. Biblical prophecy, including from Revelation, from an older dispensational standpoint.

Yamauchi, Edwin M. *The Archaeology of New Testament Cities in Western Asia Minor.* Grand Rapids: Baker, 1980. Includes an updating of some of Ramsay's archaeological data on the seven churches of Asia Minor.

Revelation 1:1–3

❧

T HE REVELATION OF Jesus Christ, which God gave him
to show his servants what must soon take place. He
made it known by sending his angel to his servant
John, ²who testifies to everything he saw—that is, the word of
God and the testimony of Jesus Christ. ³Blessed is the one
who reads the words of this prophecy, and blessed are those
who hear it and take to heart what is written in it, because the
time is near.

THESE OPENING VERSES declare the ultimate
authors of the revelation (God the Father and
Jesus), its subject matter ("what must soon take
place"), its intended audience ("his servant[s]")
and its messengers (the angel of Christ and John). Because the introduction
sets the stage for the rest of the book, we, like many other commentators,
treat Revelation 1 (and to some extent the letters to the seven churches) in
greater detail than much of the rest of the book.

The Revelation of Jesus Christ (1:1a)

THE TITLE AND subject of this book is "the revelation of Jesus Christ." Ancient
writers often included titles on the outside of their scrolls, but by the middle of the second century some scribes began transcribing earlier writings into
codexes, which are essentially the kind of books we use today.[1] Consequently,
titles that often originally appeared on the outside of documents now appear
in our works as the opening line of the document;[2] this is presumably the case
with the Revelation.

A more difficult question, however, is how the word "revelation" relates
to the name "Jesus Christ": Does the entire phrase mean "the revelation about
Jesus Christ" (a Greek construction called an "objective genitive") or "the
revelation from Jesus Christ" (a "subjective genitive"), or both?[3] If it means

---

1. Bowman, *First Christian Drama*, 10. Some argue that the full title subsumes all of 1:1–
3 (Michaels, *Revelation*, 46); Aune, *Revelation*, 1:22, observes that ancient authors frequently
used their first sentence as a title.

2. E.g., *PGM*, 13.343; 36.211–12.

3. In favor of the objective genitive, see, e.g., Corsini, *Apocalypse*, 67–72; for both, see,
e.g., Peterson, *Reversed Thunder*, 26.

---

the former, Jesus will be the subject of the book of Revelation from start to finish; if the latter, then other issues may be central in the book. On the one hand, the former position is accurate theologically—Jesus is certainly the central figure in the book. The book's judgments reflect his Lordship (e.g., 6:1, 16; 8:4–6); resemblances to the plagues in Egypt remind us that Jesus is greater than Moses and greater than the original Passover lamb. The book opens with a direct revelation of Jesus to John (1:13–20) and from the start promises that its climax will be the revelation of Jesus from heaven (1:7; 19:11–16).

On the other hand, the context and the structure of the book, as well as the customary function of both apocalypses and titles, appear to offer stronger support to the latter proposal. The revelation addresses "what must soon take place" (1:1) and is conveyed from the Father to Jesus to an angel to John to the churches; hence, it comes from Jesus. Likewise, the seals, trumpets, and bowls, which fill much of the book, detail impending judgments on the world. This is typical subject matter for apocalyptic writings, although John clearly emphasizes Jesus much more than other apocalypses emphasized any character who might be vaguely compared with him. A "revelation" could focus on the Lord himself (2 Cor. 12:1) or, as we think here, on his message (Rom. 16:25). Finally, book titles often listed the purported author, as in "the book of the words of Tobit" (lit. trans. of Tobit 1:1); or "the word of the LORD that came to Hosea" (Hos. 1:1). Jesus Christ is the author, not merely the subject; he revealed his message through his angel to John.

In the final analysis, however, the original, Greek-speaking audience of the book may not have worked as hard as we do to differentiate the two concepts (the grammar itself does not clarify any difference). The message is from Jesus Christ, but ultimately Jesus is the focus of everything in the New Testament, whether directly or indirectly. His purposes in history also reveal his character and invite us to worship him.

The Agents of Revelation (1:1b–2)

JOHN AND THE angel. Authors of most traditional Jewish apocalypses used pseudonyms borrowed from famous ancient servants of God, perhaps because many of their contemporaries believed that prophecy was no longer as active in their own day. By contrast, John seeks no famous name from earlier centuries, instead openly stating his identity.[4] That he does not need to qualify which John he is may suggest that he is the most obvious John among the

---

4. So, e.g., Leon Morris, *Apocalyptic* (Grand Rapids: Eerdmans, 1972), 52; M. A. Knibb, *The First and Second Books of Esdras* (Cambridge: Cambridge Univ. Press, 1979), 106–7; Hill, *New Testament Prophecy*, 72.

early Christians, namely, John the apostle, son of Zebedee, who had personally known Jesus in the flesh (cf. John 21:22).[5] Until the mid-third-century writer Dionysius, the external evidence for Revelation among orthodox Christians is unanimous, and even detractors admit that this evidence is some of the best available for any New Testament work.[6]

Though he is an apostle, however, he does not identify himself in terms of his authority over the churches; rather he identifies himself as a "servant of God," a title often applied to the Old Testament prophets (cf. Jer. 29:19; 35:15). This title can reflect honor as well as submission: In the ancient world the servant of a powerful master like Caesar might hold more prestige than even a Roman aristocrat.[7] But John does not exalt himself; as a servant of the Lord Christ, he writes to his fellow servants (1:1), his companions in suffering for Jesus (1:9). Likewise, in contrast to a few apocalyptic seers like one who identifies himself as "Ezra" (4 Ezra 10:38–39; 13:53–56), John does not attribute his revelation to any special merit of his own.

As in 1:1 and elsewhere (10:9; 17:1, 7; 21:9; 22:6, 8, 16), apocalyptic literature often reports God's sending revelations through angels;[8] this is not surprising, since God had sent some revelations this way in the Bible (Dan. 9:21–22; Zech. 1:9, 14, 19; 2:3; 4:1, 4–5; 5:5, 10; 6:4–5). In ancient Jewish apocalypses, angels sometimes accompanied the person receiving the visions, providing oral explanations of the strange sights the person would receive in heaven.[9]

John's testimony. John testifies "to everything he saw," which was "the word of God and the testimony of Jesus Christ" (1:2). These titles are not surprising; the Old Testament employed the phrase "God's word" not only for

5. Some doubt that one of the Twelve would have written Rev. 21:14 (e.g., Michaels, *Revelation*, 19), but John there writes of the Twelve as a group in a manner already well established in apostolic tradition, e.g., Eph. 2:20; see Feuillet, *Apocalypse*, 107–8. John does not identify himself as an apostle, but sometimes Paul also does not (Phil. 1:1; 1 Thess. 1:1; 2 Thess. 1:1; Philem. 1).

6. See the summary in Mounce, *Revelation*, 27–28. For fuller evidence for Johannine authorship (yet recognizing the problems in the evidence), see Donald Guthrie, *New Testament Introduction*, 4th rev. ed. (Downers Grove, Ill.: InterVarsity, 1990), 932–48; D. A. Carson, Douglas J. Moo, and Leon Morris, *An Introduction to the New Testament* (Grand Rapids: Zondervan, 1992), 468–73. But even some evangelical scholars remain unsure which John is in view (Aune, *Revelation*, 1:xlvii–lvi; Beale, *Revelation*, 34–36).

7. Epictetus, *Disc.* 1.19.19; 4.7.23; see further comments in Dale B. Martin, *Slavery As Salvation* (New Haven: Yale Univ. Press, 1990), 49, 55–56.

8. E.g., 1 Enoch 1:2; 72:1; 74:2; 75:3; Jub. 1:27; 2:1; 32:21; 4 Ezra 4:1; 3 Bar. 1:8; 5:1; 6:1; also later Gnostic texts in *TNHL*, 308–28, 453. Cf., e.g., James C. VanderKam, "The Putative Author of the Book of Jubilees," *JSS* 26 (Autumn 1981): 209–17 (p. 217).

9. Ford, *Revelation*, 373–74.

the written law but also for God's revelation through his prophets (1 Sam. 3:1, 7). That the message is also called Jesus' "testimony" means either John's testimony *about* Jesus (19:10) or that Jesus himself (1:5; 22:20) testified of his message through his angel to John, who in turn testifies to others. "Testify" is often courtroom language—appropriate for John and other early Christians, who would face law courts (cf. 1:9; John 16:2); Roman law always permitted the accused to speak in his defense, and Christians could use their hearings as an opportunity to proclaim Christ regardless of the consequences (Mark 13:9). The language could, however, refer more broadly to any kind of public attestation. In time the term for "testify" (*martyreo*) even began to take on the meaning "martyr"; but while witness often invited martyrdom, it is unlikely that the term itself implied this as early as the book of Revelation.[10]

Those Who Read and Hear (1:3)

BEFORE PRINTING PRESSES were available, well-to-do people often "published" works especially in public readings, perhaps most often at banquets.[11] But that the book of Revelation was read in churches alongside Old Testament Scripture suggests that the early Christians began treating it as Scripture then or soon afterward (cf. also 22:18–19).[12] That one person would read the work ("blessed is the one who reads") and the whole congregation would hear it ("blessed are those who hear it") fits what we know of the time; even in urban areas, many people could not read much.

"Blessed are" is the familiar ancient literary form "beatitude," which is especially prominent in the Hebrew Bible and Jewish texts (e.g., Ps. 1:1; Prov. 8:34).[13] The "blessing" form itself is general, but the context specifies the blessings of the end (Rev. 21–22) for which only the listener will be prepared ("the time is near," 1:3). In biblical idiom, "hearing" also often meant "heeding," i.e., obedience (e.g., the Hebrew of Gen. 26:5; 27:8), but John allows no ambiguity, adding "take to heart" (lit., "keep"); one used this language for

---

10. Other apocalyptic writers also "testified" of what they saw (e.g., 1 Enoch 104:11), and early Christians regularly "testified," or "bore witness," to what God had revealed to them (e.g., John 15:27; Acts 1:8). For the "witness" theme in Revelation, see Allison A. Trites, *The New Testament Concept of Witness*, SNTSM 31 (Cambridge: Cambridge Univ. Press, 1977), 154–74.

11. E.g., Richard A. Burridge, *Four Gospels, One Jesus?* (Grand Rapids: Eerdmans, 1994), 20; Aune, *The New Testament in Its Literary Environment*, 171. Wayne A. Meeks, *The Moral World of the First Christians*, LEC 6 (Philadelphia: Westminster, 1986), 62, estimates a 10 percent literacy rate, though we may suppose moderate reading literacy somewhat higher in the cities.

12. See Caird, *Commentary on Revelation*, 287.

13. See further Craig Keener, *A Commentary on the Gospel of Matthew* (Grand Rapids: Eerdmans, 1999), 165–66.

observing commandments. Though Revelation is not a collection of laws, its message provides us demands no less serious (Rev. 12:17; 14:12; 22:7).

HOW DOES ONE apply a statement of authorship like "his servant John, who testifies to everything he saw" (1:1–2)? Two ways are possible, though the second may yield more profit than the first.

Identification. One way some readers approach texts like 1:1 is to identify personally with John's calling and to contemplate what God has called them to do. Other readers object to this approach. After all, they respond, God does not reveal himself today the way he revealed himself to John. This objection relies on a disputed premise; most Christians today believe that God continues to speak and guide his church by the Spirit, and many believe in dramatic, supernatural revelations.[14] Nevertheless, the objection does have some force in a more general sense: The vast majority of Christians agree that the "canon" of Scripture—the measure by which we evaluate all other revelation—is closed. Most of us believe that God still speaks, but most doubt that this requires an additional revelation so forceful as the book of Revelation today!

There is a difference, however, between claiming that our situation is the same as John's and drawing an analogy between his situation and our own. (If we could not apply biblical principles by drawing analogies, much of the Bible could no longer speak to our contemporary situation.) Identifying with John's calling does not violate the spirit of the text; John receives exactly the same title as other believers—a "servant" of Jesus Christ, which is precisely what this passage calls all other Christians (1:1). John himself recognizes that he is a sharer in the experiences of the rest of Jesus' followers (1:9), and that all believers must share the same prophetic Spirit in proclaiming the gospel of Jesus Christ (19:10). In other words, John's receptivity to the Spirit, humility as God's servant, and obedience in speaking a less-than-popular message do provide a model for us.

Grasping the whole. But while it is valid for us as Christ's servants to identify with John, another approach to the text also provides some necessary insight and balance. The first audience of Revelation, the seven churches of Asia Minor (1:4), would identify with the servants to whom God was sending his revelation of Jesus Christ more than they would identify with

---

14. For an argument for the continuing of a variety of supernatural revelations, see especially Jack Deere, *Surprised by the Voice of God* (Grand Rapids: Zondervan, 1996); cf. also Craig S. Keener, *3 Crucial Questions About the Holy Spirit* (Grand Rapids: Baker, 1996), 131–80.

John himself. They would receive the mention of John first of all as a certification of the book's authority, hence an invitation to pay careful attention to the rest of the book that would follow.

This means that in order to hear these opening verses the way the seven churches would have heard them, we must try to summarize the rest of this book the way they would have heard it. This approach works more easily when we study Revelation in our private quiet time than when we teach it publicly, because most congregations and Bible studies today, in contrast to the seven churches of Asia, will not let us read the whole book to them in one setting (1:3)! (The exception might be if we could design exceptional video graphics to accompany the book.) But we must do our best to convey the whole work the way its first hearers would have heard it. After all, how can someone "take to heart"—i.e., "keep" or "obey"—the book's message (1:3) unless we have at least summarized what that message might be?

Thus we must beware of the danger of taking the introductory verses out of context. Many Christians take isolated verses out of context to defend particular views, but even if we preach entire paragraphs of Scripture, it is possible to take them out of context. These introductory verses introduce the entire book of Revelation and make their fullest sense only when attached to the rest of the book. But even if most congregations and Bible studies today will not let us read them the entire book, we can summarize its main themes in ways they can understand (see "Message of Revelation" in the Introduction). We can help those with whom we share the book's message to identify with the churches of Asia, that we might learn from the book what they did.

THE FATHER AUTHORIZES his Son, Jesus, to provide a revelation to his servants (1:1). This text reveals the submission of the Son to the Father and the gracious love of the Father for both the Son and humanity. Such verses provide us a model of our own submission to the Father, but also invite us to embrace afresh God's love for us. The heart of the gospel is God's gift of Jesus, and through Jesus God continues to provide us gifts we need. Among these gifts is wisdom for times of hardship experienced by his church and by individual believers (cf. James 1:2–5); the book of Revelation offers such wisdom.

The purpose of Revelation. The churches in Asia Minor were at a crossroads, impacted by persecution and wooed toward lives of compromise that might soften the persecution (2:10, 14). Although Christians in today's world often face different specific temptations, the basic temptation to succumb to the world's pressure remains the same. When we face such temptation, Christ's revelation to us can put everything back into perspective. No matter how difficult our situation, Revelation announces that God is still in control and that he will conclude this stage of history the way he has promised. He often provides happy endings to our individual trials; but even when he does not, we have the assurance that a time is coming when everything will be as it should be. Precisely because he rules history, he can assure us of its outcome.

God's revelation is both a promise and a demand. It is a promise because it gives us a new way of looking at the world. Soap operas, like ancient Greek tragedies, reflect a way of looking at the world that lacks hope for ultimate justice and healing. God's perspective, by contrast, encourages us that his justice will always prevail—often in the short run, but always in the long run. Because the book of Revelation comes to us as a promise, verse 3 declares, "Blessed is the one who reads ... and blessed are those who hear."

But this revelation also approaches us as a demand. As God's servants who receive his message, we, like John (1:2), must be "witnesses" of his message (6:9; 12:11; 17:6). Thus, for example, those who truly long for a kingdom of justice in the future must act justly in the present (Amos 5:18–24); those who look for the day when God will right all wrongs must avoid being wrongdoers. In many parts of the world Christians are actively sharing their faith and paying a heavy price for it; for example, Protestants in China multiplied from under two million believers to perhaps thirty times that number after four decades of intense persecution and the torture and martyrdom of many of their leaders.[15] The twenty-five baptized Christians in Nepal in 1960 multiplied one-thousand times over in twenty-five years—at a time when Christians faced a six-year prison sentence for baptizing others.[16]

By contrast, many North American Christians have proved timid merely witnessing to their coworkers.[17] Revelation challenges our complacency, whether by pointing us to the price true Christians must be prepared to pay

---

15. Patrick Johnstone, *Operation World* (Grand Rapids: Zondervan, 1993), 164 (despite China's "official" estimate, its State Statistics Bureau put the figure at 75 million Christians—see "Counting China's Christians," *CT* [June 21, 1993], 60; for lower estimates, see Kim-Kwong Chan, "The Miracles After Missions," *Christian History* 52 [1996]: 42–44 [p. 43]). For articles on subsequent persecution in China, see Kenneth Woodward, "Public Enemy Number One," *NW* (Aug. 26, 1991), 47; Andrew Wark, "The Bloody Seed of Chinese Persecution," *CT* (Nov. 23, 1992), 54–55, 61; Marco Restelli, "China's Secret Holy War," *WPR* (May 1994), 43.

16. Johnstone, *Operation World*, 405–6; on the Nepali church, see Barbara Thompson, "Nepal's Book of Acts," *CT* (Nov. 9, 1992), 14–18.

17. On the weakness of personal evangelism even among most North American evangelicals, see "Evangelism in the '90s," *CT* (Dec. 16, 1991), 34–45.

for following Jesus, or by revealing the dangers of compromise with a world inescapably opposed to the one we acknowledge as Lord. This is why verse 3 is not only a blessing, but a blessing specifically directed toward those who *hear*. Revelation is not good news for everyone. It should terrify those satisfied with the way things are the same way it would have terrified many ancient hearers who learned of its message (see comment on 9:14).

Because Revelation cites its pedigree of origin (God, Jesus, his angel, and a founding apostle, 1:1), it claims great authority and invites us to obey its teachings (1:3). One wishing to apply this section should therefore at least summarize what some of those teachings are. Revelation emphasizes themes such as are mentioned in the Introduction (see "Message of Revelation").

The time is near—or is it? The subject of the book is the events that "must soon take place" (1:1). But what "soon" means is a matter of great controversy since (happily for Christians today) Jesus did not come back in the late first century. Some understand all biblical references to an imminent ("soon") coming as referring to a secret return of Jesus for his followers before the final Tribulation, but most of these references in context clearly refer to Jesus' return to consummate history, not to a coming before the Tribulation (e.g., 2 Peter 3:10; Rev. 1:7; 16:15; cf. 1 Thess. 5:2–3 with 2 Thess. 2:2–4). "Soon" cannot simply mean "pretribulational."

Some take the word "soon" here to mean that once the events begin, they will proceed rapidly (cf. 11:14);[18] but it seems more natural to take them in their more frequent sense as implying that the events of the end will come swiftly. Many of the events promised in this book may actually have begun in or before John's day (see the comment on 12:5–6), but surely Jesus' return did not come "quickly," as the book might lead us to expect (3:11; 22:7, 12, 20). Some suggest that most of Revelation's descriptions of Jesus' return refer to figurative events (at least sometimes the case, e.g., 2:16), and that John refers only to Jesus' symbolic comings in the impending judgments the book portrays.[19] Yet this seems not the most obvious sense of the term in most of the references, nor of the parallel phrase that the "time" was near (cf. 11:18).[20] The exception might be if John meant that the "time" was near in the sense in which the kingdom was near in Mark: Although the consummation was future, the kingdom was also invading the present through the activity of Jesus Christ, placing its demands on our lives (Mark 1:15).[21]

---

18. Henry W. Frost, *Matthew Twenty-Four and the Revelation* (New York: Oxford, 1924), 144.

19. E.g., Caird, *Commentary on Revelation*, 12, 235–36.

20. See e.g., Rissi, *Time and History*, 22; similar wording in 4 Ezra 4:44–50; 6:18; 8:61–62.

21. Oscar Cullmann, *Christ and Time*, tr. F. V. Filson (Philadelphia: Westminster, 1950), 40; Beale, *Revelation*, 185, 1134.

Other approaches may address the nature of this prophecy. Because John wrote these words over 1,900 years ago, we may be tempted to doubt how "swiftly" his words have in fact come to pass;[22] but the delay may simply indicate that God's time is not our time (2 Peter 3:8), or that he is still waiting patiently for his children to fulfill their mission in the world (Matt. 24:14; 2 Peter 3:9, 12).[23] Or perhaps the real key may simply be what "time" is near: Within Revelation, this term can refer either to the end (11:18) or to a period of tribulation before the end (12:12), which may have already begun even by John's day (12:5–6).

Whatever else "the time is near" (1:3) might mean, it probably means that the events of the end will be unexpected and that we should be ready for them at any time (Mark 13:32–37; 1 Thess. 5:2), so that believers should live "every moment as though it were our last."[24] A summons to readiness is surely a major part of the phrase's rhetorical function, which we can apply readily today. As in John's day, Jesus' coming remains imminent, intruding on our preoccupied world, standing as a promise to the broken but a threat to Laodicean Christianity too satisfied with the present state of affairs. Jesus' return will bring the final scene of human rebellion to close—an announcement that is a happy ending to God's people, but a tragic one for all who chose to reject his way. Because the specific time is unknown and near, no one dare postpone repentance. There is never a good time for Christians to be attached to worldly possessions or allegiances, because there is never a time when testings or the Lord's literal return may not call us to account for all our choices.

By the same token, the unpredictability of the Lord's return means that no one should impose deadlines for the Lord's return. Columbus, for example, sailed to the New World partly because he believed God called him to be an instrument in bringing about the imminent new heaven and earth prophesied in Scripture.[25]

The Reformation period proved rife with apocalyptic expectation. Like many before him, Luther believed that he was in the end time and expected the world to end within about a century; early Puritans thought that the

---

22. Some less conservative commentators thus opine that John was simply mistaken (Boring, *Revelation*, 73).

23. Note further comments in Gordon D. Fee and Douglas Stuart, *How to Read the Bible for All Its Worth*, 2d ed. (Grand Rapids: Zondervan, 1993), 243–44.

24. Michaels, *Revelation*, 48; cf. p. 52.

25. Kevin A. Miller, "Why Did Columbus Sail?" *Christian History* 35 (1992): 9–16 (p. 10); Steven J. Keillor, *This Rebellious House: American History and the Truth of Christianity* (Downers Grove, Ill.: InterVarsity, 1996), 37; Reginald Stackhouse, "Columbus's Millennial Voyage," *Christian History* 61 (1999): 19.

Millennium ended in 1300, so expected the world to end within a century after them.[26] Anabaptist Melchior Hoffman courageously returned to Strassburg, accepting his arrest, because he expected it to become the new Jerusalem; he died there ten years later. An extremist then announced that Münster would become the new Jerusalem, crowned himself David, and reestablished polygamy, leading to the rapid slaughter of everyone in the city by Lutherans.[27] Thomas Müntzer took part in the Peasants' Revolt of 1524, expecting this to be the final judgment; but after six thousand peasants died he was captured and executed.[28] In those days end-time miscalculations often died hard, unfortunately quite literally.

Such ideas continued unabated in the following centuries. Thomas Helwys, leader among the first generation of Baptists, believed he and his followers had entered the "days of great tribulation spoken of by Christ" through the persecutions of King James I (1603–1625).[29] In 1694 forty German Pietists settled in a cave outside Philadelphia to meditate and prepare for Christ's return, though they also cared for the sick and evangelized.[30] In the 1700s some Quaker enthusiasts predicted imminent catastrophe and Christ's return.[31] Jonathan Edwards believed that God "might now be using the Awakening [of his day] as the last ingathering of the elect before the end time."[32]

A generation later, many Americans felt that the Revolutionary War was the final war, and that King George III was the final Antichrist.[33] (King George actually had evangelical sympathies, and Wesley opposed the Revolution.)[34] During the Revolution, some in a sort of postmillennial vein thought the Millennium imminent; when Jefferson later became president, a more premillennial sort of apocalyptic fear of the new president's Deism spread.[35]

---

26. Kyle, *The Last Days*, 55, 61–62, 65; Eric W. Gritsch, "The Unrefined Reformer," *Christian History* 39 (1993): 35–37. Reacting against apocalyptists' excesses, Reformers like Calvin and Zwingli became antiapocalyptic (*The Last Days*, 60).

27. Walter Klaasen, "A Fire That Spread: Anabaptist Beginnings," *Christian History* 4 (1985): 7–9 (p. 9); Robert L. Wise, "Münster's Monster," *Christian History*, 61 (1999): 23–25.

28. "A Gallery of Factions, Friends and Foes," *Christian History* 4 (1985): 13–16 (p. 14).

29. Roger Hayden, "To Walk in All His Ways," *Christian History* 4 (1985): 7–9, 35 (p. 8). In 1600s England, cf. also the Fifth Monarchists' belief that Daniel's fifth kingdom (the kingdom of God) was near ("The Fifth Monarchy Movement," *Christian History* 5 [1986]: 10).

30. "The Wissahickon Hermits," *Christian History* 5 (1986): 27.

31. Bruce L. Shelley, "Counter-Culture Christianity," *Christian History* 45 (1995): 32–34 (p. 33).

32. "God's Wonderful Working," *Christian History* 23 (1989): 12–18 (p. 15).

33. Harry S. Stout, "Preaching the Insurrection," *Christian History* 50 (1996): 11–17 (p. 14).

34. For Wesley's complaint about the Colonies' inconsistent standard of justice and freedom (denouncing British policy while exploiting African slaves), see "Selfish, Ungrateful Rebels," *Christian History* 50 (1996): 39–41 (p. 39).

35. See Mark Noll, "A Revolution in Religion, Too," *Christian History* 50 (1996): 42–44 (p. 43).

Likewise, many northern ministers on the eve of the Civil War expected the war to usher in God's kingdom; some southern ministers agreed, although expecting God to weigh in on the other side.[36] Tens of thousands earlier expected Jesus' return in the 1840s.[37] In the late nineteenth century the great urban evangelist William Booth thought that his Salvation Army "had been chosen by God as the chief agency to finally and fully establish" God's kingdom on earth.[38] The fanfare over the turn of the Millennium in 1999 is not new; a century earlier, on Dec. 31, 1899, "people took out full-page ads in New York and Chicago newspapers, anticipating the Second Coming of Jesus Christ."[39] Even when Jesus supposedly appeared to someone and commissioned him to share end-time truth, as in the disastrous Children's Crusade of the Middle Ages, one could be deceived.[40] Early and modern voices predicting times and seasons have all shared one, major common flaw: All of them have proved mistaken.

The twentieth century added significantly to such predictions. Clarence Larkin, one of the most popular representatives of the older dispensational school, concluded from his Bible interpretation that Christ would probably return by the end of the twentieth century. Some other prophecy teachers, however, apparently considered such claims too vague. Some Christian bookstores in 1988 stocked large quantities of Edgar Whisenant's bestselling book, 88 *Reasons Why the Rapture Could Be in 1988* (over three million copies were distributed).[41] (If one supposes that Jesus must return within one forty-year generation after Israel became a nation in 1948, this deadline makes sense. But this is neither the likely sense of the text on which it is based [Matt. 24:32–34], nor—we might note—did it happen.)[42] In December 1988 a friend who worked in one bookstore told me that the manager told her to sell as many of the books as possible, since they would not be able to sell them

---

36. James H. Moorhead, "Preaching the Holy War," *Christian History* 33 (1992): 38–41 (p. 39).

37. Bruce Shelley, "The Great Disappointment," *Christian History* 61 (1999): 31–33.

38. Roger J. Green, "William Booth's Theology of Redemption," *Christian History* 26 (1990): 27–30 (p. 28).

39. "1899: The Names Have Changed, but the Worries Remain," *NW* (Jan. 11, 1999), 10.

40. Cf. the Crusaders' belief that the sea would miraculously part; instead the shipowners sold the children as slaves to Muslims (Sir Steven Runciman, "The Children's Crusade," *Christian History* 40 [1993]: 30–31).

41. Cf. Christian Research Institute's wiser response, 99 *Reasons Why No One Knows When Christ Will Return*, by B. J. Oropeza.

42. Cf., e.g., Jack T. Chick, "The Last Generation" (Chino, Calif.: Chick Publications, 1972), 4. For a different and more careful reading of the passage's context, see Craig L. Blomberg, *Matthew* (Nashville: Broadman, 1992), 354–64; Craig S. Keener, *Matthew* (Downers Grove, Ill.: InterVarsity, 1997), 347–53.

in 1989. We should not think such failed predictions went unnoticed by the world; one university newspaper's weather report mocked that we must all be "sinful, depraved people" to still be on earth, because "the rapture was scheduled for last night."[43]

In 1989, the book's author reportedly revised his calculations and issued a new edition, offering 89 reasons why Jesus would come in 1989. The revised edition did not sell as well as its predecessor; let it never be said that contemporary Christians are easily deceived! Some things Christians fail to learn from the Bible we learn from experience instead.[44] Our focus on the "now" at the expense of the broad sweep of history renders us susceptible to such passing fashions. Thus a more nuanced prophecy book that seemed relevant to headlines about Saddam Hussein naturally proved popular during the Persian Gulf War, but some distributors who had overstocked later had to give away copies of the book free or sent them back to the publisher for refunds.[45]

Various prophecy teachers have suggested that the Lord will probably come around the year 2000.[46] Still less responsibly, the tabloid media, reflecting popular views that would surprise many readers of this commentary, exploit hysteria concerning the turn of the millennium; one article in the *Weekly World News* has suggested the world's end in the year 2000.[47] Another has claimed that 91 percent of "experts" now "expect the Apocalypse, stun-

---

43. *Duke Chronicle* (Sept. 14, 1988), 1 (circulation: 25,000).

44. Cf. also "Rapture Seer Hedges on Latest Guess," *CT* (Oct. 21, 1988), 43. For a history of failed predictions among popular Bible prophecy teachers, see Dwight Wilson, *Armageddon Now! The Premillenarian Response to Russia and Israel Since 1917* (Grand Rapids: Baker, 1977); see also Paul Boyer, *When Time Shall Be No More: Prophecy Belief in Modern American Culture* (Cambridge, Mass.: Belknapp of Harvard Univ., 1992); Russell Chandler, *Doomsday: The End of the World—A View Through Time* (Ann Arbor, Mich.: Servant, 1995).

45. John F. Walvoord, *Armageddon, Oil and the Middle East Crisis*, rev. ed. (Grand Rapids: Zondervan, 1990), with over one million copies in print; see the critique by Edwin Yamauchi, "Updating the Armageddon Calendar," *CT* (April 29, 1991), 50–51. Although Walvoord did not engage in this speculation, about 15 percent of Americans thought the brief Gulf War was the beginning of Armageddon ("Goodbye, Armageddon," *CT* [May 27, 1991], 57).

46. Kyle, *The Last Days*, 120, cites the approximations of Grant R. Jeffrey, *Armageddon: Appointment with Destiny* (Toronto: Frontier Research, 1988), 193; and Jack Van Impe (who also urged in 1975 that the "Soviet flag would fly over Independence Hall in Philadelphia by 1976"). The fixation on this time frame in some occult circles (see *The Last Days*, 151–56) may reveal something about Satan's plans (Matthew Fox expects the coming of the cosmic Christ then; see Steven Keillor, *This Rebellious House* [Downers Grove, Ill.: InterVarsity, 1996], 303) but should not prove influential for Christian thinking (Rom. 16:19).

47. "Will God Destroy the World in the Year 2000?" *Weekly World News* (Dec. 29, 1998), 10–11.

ning new research shows."[48] Fortunately, the issue also provided practical guidance, such as how one could make it to safety on the ark currently being constructed by space aliens.[49] An edition the year before claimed that "secret government tapes prove" that Jesus is already on earth, ready for the world's end (despite the explicit warning to the contrary in Matt. 24:26–28; Mark 13:21–22); the paper alleged a cover-up.[50] In preparation for Judgment Day, the paper invites readers to salvation—by summarizing Billy Graham's moral teachings in such a way as to mislead the reader into thinking that Graham promotes salvation by works.[51]

But those who made such predictions, expecting his coming 2000 years after his first birthday, were running a little late: Jesus was probably born around 7 B.C., so his bimillennial celebration should have been around 1993.[52] Setting deadlines—or predicting the signs that suggest such deadlines— misses the point. With or without such signs, we should always be ready.

48. Lisa Merakis, "The Millennium Countdown Has Begun!" *Weekly World News* (Dec. 29, 1998), 36.

49. Lila Schvandt, "Space Aliens Building New Noah's Ark . . . and Here's How You Can Get on It, Says Expert!" *Weekly World News* (Dec. 29, 1998), 35. The same issue reports an apparition of Mary in Egypt ("Glowing Image of Virgin Mary Dazzles Thousands!" *Weekly World News* [Dec. 29, 1998], 15).

50. George Sanford, "Jesus Is Back on Earth AND the End of the World Is Near!" *Weekly World News* (Aug. 12, 1997), 8–9.

51. R. Neale Lind, "Judgment Day—Are You Prepared?" *Weekly World News* (Dec. 29, 1998), 38–39. In another article, Beatrice Dexter, "Simple 12-Point Plan That Will Get You Into Heaven!" *Weekly World News* (Dec. 29, 1998), 38–39, includes as pointers for eternal life cherishing all God's creatures ("You might even consider becoming a vegetarian," 38), wearing "religious symbols," and giving "to the church."

52. Herod the Great wanted to kill Jesus, who by then was as old as two (Matt. 2:16), and Herod died in 4 B.C. Our calendars are off. Pastor Lee Chang-rim announced the Rapture for Oct. 28, 1992, though he did apologize when it failed to occur (*CT* [Jan. 11, 1993], 54). Slightly more wisely, Harold Camping did not expect it until Sept. 1994 ("Rapture Date Set—Again," *CT* [Nov. 23, 1992], 48; "End-Times Prediction Draws Strong Following," *CT* [June 20, 1994], 46–47; "Are You Ready?" [tract from Year of Jubilee Ministries]; "Camping Misses End-Times Deadline," *CT* [Oct. 24, 1994], 84).

Revelation 1:4–8

J OHN,

To the seven churches in the province of Asia:

Grace and peace to you from him who is, and who was, and who is to come, and from the seven spirits before his throne, ⁵and from Jesus Christ, who is the faithful witness, the firstborn from the dead, and the ruler of the kings of the earth.

To him who loves us and has freed us from our sins by his blood, ⁶and has made us to be a kingdom and priests to serve his God and Father—to him be glory and power for ever and ever! Amen.

> ⁷Look, he is coming with the clouds,
>   and every eye will see him,
>   even those who pierced him;
>   and all the peoples of the earth
>   will mourn because of him.
>   So shall it be! Amen.

⁸"I am the Alpha and the Omega," says the Lord God, "who is, and who was, and who is to come, the Almighty."

Original Meaning

IF 1:1–3 PROVIDES an appropriate title for and introduction to an apocalyptic revelation, 1:4–8 provides an epistolary introduction, specifying the audience (from "servants" in 1:1 to the "seven churches ... of Asia" in 1:4). Most important, it expounds the identity of the God who sends the revelation and in so doing encourages suffering Christians that God is greater than their tests.

Churches in Asia (1:4a)

"ASIA" WAS A common designation for the Roman province of western Asia Minor (modern western Turkey), where Christianity was flourishing by the end of the first century. A governor of Bithynia (in northern Turkey) early in the second century even complained to the emperor that the pagan temples

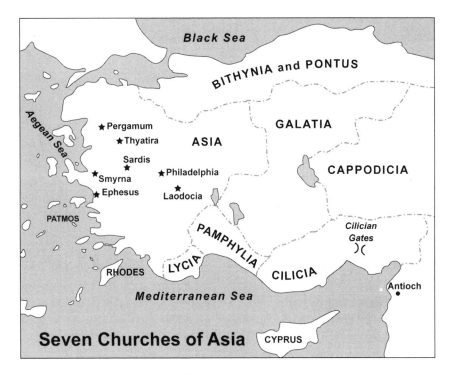

Seven Churches of Asia

were being forsaken because Christians were spreading so quickly.[1] But other strengths of the churches did not exempt them from the need for a message from God, whether warning them of further suffering (2:10) or summoning them to deeper holiness (2:14–16).

Churches had spread throughout the province of Asia and were not limited to the cities mentioned in Revelation (Acts 19:10). But John writes to the most prominent and strategic seven cities in the region, from which word would quickly spread to outlying areas. The leading council of Asiarchs (Acts 19:31, "officials of the province") met each year in a succession of seven cities, which are exactly the same seven cities to which John writes—except that John replaces Cyzicus, far to the north, with the more centrally located Thyatira.[2] Ephesus, the first city he mentions, was the most important city in the province, but also the first of the seven cities to which a messenger from Patmos, just forty to fifty miles away in the Aegean Sea, would have come.

---

1. Pliny, *Ep.* 10.96. Given the large number of Christians by the late second century, Tertullian ridicules the rhetorical inaccuracy of those who call for Christians to be thrown to the lion: "What, all of them to one lion?" (Tertullian, *Apol.* 40.2).

2. Bo Reicke, *The New Testament Era: The World of the Bible from 500 B.C. to A.D. 100*, tr. D. E. Green (Philadelphia: Fortress, 1974), 231.

Because John did not have seven secretaries to whom he could have dictated the book simultaneously, and because it would have to be recopied by hand, he did not start with seven copies of the book, one for each of the churches (although people in the churches may well have copied it down after it arrived). John's messenger probably carried the scroll from one congregation to another until all seven had heard the call to awaken that Christ had sent them.

Meanwhile, word would spread from these seven churches; for instance, other important cities, like Hierapolis, Trallis, and Magnesia, were actually on the same road that messengers would likely follow to bring the Revelation to the seven churches.[3] More important, each of the churches was strategically located to reach various populations in Asia. From Pergamum one could reach the northern coastal areas; from Thyatira, the inland area to the northeast and east; from Sardis, the broad central Hermus Valley; from Philadelphia, upper Lydia; from Laodicea, the Lycus Valley and central Phrygia; from Smyrna, the lower Hermus Valley and the north Ionian coasts; and from Ephesus, the Cayster and lower Maeander Valleys and its own metropolitan area.[4] The seven churches thus would spread the message to all of Roman Asia.

From God With Love (1:4b)

AFTER HIS "APOCALYPTIC" preface (1:1–3), John opens with an epistolary introduction that to our ears sounds much like Paul. Ancient letters customarily opened with the name and sometimes title of the sender, then listed the addressees, and typically included a prayer or thanksgiving concerning the addressees.[5] "Grace and peace" is an example of a special kind of prayer in which one directly addressed one's hearer or reader rather than God, yet actually intended these words as a prayer to God, invoking a blessing on the recipient.[6]

"Grace" (*charis*) is related to the typical Greek greeting, "greetings" (*charein*),[7] and "peace" translates the typical Jewish greeting, *shalom*. Some Greek-speaking Jewish writers had already combined such greetings (2 Macc. 1:1; 2 Bar. 78:2–3), and this combination had become standard in many

---

3. Ramsay, *Letters to the Seven Churches*, 188.

4. Ibid., 191.

5. See Stanley K. Stowers, *Letter Writing in Greco-Roman Antiquity*, LEC 5 (Philadelphia: Westminster, 1986), 20.

6. E.g., *Ep. Arist.* 185; Aune, *The New Testament in Its Literary Environment*, 193.

7. *P. Eleph.* 13.1; *P. Oxy.* 292.2; 299.1; *B.G.U.* 1079.2; Demosthenes, *Letter* 1.1; 3 Macc. 7:1; Acts 23:26. Jewish writers in Greek often maintained the Greek custom (e.g., 1 Macc. 10:18; 12:6; T. Abr. 16A; 13B; Acts 15:23; James 1:1).

early Christian letters (e.g., Rom. 1:7; 1 Peter 1:2; 2 Peter 1:2; 2 John 1:3). What is most significant in early Christian letters is not that believers invoked God the Father to bless their readers, but that they invoked the Lord Jesus alongside him, almost certainly implying their faith in his deity.[8]

The preface, or exordium, of a work sets the tone for a work (Quintilian, *Inst. Or.* 6.1.5); expansions on any part of the traditional letter introduction, including the blessings, often provide clues to themes in the rest of a letter.[9] That John expounds so fully on Jesus' roles in 1:5—6 suggests the central place that Christology will play in this book. That God "is, and . . . was, and . . . is to come" frames the source of the blessing (1:4, 8), hence is a point that John certainly wishes to underline. Some pagans understood the concept of a supreme deity's self-existence,[10] but the language here appears to have been a more common ancient Jewish interpretation of God's claim in Exodus 3:14: "I AM WHO I AM."[11]

The identity of the "seven spirits" (1:4) is not fully clear.[12] Early Judaism thought in terms of seven archangels before God's throne,[13] and especially given the angels of the seven churches (1:20), many of John's readers may at first have assumed that this was what he meant. Angels are sometimes listed elsewhere with the Father and Son (14:10; see also Mark 8:38; 1 Tim. 5:21). But sevens are common in the book of Revelation, so the "seven spirits" before God's throne need not refer to the seven angels he mentions elsewhere. Indeed, Revelation does not use "spirits" to refer to angels, and because in Greek each group has its own article, the "seven spirits" appear to be explicitly distinguished from the seven angels in Revelation 3:1. Thus most

---

8. See A. M. Hunter, *The Epistle to the Romans* (London: SCM, 1955), 26.

9. Wilhelm Wuellner, "Paul's Rhetoric of Argumentation in Romans: An Alternative to the Donfried-Karris Debate Over Romans," *CBQ* 38 (July 1976): 335–36; cf. Stowers, *Letter Writing*, 20–21.

10. E.g., Plutarch, *E at Delphi* 17, *Mor.* 392A; see further Aune, *Prophecy in Early Christianity*, 280–81. Commentators cite Plutarch, *Isis* 9, for a closer verbal parallel to a deity encompassing all that matters in past, present, and future; Aune, *Revelation*, 1:30–32, provides many parallels, suggesting that the Jewish expansion cited below may reflect Hellenistic influence in its wording.

11. Sib. Or. 3.15–16. See also the Jerusalem Targum at Ex. 3:14 and esp. Deut. 32:39 (Beasley-Murray, *Revelation*, 54; see further Ford, *Revelation*, 376; Beale, *Revelation*, 187). John's awkward Greek expression in "who is, and who was, and who is to come" probably reflects an attempt to render a Semitic original (Tenney, *Revelation*, 14).

12. Adding to the possible confusion, some early Jewish texts linked angels with God's Spirit (cf. Asc. Isa. 9:36); some early Christians also mentioned angels alongside the Trinity, though usually maintaining the distinction (Justin, *First Apol.* 6). Talbert, *Apocalypse*, 14, thinks John portrays the Holy Spirit in angelic imagery here.

13. Tobit 12:15; 1 Enoch 20:1–8; 2 Enoch 19:1–3; 4QSerek. See different groups of seven spirits in T. Reub. 2; 2 Enoch 19:6. Aune, *Revelation*, 1:34–35 argues this view.

commentators take "the seven spirits" as the "sevenfold Spirit" of Isaiah 11:2 or some other analogy for the Spirit of God,[14] a view that allows interpreters to understand the "seven spirits" here as the third person of the Trinity.

In Revelation the seven spirits "before his throne" (1:4; cf. 4:5) are the seven eyes that belong to the Lamb (5:6). The "seven eyes" reflect the eyes of God in Zechariah (Zech. 3:9; 4:10), which one might take as God's angels sent to patrol the four corners of the earth (1:8–11; but see comment on Rev. 6:1–8), who are the "four spirits of heaven" (Zech. 6:5, cf. 6:1–7); but in context the eyes could refer to God's Spirit (4:6).

If we read the seven spirits as God's Spirit here, 1:4–5 invokes a blessing from the Trinity: Father, Spirit, and the Son. Regardless of whether John invokes the Trinity here, he closes with Jesus because his role is the central focus. It is especially because of their allegiance to Jesus that John's readers face opposition from the synagogue community and hence from Rome (see the Introduction).

Jesus the Deliverer (1:5–6)

JOHN PROVIDES THREE titles that describe Jesus' person in 1:5 and three statements about his work in 1:5–6. Each of Jesus' titles in 1:5 provides special encouragement to a suffering church: Jesus had testified (and so suffered like many of John's first audience), had risen from the dead (a promise of hope to that audience), and now reigns (an assurance against their persecutors).

Jesus is the "faithful witness," who provided the ultimate witness of the Father (John 3:11) and stood faithful in his witness when on trial before Pilate (1 Tim. 6:13). Because he is the "faithful and true witness" (Rev. 3:14), believers can depend on his promises (Prov. 14:5, 25); in fact, he fulfills a divine role (Jer. 42:5).[15] But more important here, Jesus provides the perfect model for Christians who will bear witness for him (Rev. 19:10) and suffer for that witness (17:6).[16] Thus the only named martyr in the book of Revelation is likewise called a "faithful witness" (2:13).

That Jesus is the "firstborn from the dead" recalls a standard early Christian way of expressing the fact that Jesus was the first person to rise from the

---

14. Caird, *Commentary on Revelation*, 15; Beasley-Murray, *Revelation*, 55; Metzger, *Breaking the Code*, 23; Rissi, *Time and History*, 58; cf. F. F. Bruce, "The Spirit in the Apocalypse," 333–36 (esp. 336). Fekkes, *Isaiah*, 108–10, is more skeptical of a use of Isaiah here; the Spirit is sevenfold only in the LXX, unless one includes "Spirit of the LORD." Cf. a sevenfold spirit in 1 Enoch 61:11 and the messianic interpretation of Isa. 11:2 in *b. Sanh.* 93b; *Ruth Rab.* 7:2.

15. Cf. Moses as the "witness without falsehood" in Philo, *That the Worse Is Wont to Attack the Better* 138.

16. Mitchell G. Reddish, "Martyr Christology in the Apocalypse," *JSNT* 33 (1988): 85–95, notes that Jesus' various roles in Revelation emphasize his martyrdom, reminding the audience that martyrdom is victory, not defeat.

dead (Col. 1:18; Heb. 1:6; cf. Rom. 8:29), but was especially relevant to Christians who might soon face death for his name. Most Jewish people expected all the righteous dead to rise at the end of the age (Dan. 12:2); the early Christians believed that Jesus had actually inaugurated that future event in the midst of history (thus they preached "in Jesus the resurrection," Acts 4:2). As the "firstborn," Jesus' resurrection was the guarantee that his dead followers would also be raised (1 Cor. 15:20)—hence they had nothing to fear, even from death itself (see also Rev. 1:18). In Jewish teaching, angels hostile to Israel's interests ruled the nations,[17] but here Jesus rules over the kings of the earth. The language alludes to Psalm 89:27, where God's "firstborn" rules over the other "kings of the earth." To believers suffering under agents of mighty Caesar, this title of Jesus would encourage them indeed!

As John lists three titles of Jesus in 1:5, he also lists three works of Jesus in 1:5–6 (though not quite parallel grammatically): He "loves us"; he "freed us from our sins"; and he "made us ... a kingdom and priests." Jesus' love for us is expressed in his death on our behalf, as elsewhere in the New Testament (John 3:16; Rom. 5:5–8; Gal. 2:20). This assurance of Christ's love would encourage the suffering believers among John's readers; his death also provides an example for those called to join in the Lamb's sacrifice on behalf of God's mission in the world (Rev. 6:9).

In declaring that Jesus made us a "kingdom and priests," John reminds his audience that salvation is not just what God saves us from (our sins, 1:5), but what he saves us for—for a destiny as his agents and worshipers (1:6). Exodus 19 reminded Israel that they were to be holy, or separate to God, and that they were God's special and treasured possession (Ex. 19:5–6). But that passage especially declared that Israel's mission was to be a kingdom of priests (19:6). Like other early Christian writers (1 Peter 2:9), John applies this title and mission to all believers (Rev. 1:6; 5:10; 20:6), who have been grafted into the heritage of Israel. For John's audience, such an application is no small matter: Many are probably Jewish believers expelled from their synagogues for faith in Jesus (see comment on 3:8–9). Jews were exempt from worshiping the emperor, but some were accusing Christians of being no longer Jewish, hence subject to reprisals for their failure to worship Caesar (see the Introduction). By reaffirming that his audience remained attached to Israel's heritage, John encourages them of the rightness of their claims.

John adapts the wording slightly: a kingdom and priests (1:6).[18] Although a "kingdom" normally meant a ruler's right to reign (Ps. 145:11–14), it sometimes

---

17. E.g., Dan. 10:13, 20; Jub. 15:21–32, 35:17, 49:2–4; 1 Enoch 40:9; 3 Enoch 26:12; 29:1; 30:1–2; *Mek. Shir.* 2:112ff; *Sifre Deut.* 315.2.1.
18. Cf. other early Jewish sources in Beasley-Murray, *Revelation,* 57–58.

meant the people over whom he reigned (105:13), and in this case the word implies delegated authority, as when Adam and Eve ruled creation for God (Gen. 1:26–27). This kingdom will "reign" with Jesus (Rev. 5:10; 20:6), as in the biblical promises (Dan. 7:22, 27).[19]

Their title as "priests" is also significant. The Qumran community saw its own mission as priestly, and its community included many priests.[20] But the sort of priesthood John means here is a spiritual priesthood like that of ancient Israel as a whole (cf. Isa. 61:6). As priests Jesus' followers will offer worship (Rev. 4:10–11; 5:8–10; cf. 22:3) and offerings, both the incense of prayer (5:8; 8:4) and the sacrifice of their own lives (6:9).[21]

After John expresses his prayer for grace and peace from the triune God, he pauses to offer a doxology of praise to Jesus (1:6). (This is not surprising behavior for a writer who is part of the priesthood he just mentioned.) Whereas traditional Jewish texts praised God the Father, here the praise is apparently directed toward Jesus (cf. also Rom. 9:5), the one who died for us (Rev. 1:5) and made us priests to his Father (1:6).[22]

Concluding Promise and Affirmation (1:7–8)

JOHN'S INTRODUCTORY WORDS climax in a promise before concluding with another affirmation of God's eternality (1:8): Jesus is coming (1:7). That Jesus would return in the clouds (probably of divine glory) reflects Daniel 7:13; that those who pierced him would see him and mourn reflects Zechariah 12:10. Because the language of Matthew 24:30 reflects the same texts, it is likely that John here echoes an earlier saying of Jesus.[23] The "peoples [lit., tribes] of the earth" may reflect the organization of local citizens in the cities of Asia, where they were divided into tribes; Philadelphia, for

---

19. Israel's future exaltation to rule the nations became a popular Jewish tradition (Wisd. Sol. 5:16; 1QM 1.5; 12.16; CD 6.5–6; Jub. 22:11–12; 32:19; Sifre Deut. 47.2.8).

20. Emphasized by William H. Brownlee, "The Priestly Character of the Church in the Apocalypse," NTS 5 (April 1959): 224–25. A number of actual Jewish priests also became Christians (Acts 6:7).

21. Andrew J. Bandstra, "'A Kingship and Priests': Inaugurated Eschalogy in the Apocalypse," Calvin Theological Journal 27 (1992): 10–25, emphasizes present intercession and mediation of Christ's message.

22. Jesus continues to be hailed explicitly as deity even more often in early patristic texts, e.g., Justin, First Apol. 67; Second Apol. 13; also reported in Pliny, Ep. 10.96. Cf. Larry W. Hurtado, One God, One Lord: Early Christian Devotion and Ancient Jewish Monotheism (Philadelphia: Fortress, 1988).

23. Cf. Mark 13:26; 14:62; see further Beale, "Use of Daniel in the Synoptic Eschatological Discourse," 138–39; cf. Bauckham, Climax of Prophecy, 319–21. For John, Jesus' "piercing" probably means the spear-thrust of John 19:37; Rev. 1:7 is closer in wording to John 19 than to the LXX of Zech. 12:10.

---

instance, had seven.[24] No assurance could better encourage suffering believers than the knowledge that Jesus will come to set matters right, and the church's oppressors will have to acknowledge the wrong they have done to God's servants. It is not altogether clear from Revelation 1:7 whether the "mourning" implies repentance (cf. 11:11–13) or—more likely in the case of the Gentiles implied here (cf. Matt. 24:30)—fear (Rev. 6:16), but the note of vindication is unambiguous.

Finally, John confirms once again that all history is in God's hands—the future as well as the present (1:8); thus, his people need not fear as if something will happen to them apart from God's plan. The title "the Alpha and the Omega," like the one "who is, and who was, and who is to come," indicates God's eternality, that all of history from beginning to end is the same to him. Greeks sometimes used symbolic letters to describe their deities,[25] but John uses the first and last letters of the Greek alphabet to describe God as the "first" and the "last"; some Jewish writers used the first and last letters of the Hebrew alphabet (Aleph and Tav) to make the same point.[26] In both cases the writers allude to the book of Isaiah, where God declares that he is both the first and the last (Isa. 41:4; 44:6; 48:12). Pagans also might recognize that "the first" depicts a supreme deity,[27] or even used "the first and the last" in this manner;[28] but Jewish people in particular described God as first and last,[29] as well as the "beginning and the end of all."[30]

God not only is Lord over time, but he rules the entire universe: he is *pantokrator*, "Almighty," a common title for God in this book (1:8; 4:8; 11:17; 15:3; 16:7, 14; 19:6, 15; 21:22; elsewhere in the New Testament only at 2 Cor. 6:18).

---

24. Ramsay MacMullen, *Roman Social Relations: 50 B.C. to A.D. 284* (New Haven, Conn.: Yale Univ. Press, 1974), 131–32. Greek readers also could envision distinct peoples elsewhere, e.g., the estimated 118 "peoples" of India (Arrian, *Ind.* 7.1).

25. E.g., Plutarch, *E at Delphi*, passim. For the use of vowels in magic, see Aune, *Revelation*, 1:57–59.

26. Cf. Robert Hayward, *Divine Name and Presence: The Memra* (Totowa, N.J.: Allanheld, Osmun & Co., 1981), 34. Often they also included the middle letter (Mem) to depict God as "truth" or "faithfulness" (Aleph-Mem-Tav), *p. Sanh.* 1:1, §4; *Gen. Rab.* 81:2).

27. Plutarch, *Isis* 2, 75; *Mor.* 352A, 381B; other deities in Apuleius, *Metam.* 4.30. In some unrelated cultures, see John S. Mbiti, *African Religions and Philosophies* (Garden City, N.Y.: Doubleday, 1970), 43.

28. Zeus in *Orphic Hymns* 15.7; the beginning and end belong to Apollo in *Orphic Hymns* 34.15. The use of "Alpha" and "Omega" in magical texts (e.g., *P. Köln*, 6; citations in David E. Aune, "The Apocalypse of John and Greco-Roman Revelatory Magic," *NTS* 33 [1987]: 481–501) might reflect Christian influence.

29. E.g., Philo, *Noah's Work As a Planter* 93.

30. Josephus, *Ant.* 8.280; in *Apion* 2.190 he adds also the "middle."

Jewish texts written in Greek regularly use this title for God;[31] later rabbis continued to employ the equivalent Hebrew and Aramaic terms.[32] Some Roman writers also describe the supreme deity in the equivalent Latin title.[33] But in the old Greek stories most widely told, deities often appeared pathetic. Such deities could be captured and interrogated by mortals, or proved unable to protect a mortal relative;[34] their power was a far cry from that of the living God of ancient Israel.

For Christians suffering under Caesar, the *autokrator* or emperor,[35] knowing that they served the "Almighty" must have provided strength. Caesar might rule citizens of an empire in limited ways, but God rules the cosmos; and God, who is the beginning and the end, will guide the course of history long after Caesar's death and the cremation of his body in Rome.

Bridging
Contexts

MISINTERPRETATIONS OF REVELATION 1–3. This passage has raised various interpretive issues for modern readers, especially in circles heavily influenced by some popular prophecy teachers. One issue raised by the older view is that the seven churches are symbolic. To be sure, most of Revelation belongs to a mixture of apocalyptic and prophetic genres, some of whose symbols have proved more difficult to fathom than others; letters, however, are usually a different kind of literature. Most apocalyptic writings used pseudonyms for their authors and did not explicitly address a particular audience. But Revelation is different, framed as a letter.[36] That it is a letter to specific first-century churches suggests the degree to which we should interpret the symbolism of this book in light of symbols these churches would have understood.

Some early dispensationalists have interpreted the seven churches of Asia (1:4) symbolically as seven "church ages," or stages of church history, though few hold this view today.[37] For a number of reasons, this line of interpreta-

---

31. E.g., Wisd. Sol. 7:25; 2 Macc. 6:26; 3 Macc. 5:7; Ep. Arist. 185; Sib. Or. 1.66. The LXX employs the title over 150 times, usually for the Lord "of hosts."

32. E.g., *b. Shab.* 88b; *Yeb.* 105b; *Yoma* 12a.

33. E.g., Virgil, *Aen.* 7.141, 770; 9.625; *Georg.* 2.325; Ovid, *Metam.* 1.154; 2.304 (I cite here only a small percentage of the references I collected in my own random survey of the sources). For the Greek term, cf. *Orphic Hymn* 18.17.

34. E.g., Homer, *Od.* 4.459–61; Euripides, *Electra* 1298–1300.

35. E.g., Josephus, *Ant.* 14.199.

36. Fiorenza, *Revelation*, 35; Aune, *The New Testament in Its Literary Environment*, 240. No one would be troubled by the mixing of such different blends of literature, however; thus, for example, a work of history could also open with a letter introduction (2 Macc. 1:1–6).

37. For critique, see Michaels, *Revelation*, 24; Robert L. Thomas, "The Chronological Interpretation of Revelation 2–3," *BibSac* 124 (1967): 321–31; Lewis, *Questions*, 74–76; a

tion is no more feasible than allegorizing the churches addressed in Paul's letters. (1) Abundant evidence suggests that Revelation addresses seven literal church communities, including items of local color that fit each of the seven letters (see comments on the letters).

(2) A map shows that Revelation addresses the seven churches in the very sequence that a messenger from John, arriving first in Ephesus near the sea, would travel to each of the cities listed, presumably along the main roads of Asia (see the Introduction). The average distance between each city was about thirty to forty-five miles.[38]

(3) Only a forced reading of church history (regularly revised with the passing of time) has allowed this interpretation.

(4) Finally, if Revelation requires the completion of seven church ages before Jesus' return, then in most centuries of church history Christians had no right to expect the imminent return of the Lord! This would be a curious conclusion for advocates of the seven church ages view, most of whom vehemently emphasize the imminence of Christ's return.

Modern doctrinal agendas. Another danger in reading biblical texts is that we read our modern doctrinal agendas into them. For instance, some writers have sought to distinguish a pretribulational rapture from a posttribulational second coming by arguing that Jesus "comes in the clouds" at the Rapture (cf. 1 Thess. 4:17) but touches down on earth at the Second Coming (Zech. 14:4). Whatever one's view of that doctrine, an argument based solely on such a distinction inevitably fails. Most of the texts about Jesus' return in judgment do not mention the detail of him landing on earth; further, most of the texts about Jesus' coming with clouds refer plainly to his coming visibly to the entire world, as here (1:7; cf. Dan. 7:13; Mark 13:26; 14:62).[39] Nor ought we to read other modern doctrinal controversies into texts that were not written to address them. John writes not as a modern theologian but as a prophet and pastor, encouraging suffering believers and exhorting complacent ones.

---

modern example is Lindsay, *New World Coming*, 38. Corsini, *Apocalypse*, 103–9, finds the history of salvation in the letters.

38. See Ramsay, *Letters to the Seven Churches*, 183–86; Hemer, *Letters to the Seven Churches*, 15; Ford, *Revelation*, 382. Some of Ramsay's details regarding the road system appear to be inferences, though some of the roads are attested by milestones (Aune, *Revelation*, 1:131). When sequence differed from what one would expect, ancients often noticed (e.g., Plutarch, *T.T.* 4.7, *Mor.* 672). Bowman, *First Christian Drama*, 23, suggests that the churches were arranged like a Herodian menorah, but even if true, this suggestion would require more cartographic skill on the part of John's ancient audience than is feasible.

39. Probably also Acts 1:9–11. Clouds often accompanied divine judgment, especially in the final time (Ezek. 30:3, 18; 32:6–7; Joel 2:2).

Does this passage speak to today? But if we seek to approach this passage on its own terms, how relevant does it prove for today? If John emphasizes Jesus' triumph over death (1:5) and God's sovereign rule over history (1:8) to encourage believers threatened by a hostile Roman government, does his message have anything to say to modern readers one and a half millennia after Rome's fall?

That question is not difficult to answer. All believers face death (Heb. 9:27), and all witnessing believers face opposition of some sort (2 Tim. 3:12). Jesus' words come as an encouragement to us in our various personal trials that God has a plan larger than the details that we can see, and that we fit into his plan for history, the goal of which is a people who will constitute a kingdom and priests.

Such words especially set our corporate sufferings as the church in broader perspective. Apart from the eyes of faith, no one could have guessed that the struggling Christian movement would have outlived the mighty Roman Empire. Likewise, apart from the eyes of faith, who would have guessed a century ago that believers in the Two-Thirds World would easily outnumber believers in the West? Or that the Berlin Wall would have fallen? Or that apartheid would have died in South Africa without a civil war?[40]

Today's persecutors of the church are often different, but the principle is the same. Radical Islamic regimes in Iran[41] and especially the Sudan[42] have martyred many Christians, but knowing the Lord of history summons us to look beyond the present to God's ultimate plan. Because much of Revelation is most relevant to believers experiencing or anticipating state persecution, it reminds us of our participation in the universal body of Christ and invites us to pray with faith for our suffering brothers and sisters, as we would hope they would do for us when our time comes (Matt. 24:9).

---

40. For Christian influence in the collapse of totalitarian states in Eastern Europe, see Bud Bultmann, *Revolution by Candlelight* (Portland: Multnomah, 1991); for Christian resistance to apartheid, see, e.g., Albert Luthuli, postscript to "Let My People God," 409–26 in *Classics of Christian Missions*, ed. Francis M. DuBose (Nashville: Broadman, 1979); Caesar Molebatsi with David Virtue, *A Flame for Justice* (Batavia, Ill.: Lion, 1991).

41. See "The Church Triumphant in Iran," *Mountain Movers* (May 1995), 6–8; "Prominent Church Leaders Slain," *CT* (Aug. 15, 1994), 54; "Protestants Live with Fear, Insecurity," *CT* (Feb. 6, 1995), 58.

42. See Charles Colson, "Tortured for Christ—and Ignored," *CT* (March 4, 1996), 80. On the Islamic north's repression of the largely Christian and traditionalist south, see Jeffrey Bartholet, "Hidden Horrors in Sudan," *NW* (Oct. 12, 1992), 49; Shyam Bhatia, "A War's Living Booty," *WPR* (Aug. 1995), 40; "Sudan: The Ravages of War" (New York: Amnesty International USA, 1993); Marcus Mabry, "The Price Tag on Freedom," *NW* (May 3, 1999), 50–51.

MISSION STRATEGY AND **church reality.** That the book was sent first to the most strategic cities of Asia Minor, trusting that its message would spread from there (1:4), invites us to think strategically in our plans to spread God's message to our communities and the world. We should think as strategically as possible as we mobilize believers for world missions,[43] develop strategies for serving our communities,[44] organize target-group evangelism,[45] and so forth.

Yet our vantage point in history may also allow us to draw an additional application that would have been less clear in John's day. When Revelation was written, Christianity flourished in western Turkey, but over the centuries each of these churches gradually succumbed to pressures until the last was virtually stamped out by Islam. The regions where the early church was strongest (Turkey, Syria, and North Africa) are now Islamic strongholds.

Yet by and large it was the church rather than Islam that destroyed the church; Muslim invaders simply mopped up after them. In North Africa, Christianity weakened itself through internal doctrinal and ethnic divisions, heresies, and the insensitivity of Byzantine and Latin Christians to local culture. Nubia remained a richly Christian African culture until its growing weakness in both missions and Christian education led to its collapse to Islam in the fourteenth through the sixteenth centuries.[46] The disunity of the church led to the demise of a glorious Eastern Orthodox culture before Islam.[47] Regions relatively barren of the gospel two centuries ago are now flourishing with the gospel, while parts of the Western world struggle to maintain a Christian voice. Lampstands can be moved from their place (2:5), and this should serve as a warning to believers in various parts of the world today: We dare not take our role in God's plan for granted. When part of the church abandons its mission, God will raise up others to fulfill it.

Assurance of God's help and presence. More important to the point of the book is the God who assures his people of help in their troubles. Because

---

43. Beginning with prayer; see David Bryant, *In the Gap* (Ventura, Calif.: Regal, 1984); Johnstone, *Operation World.*

44. One brief but extremely practical manual on serving our communities, which I have used for some of my classes, is Joy Bolton, *Ideas for Community Ministries* (Birmingham: Women's Missionary Union, 1993).

45. See Ralph W. Neighbour Jr. and Cal Thomas, *Target Group Evangelism* (Nashville: Broadman, 1975); one example of this is the DivorceCare video series (1994), targeted for small groups in local congregations.

46. Craig S. Keener and Glenn J. Usry, *Defending Black Faith* (Downers Grove, Ill.: InterVarsity, 1997), 15–16, 19.

47. Mark Galli, "Better the Infidel," *Christian History* 54 (1997): 19.

Revelation addresses some churches that were experiencing or were on the verge of impending suffering, it emphasizes the sufficiency of their keeper. The title of the one "who is, and who was, and who is to come" frames this paragraph (1:4, 8), encompassing all the other titles in it. As George Caird puts it, this elaboration of Exodus 3:14 "sets the church's coming ordeal against a background of God's eternity, but it also brings God down into the arena of history. He is Lord of past, present, and future." Yet the sequence is also important: The past and future are embraced in God's eternal present.[48] Christians can be assured because, as one early Christian hymnist observed, God saw the end clearly at the very beginning (Odes Sol. 4:12, 14). God saw our own generation and all the martyrs of history at the same time; the church of all ages is part of his plan, and we are part of a purpose that is bigger than us individually and which will not fail.

Suffering Christians, such as those in Smyrna and Philadelphia and many today, need reminders of God's great compassion for them; sometimes when we suffer we do not feel as if the sovereign God loves us, unless we can recognize his sharing our suffering in the cross. The assurance of Jesus' love (1:5) goes deeper than mere words. Just as a husband and wife should practically demonstrate their love as well as announcing, "I love you," so the New Testament portrays Christ's love for us as intimately bound up with his sacrifice for us (1:5; Rom. 5:5–9). God's love in the familiar verse John 3:16 is in the aorist tense, which may suggest a concrete past demonstration of his love coinciding with the time he "gave" his Son (on the cross, 3:14–16).

In my times of deepest brokenness, when no sophisticated theological argument could comfort me, my deepest assurance of God's love has been to look at the cross and remember that God himself has shared my pain with me. Revelation 1:5 uses the present tense, "loves," perhaps because the suffering church here needs assurance that God's love for them continues, that he has not forgotten them.

Christ's freeing believers from their sins reminds them of the distinction between themselves and the world system that persecutes them or lures them to compromise. Although verb tenses in Revelation are not always consistent, the tense of "freed" may well point to a decisive, past liberation from sin.[49] We do not gradually relinquish our sins to make ourselves acceptable to God; Jesus liberates us into a new life at the new birth (John 3:3–5). Whether we immediately translate all of that transformation into behavior depends on

---

48. Caird, *Commentary on Revelation*, 16.
49. Vincent Taylor, *The Atonement in New Testament Teaching* (London: Epworth, 1945), 39. The later variant, "washed," reflects a difference of one Greek letter, but the idea appears in 7:14; cf. 1 John 1:7.

the degree to which we embrace by faith the transformation Christ himself has accomplished in us in that new birth (Rom. 6:11). But as much of John's first audience may have understood, suffering does seem to help the process (1 Peter 4:1).

God has everything under control. That God is both beginning and end, that he is eternal, invites us to remember that nothing can happen to us apart from his plan. That God judges sinful nations is a recurrent biblical principle, a principle that inevitably includes our own nation. But while such judgments can appeal to our sense of God's justice and holiness, they also can unnerve us, because we are part of the same world that is shaken by his judgment. Yet biblical principles are no less emphatic in their assurance: God has everything under control.[50] This message, too, accords with a strand of hope that runs through the whole of Scripture. Judgment is coming, but God will watch over his servants (Gen. 19:16; cf. Hab. 2:4); even at the hands of their enemies, nothing can overtake them apart from God's purposes (Matt. 10:28–31; 1 Peter 2:15; 3:17; 4:19).

Calling God "Alpha" and "Omega" and the one "who is, and who was, and who is to come" shows just how "Almighty" God must be (1:8). Because of the properties of recently discovered particles, many late twentieth-century physicists have argued for the necessity of at least nine dimensions at the creation event, not simply the four we experience. The creation event involved all those dimensions and necessarily originated with a source outside those dimensions. This discovery is just one reminder that God our Creator is bigger than space and time, and no point in the history of the universe—whether beginning or end—is ever inaccessible to him.[51] The concept of an all-powerful supreme deity exists in many traditional religions, generating awe as in the Bible.[52] But the Bible reminds us of God's power not only to generate awe, but also that this all-powerful God is our Father, who cares for us.

Remembering that God is Lord of history puts our lives in perspective. No situation we encounter takes God by surprise. Many of Israel's contemporaries told stories in which one side could lose a battle while their patron deity slept;[53] Elijah mocked the prophets of Baal with their own traditions that Baal might be sleeping or out chasing women (1 Kings 18:27); but Israel's God neither slumbers nor sleeps (Ps. 121:3–4)! Rare will be the community, the

---

50. Graham, *Approaching Hoofbeats*, 23; cf. also David Wilkerson, *The Vision* (Old Tappan, N.J.: Revell, 1974), 113–21.

51. See most fully Hugh Ross, *Beyond the Cosmos* (Colorado Springs: NavPress, 1996).

52. See Mbiti, *Religions*, 40–41.

53. E.g., Homer, *Il.* 14.352–60; Mesopotamian deities in "Prayer to the Gods of Night," *ANET*, 391. The Egyptians held a higher view of the chief deity Amon-Re ("Hymn to Amon-Re," *ANET*, 366).

congregation, or the individual working for God who is not faced with difficult challenges to faith—the death of loved ones, obstructions in what one feels is God's plan, setbacks in preaching the gospel. Yet in the scope of God's entire plan, we are assured that he will work these situations for our good (Rom. 8:28), even if sometimes that working focuses primarily on ultimately conforming us to Christ's image (8:29).

Revelation 1:9–12

I, JOHN, YOUR BROTHER and companion in the suffering and kingdom and patient endurance that are ours in Jesus, was on the island of Patmos because of the word of God and the testimony of Jesus. ¹⁰On the Lord's Day I was in the Spirit, and I heard behind me a loud voice like a trumpet, ¹¹which said: "Write on a scroll what you see and send it to the seven churches: to Ephesus, Smyrna, Pergamum, Thyatira, Sardis, Philadelphia and Laodicea."

¹²I turned around to see the voice that was speaking to me. And when I turned I saw seven golden lampstands.

Original Meaning

AFTER COMPLETING HIS epistolary or letter introduction (1:4–8), John turns to a narrative introduction (1:9–20). Ancient treaties, speeches, and letters often began with a narrative introduction (in speeches, called the *narratio*), which led up to the heart of the communication. After setting the scene for its occasion (1:9–10), John recounts his vision of the glorified Christ (1:11–16) and the beginning of Jesus' message to the seven churches (1:17–20). We begin with the setting that introduces the vision of Jesus (1:9–12)—a setting he shares with the seven churches to whom the revelation is sent: persecution (1:9) and (most likely) worship (1:10). When he sees the risen Christ (1:13–16), he also sees the context in which Jesus appears: in the midst of the lampstands (1:12), which are the churches (1:20).

Setting the Scene (1:9–10)

JOHN WAS A "brother" and a "companion in the suffering"—that is, a fellow sufferer with these churches for the gospel (6:11; 12:10). "Suffering" and the "kingdom" are inseparable parts of our inheritance in Jesus. "Endurance" requires fortitude in view of God's promises (13:10; 14:12) during present tribulation (*thlipsis* in 1:9; 2:3, 9–10; 3:10; 7:14). A North African theologian records one saying of Jesus reportedly still circulating in his day: "No one can obtain the kingdom of heaven without first passing through testing."[1]

---

1. Tertullian, *Baptism* 20, in Joachim Jeremias, *Unknown Sayings of Jesus*, 2d ed., tr. R. H. Fuller (London: SPCK, 1964), 73.

When John, in the context of speaking of "suffering," declares that he was on the island of Patmos "because of the word of God and the testimony of Jesus," he does not imply that Patmos was a vacation stop on a pleasure cruise. Literally he was there "on account of" God's word—as a punishment by the state for preaching and testifying about Jesus (cf. 6:9; 12:11). Whereas Ezekiel saw his vision of the Lord while exiled near literal Babylon (Ezek. 1:1), John has a vision while exiled by an empire that resembled the earlier Babylon. Although different kinds of exile existed, usually exile involved banishment to an island;[2] a later writer charges that the islands were full of exiles during the reign of the emperor Domitian.[3] Often people of lower social status were executed, enslaved, or banished to the mines or to die in gladiatorial combat;[4] but John was aged, and sometimes those in authority sentenced persons more lightly on account of their age.[5]

But while banishment was a lesser penalty than execution, we should hardly think John's sentence light. He may have been treated less harshly than others on account of his age or because the governor rather than the emperor sentenced him, but in any case banishment involved loss of honor.[6] The severest form of banishment—probably not what John experienced—involved loss of one's civil rights, including the forfeiture of nearly all one's property to the state. Unless the government lifted the ban, those banished to an island remained there until they died. Those of higher social status could work on the island and earn some money; those of lower status were scourged (a punishment that is known to have laid a person's bones bare), chained, given little food or clothing, left to sleep on the bare ground, and sentenced to hard labor.[7]

Because this severer penalty (*deportatio*) required the emperor to pass judgment, probably we should think of John as enduring a lighter form of punishment (*relegatio*) ordered by the governor of his local province, who did

---

2. Plutarch, *Exile* 12, *Mor.* 604B; Juvenal, *Sat.* 1.73; Tacitus, *Ann.* 1.53; 3.68–69; 4.13, 30; 13.43; Suetonius, *Aug.* 19; *Gaius* 14–15; *Galba* 10. Life on such islands was normally unpleasant (Epictetus, *Disc.* 1.25.20; 2.6.22).

3. Philostratus, *V.A.* 8.5.

4. Paulus, *Sententiae* 5.23.14, 19; John E. Stambaugh and David L. Balch, *The New Testament in Its Social Environment*, LEC 2 (Philadelphia: Westminster, 1986), 35.

5. Compare *Digest* 47.21.2; Sophocles, *Oed. Rex* 402–3, 1153; Dionysius of Halicarnasus, 10.29.1; Herodian 2.5.8; Cornelius Nepos, 19 (Phocion), 4.1.

6. Apuleius, *Metam.* 7.6. Philosophers might reject concern over such matters (Epictetus, *Disc.* 1.29.7; 1.30.2–3; 3.24.100, 109, 113; 4.4.34; 4.7.14; Dio Chrysostom, 13th Disc., *In Athens* 4–5; Wayne A. Meeks, *The Moral World of the First Christians*, LEC 6 [Philadelphia: Westminster, 1986], 49).

7. Ramsay, *Letters to the Seven Churches*, 83–85.

---

not seize all his property.[8] It is also difficult to imagine John as a working convict who had to receive his entire vision before going off to work Sunday morning! But though he probably experienced the more lenient form of banishment, his conditions would be harsh for someone of his age.

Rome especially used two groups of islands in the Aegean Sea near Asia Minor to detain political prisoners, namely, the Cyclades and the Sporades; Patmos was in the Sporades, and the older Pliny can be understood as naming this a place of exile.[9] The island was not deserted; it included a Greek gymnasium and a temple and cult of Artemis (though it would not have been as pervasive as the veneration of Artemis in nearby Ephesus).[10] Since John would be permitted visitors, the churches of Asia would undoubtedly send him messengers; Patmos was only forty to fifty miles southwest of Ephesus.

Some people in Asia Minor celebrated a monthly "emperor's day" (Sebaste, Augustus Day) in honor of the divine emperor.[11] By contrast Christians, who might suffer for their refusal to worship the emperor, celebrated a different day in honor of the true and ultimate king—*kyriakos* (lit., "Lord's"), which was a term Romans used to designate what belonged to Caesar, but which Christians applied to the ultimate *kyrios* or Lord (1:10).

Most likely the "Lord's Day" refers to the first day of the week, Sunday.[12] The phrase also appears in Did. 14.1 for the day on which Christians gathered to break bread, and Roman officials also recognized that Christians gathered on a fixed day (Pliny, *Ep.* 10.96). Christians seem to have assembled together on Sunday from an early period (Acts 20:7; 1 Cor. 16:2), probably to commemorate Jesus' resurrection (John 20:19, 26).[13] Because the first

---

8. Caird, *Commentary on Revelation*, 21–23. On forms of banishment, see Aune, *Revelation*, 1:80–81.

9. Pliny, *N.H.* 4.12.69; 4.23; Talbert, *Apocalypse*, 3; J. N. Sanders, "St. John on Patmos," *NTS* 9 (Jan. 1963): 75–85 [76]; though cf. Aune, *Revelation*, 1:78–79. Some cite the (unlikely) view of Victorinus of Petau (*Comm. on Rev.* 10.3) that Domitian condemned John to the mines on Patmos. Some thus claim that prisoners there worked the marble quarries (Bowman, *First Christian Drama*, 23), others that Patmos appears to have lacked mines (Sanders, "Patmos," 76).

10. H. D. Saffrey, "Relire l'apocalypse à Patmos," *RB* 82 (1975): 385–417.

11. See G. Adolf Deissmann, *Light From the Ancient East* (Grand Rapids: Baker, 1978), 358–59. Most scholars today accept this background (Ford, *Revelation*, 382; Beasley-Murray, *Revelation*, 65).

12. With most scholars (e.g., Arthur Darby Nock, *St. Paul* [New York: Harper & Row, 1963], 58; Oscar Cullmann, *Early Christian Worship* [Philadelphia: Westminster, 1953], 10–11; Rissi, *Time and History*, 28; Ugo Vanni, "Il 'Giorno del Signore' in Apoc. 1,10, giorno di purificazione e di discernimento," *Rivista Biblica* 26 [1978]: 187–99; Beale, *Revelation*, 203), although some have preferred other views (e.g., Kenneth A. Strand, "Another Look at 'Lord's Day' in the Early Church and in Rev. I.10," *NTS* 13 [Jan. 1967]: 174–81).

13. Cf. Ep. Barn. 15.9; Justin, *First Apol. 67; b. Taan.* 27b. In time Sunday came to be viewed as a "little Easter."

Christians were Jewish, they may have also avoided assembling on Friday evening or Saturday morning to avoid conflict with their synagogue services. "The Lord's Day" here may also involve a play on words: In worship, John was experiencing a foretaste of the future day of the Lord, when believers' suffering would give way to the kingdom (1:9).[14]

John's contemporaries most often associated the Spirit with prophetic inspiration, and John's audience would therefore have naturally understood John's being "in the Spirit" in terms of prophetic inspiration (see Ezek. 2:2; 3:12–14; 11:5, 24).[15] But because John was already in the Spirit when the vision began, perhaps "in the Spirit" begins here not with a visionary state, as in 4:2 and 21:10, but initially in worship that led to a visionary state.[16] Such an interpretation helps explain John's mention of "the Lord's Day," likely used for corporate worship (see comment above). Given the usual sense of "in the Spirit" among John's contemporaries, "worship in the Spirit" (cf. John 4:24; Phil. 3:3) undoubtedly meant Spirit-guided and Spirit-empowered worship. Prophetically inspired worship characterized early Christianity (1 Cor. 14:15, 26; Eph. 5:18–19) and existed in ancient Israel (1 Sam. 10:5; 1 Chron. 25:1–5). John, whose message will be read when the Asian churches assemble on the "Lord's Day," probably was himself in worship on that day when the vision came.[17]

Among the Lampstands (1:11–12)

JOHN TURNS WHEN he hears a voice "like a trumpet" (1:10). This expression presumably refers to the clarity of Jesus' voice, a voice that could therefore strike terror into the hearts of the unprepared.[18] Several scholars argue that some Jewish people understood God's "voice" as itself a divine being and note that when John turns, he sees the "voice" (1:12), perhaps linked with

---

14. Cf. Shepherd, *Paschal Liturgy*, 78. Some Jewish eschatological schemes envisioned a future Sabbath era (cf. *Mek. Shab.* 1.38ff.; Life of Adam 51.1–2; Samuele Bacchiocchi, "Sabbatical Typologies of Messianic Redemption," *JSJ* 17 [1986]: 153–76), sometimes a millennium in length (2 Enoch 33:1–3, rec. J, possibly Christian material), and some later Christians followed this with an "eighth" era typified by Christ's resurrection on the first (eighth) day (Ep. Barn. 15.8–9).

15. On the Spirit and inspiration, see Craig S. Keener, *The Spirit in the Gospels and Acts* (Peabody, Mass.: Hendrickson, 1997), 10–13.

16. Cf. also Hill, *New Testament Prophecy*, 90. Less likely, some interpret "in the Spirit" as "in the believing community" (Richard L. Jeske, "Spirit and Community in the Johannine Apocalypse," *NTS* 31 [1985]: 452–66).

17. See Cullmann, *Early Christian Worship*, 7.

18. Like that of Achilles, "clear as a trumpet," in Homer, *Il.* 18.219; cf. Isa. 58:1.

Jesus' title as the "Word" (19:13).[19] More likely, however, the voice's near personification is simply Semitic idiom (Ex. 20:18; Josephus, *War* 6.301).

Sometimes visionaries wrote by dictation as they saw their visions; this may be the case here (1:11). Sometimes they wrote shortly after their vision, as in 10:4. John does not, however, need to wait until the completion of his visions (which happened in some Jewish texts; Tobit 12:20; Jub. 32:25–26). And "I saw" (1:12; 5:1) is typically visionary language, not only in the Bible (Ezek. 1:1; 23:13; Dan. 8:7) but also in apocalyptic literature.[20]

What is most significant is that Jesus appears among the lampstands (1:12–13; 2:1), which represent the seven churches (1:20), probably suggesting Jesus' presence with his church (cf. John 20:19). Because priests needed light to function in the sanctuary concealed from the light of the external world, the temple included a golden lampstand (Ex. 25:31–35; 37:18–21; 2 Chron. 4:7, 20), never extinguished by night or day.[21]

Throughout the ancient Mediterranean world, this seven-branched lampstand, or menorah, stood as the most common symbol of Israel and Judaism,[22] including in Asia Minor.[23] Those who believed themselves the true heirs of Israel's heritage, such as the Samaritans, naturally appropriated the symbol for themselves.[24] John encourages Jewish Christians excluded from their synagogues that it is not they but their opponents who are severed from their Jewish heritage (see comment on 2:9). But whereas the lampstand in Jewish iconography may stand for Israel as a whole, for John each local congregation is a lampstand, perhaps because it embodies "the church universal in all its fulness."[25]

---

19. T. Abr. 14; 15; 20A; *Apoc. Sedr.* 2:2; James H. Charlesworth, "The Jewish Roots of Christology: The Discovery of the Hypostatic Voice," *SJT* 39 (1986): 19–41; idem, *The Old Testament Pseudepigrapha and the New Testament*, SNTSM 54 (Cambridge: Cambridge Univ. Press, 1985), 128–30; Ellul, *Apocalypse*, 104. For "behind him," cf. John 20:14.

20. E.g., 1 Enoch 17:3–8; 18:1–12; 2 Enoch 20:1; 3 Enoch 42:3; 44:7.

21. Josephus, *Apion* 1.198–99. Menorah symbolism was common in Palestine; e.g., *CIJ* 2:165, §980; 2:234–35, §1197–98; G. Foerster, "Some Menorah Reliefs from Galilee," *IEJ* 24 (1974): 191–96; Zvi Uri Ma'oz, "Ancient Synagogues and the Golan," *BA* 51 (June 1988): 116–28 (p. 123).

22. E.g., *CIJ* 1:8, §4; 1:16, §14 (*CIJ* altogether contains about 200 examples); Harry J. Leon, *The Jews of Ancient Rome* (Philadelphia: Jewish Publication Society of America, 1960), 49, 196–97; Erwin R. Goodenough, *Jewish Symbols in the Greco-Roman Period*, 13 vols (New York: Pantheon Books, 1953–1965), 12:79–83.

23. E.g., *CIJ* 2:12, §743; 2:32, §771 and passim through 2:53, §801; Andrew R. Seager, "The Synagogue and the Jewish Community: The Building," pp. 168–77 in *Sardis from Prehistoric to Roman Times*, ed. George M. A. Hanfmann (Cambridge: Harvard Univ. Press, 1983), 171, 176; Goodenough, *Symbols*, 2:77–78.

24. Goodenough, *Symbols*, 1:262–63; S. Dar, "Three Menorot From Western Samaria," *IEJ* 34 (1984): 177–79.

25. Caird, *Commentary on Revelation*, 24; cf. also Beale, *Revelation*, 207, on the Israel symbolism of the lampstands representing the church.

IN THIS SECTION we will examine issues such as various views concerning the "Lord's Day," Spirit-filled worship, and some aspects of the relationship between Judaism and Christianity.

Sharing in sufferings. Believers in many parts of the world as well as some ministry situations here can identify with the shame and persecution John endured for Christ. Most of us in the West, however, at the moment are tested more by materialism than by persecution, and John's own suffering was persecution. This does not suggest, however, that analogies cannot be drawn. If John's suffering is more serious than ours, we should reason: If God enabled John and his companions in persecution to stand, how much more should we stand firm in the face of less severe testing?

Furthermore, even in the West today we have plenty of reminders that the world does not embrace the church as an ally (cf. John 15:18–25). Many of us have been denied jobs or otherwise maligned on account of our obedience to Christ; some of us have even suffered "friendly fire" within the church because we sought to do God's will. Yet as John stood boldly as a model for believers then, he stands also as an example for us.

The Lord's Day, church, and the Sabbath. The meaning of "the Lord's Day" is important for the setting of this section, but has been reapplied in some ways that shed little light on John's point. Yet our own traditions can lead us to read illegitimate ideas into this text.[26] One area of potential misinterpretation concerning the "Lord's Day" is that some believe that Sunday is a new Sabbath. When I was in Bible college, my hometown newspaper ran a debate between a traditional pastor and a Seventh-Day Adventist layperson as to the day of the week on which the Sabbath should be honored. The Adventist argued predictably for Saturday, to which the pastor responded, "We're not under the law, so the Sabbath is on Sunday." The pastor's conclusion certainly did not follow from his argument, first because the Sabbath teaching precedes the Law of Moses (Gen. 2:2–3), second because the pastor did not define how he meant "under the law" (a matter of considerable debate today), and worst of all because he simply assumed that not being under the law meant moving the Sabbath one day forward!

As early as the second century some Gentile Christians may have contrasted the "Lord's Day" with the Jewish Sabbath (Ignatius, *Magn.* 9.1).[27] But

---

26. Fortunately, few of us are likely to fall into the mistaken interpretation of Jehovah's Witnesses, who, to preserve their tradition, understand the "Lord's Day" as the period from 1914 forward (*Revelation: Grand Climax*, 22, 24).

27. Though R. B. Lewis, "Ignatius and the 'Lord's Day,'" *AUSS* 6 (1968): 46–59, is correct that the term "day" is lacking in the Greek original.

within the New Testament itself there is no evidence that the Sabbath was "changed" from Saturday to Sunday. The custom of Sunday as a Christian "Sabbath" became widespread only in a later period, probably after A.D. 321, as church historian Henry Chadwick points out:

> An inscription found near Zagreb records that Constantine changed the old custom of working for seven days and holding a market-day every eighth, directing farmers to hold their market-day each Sunday. This is the earliest evidence for the process by which Sunday became not merely the day on which Christians met for worship but also a day of rest, and it is noteworthy that in both law and inscription Constantine's stated motive for introducing this custom is respect for the sun.[28]

Some Christians argue that no weekly day of rest remains necessary; we should celebrate every day alike (Rom. 14:5–6) and enjoy Jesus' Sabbath-rest continually (Heb. 4:9). Others argue that because God built a day of rest into the nature of creation (Gen. 2:2–3), we will function in much better physical and emotional health if we take a day away from our work each week, though the particular day is less important.[29] Those who insist on a particular day, however, cannot insist from the authority of Scripture that the day must be Sunday.[30] Likewise, some of those who argue that the particular day in Scripture is Saturday and was never changed insist that one should attend church on Saturday; but Scripture does not require one to hold church on one's day of rest. The connections between the "Lord's Day" and the Sabbath on the one hand and between the Sabbath and church services on the other are postbiblical, and we should be charitable for differences of practice on this point.

In which Spirit? If we have correctly understood this verse as including a reference to Spirit-filled worship, we must be careful in applying it today. Different churches and cultures have different understandings of what "Spirit-filled" worship is. Some prefer lively Scripture choruses; others prefer

---

28. Henry Chadwick, *The Early Church* (New York: Penguin, 1967), 128. Constantine may have also chosen the date for Christmas to subsume worship of the sun under worship of Christ (see E. Glenn Hinson, "Worshiping Like Pagans?" *Christian History* 37 [1993]: 16–20 [p. 20]). For a second-century date, see in more detail Samuele Bacchiocchi, *From Sabbath to Sunday: A Historical Investigation of the Rise of Sunday Observance in Early Christianity* (Rome: Gregorian Univ. Press, 1977).

29. On the importance in general of consecrating some weekly day, see Eugene H. Peterson, "Confessions of a Former Sabbath Breaker," *CT* (Sept. 2, 1988), 25–28; idem, "The Good-for-Nothing Sabbath," *CT* (April 4, 1994), 34–36.

30. See "Consider the Case for Quiet Saturdays," *CT* (Nov. 5, 1976), 42.

---

traditional church hymns that sometimes reflect a deeper contemplation of Scripture than songs that merely quote Scripture (sometimes out of context, like "This is the day" in Ps. 118:24). Some preferences in worship style reflect cultural or generational differences rather than the presence or absence of the Spirit and are best tailored to those we invite to worship. I know some aging churches that cannot understand why they are not attracting younger worshipers, yet nothing in the style of music reveals their commitment to younger worshipers' culture!

At the same time, the content of the worship songs may be significant: Do they invite us to worship our awesome God, or simply to enjoy the music (not that bad music is necessarily more conducive to good worship)? Do they provide simply nostalgic feelings of security for traditional believers, or do they provide us the opportunity to transcend our feelings in obediently glorifying God? In any case, we need to depend on the power of God's Spirit to lead us deeper in our intimacy with him; we cannot achieve that by merely "fleshly" or mechanical means. Only by depending on God's power can we offer worship truly worthy of his honor.

One should also be careful in applying this text to not promise too much. Jewish mystics and apocalyptists in John's day sometimes offered formulas for how one could be caught up into heaven to receive visions or revelations; some of these techniques were magical and involved spirits other than God's Spirit. Like the biblical prophets, however, John was simply spiritually prepared when Jesus came to him (cf. Isa. 6:1, 5; 2 Cor. 12:2–4); he was not trying to induce a vision.[31] Scripture does allow that prophets could seek God for guidance (Dan. 2:18–19), but the means were always prayer, not magical manipulation, and God could also speak to those who were not seeking a revelation (e.g., Judg. 6:11–12; Acts 10:9–13).

We cannot promise how God will meet his people in worship or other experiences in the Spirit. But we can promise that when they turn their eyes to him, they will find his presence, and in his presence they will begin to learn the answers they need. The answers we need are not always the answers we want (John promises greater hardship), but they are also often better than we can guess (compare the picture of the new Jerusalem).

Lampstands, Judaism, and the church. How should we apply today John's application of the lampstand, a standard symbol of Judaism, to the

---

31. Due to his verbal lucidity, many are skeptical that John's state is ecstatic (Hill, *New Testament Prophecy*, 90; M. Eugene Boring, *Sayings of the Risen Jesus*, SNTSM 46 [Cambridge: Cambridge Univ. Press, 1982], 83). For requests for revelation, see Norman B. Johnson, *Prayer in the Apocrypha and Pseudepigrapha*, JBLMS 2 (Philadelphia: Society of Biblical Literature and Exegesis, 1948, 34–36); on unsolicited visions, see Aune, *Prophecy In Early Christianity*, 118.

churches in 1:12, 20? We cannot suppose that he is addressing only ethnically Jewish Christians in the seven churches; long before this period Gentiles had become Christians in some of these cities (e.g., Acts 19:10, 17). Some Christians have responded to this and other New Testament passages by claiming that the church has replaced Israel in God's plan; Jewish scholars tend to react with hostility to such claims, especially since the Nazi Holocaust in "Christian" Europe.[32] Has the "church" replaced Israel?

To understand John's perspective requires us to set aside for a few moments nineteen centuries of subsequent interpretation and imagine ourselves among first-century Christians. Jewish Christians proclaiming a Jewish Messiah, the fulfillment of ancient promises to Israel, won pagan, usually polytheistic converts to faith in Israel's one God. Unlike most other Jews, Jewish Christians in Paul's circle did not require Gentile converts to be circumcised, but they nevertheless embraced them as new participants in their Jewish faith in Jesus, spiritual children of Abraham (Gal. 3:29), inwardly circumcised (Rom. 2:28–29). They viewed such Gentile converts as grafted into Israel, while unbelieving branches were broken off (11:17).

Although people rarely understood this perspective before Jesus came, the principle was already available in the Old Testament (cf. Rom. 16:25–26). God had cut off disobedient Jewish individuals from the blessings of his covenant; in some generations, this involved even the majority of the nation (Deut. 1:35–38), though in other generations it involved only a small minority (Josh. 1:16–18). Likewise, Gentiles sometimes became members of the covenant community (e.g., Josh. 6:25; Ruth 1:16; 2 Sam. 8:18), though they had always been a minority.

John's circle of Christians believed that they were the heirs of the Old Testament promises, but probably did not think in terms of a largely Gentile church "replacing" Israel. Instead, they most likely saw the Jewish people who rejected Jesus as apostate from Israel (2:9; 3:9), just as the Dead Sea Scrolls viewed Jewish people who rejected their teaching; they probably saw Gentile Christians as converts to the truest form of Judaism. In other words, John uses the "lampstand" image to stress the Jewishness of faith in Jesus and the continuity of believers' faith with the heritage of ancient Israel.[33] In our less polemical situation today, Gentile Christians should continue to

---

32. Many Christians did seek to protect Jews from Hitler's agents (see esp. David P. Gushee, *The Righteous Gentiles of the Holocaust: A Christian Interpretation* [Minneapolis: Fortress, 1994]); but these were only a small percentage of professing Christians.

33. Because Jews were exempted from worshiping the emperor, appealing to the Jewishness of their faith also provided a strategy for combating persecution by the governing authorities—though in the end it seems not to have persuaded them (see comment on 2:9).

see themselves grafted into the spiritual heritage of Israel, yet we should do so by recognizing, as we often have failed to do, that it was we and not the heritage that changed.[34]

SHARING IN SUFFERINGS. Sometimes we pontificate too easily about the sufferings of others that we have not shared, and our insensitivity becomes obvious. This can happen with all kinds of deprivation, not simply the persecution John shared. I attended a singles meeting where a pastor who had been married since his early twenties lectured his hearers on how they ought to be content with their singleness. Although I agreed with his premise, I saw no proof from his own life that he understood the heaviness of his demand, how much some singles had to pray and fast and seek God's strength to rest content while waiting for something that mattered to them very much. He may have been more persuasive if he could have better identified with his hearers' situation.

Those who share in sufferings or in the world's opposition often are unified in ways that surmount other barriers. In Bible college some of us nearly broke fellowship over details about the end times, though most of us belonged to the same denomination. By contrast, in the high school and secular universities I attended, as well as at secular jobs I worked, committed Christians stuck together regardless of denominational differences.[35]

We should also notice John's point that "suffering" is "ours in Jesus"; one cannot follow Christ and not experience affliction. Some churches today teach prospective converts that God will solve all their problems and bless them with abundance if they become Christians, but this was not what the apostles taught new converts (Acts 14:21–22), nor was it the life that the apostles themselves experienced (1 Cor. 4:11–12). With proclamation comes persecution and sometimes deprivation; banishment often could include seizure of any assets one had. The leaders of John's society cut him off from everything else familiar to him, but the aged prophet still retained his greatest security: God is sovereign in testing (1:8), and just as he suffered with Christ, he would also reign with him (Rom. 8:17; 2 Tim. 2:12). If he shared

---

34. Paul may have viewed Gentiles as in some sense proselytes to spiritual Judaism; see Terence L. Donaldson, "'Riches for the Gentiles' (Rom 11:12): Israel's Rejection and Paul's Gentile Mission," *JBL* 112 (1993): 81–98.

35. For the same sort of reason, many North American evangelical leaders today have argued that in an increasingly secular society, conservative Catholics and evangelicals often share a common voice on moral and spiritual issues despite our differences; see Charles Colson and Richard John Neuhaus, eds., *Evangelicals and Catholics Together* (Dallas: Word, 1995).

with his fellow believers the sufferings of Christ, he also shared Christ's perseverance and ultimately his kingdom, as this passage declares (1:9). As F. F. Bruce puts it,

> [John's] placing of "the kingdom" between "the tribulation" and "the patient endurance" underlines a recurrent New Testament theme—that the patient endurance of tribulation is the way into the kingdom of God. If, then, John encourages his friends in the churches of Asia to stand firm, he is not cheering them on from the sidelines; he is involved with the same struggle.[36]

John's response to his suffering may also be instructive to some believers today who feel that an easy life is our birthright and prove hostile to those who threaten it. Some of John's contemporaries advocated violent resistance against Rome, but John is among those who wait on God for deliverance. At the same time, John is not completely passive; he believes, like some of his Jewish contemporaries, that suffering and martyrdom for God's word hastens the end (6:9; cf. Col. 1:24).[37]

Revelation in the context of worship. If John was worshiping "in the Spirit" as we have suggested (or in any case overwhelmed by God's Spirit), this passage suggests to us that we are apt to hear from God most clearly when it is his face and glory we are seeking. My first year in Bible college a student named Lillian prayed for many hours each day—her life so anointed for prayer that every time I even saw her, I felt an urge to run somewhere and pray. Some of her witnessing partners told me stories about her witnessing methods: For example, when a man was mocking her witness, she began listing his secret sins, leading quickly to his repentance. We each have different gifts; Lillian told me whenever she saw me, it made her want to run and read her Bible. But devotion to prayer and worship often opens our hearts more fully to other aspects of the Spirit's testimony.

Throughout Revelation we see the saints in heaven engaged in worship (4:10; 5:14; 7:11; 11:16; 19:4), while saints are being slaughtered on earth and followers of the beast worship the beast (13:4, 8, 12, 15; 14:9–11). The scenes of heaven are intended as scenes of worship, for heaven's furniture is the furniture of the Old Testament temple: the ark (11:19), the tabernacle (15:5), the altars of incense and sacrifice (6:9; 8:3–5; 9:13), the sea (4:6; 15:2; cf. 1 Kings 7:23–25, 39, 44)—and, of course, the lampstands (Rev.

---

36. F. F. Bruce, *The Message of the New Testament* (Grand Rapids: Eerdmans, 1981), 85.

37. Adela Yarbro Collins, "The Political Perspective of the Revelation to John," *JBL* 96 (June 1977): 241–56 (esp. 255–56); S. Légasse, "Les chrétiens et le pouvoir séculier d'après l'Apocalypse johannique," Bulletin de Littérature Ecclésiastique 80 (1979): 81–95; cf. also a noneschatological equivalent in 4 Macc. 6:28–29; 17:20–21.

1:12–13; 2:1, 5). The church on earth is never closer to heaven than when we are offering God and the Lamb the glory they deserve; it is then that we experience "in the Spirit" a foretaste of heaven (cf. 1 Cor. 2:9–10; 2 Cor. 5:5).[38] A church that is suffering in this world will long for heaven, and in turning our hearts toward our heavenly king we will find strength to remember that the future world belongs to us.

The book of Revelation is a book of worship that summons us to recognize the awesome majesty of our Lord. The congregation I pastored used a number of worship choruses from the this book, so in one of my first sermons I interspersed these worship choruses with the sermon as a way to both explain the contextual significance of the subject of our songs and respond to the message of Scripture by adoring the God who had spoken to us in it.[39]

Jesus among the churches. One of Revelation's most important declarations is that Jesus appears among the lampstands (1:12; 2:1), which represent the seven churches (1:20). One need only skim the letters to these churches in chapters 2 and 3 to realize that five of them needed serious correction. Nevertheless, until a church has gone so far as to be withdrawn from its place (2:5), it remains the place where Christ's presence is found.[40] One might remember the Corinthian Christians, "sanctified in Christ Jesus" (1 Cor. 1:2); despite their lifestyle (3:3; 5:2), God still viewed them according to his finished work in Christ (6:11). We see here in Revelation Christ's faithfulness to the church, including the local church. When we see the flaws in churches, our tendency is sometimes to react with disdain; but we must never give up on the spiritual life that remains in the church, for the Lord of the churches, who offered his blood to redeem them, still loves them and walks among them (cf. 1:5; 3:4).

Because John portrays the churches symbolically as "lampstands," a traditional Jewish image, he emphasizes the Jewishness of our faith. We Gentile Christians too often treat the Old Testament like a mere prolegomenon to the New Testament, or its history as a boring and irrelevant story with no relevance to our lives today. Nothing could be further from Scripture's intention![41] We

---

38. On recognizing "worship in the Spirit" as a foretaste of the future world, see David E. Aune, *The Cultic Setting of Realized Eschatology in Early Christianity*, NovTSup 28 (Leiden: Brill, 1972), 12–16.

39. D. L. Barr, "The Apocalypse of John as Oral Enactment," *Interp* 40 (1986): 243–56, suggests that John designed Revelaton for oral enactment, most likely during the Eucharistic liturgy.

40. See Bowman, *First Christian Drama*, 25.

41. For various views on the relevance of the Old Testament for believers today, see Walter C. Kaiser Jr., *The Old Testament in Contemporary Preaching* (Grand Rapids: Baker, 1973); Daniel P. Fuller, *Gospel and Law: Contrast or Continuum?* (Grand Rapids: Eerdmans, 1980); David

should read the stories of patriarchs and prophets as the stories of our spiritual ancestors, and ourselves as grafted by mercy into God's single plan in history for his people running from Abraham forward. We should learn from Judaism an appreciation for a heritage that Jewish tradition has often preserved with greater reverence than we have (cf. Rom. 11:16–18, 24). At the same time, the New Testament witness is unanimous that no heritage or tradition is adequate to make us right with God; only faith in his Son, Jesus, can do this (John 14:6; Acts 4:12).[42]

Applying this lesson will be easier in some contexts than in others. Many Christians in the urban areas of the United States have Jewish friends and may be inclined from the start to reclaim the Jewishness of their faith; by contrast, presenting faith in Jesus as conversion to Israel's heritage in the Arab world could lead to serious misunderstandings without careful explanation of biblical teaching about the role of Arab peoples in God's plan (cf., e.g., Isa. 19:24–25). Ultimately, it was God's plan from the start to bless all peoples; but he chose the history of a particular people as the channel through which that blessing would come (Gen. 12:3).

L. Baker, *Two Testaments, One Bible*, rev. ed. (Downers Grove, Ill.: InterVarsity, 1991); Wayne G. Strickland, ed., *The Law, the Gospel, and the Modern Christian: Five Views* (Grand Rapids: Zondervan, 1993).

42. See Keener and Usry, *Defending Black Faith*, 108–35.

Revelation 1:13–20

🌿

AND AMONG THE lampstands was someone "like a son of man," dressed in a robe reaching down to his feet and with a golden sash around his chest. [14]His head and hair were white like wool, as white as snow, and his eyes were like blazing fire. [15]His feet were like bronze glowing in a furnace, and his voice was like the sound of rushing waters. [16]In his right hand he held seven stars, and out of his mouth came a sharp double-edged sword. His face was like the sun shining in all its brilliance.

[17]When I saw him, I fell at his feet as though dead. Then he placed his right hand on me and said: "Do not be afraid. I am the First and the Last. [18]I am the Living One; I was dead, and behold I am alive for ever and ever! And I hold the keys of death and Hades.

[19]"Write, therefore, what you have seen, what is now and what will take place later. [20]The mystery of the seven stars that you saw in my right hand and of the seven golden lampstands is this: The seven stars are the angels of the seven churches, and the seven lampstands are the seven churches.

AFTER INTRODUCING THE setting for his vision of Christ (1:9–12), John turns to the vision (1:13–16) and the beginning of Jesus' message to the churches (1:17–20), followed by the letters to the seven churches (2:1–3:22).

John's Vision of the Son of Man (1:13–16)

THE FOCUS OF many reported visions by Jewish mystics and apocalyptic seers was God on his throne,[1] but Revelation opens with Jesus as the revealer. The robe and girdle may recall the biblical high priest (Ex. 28:4; 39:29; Lev. 8:7)[2] and suggest that Jesus is his people's high priest (cf. the similar garb of

---

1. See Ira Chernus, "Visions of God in Merkabah Mysticism," *JSJ* 13 (1982): 123–46.

2. So Caird, *Commentary on Revelation*, 25. Others object that the image need not be so specific; the girdle is worn high to contrast with a laborer whose work remains incomplete (Beasley-Murray, *Revelation*, 66–67).

Jesus' bride in 21:19–20; she is a kingdom and priests). Though the girdle might also recall Daniel 10:5, which is relevant in this context, it may still derive its symbolic meaning from priestly imagery; the only other occurrence of girdles in Revelation is 15:6 (also "golden"), where it is priestly imagery for angels in the heavenly temple. Thus Jesus appears not only as king, but as priest, a combination of images that grew familiar to Jewish people in the Maccabean period.[3]

The image of Jesus in this passage weaves together imagery from three sources in the book of Daniel. The first (the least important) is the angelic revelation in Daniel 10:5–6, but the two most important stem from the same passage: the reigning son of man (7:13–14) and the Ancient of Days (God), before whom the son of man appears (7:9).

The angelic features in John's vision of Jesus (eyes like fire and limbs like bronze in Dan. 10:6,[4] though bronze limbs may also recall Ezek. 1:7) do not reduce Jesus to an angelic level, but probably simply suggest Jesus' great glory; he cannot be portrayed as less glorious than a glorious angel. Eyes like fire describe passionate eyes in Greek literature,[5] but they can also depict the supernaturally flaming eyes of divine beings or angels;[6] glowing metal may also depict God's glory in Ezekiel 1:27.

Yet other features suggest that while John portrays Jesus' glory as no less than that of an angel, it is certainly *more* than that of an angel. The voice like "the sound of rushing waters" (1:15; cf. 19:6) may recall the voice like a multitude in Daniel 10:6, but especially recalls the sound of God's own voice as many waters in Ezekiel 1:24; 43:2 (cf. 4 Ezra 6:17).[7] Jesus' title ("someone 'like a son of man,'" Rev. 1:13) recalls the figure who would reign as God's agent in Daniel 7:13–14; the hair like wool and comparison with white snow (1:14) allude to God himself, the "Ancient of Days" in the same Daniel passage (Dan. 7:9–10).[8]

---

3. See further Beale, *Revelation*, 208–9, who associates Daniel's images with the priesthood as well. Aune, *Revelation*, 1:94, parallels gold tunics in Hellenistic epiphanies.

4. Cf. Christopher Rowland, "The Vision of the Risen Christ in Rev. i.13ff.: The Debt of an Early Christology to an Aspect of Jewish Angelology," *JTS* 31 (1980): 1–11; idem, "A Man Clothed in Linen: Daniel 10.6ff. and Jewish Angelology," *JSNT* 24 (1985): 99–110. Cf. angelophanies in 3 Enoch 22:4–9; 26:2–7; 35:2; the similar angelophany in Apoc. Zeph. 6:11–15 may be an Ebionite response to the Christology of Rev. 1:13–16.

5. Fury in Homer, *Il.* 1.104; 12.466; 19.16–17, 365–66, 446; passion in Ovid, *Metam.* 4.348–50; beauty in Herodian 1.7.5.

6. *PGM*, 4.703–4; 3 En. 18:25; 35:2; Jos. and Asen. 14:9; perhaps Homer, *Il.* 1.200, 206.

7. Later Jewish tradition comments on these waters in its portrayals of heaven; see comment on 4:6.

8. The Old Greek version of Dan. 7:13 also conflates the two figures; see Loren T. Stuckenbruck, "'One Like a Son of Man As the Ancient of Days' in the Old Greek Recension of Daniel 7,13: Scribal Error or Theological Translation?" *ZNW* 86 (3–4, 1995): 268–76.

Jesus' face also shines like the sun (1:16). Greek texts sometimes portrayed deities shining like the sun or lightning;[9] Jewish texts did the same for angels (cf. 10:1) and others,[10] but also for God himself.[11] The point of Jesus' fiery eyes, white hair, and bronze feet (1:14–15) is that he was radiating light or fire (the bronze is said to be "glowing" in 1:15)—like some visions of God in the Bible (Ezek. 1:27; Dan. 7:9–10; cf. Rev. 21:23; 22:5).[12] Other deities were portrayed as bearing swords,[13] but this image is an allusion to Isaiah 11:4 ("He will strike the earth with the rod of his mouth; with the breath of his lips he will slay the wicked")[14] and Jewish images of God's Word as a warrior with a sword (Wisd. 18:15; cf. Rev 19:15).

Jesus' Message (1:17–20)

JOHN RESPONDS TO this revelation of Jesus' glory by falling down prostrate at his feet "as though dead" (1:17). Other prophets had responded this way to divine and angelic glory (Ezek. 1:28; 3:23; 43:3; 44:4; Dan. 8:17; 10:9), so this came to be a standard response in Jewish tradition based on Scripture.[15] Falling as if one were "dead" simply drives home how completely John is overwhelmed; such language is again familiar as a response to traumatic revelations or news (Matt. 28:4).[16] When recipients of a traumatic revelation respond in such a manner, the revealer often raises the recipient on his feet or declares, "Do not be afraid" (Dan. 10:11–12; cf. Matt. 17:7).[17]

---

9. Aristophanes, *Lysis.* 1285; *PGM*, 4.635–38. Of a divinely terrifying mortal in Homer, *Il.* 18.205–6.

10. Angels: e.g., in Dan. 10:6; 2 En. 1:5; 19:1; T. Abr. 2; 7A; Jos. & Asen. 14:9; cf. further Mark S. Smith, "Biblical and Canaanite Notes to the *Songs of the Sabbath Sacrifice* from Qumran," *RevQ* 12 (1987): 585–88. Angels were typically thought to consist of fire (1 Enoch 17:1; 2 Enoch 20:1; 29:3; 4 Ezra 8:22). Cf. Abel in T. Abr. 12A; Moses in *b. B.B.* 75a; Zion in 4 Ezra 10:25.

11. E.g., Dan. 7:9–10; 1 Enoch 14:18–20; 46:1; 71:10; 3 Enoch 28:7.

12. That he is likely barefoot (1:15) would not surprise John's audience, who may have seen the common portraits of the deified emperor as barefoot (Aune, *Revelation*, 1:95).

13. E.g., Apollo (*Ap. Rhod.* 3.1283).

14. Cf. also judgment from God's mouth in 1 Enoch 62:2; the Messiah's in Ps. Sol. 17:35; 4 Ezra 13:10. Cf. the sword as a metaphor for speech in early Jewish texts (Prov. 12:18; 25:18; further, Aune, *Revelation*, 1:98–99).

15. E.g., Tobit 12:16; 1 Enoch 14:13–14; 60:3; 71:2, 11; 2 Enoch 21:2; 22:4; 4 Ezra 4:12; 10:30; Jos. & Asen. 14:10–11; T. Job 3:4/5; Apoc. Zeph. 6:9–10. Compare also the fear in Gen. 15:12; 1 Enoch 89:30–31; 102:1; Ach. Tat. 1.3.4–5.

16. See also 1 Sam. 25:37; Josephus, *Ant.* 6.306; 4 Macc. 4:11; Diodorus Siculus, 4.24.5; Petronius, *Sat.* 62; weakness in response to a revelation also appears in *PGM*, 4.725. But John meets the one who was truly dead and now lives (1:18).

17. Compare also Tobit 12:17; 1 Enoch 60:4; 71:3; 2 Enoch 1:8; 20:2; 21:3; 22:5; 3 Enoch 1:7, 9; 4 Ezra 5:14–15; Jos. & Asen. 14:11; *PGM*, 1.77–78; the command to stand in 2 Bar. 13:1–2.

Most important, Jesus is "the First and the Last" (1:17). This means more than simply "firstborn from the dead" (1:5); its sense is exactly equivalent to "the Alpha and the Omega," a title appropriate only to God (1:8; 21:6), probably applied to Jesus also in 22:12–13. Because it is precisely the same title that identifies deity in the same context (cf. Isa. 41:4; 44:6; 48:12), Jesus thus opens his revelation to John by announcing his deity. The state might demand worship of Caesar and many synagogues demand renouncing Jesus' deity, but if Jesus is truly Lord of the universe, he is worth suffering and even dying for.

All the claims of 1:18 involve Jesus' triumph over death. In the Bible and Jewish tradition, God is the "Living God" or the "Living One" (cf. also 7:2; 15:7), but Jesus is specifically called the "Living One" here because, though he had died, he is alive forever. Jewish people believed in a resurrection of the righteous at the end of time; the early Christians recognized Jesus' resurrection as the actual firstfruits, or first installment, on the future resurrection (see comment on 1:5). Thus by rising from the dead, Jesus guaranteed eternal life to all his followers, even if they faced death for his name (20:4)— a promise to the churches quite relevant in view of the rest of the revelation that follows.

Because of his victory over death, Jesus held the "keys of death and Hades" (1:18). In ancient palaces, the one who held the keys was an important official, able to admit or shut out people from the king's presence (see comment on 3:8). Hades was a Greek deity who ruled over the realm of the dead, the "house of Hades,"[18] but by this period his territory was widely known as "Hades."[19] "Death and Hades" together represent death's power; as Jesus had told Peter, the gates of Hades will not prevail against the church (Matt. 16:18). Greek texts spoke of coming to the realm of the dead as coming to the "gates" of Hades;[20] some Jewish texts likewise spoke of the "gates of [Sheol]" (Isa. 38:10) or the "gates of death" (Job 38:17; Ps. 9:13; 107:18), which appeared in Jewish texts written in Greek as the "gates of Hades" (e.g., Isa. 38:10 LXX; 3 Macc. 5:51).

Greeks told stories of heroes like Orpheus, who sought to bring his deceased wife from Hades but failed, and of Heracles, who succeeded in bringing some people up (e.g., Diodorus Siculus, 4.25.4; 4.26.1); but none of these heroes held the power to restore the dead in general. Pagans assumed that their god of the underworld (Hades, Pluto, or Anubis) held the keys to

---

18. Widespread as early as Homer (e.g., *Il.* 22.52, 213, 425, 482).

19. E.g., Homer, *Il.* 11.263, 445; Sophocles, *Ajax* 635; Euripides, *Ch. Her.* 218; *Electra* 142–43; Apollonius Rhodius, 2.609; 3.810..

20. Homer, *Od.* 14.156; Euripides, *Hippol.* 56–57, 1447; similar expressions in Euripides, *Hec.* 1.

that underworld.[21] In reality, however, only the truly risen and Living One, "the firstborn from the dead" (1:5), could release people from Hades, the realm of death. Jewish texts attributed this authority to God alone: "You have the power over life and death; you lead mortals down to the gates of Hades and back again" (Wisd. Sol. 16:13). The one who knows Jesus' identity, however, will not be surprised that he functions in this divine role (Rev. 1:17).

Others like the emperor, employing the brute power of the state, could have persons executed even if they could not restore the dead. Yet because Jesus holds the keys to death and Hades, he—rather than the Roman emperor or believers' other persecutors—controls who lives and dies. No hair of theirs will fall to the ground apart from his knowledge and will (Matt. 10:29–31), so those who trust his loving care do not need to fear. Death will not come to them by accident; when it comes, it comes only in the time our loving Lord permits it.[22]

When Jesus tells John to write "what you have seen, what is now and what will take place later" (1:19), he casts John in the typical role of a "witness" (1:2), one who must testify of what one has personally seen (Acts 22:15; 1 John 1:1–2).[23] (For "writing" apocalyptic visions, see comment on Rev. 1:11.) The combination of past, present, and future revelation in this verse reminds us again that Jesus is Lord of history (1:17): God is, was, and is to come (1:8). Pagans spoke of prophetic diviners and deities who recounted the past, present, and future,[24] but Jewish people and Christians recognized that only the true God reveals past, present, and future to his servants (Isa. 42:9; 48:5–7).[25] John encourages the persecuted part of his audience that the true Lord is genuinely in charge of history, hence of their heritage, their present situation, and their destiny.

---

21. Anubis in *PGM*, 4.340–41, cf. Apollodorus, 3.12.6. In Jewish tradition, of course, God or one of his chief angels held the keys (e.g., 3 Bar. 11:2; 4 Bar. 9:5; *b. Sanh.* 113a; but demons in 2 En. 42:1).

22. The now-common homiletical portrayal of Jesus as defeating Satan and rescuing the dead in Hades, however, is post–New Testament; see "Christ's Descent Into Hell" (tr. F. Scheidweiler in *New Testament Apocrypha,* 1:470–76).

23. One could take the "now" and "later" clauses as explaining "what you have seen" (Mounce, *Revelation*, 82), but this is less likely; all three clauses are parallel in formulation. Beale, *Revelation*, 152–60, finds an allusion to Dan. 2:28–29, 45 (probable at least in "what is to come").

24. E.g., Homer, *Il.* 1.70; Plutarch, *E at Delphi* 6, *Mor.* 387B; *Egyptian Book of the Dead*, spell 172.S–3. Gentiles divided time into past, present, and future (Seneca, *Dial.* 10.10.2) and debated whether oracular deities genuinely ruled or merely predicted the future (Lucan, *C.W.* 5.91–93).

25. They customarily used language about past, present, and future revelation similar to John's here (Jub. 1:4; Sib. Or. 1.3–4; 11.319–20; Ep. Barn. 1.7; incomplete but analogous, 2 Bar. 14:1).

The "mystery" in 1:20 is not one which God wishes to keep secret (cf. 17:7); God sometimes revealed his "mysteries" to seers in both the biblical (Dan. 2:27–30, 47) and apocalyptic (1 En. 103:2) traditions. That the stars in Jesus' hand represent the angels of the churches and the lampstands among which he stands represent the churches indicates Jesus' intimate care for his people: He is among them (cf. 21:3), and their future lies in his hand (cf. John 10:28–29). The star (of David) occasionally appears as a Jewish symbol in Roman inscriptions, but nowhere as early or as frequently as the lampstand.[26] More important, astrology pervaded Mediterranean thought by this period; people felt that fate controlled their future, guided or revealed through the stars. Even most Jewish people believed that God revealed the Gentiles' future through the stars.[27] By contrast, Jesus' followers have nothing to fear: Jesus holds the stars of the churches in his hand.

The more difficult question is: What are the angels of the seven churches? In Greek, the term used here (*angelos*) can mean simply "messenger,"[28] sometimes used for "messengers" of the gods.[29] Thus some interpret them as prophetic messengers bearing John's message.[30] Others apply the term to readers of the message in the congregations, that is, leaders whose title could also be translated "messengers."[31] Because a public reader in a congregation functioned as its "messenger" or agent before God, a reader who executed his task inappropriately could bring trouble on the entire congregation (*m. Ber.* 5:5). Some even apply them to bishops of local communities.[32]

---

26. E.g., *CIJ* 1:444, §621; 1:474, §661.

27. E.g., Josephus, *Ant.* 1.69; 18.216–17; Philo, *Creation* 58–59; *tos. Kid.* 5.17. Of relevance here, some also used the temple's seven lampstands to symbolize the "seven planets" (Josephus, *War* 5.217; *Ant.* 3.144–45; Philo, *Heir* 221; *Moses* 2.103). Some viewed literal stars as angels (1QM 10.11–12; 1 Enoch 18:14; 2 Enoch 4:1; 3 Enoch 46:1). Michal Wojciechowski, "Seven Churches and Seven Celestial Bodies (Rev 1,16; Rev 2–3)," *BibNot* 45 (1988): 48–50, suggests the sun, moon, and five planets, finding specific parallels in the church letters. For astronomical data about seven celestial bodies, see Aune, *Revelation*, 1:97–98.

28. E.g., Homer, *Il.* 22.438; Euripides, *Medea* 1120–1230; 1 Macc. 1:44.

29. Divine messengers, e.g., Homer, *Il.* 4.121; 24.169; Euripides, *Electra* 462; *PGM* 1.76–77, 172; occasionally for a human messenger of the gods (Epictetus, *Disc.* 3.22.23).

30. E.g., Aune, *Prophecy in Early Christianity*, 197; cf. perhaps Josephus, *Ant.* 15.136. The Hebrew term for "messenger" replaces "prophet" in the latest biblical prophets (Naomi G. Cohen, "From *Nabi* to *Mal'ak* to 'Ancient Figure,'" *JJS* 36 [1985]: 12–24).

31. Cf. Talbert, *Apocalypse*, 17. But this usage seems limited to rabbinic texts (cf. *b. Ber.* 7b), and even there the leaders of congregations probably doubled as readers only rarely (*tos. Meg.* 3:21). Brownlee, "Priestly Character," 224, suggests a priestly background for the image.

32. Fréderic Manns, "L'évêque, ange de l'Église," *Ephemerides Liturgicae* 104 (1990): 176–81, noting Jewish texts comparing priests with angels.

But Revelation, like other apocalypses, is full of angels; early Christian texts rarely use "angel" for a human being, and it is thus more natural to read the text as a reference to angels of some sort. The book of Daniel (Dan. 10:13, 20–21) and most of early Judaism recognized that heavenly angels guided the activities of earthly rulers, and in some Jewish traditions these angels shared the responsibility for the earthly rulers' behavior.[33] Thus these angels most likely represent guardian angels of the congregations.[34] Alternatively, one might view them as the heavenly representatives of congregational leaders, again functioning like guardian angels but of individuals (cf. Matt. 18:10).[35]

JESUS' APPEARANCE IN 1:13–16. Some interpreters have misapplied the image of Jesus in this passage, although sometimes with good intent. A pitfall that occurs in some circles is the attempt to identify the glorified Jesus' ethnic features. Some have pointed to the hair "like wool" (1:14) and argued that Jesus must have been African.[36] To be sure, Greeks and Romans described African hair as "wooly";[37] Daniel 7:9 compares God's clothing with the whiteness of snow (also 1 En. 14:20) but describes his hair only as being "like wool" (also 3 En. 28:7). But John specifically calls the hair "white like wool" (Rev. 1:14; also 1 En. 46:1; 71:10). Lest anyone miss the point, John clarifies further: "as white as snow" (Rev. 1:14), which was an even more common ancient way of describing whiteness.[38] The white hair, of course, means neither that Jesus was blond (as in some portrayals) nor that he was on the verge of dying from old age; it recalls the symbolically "aged" hair of the "Ancient of Days" (Dan. 7:9), reminding us that Jesus is God in the flesh.

These reservations hardly mean that Jesus was a white European. One would not expect to measure his pigment level while he was glowing, but during Jesus' earthly ministry he could blend into a crowd (John 7:10–11, 25),

---

33. See documentation in Craig S. Keener, *Paul, Women and Wives* (Peabody, Mass.: Hendrickson, 1992), 41–42 and notes.

34. Caird, *Commentary on Revelation*, 24.

35. Beasley-Murray, *Revelation*, 69 (citing the Persian *fravashis*).

36. For Christian groups, see some mentioned in Walter J. Hollenweger, *The Pentecostals*, tr. R. A. Wilson (Peabody, Mass.: Hendrickson, 1988), 294; Gayraud S. Wilmore, *Black Religion and Black Radicalism: An Interpretation of the Religious History of Afro-American People*, 2d rev. ed. (Maryknoll, N.Y.: Orbis, 1983), 153–54; in addition to Nation of Islam.

37. See Frank M. Snowden Jr., *Blacks in Antiquity: Ethiopians in the Greco-Roman Experience* (Cambridge, Mass.: Harvard Univ. Press, 1970), 6, 264.

38. E.g., Homer, *Il.* 10.437; Virgil, *Aen.* 11.39; *Ecl.* 2.20; Ovid, *Metam.* 13.789; Babrius, 45.3; Phaedrus, 5.7.36–37; Jos. & Asen. 5:4/5; 16:18/13; 22:7. Noah is so described in 1 Enoch 106:2; 1QpGen Apoc col. 2; angels in 1 En. 71:1.

suggesting an appearance compatible with most of his Jewish contemporaries. Jews were not Europeans and included a mixed ethnic heritage of primarily Middle Eastern but also some northern African blood.[39] Of far greater importance for Christians of any race or culture is Jesus' appearance in this glorified state: The risen Lord is powerful, even deity, and therefore can protect and empower his people in the face of their oppressors. As one charismatic Catholic writer remarks, the symbolic language of this passage does not give us an exact portrait of what Jesus always looks like; "it would be a horrible picture of a man with a sword sticking out of his mouth to begin with."[40] Instead, it teaches us about who he is.

Content of the revelation. One of the most blatant examples of reading something into a biblical text in this section is that committed by Jehovah's Witnesses, who try to evade the clear implications of Jesus' divine title "the First and the Last" in 1:17 (cf. 2:8).[41] Exactly this title is a divine title in Isaiah (Isa. 41:4; 44:6; 48:12) and is applied to God elsewhere in Revelation (21:6), especially in the form "the Alpha and the Omega" (1:8), which is equivalent (21:6; 22:13; see comment on 1:8) and also applies to Jesus (22:13). The book repeatedly applies Old Testament images concerning God to Jesus (e.g., 7:16–17). But such evasive interpretation may serve the helpful purpose it served me as a young Christian when I debated with Jehovah's Witnesses: It can force us to recognize our own evasive tactics in trying to get around various texts that conflict with our prejudices on various issues.

Some interpreters, for example, find in 1:19 ("what you have seen, what is now and what will take place later") a structuring device for the rest of Revelation: Beyond what John has already seen, he will report on the present (the seven churches) and things to come (the future in the rest of Revelation).[42] Clearly the verse promises revelation about both present and future, but it does not specify which passages in Revelation represent his own day and which represent the future.[43] One might argue from 12:5–6 that much more

---

39. See Glenn J. Usry and Craig S. Keener, *Black Man's Religion* (Downers Grove, Ill.: InterVarsity, 1996), 60–75; see also W. E. B. DuBois, *The World and Africa* (New York: International Publishers, 1965), 143.

40. John Randall, *The Book of Revelation: What Does It Really Say?* (Locust Valley, N.Y.: Living Flame, 1976), 45.

41. They claim it is a title merely "bestowed" by Jehovah and that the "Last" means the last one resurrected "by Jehovah personally" (*Revelation: Grand Climax*, 27–28), an idea for which Revelation provides no hint.

42. Cf. Ryrie, *Revelation*, 118.

43. Thus Aune, *The New Testament in Its Literary Environment*, 241, complains that even if it is a structuring device, this insight is not very illuminating. Gregory K. Beale, "The Interpretive Problem of Rev. 1:19," *NovT* 34 (1992): 360–87, argues that each of the clauses apply to the entire Apocalypse.

of Revelation than the letters to the seven churches includes John's own day; certainly many promises and warnings in the letters to the seven churches also involve the future.

Interpreters concerned with the symbols in Revelation should pay special attention to 1:20, where two of the key symbols are explicitly interpreted. As Gordon Fee emphasizes, "When John himself interprets his images, these interpreted images must be held firmly and must serve as a starting point for understanding others."[44] Jesus' triumph over death (1:18) is likewise relevant to his church as we face opposition today, but remains applicable to all believers, who will ultimately face death if they do not live until Jesus' return.

JESUS' APPEARANCE IN 1:13–16. One could feel the tension as I began to read from this passage in a Sunday morning service in a black Baptist church in North Carolina, the church in which I had been ordained some years earlier. In recent months white supremacists had burned a number of churches across the South, and this church had received threats that they would be next after the pastor had publicly taken a courageous stand against the burnings.[45] The threats had become so severe that a local rabbi had even promised to surround the church with his members to protect it—though I doubt that white supremacists would have considered Jewish volunteers a less appealing target.

Before the burnings had become a threat to us, I had already felt that the Lord wanted me to speak from this text when I would visit my church again. Now I explained that the point of Jesus' description here was not to tell us his complexion—but to declare his power. He was the reigning Lord of the universe, the one with the power over life and death (1:18). John was writing to persecuted Christians, reminding them that God was bigger than their trials; and that day John's message spoke across the centuries to our church in our trials. Our tension quickly gave way to celebration as we recognized the awesome power of our faithful Lord.

Jesus' message. In contrast to some passages in Revelation, this one requires little work to translate from John's setting to our own. John's audience included those suffering directly for their faith (2:10; 3:8–10), those fac-

---

44. Fee and Stuart, *How to Read the Bible*, 237.

45. For one example of racist instigation of many of the church burnings, the Southern Poverty Law Center eventually won a successful suit against a Klan group for the burning of Macedonia Baptist Church in South Carolina in 1995 ("'Day of Reckoning': Record Judgment Cripples Klan Group," *SPLC Intelligence Report* [Summer 1998], 6–7).

ing economic testing (13:17), those facing invitations to compromise (2:14, 20), and other sorts of challenges that continue today. Both we and the people in our churches face daily challenges that render relevant the reminder of Jesus' triumph over death and his lordship over human history. Specific applications will vary, depending on the experiences people among whom we minister face (such as unemployment, abandonment by a spouse or parent, bereavement, or harassment on the job for religious, sexual, or other reasons).

Most of all we must hear the promise that no matter what Christ's church faces, the future belongs to us. Some older North American Christians recall a time when symbols of Christianity were widely accepted as part of the fabric of our culture. Times have changed; in some parts of the United States, "freedom of speech" is held to uphold artwork insulting to Christ or a "cultural" statue of a pagan deity, whereas arguably "cultural" public nativity scenes at Christmas are banned as an insult to religious pluralism![46]

But such a situation should not alarm Christians into paranoid responses; Revelation addressed churches in a much harsher situation. In the Roman Empire Christians were a small and persecuted minority; no one but those who trusted Christ could have imagined that we would outlive that empire. In many parts of the world Christians today are advancing the gospel in the face of tremendous opposition;[47] the future of the church is bigger than any of us singly, but the future belongs to the church and to all its members, who share its hope and destiny (21:2–7). Like Jesus' triumph over death (1:18), the fact that Jesus holds the churches in his hands (1:20) reassures us that in the end God's benevolent purposes will triumph.

---

46. See Stephen V. Monsma, "Yelling 'Fire' in a Crowded Art Gallery," *CT* (Oct. 22, 1990), 40–41; Mark A. Kellner, "City Erects Pagan Sculpture," *CT* (Sept. 12, 1994), 62–63.

47. See, e.g., the conversion of thousands of Bihals in a largely Hindu region of India, and Muslim responses to the Jesus video in Jordan and the southern Philippines ("International Year 1997: Popcorn Testimonies, Various Individuals," Campus Crusade cassettes, 1997); on Muslim conversions, see, e.g., Stan Guthrie, "Muslim Mission Breakthrough," *CT* (Dec. 13, 1993), 20–26.

Revelation 2:1–7

T O THE ANGEL of the church in Ephesus write:

These are the words of him who holds the seven stars in his right hand and walks among the seven golden lampstands: ²I know your deeds, your hard work and your perseverance. I know that you cannot tolerate wicked men, that you have tested those who claim to be apostles but are not, and have found them false. ³You have persevered and have endured hardships for my name, and have not grown weary.

⁴Yet I hold this against you: You have forsaken your first love. ⁵Remember the height from which you have fallen! Repent and do the things you did at first. If you do not repent, I will come to you and remove your lampstand from its place. ⁶But you have this in your favor: You hate the practices of the Nicolaitans, which I also hate.

⁷He who has an ear, let him hear what the Spirit says to the churches. To him who overcomes, I will give the right to eat from the tree of life, which is in the paradise of God.

Original Meaning

BECAUSE THE LETTERS to the seven churches (chs. 2–3) are the most frequent source of preaching and provide so much of direct significance to the life of today's church, we will focus some special attention on this section. In this chapter, we will provide both general comments on the letters as a whole and specific comments on the letter to Ephesus.

The Letters in General

LIKE ALL LETTERS not carried by imperial couriers, the book of Revelation would have been carried by travelers or (in this case) personal messengers; apart from official business of the empire, no public postal service existed.[1] The letters to the seven churches are "prophetic letters," a sort of writing

---

1. William M. Ramsay, "Roads and Travel (in NT)," 5:375–402 in *The Dictionary of the Bible*, 5 vols., ed. James Hastings (New York: Charles Scribner's Sons, 1904); S. R. Llewelyn, *New Documents Illustrating Early Christianity*, vol. 7 (North Ryde, N.S.W.: Ancient History Documentary Research Centre, Macquarie University, 1994), §1 (pp. 1–25). Mail could thus take a long time (Seneca, *Ep. ad Lucil.* 50.1; M. P. Charlesworth, *Trade-Routes and Commerce of the Roman Empire*, 2d rev. ed. [New York: Cooper Square, 1970], 86).

that appeared earlier in the Bible (2 Chron. 21:12–15; Jer. 29), early Jewish literature (including 2 Bar. 77:17–19, 78–87; Ep. Jer. 1), and in some ancient Near Eastern sources (Mari letters). Given the authority of these letters, they also bear some resemblance to "ancient royal and imperial edicts."[2] But they resemble even more closely the biblical format of oracles concerning various peoples (Isa. 13–23; Jer. 46–51; Ezek. 25–32; Amos 1–2), here applied more specifically to God's people dispersed in different cities.[3]

Each letter is a prophetic word from Jesus (e.g., Rev. 2:1) through the Spirit (e.g., 2:7), who is inspiring John (1:10).[4] "These are the words" (2:1) is literally, "Thus says," a standard biblical prophetic messenger formula (e.g., Acts 21:11; hundreds of times in the Old Testament prophets). Each letter follows a similar pattern, balancing praise and reproof:[5]

- To the angel of the church in a given city, write:
- Jesus (depicted in glory, often in terms from 1:13–18) says:
- I know (in most instances offers some praise)
- But I have this against you (offers some reproof, where applicable)
- The one who has ears must pay attention to what the Spirit says
- Eschatological promise[6]

That the message is from Jesus, following the same form as oracles in the Old Testament (also T. Abr. 8A), plainly implies Jesus' deity.[7] Indeed, the descriptions of Jesus' glory formally resemble the sort of epithets with which Greeks often addressed their deities (e.g., Homer, *Il.* 1.37–38, 451–52).

Letter to Ephesus

THAT EPHESUS IS addressed first makes sense not only from a geographical perspective (if a messenger brought Revelation from Patmos) but from the perspective of its prominence in the province. Despite competition with

---

2. For edicts, see Aune, *The New Testament in Its Literary Environment*, 159, 242; idem, "The Form and Function of the Proclamations to the Seven Churches (Revelation 2–3)," *NTS* 36 (1990): 182–204; idem, *Revelation*, 1:126–28; Deissmann, *Light From the Ancient Past*, 374.

3. Cf. Mic. 1:6–16; for oracles concerning different peoples or places in the early Christian period, see Matt. 11:21–24; Sib. Or. passim (e.g., 5.447–67).

4. "This is what the Spirit says" characterized other Christian prophecies (Acts 21:11). Prophecies from Christ also appear in Odes Sol. 8:8–19; 17:6–16; 22:1–12; 28:9–20; 31:6–13; 36:3–8; 41:8–10; 42:3–20.

5. As recommended by ancient rhetoricians (Stowers, *Letter Writing*, 80–81).

6. William H. Shea, "The Covenantal Form of the Letters to the Seven Churches," *AUSS* 21 (1983): 71–84, compares biblical covenant patterns. Most biblical prophets concluded with a message of hope (as noted also by many ancient interpreters, e.g., *Pes. Rab Kah.* 13:14).

7. The form was also used in messenger formulas (e.g., 2 Kings 18:19; T. Job 7:10/8), but oracles imply a divine source.

both, Ephesus had proved more powerful than Pergamum politically and more favored than Smyrna for the imperial cult.

The portrait of an evil world ruler demanding worship (13:12–15) would certainly be relevant to Christians in Ephesus, who found themselves surrounded by symbols of civil religion. Augustus had allowed Ephesus to build two temples in his honor, and Domitian had named Ephesus "guardian" of the imperial cult, making it the foremost center of the imperial cult in Roman Asia. Ephesus, in fact, hosted a new cult of the emperors that had opened only about half a decade before Revelation was written. Ephesus honored Domitian at Olympic games just shortly before this book was written.[8] Nor was the emperor cult the only prominent element of paganism there: Ephesus was known for the worship of Artemis (Acts 19:23–40) and the practice of magic (19:13–19). It also had a large Jewish community (19:8–9).[9] All these elements would help make various features of the book relevant to them.

The presence of false teachers in Ephesus is hardly surprising (Acts 20:29–30; 1 Tim. 1:3–7); but Revelation 2:2 indicates that the church appears to have improved in discernment since Paul's day (2 Tim. 1:15), a practice they seem to have continued in the decades that followed (Ignatius, *Eph.* 6.2; 8.1).[10] That these teachers are self-styled apostles (2:2) need not mean that they claimed to be sent from Jerusalem per se (cf. 2 Cor. 11:13, 22), but probably implies that they have arrived from outside Ephesus (Ignatius, *Eph.* 9.1).[11]

Yet all that the Ephesian Christians are doing right is not sufficient to excuse what they are doing wrong. The fatal flaw in their behavior is their lack of love. Some interpreters have understood "forsaken your first love" to refer to a diminished love for God (cf. 12:11); more commentators today understand the phrase as love for one another (as likely in 2:19; cf. Eph. 1:15; Col. 1:4; 2 Thess 1:3). Both objects of love are possible (cf. Heb. 6:10), but surely the latter is included, given the ringing contrast between "hatred" of the Nicolaitans' works (2:6) and the lack of "love" in 2:4.[12]

---

8. For details, see Kraybill, *Imperial Cult and Commerce*, 27–28; Steven Friesen, "Ephesus: Key to a Vision in Revelation," *BAR* 19 (1993): 24–37.

9. On the Jewish community there, see *CIJ* 2:13–14, §§745–47; Kraabel, "Judaism," 51–60. Some Jewish oracles anticipated judgment on Ephesus and Smyrna (Sib. Or. 3.343–44). For magic there, see Floyd V. Filson, "Ephesus and the NT," *BA* 8 (Sept. 1945): 73–80 (p. 78); Clinton E. Arnold, *Ephesians: Power and Magic*, SNTSM 63 (Cambridge: Cambridge Univ. Press, 1989), 14–16; Paul Trebilco, "Asia," 291–362 in *The Book of Acts in Its Graeco-Roman Setting*, ed. D. W. J. Gill and C. Gempf (Grand Rapids: Eerdmans, 1994), 314.

10. Ignatius praises the Ephesian Christians highly, but for different works than in Revelation (Ramsay, *Letters to the Seven Churches*, 240–41).

11. See Michaels, *Revelation*, 70.

12. Many commentators apply it to love of fellow Christians (Ray Frank Robbins in George, *Revelation: Three Viewpoints*, 160; Beasley-Murray, *Revelation*, 75) or to both (Hemer,

Those who once knew what was right should "remember" that they can repent and return (2:5; cf. 3:3; Deut. 9:7; 16:3).[13] Some have understood the removal of the Ephesian church from its place (Rev. 2:5) as an allusion to the silt deposits of the Cayster River, which eventually forced the literal relocation of the city.[14] More likely Jesus directly threatens the church alone: The removal of its lampstand from before Christ means that it will cease to exist as a church—whatever else, if anything, it may continue to be.

We can only guess the identity of the Nicolaitans. The second-century identification with the biblical Nicolas (Acts 6:5) in Irenaeus (1.26.3; 3.11.1) is probably no more than a guess, as is the association with antinomian Gnosticism (Epiphanius, *Haer.* 1.2.25; Hippolytus, *Haer.* 7.24).[15] Nor do these heretics persecute from the outside, like the "Jews" of Revelation 2:9 and 3:9. The most reasonable guess is that they offer views similar to (but not identical with) those of "Balaam"—hence condone immorality and the eating of food offered to idols (2:14–15), apparently common areas of assimilation among early Christians (cf. 1 Cor. 6; 8–10).[16]

For the church in Ephesus, "overcoming" or "conquering" (2:7) requires more than the vigilance of theological watchmen; it requires the internal unity of love. The reward of such overcoming is eating "from the tree of life," a familiar image in ancient Judaism.[17] Ancient Jewish writers portrayed as a "tree of life" the righteous (Ps. Sol. 14:3–4), God himself (4 Macc. 18:16), edifying speech (Prov. 11:30; 15:4), and most frequently among teachers of the law, God's law (*Sifre Deut.* 47.3.2; *b. Ab.* 6:7). But here as in some Jewish end-time texts (e.g., 4 Ezra 8:52), the tree of life performs its original function in Genesis as a source of eternal life (Gen. 3:22; Rev. 22:2); it is the tree

---

Letters to the Seven Churches, 41). Beale, *Revelation,* 230–31, applies it to loss of zeal for witness, but this does not appear clear in the text.

13. "Remember" is common language in biblical (Deut. 4:10; 8:18; 16:12) and Hellenistic (see Aune, *Revelation,* 1:147) moral exhortation.

14. Ramsay, *Letters to the Seven Churches,* 243–45; somewhat differently, Hemer, *Letters to the Seven Churches,* 53.

15. The longer recension of Ignatius, *Trall.* 11 and *Philad.* 6 accuses Nicolaitans of loving pleasure, but these are not part of the original text.

16. Cf. similarly Fiorenza, *Revelation,* 195; Aune, *The New Testament in Its Literary Environment,* 245; Tenney, *Revelation,* 61; Panayotis Coutsoumpos, "The Social Implication of Idolatry in Revelation 2:14: Christ or Caesar?" *BTB* 27 (Spring 1997): 23–27; cf. the etymological connection with Balaam in Beale, *Revelation,* 251. The link with Balaam and Jezebel is, however, by no means certain (cf. W. M. Mackay, "Another Look at the Nicolaitans," *EvQ* 45 [1973]: 111–15).

17. See Erwin R. Goodenough, *Jewish Symbols in the Greco-Roman Period,* 13 vols. (New York: Pantheon, for Bollingen Foundation, 1953–1968), 7:87–134 (esp. 134).

in "paradise," God's garden.[18] Even apart from Scripture, Ephesian Christians will not find such an image unfamiliar; both traditional royal gardens in Asia and the garden estates of the Ephesian cult of Artemis boasted trees, and in the latter case also tree-shrines, which functioned as a place of asylum for suppliants.[19]

THE LETTERS IN general. Some commentators have noted that the churches are each invited to read the others' mail (undoubtedly a matter of some embarrassment to members of the churches addressed most harshly; cf. Col. 4:16). This interpretive principle is implied clearly enough in the text: Each church is called to hear "what the Spirit says to the churches" (note the plural). To what degree are the messages to the particular churches distinctive, and to what degree should they be read as samples of what is addressed to all the churches?

There is surely a sense in which each church receives the letter appropriate to it. In the early twentieth century William Ramsay (and more recently Colin Hemer) emphasized how the message to each church resembles what we know of the cities in which the churches existed. Some of Ramsay's parallels carry little weight by themselves, since some parts of the message would have fit a number of ancient cities; but some of his other parallels are stronger, and the cumulative weight of these is sufficient to support a connection in many cases.

Yet each church also receives the entire book of Revelation. Like all John's audience (1:3; 13:9; 22:17), each church must "hear," common enough language in both Jewish and Greek ethical exhortations;[20] the particular expression likely echoes Jesus' original teachings (Mark 4:9). Each church is also summoned to "overcome," which implies endurance in the coming trial depicted in much of the book (Rev. 21:7); the invitation probably also suggests the term's nuance of "conquer," especially if believers appear as God's end-time army (cf. comment on 14:3–4).[21] Each church shares the hope

---

18. Cf. "Tree of Life," 889–90 in *Dictionary of Biblical Imagery*, ed. Leland Ryken et al. (Downers Grove, Ill.: InterVarsity, 1998). The tree of life may symbolize resurrection in the Dead Sea Scrolls (Marc Philonenko, "Un arbre se courbera et se redressera [4Q 385 2 9–10]," *RHPR* 73 [1993]: 401–4). It probably represents eternal life in 1 Enoch 25:4–5.

19. Hemer, *Letters to the Seven Churches*, 44–51.

20. See Deut. 6:4; 9:1; Epictetus, *Disc.* 2.19.12; 3.24.68; Plutarch, *Lectures* 14, *Mor.* 45D.

21. For some further synthetic comments on "overcoming," see also Stephen L. Homcy, "'To Him Who Overcomes': A Fresh Look at What 'Victory' Means for the Believer According to the Book of Revelation," *JETS* 38 (June 1995): 193–201.

promised to the other churches; when the churches have heard this through to the end, they will recognize that the promises to all the churches are fulfilled in the book's closing vision of the coming world (chs. 21–22).[22]

The basic principle for applying these letters to ourselves and others today thus seems to be: If the shoe fits, wear it. To whatever degree our lives or churches reflect symptoms analogous to any of the churches the risen Lord addresses in these letters, we must take heed to "what the Spirit says to the churches."

The letter to Ephesus. A serious danger in hearing Jesus' message to the Ephesian church's weakness in love is that we will simply dismiss it from any relevance to ourselves. Yet dismissing the church in Ephesus is somewhat like reading the story of the Pharisee and the tax collector (Luke 18:9–14) and concluding, "Thank God I'm not like that Pharisee!" We need to hear the warning this church presents to us.

Another danger is for us to assume from the condemnation of false apostles that true apostles (except for John) had ceased. But do the false Jews of 2:9 and 3:9 imply that genuine Jews had ceased to exist? Like the false Jews, this counterfeit was potentially believable probably because genuine apostles also continued to exist (cf. 18:20; Eph. 4:11–13).[23]

Some matters are hard to apply or recontextualize because we do not know what they originally meant. Who were the Nicolaitans? Even though Scripture is God's Word, some understanding is missing to us today because we do not understand the immediate background known to the first audience (e.g., 2 Thess. 2:5).[24] But even if we do not know the specific nature of the error, the warning against the Nicolaitans retains for us its basic lesson that we should guard against false teachers—a lesson with a wide range of potential applicability.

THE LETTERS IN GENERAL. That the letters to the seven churches often betray characteristics of the cities in which these churches flourished reminds us how easily churches can reflect the values of their culture if we do not remain vigilant against those values. (This is especially

---

22. See G. R. Beasley-Murray, "The Contribution of the Book of Revelation to the Christian Belief in Immortality," *SJT* 27 (1974): 76–93.

23. I have argued elsewhere that there is no adequate biblical grounds to argue for the cessation of any gifts, even if in practice we may see little evidence of some of them in our circles (*3 Crucial Questions About the Holy Spirit* [Grand Rapids: Baker, 1996], 81–107).

24. This could happen with a variety of ancient works where we are too far removed from the ideal reader (e.g., Phaedrus, 3.1.7); ancients also understood that they could become too far removed from texts historically to understand them fully (Aulus Gellius 20.1.6).

true of the less persecuted churches.) Such parallels are noted at relevant points in the commentary, but one of Ramsay's other observations should be summarized here: The two cities that are now completely uninhabited belong to two of the churches most severely rebuked (Sardis and Laodicea); the two cities that held out longest before the Turkish conquest are the only two churches fully praised (Smyrna and Philadelphia); and the city of Ephesus was later literally moved to a site about three kilometers from where it was in John's day, just as the church was threatened with removal from its place (2:5).[25]

Such parallels may be coincidence, but they might also illustrate a pattern in history: The church, no matter how powerless in a given society, is a guardian of its culture. Just as the presence of the righteous in Sodom was the only factor that could have restrained judgment (Gen. 18:20–32), the fate of a culture may depend ultimately on the behavior of the believers in that culture. Given the high degree of assimilation of North American Christians to our culture's values—more time spent on entertainment than on witness, more money spent on our comfort than on human need—the prognosis for the society as a whole is not good. (On dangers of some forms of modern entertainment, see comment on 13:14.)

When pagans charged that Rome fell because of its conversion to Christianity, Augustine responded that it fell rather because its sins were piled as high as heaven and because the commitment of most of its Christian population remained too shallow to restrain God's wrath. Naturally we recognize that not all suffering reflects judgment; but some does, especially on the societal level. Is Western Christianity genuinely different enough from our cultures to delay God's judgment on our societies?

The letter to Ephesus. Positive models provided by the Ephesian church include testing of prophets; as relativism increases in our culture, discernment and backbone to stand against error become both increasingly unpopular and increasingly vital (see comment on 2:20).[26] The current postmodern culture of the universities encourages the sharing of diverse beliefs (welcoming Christians in some new ways and providing opportunities previously unavailable to us). But it also forbids us to try to convert anyone as if we have

---

25. Ramsay, *Letters to the Seven Churches*, 432–33.

26. For application, see Osei-Mensah, *God's Message*, 47–49. For some critiques of relativism today, see Joe Klein, "How About a Swift Kick?" *NW* (July 26, 1993), 30; George Will, "A Trickle-Down Culture," *NW* (Dec. 13, 1993), 84; Tim Stafford, "'Favorite-Song' Theology," *CT* (Sept. 14, 1992), 36–38; Christina Hoff Sommers, "How to Teach Right and Wrong," *CT* (Dec. 13, 1993), 33–37; Charles Colson, "Postmodern Power Grab," *CT* (June 20, 1994), 80; Peter Bocchino, "Words Without Meaning," *Just Thinking* (Ravi Zacharias Ministries; Winter 1995), 4–7; articles in *Worldwide Challenge* (July 1997).

absolute truth; "yet this is precisely what Christians aim to do."[27] We want people to understand the gospel, but we also seek for them to embrace it. Even many Christians, however, are growing uncomfortable with the idea of absolute truth.

If there were in John's day self-styled "apostles" (2:2) and prophets (2:20), preaching falsely called "deep secrets" (2:24), their number does not seem to have declined in our own, and the need for vigilance against infiltration by false teachers has not decreased. Thus, for example, a few charismatics have closed ranks against noncharismatic critics of excesses in Word-of-Faith circles, rather than carefully examining the challenges to see which are cogent.[28] Yet some of the Word-of-Faith teachings originally began with E. W. Kenyon, a non-Pentecostal whose thinking was heavily influenced by the New Thought movement, which also produced Christian Science; writers have shown that the Modern Faith movement's founder copied, at some points nearly word for word, from Kenyon.[29]

As a prophet and an apostle, John surely was not against prophets or apostles in general; but he demanded discernment in his day and would demand it no less in ours. If the Nicolaitans (2:6) supported the popular cultural values of sexual and/or religious compromise, they also serve as a warning to us to beware of modern purveyors of what people simply want to hear. Indeed, in talking with some members of churches that preach biblical holiness I have been struck by the number of people who embrace what their pastor says on matters that comfort them but prefer other, more worldly sources for instruction on morality.

Yet part of discernment involves knowing what we must discern, and the tragedy of the Ephesian church's failure on this count is a tragedy of human

---

27. Ajith Fernando, *Acts* (NIV Application Commentary; Grand Rapids: Zondervan, 1998), 59, citing as introductions to postmodernism Stanley Grenz, *A Primer on Postmodernism* (Grand Rapids: Eerdmans, 1996); J. Richard Middleton and Brian Walsh, *Truth Is Stranger Than It Used to Be* (Downers Grove, Ill.: InterVarsity, 1995); and Gene Edward Veith Jr., *Postmodern Times* (Wheaton: Crossway, 1994). For other various, mostly nuanced, responses to postmodernism, see *Christian Apologetics in the Postmodern World*, ed. T. R. Phillips and D. L. Ockholm (Downers Grove, Ill.: InterVarsity, 1995); *The Challenge of Postmodernism*, ed. David S. Dockery (Wheaton: Bridgepoint, 1995).

28. For a noncharismatic critique, see, e.g., Hank Hanegraaf, *Christianity in Crisis* (Eugene, Ore.: Harvest House, 1993); John F. MacArthur Jr., *Charismatic Chaos* (Grand Rapids: Zondervan, 1992), 264–90; from a charismatic perspective, see Gordon D. Fee, "The Disease of the Health and Wealth Gospels" (Costa Mesa: Word for Today, 1979); Bruce Barron, *The Health and Wealth Gospel* (Downers Grove, Ill.: InterVarsity, 1987); D. R. McConnell, *A Different Gospel* (Peabody, Mass.: Hendrickson, 1988); Charles Hummel, *The Prosperity Gospel* (Downers Grove, Ill.: InterVarsity, 1991). Cf. also Larry Bishop, "Prosperity," *Cornerstone* (Jesus People USA) 10 (May 1981): 12–16.

29. See in some detail McConnell, *Gospel*, 8–12, 21–50.

nature that recurs through history and in our own time. The same church that rightly "hated" the works of the Nicolaitans (2:6) wrongly abandoned their earlier commitment to "love" (2:4); like many Christians today, they may have neglected the adage that we should "hate the sin but love the sinner."[30] Today, in fact, our hatred of what we disapprove has sometimes carried beyond sin and those who commit it. Not all doctrines are at the heart of the gospel, not all errors are properly labeled heresy, and not all disagreements are worth fighting about.[31]

Yet despite important, notable exceptions, many of the churches most firmly committed to the truth of the gospel are also those churches that have drawn boundaries too tightly on secondary issues. Countless times we have witnessed committed Christians marginalized for their views on gender roles, their different cultural or political perspectives, or for other reasons.[32] In many of these cases those we have marginalized have naturally found circles where they were more accepted—even though many of those circles proved lax on matters that were close to their hearts (circles with the sin of Thyatira—see below).

In some of those cases I have also watched these wounded Christians react against the rejection they experienced in their more traditional background in ways that discarded the proverbial baby with the bath water. For example, a professor marginalized by her evangelical campus ministry years ago because she held different views on gender roles now reportedly multiplies her hostility toward the Bible among her students.

Often we have marginalized people by careless thinking—for example, in our biblically correct opposition to divorce we have sometimes condemned faithful spouses abandoned and divorced against their will (about as sensible as condemning a rape victim because we oppose rape).[33] When they then

---

30. See Darrell L. Bock, "Arrogance Is Not a Family Value," *CT* (Nov. 9, 1992), 10; Charles Colson, "Wanted: Christians Who Love," *CT* (Oct. 2, 1995), 112. Many address the specific issue of homosexual behavior, e.g., Stanton L. Jones, "The Loving Opposition," *CT* (July 19, 1993), 18–25; Tim Stafford, "Ed Dobson Loves Homosexuals," *CT* (July 19, 1993), 22; Thomas Schmidt, *Straight and Narrow?* (Downers Grove, Ill.: InterVarsity, 1995); Mindy Michels and Jenell Williams, "'Finding Common Ground': Anti-Gay Violence and Public Discourse," *The Graduate Review* (American University, 1996), 18–27.

31. For what a Calvinist and Arminian learned through their separation and reconciliation, see J. D. Walsh, "Wesley vs. Whitefield," *Christian History* 38 (1993): 34–37.

32. Note that a generation ago the fighting topics were more frequently end-times views or spiritual gifts. In contrast to this is the irenic tone in many multiple views books (e.g., Darrell Bock, ed., *Three Views on the Millennium;* Wayne Grudem, ed., *Are Miraculous Gifts for Today? Four Views* [Grand Rapids: Zondervan, 1996]; Zondervan's forthcoming four-views work on gender roles, ed. Craig Blomberg and James Beck); or the public dialogue in which Darrell Bock and I engaged on women's roles at Dallas Seminary in March 1999.

33. See Craig Keener, "Divorce as a Justice Issue," *Prism* 5 (Nov. 1998): 6–8, 20; idem, *... And Marries Another* (Peabody, Mass.: Hendrickson, 1991), 1–11; idem, "Some Reflections

leave our church, we sometimes feel confirmed in our suspicion that they must have been unspiritual to begin with!

Even when we are dealing with clear cases of sin and error, does not Scripture call us to offer correction with love and grace (Luke 15:1–2; 2 Tim. 2:24–26)? Meanwhile, as J. I. Packer rightly notes, many of us Western evangelicals "can smell unsound doctrine a mile away," and yet the fruit of personal experience of God often proves rare among us.[34]

A church where love ceases can no longer function properly as a local expression of Christ's many-membered body. This is one of the offenses for which a lampstand can be moved from its place (2:5), through which a church can ultimately cease to exist as a church. Some churches die from lack of outreach, lack of planning for the rising generation, or lack of courtesy to visitors; some churches, like the church in Ephesus, may risk simply killing themselves off by how they treat others.

---

on Justice, Rape, and an Insensitive Society," 117–30 in *Women, Abuse and the Bible: How Scripture Can Be Used to Hurt or Heal*, ed. C. C. Kroeger and J. R. Beck (Grand Rapids: Baker, 1996).
    34. J. I. Packer, *Knowing God* (Downers Grove, Ill.: InterVarsity, 1973), 25.

Revelation 2:8–11

TO THE ANGEL of the church in Smyrna write:

These are the words of him who is the First and the Last, who died and came to life again. ⁹I know your afflictions and your poverty—yet you are rich! I know the slander of those who say they are Jews and are not, but are a synagogue of Satan. ¹⁰Do not be afraid of what you are about to suffer. I tell you, the devil will put some of you in prison to test you, and you will suffer persecution for ten days. Be faithful, even to the point of death, and I will give you the crown of life.

¹¹He who has an ear, let him hear what the Spirit says to the churches. He who overcomes will not be hurt at all by the second death.

Original Meaning

JESUS' MESSAGE TO Smyrna highlights contrasts: The one "who is the First and the Last," who was dead but came to life, speaks to those who are impoverished yet rich, persecuted by those who claim to be Jews but are not, and will, like Jesus, find life in death.[1]

For three centuries Smyrna had been one of the most important cities in Asia Minor; this as well as its location may have merited its second place listing among the churches. Along with Pergamum (2:12), Smyrna vied with Ephesus for preeminence, though Ephesus remained the most powerful city in the province. Like Ephesus, Smyrna was an important center of the imperial cult in Asia, the second city to receive from an emperor this "privilege."[2] As noted earlier, only Jews were exempt from worshiping the emperor, for Rome knew that Jews were monotheistic and were an ancient, ethnic religion that merited tolerance. The recognition that Christians were a part of Judaism (they claimed that Jesus fulfilled biblical promises to ancient Israel) thus protected Christians (at least initially) from unnecessary persecution. Unfortu-

---

1. With Ford, *Revelation*, 394. "Poverty" sometimes appears as a title of piety in the Qumran Scrolls, but its contrast with true wealth suggests here genuine affliction.

2. Tacitus, *Ann.* 4.55–56. For other forms of paganism there, see Giulia Sfameni Gasparro, *Soteriology and Mystic Aspects in the Cult of Cybele and Attis* (ÉPROER 103; Leiden: Brill, 1985), 71–72.

nately, many synagogue leaders seem to have felt it necessary to distinguish themselves sharply from Christians or even to make the Jewish Christians unwelcome in the synagogues.

Smyrna's ruling class was predominantly Asian Greeks, with whom the Jewish community had less secure relations than, say, in Sardis.[3] The Jewish community in Smyrna seems to have been substantial, and they seem to have been on more positive terms with the Roman government.[4] At the same time, they could not afford to take chances; after the Judean war against Rome two decades earlier, which resulted in a special tax Jews everywhere in the empire had to pay, many Asian Jewish leaders were probably nervous about being associated with prophetic, messianic movements like Christianity.

Local Jewish repudiation of Christians apparently continued for several decades after this time. In the early second century some Jewish accusers participated in betraying to the Romans Polycarp, a disciple of the apostle John and bishop of Smyrna, leading to his execution.[5] Such conflicts help explain "the slander of those who say they are Jews and are not, but are a synagogue of Satan" (2:9). Public accusations within the Jewish community had earlier led to persecution of Jewish Christians, sometimes by Gentiles (Acts 13:50; 14:2, 19; 17:5; 18:12; 24:5; 1 Thess. 2:14–15). The synagogue of "Satan" also suggests involvement with "the devil," who would cast believers into prison (2:9–10). Many commentators thus recognize the likelihood that at least some members of the local Jewish community were collaborating with local officials to repress the Christian minority.[6]

Scholars have proposed other interpretations of the false Jews of this passage, but none of these proposals has gained any consensus, and none adequately explains the "slander" of these Jews that appears associated with the

---

3. While promising peace to Asia, a Jewish mantic could threaten Smyrna's demise (Sib. Or. 3.365–67; cf. 5.122–23, 306).

4. See Claudia J. Setzer, *Jewish Responses to Early Christians: History and Polemics, 30–150 C.E.* (Minneapolis: Fortress, 1994), 114. For the Jewish presence, see *CIJ* 2:9–12, §§739–43; *New Documents Illustrating Early Christianity*, vol. 3, ed. G. H. R. Horsley (North Ryde, N.S.W.: The Ancient History Documentary Research Centre, Macquarie University, 1983), 3:52, §17 (further, Goodenough, *Symbols*, 2:79–81; Colin J. Hemer, "Unto the Angels of the Churches," *Buried History* 11 [1975]: 62). Kraybill, *Imperial Cult and Commerce*, 170–94, suggests that the issue in the letters was Jewish but not Christian exemptions in pagan commerce.

5. *Mart. Polyc.* 13.1; 17.2. For later Jewish slanders against Christians claimed by Justin, Tertullian, and Origen, see Aune, *Revelation*, 1:162; see further discussion in Kraabel, "Judaism in Western Asia Minor," 32–40. For later martyrdoms in Smyrna, see James Parkes, *The Conflict of the Church and the Synagogue: A Study in the Origins of Antisemitism* (New York: Atheneum, 1979), 137.

6. E.g., Setzer, *Responses*, 101; Hemer, *Letters to the Seven Churches*, 67.

---

persecution Smyrnean Christians must be prepared to undergo. This slander most likely refers to "informers," what the Romans called *delatores*. Roman officials normally depended on informers as accusers before they would prosecute a case, and this was true for prosecution of Christians in Asia in the decades immediately following Revelation's publication.[7] Once admitted, however, such accusations often became excuses for destroying others on flimsy evidence if the officials would permit it.[8]

The passage envisions official persecution on the local level. Imprisonment (2:10), a Roman punishment, was usually a temporary detention until a trial and then either official punishment or release.[9] The punishment that the text suggests believers must prepare for is execution ("Be faithful, even to the point of death"); the Smyrnean Christians would thus understand what it meant to achieve victory while not loving their lives to the death (cf. 12:11).

One might object that the specific duration of the imprisonment ("ten days") suggests an emphasis on detention rather than on a later punishment; but this time period, like many others in Revelation, is probably a symbolic allusion to the Old Testament. Like Daniel and his colleagues (Dan. 1:12–14), the believers in Smyrna would be "tested" for ten days by others—but so that God might ultimately exalt them to fulfill his purposes in history. The duration of their detention might include torture in an attempt to secure information against others. The very knowledge that imprisonment could include such torture demanded faithfulness.[10]

Some commentators find significance in the particular title of Jesus in 2:8. Centuries before, Smyrna had nearly vanished but had recovered to become a prominent and beautiful city (Strabo, 14.1.37), allowing some to compare it with the mythical phoenix, a symbol of resurrection;[11] Jesus, by contrast, truly rose from death. Whatever the merit of this proposal, the primary emphasis on Jesus' resurrection here is the promise to the Smyrnean Christians, who may face death, yet dare hope in a crown of life to follow (2:10), and whose experience of martyrdom would spare them the horror of the

---

7. For delation in general, see W. J. O'Neal, "Delation in the Early Empire," *Classical Bulletin* 55 (1978): 24–28; E. A. Judge, *The Social Pattern of the Christian Groups in the First Century* (London: Tyndale, 1960), 71.

8. E.g., Herodian 7.3.2. Personal or factional causes may have generated many of the accusations (cf. Gary J. Johnson, "De conspiratione delatorum: Pliny and the Christians Revisited," *Latomus* 47 [1988]: 417–22).

9. See e.g., Hemer, *Letters to the Seven Churches*, 68.

10. Cf. *Digest* 48.19.29 in Aune, *Revelation*, 3:1166.

11. See further Hemer, *Letters to the Seven Churches*, 58–59, 63–64, 76. For prominence, see Dio Chrysostom, *40th Disc.* 14.

"second death" (2:11).[12] Many Smyrnean Christians were presumably familiar with Jewish martyrdom traditions that stressed faithfulness in facing death
(4 Macc. 7:15–16), the promise of eternal life for martyrs (16:25; 17:12),
and the crown of victory for those who overcome in martyrdom (17:15).

Crowns (wreaths of olive, laurel, pine, or celery) were appropriate to victory in battle and more often in athletic competition; hence, they became a
familiar symbolic image to all adults and most children in Roman Asia.[13]
People also gave crowns as other honors (Sir. 32:1–2), and the term *crown*
came to apply figuratively to any sort of honor or award.[14] Jewish end-time
reflection also spoke of crowns as rewards for the righteous, a tradition widely
circulated among early Christians as well.[15] In this passage the "crown" might
also represent a subtle contrast with the city's claims to power: Smyrna's
citadel was often compared with a crown, and nearly 20 percent of the
inscriptions from earlier centuries contain the wreath emblem.[16]

Whereas "overcoming" in Ephesus required restoration of love (2:4), in
Smyrna it demanded withstanding persecution. Popular Jewish teaching on
martyrdom already could identify martyrdom with overcoming (4 Macc.
9:24; 17:15), so no one could miss the point. But Revelation especially underlines the point in the image of the triumphant lion as a slain lamb in 5:5–6:
We overcome not by returning hostility but by laying down our lives in the
confidence that God will vindicate us.

---

12. In some early Jewish texts "second death" refers to annihilation (I. Abrahams, *Studies in Pharisaism and the Gospels* [2d ser.; Cambridge: Cambridge Univ. Press, 1924], 44; cf. Martin McNamara, *Targum and Testament* [Grand Rapids: Eerdmans, 1972], 123; perhaps *Gen.
Rab.* 96:5), but in Revelation the same phrase (20:6, 14; 21:8) refers to a resurrection to eternal torment (14:11; 20:10). The conception would be familiar even without a precise allusion to Jewish usage; one could even speak of added torment during death as a "second
death" (Phaedrus, 1.21.11).

13. For battle, see, e.g., Dionysius of Halicarnassus, 6.94.1; Arrian, *Alex.* 7.5.4; Aulus
Gellius, 5.6; for athletic competition, see Pausanius, 6.8.4; 6.14.11; Diodorus Siculus,
16.79.3; for the symbolic use, see Dio Chrysostom, *9th Isthmian Disc.* 10–12; Wisd. Sol. 4:2;
Josephus, *Apion* 2.217–18; T. Job 4:10/8; for posthumous awarding of wreaths, see Aune,
Revelation, 1:168–69.

14. E.g., Apuleius, *Metam.* 10.12; fig., Job 19:9; Prov. 4:9; 12:4; 16:31; 17:6; Isa. 28:1–
3; Ep. Arist. 280; *m. Ab.* 4:13; *Ex. Rab.* 34:2. It represents prosperity and ease in Prov. 14:24;
Lam. 5:16; Sib. Or. 5.100; celebration in Jub. 16:30 (esp. at weddings, Song 3:11; *Koh. Rab.*
10:5, §1; *Lam. Rab.* 5:16, §1); later Jewish tradition applied it to the Israelites at Sinai (*b. Shab.*
88a; *Pes. Rab Kah.* 16:3; *Song Rab.* 4:4, §1; *Lam. Rab.* 2:13, §17). Cf. also discussion in Aune,
Revelation, 1:172–75.

15. See Isa. 28:5; 1QS 4.7; Wisd. Sol. 5:16; 2 Bar. 15:8; Sib. Or. 2.153–54; T. Job
40:3/5; Gr. Ezra 6:17; *b. Ber.* 17a; *Meg.* 15b; *Deut. Rab.* 3:7; 1 Cor. 9:25; Phil. 4:1; 1 Thess.
2:19; 2 Tim. 4:8; James 1:12; 1 Peter 5:4.

16. See *New Documents*, 3:52, §17; Ramsay, *Letters to the Seven Churches*, 205; Hemer, *Letters
to the Seven Churches*, 59–60, 72–74.

Bridging Contexts

"SYNAGOGUE OF SATAN" (2:9) is strong language, and such words proved easy to exploit in the later history of the church.[17] While originally uttered as a protest against a dominant Jewish community oppressing a Christian minority, the language was recycled in the interests of later "Christian" regimes to persecute Jewish minorities, and it continues to figure prominently in the propaganda of violent Aryan supremacists in the United States today. Contemporary white supremacists aligned with the Christian Identity movement claim that people of color are mud people and Jews are the literal offspring of Satan and Eve (though a growing "moderate" faction claims that they are satanic, while not his literal descendants). The extreme white supremacists keep heavily armed, awaiting their Armageddon against the Jewish-controlled government of the United States, after which they will establish a new Jerusalem here.[18] As long as such views circulate, it remains important for genuine Christians to articulate what we do and do not mean.[19]

What is the proper way for Christian readers of Revelation today to take Jesus' words to Smyrnean Christians to our very different modern setting? The first step is to understand the circumstances Jesus is addressing. John's audience regard their congregations as Jewish; that is why they are portrayed as lampstands (see comment on 1:12). The earliest Christians were Jewish, and their earliest Gentile converts naturally regarded themselves as converts to the truest form of Judaism. In a world where most people venerated multiple deities and sacrificed before idols, and where Jewish sexual ethics and biblical history were disdained, Christians who worshiped Israel's God, embraced Israel's Messiah and Scriptures, and practiced sexual fidelity appeared as Jews. Unlike other Jews, however, they believed that obedience to Jesus was as nec-

---

17. For applications, see González, *Revelation*, 27. For the history of anti-Semitism in the church (though its roots are pre-Christian), see Edward H. Flannery, *The Anguish of the Jews: Twenty-Three Centuries of Anti-Semitism* (New York: Macmillan, 1965); James Parkes, *The Conflict of the Church and the Synagogue: A Study in the Origins of Antisemitism* (New York: Atheneum, Temple Books, 1979).

18. "Racist Identity Sect Fuels Nationwide Extremist Movement," *Klanwatch Intelligence Report* (Aug. 1995), 1–5 (pp. 3–4); "Mistaken Identity," *Intelligence Report* (Winter 1998), 8–9; Richard Abanes, *American Militias: Rebellion, Racism and Religion* (Downers Grove, Ill.: InterVarsity, 1996), 162–62; Richard Kyle, *The Last Days Are Here Again: A History of the End Times* (Grand Rapids: Baker, 1998), 160–61; Leonard Zeskind, "Justice vs. Justus," *Intelligence Report* (Spring 1988), 14–17 (p. 17).

19. Although not currently dominant, these white supremacists have sought to build "common ground" with nonracist fundamentalists who share some conservative agendas ("Racist Sect," 5); for the reality of the danger, see Abanes, *American Militias.*

essary in their own time as obedience to Moses' revelation had been in centuries past; consequently, they regarded Jews who rejected Jesus as apostate from the true faith of Israel. Note too that Christians were not the only Jewish movement to regard the rest of Israel as unfaithful or apostate; the same rhetoric appears in the Dead Sea Scrolls.[20]

When Jewish leaders in places like Smyrna denounced the Christians as no longer truly Jewish, it is not surprising that the Jewish Christians would respond, "It is you who have cut yourselves off from your heritage in God's covenant."[21] Some first-century Jewish people actually used "Jew" in a pejorative sense; here, however, it applies to those who truly fulfill their role as members of the covenant people.[22] The phrase "synagogue of Satan" is deliberately disjunctive and shocking and reflects the same sort of sentiments expressed by the Jewish author of a hymn found at Qumran, which labels Israel outside the Dead Sea sect the "congregation of Belial," or Satan (1QH 2.22–23).[23]

Christians today should not recycle first-century Jewish-Christian denunciations of their higher-class Jewish opponents in an anti-Jewish way. In today's society we have an opportunity—perhaps unique in human history—to dialogue in mutual respect with those with whom we disagree, trusting the Holy Spirit to use his truth to transform hearts. Christian anti-Semitism has erected the largest barriers to belief in Jesus that many modern Jewish people face; the largest consequent barrier may be the widespread premise that a Jewish person cannot be faithful to their ancestral heritage and believe in Jesus. Polemic reinforces that barrier, whereas love and appreciation for their—and our—heritage in biblical Judaism can reduce it.

The threat of death, though only realized among the Asian churches occasionally so far (2:13), proved genuine over the following centuries. It is too easy for North American Christians to pass over such texts as irrelevant to the challenges most of us currently face, especially for middle-class believers in the suburbs. But we need only ask some hypothetical "What if?"

---

20. Luke Timothy Johnson, "The New Testament's Anti-Jewish Slander and Conventions of Ancient Rhetoric," *JBL* 108 (1989): 419–41; cf. Craig Keener, *A Commentary on the Gospel of Matthew* (Grand Rapids: Eerdmans, 1999), 536.

21. Cf. Setzer, *Responses*, 100. Turning charges around was an accepted form of ancient conflict rhetoric (1 Kings 18:17–18; Matt. 12:24, 45; Cornelius Nepos, 7 [Alcibiades].4.6). For its social function in Christian self-definition, cf. Adela Yarbro Collins, "Vilification and Self-Definition in the Book of Revelation," *HTR* 79 (1986): 308–20.

22. For one discussion of the use of this language, see Craig S. Keener, "The Function of Johannine Pneumatology in the Context of Late First Century Judaism" (Ph.D. diss.: Duke University, 1991), 330–49.

23. Cf. true and false Greeks in Diogenes, *Ep.* 28, to the Greeks.

---

questions to bring the matter closer to home. The martyrdom of our brothers and sisters in the past as well as many in other locations in the present must challenge us to count the cost: How much is Jesus worth to us?

OF THE SEVEN churches, the only two that are unequivocally commended are the suffering churches in Smyrna and Philadelphia. Suffering has a way of reminding us which things in life really matter, forcing us to depend radically on God, and thus purifying our obedience to God's will.

But it is important to know God's heart before we face suffering, so that we may understand our suffering in light of his love for us, in light of his sharing our suffering in the cross, rather than interpreting his heart toward us on the basis of our suffering. As Billy Graham points out, "suffering has a mysterious, unknown component"; whereas Smyrna would face greater suffering (2:10), the other persecuted church (Philadelphia) would be delivered (or on our view, strengthened) through theirs (3:10). In the same way, James was executed but Peter was released (Acts 12:2–7); some experienced miraculous release while others died (Heb 11:35); Corrie ten Boom survived the Nazi prison camp but her sister died there. We cannot explain why some suffer much more than others. "All I know from the short letters in Revelation," Graham concludes, "is this: Christ commands us to 'Overcome!' in the strength He alone can supply...."[24]

I have close friends from other parts of the world who face sufferings more intensely than the vast majority of Westerners can identify with. For instance, I have listened to some of my Nigerian friends as they mourned how radical Muslims in their part of the country had rioted, murdering Christian pastors who were friends of theirs; they also noted that the murderers would never be brought to justice by the Muslim government then in power.[25] An African commentator lists many prominent African martyrs, including many under the Muslim Idi Amin in Uganda and during a revival of traditional religions in Chad—suffering that they "endured joyfully for Jesus' sake." The East African revival likewise prepared many Kenyan pastors to refuse the

24. Graham, *Approaching Hoofbeats*, 60–62.

25. For news reports, see "Did Muslims Plan Religious Violence?" *CT* (July 10, 1987), 43; Sharon Mumper, "Global Report: Nigeria," *EMQ* 24 (Jan. 1988): 86–87; "Riots Kill Hundreds," *CT* (June 24, 1991), 56; "Christian-Muslim Tensions Prompt Riots," *CT* (Nov. 25, 1991), 58; "Intolerance," *World Press Review* (July 1991), 38; Randy Tift, "More Bloodshed Feared in Religious Fighting," *CT* (June 22, 1992), 67; "The Fight for African Souls," *World Press Review* (June 1992), 48.

Mau Mau oath to hate whites or venerate idols, and many were converted through their triumphant funerals.[26]

To bring the matter closer to home for some of us, the prospect of martyrdom need not necessarily require relocation. Even at the beginning of my Christian life as I witnessed on streets in the United States in the late 1970s, I was beaten and had my life threatened on several occasions. It has been some years now since my last beating, but I have received additional death threats since then for my witness, and faced other dangerous situations because of places I chose to live for the sake of my witness. The reader may well presume that I have not been killed, but even in the United States martyrdom is a viable possibility, and it may become more so in time: Jesus promised that we would be hated by all nations (Matt. 24:9). Many believers have chosen to relocate to or remain in drug- or murder-infested areas for the sake of a witness for Christ, and this, too, reveals commitment to die for Christ if that is his call.

If we have not prepared ourselves and our congregations to die for Christ's name if necessary, we have not completed our responsibility of preparing disciples (Mark 8:34–38). Like Daniel and his friends, we prepare best for more strenuous future tests by passing the ones we are given in the present. But when we remain faithful in the face of rejection and persecution, Jesus promises us a reward far greater than the power and status our oppressors now enjoy.

---

26. Osei-Mensah, *God's Message*, 25.

Revelation 2:12–17

TO THE ANGEL of the church in Pergamum write:

These are the words of him who has the sharp, double-edged sword. ¹³I know where you live— where Satan has his throne. Yet you remain true to my name. You did not renounce your faith in me, even in the days of Antipas, my faithful witness, who was put to death in your city—where Satan lives.

¹⁴Nevertheless, I have a few things against you: You have people there who hold to the teaching of Balaam, who taught Balak to entice the Israelites to sin by eating food sacrificed to idols and by committing sexual immorality. ¹⁵Likewise you also have those who hold to the teaching of the Nicolaitans. ¹⁶Repent therefore! Otherwise, I will soon come to you and will fight against them with the sword of my mouth.

¹⁷He who has an ear, let him hear what the Spirit says to the churches. To him who overcomes, I will give some of the hidden manna. I will also give him a white stone with a new name written on it, known only to him who receives it.

PERGAMUM WAS A famous city that had long prospered; it included between 120,000 and 200,000 inhabitants.[1] Its citizens had also proved foresighted enough to take the lead in joining Rome to defeat the other kings of the eastern Mediterranean, thereby securing for themselves special favor. The image of the "sword" may allude to the Roman government's *ius gladii*, the right to execute capital punishment, in which case Jesus is reminding Christians that he, not the Roman governor, holds the power of life and death (1:18).[2] Such words would encourage the persecuted (2:13). Yet this letter focuses on false teachers in the church, so the "sword" may refer to the judgment of war, as often in the biblical prophets—but here with reference to the Lord Jesus, who will war against false teachers corrupting his church (2:15–16).[3]

---

1. On its prosperity, see Strabo, 13.4.1–3; for the population, see the Galen citations in Aune, *Revelation*, 1:181.

2. Ramsay, *Letters to the Seven Churches*, 292–93; Hemer, *Letters to the Seven Churches*, 85.

3. Beale, *Revelation*, 250–51, cites here Num. 22:23, 31 and later Jewish tradition specifically concerning the threat to "Balaam."

This church faced external as well as internal opposition. Although its general sense is clear enough, the precise referent of "Satan's throne" (2:13) is disputed. The healing cult of Asclepius was famous at Pergamum; Christians from this city may recognize in Revelation's serpent (12:9) the chief symbol of their city's deity.[4] More often scholars think of the famous huge throne-like altar of "Zeus the Savior," whose sculptures included serpents; it was "a monumental colonnaded court in the form of a horseshoe, 120 by 112 feet," whose podium "was nearly 18 feet high."[5]

Other pagan connections likewise remained prominent in Pergamum, especially surrounding Demeter, Dionysius, Athena, and Orpheus.[6] Any or all of these connections with "Satan's throne" is possible. If a specific allusion to paganism is in view, however, the greatest immediate threat to believers would have been the cult of the emperor; the old temple of Augustus stood on the lofty rock citadel, conspicuous to anyone who approached the city.[7] As a center of the provincial imperial cult, Pergamum warranted Revelation's apt condemnation as Satan's "throne."[8] Pergamum not surprisingly appears among the cities some Jews thought slated for divine destruction (Sib. Or. 5.119).[9]

Given the context, paganism in general or, more likely, the imperial cult in particular led to the martyrdom of Antipas mentioned in 2:13. As a "faithful witness" he is like his Lord (1:5; cf. 3:14). Others in the church have survived but have nevertheless suffered, and Jesus commends them for their "faith" in him (2:13), which probably means faithfulness to him (cf. 2:10; 14:12).[10] But

---

4. For Asclepius's cult there, see Pausanius, 2.26.9; Herodian, 4.8.3. Associations with healing there appear as early as Homer, *Il.* 5.446–448 (Apollo). For information on Asclepius, who was particularly popular in this period and centered in this city, see Howard Clark Kee, *Miracle in the Early Christian World: A Study in Sociohistorical Method* (New Haven: Yale, 1983), 78–104.

5. Yamauchi, *The Archaeology of New Testament Cities*, 35. For the view that this might be "Satan's throne," see Stambaugh and Balch, *Environment*, 153; Beasley-Murray, *Revelation*, 84; a few have applied the title instead to the entire acropolis (Peter Wood, "Local Knowledge in the Letters of the Apocalypse," *ExpT* 73 [1962]: 263–64).

6. See W. K. C. Guthrie, *Orpheus and Greek Religion*, 2d ed. (New York: W. W. Norton, 1966), 260–61; W. W. Tarn, *Hellenistic Civilisation* (London: E. Arnold, 1952): 354; Ramsay, *Letters to the Seven Churches*, 284–85; Yamauchi, *The Archaeology of New Testament Cities*, 31.

7. Hemer, *Letters to the Seven Churches*, 82–85; Ford, *Revelation*, 398; Fiorenza, *Revelation*, 193. Pergamum's own earlier rulers were not worshiped while alive (Tarn, *Civilisation*, 51). Aune, *Revelation*, 1:182–84, applies the designation more generally to local Roman opposition to Christians.

8. Bowman, *First Christian Drama*, 31.

9. For archaeological evidence of a synagogue at Pergamum, see Goodenough, *Symbols*, 2:78–79.

10. See Donald S. Deer, "Whose Faith/Loyalty in Revelation 2.13 and 14.12?" *Bible Translator* 38 (1987): 328–30.

despite Jesus' special sensitivity for a suffering church (2:8–11; 3:7–12), having suffered does not automatically validate everything we do or believe (2:14).

In addition to opposition from the outside, Pergamum is also experiencing internal problems. Like "Jezebel" in Thyatira (2:20), "Balaam" (2:14) is undoubtedly not the prophet's own preferred name, but a code name signifying that this prophet is a false one, leading astray the people of God. In the Bible and more clearly in Jewish tradition, Balaam acted out of greed for money (Num. 22:19; Deut. 23:4; Neh. 13:2; 2 Peter 2:15; Jude 11).[11] He led Israel into sin in order to take them out of God's favor, recognizing that this was the only way to destroy them (Num. 31:16). Others also acknowledged that Israel could only be crushed if first lured into disobedience to God (Judith 5:20–21; 11:10).[12] The particular sins of Israel in connection with Balaam were sexual immorality and food offered to idols (Num. 25:1–2; cf. 31:8, 16), sins that remained temptations in later pagan society and brought judgment on Christians (1 Cor. 10:7–8; Did. 6.3).[13]

Scholars debate whether "sexual immorality" in Revelation 2:14 refers to literal prostitution, such as the prostitution sometimes conducted in pagan temples, or to a spiritual adultery that leads astray from God.[14] Sexual immorality was rife in the eastern Mediterranean—no less common than today. Nevertheless, in view of the frequent use of the image in the Hebrew Bible (e.g., 2 Kings 9:22; Jer. 3:9; 13:27; Ezek. 16:15–36; 23:7–35; Hos. 1:2; 4:12; 5:4; Nah. 3:4) and especially in view of the "prostitute" later in this book (Rev. 17:1, 15–16), the spiritual sense seems more likely here and in 2:20.[15]

Balaam's promotion of food offered to idols means promotion of syncretism, in which God's people were lured into participating in the cults of other deities.[16] The most conservative Jewish people would resist eating food offered to idols even under the pain of death (4 Macc 5:2–3). Much of the meat sold in the marketplaces of ancient cities had been offered to pagan

11. Also *Ps-Philo* 18:13. Many considered him the best pagan prophet (Josephus, *Ant.* 4.104; *Sifre Deut.* 343.6.1; 357.18.1–2), and later rabbis viewed him as the best pagan "philosopher" (*Pes. Rab Kah.* 15:5; *Gen. Rab.* 65:20; 93:10; *Lam. Rab* Proem 2). In general, see John T. Greene, "The Balaam Figure and Type Before, During, and After the Period of the Pseudepigrapha," *Journal for the Study of the Pseudepigrapha* 8 (1991): 67–110.

12. Later rabbis regarded leading another into sin as worse than killing him (*Sifre Deut.* 252.1.4). They understood that this was how Balaam caused Israel trouble (*p. Sanh.* 10:2, §8; *Taan.* 4:5, §10), and some associated him with denial of judgment (*Pes. Rab.* 41:3).

13. For Balaam's association with immorality, see also Josephus, *Ant.* 1.129–48; 4.157; Philo, *Moses* 1.296–97; *Ps-Philo* 18:13.

14. For spiritual prostitution, see Caird, *Commentary on Revelation*, 39, 44.

15. For a figurative use of the image, see 4QpNah 3.4; probably Wisd. 14:12.

16. Jewish tradition amplified the account of this idolatry (Josephus, *Ant.* 4.130, 141, 149; Philo, *Moses* 1.298–99).

gods, but because such meat was not distinguished from meat that had not been offered, it might not be in view here.[17]

More to the point are the sorts of occasions where the meat was specifically known to have been sacrificed for a pagan deity, such as free food doled out at pagan festivals and dining in an idol's temple (1 Cor. 8:10; *m. A.Z.* 2:3; 3:4), or, more likely for Christians here, participating in a guild banquet. The prophets could thus advocate compromise with the imperial cult, sharing food offered to Caesar; this would fit the experience of persecution in Pergamum (2:13).[18] Yet because the same teaching appears in Thyatira with little hint of persecution, the temptation may be more subtle; it may reflect the general tendency to eat food offered to idols.

One of the most difficult forms of this temptation may have been its challenge to the Christians' livelihood by denying their ability to participate in trade guilds. Trade guilds involved meals honoring a patron deity at their meetings,[19] and especially in Thyatira it would be difficult to evade the trade guilds that so dominated city life. On the theological level, compromise with the imperial cult to save one's life and compromise with the pagan activities of trade guilds to save one's livelihood are all of one piece (cf. 13:17); they represent accommodation to the world at the expense of one's total devotion to God's standards. One who advocates such accommodation, like ancient Israel when unfaithful to Yahweh, is a "prostitute" (cf. 2:20; 17:1–2). By the early second century, Roman officials recognized Christian influence in refusal to eat sacrificial meat and responded harshly (Pliny, *Ep.* 10.96).

For Christians in Pergamum, to "overcome" means to continue steadfast in the face of opposition (2:13), but especially to stand against teachings of compromise with the world and to do their best to purge such teachings from their ranks (2:14–16).

To those who overcome Jesus promises both the "hidden manna" and a "white stone with a new name written on it" (2:17). The hidden manna probably alludes to a Jewish tradition that the manna deposited in the ark would

---

17. For meat in the marketplace, see E. P. Sanders, *Jewish Law From Jesus to the Mishnah: Five Studies* (London: SCM; Philadelphia: Trinity Press International, 1990), 280; Wendell Lee Willis, *Idol Meat in Corinth: The Pauline Argument in 1 Corinthians 8 and 10* (SBLDS 68; Chico, Calif.: Scholars, 1985), 63; Gerd Theissen, *The Social Setting of Pauline Christianity*, tr. J. H. Schütz (Philadelphia: Fortress, 1982), 124–27; Aune, *Revelation*, 1:191–94.

18. Such sacrificial meals in the imperial cult are probably implied in *CIL* 3.550 and reflect the more general pagan custom. Some scholars suggest meat from that cult here (Bowman, *First Christian Drama*, 31).

19. See E. A. Judge, *The Social Pattern of the Christian Groups in the First Century: Some Prolegomena to the Study of New Testament Ideas of Social Obligation* (London: Tyndale, 1960), 40; Ramsay Mac-Mullen, *Roman Social Relations: 50 B.C. to A.D. 284* (New Haven: Yale, 1974), 77, 82.

be restored when the ark was restored in the end time (*tos. Kip.* 2:15). Although Jeremiah had explicitly declared that the original ark would never be restored (Jer. 3:16), early Jewish tradition declared that the ark and the temple vessels were hidden and would be recovered in the messianic era.[20] John soon learns that the heavenly ark will be revealed (11:19), but for him the manna probably symbolizes especially the new exodus (cf. 12:6, 14) and God's promise of eternal sustenance without labor (7:17; 22:2).[21] This promised manna also contrasts starkly with the idolatrous food for which Balaam's followers seem prepared to compromise their future reward (2:14).[22]

The meaning of the white stone is more debated, because people used stones in various symbolic ways; often such a *tessera* or small block of stone or ivory contained inscribed words or symbols.[23] Revelation could draw here on a variety of nuances (cf. 17:9–10), but its setting may help us decide which are most likely. A contrast with Asiatic paganism is possible; the sacred totem of Cybele, the prominent Phrygian Mother Goddess, was a black stone.[24] More likely, however, people used pebbles as admission tokens for public assemblies or festivities; the occasion here would be the celebration of heaven and the new manna of the messianic banquet (7:9; 19:9).[25] Perhaps the most significant allusion is a reference to some ancient courtrooms, where jurors voted for acquittal with a white stone and for conviction with a black one. Here a capital case is probably in view (2:13), and Jesus will overturn the verdict of the Pergamum Christians' persecutors at the final judgment when he declares both life and the second death (2:13; 20:12–14; cf. Acts 7:56–60).[26]

---

20. See 2 Macc. 2:4–8; 2 Bar. 6:7–9; 4 Bar. 3:10, 19; 4:4; *Lives of Prophets* 2:15 (Greek in §25, Jer.); *m. Shek.* 6:1–2; *Yoma* 5:2. For related Samaritan ideas, cf. Josephus, *Ant.* 18.85; M. F. Collins, "The Hidden Vessels in Samaritan Traditions," *JSJ* 3 (1972): 97–116; Isaac Kalimi and James D. Purvis, "The Hiding of the Temple Vessels in Jewish and Samaritan Literature," *CBQ* 56 (Oct. 1994): 679–85.

21. See also eschatological manna in 2 Bar. 29:8; *Mek. Vayassa* 3.42–45; 5.53–65; cf. *Ex. Rab.* 47:5; Christian tradition in Sib. Or. 7.149. For manna as angelic food, see *b. Yoma* 75b.

22. Ancient readers would probably recognize the contrast quickly; for an analogous contrast, see the later *Num. Rab.* 21:21.

23. Ramsay, *Letters to the Seven Churches*, 302. The majority of views recited below were proposed by or before Ramsay, prior to being developed by other scholars.

24. Stambaugh and Balch, *Environment*, 136. At Sardis the Kore also appears as a rock (David J. Gill, "Religion in a Local Setting," 79–92 in *The Book of Acts in Its Greco-Roman Setting* [ed. D. W. J. Gill and C. Gempf; Grand Rapids: Eerdmans, 1994], 88).

25. Caird, *Commentary on Revelation*, 42; Ford, *Revelation*, 399–400; Beasley-Murray, *Revelation*, 88; Hemer, *Letters to the Seven Churches*, 98–99.

26. Beasley-Murray, *Revelation*, 88; Ford, *Revelation*, 399–400; fuller documentation in Hemer, *Letters to the Seven Churches*, 97. But voters also sometimes wrote on potsherds (Cornelius Nepos 2 [Themistocles], 8.1; 5 [Cimon], 3.1).

This pebble may also be white to symbolize eternal life or purity from sin (Rev. 3:4–5, 18; 4:4; 6:11; 7:9, 13–14). Practical considerations also support a white stone for inscribing a name; although most building materials in Pergamum were of dark brown granite, that city used white marble for its inscriptions.[27] Pagan deities sometimes gave worshipers new names to signify a new identity (just as parents named children shortly after birth).[28] In Israel's own history, a change of name was often associated with a promise (see, e.g., Gen. 17:5, 15; cf. 17:4, 9, 20).

The new name alludes here to Isaiah 56:5 and especially 62:2, which promises that God will give his people a new name, removing their shame (62:4); this fits the time of the new Jerusalem and new creation (65:15–19). The new name may represent a new description of a person's identity (cf. Rev. 3:1, 5), but in the context of Revelation more likely the hidden name of God (3:12; cf. 2:13; 3:8; Isa. 43:1) and the Lamb (14:1; 19:12–13, 16), which they will bear forever (22:4).

A WARNING AGAINST assimilation. Although the issue of persecution is central to Revelation, those who emphasize that the book as a whole warns against assimilation with the world are also correct. As one scholar notes, "The Apocalypse of John has pastoral relevance in any context where Christian assimilation into a culture with a non-Christian ethos is an issue."[29]

We should be careful, of course, to distinguish between appropriate interaction with culture and compromise with it. Paul as a first-century missionary readily spoke the language of his culture (adapting, for instance, Stoic models to promote his case in Rom. 1:19–32), and had friends who were high-ranking citizens regularly involved in pagan civic religion (Acts 19:31). The warnings against intimate relations with unbelievers (Ps. 1:1; Prov. 13:20) caution against imbibing the world's values, not against being with others to promote Christ's values (Matt. 11:18–19; Luke 15:1–2). Joseph (Gen. 41:45; 47:22, 26) and Daniel (Dan. 2:24; 4:19) both worked within and showed

---

27. Hemer, *Letters to the Seven Churches*, 101–2. That a particular white curative stone was called the "Judean stone" (Galen 9.2.5; Dioscurides, *Materia Medica* 5.137) is probably irrelevant; calcareous white stone characterized some regions of Asia (cf. J. B. Lightfoot, *Saint Paul's Epistles to the Colossians and to Philemon* [n.p.: Macmillan & Company, 1879], 10).

28. Talbert, *Apocalypse*, 19; Hemer, *Letters to the Seven Churches*, 99–100, citing Aelius Aristides, *Hymn to Ascl.* 6.69. Children generally received names eight to nine days after birth (Plutarch, *R.Q.* 102, *Mor.* 288BC; Luke 1:59). Cf. figurative renaming in 1QpHab 8.9.

29. Talbert, *Apocalypse*, 111.

respect for their colleagues and kings in a pagan culture, and Jeremiah told the exiles to seek the good of the land where God had placed them (Jer. 29:7). But we need to make sure that we are influencing the world with the kingdom's values, not embracing the world's values where they conflict with those of the kingdom.

In some parts of the world, Christian parents (sometimes taught by Western missionaries that God no longer heals today) take their children to witch doctors to secure healing.[30] Although most Western Christians today do not have to deal with literal idols, the analogy with the temptations we face is so straightforward as to be almost transparent—if we have the courage to face it. The problem with an idol is not the artwork, monotheism is not "one God or less," and pagan ideologies can include the atheistic premises of secular materialism no less than the blatant naming of other gods. In North America we do not confront emperor worship per se, but we have plenty of idols, whether materialism (Matt. 6:24) or celebrities who receive more attention than many people give to God.[31]

When we seriously examine Jesus' teachings and parts of Acts to discern ideal models for the church, we find there Christians intensely committed to evangelism and other ministry, using all their resources and paying whatever price necessary to accomplish the task (e.g., Luke 14:26–35; Acts 4:32). When we compare most of North American Christianity today, we see Christians deeply committed to their own material advancement, spending countless hours each week on entertainment, yet far less on learning God's Word. Studies indicate that the vast majority of "evangelical" Christians today never share their faith with non-Christians in the sense of explaining salvation to them.[32] If we read our culture in light of Scripture rather than the reverse, dare we doubt that the church is sorely in need of spiritual awakening? Balaam and Jezebel no longer represent factions within the church; they dominate it, and Revelation's only solution for us is repentance (2:16, 21–22).

Although only a faction of the church has succumbed to such teachings (2:14–15), Jesus tells the entire church that he has this against them and then calls on it to repent (2:16). In other words, if we choose to look the other way when apostasy is occurring, then we must share the Lord's reproof.

---

30. See Osei-Mensah, *God's Message*, 28; Madame Nanan, "The Sorcerer and Pagan Practices," 81–87 in *Our Time Has Come: African Christian Women Address the Issues of Today*, ed. Judy Mbugua (Grand Rapids: Baker, 1994).

31. For fan clubs surrounding entertainers, see Ned Zeman, "The Adoration of the Elvii," *NW* (Apr. 22, 1991), 82–83; for troubles fame creates for celebrities, see Walter Leavy, "The Price of Fame," *Ebony* (Sept. 1994), 54–59.

32. See the statistics in James F. Engel, "Who's Really Doing Evangelism?" *CT* (Dec. 16, 1991), 35–37.

ANTIPAS AND CHRISTIAN **suffering today.** Because Revelation mentions only the martyrdom of Antipas, probably few Christians had already been martyred when Revelation was being written. If the churches of Asia were like many of us, they may have been hoping and praying that Antipas would prove the final martyr. But Revelation warns that suffering is coming; the gospel always involves suffering (Mark 13:9–10; 2 Tim. 3:12). If we pray for the Lord's return we must also be ready to spread the gospel, a prerequisite for that return (Matt. 24:14; Rom. 11:25; cf. 2 Peter 3:9, 12, 15); yet with cutting-edge evangelism inevitably comes suffering (Matt. 10:16–39; Col. 1:23–24), right through the final generation (Rev. 6:9). Revelation prohibits us loving our lives more than his gospel; it summons us to follow the model of Antipas as faithful witnesses, no matter what the cost.

As noted above, Jesus seems especially patient with and encouraging to a suffering church (2:8–11; 3:7–12), but having suffered does not automatically validate everything we do or believe. The churches in Pergamum and Thyatira, tolerating invitations to compromise, merited Jesus' rebuke. Yet their temptations were all too like the sorts of choices all Christians living in non-Christian societies must make.

If my brother's wedding banquet is catered by priests from the adjoining idol's temple, do I eat the idol meat or offend my brother? Do I publicly refuse food offered to some deity for Caesar, thereby incurring the suspicion of disloyalty to the state? Because potential applications of this passage's warning against compromise are so many, we can at most provide samples; each pastor, Bible study leader, and individual guided by God's Spirit will recognize the most appropriate applications for his or her own settings.

The temptation to compromise. Once we move past the particulars of the situations in Pergamum and Thyatira, the principle of compromise can be expressed in innumerable situations. When I taught Revelation for a college Sunday school class roughly a decade ago, the churches in Pergamum and Thyatira generated more discussion than all the rest of Revelation combined. Students identified with the pressures to compromise in areas of sexual morality, chemical addictions, silent accommodation of the reigning secularism of their campus, and so forth. Whether Revelation employs the image of sexual immorality literally or figuratively, the image still serves as a warning against literal immorality: Sexual immorality, like any other sin, compromises God's will, and in our culture certainly accommodates the values of the world.[33]

---

33. On sexual immorality, see Andrés Tapia, "Abstinence: The Radical Choice for Sex Ed," *CT* (Feb. 8, 1993), 25–29; Katherine Bond, "Abstinence Education: How Parents Are Making It Happen," *Focus on the Family* (Sept. 1998), 12–13; Craig Keener, "Sexual Infidelity As Exploitation," *Priscilla Papers* 7 (Fall 1993): 15–18; see other sources cited in the Contemporary Significance section of 21:8.

The Bible is firm against all premarital or extramarital sex and often uses the term "prostitute" to describe one who practices any such behavior (17:5); after all, if it is despicable for a person (even one in great need) to sell his or her sexuality for a little money, is it any better to give it away without charging anything?[34] Biblical sexual ethics require us to save our bodies for those who will value us not for a small fee but who will regard us as persons of worth equal to themselves and commit their lives to us.

But we also need to be sensitive to those who have lived differently before they met Jesus, because all of us are dependent on his forgiveness for our sins, whatever our sins have been (Mark 2:14–17; Luke 7:47–50; 15:1–32; John 4:16–26). Those still involved in immorality must also be reached in Christian love; they must learn how much God thinks they are worth. Contrary to the approval of his most religious contemporaries, Jesus ministered to prostitutes (Matt. 21:31–32); a Christian woman I know with the same ministry has encountered the same sorts of criticisms from some Christians today. Thus, when we expound on sexual immorality in this passage, we should, as with other sins, make clear that we are warning against the sin rather than denying the efficacy of Christ's blood for the past.

Sanctifying the world's values. As a religious "prophet," "Balaam" probably sanctified the values of the culture by providing theological justifications for them, such as, "Since an idol is really nothing, my worshiping it does no harm" (e.g., 1 Cor. 8:4). Like Balaam and Jezebel, we can sanctify worldly values by attributing them to God. During the Civil Rights Movement, the Bible and Christianity were exploited by Klan leader Sam Bowers to justify violent Klan activity, while popular Baptist pastor Douglas Hudgins used them to ignore the segregation and violence being promoted even by members of his church.[35] By contrast, the civil rights struggle revealed Christians committed to stand against the values of their culture: Black activist Fannie Lou Hamer both forgave her white persecutors and stood for justice in Jesus' name, and white Mississippian Ed King shared in the suffering of his black

---

34. Most ancient prostitutes were reduced to their situation by financial need (Terence, *Lady of Andros* 73–79) or, in Paul's day, were often slaves forced into prostitution against their will (Martial, *Epig.* 9.6.7; 9.8; Apuleius, *Metam.* 7.9; *ARN* 8A), which (in the case of slavery) surely placed the onus of sin on those who exploited them.

35. Lest one think no one would use the Bible to justify racism today, a minister in the white supremacist "Church of the Creator," George Loeb, urged fellow racists to kill large numbers of blacks, whom he stated were subhuman. After his arrest for murdering a black man, he received an "Award of Honor" from leaders in his movement. On George Loeb, see Morris Dees, Southern Poverty Law Center mailing (April 13, 1995); "National Alliance Leader William Pierce Sued in Connection with Church of the Creator Case," *Klanwatch Intelligence Report* (March 1995), 9.

colleagues, recognizing that "if a person calls himself a Christian, he must give up everything and follow Christ."[36]

In short, when we value what the world does instead of valuing the kingdom, we forfeit our role as witnesses for Christ's kingdom in this world. Too much of Western Christianity has become indistinguishable from our culture, too much of our "evangelistic" effort geared toward persuading the world that we are acceptable because we are just like them. If we affirm what the world affirms, or, more often, live as the world does, to what then do we invite them in conversion that differs from what they already experience?

Revelation called the churches in Asia to wake up to the reality that the world and the church were locked in a fight to the death, and that the church could "overcome" only by rising to the battle and risking martyrdom in its uncompromising witness for Christ. In modern Western Christendom one is almost tempted to wonder if the battlefield has shifted, so that the line now lies between a remnant of radical, witnessing Christians on the one hand, and the rest of the church with the world on the other. Many disciples suffering for the gospel in other parts of the world mourn how quickly the United States has shifted from what was in many respects a source of spiritual blessing to the world to a self-centered mission field exporting sexual promiscuity and greed through its entertainment media far more than its Christians are exporting the gospel.

The very image of "Balaam" reminds us that it was compromise with paganism that brought ancient Israel defeat, and compromise with pagan values will do the same for us. But wherever possible, biblical prophets ended on a note of encouragement. Perhaps not all Pergamum Christians will "overcome," but those who do and avoid the idol food will be admitted to a heavenly banquet with an unlimited supply of manna. It is easier for Christians to avoid compromise with the seductive values of the world when we keep in mind the much better world God has in store for us someday. Whatever we must overcome, he has a better hope in store for us.

---

36. See Charles Marsh, *God's Long Summer: Stories of Faith and Civil Rights* (Princeton: Princeton Univ. Press, 1997), 131.

Revelation 2:18–29

TO THE ANGEL of the church in Thyatira write:

These are the words of the Son of God, whose eyes are like blazing fire and whose feet are like burnished bronze. ¹⁹I know your deeds, your love and faith, your service and perseverance, and that you are now doing more than you did at first.

²⁰Nevertheless, I have this against you: You tolerate that woman Jezebel, who calls herself a prophetess. By her teaching she misleads my servants into sexual immorality and the eating of food sacrificed to idols. ²¹I have given her time to repent of her immorality, but she is unwilling. ²²So I will cast her on a bed of suffering, and I will make those who commit adultery with her suffer intensely, unless they repent of her ways. ²³I will strike her children dead. Then all the churches will know that I am he who searches hearts and minds, and I will repay each of you according to your deeds. ²⁴Now I say to the rest of you in Thyatira, to you who do not hold to her teaching and have not learned Satan's so-called deep secrets (I will not impose any other burden on you): ²⁵Only hold on to what you have until I come.

²⁶To him who overcomes and does my will to the end, I will give authority over the nations—

²⁷'He will rule them with an iron scepter;
he will dash them to pieces like pottery'—

just as I have received authority from my Father. ²⁸I will also give him the morning star. ²⁹He who has an ear, let him hear what the Spirit says to the churches.

Original Meaning

IF EPHESIAN CHRISTIANS were tempted by rigidity and lovelessness, Smyrnean Christians by persecution, and Pergamum's Christians by persecution and prophets of compromise, economic pressures were inviting compromise on the part of Thyatira's Christians. The Asian churches may well hear in Jesus' biblical title "Son of God" (2:18) a direct challenge to the imperial cult. Emperors claimed to be deities and saviors in Asia; some commentators have further suggested a specific contrast with Zeus's son Apollo, a patron deity of Thyatira, with whom the deified emperors were linked.[1] Apollo's link with Helios, the sun god, also could amplify the contrast implicit in Jesus' fiery features here, though these would be relevant to any readers familiar with the biblical prophets (cf. 1:14–16). Although the matter is uncertain, it may be more than coincidence that Jesus reminds hearers of his feet like bronze (1:15) specifically in a city where metal-working was a prominent industry.[2]

Jesus knows that the Christians in Thyatira, in contrast to those in Ephesus, are doing his works more than they have before (2:5, 19), but one flaw in the congregation proves serious enough to offset this praise: Unlike Ephesus, they are tolerating a false teacher of compromise (2:2, 20). Thyatira was known for its merchants, crafts, and their guilds (cf. also Acts 16:14).[3] Those who participated in this aspect of public economic life would risk a substantial measure of their livelihood by refusing to join trade guilds. The guild meetings, however, included a common meal dedicated to the guild's patron deity—a meal thereby off-limits to more traditional Christians (Acts 15:20; 1 Cor. 10:19–22). Starting in this general period, aspects of the imperial cult also began to affect nearly every trade guild.

A large number of commentators envision this situation as a primary contributor to "Jezebel's" appeal.[4] Not surprisingly, a prophet or prophetess who tells people what they want to hear can become readily popular (cf. 2 Tim. 4:3–4). Yet as some in Ephesus falsely claimed to be apostles (Rev. 2:2), some in Smyrna and Philadelphia falsely claimed to be Jews (2:9; 3:9), and the Laodicean Christians claimed to be rich (3:17), this Jezebel falsely claims to be a prophetess (2:20) and to offer "deep secrets" (2:24). Like Satan (12:9; 20:2, 8, 10) and the world system (13:14; 18:23; 19:20), she is a deceiver who misleads God's servants.

Like "Balaam," this false prophetess receives a nickname undoubtedly not of her own choosing. Jesus' title for her, "Jezebel," immediately calls to mind multiple associations. The biblical Jezebel was not a "prophetess," but sponsored

---

1. Hemer, *Letters to the Seven Churches*, 86–87; Fiorenza, *Revelation*, 193; Caird, *Commentary on Revelation*, 43. For Thyatira's Macedonian links, see Strabo, 13.4.4.

2. See Hemer, *Letters to the Seven Churches*, 111–17, including comments on the rare Greek terms most specifically intelligible there; cf. Caird, *Commentary on Revelation*, 43.

3. Their location at the "most important junction of roads between Lydia and Mysia" (Aune, *Revelation*, 1:213) may have also helped position them in commerce.

4. See Kraybill, *Imperial Cult and Commerce*, 110–23; Beasley-Murray, *Revelation*, 89–90; Collins, *Crisis and Catharsis*, 88; Talbert, *Apocalypse*, 20; Beale, *Revelation*, 261. On the appeal and dangers of commerce for Judaism and the churches, see especially and most thoroughly Kraybill, *Imperial Cult and Commerce*, 87–99, 184–93.

850 false prophets (1 Kings 18:19; Josephus, *Ant.* 8.318); she also sought to take the lives of God's true prophets (1 Kings 18:13; 19:2; Josephus, *Ant.* 8.334, 347). She is never accused of literal harlotry, but she sponsored spiritual harlotry by leading Israel away from its God (2 Kings 9:22, where her religious activity is also compared with witchcraft; cf. Rev. 9:21; 18:23). Babylon the prostitute later in this book is probably modeled partly on "Jezebel," Thyatira's local embodiment of the larger system of "Babylon," because she advocated participation in local civic and commercial life even where they demanded compromise with paganism.[5]

Early Christians were familiar with godly prophetesses (Acts 2:17–18; 21:9; 1 Cor. 11:5), and as early as the mid-second century writers speak of a first-century prophetess named Ammia in the Asian church of Philadelphia.[6] But they also knew of both false prophetesses and false prophets (Neh. 6:14; Ezek. 13:17); pagan and Jewish religion in Asia also respected female prophetic figures.[7]

The primary female prophetic model in Asia was the ancient, mythical Sibyl (often associated with Asia, cf. Strabo, 14.1.34), who supposedly had been granted both oracular abilities and a long life without perpetual youth.[8] Sometimes ancient writers associated other women developed in oracular arts with Sibyls or even gave them this title. Both Roman and Jewish Sibyl traditions located a significant number of Sibyls in Roman Asia, and some scholars have argued that the local goddess Sambathe was identified with Sibyls, providing a local prophetic cult with possible Jewish involvement that may have affected how some Christians in Thyatira understood prophetism.[9] For John, the true prophets are those who confess the truth

---

5. See Bauckham, *Climax of Prophecy,* 377–78; C. S. Keener, "Woman and Man," 1205–15 in *Dictionary of the Later New Testament and Its Developments,* ed. R. P. Martin and P. H. Davids (Downers Grove, Ill.: InterVarsity, 1997), 1211.

6. See Eusebius, *H. E.* 5.17.3–4. For Ammia see Catherine Kroeger, "The Neglected History of Women in the Early Church," *Christian History* 17 (1988): 6–11 (p. 7).

7. For women in the Asian imperial cult, see Mary R. Lefkowitz and Maureen B. Fant, *Women's Life in Greece and Rome* (Baltimore: Johns Hopkins Univ. Press, 1982), 157 (§159); in the trade guilds, see Hemer, *Letters to the Seven Churches,* 121. Thyatira later succumbed heavily to Montanism, in which prophetesses played a significant initial role.

8. E.g., Ovid, *Metam.* 14.129–53. On Jewish Sibyllism, see especially John J. Collins, *The Sibylline Oracles of Egyptian Judaism,* SBLDS 13 (Missoula: SBL, 1972); for the Jewish Sibyl see Sib. Or. 1.287–90; 3.827; *CPJ* 3:47–51; among Christians, see Herm. 1.2.4; Theophilus, 2.36; a reading of Tertullian, *Apol.* 19.1.

9. Hemer, *Letters to the Seven Churches,* 119; Ford, *Revelation,* 405; but contrast Ramsay, *Letters to the Seven Churches,* 337; Moffatt, "Revelation," 360. On the Jewish population in Lydia, esp. Thyatira (though this letter lacks direct reference to them), see *CIJ* 2:17–18, §752; Kraabel, "Judaism in Western Asia Minor," 155–97; for God-fearers, see Acts 16:14. There is also

about Jesus (Rev. 19:10; cf. 1 John 4:1–2); signs are less decisive, because they may accompany prophets true (11:5–6) or false (13:13–14).

But the Lord will not allow those leading his people astray to go unchallenged; he will strike "Jezebel" with sickness (2:22). (The punishment probably fits the crime: a "bed" often described the place of intercourse [cf. Heb. 13:4], but it was also the place of one bedfast from sickness.) He will also kill her "children" (2:23)—undoubtedly her disciples, perhaps members of house churches under her guidance (cf. 2 John 1:1).[10] Killing with "death" (the phrase rendered in the NIV "strike . . . dead") reflects a familiar Greek translation of a Hebrew expression for the divine judgment of a plague or pestilence, a judgment sometimes associated with blasphemy (Num. 14:36–38).[11] Repayment according to one's deeds will also occur at the Lord's return (Rev. 22:12).

The presence of this false teaching in the church at Thyatira is the Lord's only criticism here (2:23; for "not . . . any other burden" in 2:24; cf. Acts 15:28), but this challenge alone is substantial enough to require warning that the believers must hold firm their faith until Jesus comes (Rev. 2:24). As searcher of hearts and minds—that is, as God—Jesus knows what is in their hearts (2:23; cf. John 2:24).[12] By "deep secrets" (lit., "deep things") Jezebel and her followers undoubtedly mean "profound things" likely obtained by revelation (1 Cor. 2:10; 1 En. 63:3; 3 En. 11:1).[13] But as the true searcher of hearts, Jesus notes the source of their revelations: Satan (2:24), who has also authored opposition from the synagogue community (2:9; 3:9).

Jesus promises those who overcome this threat of false teaching that they will share with him in his reign over the nations (2:26); they are not

some evidence for Jewish metalworkers in first-century Asia (S. Applebaum, "The Social and Economic Status of the Jews in the Diaspora," 701–27 in *Jews in Palestine in the First Century*, 717–18).

10. Some Jewish tradition emphasized divine judgment on offspring of adultery (Wisd. Sol. 3:13, 16; cf. 2 Sam 12:14) or other children of wicked parents (Jub. 5:7; T. Jud. 11:3–5), but Rev. 2:23 employs the image figuratively as an insult (cf. Isa. 57:3, 8); her children perpetuate her spirit of prostitution (cf. Rev. 17:5; also John 8:41). For sickness as judgment, see 1 Cor. 11:30; T. Reuben 1:7–8; T. Zeb. 5:2, 4.

11. See Matthew Black, "Some Greek Words with Hebrew Meanings in the Epistles and the Apocalypse," 135–46 in *Biblical Studies: Essays in Honor of William Barclay*, ed. J. R. McKay and J. F. Miller (Philadelphia: Westminster, 1976), 136. NIV's "repay" here accurately renders the Semitic nuance of the Greek (Black, "Greek Words," 145).

12. For God as "searcher of hearts and minds," see 1 Chron. 28:9; Rom. 8:27; Heb. 4:13; tos. Sanh. 8:3; Epictetus, *Disc.* 2.14.11; A. Marmorstein, *The Old Rabbinic Doctrine of God: The Names and Attributes of God* (New York: KTAV, 1968), 73.

13. *Bathos* ("deep") can mean "profound" in Greek (e.g., Longinus, *Sublime* 2.1; Philo, *Posterity of Cain* 130), and sources ranging from mystery cults to Qumran emphasized mysteries revealed to a special group.

only a kingdom and priests (1:6; 5:10) but those who will reign with him (5:10), both during the thousand years (20:6) and eternally (22:5). They will share in Jesus' rule with an iron rod (2:27), a hope derived from the messianic promise of Psalm 2:9. Like the most popular Greek version of the Old Testament, Revelation speaks not merely of "ruling" the nations with an iron rod but of "shepherding" them, emphasizing again that they will share Jesus' authority (Rev. 7:17).[14] The frequency of "giving" language in the Greek text of these letters underlines the promises to overcomers (2:7, 10, 17, 26, 28; 3:9, 21).

Although Psalm 2 addressed God's messianic viceroy alone (see also Ps. Sol. 17:23–25), Jesus shares his rule with his people, for God has delegated rule over the earth to humanity (Gen. 1:26–27; Ps. 8:6; cf. Dan. 7:14, 22). Jesus will also give those who overcome the morning star (Rev. 2:28). Ancients emphasized the glory of the planet Venus, the "morning star" (Sir. 50:6–7), and could apply the image to magnificent rulers (Isa. 14:12).[15] Romans associated Venus with triumph and reign, hence praised this goddess for their conquests.[16] In Revelation, however—although one might not catch this until one's second time through the book—Jesus is himself the morning star (Rev. 22:16), probably alluding to the promised star of Numbers 24:17, which many ancient Jews understood messianically.[17]

In other words, Jesus' promise to the church in Thyatira suggests that he will share not only victory in an abstract sense (2:26) but himself as the morning star with his people (2:28). He is greater than the stars, who are angels of the churches (1:20).

---

14. Even a child with a "rod" could drive a flock of sheep (Epictetus, *Disc.* 1.16.5); ancient texts also portray God or deities investing faithful agents with their scepter or crown (ibid., 4.8.30; *Ex. Rab.* 8:1; cf. 26:2); for the Messiah, see Ps. Sol. 18:7.

15. Some identified morning and evening stars (Diogenes Laertius, 8.1.14), but a "star" in general could symbolize conquest (Sophocles, *Electra* 66); it probably functions eschatologically in 2 Peter 1:19.

16. On this point see Beasley-Murray, *Revelation*, 93–94, for further detail. This background would present Christ (22:16) as the true world ruler (Beale, *Revelation*, 269).

17. Early second-century rabbis wrongly applied Num. 22:16 to the messianic pretender Bar Kochba. Ps. 2:9 and Num. 24:17 in Rev. 2:26–28 represent two of the book's four messianic passages that use the word "scepter": Rev. 22:16 links Num. 24:17 with Isa. 11:10; Rev. 5:5 links Gen. 49:9 and Isa. 11:10; and Rev. 19:15 links Ps. 2:9 with Isa. 11:4. Bauckham, *Climax of Prophecy*, 323, cites associations in Ps. Sol. 17:24–27; 4QPBless. Michael S. Moore, "Jesus Christ: 'Superstar' (Revelation xxii 16b)," *NovT* 24 (1982): 82–91, suggests some Mesopotamian background for the morning star image.

Bridging Contexts

SOME MERCHANTS IN Thyatira, certain that God did not want to limit their ability to function within society, apparently dismissed the concerns of more traditional Christians about participation in guilds and associations dedicated to pagan deities. It "was economic suicide to reject the minimum requirements for guild membership," and "every generation of Christians must face the question: How far should I accept and adopt contemporary standards and practices?"[18] Do we look ultimately to the world for our survival, or to the God who supplies manna in the desert (12:6, 14; 13:17)?

Another social aspect of this conflict remains no less familiar to us today. Who of us has not been tempted to dismiss warnings from more traditional Christians on some matter or another as simply culturally naive, whether over music styles, dress codes, or excessive rigidity in relating to other believers? At the same time, we often find ourselves on the other side of the equation, warning Christians we think are straying from the central truth of the gospel into the uncertain reefs of liberal relativism. What one group regards as a legitimate, compassionate concern another regards as legalism and cultural irrelevance. Where should we draw the lines?

The Bible is clear that we do not have to draw the line on matters of cultural preferences, even when they may be theologically informed (Rom. 14:3–10). Moreover, even the apostles did not agree among themselves on every point beyond the gospel, although they seem to have reserved public rebukes only for the most serious matters (Gal. 2:11, in this case rebuking an apostle for valuing the cultural sensitivities of his colleagues over those of Gentile converts, who were being treated as second-class Christians). No matter how strongly Christians feel on various sides of the debates on end-times teachings, women's ministry, spiritual gifts, and other such matters, we must recognize and publicly affirm that those who sincerely hold different views can be committed Christians, brothers and sisters for whom we should lay down our lives.

At the same time, other matters involve spiritual life and death, such as participation in idolatry. Jesus' deity, for instance, is an implication of his lordship, a teaching central to the original apostolic proclamation of Christ recorded in the New Testament. To my knowledge, this view is not disputed in many churches today, certainly not in evangelical ones. But other matters do involve life and death issues and are becoming increasingly matters of concern in our churches, matters that can no longer be ignored (see Contemporary Significance section).

---

18. Metzger, *Breaking the Code*, 37.

Jesus' promise to this church would hearten all the churches in Asia Minor: They would shepherd or rule the nations with an iron rod (2:27). In their day, Rome ruled the nations, and the church suffered accordingly.[19] To apply this promise most relevantly, we should consider the various ways that today's world inhibits the spread of the gospel and practices injustice; we should remind ourselves and our fellow believers that in the end God will reward those found faithful to his Word.

ECONOMIC TEMPTATIONS. BECAUSE part of the temptation to compromise in Thyatira may have been economic, we may wish to consider applications first of all with an economic component. Of course, every time we buy groceries, we participate in an international economic system that includes inequities; in many Caribbean countries banana workers have been paid less per day than what is necessary merely to feed their families a survival diet, in order to provide more competitive prices for North American consumers. In 1954 the U.S. government responded to a perceived threat to one of its fruit companies by helping to overthrow a democratically elected government in Guatemala. When banana workers in 1975 demanded fairer wages for their workers, the large companies that controlled 90 percent of the banana market starved most of them into submission, bribing a government to silence the rest.[20]

But boycotting bananas would probably only make the situation worse, and even if all consumers united and demanded a rise in banana prices (an unlikely event!), we would have little guarantee that the extra profits would go to the banana workers. It is right to address such inequities by whatever ethical means possible, but for individuals not politically adept, perhaps it is most practical to use the economic advantages we have as North American consumers to invest in Christian economic development programs that will alleviate the need to work for substandard wages (hence require banana companies to pay more competitive wages).

On the personal level, however, the implications of economic temptations become still clearer. To whom do we ultimately look for our well-being? In many of the projects, a young man can make hundreds of dollars more in a day dealing drugs on the corner than working at McDonald's, often the next best-paying alternative. In some corporations one can advance only by sac-

---

19. Ramsay, *Letters to the Seven Churches*, 333, points out that Thyatira was one of the least significant of the cities, hence reinforcing the irony of this promise of future rule.

20. Ronald J. Sider, *Rich Christians in an Age of Hunger*, 3d ed. (Dallas: Word, 1990), 143–44.

rifices likely to destroy one's family or credibility as a Christian witness. Certainly in academia those who do not toe the correct party line of an institution risk their job (not only in some conservative schools but also in some allegedly open-minded secular university religion departments). Jesus' approval on the Day of Judgment has to matter more to us than wealth or status in this life, or we will succumb to the temptation of the Thyatiran believers.[21]

The gospel and modern pluralism. In a broader sense, the principles of temptation to compromise here go beyond economic temptations, and many applications we note here continue the basic themes evident in the letter to the Pergamum Christians. Rome was tolerant of religions as long as they did not make universal claims that might ultimately compete with loyalty to the state; but a universal religion was a threat to Rome, and "such a religion must conquer or die."[22] A praiseworthy aspect of modern pluralism is that it provides more of a voice for minorities—whether for ethnic minorities, religious minorities like committed Christians, or others.

A danger of modern pluralism, however, like that in the Roman empire, is that it can inadvertently appear to lend credibility to the claims of philosophic, moral, or religious relativism.[23] Seventy-two percent of Americans in the 18–25 age bracket believe there is no such thing as absolute truth; this view appears to be shared by over half of those who claim to be born-again Christians.[24] Much of our society has absolutized relativism (how is that for oxymoronic thinking?) as the only nonnegotiable truth, in essence arguing that everyone is right unless one claims to be. One commentator cautions, "For some people today tolerance is the only real virtue and intolerance the only vice";[25] another that "while the message to Ephesus warns the church

---

21. For fuller examples, see how caring for the needy and prisoners could alienate Dave Chapman's clients (Charles Colson, *Loving God* [Grand Rapids: Zondervan, 1987], 217–44), and Judge Bill Bontrager lost his job by obeying what he believed God demanded (ibid., 147–64).

22. Martin Persson Nilsson, *Greek Piety*, tr. H. J. Rose (Oxford: Clarendon, 1948), 185.

23. For example, genetic classes (race or gender) should not be interchanged with immoral behavior (such as homosexual behavior—or, for that matter, mistreatment of gays and lesbians), though they are often grouped together (e.g., the artists reported in Peter Plagens, "Fade From White," *NW* [March 15, 1993], 72–74); see Jo Kadlecek, "Blacks, Latinos, Native Americans, Asians—and Gays?" *Urban Family* (Spring 1993), 34; David Neff, "Two Men Don't Make a Right," *CT* (June 19, 1993), 14–15; Matthew James Jr., "Who's Leading the Choir?" *Urban Family* (Fall 1995), 18–19. Relativism has been used to justify or deny the reality of even the Nazi holocaust (cf. Laura Shapiro, "Denying the Holocaust," *NW* [Dec. 20, 1993], 120).

24. George Barna, *What Americans Believe* (Ventura, Calif.: Regal, 1991), 83–85.

25. Michaels, *Revelation*, 78.

about the dangers of loveless orthodoxy, the message to Thyatira warns against the dangers of a 'soft' love that tolerates all things and judges none."[26] Many non-Christians no longer deny the possibility of miracles or of Jesus being a way to God. But to them the Christian way is only one way among many; they bristle at the claim that Jesus is the only true way.

Yet the world is not alone in its excessive tolerance. Like the Thyatiran Christians, we may tolerate some who falsely claim "deep" teachings that directly undermine the gospel or Christian ethics. As noted above, few evangelicals today are tempted to question some cardinal Christian teachings like Jesus' deity or resurrection. But because relativism has become increasingly popular in our culture, the absolute necessity of faith in Christ for salvation has become a more uncomfortable position for many to hold. "Over nineteen centuries of Christian missionary activity hinged on this belief alone," but studies reveal that this remains "the single most socially offensive aspect of Christian theology," and that this has been the most prominent impact of theological liberalism.

This trend toward accepting relativism is likely to take its toll in evangelical circles and will probably become a primary battleground of early twenty-first century evangelicalism. Among students at "elite" evangelical liberal arts colleges and seminaries, one third believe that other ways of salvation may be possible for those who have never heard of Jesus Christ.[27] Most will not go so far as a Hindu acquaintance of mine who acknowledged Jesus as a legitimate but not the only path of salvation; they simply claim that God may have a special plan for those who have never heard the gospel.

Yet even this more modest claim guts the very heart of the saving gospel. The standard Jesus-is-the-only-way texts aside (e.g., John 14:6; Acts 4:12), what kind of heavenly Father would send his own Son to the cross if the plan of salvation was actually multiple choice (Gal. 2:21)? The New Testament presents the apostolic preaching of salvation from a variety of complementary angles: rebirth by the Spirit, justification by faith, passing from death to life or from darkness to light, and so forth. Yet all these models share the common element that the criterion for transition from one state to another is dependence on Christ; all humanity remains alienated from God until saved through this gospel (John 3:17–18; Rom. 10:13–17). In practice, the apostolic gospel demands from us a nonnegotiable commitment to missions.

---

26. González, *Revelation*, 31. By "tolerance" here we mean not the biblical virtue of loving those who disagree with us but the intellectual paralysis that comes from fear to disagree.

27. James Davison Hunter, *Evangelicalism: The Coming Generation* (Chicago: Univ. of Chicago Press, 1987), 34–35. Roughly half of self-identified born-again Christians believe that Christians and Buddhists share the same God (Barna, *What Americans Believe*, 212; the question can be interpreted in more than one way, however).

To suggest that God has other means of salvation in addition to faith in the message about Christ, then, runs counter to the center of the Christian faith. While Christians may divide from one another on many issues (see comments on 2:4), some of us have proved too tolerant—or too lacking in backbone (Prov. 25:26)—on matters that directly affect people's salvation. Jews suffered in the Roman world for insisting that God is one; Christians merely compounded the offense by insisting that even their fellow monotheists were unsaved if they did not come through Christ.[28] The ancient challenge of idolatry was a denial that God is one and demands correct worship; that challenge has appeared in a new guise today, and Christians must be ready to fight it even at the cost of our lives.

Remaining faithful to the end. The necessity of remaining faithful until the end (2:26) fits historic Calvinist and Arminian belief: The former argue that those who fall away were never converted, whereas the latter argue that they have lost their salvation—but both concur that they will not be saved. Verses such as this one and countless others (Acts 14:22; 1 Cor. 9:27; 2 Cor. 13:5; Col. 1:23; 1 Thess. 3:5; 1 Tim. 4:1; Heb. 2:1–4; 4:1–2; 6:4–8; 10:19–31; 12:14–17; James 5:19–20; see comment on Rev. 3:5), however, may prove uncomfortable to those who think that merely praying a prayer without truly persevering in Christian faith is adequate for salvation.[29] The threats to perseverance vary among the churches, however, from persecution to lovelessness to compromise with paganism—enough warnings to summon the entire church worldwide to spiritual vigilance.

---

28. For a fuller argument, see "Why Does It Matter?" the closing chapter in Keener and Usry, *Defending Black Faith*, 108–35. For one excellent and balanced presentation, see Ajith Fernando, *The Christian's Attitude Toward World Religions* (Wheaton, Ill.: Tyndale House, 1987). For various views, see the essays in William V. Crockett and James G. Sigountos, *Through No Fault of Their Own? The Fate of Those Who Have Never Heard* (Grand Rapids: Baker, 1991); Dennis Okholm and Timothy Phillips, *More Than One Way? Four Views on Salvation in a Pluralistic World* (Grand Rapids: Zondervan, 1995).

29. See I. Howard Marshall, *Kept by the Power of God: A Study in Perseverance and Falling Away* (Minneapolis: Bethany Fellowship, 1974); from an Arminian perspective, Robert Shank, *Life in the Son: A Study of the Doctrine of Perseverance*, 2d ed. (Springfield, Mo.: Westcott, 1961).

Revelation 3:1–6

TO THE ANGEL of the church in Sardis write:

These are the words of him who holds the seven spirits of God and the seven stars. I know your deeds; you have a reputation of being alive, but you are dead. ²Wake up! Strengthen what remains and is about to die, for I have not found your deeds complete in the sight of my God. ³Remember, therefore, what you have received and heard; obey it, and repent. But if you do not wake up, I will come like a thief, and you will not know at what time I will come to you.

⁴Yet you have a few people in Sardis who have not soiled their clothes. They will walk with me, dressed in white, for they are worthy. ⁵He who overcomes will, like them, be dressed in white. I will never blot out his name from the book of life, but will acknowledge his name before my Father and his angels. ⁶He who has an ear, let him hear what the Spirit says to the churches.

Original Meaning

THIS LETTER ADDRESSES Sardis, a "dead" church (3:1). Jesus' oracle to Ephesus challenges a loveless church; his oracle to Smyrna encourages a persecuted church; his oracle to Pergamum addresses both persecution and compromise; his oracle to Thyatira challenges compromise. But Jesus' word to Sardis summons a sleeping church to wake up.[1]

Sardis was full of sophisticated paganism; for example, Greeks had identified the early Asiatic mother goddess with their Demeter, and early in the first century Romans had identified this goddess with the deified empress Livia.[2] That no mention of persecution against Christians is mentioned in

---

1. Cf. similar exhortations in Rom. 13:11; 1 Thess. 5:6; among moralists and seers, see Seneca *Ep. Lucil.* 20.13; Marcus Aurelius, 6.31; 1 Enoch 82:3.

2. See Caird, *Commentary on Revelation*, 47; on Demeter and Kore, see Hanfmann, *Sardis*, 147. Some excavators believe they have found an imperial temple as well (C. Ratté, T. N. Howe and C. Foss, "An Early Imperial Pseudodipteral Temple at Sardis," *American Journal of Archaeology* 90 [1986]: 45–68).

such a city is significant; it probably reflects the secure position that the Jewish community, which rejected pagan worship, had attained, and suggests that Christians shared this benefit of toleration.[3]

Sardis had a significant and powerful Jewish community.[4] When they later built a new synagogue next to the city gymnasium (a center of pagan Greek culture), the synagogue was roughly the length of a football field, certainly one of the largest in antiquity.[5] In contrast to churches in Smyrna and Philadelphia, however (cf. 2:9; 3:9), Jesus' followers seem to have coexisted peacefully with the synagogue community, and therefore likely coexisted peacefully with the city establishment as a whole. Lacking the world's opposition, they may have grown comfortable in their relationship with the world.[6]

Jesus' reproof of a church with a name that is alive yet it is dead (3:1) may have evoked a variety of local associations. For instance, some of the most prominent local pagan religion focused on seasonal renewal of life.[7] Perhaps less likely, some have also suggested an allusion to the opposing hills of Sardis, the Acropolis and Necropolis, so that the Christians there appear lively like the Acropolis but are actually dead like the city's almost equally visible necropolis.[8]

But local Christians would more likely recall other images of dead and alive relevant to their region. For instance, several decades before Revelation was written, Sardis had been devastated by an earthquake,[9] and its architecture

---

3. Iconography in Sardis's synagogue suggests they were at home with Gentile culture; see Eric Meyers and A. Thomas Kraabel, "Archaeology, Iconography, and Nonliterary Written Remains," 175–210 in *Early Judaism and Its Modern Interpreters*, ed. R. A. Kraft and G. W. E. Nickelsburg, SBLBMI 2 (Atlanta: Scholars, 1986), 192.

4. See Josephus, *Ant.* 14.235, 259–61; *CIJ*, 2:16, §§750–51; Kraabel, "Judaism in Western Asia Minor," 198–240.

5. See David Gordon Mitten, "A New Look at Ancient Sardis," *BA* 24 (May 1966): 38–68 (esp. 65); George M. A. Hanfmann, "The Tenth Campaign at Sardis," *BASOR* 191 (Oct. 1968): 2–41; Marianne Palmer Bonz, "Differing Approaches to Religious Benefaction: The Late Third-Century Acquisition of the Sardis Synagogue," *HTR* 86 (April 1993): 139–54. Helga Botermann, "Die Synagoge von Sardes: Eine Synagoge aus dem 4. Jahrhundert?" *ZNW* 81 (1990): 103–21, dates the evidence later.

6. Pilch, "Lying," 132, suggests the Christians had accommodated themselves to the synagogue establishment to avoid conflict. For Christianity in Sardis in a later period, see George M. A. Hanfmann and Hans Buchwald, "Christianity: Churches and Cemeteries," 191–210 in *Sardis*, ed. Hanfmann.

7. See Hemer, *Letters to the Seven Churches*, 138–40; Ramsay, *Letters to the Seven Churches*, 363–65, on Demeter and Persephone.

8. Peter Wood, "Local Knowledge in the Letters of the Apocalypse," *ExpTim* 73 (1962): 263–64.

9. Strabo, 12.8.18; Tacitus, *Ann.* 2.47.

after the rebuilding suggests continuing fear of another one.[10] Likewise, Sardian Christians are perhaps identifying with the widely known ancient tradition of their city. Sardis maintained an ancient "reputation" (lit., "name") as a great city from the time of its most famous ruler, Croesus, but at the time Revelation is written, Sardis had little more than its ancient name.[11] To be sure, Jesus addresses the church and not the history of the city.[12] But cities had enduring reputations, and local inhabitants grew up aware of such reputations. Whatever the specific basis for the image used here, however, its most important function is a deliberate contrast with the Lord himself, who was dead and is now alive (1:18; 2:8). The spiritual state of the believers in this city is hindering them from appropriating Jesus' own resurrection power.

Jesus' warning that he will come on them as a "thief" (3:3), presumably unexpectedly as in the night, recalls Jesus' words about the end times (Matt. 24:43; cf. Luke 12:39) often repeated by early Christians (1 Thess. 5:2; 2 Peter 3:10; Rev. 16:15).[13] But this warning would also prove especially alarming to proud Sardians schooled from youth in the history of their city. Conquerors had never overtaken Sardis by conventional war, but had twice conquered it unexpectedly because Sardians had failed to watch adequately.[14] (The Greek word behind NIV's "wake up" is translated "watch" in other texts, e.g., Matt. 24:42–43.) Indeed, a city that appeared powerful yet was easily captured provided a ready target for derision (Sib. Or. 4.93).

That those who have not "soiled" their clothes will walk with Jesus "dressed in white" (3:4) is significant. In the temples of Asia and elsewhere, worshipers dared not approach deities with soiled clothes; the normal apparel for approaching the gods in temples was white or linen.[15] Jesus presumably

---

10. Mitten, "Look," 61–62; cf. Ramsay, *Letters to the Seven Churches*, 375. Sib. Or. 5.289 targets Sardis, among other Asian cities, for judgment by earthquake, but this probably reflects historical events.

11. See Herodotus, 1.26–28; Strabo, 13.4.5; Colin J. Hemer, "The Sardis Letter and the Croesus Tradition," *NTS* 19 (Oct. 1972): 94–97. It was long known for its red dye (Aristophes, *Acharnians* 112). Gold dust was often found in rivers (Strabo, 15.1.69), but the supply in the nearby Pactolus had given out (Strabo, 13.4.5); nevertheless, Sardis remained relatively wealthy in the first century (Philostratus, *V.A.* 1.11).

12. Michaels, *Revelation*, 82.

13. See more fully, Richard Bauckham, "Synoptic Parousia Parables Again," *NTS* 29 (1983): 129–34.

14. See Caird, *Commentary on Revelation*, 47; Richard, *Apocalypse*, 59. For conquests of Sardis, see Herodotus, 1.47–91; 7.11; cf. Cornelius Nepos 1 (Miltiades), 4.1. Cyrus's unexpected conquest of Sardis became a source for moral lessons mined by later writers (see Aune, *Revelation*, 1:220).

15. See Josephus, *War* 2.1; *Ant.* 11.327; Philo, *Cont.* 66; Euripides, *Bacch.* 112; Pausanius, 2.35.5; 6.20.3; Diogenes Laertius, 8.1.33; for priests, see Josephus, *War* 5.229; *Pes. Rab.*

promises here that his followers who have not polluted themselves with the paganism of their culture will participate in the new Jerusalem; though that city will have no specific temple (21:22), it will be a temple city, the dwelling of God (21:3, 16). Those who fail to watch will be found naked (16:15).

The promise that the overcomers in Sardis will not be blotted out "from the book of life" (3:5) implies the obverse, namely, that much of the church in Sardis is close to spiritual death (3:2) and will not see the kingdom. The image of blotting out stems from Exodus 32:32–33, which came to be applied to a heavenly book of life (Ps. 69:28; Dan. 12:1; Luke 10:20; Phil. 4:3).[16] An ancient audience in Asia may have heard this image against the citizen-registers known throughout Asia Minor; in an earlier period Sardis was known for its royal archives. In some places (best documented from Athens), names of errant citizens were deleted from the register immediately prior to their execution.[17] The promise that Jesus will confess the faithful remnant before his Father echoes what he told his disciples (Matt. 10:32; Luke 12:8).

Bridging Contexts

SOME ELEMENTS OF the letter speak concretely to Sardis, but this no more makes the exhortations irrelevant to modern readers than concrete local color does in Paul's letters. All the churches are invited to learn from Jesus' warnings to the others (2:7, 11, 17, 29; 3:6, 13, 22), and the exhortation to "watch" or "wake up" (3:2) applies to all (16:15; cf. 1 Thess. 5:2). We can apply this to everyone, for we must all be ready for the Lord's return or judgment. But we should apply the point of the text most securely where analogies are closest, so that the warning to "wake up" is especially relevant to sleeping churches—that is, to those that are guided more by their culture than by Jesus' voice or any sense of future reckoning before him.

Also, it is important to hear the blunt warning of the text and not to reduce it on the basis of our more comfortable theological presuppositions. Our faith in the Bible as God's Word requires us to revise our thinking to fit

---

33:10; Appian, *C.W.* 4.6.47; Plutarch, *Isis* 3–4, *Mor.* 352C; Apulius, *Metam.* 11.10, 23. Cf. Ramsay, *Letters to the Seven Churches*, 386–87; Hemer, *Letters to the Seven Churches*, 146–47, though they prefer the image of a Roman triumph here.

16. See further 1 Enoch 10:8; 47:3; 104:1; Jub. 30:18–23; 36:10; 1QM 12.1–2; Hermas 1.1.1; Jean Daniélou, *The Theology of Jewish Christianity* (London: Darton, Longman & Todd, 1964), 192–204; perhaps Isa. 4:3; also the curse against the schismatics in the Eighteen Benedictions. See esp. sinners' names being erased from the heavenly books in 1 Enoch 108:3.

17. Hemer, *Letters to the Seven Churches*, 148; Ramsay, *Letters to the Seven Churches*, 385; Aune, *Revelation*, 1:225.

the text, not the reverse. Take, for example, the implication of lostness for those who fail to overcome (3:5, see next section).

WARNING TO A **dead church.** The Sardian Christians were different from the other churches discussed so far. Satan did not have to pressure them with persecution or temptation; their church was already dead. They had become comfortable with the world, had no price to pay for their faith in Jesus Christ, and would therefore be taken by surprise (3:3). Such a warning should generate introspection for modern Western Christians: As a church, the believers in Sardis undoubtedly dreamed that they were awake. Jesus may not be satisfied with the status quo in our lives or our churches.

Staying awake is difficult when the world around us remains asleep (cf. 16:15). In Nazi Germany some 7,000 of 18,000 pastors in the state church opposed the Aryan clause that excluded Christians of Jewish descent from working in the church.[18] In time, the Confessing Church formed to protest the state church's compromises with Hitler, but gradually Hitler began to woo this very church. He allowed some of their distinctives and provided legitimacy for them if they would simply acquiesce to his expansionist plans. Dietrich Bonhoeffer fought this compromise, but became an increasingly isolated minority voice in view of the "practical realities" of the church's situation.[19] He claimed "that the failure of German Christians to resist the Nazi rise to power stemmed from their lack of moral clarity"; the only people who can stand firm in such situations are those whose standard is not reason or conscience but God and his Word.[20] Whether we are seeking to win resistant converts or fighting for justice for the poor or unborn, it is always easy to grow weary in well-doing and follow the crowd—especially when the church around us has become part of it.

Further, like both the city of Sardis and the Sardian Christians, it is too easy for us to depend on past achievements instead of looking to God's call for us in the future (cf. Phil. 3:12–14). We may recall the example of Gideon, who made a golden ephod to commemorate his victory, yet failed to destroy

18. Richard V. Pierard, "Radical Resistance," *Christian History* 32 (1991): 30–33 (p. 31).

19. See Geffrey B. Kelly, "The Life and Death of a Modern Martyr," *Christian History* 32 (1991): 8–17 (pp. 13–14). Despite state pressures, however, the Confessing Church did eventually officially condemn the state's murder of the mentally ill and non-Aryans (Pierard, "Resistance," 32).

20. Gary Haugen, *Good News About Injustice: A Witness of Courage in a Hurting World* (Downers Grove, Ill.: InterVarsity, 1999), 91.

this ephod even when his people began worshiping it (Judg. 8:27). By lowering the standards, he set the stage for the return to Baal worship after his death and the disintegration of his spiritual legacy in Israel, and he effectively undercut the good he had achieved earlier in his life (8:33). Gideon looked back to his past victory, but should have made better plans for the future.

Changing from within. That a minority in Sardis remained unsoiled (Rev. 3:4) may challenge the presuppositions that some faithful Christians outside churches like Sardis's church may hold. It is noteworthy that Jesus does not call the righteous believers in the church of Sardis to migrate to another city or even start an alternative church elsewhere in town. There are genuine Christians in many "sleeping" (and drowsy) churches today, at least in churches that many other Christians would consider "asleep." Some conservative Christians look down on biblically faithful Christians in denominations that have strayed from their biblical roots; but God calls some Christians to remain in those denominations to call them back to faithfulness. There does come a point when a church is no longer a church (2:5) and separation (either into a distinct witnessing minority or by departure) may be necessary (18:4), but it is not wise for those of us in more spiritually comfortable situations to judge our colleagues who have remained to fight a battle we judged not our own.

On those who do not persevere. The implicit warning of 3:5 (that those who do not overcome will be blotted from the book of life) challenges some popular ideas in traditional North American religion. Arminians teach that apostasy can reverse the results of conversion; historic Calvinists teach that people who fail to persevere were never converted to begin with. What is most important is that both agree on the end result: Those who do not persevere are lost. But many (especially in my own Baptist tradition) have wrongly reinterpreted the Calvinist teaching so as to allow into heaven anyone who once professed salvation, an idea refuted both here and regularly throughout the New Testament (e.g., Mark 4:16–19; John 8:30–32; 15:6; Rom. 11:20–22; Gal. 4:19; 5:4; 2 Peter 2:20–22; see also comment on Rev. 2:26).

In personal evangelism, I have often encountered nominal evangelicals who rarely give thought to the Lord Jesus Christ, yet suppose that they are bound for heaven because they once were baptized or followed someone in the sinner's prayer. The promise that those who persevere will not be blotted from the book of life also offers a serious warning to many nominal Christians in our culture who depend purely on a past profession of faith to ensure their salvation.

When Mickey Cohen, a famous Los Angeles gangster of the late 1940s, made a public profession of faith in Christ, his new Christian friends were elated. But as time passed, they began to wonder why he did not leave his gangster lifestyle.[21] When they confronted him concerning this question, however, he protested, "You never told me I had to give up my career. You never told me that I had to give up my friends. There are Christian movie stars, Christian athletes, Christian businessmen. So what's the matter with being a Christian gangster? If I have to give up all that—if that's Christianity—count me out."[22] Cohen gradually drifted away from Christian circles and ultimately died lonely and forgotten. As Chuck Colson notes:

> Cohen was echoing the millions of professing Christians who, though unwilling to admit it, through their very lives pose the same question. Not about being Christian gangsters, but about being Christianized versions of whatever they already are—and are determined to remain.[23]

21. Charles Colson, *Loving God* (Grand Rapids: Zondervan, 1987), 81–92.
22. Ibid., 92.
23. Ibid., 94.

Revelation 3:7–13

TO THE ANGEL of the church in Philadelphia write:

These are the words of him who is holy and true, who holds the key of David. What he opens no one can shut, and what he shuts no one can open. ⁸I know your deeds. See, I have placed before you an open door that no one can shut. I know that you have little strength, yet you have kept my word and have not denied my name. ⁹I will make those who are of the synagogue of Satan, who claim to be Jews though they are not, but are liars—I will make them come and fall down at your feet and acknowledge that I have loved you. ¹⁰Since you have kept my command to endure patiently, I will also keep you from the hour of trial that is going to come upon the whole world to test those who live on the earth.

¹¹I am coming soon. Hold on to what you have, so that no one will take your crown. ¹²Him who overcomes I will make a pillar in the temple of my God. Never again will he leave it. I will write on him the name of my God and the name of the city of my God, the new Jerusalem, which is coming down out of heaven from my God; and I will also write on him my new name. ¹³He who has an ear, let him hear what the Spirit says to the churches.

Original Meaning IN CONTRAST TO churches strong in their own sight (3:17), but like the Smyrnean Christians who acknowledged their poverty (2:9), the Philadelphian church has only a "little strength," but has proved successful in standing in that strength (3:8). Although closer in location to Sardis, the Philadelphian Christians' situation resembles that of their fellow believers in Smyrna, roughly sixty miles to the west.

Jesus is the one "who holds the key of David," with the authority to open and shut. This means that Jesus is not only the "root of David" (5:5; 22:16), but the majordomo, the one who controls entrance into the royal palace, a position of the highest authority in the kingdom (Isa. 22:15–25, esp. 22:22;

Isa. 45:1–2; Ezek. 44:2).[1] As such Jesus determines who may enter his household and who may not.

As in Smyrna, believers in Philadelphia experienced conflict with the local synagogue.[2] Probably they were like the Jewish Christians for whom John first wrote his Gospel, many of whom were likely expelled from their synagogues (similar to the formerly blind man of John 9:34). But Jesus defended that man as one of his sheep, noting that he as the divine shepherd had the right to determine who belonged to his people and who did not (10:1–15). In the same way here, though these synagogues may have expelled Jewish Christians from their houses of worship, Jesus welcomes the believers into his own household.

Though the authorities believe they have excluded these believers from God's people, Jesus is the one who truly provides access to the new Jerusalem (21:12–14). This is the likeliest sense of opening and shutting the door here.[3] Some Jewish leaders in the late first century apparently felt they had the authority to control access to the synagogue and God's people (Matt. 23:13). The text probably also alludes to a door to heaven (4:1), or more likely to the gates of the new Jerusalem (3:12; 21:12–15, 21, 25; 22:14) or the entrance to the temple (11:19; 15:5), to presently available fellowship with Jesus (3:20), or to Jesus as completed salvation (cf. Luke 13:24–25; John 10:7–9; 14:6).[4]

The biblical prophets had promised God's people that the Gentiles would one day bow down to them (Isa. 60:14; cf. 45:14; 49:23; cf. 45:23; 49:7; 66:23), as Jewish tradition also recognized (1 Enoch 90:30; 1QM 12.14). But here unbelieving Jews join unbelieving Gentiles in bowing down before the faithful believers (Rev. 3:9).[5] They must recognize that God has chosen his people (Isa. 49:7)

---

1. One who held the keys of gates, royal treasuries, etc., wielded considerable authority; see also 9:1; 20:1; and esp. comment on 1:18. See Livy, 24.23.1; 24.37.8; Boaz Cohen, *Jewish and Roman Law: A Comparative Study*, 2 vols. (New York: Jewish Theological Seminary of America, 1966), 538–39. Because most doors had just one key, its bearer had significant authority (E. F. F. Bishop, *Apostles of Palestine: The Local Background to the New Testament Church* [London: Lutterworth, 1958], 232).

2. On Philadelphian Judaism, see *CIJ* 2:18–19, §754; Ignatius, *Philad.* 6.1; Kraabel, "Judaism in Western Asia Minor," 181–90.

3. Cf. Beasley-Murray, *Revelation*, 100; Mounce, *Revelation*, 116–17; against Caird, *Commentary on Revelation*, 51–53, who envisions opportunities for evangelism here (the typical Pauline sense: 1 Cor. 16:9; 2 Cor. 2:12; Col. 4:3). "Opening" a "door" was a frequent figurative expression in Greek (e.g., Plutarch, *Reply to Colotes* 3, *Mor.* 1108D); cf. also God's "door of hope" for a fearful heart (1QM 11.9).

4. Cf. Michaels, *Revelation*, 84. Cf. gates of heaven (Jub. 27:25); God's opening gates of salvation (1QM 18.7) or heavenly portals (4:1; 1 Enoch 14:15; 3 Macc. 6:18; T. Levi 2:6).

5. Fekkes, *Isaiah and Prophetic Tradition*, 134–35, emphasizes the link between God's oppressed community in Isaiah and that in Revelation.

---

and that he loves them (43:4; esp. Mal. 1:2). As those whom Jesus loves, they are the destined inhabitants of "the city he loves" (Rev. 20:9). What marks them as Christ's people is that they have "kept" or guarded his word (3:10; cf. 1:3; 2:26; 3:3, 8; 12:17; 14:12; 16:15; 22:7, 9); he will thus guard them.[6]

Revelation 3:10 first introduces Revelation's typical contrast between "those who live in heaven" and "those who live on the earth." The earth-dwellers are normally the wicked who invite judgment (6:10; 8:13; 11:10; 13:8, 12, 14; 17:2, 8), whereas the heaven-dwellers refer to the righteous (12:12; 13:6). That the term *earth-dweller* does not normally include the suffering saints on earth (though cf. 2:13) may suggest that though these people suffer temporarily on earth, their long-term home is heaven.[7] The hour of testing is designed to test unbelievers; believers will be protected during it (see comment on 7:1–8).[8]

Despite Jesus' praises for the Philadelphian Christians' perseverance to this point, however, "it's not over till it's over." They must continue to hold fast what they have (3:11), that is, to continue to keep the message that demands their perseverance (3:10), lest their persecutors seize from them their crown (3:11; cf. 2:25). The "crown" is a victor's wreath appropriate to overcomers (see comments on 2:10, where the crown of life contrasts with the second death in 2:11), and losing it means roughly the same as the warning to the preceding church: exclusion from the kingdom (3:5).

Those who do overcome, however, will not only be welcome in Jesus' household, God's temple; they will constitute a part of it (3:12). Thus, though expelled from "Satan's synagogue" (3:9), they remain in God's temple. This image directly recalls Isaiah 56:5, in which foreigners and eunuchs will have a place and an eternal name within God's house, better than that of Israelites. Although Gentiles were permitted in the Old Testament temple (1 Kings 8:41–43), the architecture of the second temple (destroyed a few decades before Revelation's writing) had separated even Israelite women from Israelite men. It placed the women on a lower level than Jewish men and placed Gentiles even further from the sanctuary (see Acts 21:29).

Meanwhile, eunuchs had always been excluded from God's people (Deut. 23:1). Yet God promised the Gentiles and eunuchs who obeyed his

---

6. Besides Old Testament references, cf. similar expressions for keeping commandments in Jub. 2:28; 20:2; 1QS 5.9; 8.3; CD 6.18; 10.14, 16; 20.17; 1 Macc. 2:53; Sib. Or. 1.52–53, 170. For God's keeping those who "keep" his Word, see *Midr. Ps.* 17.8.

7. For "earth-" and "heaven-dwellers," cf. also Nah. 1:5; Luke 21:35; 1 Enoch 40:6–7; 54:6; 65:12; 80:7; 104:6; 4QpNah prologue 9; Wisd. Sol. 9:18; 4 Ezra 5:6; 7:72; 13:30–31; 2 Bar. 25:3; 27:15; T. Abr. 3 A; T. Job 36:3–6. "Heaven-dwellers" can refer to deities in pagan texts (Frederick C. Grant, *Hellenistic Religions* [Indianapolis: Bobbs-Merrill, 1953], 136; Cicero, *De Legibus* 2.8.19).

8. Cf. here Guthrie, *Relevance*, 97.

commandments a better place than that of his own people who did not obey (Isa. 56:3–6), thereby making his new temple a "house of prayer for all nations" (56:7; cf. Mark 11:17). That Christ had established his people as one new temple made of both Jew and Gentile was familiar imagery for Christians in Asia by this time (Eph. 2:18–22; 1 Peter 2:5). Everyone would expect this new temple to include pillars (Ezek. 40:9–41:3; 1 En. 90:29) just as the old one did (Ex. 27:10–17; 38:10–28; 1 Kings 7:2–6, 15–22), and personified pillars specifically functioned as an image of strength or blessing (Ex. 24:4; Ps. 144:12; Jer. 1:18; Gal. 2:9; 1 Clem. 5.2).[9]

That such pillars would bear the name of God, of the new Jerusalem, and Jesus' new name (3:12) merely confirms that they belong in the holy city. Ancient pillars frequently bore honorary inscriptions,[10] and one might expect the same for eschatological pillars.[11] Further, earlier prophets had already announced the significance of the new Jerusalem's future name (Jer. 33:16; Ezek. 48:35; cf. *b. B.B.* 75b). God had also promised his people a new name in the time of their end-time vindication (Isa. 62:2; see comment on Rev. 2:17). Perhaps because Philadelphia had adopted two new names in the first century, Philadelphian Christians would be particularly sensitive to the promise of a new name. But such honorary names appear in some other locations, and of course all believers will have a new name.[12]

---

9. On people as strong "pillars," see also 2 Bar. 2:1; 4 Bar. 1:2; *ARN* 25A; certain manuscripts of Jos. and Asen. 17:6; the patriarchs in *Gen. Rab.* 43:8; 75:5; cf. Greek sources in Aune, *Revelation*, 1:241. Beale, *Revelation*, 295, compares some Greek versions of Isa. 22:23. For eschatological pillars, cf. Sib. Or. 2.240 (though possibly part of a Christian interpolation). The old temple's pillars may contrast with the pagan use of pillars (e.g., Ex. 23:24; 34:13; Deut. 7:5; 12:3; 1 Kings 14:23; 2 Kings 10:26; 17:10; 18:4; 23:14; 2 Chron. 31:1; Hos. 10:1–2; Mic. 5:13; Homer, *Il.* 17.434; *Od.* 12.14; Cornelius Nepos, 7 [Alcibiades], 3.2). Association with the "royal pillar" of Solomon's temple (Richard H. Wilkinson, "The *STULOS* of Revelation 3:12 and Ancient Coronation Rites," *JBL* 107 [1988]: 498–501) may thus be too narrow. But one cannot press "in the temple" to exclude Solomon's external pillars (so Aune, *Revelation*, 1:241), which were part of the temple complex.

10. E.g., Diogenes Laertius, 7.1.11–12; Josephus, *Ant.* 16.165; cf. 2 Sam. 18:18; 1 Macc. 14:27; also curse inscriptions (Cornelius Nepos, 7 [Alcibiades], 6.5) and laws (Lysias, *Murder of Eratosthenes* 30). The synagogue pillars at Capernaum contain names (M. Avi-Yonah, "Archaeological Sources," 46–62 in *JPFC*, 53). For figurative use of this image, see Philo, *Abraham* 4.

11. For inscriptions on Israel's eschatological standards, see Michael Avi-Yonah, "The 'War of the Sons of Light and the Sons of Darkness' and Maccabean Warfare," *IEJ* 2 (1952): 1–5 (p. 3); Yigael Yadin, *The Scroll of the War of the Sons of Light Against the Sons of Darkness* (Oxford: Oxford Univ. Press, 1962), 61–64 (though cf. K. M. T. Atkinson, "The Historical Setting of the 'War of the Sons of Light and the Sons of Darkness,'" *BJRL* 40 [1957–1958]: 272–97 [p. 291]).

12. Mounce, *Revelation*, 121, is skeptical that Philadelphia's new names (Neocaesarea and Flavia) are relevant to the verse.

The new Jerusalem "is coming down out of heaven" (3:12); some take this as an iterative present, suggesting that the new Jerusalem always meets believers in the present as they submit to God's reign. More likely, the present tense merely vividly emphasizes the origin of this city as from above (21:2), which contrasts it with the merely human Jerusalem in which Israel's hopes were recently shattered and the synagogue community from which Philadelphian Christians have been expelled (3:9).

IF JESUS' PROMISE to excluded Christians tempts any of us toward unnecessary separatism, it is helpful for us to remember the reasons for that exclusion. The Christians here are not excluding others or seceding from their public witness in a difficult arena, but are excluded against their will on account of their witness.

Because our Bridging Contexts section often addresses dangers in interpretation, it may be helpful to address one popular application of 3:10. Many North American interpreters have argued that this verse supports the doctrine that the church will be raptured out before the final three-and-a-half or seven-year Tribulation.[13] Thus, for example, one notes that one is kept not merely from suffering but from the "hour" of suffering.[14] Such a reading of this text is not impossible grammatically, but this verse by itself is not a good foundation for the doctrine, as both the words employed and the broader context of Revelation suggest.[15]

---

13. E.g., Jeffrey L. Townsend, "The Rapture in Revelation 3:10," *BibSac* 137 (1980): 252–66; Lindsey, *New World Coming*, 77; more cautiously, Walvoord, *Revelation*, 87. For those readers unfamiliar with the doctrine, it appears to have originated in 1830 as a corollary of John Nelson Darby's original form of dispensationalism, which contended that God would not deal with both Israel and the church simultaneously (see summaries in J. Barton Payne, *The Imminent Appearing of Christ* [Grand Rapids: Eerdmans, 1962], 11–42; Robert H. Gundry, *The Church and the Tribulation* (Grand Rapids: Zondervan, 1973), 172–88; Arthur Katterjohn with Mark Fackler, *The Tribulation People* (Carol Stream, Ill.: Creation House), 104–115; Timothy Weber, "The Dispensationalist Era," *Christian History* 61 (1999): 34–37 (esp. 35). Walvoord, *The Rapture Question* (Grand Rapids: Zondervan, 1972), 52–56, responds by appealing to progressive revelation in church history. The earliest postapostolic interpreters appear to have been posttribulational (e.g., Herm. 1.2.2; 1.4.2–3; Irenaeus, 5.28.4; 5.29.1; 5.35.1).

14. So Ryrie, *Revelation*, 29–30.

15. For grammatical arguments favoring a pretribulational rapture here, see Thomas R. Edgar, "R. H. Gundry and Revelation 3:10," *GTJ* 3 (1982): 19–49; David G. Winfrey, "The Great Tribulation: Kept 'Out of' or 'Through'?" *GTJ* 3 (1982): 3–18; J. F. Strombeck, *First the Rapture* (Eugene, Ore.: Harvest House, 1982), 172–75; for some posttribulational arguments, see Gundry, *The Church and the Tribulation*, 55–60; Payne, *Imminent Appearing*, 78; Mounce, *Revelation*, 119; Beale, *Revelation*, 290–92.

The "hour of trial" does not settle the issue. In Revelation "hour" can refer to either testing before the end (9:15; 17:12) or to the final hour at our Lord's return (3:3; 14:7, 15).[16] In either case, references to time in Revelation are often qualitative, addressing the kind rather than duration of time (see comment on 12:6). "Trial" more likely refers to tribulation before Jesus' return (cf. 2:10), but the sample size for Revelation's use of the term is too small to be sure.

The phrase "keep ... from," however, may prove more suggestive. Elsewhere in Revelation "keep" refers to guarding God's commandments. The expression "keep ... from" appears only here in Revelation, but it occurs in one other New Testament instance, where John also records Jesus as speaking and where the meaning is clear: not removal from trial, but protection through it (John 17:15; cf. 1 John 5:18).[17] This may fit the image of eschatological survivors found in some end-time texts (Mark 13:20; 4 Ezra 6:25; 7:27). In the Bible God generally delivers his people after they are already in testing (e.g., Ps. 34:19; 107:6; Jer. 30:7). Interestingly, persecution did continue for Philadelphian Christians (Mart. Polyc. 19.1).

More important is the broader context of Revelation. No description of Jesus' return precedes 19:11–16, and no clear mention of any corporate resurrection precedes the "first" resurrection in 20:4–6, at the beginning of the thousand years. Although saints are slaughtered throughout Revelation, they are also protected from God's anger in 7:1–8, an activity that would fulfill the promise of 3:10 to Philadelphia and Christians like them. One commentator complains that the "effect of this 'pretribulation rapture' is to dissociate Christian readers from any persecution and suffering at the hands of the Beast and to deny the church's identity as a martyr church."[18] Those who, for whatever reasons, dissociate Christians from the suffering saints in Revelation miss much of the relevance of the book's primary warnings. But in the final analysis, it is possible that Revelation may not refer to the specific three-and-a-half or seven-year Tribulation emphasized in modern prophecy teaching anyway (see discussion of 12:5–6); if it does not, it might not even comment directly on such a question as we have addressed here.

---

16. Some examples can be counted either way, depending on one's interpretation of the context (11:13; 18:10, 17, 19); most of Jesus' warnings in the context do, however, involve the hour of his return, whether fig. or lit. (2:5, 16; 3:11). For the testing time as the final day of judgment, see 2 Enoch 50:5–6, rec. A; Lucan, *C.W.* 1.73; for the Tribulation here, see Schuyler Brown, "'The Hour of Trial' (Rev 3:10)," *JBL* 85 (Sept. 1966): 308–14; Rissi, *Time and History*, 28–29; Bauckham, *Climax of Prophecy*, 83.

17. With most commentators, e.g., Brown, "Hour," 310; Tenney, *Revelation*, 65; Beasley-Murray, *Revelation*, 101. For "keep" as "protect," cf. 1 Enoch 100:5; 1QM 14.10.

18. Michaels, *Interpreting Revelation*, 140.

DEPENDENCE ON GOD'S **power.** That the Christians have little power (3:8) counts in their favor before God; power is easily abused, but weakness often leads to dependence on God's power.[19] Although theologians debate some of the more radical proposals of liberation theologians, one insight of liberation theology clearly draws on the biblical perspective: God's special concern for the broken. God promises to live with and embrace especially the broken and humble, just as he is far from the proud and self-sufficient (Ps. 51:17; Isa. 57:15; 66:2; James 4:6). Each of us comes from a different background, some with more advantages and some with less, but God judges us not on what power we start with, but on what we do with what he has given us.

The Christians in Philadelphia have become broken by their exclusion from the synagogue, hence from their heritage. Faithfulness often means being excluded from circles that mean much to us—sometimes even from family. Those who have grown up in Christian homes or have families in a church may not recognize the need of single Christians or Christians in religiously mixed marriages to experience Christian family ties in the church, especially if such people have experienced rejection for the gospel's sake from their family of origin. I have witnessed this familial rejection among some messianic Jewish friends or those converted from nominal, "culturally" Christian homes, and felt something like it in the earliest days of my own witness.[20]

Jesus will preserve his people through their trial, which they share with the world (3:10), and will vindicate them (3:9), presumably at his coming (3:11). Even in the worst situations, hope provides believers strength to endure.[21] But perseverance is mandatory for participating in that hope (3:11; see comment on 3:5). Each of the images of reward in 3:12 emphasizes the depth of God's love for his faithful people. Many people attend larger churches without knowing other members personally, but Jesus promises fellowship and recognition to those otherwise excluded. Some Christians today are embarrassed to wear explicitly Christian markings (such as church sweatshirts) or speak openly for their faith, but those excluded today for their faith will wear the name that identifies them as citizens of the promised future world.

---

19. See similar comments by Ellul, *Apocalypse,* 138.

20. This persecution can become even more dramatic in some contexts, e.g., a Hindu convert in Nepal may face death threats from his own family (Barbara Thompson, "Nepal's Book of Acts," *CT* [Nov. 9, 1992], 14–18 [p. 16]).

21. For an excellent perspective on our hope "as the ultimate form of deferred gratification," see Philip Yancey, "Why Not Now?" *CT* (Feb. 5, 1996), 112. But endurance for deferred gratification demands faith that the promiser has spoken the truth.

Participation in God's eternal temple. That Christians will participate eternally in God's temple indicates that we will always live in his presence (cf. 21:3, 22–25). Revelation is full of allusions to the heavenly temple: the ark (11:19), the tabernacle (15:5), the altars of incense and sacrifice (6:9; 8:3–5; 9:13), the sea (4:6; 15:2; cf. 1 Kings 7:23–25, 39, 44)—and of course the lampstands (1:12–13; 2:1, 5). Because throughout Revelation heaven appears as a temple and the primary focus of its activity is worship, we also recognize that our function in God's temple will include worship.

Never are we as close to our eternal destiny as when we are glorifying God by worship or by inviting others to recognize his greatness. Of course, worship is not merely what often passes for it in our churches; we can easily mistake a sense of awe in majestic hymns or a sense of excitement in familiar praise choruses for worship, while ignoring the true object of worship to which such songs summon us. Worship involves recognizing God's and Christ's true identity and work (cf. 5:9–10, 12), so that we are in awe of not merely sublime sounds but of the Lord himself. When we know what God is truly like, we cannot withhold the honor due him.

Revelation 3:14–22

TO THE ANGEL of the church in Laodicea write:

These are the words of the Amen, the faithful and true witness, the ruler of God's creation. ¹⁵I know your deeds, that you are neither cold nor hot. I wish you were either one or the other! ¹⁶So, because you are lukewarm—neither hot nor cold—I am about to spit you out of my mouth. ¹⁷You say, 'I am rich; I have acquired wealth and do not need a thing.' But you do not realize that you are wretched, pitiful, poor, blind and naked. ¹⁸I counsel you to buy from me gold refined in the fire, so you can become rich; and white clothes to wear, so you can cover your shameful nakedness; and salve to put on your eyes, so you can see.

¹⁹Those whom I love I rebuke and discipline. So be earnest, and repent. ²⁰Here I am! I stand at the door and knock. If anyone hears my voice and opens the door, I will come in and eat with him, and he with me.

²¹To him who overcomes, I will give the right to sit with me on my throne, just as I overcame and sat down with my Father on his throne. ²²He who has an ear, let him hear what the Spirit says to the churches."

Original Meaning

PERHAPS MOST CONCRETE in local color is the message of Jesus to the church at Laodicea. Laodicea lay in Phrygia's Lycus Valley, ten miles west of Colosse (Col. 2:1; 4:15–16) and six miles south of Hierapolis (Col. 4:13). Pagan worship, especially of Zeus but also of numerous other deities (such as Dionysus, Helios, Hera, and Athena) flourished there.[1] A significant Jewish community lived in Phrygia (Acts 13:14–50; 14:1–5, 19), but they seem to have blended into Greek culture in many respects.[2]

---

1. Yamauchi, *The Archaeology of New Testament Cities*, 143–44; J. B. Lightfoot, *Saint Paul's Epistles to the Colossians and to Philemon* (Grand Rapids: Zondervan, 1959; reprint of 1879 ed.), 8–9.
2. Kraabel, "Judaism in Western Asia Minor," 82–86, 146; cf. Craig A. Evans, "The Colossian Mystics," *Biblica* 63 (1982): 188–205; F. F. Bruce, "Colossian Problems. Part 1: Jews and Christians in the Lycus Valley," *BibSac* 141 (1984): 3–15.

By the third century illustrations on some coins had mixed together Jewish and pagan versions of the Flood stories.[3]

Jesus pulls no punches when he addresses the Laodicean church. He is the "Amen" (3:14), a Hebrew term of confirmation (e.g., Jer. 11:5; 28:6) that suggests the assurance of all his promises (cf. 2 Cor. 1:20).[4] Likewise he is "faithful and true" (3:14), a way of emphasizing again the certainty of his promises (19:11; 21:5; 22:6). Yet for the Laodicean Christians this was not exclusively good news. Jesus was also "the ruler" (3:14; lit., "the beginning"). Elsewhere in Revelation "beginning" is an explicitly divine title linked with "first" (21:6; 22:13), a clear divine title in Isaiah 41:4; 44:6; 48:12. Cognates of the Greek word used here (*archē*) denote "ruler"—a word that can denote rule or power; the Roman emperor in fact called himself the *princeps*, or "first" among Romans, but was worshiped as a deity.

Laodicea boasted great resources (3:17), but while the Laodicean Christians likely shared their Laodicean neighbors' pride over their self-sufficiency in many respects, they presumably also shared a common dislike for their water supply (3:15–16). The bad situation of Laodicea's water was well known. Ancient sources are explicit that, though it was more drinkable than that of Hierapolis, it was full of sediment.[5] Excavation of the city's terra cotta pipes reveal thick lime deposits, which suggest heavy contamination in the water supply; lime deposits on the waterfall cliff just opposite Laodicea would provide a constant visible reminder of their water supply.[6]

Laodicea lacked its own water supply, having no direct access to the cold water of the mountains or the hot water of the nearby springs in Hierapolis to the north. In contrast to its claims to self-sufficiency (3:17), it had to pipe in its water; though much of the aqueduct from the south was underground, nearer the city it came through stone barrel pipes, thus remaining vulnerable to any intended besiegers who wished to cut off the city's water supply.[7] More important, this water had grown lukewarm by the time of its arrival.

---

3. Eric M. Meyers and A. Thomas Kraabel, "Archaeology, Iconography, and Nonliterary Written Remains," 175–210 in *Early Judaism and Its Modern Interpreters*, ed. R. A. Kraft and G. W. E. Nickelsburg, SBLBMI 2 (Atlanta: Scholars, 1986), 191.

4. Some commentators suggest a parallel with oath formulas (cf. Jesus' familiar, "Truly [lit., "Amen"] I say to you"); hence Fekkes, *Isaiah*, 137–39, suggests possible background in Isa. 65:16, which would fit the comment about "creation" in 3:14 (Isa. 65:17; see further Beale, *Revelation*, 298–300).

5. See Strabo, 13.4.14.

6. See Sherman E. Johnson, "Laodicea and Its Neighbors," *BA* 13 (Feb. 1950): 1–18 (p. 10); Beasley-Murray, *Revelation*, 105.

7. Ramsay, *Letters to the Seven Churches*, 415; Johnson, "Laodicea," 10. Ancient engineers were more skillful than we might think. To reduce the likelihood of pipes bursting, Roman engineers often tunneled through hills and spanned valleys with high arcades, so the water

The point of lukewarm water is simply that it is disgusting, in contrast to the more directly useful "hot" and "cold" water; all the churches would plainly understand this warning.[8] Hot water (as long as it was not too hot) was useful for bathing; waters at hot springs like nearby Hierapolis or other sites was considered helpful for relieving ailments. Of course, Laodiceans could have reheated the water themselves, but this was extra work, a matter some may have regarded as drudgery.[9] Cold water was useful for drinking and available in nearby locations like Colosse, but Laodicea's water did not arrive in this state. Most people preferred cold drinks, but hot drinks were also common at banquets.[10]

Jesus thus finds the church in Laodicea to be other than what he desires (cf. Isa. 5:2–6). In today's English, he is telling the self-satisfied church in Laodicea: "I want water that will refresh me, but you remind me instead of the water you always complain about. You make me want to puke." Earlier prophets also used images of rotten food to describe God's rejection of people who had grown disgusting to him (Jer. 24), but Jesus contextualizes the image for Laodicea. Ancients also applied to people the analogy of spitting out bitter water.[11]

Jesus' challenge to the Laodicean Christians' self-sufficiency (3:17–18) reminds us how readily we Christians absorb the attitudes of our culture without pausing for critical reflection on this behavior.[12] Laodicea was known

---

could flow at a relatively uniform speed even over a distance of up to fifty miles (M. Cary and T. J. Haarhoff, *Life and Thought in the Greek and Roman World*, 4th ed. [London: Methuen & Company, 1946], 105–6).

8. Cf. M. J. S. Rudwick and E. M. B. Green, "The Laodicean Lukewarmness," *ExpTim* 69 (March 1958): 176–78; Hemer, *Letters to the Seven Churches*, 188–91 (on the quality, not temperature, of the water); Stanley E. Porter, "Why the Laodiceans Received Lukewarm Water (Revelation 3:15–18)," *TynBul* 38 (1987): 143–49; cf. Aune, *Revelation*, 1:258.

9. Ancients sought to mix the appropriate amounts of hot and cold water when washing one's feet (Homer, *Od.* 19.386–89). Ancients often heated water for baths (Apollonius Rhodius, 3.272–73; Petronius, *Sat.* 72; *tos. Shab.* 3:3–4), though too much hot water was dangerous (Diodorus Siculus, 4.78.2); accidentally adding too much hot water in a bath house, hence scalding a patron, could invite a lawsuit (*P. Enteuxis* 82). Romans typically heated baths by furnaces and subterranean ducts. Water in hot baths was less likely to incur uncleanness (*p. Ter.* 8:5); but some today think excessively hot water lowered male fertility (A. M. Devine, "The Low Birth-Rate in Ancient Rome: A Possible Contributing Factor," *Rheinisches Museum für Philologie* 128 [3–4, 1985]: 313–317).

10. On the usefulness of cold water for drinking, see Achilles Tatius, 4.18.4; Diogenes Laertius, 6.9.104; of hot water mixed with wine, Martial, *Epig.* 1.11.3; on the inappropriateness of hot drinks at times, see Dio Cassius, 57.14.10; 59.11.6; 60.6.7; on the disgusting character of lukewarm water, Seneca, *Dial.* 4.25.1.

11. *Ahîquar* 148, saying 59; more explicitly, *Armenian Ahîquar* 2:8.

12. For analogous critiques of self-sufficiency, see Luke 12:19; Epictetus, *Disc.* 3.7.29. For the Stoic motif of lacking possessions that frees one to possess what matters, see in some detail Victor Paul Furnish, *II Corinthians*, AB 32A (Garden City, N.Y.: Doubleday, 1984), 348.

as a wealthy banking center, and it had flourished especially under the imperial dynasty that remained in power in John's day.[13] The city hosted gladiatorial games as early as 50 B.C. and boasted a theater.[14] More important, it was the capital of the Cibryatic convention, which included at least twenty-five towns.[15] Local civic pride grew fierce in some cities of Asia, and Laodicea vied for power with Antioch, its primary rival in Phrygia.[16] So arrogant was Laodicea about its wealth that when the emperor proposed to help rebuild Laodicea along with other Asian cities destroyed by an earthquake in A.D. 60, Laodicea refused what we would call the "federal disaster relief funds."[17]

Laodiceans would doubt that they were "naked"; their city was famous for its production of textiles, especially cloth and carpets woven from black wool.[18] Thus some commentators observe that Jesus' offer of "white clothes" probably provides a stark contrast with this notorious black wool of Laodicea. They may also experience surprise that they need Jesus to supply them spiritual eye salve. Ancient sources report a first-century medical school located in Laodicea, ear ointment made there, a famous eye doctor practicing there, and eye salve made of Phrygian powder (probably abundantly available there).[19] Yet most Laodiceans would acknowledge the usefulness of divine help alongside their medical establishment.[20] Thus the city greatly revered both Apollo, god of prophecy, and Asklepios, god of healing.[21]

---

13. Various commentators cite Cicero, *Ep. Fam.* 3.5; *ad Att.* 5.15; see further Hemer, *Letters to the Seven Churches*, 191–92. Nearby Hierapolis was also wealthy (Sib. Or. 5.318).

14. Yamauchi, *The Archaeology of New Testament Cities*, 142–43.

15. See Lightfoot, *Colossians*, 6–7.

16. Herodian, 3.3.3; 3.6.9.

17. See Tacitus, *Ann.* 14.27. An earlier generation had accepted imperial help (Strabo, 12.8.18). For Laodicea's destruction and rebuilding, see Sib. Or. 4.107–8; cf. other prophecies of judgment in Sib. Or. 5.289–91 (by earthquake); 7.22 (probably Christian material).

18. See Strabo, 12.8.16; Vitruvius, 8.3.14; see Ramsay, *Letters to the Seven Churches*, 429.

19. See Galen, *De san. tuenda* 6.4.39; Strabo, 12.8.20; see the appropriately cautious approval in Hemer, *Letters to the Seven Churches*, 196–99; Horsley, ed., *New Documents*, 3:56, §17; Aune, *Revelation*, 1:260. Eye salve was useful when used properly (Epictetus, *Disc.* 2.21.20; 3.21.21), but the wrong ointment applied to the eyes could actually produce blindness (Diodorus Siculus, 22.1.2; Dionysius of Halicarnasus, 20.5.2–3; Appian, *R.H.* 3.9.2).

20. Deities could employ eye medicine (Epidauros inscr. 4, 9), and Jewish sources report miraculous eye salve (Tob. 6:8; 11:11–13), resembling some ancient medicinal custom (Bernd Kollmann, "Göttliche Offenbarung magisch-pharmakologischer Heilkunst im Buch Tobit," *ZAW* 106 [1994]: 289–99). Some Jewish sages used medicines as a symbol for God's law (*Sifre Deut.* 45.1.1–2; *Lev. Rab.* 12:3; *Deut. Rab.* 8:4); for Jewish eye salves in general, cf. P. R. Berger, "Kollyrium für die blinden Augen, Apk. 3:18," *NovT* 27 (April 1985): 174–95; in addition, *b. Shab.* 108b; *Lam. Rab.* 4:15, §18.

21. Yamauchi, *The Archaeology of New Testament Cities*, 145; for Hierapolis, see Lightfoot, *Colossians*, 11–12; for its healing springs, Strabo, 13.4.14.

The language of 3:17–18 employs the technique of irony common in ancient texts: thus, for example, a blind seer tells a sighted king that he sees but will be blind, and is rich but will become poor;[22] but the metaphor is especially common in the biblical prophets (Isa. 6:10; 29:9; 42:19; 43:8; 56:10; Jer. 5:21; Ezek. 12:2; cf. John 9:39–41). The Laodicean Christians, reflecting the values of their prosperous society, boast, "I am rich and wealthy," as had Israel of old (Hos. 12:8).[23] Jesus advises them to buy true wealth and garments from him (Rev. 3:18; 21:18, 21; cf. Isa. 55:1), which contrast starkly with the grandeur of the world (Rev. 17:4; 18:12, 16).

Lest anyone misunderstand the tone and motivation of Jesus' rebuke, he makes clear that its purpose is love (3:19, using the language of Prov. 3:12; cf. Heb. 12:6; 1 Clem. 56.4).[24] Indeed, not only does Jesus not reject them, but he wants to have dinner with them (Rev. 3:20), a familiar image for intimacy in antiquity;[25] inviting Jesus in for a meal was the least sort of hospitality one would expect of even an acquaintance. Can a Christian who calls Jesus Lord do any less? The personalized nature of the invitation suggests that not only the future messianic banquet (2:17; 19:9) but a present foretaste of the intimacy available to those who respond to Jesus' call; hearing Jesus' "voice" may perform the same function as in John 10:3–4. Jesus is inviting the Laodicean Christians to realize how they have shut him out of their lives with their own self-sufficiency.

Jesus provides a promise of sharing his reign to those who like him "overcome" (3:21). This is a familiar promise for the future in Revelation (2:26–27; 5:10; 20:6; 22:5); although in the present believers share Christ's exaltation over the demonic powers (Eph. 1:20–23; 2:6), early Christian litera-

---

22. Sophocles, *Oed. Tyr.* 454–55.

23. See Beale, *Revelation*, 304; for extrabiblical parallels, particularly the Stoic emphasis on the true wealth of the wise, see Aune, *Revelation*, 1:258–59. Nakedness is elsewhere used figuratively (4QpNah 2.8–3.1).

24. The idea of God "disciplining" the righteous or his children appears frequently in early Jewish texts (Ps. Sol. 3:4; 8:26; 10:1–3; 13:9–10; 14:1–2; 18:4; Wisd. Sol. 3:5; 12:22; 2 Macc. 7:32–35; *Sifre Deut.* 32.5.6–7).

25. It is thus unclear whether this saying refers back to the parable of the doorkeeper (Matt. 24:42; Mark 13:33–37; Luke 12:37b; James 5:9), as Joachim Jeremias (*The Parables of Jesus*, 2d rev. ed. [New York: Scribner's, 1972], 55) thinks. Others find an allusion to Song 5:2, especially as understood in Jewish tradition (André Feuillet, "Le Cantique des Cantiques et L'apocalypse. Étude de deux réminiscences du Cantique dans l'Apocalypse johannique," *RSR* 49 [1961]: 321–53; Enric Cortès, "Una interpretación judía de Cant 5,2 en Ap 3,19b–20," *Revista Catalana de Teologia* 4 [1979]: 239–58); this would fit the bridegroom's invitation to his banquet (Rev. 19:9; cf. Luke 12:36–37). A connection with Jesus' eating with sinners (see Tim Wiarda, "Revelation 3:20: Imagery and Literary Context," *JETS* 38 [June 1995]: 203–12) is possible. For knocking, see Callimachus, *Hymn* 2.1–8.

ture indicates that the fullness of our reign awaits Christ's return (Matt. 5:5; Rom. 5:17; 8:32; 2 Tim. 2:12). The eschatological enthronement and reign of the righteous is a familiar Jewish concept (Dan. 7:22; 1 En. 108:12).[26]

WE MUST NOT allow theological presuppositions to control our reading of the text. An extreme example of doing this is the cult that takes "beginning of God's creation" in 3:14 (which the NIV interprets as "ruler of God's creation") as an admission that Jesus is a created being, albeit the first one created.[27] But such interpretation is an attempt to force biblical texts into a prior theological commitment. "Beginning" is in fact a divine title in Revelation, identical with "the First and the Last" (21:6; 22:13)—explicit divine titles in Isaiah (Isa. 41:4; 44:6; 48:12). In view of this usage, Jesus is the source of creation here rather than its first sample; the text implies his deity rather than the opposite. "'God has no origin,' said Novatian, and it is precisely this concept of no-origin which distinguishes That-which-is-God from whatever is not God."[28]

Some writers have overstated our future spiritual privileges by affirming that Christians will share "equality" with God.[29] Although the idea runs counter to the entire tenor of Scripture, one text in which they might find most ready support for such an assertion is 3:21. One can argue that sharing a throne may connote the equality of those who share it.[30] The point of the image, however, is the believers' exaltation to reign with Christ (5:10; 20:6; 22:5); the rest of the book clearly qualifies this reign as subject to God for all eternity (4:10; 22:2—4).

---

26. Cf. the more generic wisdom saying in Sir. 40:3. If Rev. 3:21 at all reflects Jesus' saying in Matt. 19:28 and Luke 22:30 (Roloff, *Revelation*, 65), it democratizes a saying to the Twelve.

27. E.g., *Revelation: Grand Climax*, 66, though with little comment. See also the earlier Arian position held by some of the Eastern clergy in Robert Payne, "A Hammer Struck at Heresy," *Christian History* 51 (1996): 11—19 (p. 17).

28. A. W. Tozer, *The Knowledge of the Holy* (New York: Harper and Row, 1961), 32.

29. According to some popular teachers today, Christians are Christ (Kenneth Hagin, *Authority of the Believer*, 11—12; "Understanding Confession," 25—27; *Zoe: The God-Kind of Life* [1981], 41; *The Name of Jesus*, 105—6); humanity belongs to God's class of being (Hagin, *Zoe*, 36; Kenneth Copeland, "The Decision Is Yours" [1978], 6) and "was never made to be a slave. . . . He was created on terms of equality with God, and he could stand in God's presence without any consciousness of inferiority" (*Zoe*, 35).

30. Aune, *Revelation*, 1:262, who argues that the image in 3:21 may be that of the *bisellium*, or double-throne, known in antiquity.

Of course, orthodox Christians are also capable of misapprehending other aspects of texts on the basis of our traditions of interpretation, even if on a lesser level. Sometimes the way we have heard a text applied misleads us in interpretation. Some interpreters regard "hot" as good, symbolizing fiery zeal for God, whereas "cold" refers to spiritual deadness and "lukewarm" to those who try to play both sides of the spiritual fence.[31]

While God certainly opposes any attempt to play both sides of a spiritual fence (cf. James 4:4, 7–8), this interpretation misses the point of Jesus' analogy. Heat is not always a positive symbol in the Bible, nor is cold always a negative one (cf. fire as judgment in Matt. 3:10–12); and in the case of water cold is more often a positive symbol in ancient literature than hot is (cf. Matt. 10:42). The real point is that whereas hot and cold water both serve important functions, even at times in drinking, lukewarm water does not; it must be either heated or left somewhere in the shade to cool off. As some pampered Laodiceans might complain that their water made them sick, Jesus tells the pampered Laodicean Christians that this is just how he feels about them.[32]

Contextualizing the message for today's church does not mean sugarcoating it, because when Jesus addresses the Laodicean Christians harshly, he addresses a church that is in many respects like many churches today (see below).

LISTENING TO JESUS' rebuke. Jesus' words to the church in Laodicea are uncomfortable not only because of the issues they address but simply because they constitute a rebuke (3:19). In the therapeutic mode of modern Western Christianity, we do not want to hear from a God who will speak harshly to us. Many Christians feel victimized (some for good reasons) and regard as insensitive any criticism of their own or anyone else's values. But Christ has a harsh word for many of us.

To be sure, Jesus speaks tenderly to those who have truly been broken—to the weak and marginalized, to those who have suffered (2:9–10; 3:8–10). We should not be callous in applying Jesus' forthright rebukes to Laodicea to our brothers and sisters working through genuine pain in their lives. But Jesus' words strike like thunder those churches that are self-satisfied and

---

31. E.g., Walvoord, *Revelation*, 91–92; Richard, *Apocalypse*, 62; cf. Meeks, *Moral World*, 147. By contrast, Aune, *Revelation*, 1:257, suggests "hot" as bad (Prov. 15:18), "cool" as good (Prov. 17:27, NRSV), which at least does not read modern figures of speech into Revelation.

32. Spitting out may even imply, as John Piper suggests (*Desiring God: Meditations of a Christian Hedonist* [Portland, Ore.: Multnomah, 1986], 261), that "eternity is at stake" when we lose our desire for God.

secure in their own endowments—those who like the Laodicean society and its church feel little need for help from outside themselves.

Yet even when Jesus rebukes complacent, self-satisfied Christians, we must not miss the tone of his voice. His cries of reproof flow not from irrational anger but from a broken heart: "Those whom I love I rebuke and discipline" (3:19). Then he invites us over for dinner (the current Western idiom "do lunch" may not be quite strong enough in this instance) if we will but open the door to him (3:20). God desires intimacy with us in the deepest recesses of our lives.[33] The focus of this text is Jesus' reproof and summons to unrepentant Christians.[34]

The danger of physical wealth and spiritual poverty. The church in Laodicea reflected the values of its culture: proud, self-sufficient, not needing any outside help, including much from the Lord (3:17). They contrasted with suffering churches that recognized their own desperation for God's intervention (cf. 2:9; 3:8). Comparing the church in North America with churches in many other parts of the world, I fear that the problems of Laodicea's Christians are most like our own.[35] We hear of massive suffering elsewhere and often find theological or sociological explanations for it to avoid the thought that we could experience the same hardships. Many of us are eager to export the profound learning of North American Christianity without humbly listening first to the lessons learned by other churches who have suffered far more than we have.

Prayerlessness or dry devotional times, so typical of many of our lives in the West, often stem from a lack of sense of need before God. Our material abundance can, if we are unwary, prove a source of spiritual poverty as it did for the Christians of Laodicea. Our indifference to persecution, political oppression, and other forms of suffering pervasive among our spiritual siblings in many regions likewise betrays our contentment with the world as we experience it. As in Laodicea, our prosperity may blind us. Note this com-

---

33. On this intimacy in prayer, see Richard J. Foster, *Prayer: Finding the Heart's True Home* (New York: HarperCollins, 1992), 1. For discussion of hearing God's voice, see from somewhat different (but not contradictory) angles, Jack Deere, *Surprised by the Voice of God* (Grand Rapids: Zondervan, 1996); and Craig S. Keener, *3 Crucial Questions About the Holy Spirit* (Grand Rapids: Baker, 1996), 131–80.

34. A secondary application to evangelism is not necessarily wrong if made along the lines of applying the principle of how Jesus approaches people (Wiarda, "Revelation 3:20," 212); cf. Paul's application of evangelistic language to unrepentant Christians in 2 Cor. 5:20–6:2.

35. So also some other observers, e.g., Karen M. Feaver, "Chinese Lessons," *CT* (May 16, 1994), 33–34; J. I. Packer, *Knowing God* (Downers Grove, Ill.: InterVarsity, 1973), 174, on some Western churches, and adding that we must repent "before judgment falls" (175).

ment from Richard Stearns of World Vision, former CEO of Lenox, Inc. (a manufacturer of fine china): "If the Book of Revelation were written today, and there was a letter to the church in America, I think it would decry the fact that our materialism and wealth have deafened our ears and blinded our eyes to the cause of the poor."[36]

Some of us learn such comparisons the hard way. Thus one minister registered his shock when a member of a delegation of Russian visitors lamented their disappointment in American Christian youth. "Since they are Christians, I expected that they would be concerned about spiritual things. Instead, they are more materialistic than the Marxist youth in my country."[37] Perhaps somewhat hyperbolically, a Jewish student who had recently become a Christian complained to the same minister, "If somebody took Jesus' teachings in the Beatitudes (Matt. 5:3–12) and decided to create a religion that contradicted those teachings, then he'd probably come up with the Protestant church."[38] In prison, former televangelist Jim Bakker realized to his horror that he had been teaching the exact opposite of what Jesus had taught.[39] We have a long way to go to fulfill God's calling.

Some churches are weak, yet endure (3:8); some are poor, yet rich (2:9), like the Nepalese Christians, who have multiplied so many times over through much suffering and poverty. But some churches think that they are rich, yet do not know how devoid they are of true spiritual power (3:17–18). We do not think of ourselves as arrogant or uncommitted, yet as our own brothers and sisters in Christ suffer and die for their faith in many lands, we share little of our resources to help them, and most North American Christians do not even pray for them. While our economy is comparatively strong, we have opportunities to multiply our resources many times over; but our time, like every other nation's time, will run out. May we have wisdom to sow for eternal things while we have opportunity.

"It used to be tough [to be a Christian] because it cost so much," one commentator remarked. "Now it's tough because it pays. Of the two, the latter is by far the most insidious."[40] "I do not see how it is possible ... for any revival of religion to continue long," Wesley complained; for true religion produces hard work and thrift, which produce wealth, but wealth in turn

---

36. *World Vision News* (Summer 1998), 5.

37. Tony Campolo, *Wake Up America!* (Grand Rapids: Zondervan, 1991), xii.

38. Ibid., 96.

39. Jim Bakker with Ken Abraham, *I Was Wrong* (Nashville: Thomas Nelson, 1996), 531–44. The profound lessons available in Bakker's candid and repentant revelations in that chapter are worth the price of the book.

40. John Fischer, "When Christianity Pays," *Contemporary Christian Magazine* 8 (Dec. 1985): 46.

produces "love of the world in all its branches."[41] A warning of Dr. Martin Luther King Jr., originally uttered in a context of the church's silence on racial segregation, remains appropriate today regarding many other areas of the church's isolation from today's issues:

> But the judgment of God is upon the Church as never before. If the Church of today does not recapture the sacrificial spirit of the early Church, it will lose its authentic ring, forfeit the loyalty of millions, and be dismissed as an irrelevant social club with no meaning for the twentieth century. I am meeting young people every day whose disappointment with the Church has risen to outright disgust. Maybe again I have been too optimistic. Is organized religion too inextricably bound to the status quo to save our nation and the world?[42]

This was not a new problem in King's day; many of the abolitionists "ended up disillusioned and disgusted" by the halfhearted response of most of the church to their cries for justice, "and some of them lost their faith."[43] Such disillusionment helped set the stage for an increasing secularism in the United States.

Experiencing the Tribulation. On a practical level, Western Christianity has sometimes misrepresented the cost of the gospel even to others. In a memo celebrating the spread of Christ's message in China, an American denomination's missions director also noted that during Mao Tse Tung's purges, which led to millions of deaths, many Chinese Christians believed that "the Great Tribulation had begun, that they had missed the awaited rapture of the Church, and were now committed to the cold possibilities of martyrdom."[44] Yet if we catch the whole context of Revelation, all Christians should be prepared for martyrdom and should teach accordingly. As Brother Andrew put it, urging North American Christians to lay their lives on the line for the gospel, many Chinese Christians did not want the missionaries to return, because "we've gone through the great tribulation and there was no Rapture. You were liars."[45]

---

41. Nathan O. Hatch and Michael S. Hamilton, "Can Evangelicalism Survive Its Success?" *CT* (Oct. 5, 1992), 20–31 (p. 31). For Wesley's views on Christians' resources, see Theodore W. Jennings Jr., *Good News to the Poor: John Wesley's Evangelical Economics* (Nashville: Abingdon, 1990); on living simply in general, see Frank Martin, "Lighten Your Load," *Discipleship Journal* 78 (Nov. 1993): 28–31.

42. Martin Luther King, Jr., "Letter from the Birmingham City Jail" (April 16, 1963 [p. 12 in my edition]).

43. Tim Stafford, "The Abolitionists," *Christian History* 33 (1992): 21–25 (pp. 24–25).

44. General letter from G. Edward Nelson, Secretary of U.S. Relations, Assemblies of God Division of Foreign Missions (Feb. 1986), 1.

45. Michael Maudlin, "God's Smuggler Confesses," *CT* (Dec. 11, 1995), 45–46, in which Brother Andrew argues that pretribulationism is wishful thinking and must be confronted.

Nor have Christians felt that they experienced the Great Tribulation only in this century; like the early church fathers, for example, the first Anabaptists, a Protestant group hated by Catholics and other Protestants alike, believed that they were in the Tribulation directly preceding the Second Coming.[46] Today our increasing vulnerability to international terrorism is beginning to get our attention, reminding us that the United States, like every other nation and empire of history, has only its season in God's plan.[47] We who are Christians should use what remains of that season not to increase our luxury but to serve God's purposes among the nations.

The solution to Laodicean Christianity is repentance (3:19)—admitting that we consume our fabulous dinners without the presence of Jesus (3:20), who dwells only with the contrite and broken (Isa. 57:15; 66:2; James 4:6). We eat without him because our self-glorification, which resembles that of the world (Rev. 18:7), nauseates him (3:16). If we humble our hearts and listen to his voice in the Scriptures and through the churches elsewhere, we may yet overcome.

---

46. Walter Klaasen, ed., *Anabaptism in Outline: Selected Primary Sources* (Scottsdale, Pa.: Herald, 1981), 317—21. For Christian suffering during the Tribulation in the church fathers, see Hermas 1.4.2–3; Irenaeus, *Her.* 5.28.4; 5.29.1; 5.35.1; Clementine, *Homilies* 2.17; Ambrose, *Comm. Luke* 10; cf. Did. 10.

47. See comments on terrorism under 6:4.

Revelation 4:1–11

FTER THIS I looked, and there before me was a door standing open in heaven. And the voice I had first heard speaking to me like a trumpet said, "Come up here, and I will show you what must take place after this." ²At once I was in the Spirit, and there before me was a throne in heaven with someone sitting on it. ³And the one who sat there had the appearance of jasper and carnelian. A rainbow, resembling an emerald, encircled the throne. ⁴Surrounding the throne were twenty-four other thrones, and seated on them were twenty-four elders. They were dressed in white and had crowns of gold on their heads. ⁵From the throne came flashes of lightning, rumblings and peals of thunder. Before the throne, seven lamps were blazing. These are the seven spirits of God. ⁶Also before the throne there was what looked like a sea of glass, clear as crystal.

In the center, around the throne, were four living creatures, and they were covered with eyes, in front and in back. ⁷The first living creature was like a lion, the second was like an ox, the third had a face like a man, the fourth was like a flying eagle. ⁸Each of the four living creatures had six wings and was covered with eyes all around, even under his wings. Day and night they never stop saying:

"Holy, holy, holy
is the Lord God Almighty,
who was, and is, and is to come."

⁹Whenever the living creatures give glory, honor and thanks to him who sits on the throne and who lives for ever and ever, ¹⁰the twenty-four elders fall down before him who sits on the throne, and worship him who lives for ever and ever. They lay their crowns before the throne and say:

¹¹"You are worthy, our Lord and God,
to receive glory and honor and power,
for you created all things,
and by your will they were created
and have their being."

SCHOLARS HAVE READ in various ways the section of Revelation following the letters to the churches.[1] But most likely chapters 4–5 introduce the heavenly events that precede and explain the seals, trumpets, and vials of chapters 6–16; events in heaven affect and are affected by events on earth (12:7–12).

John's throne vision in Revelation 4, like most of this book, resembles visions in the biblical prophets (esp. Isa. 6:1–5; Ezek. 1:4–28; Dan. 7:9–14).[2] Yet while Revelation is biblical, it is also relevant to the issues and language of its day: John frequently emphasizes the themes most dominant in the literature of his contemporaries, which we call *apocalyptic literature*. From an early period, Jewish apocalyptic texts focused on and developed particularly the throne visions of Ezekiel and Isaiah.[3] John's language regularly echoes Scripture, but he shares this feature with some of his contemporaries: "And I looked and behold" (lit. trans. of 4:1) is standard language from Ezekiel (e.g., Ezek. 1:4, 15; 2:9; 8:2, 7, 10; 44:4) and Daniel (Dan. 8:3, 15; 10:5; 12:5), which also becomes characteristic of apocalyptic visions (e.g., 1 Enoch 14:14–15, 18; 85:3).[4]

The similarity of subject matter between Revelation and other apocalyptic visions makes some of the differences in detail all the more striking. Apocalyptic texts frequently narrate the visionary's arduous journey through various heavenly gates to reach God's throne (e.g., 1 Enoch 14:9–13); some suggest dangers involved in this journey.[5] By contrast, yet like his biblical

---

1. Corsini, *Apocalypse*, 120–21, reads Rev. 4:1–8:1 as an allegory of salvation history beginning with the fall; André Feuillet, *Johannine Studies*, tr. Thomas E. Crane (Staten Island, N.Y.: Alba House, 1964), 256, suggests that Rev. 4–11 explains the Synoptic Apocalypse, starting with A.D. 70.

2. I see Ezek. 1 as a primary source here, but cf. G. K. Beale, "The Use of Daniel in the Synoptic Eschatological Discourse and in the Book of Revelation," 130–37 in *The Jesus Tradition Outside the Gospels*, ed. D. Wenham (Sheffield: JSOT, 1984), 134, who argues for the priority of Dan. 7. In any case Merkabah texts harmonize elements from all three sources (P. Alexander, "Introduction" to 3 Enoch, *OTP*, 1:247).

3. E.g., D. Dimant and J. Strugnell, "The Merkabah Vision in Second Ezekiel (4Q385 4)," *RevQ* 14 (1990): 331–48; see further Aune, *Revelation*, 1:276–78.

4. See also 4 Ezra 11:2, 5, 7, 10, 12, 20, 22, 24–26, 28, 33, 35, 37. It is a common enough Semitic idiom, occurring some fifty times in the Old Testament but in the New Testament only seven times, all in Revelation (4:1; 6:2, 5, 8; 7:9; 14:1, 14).

5. No mystic transformation is found here as in some texts (on which see 1 Enoch 71:11; 2 Enoch 22:8–10; 3 Enoch 15:1; C. R. A. Morray-Jones, "Transformational Mysticism in the Apocalyptic-Merkabah Tradition," *JJS* 43 [1992]: 1–31). Later apocalypses (e.g., T. Jacob) also often include tours of heaven and hell, as in Milton; cf. Richard J. Bauckham, "Early Jewish Visions of Hell," *JTS* 41 (1990): 355–85. "Tours of hell" originally reflect a Greek genre (e.g., *Select Papyri* 3:416–21) with roots no later than the interviews with the netherworld spirits in Homer's *Odyssey*.

predecessors, John is simply transported there by God's sovereign summons (Rev. 4:1) and the Spirit's inspiration (4:2; cf. 17:3; 21:10). Some texts provide angelic help for the ascent (e.g., 1 Enoch 71:5; 87:3; 2 Enoch 7:1; 2 Bar. 6:3–4), but John ascends simply by the Spirit, as did Ezekiel (Ezek. 2:2; 3:12, 14, 24; 8:3; 11:1, 5, 24; 37:1; 43:5).[6]

The "open" door in heaven (4:1) signifies what openings in heaven often signify, namely, God's revelation (11:19; 15:5; cf. Ezek. 1:1; Mark 1:10; John 1:51).[7] John does not have to force his way into heaven, as some of his contemporaries thought they did; he is invited, in language that recalls God's call to Moses to receive his revelation: "Come up here" (Rev. 4:1; cf. Ex. 19:20, 24; 24:12; 34:2) recalls the Bible's first throne vision (Ex. 24:10–12; cf. also 19:24). Jewish tradition acknowledged (Jub., title; Ps-Philo 11:2) and further developed God's summons to Moses, eventually to the extent that many averred that it included an ascent to heaven.[8] Jewish writers applied the same language to other heavenly visions as well.[9]

If John's mode of entry into heaven (4:1–2) differs strikingly from the apocalyptic visions of his contemporaries, so does his vision of the heavenly court (4:3–11). Chief deities of surrounding cultures, understood as rulers, were naturally portrayed as enthroned. Thus Jewish people naturally recognized that God was enthroned, and biblical visions elaborated this image (1 Kings 22:19; Isa. 6:1; 66:1; Ezek. 1:26; 10:1); but visions of the throne especially characterized Jewish apocalypses and mysticism.[10] Beholding the throne was actually the goal of some forms of Jewish mysticism (e.g., 3 Enoch 1).

---

6. One could contrast an ascent "in spirit" with a "bodily" ascent as in some texts (1 Enoch 71:1; T. Abr. 8B; 2 Cor. 12:2–3), but in the context of Revelation "Spirit" here must refer to the Spirit of God, who inspires prophets (Rev. 1:10; 2:7; 19:10; cf. Odes Sol. 36:1–2; Hermas 1.1.1; 1.2.1; Craig S. Keener, *The Spirit in the Gospels and Acts* [Peabody, Mass.: Hendrickson, 1997], 10–13).

7. For opened heavens in Jewish epiphanies, see 1 En. 14:8; 2 Bar. 22:1; Test. Levi 2:6; 5:1; F. Lentzen-Deis, "Das Motiv der 'Himmelsöffnung' in verschiedenen Gattungen der Umweltliteratur des Neuen Testaments," *Biblica* 50 (1969): 301–27. Both Jews and others could also understand the parting of the sky to send or receive bearers of divine revelation (Virgil, *Aen.* 9.20–21; T. Abr. 7 A). Ancient texts frequently envision heavenly "gates" or "doors" (e.g., *PGM*, 4.662–63).

8. E.g., *Sifre Deut.* 49.2.1; *Ex. Rab.* 28:1; 47:5; *Lev. Rab.* 1:15; *Pes. Rab.* 20:4. Whether this tradition is as early as John's day is unclear, though cf. Deut. 30:12.

9. E.g., 1 Enoch 14:24–25; 15:1; 2 Enoch 21:3; 3 Enoch 41:1; 42:1; 43:1; 44:1; 47:1; also *b. Hag.* 14b (a rabbi repeating Moses' experience); cf. Plutarch, *Divine Vengeance* 33, *Mor.* 568A. "Come and hear" or "Come and I will teach you" were common ways to invite hearers to contemplate a teaching (e.g., *b. Ber.* 19b; *Men.* 109b), but "Come and I will show you" could also function as an invitation to see something (*b. B.B.* 46a; 73b–74a; *Bek.* 28b).

10. For God enthroned, see Sir. 1:8; 1 Enoch 9:4; 18:8; 2 Enoch 1a:4; 20:3; T. Moses 4:2; *CIJ*, 2:54, §802; for apocalyptic and mystic portraits, see Life of Adam 25:3–4; T. Levi 5; Gershom G. Scholem, *Major Trends in Jewish Mysticism*, 3d rev. ed. (New York: Schocken,

Some apocalypses elaborate the character of God's throne in great detail to amplify his majesty; being more ready to acknowledge the inadequacy of human language to communicate God's grandeur, John presents his vision of God's throne without such adornment.[11] The heavenly court also provides a harsh contrast with the pretense of merely earthly grandeur in the court of the Roman emperors worshiped in Asia.[12] The heavenly worship thus contrasts starkly with earthly worship of the beast (13:4–8, 15).[13] As a Greek chorus would explain the action of a Greek drama, so the heavenly songs in Revelation provide the true picture of the events of the book: No matter what is experienced on earth, God is truly in charge of it all.[14]

The "rainbow" (4:3) recalls the radiance of God's throne in Ezekiel 1:28. "Jasper" (4:3) was also crystal clear and brilliant, so John's audience will later recognize the new Jerusalem as the place of his glorious dwelling (21:11, 18–20); in Ezekiel God's throne appeared like sapphire (Ezek. 1:26; 10:1).

The twenty-four elders around the throne (4:4), like other worshipers in heaven (4:7–9; 5:11–14), illustrate the appropriate response to God's glory: worship (4:10–11; 5:8–10, 14).[15] While their literary function in this sense is difficult to dispute, their exact identity does not share the same accessibility. Some regard them as angels, others as Old Testament saints.[16] But most likely

---

1971), 44. Temples in Asia, as elsewhere, often included thrones for their deities (cf. David W. J. Gill, "Religion in a Local Setting," 79–92 in *The Book of Acts in Its Greco-Roman Setting*, ed. D. W. J. Gill and C. Gempf [Grand Rapids: Eerdmans, 1994], 89).

11. Some texts develop biblical imagery in ways similar to Revelation here, though often more fully (e.g., 1 Enoch 14:18–20; 71:5–9). For the magnitude of heavenly realities in later sources, however, see 3 Enoch 9:2–3; *Pes. Rab.* 20:4.

12. See David E. Aune, "The Influence of the Roman Imperial Court Ceremonial on the Apocalypse of John," *Biblical Research* 28 (1983): 5–26; Meeks, *Moral World*, 145.

13. See Paul S. Minear, "The Cosmology of the Apocalypse," 23–37 in *Current Issues in New Testament Interpretation: Essays in honor of Otto A. Piper*, ed. W. Klassen and G. F. Snyder (New York: Harper & Row, 1962), 31.

14. See Tenney, *Revelation*, 36; cf. Gerhard Delling, "Zum Gottesdienstlichen Stil der Johannes-Apokalypse," *NovT* 3 (1959): 107–37.

15. They surround the throne like a royal court (some also cite the tradition of the Sanhedrin—Bowman, *First Christian Drama*, 43), but also like a Greek chorus (cf. Callimachus, *Hymn* 4.301; 4 Macc. 8:4; 13:8; 14:7–8; they could have 24 members), whose function as a composite, usually reliable character they perform here. In Jewish visions both angels (T. Abr. 7 A) and martyrs (4 Macc. 17:18–19) could stand by God's throne.

16. Mounce, *Revelation*, 135–36, prefers angels. Feuillet, *Studies*, argues against angels (185–94) and in favor of Old Testament saints (194–214; idem, "Les vingt-quatre vieillands de l'Apocalypse," *RB* 65 [1958]: 5–32; idem, "Quelques énigmes des chapitres 4 à 7 de l'Apocalypse: Suggestions pour l'interprétation du langage imagé de la révélation johannique," *Esprit et Vie* 86 [1976]: 455–59); A. Geyser, "The Twelve Tribes in Revelation: Judean and Judeo-Christian Apocalypticism," *NTS* 28 [1982]: 388–99 (p. 396 argues for the ideal Israel). Angels characteristically appear in white (1 Enoch 71:1; 87:2); later Jewish tradition also associated crowns with Israel at Sinai (*ARN*, 1A). For a survey of views, see Aune, *Revelation*, 1:288–92.

they represent all believers. The doubling of the twelve could represent the Old and New Testament peoples of God together (see 21:12–14). But given their function in worship they probably represent the twenty-four courses of priests in the Old Testament (1 Chron. 24:4).[17]

White robes characterized priests and worshipers in a variety of Mediterranean religions.[18] Further, some Jewish traditions envision special priestly access to the throne (3 Enoch 2:3–4) or a priestly model of worship in heaven (2 Enoch 22:3 A). Because crowns were appropriate to victors or "overcomers" in athletic competitions, their crowns may signify that these are Christians who have persevered to the end, as each of the letters to the churches demands. But crowns were more often "golden" when won in games sacred to a deity, and most often golden when worn by priests approaching a deity.[19]

But we should hardly take this to limit this number to the leaders of God's people. In Asiatic art a small number of priests have represented a much larger number of worshipers.[20] Elders were leaders of the people and stood as their representatives before God's glory at Sinai (Ex. 24:9–10) as they would in the eschatological time (Isa. 24:23). Thus these elders represent God's people as a whole, all of whom together are a "kingdom and priests" (Rev. 1:6; 5:10).[21]

The thunders around God's throne (4:5; 8:5; 11:19; 16:18) reveal his sovereignty. This would have been clear to Revelation's first readers; not only Jews (Ps. 29:3) but other prominent Mediterranean religions portrayed the supreme deity associated with lightning and thunder.[22] Lightnings were also characteristic of the heavens, as one might expect (cf. 1 Enoch 14:8; 17:3;

---

17. These remained in later times, cf. Luke 1:5, 8; Josephus, *Life* 2; *Ant.* 7.366; *tos. Suk.* 4:26–27; *Taan.* 2:1; 3:1; cf. 26 divisions in 1QM 2.2.

18. E.g., Jerusalem worship (Josephus, *War* 2.1; *Ant.* 11.327); the imperial cult (*SEG*, 11.923); pagan worship in general (Diogenes Laertius, 8.1.33; Athenaeus, 4.149d); Isis' priests (Apuleius, *Metam.* 11.10); worshipers of Artemis (Acts of John 38). But white also symbolizes good (Diogenes Laertius, 8.1.34), joy (*p. R.H.* 1:3, §27), or burial garments of those who anticipate resurrection (Ps-Philo 64:6).

19. See Gregory M. Stevenson, "Conceptual Background to Golden Crown Imagery in the Apocalypse of John (4:4, 10; 14:14)," *JBL* 114 (1995): 257–72 (pp. 259, 261–65), although he does not settle on the priestly interpretation here (269).

20. Ramsay, *Letters to the Seven Churches*, 62–63.

21. The Targum understood the elders in Isa. 24:23 as Israel's leaders (Beasley-Murray, *Revelation*, 113); Jewish tradition commonly viewed them as the heavenly court of which the Sanhedrin was an earthly replica (Joseph M. Baumgarten, "The Duodecimal Courts of Qumran, Revelation, and the Sanhedrin," *JBL* 95 [March 1976]: 59–78 [pp. 67–70, 78]).

22. Homer, *Il.* 7.443; 15.377; *Od.* 5.4; Aristophanes, *Lysis.* 773; Pausanias, 10.9.11; among Diaspora Jews, Sib. Or. 1.323; 4.113; 5.302–3. See further John Pairman Brown, "Yahweh, Zeus, Jupiter: The High God and the Elements," *ZAW* 106 (1994): 175–97. Some ancient thinkers did, however, offer purely naturalistic explanations for storms (Pliny, *N.H.* 2.18.82).

69:23); some Jewish texts delegated lightnings to the high angels (3 Enoch 29:2).[23] Most important, however, the thunders and lightnings around the throne recall the revelation of God's majesty when he gave the law at Mount Sinai (Ex. 19:16; 20:18).[24]

The "sea" (4:6) merits special comment; it probably suggests to readers the great glory of the heavenly temple. Mighty waters (cf. 1:15) also appear in apocalyptic visions of heaven or paradise, perhaps developing Psalm 104:3; 148:4; and especially Ezekiel 1:24; note too that rain and lightning fall from heaven.[25] Thus some texts of uncertain date portray a vast ocean in the lowest heaven (2 Enoch 3:3 J; 4:2 A) or a heavenly sea of fire (Apoc. Zeph. 6:1–2). John's most direct source here, however, is the bronze "sea" of Solomon's temple for the priests to wash in (1 Kings 7:23–44; 1 Chron. 18:8; 2 Chron. 4:2, 6), because heaven in Revelation appears like a temple (Rev. 7:15; 11:19; 14:15, 17; 15:5–16:1; 16:17; for temple apparatus in heaven, see Contemporary Significance section of Rev. 1:10). Solomon's temple probably included a "sea" for the same reason that ancient Egyptian temples depicted heaven on their ceilings: to testify that their deity ruled the entire cosmos.[26]

That the sea is of "glass, clear as crystal" reflects the sapphire that was "clear" in God's revelation to Israel at Sinai (Ex. 24:10), but especially the crystalline, heavenly expanse beneath God's throne and above the throne angels in Ezekiel 1:22. That it is like "crystal" links it with the new Jerusalem, clear enough for God's great glory to shine through it (Rev. 21:11, 18, 21). It is thus probably not a symbol of subdued cosmic evil, as some commentators have suggested.[27]

---

23. Fire is associated with God's throne in Aramaic incantation text 12.14; with Abel's judgment throne in T. Abr. 12 A.

24. This continued to be emphasized in Jewish (Josephus, *Ant.* 3.80; Ps-Philo 11:4–5) and Samaritan (John Bowman, ed., *Samaritan Documents Relating to Their History, Religion & Life*, POTTS 2 [Pittsburgh, Pa.: Pickwick, 1977], 48) tradition. Cf. also the stormy revelation in Ezek. 1:4, 13.

25. See 1 Enoch 14:10; Life of Adam 28:4; 29:2. Moisture fell through "doors" of heaven (Martial, *Epig.* 4.2; cf. Gen. 7:11; 1 Kings 8:35; Mal. 3:10).

26. See Manfred Lurker, *The Gods and Symbols of Ancient Egypt: An Illustrated Dictionary* (London: Thames & Hudson, 1980), 120; Alexander Badawy, *A History of Egyptian Architecture: The Empire (1580–1085 B.C.)* (Berkeley: Univ. of California Press, 1968), 161. This reflects the later, not earlier, period of temples (Harold H. Nelson, "The Egyptian Temple," 147–58 in *The Biblical Archaeologist Reader*, ed. G. E. Wright and D. N. Freedman [Chicago: Quadrangle, 1961], 150–52). On the tabernacle in its cultural context, see Keener and Usry, *Defending Black Faith*, 139–46; "Tabernacle," 837–40 in *Dictionary of Biblical Imagery*, ed. Leland Ryken et al. (Downers Grove, Ill.: InterVarsity, 1998).

27. Michaels, *Revelation*, 92–93; against Caird, *Commentary on Revelation*, 65–68 (despite 13:1; 21:1). Crystal stones or apparatus appears in heaven, e.g., in 1 Enoch 71:5; T. Abr. 12 A. Exodus's sapphire probably reflects the transparent blue of heaven (with *b. Men.* 43b, bar.); later teachers (rightly) linked the blue of the sea with the blue of heaven (*Sifre Num.* 115.2.8).

That the glass was "clear" contrasts with most of the glass available in John's day.[28]

In view of descriptions of heavenly worship in Isaiah 6:1–4; Ezekiel 1:4–28; and Daniel 7:9–14, it is not surprising that John's contemporaries believed that worship was a major feature of heavenly activity (see 1 En. 12:3; 39:7; Ps-Philo 19:16). The people who wrote the Dead Sea Scrolls even tried to align their earthly worship with heavenly worship so they could worship God along with the angels; the first Christians who heard John's descriptions of worship during their own worship services undoubtedly would have identified with the heavenly chorus.[29]

Again, because Jewish descriptions of heaven nearly always started with what Scripture already said, it is not surprising that most emphasize the living creatures around the throne, Isaiah's fiery "seraphim" (Isa. 6:2–3), or Ezekiel's cherubim supporting God's throne (Ezek. 1:5–21; 10:1–20; 11:22).[30] The cherubim probably functioned as a throne pedestal from the start (cf. 1 Sam. 4:4; 2 Sam. 6:2; 2 Kings 19:15; 1 Chron. 13:6; Ps. 80:1; 99:1).[31] Like the portraits of most of his contemporaries, John's probably come directly from Ezekiel; the lion, bull (here a calf), eagle, and human faces were also on Ezekiel's creatures (except that in Ezekiel each creature had all four faces). Ezekiel's vision probably employed the most powerful and regal of animals to communicate the majesty of the creatures that carry God's throne.[32] That

---

28. Cf. James Moffatt, *The First Epistle of Paul to the Corinthians*, MNTC (London: Hodder & Stoughton, 1938), 201. On the rare use of glass windows, see S. Safrai, "Home and Family," 728–92 in *JPFC*, 734; M. Cary and T. J. Haarhoff, *Life and Thought in the Greek and Roman World*, 4th ed. (London: Methuen, 1946), 101, 116.

29. For Jewish worship with angels, cf. also *Sifre Deut.* 306.31.1; probably also Ps. 148:2; 1QS 10.6; 1QM 12.1–2; Jub. 30:18; 31:14; Prayer of Manasseh 15; see further Fred O. Francis, "Humility and Angelic Worship in Col 2:18," 163–95 in *Conflict at Colossae*, ed. F. O. Francis and W. A. Meeks, SBS 4 (Missoula, Mont.: Society of Biblical Literature, 1973), 178–80.

30. E.g., Sib. Or. 3.1–2; 1 Enoch 61:10; 71:7; 2 Enoch 1a:6; 21:1; 22:2; 3 Enoch 1:7–8; 21:1–2; 22:13–16; 26:9–12; 2 Bar. 51:11; Apoc. Abr. 18:3–12; *b. Hag.* 13b. Archangels apparently fill this role in 1 Enoch 20:7; 40:2–10. Contrary to some later distinctions between Ezekiel's "living creatures" and cherubim (*Ruth Rab.* 5:4), Ezekiel identifies them (Ezek. 10:1–20; 11:22). Western Christian iconography conflated Ezekiel's cherubim and Revelation's creatures (Robin M. Jensen, "Of Cherubim & Gospel Symbols," *BAR* 21 [July 1995]: 42–43, 65).

31. Thus these creatures are part of the throne (hence "in the center"); see Robert G. Hall, "Living Creatures in the Midst of the Throne: Another Look at Revelation 4:6," *NTS* 36 (1990): 609–13.

32. Cf. *m. Ab.* 5:20. Cf. also Roloff, *Revelation*, 71–72, who with others (e.g., Caird, *Commentary on Revelation*, 64) is skeptical of the zodiacal interpretation proposed by some scholars. Mixed creatures featured in ancient imagery (e.g., Homer, *Il.* 6.179–82; Apollodorus, 2.3.1); for lions, see comment on Rev. 5:5; for eagles, on 8:13.

the creatures were "covered with eyes" (Rev 4:6; cf. Ezek 1:18; 10:12; 3 Enoch 22:8) suggests that nothing on earth is hidden from them (Zech. 4:10), with the implication, "How much less from God himself?" That they never rest from worship (Rev. 4:8) suggests both divine empowerment for worship and the worthiness of God (cf. 7:15).[33]

The climax of the presentation of the four living creatures is not their own splendor but their message. These beings, glorious beyond human conception, serve no other function than to extol the character of God: "Holy, holy, holy!" (4:8). John is familiar with the praise of these creatures from Isaiah 6:3, as are his contemporaries; Jewish tradition even adopted these words into the third benediction of a prayer that was becoming part of the synagogue liturgy.[34]

As if all this proved insufficient reminder of God's greatness, John twice in the following breath reiterates that God is the sovereign one—the one who sits on the throne—and that he lives forever and ever (4:9–10).[35] All the heavenly creatures—all beings who directly witness God's greatness—give him glory, hence summon us (and ultimately all creation in 5:13) to do the same.[36] Falling on one's face before another (4:10) was the ultimate obeisance, the supreme gesture of honoring the other far above oneself, appropriately applied to worship of God.[37] John was well aware that earthly kings might

---

33. Ability to go without rest in God's presence appears elsewhere (2 Enoch 22:3) and may be implied in Moses' revelation (Ex. 24:18; 34:28; Deut. 9:9; 10:10); ceaseless praise appears in 1 Enoch 41:7. See Beale, *Revelation*, 332, for other early Jewish texts declaring that cherubim praised without rest. For eyes, cf. Aeschylus, *Suppl. Maidens* 303–5.

34. The Amida; see W. O. E. Oesterley, *The Jewish Background of the Christian Liturgy* (Oxford: Clarendon, 1925), 67–68; Aune, *Revelation*, 1:303–7. The trisagion ("Holy, holy, holy") appears regularly in heavenly depictions (1 Enoch 39:12; 2 Enoch 21:1; 3 Enoch 1:12; 20:2; 27:3; 34:2; 35:5; 38:1; 39:1; 40:1–3; 22B:7; T. Adam 1:4) and elsewhere (4 Bar. 9:3; T. Abr. 3; 20 A; Aramaic incantation 33.5; *CIJ*, 2:373, §1448; A. L. Warren, "A Trisagion Inserted in the 4QSam[a] Version of the Song of Hannah, 1 Sam. 2:1–10," *JJS* 45 [1994]: 278–85). It was later adapted by Christian liturgy (Oesterley, *Background*, 142–47; David Flusser, "Jewish Roots of the Liturgical Trishagion," *Immanuel* 3 [1973–1974]: 37–43).

35. This reflects careful design: The title "one who sits on the throne" recurs seven times in the book, as does the title "Christ"; Jesus appears fourteen times (7 with "witness"), and "lamb" twenty-eight times (7 in phrases linked with God); see Bauckham, *Climax of Prophecy*, 33–34.

36. Many commentators think the hymns in Revelation are or, more likely, resemble early Jewish Christian worship songs; see Oscar Cullmann, *Christ and Time*, tr. F. V. Filson (Philadelphia: Westminster, 1950), 74; Archibald M. Hunter, *Paul and His Predecessors*, rev. ed. (Philadelphia: Westminster, 1961), 37; Hans Conzelmann, *History of Primitive Christianity*, tr. J. E. Steely (Nashville: Abingdon, 1973), 74.

37. For prostration to worship God, see 2 Chron. 20:18; 29:30; 1 Esd. 9:47; Judith 6:18; 9:1; 1 Macc. 4:40, 55; 3 Macc. 5:50–51; Sir. 50:21; Ps-Philo 4:5; T. Abr. 20 A; 4 B. The nations in the end would prostrate themselves before God (Isa. 66:23; Sib. Or. 3.716, 725).

demand the same obeisance—the same combination of "falling down" to "worship" appears six times in the summons to worship Nebuchadnezzar in Daniel 3:5–15; but Revelation calls Christians to respectfully reserve true worship for God alone.

God alone should receive all glory and power, for he created all things (4:11), a claim that again challenged the pretensions of Caesar in John's day as well as all human idols since then.[38] Jewish tradition often suggested that God created the world for the sake of humanity or of Israel; we as Christians see God's ultimate purpose in his saving work in Christ (cf. Eph. 1:10; Col. 1:18–22).[39] But this text reminds us that whatever God's other interests, it is also fair to say simply that all things were created for (or "on account of") God's will.

Such a dramatic statement reinforces the portrait of God's sovereignty here. John's contemporaries would have understood the connection between God as Creator and God as rightful Ruler (1 En. 9:5). The emperor Domitian expected worship as *dominus et deus*, "lord and god," and all who resisted such worship would be suspect to many agents of imperial power in Asia.[40] But as anyone who knew the ancient Scriptures of Israel would expect, the heavenly choirs of angels and redeemed people hail the true "Lord and God" (4:11), who created and rules his universe.[41]

THE GREATNESS OF GOD. One seeking to digest or communicate this chapter should not bog down in the details of most of its background, important as they are for understanding the details of John's portrait. One should instead place all the details (expounded in the context of their primary Old Testament background) in the broader

---

38. Repetition of terms (e.g., "glory," "honor") merely functions rhetorically to intensify the point, as if building to a crescendo (Ps. 150:1–6; 1 Enoch 41:7; 3 Enoch 1:12; 14:5); Jewish benedictions also praised God as Creator and Redeemer (cf. Rev. 5:9).

39. For God's creating the world for Israel, see T. Moses 1:12–13; 4 Ezra 6:59; 7:11; *Sifre Deut.* 47.3.1; for the righteous, 2 Bar. 15:7; 21:24; *Sifre Deut.* 47.3.1–2; for humanity, 2 Bar. 14:18–19; Gr. Ezra 5:19; *Koh. Rab.* 7:13, §1; for Torah, ARN, 31, §66; *Gen. Rab.* 1:4, 10; 12:2. But some tradition also averred that he created all solely for his glory (*m. Ab.* 6:11).

40. Suetonius, *Dom.* 13; see further Deissmann, *Light From the Ancient Past*, 361; G. B. Caird, *The Apostolic Age* (London: Gerald Duckworth, 1955), 19, citing Dio Cassius, 67.13; Aune, *Revelation*, 1:310–12. Cf. hymns used to honor the emperor (Herodian, 4.2.5; Yamauchi, *The Archaeology of New Testament Cities*, 42).

41. See esp. the LXX of Ps. 86:15 (85:15 in LXX). Following the Bible, Jewish sources also reserved this title for God (1 Enoch 84:5); but Christians often paid a special price for it (see comment on 2:9).

perspective of their function—to reveal the greatness of God's court, hence, his own greatness. Thus, they also reveal a striking contrast with the pretense of the earthly ruler's arrogant pomp. The text invites us to worship, today no less than at its first reading in Ephesus. It also invites us to relinquish our fear of human grandeur, which pales before the majesty of the eternal God with whom we have become intimate.

Common pitfalls and important guidelines. We must also address some common pitfalls in interpretation as well as guidelines for moving from interpretation of the original sense to application. Only an overwhelming commitment to read one's views of the end times into the text can force the vision in Revelation 4 to address our questions about the sequence of end-time details, but this has sometimes been attempted. (We comment here on the method of proving the doctrine, not on whether or not the doctrine is accurate on the basis of other texts.) Thus some who find the church age in the letters to the churches and the Tribulation in Revelation 6–16 locate the Rapture in 4:1 (specifically in the words, "Come up here"). They argue that if the church (on the basis of other Scriptures) is raptured before the Tribulation, it must either be located here or be admitted that Revelation does not provide explicit mention of a pretribulation Rapture (which some pretribulationists concede). Usually these interpreters acknowledge that 4:1 refers to John's vision, but argue that John functions here as a "type" of the church.[42]

Nevertheless, most interpreters who use 4:1 to portray the Rapture of the church before the Tribulation admit that the text does not actually *prove* their position. Strombeck, who contends that "no event recorded in Revelation can better represent the rapture of the Church" than John's experience in 4:1, admits that such a "type" cannot function as a proof, "but if one is seeking an event" in Revelation that resembles the pretribulational Rapture, "none other as good can be found."[43]

One does wonder why John's revelation in 4:1 makes a better type of the Rapture than other revelations of John elsewhere in the book. John also hears a trumpet in 1:10 and is elsewhere told, "Come" (17:1; 21:9), but these are not viewed as "raptures" because they occur at the wrong places in the book to typify a pretribulational Rapture. And even if this text were a type of the Rapture, its timing could be significant only if its context were also types; thus it might symbolize a rapture after a time of martyrdom rather than

---

42. E.g., Strombeck, *Rapture*, 185–86; see the response in Ladd, *Blessed Hope* (Grand Rapids: Eerdmans, 1956), 76.

43. Strombeck, *Rapture*, 185–86; cf. similarly Walvoord, *Revelation*, 103. The exegetical shortcomings of the doctrine can be surmounted if (but probably only if) one presupposes traditional dispensationalism (see John F. Walvoord, *The Rapture Question* [Grand Rapids: Zondervan, 1972], 19–21, 65–66).

before (see the context of the "Come up here" in 11:12). But here in 4:1, "Come up here" probably simply recalls God's call to Moses on Sinai, as we noted above. John is "in the Spirit" (4:2), caught up in visions like Ezekiel (Ezek. 8:3).

Some interpreters press too much understanding of end-time events into John's "after these things" (4:1, NASB), as if this chronological marker separated the present "church age," typified in the letters to the churches, from a distant future Tribulation (cf. 1:19). But "after these things" is a common transition device in ancient texts, including both apocalyptic literature (1 Enoch 89:30) and other writings (e.g., John 5:1; Tob. 1:1). "After these things" can refer to events that follow (Rev. 9:12; 20:3), but also to revelations that follow earlier revelations (7:9; 15:5; 18:1; 19:1); here it simply implies that after John heard from Jesus the letters to the churches, he heard a voice calling him to a heavenly vision. That is, it applies to the sequence of John's seeing, not to the sequence of historical events.[44]

Claiming that the "seven lamps" before the throne (4:5) represent the raptured church in heaven[45] might have worked (cf. 1:20), except that the text explicitly claims that these lamps represent the seven spirits of God (4:5); further, a Greek word different from that for the lampstands in 1:20 is used (the same word is translated "torch" in 8:10).

A better argument could be made for proposing that the "elders" in 4:4 refer to the saints before the throne—hence the notion that Christians have already been resurrected. This argument, however, also falters. Saints can arrive in heaven and receive white robes without being resurrected (6:11), and crowns can imply martyrdom (2:10) and can be conditionally promised before the judgment (3:11). Thus, arguing that these elders are the "saints" (as we would agree) provides no necessary evidence that they have been "raptured."[46]

To be sure, the "church" is not mentioned on earth by that name during Revelation's Tribulation, but neither is it mentioned by that name in heaven; the "saints" appear, however, in both locations.[47] Worse still, neither John nor his heavenly guides employ the word "church" to describe Christians in general even before 4:1; he speaks only of local churches. Yet to my knowledge

---

44. For events that follow, see Ep. Arist. 179; Josephus, *Life* 427; for visions that follow, see 1 En. 41:1; 2 Bar. 22:1. As Gundry, *Church and Tribulation*, 66, notes, if the phrase signifies a dispensational change, then six or seven such changes occur during the Tribulation.

45. So Lindsey, *New World Coming*, 86.

46. See also Gundry, *Church and Tribulation*, 74; Ladd, *Blessed Hope*, 96–97. The righteous in heaven (before the resurrection) wear robes, crowns, and sit on thrones in Asc. Isa. 9:24–26, but this probably reflects early Christian influence.

47. Walvoord, *Revelation*, 103, is among those who note the absence of the "church" between 4:1 and 22:16, though conceding that it is implied in 19:7.

no one argues for a rapture of specific local churches (despite 3:10)—except one nonevangelical sect in the Philippines (which reportedly argues that even the church buildings will be raptured). Further, the scene in heaven provides the logic for the judgments poured out in the seals; if it tells us anything about chronology, it probably tells us, as we will argue below, about the state of heaven before judgments that began nearly two thousand years ago.

 GOD IS IN CHARGE. Because chapters 4–5 introduce the pictures of God's judgments on the world, they summon us to a heavenly perspective that reminds us who is in charge. As Gregory Beale rightly puts it, "The pastoral purpose [of Rev. 4–5] is to assure suffering Christians that God and Jesus are sovereign and that the events that the Christians are facing are part of a sovereign plan that will culminate in their redemption and the vindication of their faith through the punishment of their persecutors."[48]

There is no evidence that John worked himself up into a vision; in contrast to the explicit testimonies of many of his contemporaries about their own experiences, he seems to have simply been available to God's Spirit (4:2). Though we should walk intimately with God and be open to his voice, we are not responsible to generate spiritual experiences, as in some circles (or to negate them, as in some others). We should give God the praise he deserves and let him bestow those experiences that he wills.[49] The focus of the revelation John receives is God's glory; even the judgments he will soon witness glorify God and explain his activity, rather than simply entertain our curiosity about the future.

Invitation to praise. If the twenty-four elders symbolize the church (and probably even if they do not), the total nature of their worship invites us to similar praise. They offer God not only their words but their own glory, casting their crowns before the throne (4:10; cf. 21:24), because they recognize God as the author and purpose of existence (4:11).[50] As one scholar notes, "In antiquity a common sign of vassalage was the taking off of the

---

48. Beale, *Revelation*, 311.

49. Seekers of mystic experiences can induce trances through natural means (e.g., J. G. Clark, "Noisy Brain in Noisy World" [NJ Psychological Association, Nov. 5, 1977]), and some activities that induce group ecstasy can produce psychophysiological changes (see Felicitas D. Goodman, Jeannette H. Henney, and Esther Pressel, *Trance, Healing, and Hallucination: Three Field Studies in Religious Experience* [New York: John Wiley & Sons, 1974]); but these do not guarantee God's blessing.

50. Jewish tradition also could extol God's greatness by envisioning an exalted one making crowns for the creator (*b. Hag.* 13b, bar.).

---

diadem (symbol of royalty) by the conquered ruler and the placing of that diadem at the feet of the conqueror (Cicero, *Sest.* 27; Tacitus, *Ann.* 15.29)." By imitating "such an act of subordination," the elders demonstrate that they do not claim the crowns as their own or the dragon's, but God's alone.[51] Humility is not simply humiliation; it is recognizing who God is and who we are, and the consequent vast difference between God and ourselves.

This passage in Revelation and others like it remind us that our primary job in heaven, like that of every other created being in heaven, is to worship God. In the present life, worship that focuses on God's worthiness—both his character (4:8) and deeds (4:11; 5:9; cf. both in Ps. 150:2)—is our nearest foretaste of heaven, an experience in the down payment of the end-time Spirit (1 Cor. 2:9–10; 2 Cor. 1:22). Worship also reminds us that whatever else our calling or gifts now, all Christians become the same as God's worshipers; the eternal future leaves little place for gifts now valued, but our devotion to God will always rise (cf. 1 Cor. 13:8–13).

The holy God. Although the praise was commonly reused in other contexts, most ancient listeners hearing the living creatures crying out, "Holy! Holy! Holy!" would think first of Isaiah 6. In Isaiah, a holy priest in the holy sanctuary among the holiest of peoples in one of the purer periods in their history cries out in utter dismay, "I am a man of unclean lips, and I live among a people of unclean lips" (6:5). He recognizes his uncleanness not because he compares himself with others but because he stands before the holy God, before whom no mortal creature is adequate (6:3); he is confronted with his uncleanness once his eyes see "the King, the LORD Almighty" (6:5). Nothing banishes pride of mortal flesh or human competition and agendas better than a taste of God's infinite greatness.

God is holy, almighty, and eternal (4:8; see comment on 1:8), in contrast to the pretense of the mortal human frame, so easily reduced to dust. Imperial choirs throughout Asia were hailing the mighty emperor as god in their own hymns.[52] Before John's portrait of the most majestic throne room of all, however, the emperor's claims fade into absurdity, and worshiping Christians find strength to withstand the falsehood of the emperor's claims.[53]

The praises of the living creatures also remind us that simply declaring truly who God is and what he is like brings him glory. God is "holy," alone

51. Stevenson, "Crown Imagery," 269. See further analogies in Aune, *Revelation*, 1:308–9.

52. E.g., Sjef van Tilborg, *Reading John in Ephesus*, NovTSup 83 (Leiden: Brill, 1996), 201–2; Aune, *The New Testament in Its Literary Environment*, 243. Ancient worship often involved choral processions singing to deities (e.g., Livy, 27.37.7; 31.12.9–10).

53. Many passages in Revelation seem to contrast the heavenly worship of God and the Lamb with the earthly worship of Caesar; see Paul Barnett, "Polemical Parallelism: Some Further Reflections on the Apocalypse," *JSNT* 35 (1989): 111–20).

in his perfection; no one else can be compared with him. Worship is not the invention of nice things to say about God; it is the recognition of who God already is (4:8), as well as what he has already done or promised to do (4:11; 5:9–12), and how worthy he is of our praise (4:11; 5:12–14).[54]

Yet worship is not mere theological information; as J. I. Packer notes, we must "turn our knowledge about God into knowledge of God" by turning "each truth that we learn about God into matter for meditation *before* God, leading to prayer and praise to God."[55] One difference between our worship and the model provided for it here is that we desperately need the model! While the creatures before God's throne worship him in the clarity of his present glory, we usually worship him in this age in faith, seeing through a glass darkly but confident that the One we worship is greater than all the work of his hands (cf. 1 Cor. 13:12).

To fall on our faces (4:10) is to make our own honor nothing in comparison with God's. Some of us are too anxious for our own honor or reputation, even when we disguise it as concern for our "call." We should, of course, do our best to retain our good reputation for the gospel's sake (1 Tim. 3:2, 7; cf. Prov 22:1), but the kind of competition and petty disputes that ministers and others often experience in the kingdom (Mark 9:34; Luke 9:46; 22:24; 1 Cor. 3:4–7; 2 Cor. 10:12; Phil. 1:15–17) should vanish into ashamed silence when we together recognize the only one who genuinely deserves any glory.

The heart of God. God is self-sufficient, but Augustine rightly declared that "God thirsts to be thirsted after." His love makes him vulnerable to those he loves, if we dare use such language to describe his desire for intimacy with us. As Richard Foster points out, "Our God is not made of stone. His heart is the most sensitive and tender of all. No act goes unnoticed, no matter how insignificant or small."[56] A cup of cold water is enough to secure his attention (Mark 9:41), like a mother delighted to receive her child's offering of dandelions. Jesus was moved by the one cleansed leper who returned to give thanks and sad about the nine who did not (Luke 17:17–18). Jesus was touched by the woman who anointed his feet (Mark 14:6–8).[57] God delights in our affection for him and in our pausing to allow him to lavish his affection on us by his Spirit.

Standing up to contemporary idols. John's vision encourages Christians in Roman Asia that the worship in the imperial cult is merely a farce, a pale

---

54. "Worthy" (*axios*) was a Greek word typically used for great benefactors in antiquity, meaning what was "appropriate" or "fitting"; here it denotes that worship is fitting to God—more than to any other—as the greatest benefactor; see Aune, *Revelation*, 1:309–10.

55. J. I. Packer, *Knowing God* (Downers Grove, Ill.: InterVarsity, 1973), 23.

56. Richard J. Foster, *Prayer: Finding the Heart's True Home* (New York: HarperCollins, 1992), 85.

57. Ibid.

imitation of the true worship in the heavenly court. And as late first-century Christians gained courage to declare that the emperor had no clothes, we must declare the same for the idols of our generation. Caesar did not create (4:11) and is not eternal (4:8), nor did he redeem us by his blood (5:9); he had no control over ultimate hope. In view of present knowledge about the narrow parameters essential for the formation of life in the universe, we can see God's loving design in creation today in greater detail than our fore-bears.[58] Only in the depths of worship, as we stand in awe of God's majestic glory, do all other competing claims for affection and attention recede into their rightful place. God alone is God, and he alone merits first place—beyond every other love, every other anxiety, every other fear that consumes us.

If God's grandeur dwarfs the emperor's majesty, it also challenges in a different way the numbing triteness of modern Western culture. God's greatness summons our attention: Who are we to be overwhelmed by the mortal emperor or our present trials? That God is Lord of history and has everything under control helps us view everything else in life the way we should. Praise puts persecution, poverty, and plagues into perspective; God is sovereignly bringing about his purposes, and this world's pains are merely the birth pangs of a new world (Rev. 21–22).

---

58. See Hugh Ross, *Creator and the Cosmos* (Colorado Springs: NavPress, 1993).

Revelation 5:1–14

THEN I SAW in the right hand of him who sat on the throne a scroll with writing on both sides and sealed with seven seals. ²And I saw a mighty angel proclaiming in a loud voice, "Who is worthy to break the seals and open the scroll?" ³But no one in heaven or on earth or under the earth could open the scroll or even look inside it. ⁴I wept and wept because no one was found who was worthy to open the scroll or look inside. ⁵Then one of the elders said to me, "Do not weep! See, the Lion of the tribe of Judah, the Root of David, has triumphed. He is able to open the scroll and its seven seals."

⁶Then I saw a Lamb, looking as if it had been slain, standing in the center of the throne, encircled by the four living creatures and the elders. He had seven horns and seven eyes, which are the seven spirits of God sent out into all the earth. ⁷He came and took the scroll from the right hand of him who sat on the throne. ⁸And when he had taken it, the four living creatures and the twenty-four elders fell down before the Lamb. Each one had a harp and they were holding golden bowls full of incense, which are the prayers of the saints. ⁹And they sang a new song:

> "You are worthy to take the scroll
>   and to open its seals,
> because you were slain,
>   and with your blood you purchased men for God
>   from every tribe and language and people and nation.
> ¹⁰You have made them to be a kingdom and priests to
>   serve our God,
>   and they will reign on the earth."

¹¹Then I looked and heard the voice of many angels, numbering thousands upon thousands, and ten thousand times ten thousand. They encircled the throne and the living creatures and the elders. ¹²In a loud voice they sang:

> "Worthy is the Lamb, who was slain,
> to receive power and wealth and wisdom and strength
> and honor and glory and praise!"

¹³Then I heard every creature in heaven and on earth and under the earth and on the sea, and all that is in them, singing:

"To him who sits on the throne and to the Lamb
be praise and honor and glory and power,
for ever and ever!"

¹⁴ The four living creatures said, "Amen," and the elders fell down and worshiped.

WHENEVER JOHN NOTES, "And I saw," he reports the next scene he sees, but its *content* may or may not follow chronologically the scene he has just reported. In this passage, however, we have no compelling reason to doubt that it follows the preceding scene (cf. 6:2; 1 Enoch 86:1, 3).

Jewish traditions often portray books or tablets in heaven containing God's heavenly moral decrees, people's destinies in life, or people's eternal destinies (1 En. 103:2). Although the book in this text is never specifically identified, it may well represent the Lamb's book of life, hence the Lamb's legacy for his people (Rev. 13:8; 17:8; 20:12, 15; 21:27; see comment on 3:5). While some could suggest that the heavenly scroll is the prototype of this book of Revelation, reporting God's decrees for history (1:11; 22:7–10, 18–19), Revelation remains unsealed (22:10).

Most ancient people wrote on only one side of a scroll, generally the "front" (the *recto*, whose fibers lay horizontally, hence making writing easier). They usually employed the back (the *verso*) only if they ran out of space on the front.[1] The scroll in the present text (recalling the scroll containing judgments in Ezek. 2:10; see comment on Rev. 10:8) clearly has a lot to say. Then the scroll's user would roll the scroll up, tying it shut with a thread or, in legal documents meant to prevent tampering, several threads.

Legal documents normally closed by listing witnesses, usually about six in number.[2] Such documents were normally sealed shut with hot wax over the threads that tied the scroll closed; then witnesses would press their personal seals (usually from signet rings) into the hot wax, making an impres-

---

1. Deissmann, *Light From the Ancient Past*, 29; George Milligan, *St. Paul's Epistles to the Thessalonians: The Greek Text with Introduction and Notes* (London: Macmillan & Company, 1908), 123. Juvenal, an ancient Roman gossip columnist, makes fun of a dramatist who proved so verbose that his work filled both sides of a scroll and was not complete even by that point! See Juvenal, *Sat.* 1.4–6.

2. See *P. Eleph.* 1.16–18; *P. Tebt.* 104.34–35.

sion that matched their distinctive seal and attested that they were the witnesses. No one could open the scroll without breaking the hardened wax seals that held the threads in place, and no one could replace such seals without the witnesses' rings; hence no one could tamper with the legal document until it was time to publicly open it.[3] While the witnesses remained alive, one could also recall them to testify to the validity of their seals, though the seals in Revelation can hardly be fabricated (6:1–17).[4]

Seals reserved the contents of a document for its rightful recipient and authenticated the document with witnesses who attested it. Some apocalyptists envisioned heavenly scrolls as sealed documents to prevent any accusation of tampering (1 En. 89:71). Some traditions allowed these seals broken only by high angels before the document was handed to God (3 En. 27:2); the opening of such books might lead to the sending of angels to execute judgment (3 En. 32:1). Thus one might think of a sealed book of judgments (Isa. 29:11). Like the scroll here, the scroll in Ezekiel 2:9–10 contains writing on both front and back, emphasizing the great quantity of suffering in judgment that the book records.

Here, however, the judgments are not the contents of the book but the attesting witnesses in the seals (6:1–17).[5] If this is the Lamb's book of life, God's judgments in history authenticate the promised inheritance of the saints. (The most likely alternative, as noted above, would be to view the seals as the outside of the book, followed by other judgments written throughout the scroll as in Ezekiel, so that the "scroll" essentially becomes the book of Revelation. Like Ezekiel in Ezek. 2:9–3:3, John finds the content of the book bitter [Rev. 10:2–10].)

God holds the book in an open hand, and one of his angels issues the invitation (or challenge) to all creation: Who can open the book (5:3)?[6] Normally a scroll should be "loosed" (have its seals broken) only by those to whom it is addressed; moreover, these seals, on a book in the right hand of the living

---

3. See Euripides, *Hippol.* 864–65; Chariton, *Chaer.* 4.5.8; *Pes. Rab Kah. Sup.* 2:4; Efrat Carmon, ed., *Inscriptions Revealed: Documents From the Time of the Bible, the Mishna and the Talmud,* tr. R. Grafman (Jerusalem: Israel Museum, 1973), 90–91, 200–201, §189. For a discussion of the specific form of document here, see esp. Beasley-Murray, *Revelation,* 120–23.

4. On recalling witnesses to testify to the validity of the seals, see *P. Oxy.* 494.31–43.

5. Beale, *Revelation,* 343, does cite testaments in which the seals of witnesses include abbreviations of the contents, but despite his objection, the use of seals to conceal in Dan. 12:4, 9, probably militates against that idea here.

6. Questions from heavenly figures or from the visionaries offer opportunities for clarification in apocalyptic texts, e.g., Dan. 10:20; Zech. 4–5; 1 Enoch 25:1; 54:4; 108:5; T. Abr. 12–13 A; 8 B; *p. Hag.* 2:2, §5; Cicero, *De Re Publica* 6.18.18. Aune, *Revelation,* 1:331, cites rhetorical "who" questions introducing praise hymns in antiquity. On scrolls being opened by addressees, see Euripides, *Iph. Aulis* 307.

God, are too strong for ordinary mortals to break. After hailing God as worthy of all power (4:11), who can presume to be "worthy" (5:2) to have strength ("could," 5:3) to open it? Not yet recognizing that the Lamb is also worthy of all power (5:12), John is traumatized with despair over the situation: The universe appears to lack a champion, and John weeps (*klaio*, a term for the most dramatic form of mourning, 5:4).

But finally one of God's worshipers, perhaps a representative of God's redeemed people (see comment on 4:4; cf. 7:13), comforts John: The Lion from the tribe of Judah is the triumphant champion, and he has conquered (5:5).[7] The image of the Lion from Judah comes from Genesis 49:9–10, which Jewish people usually applied to the Davidic Messiah (4 Ezra 12:31–32).[8] The "Root of David" is the Messiah who comes from the truncated house of David (Isa. 11:1), anointed by the Spirit (11:2) and appointed to rule all the nations with peace (11:3–10; cf. Jer. 23:5; 33:15; Zech. 3:8; 6:12; 1QH 6.15; 7.19; 8.6–10). Early Judaism recycled the imagery of this passage to represent a mighty warrior prince.[9]

But here the central paradox of Revelation and of Christian faith in general comes to the fore: Jesus conquered not by force but by death, not by violence but by martyrdom. The Lion is a Lamb! Regularly in ancient literature, lions functioned as images of great strength—the courageous, powerful rulers of the animal kingdom (cf. Rev. 9:8, 17; 10:3).[10] Even Jewish texts use the image of a lion for courage and power in general more often than specifically for the Messiah.[11] John turns, expecting to witness a powerful hero. Yet the

---

7. Confused visionaries elsewhere receive such comfort (T. Abr. 7 B) or explanations (1 Enoch 19:1; 21:5, 9).

8. Also 1QSb 5.29. For other uses of the lion symbol in early Judaism, especially surrounding the Torah shrine, see *CIJ*, 1:197, §281a; 1:378–79, §§516–17; Zvi Uri Ma'oz, "Ancient Synagogues and the Golan," *BA* 51 (June 1988): 116–28 (p. 125). Lions were an especially popular symbol in Asia, particularly in Lydia (Eric M. Meyers and A. Thomas Kraabel, "Archaeology, Iconography, and Nonliterary Written Remains," 175–210 in *Early Judaism and Its Modern Interpreters*, ed. R. A. Kraft and G. W. E. Nickelsburg, SBLBMI 2 [Atlanta: Scholars, 1986], 191).

9. Bauckham, *Climax of Prophecy*, 181, citing 1QSb 5.24; Ps. Sol. 17:27; for Isa. 11:1–10 as a messianic text see 4QFlor 1.11–12; 4QpIsaa Frag. D. "Shoot from David" and "lion of Judah" appear together in 4QPatriarchal Blessings; 1QSb 5.20–29 (Bauckham, ibid.; L. P. Trudinger, "Some Observations Concerning the Text of the Old Testament in the Book of Revelation," *JTS*, n.s. 17 (April 1966): 82–88 [p. 88]). Many view this passage as the Lamb's enthronement; some (Aune, *Revelation*, 1:332–38) relate it to his investiture (citing Dan. 7:9–18).

10. Pervasive throughout literary sources: e.g., Homer, *Il.* 10.297, 485; 11.239, 548; *Od.* 4.724; 6.130; Virgil, *Aen.* 12.6; Apollonius Rhodius, 2.26–29; Babrius, 1, 65, 90–92, 95, 97, 101, 103, 105–7, 139; Phaedrus, 1.5; 4.14.2; Seneca, *Dial.* 4.11.4; Martial, 1.60; Cornelius Nepos, 18.11.1.

11. See 1 Macc. 3:4; Sib. Or. 11.290–91; Ps-Philo 24:6; T. Abr. 17 A; *Pes. Rab Kah.* 4:2; 11:24; 13:15; *Pes. Rab Kah. Sup.* 1:8.

Lamb, by contrast, provides an image of helplessness.[12] Lambs were the most vulnerable of sheep, and sheep were among the weakest of creatures, typically contrasted with predators.[13]

Most significantly for John, this is a *slaughtered* lamb, a sacrificed lamb. Plagues will fall on the disobedient world (Rev. 6–16), but just as the blood of the Passover lamb delivered Israel from the climactic plague (Ex. 12:23), so Jesus' blood will protect his people during God's judgments on humanity (Rev. 7:3). Jesus' victory is like a new exodus (5:9–10; 15:3), and Jesus himself is the new Lamb (cf. 1 Cor. 5:7).[14]

What do the "horns" (5:6) mean? One might speak of horned lambs in apocalyptic symbolism (1 En. 90:9), but horns also appear on literal Passover lambs (*tos. Pisha* 6:7—though male lambs would grow two horns, not seven). John's reinterpretation of traditional symbolism goes beyond any models of his contemporaries, however, to communicate a uniquely Christian viewpoint. Horns in prophetic literature sometimes represent power (Dan. 7:7–24; 8:3–22), but here the power is not human power, but the seven spirits of God (Rev. 5:6); this alludes to the ancient prophecy that the Jewish king must prevail not by human strength but by the power of the Spirit (Zech. 4:6).

John identifies the horns here with seven eyes (5:6), which he probably understands as representing the Spirit in Zechariah's vision (Zech. 3:9; 4:6, 10) as well as the seven lamps (4:2; Rev. 4:5). But in Zechariah, the eyes that watch over God's purposes and his people belong to God himself; their application to Jesus the Lamb provides a clue to Jesus' true, exalted identity.[15] Jesus' location by the throne (Rev. 5:6) may also suggest a status that some texts reserve for divine Wisdom (Wisd. 9:4; cf. 3 En. 10:1); but Jesus' status is higher even than divine Wisdom, for he ultimately sits in the midst of the throne, sharing the Father's supreme reign (Rev. 7:17; 22:1, 3; though cf. also 3:21).

One of the many sorts of documents in the ancient world sealed by witnesses was a will (often sealed with six witnesses, though seven witnesses also

---

12. Some portray the lamb as an image of power related to apocalyptic lambs (1 Enoch 90:38; Talbert, *Apocalypse*, 29), but this is a single slain lamb, and the earliest Jewish sources would think especially of Passover or sacrifice. Most thus see Jesus' conquest through death and note the contrast of images (Boring, *Revelation*, 111; Bauckham, *Climax of Prophecy*, 183–84).

13. See Sir. 13:17; Diogenes Laertius, 6.5.92; Dionysius of Halicarnassus, 7.11.3; Aelian, *Animals* 7.27; Terence, *Brothers*, 534–35.

14. On Christ as paschal lamb here, see also Paul S. Minear, *Images of the Church in the New Testament* (Philadelphia: Westminster, 1960), 102–3; Norman Hillyer, "'The Lamb' in the Apocalypse," *EvQ* 39 [1967]: 228–36; C. S. Keener, "Lamb," 641–42 in *Dictionary of Later New Testament*; more speculatively, Fréderic Manns, "Traces d'une Haggadah pascale chrétienne dans l'Apocalypse de Jean?" *Antonianum* 56 (1981): 265–95.

15. See Bruce, "The Spirit in the Apocalypse," 335.

appear).[16] Once it was attested that the person who made the will was genuinely dead, the seals would be broken and the will opened, making public its contents. In this way the veracity of its contents was guarded.[17] It may be significant here that it is only after the Lamb has been slain that the book can be opened (5:6); if this book is the Lamb's book of life, his legacy for his followers, it becomes theirs through his self-sacrifice. Many interpreters thus understand the book in this passage as Jesus' testament.[18]

In any case, Jesus "took" the scroll from God's hand (5:7); the verb's perfect tense may suggest that he not only receives the book but that he still holds it, hence reigns over the events of human history. What would most astound a traditional Jewish hearer, however, was what follows: The heavenly chorus offers not to God the Father but to Jesus the prayers of the saints (5:8), prayers that directly invite the plagues he will soon release for their vindication (6:10; 8:4–6).[19] Worship apparatus like censers in heaven would not be surprising (Apoc. Mos. 33:4); incense offerings were standard in the temple, so a heavenly temple would be incomplete without them; golden bowls were considered the most exotic.[20] Harps (as in Rev. 5:8; 14:2; 15:2) also belong in the heavenly temple (cf. 1 Chron. 15:16; 16:5; 25:1, 3, 6).[21]

Furthermore, Jewish people had long envisioned one of the chief angels presenting the prayers of the saints before God (Tob. 12:15); in one line of tradition the archangel Michael presents before God a massive bowl containing the righteous deeds of the saints (3 Bar. 11:8–9).[22] The astonishing feature here is that a Lamb receives worship in God's heaven (5:12), sharing with God himself as its object (5:13).[23]

Often worshipers in the time of the first temple offered God a "new song" (5:9; 14:3), perhaps implying a freshly inspired song in addition to the reper-

---

16. Six witnesses in *P. Eleph.* 2.17–18; *P. Lond.* 1727.68–72; seven in Emmet Russell, "A Roman Law Parallel to Revelation Five," *BibSac* 115 (1958): 258–64.

17. See *B.G.U.* 326.21.

18. George E. Ladd, *A Theology of the New Testament* (Grand Rapids: Eerdmans, 1974), 623.

19. One might think of intercessions of departed saints for people on earth, as in 2 Macc. 15:12, 14; 1 En. 39:5 (though Ps-Philo 33:4–5 opposes this concept); but Revelation itself speaks of cries for vindication (Rev. 6:10; 8:4–6), which also brings judgment in 1 Enoch 97:3–5.

20. On preference for golden bowls, see Virgil, *Georgics* 2.192.

21. Though holding both harp and incense pans seems awkward, ancient art sometimes portrayed worshipers in this manner (see sources in Aune, *Revelation*, 1:355–56).

22. Greek tradition earlier portrayed human destinies as two urns before Zeus (Homer, *Il.* 24.527–33).

23. For full discussion of Jesus as an object of worship in Revelation, see Bauckham, *Climax of Prophecy*, 118–49; elsewhere in early Christianity, see Rom. 9:5; Pliny, *Ep.* 10.96.7. The Son of Man receives worship in Enoch's Similitudes (48:5–6 as rendered by Knibb but not Isaac), but these may reflect some Christian influence.

toire of praises already available (Ps. 33:3; 40:3; 96:1; 98:1; 144:9; 149:1; Isa. 42:10). Israel sang hymns to celebrate God's redemption of their people from Egypt in the Passover and Exodus (Ex. 15:3; cf. *m. Pes.* 10:5); they especially used Psalms 113–18 to commemorate that event. Further, part of what early became regular synagogue liturgy celebrates God's choosing his people "from among all nations and tongues."[24]

But the perspective of the true heavenly chorus celebrates an even more critical focus of God's activity in history: the redemption of saints from among all nations by the blood of a new Passover Lamb (5:9). Like ancient Israel (Ex. 19:6), these people will also be a "kingdom and priests" (Rev. 5:10; see comment on 1:6).[25] Those persecuted for their refusal to participate in worship of the emperor may have been struck with the contrast of the pretensions of human power. In various regions throughout the empire regional choruses sang the emperor's praises.[26] But an audience immersed in the Old Testament would be most struck by the fact that this new act of redemption encompassed believers from all peoples. John's fourfold formula describing all peoples ("tribe and language and people and nation") occurs in varying sequences seven times in Revelation and matches a threefold formula that occurs six times in Daniel (Dan. 3:4 [cf. LXX here], 7; 4:1; 5:19; 6:25; 7:14). Daniel announced the rule of the Son of Man over all these peoples (7:14), and John sees a literal fulfillment of this promise in the church.[27]

That God has so many myriads (Rev. 5:11) to worship him reinforces the text's example for us that he is worthy of worship. "Ten thousand" was simply the largest number for which the Greek language afforded a ready term, so the plural (in the Greek) of "ten thousand times ten thousand" is a handy way of saying that they were innumerable.[28] One suspects that even the

---

24. Martin McNamara, *Targum and Testament* (Grand Rapids: Eerdmans, 1972), 39.

25. This promise contrasts starkly with the pretensions of emperors who bestowed kingdoms and confirmed priestly offices (Kraybill, *Imperial Cult and Commerce*, 221–22). For other contrasts here, see Peder Borgen, "Moses, Jesus, and the Roman Emperor: Observations in Philo's Writings and the Revelation of John," *NovT* 38 (1996): 145–59. Worship appears as anticipatory eschatology also in Jewish mystic texts (P. Prigent, "Qu'est-ce qu'une apocalypse?" *RHPR* 75 [1995]: 77–84).

26. Kraybill, *Imperial Cult and Commerce*, 221; cf. Herodian, 4.2.5; Yamauchi, *The Archaeology of New Testament Cities*, 42. On the use of Christian hymns here, see Oscar Cullmann, *Early Christian Worship* (Philadelphia: Westminster, 1953), 21; A. M. Hunter, *Paul and His Predecessors*, rev. ed. (Philadelphia: Westminster, 1961), 37; for hymns' centrality in Revelation, see Tenney, *Revelation*, 36; Gerhard Delling, "Zum gottesdienstlichen Stil der Johannesapokalypse," *NovT* 3 (1959): 107–37.

27. Bauckham, *Climax of Prophecy*, 326–29.

28. The phrase likely means "an incalculable immensity" (cf. Beale, *Revelation*, 509, on 9:16).

emperor would have been impressed had he found himself privy to such a revelation. The image comes directly from Daniel 7:10, a source for later Jewish speculation on the infinite greatness of a God worshiped by an unlimited supply of such heavenly beings (see 1 En. 14:22–23; 40:1; 60:1; 71:8).[29] Not only all of heaven, but all of creation ultimately offers God glory (Rev. 5:13; cf. Ps. 148:1–13; 1 En. 69:24).[30]

IDENTIFICATION WITH BIBLICAL CHARACTERS. As we read this text, we are invited to identify with John in experiencing the grandeur of heavenly worship. Too often we fear to identify with positive characters in the Bible, supposing that they are on a spiritual level far beyond anything we can achieve. Yet some identification is essential to Bible study. Did not the apostle Paul summon members of his churches to "imitate" him (1 Cor. 4:16; 11:1)? How else can we learn moral lessons from Bible stories (2 Tim. 3:16) if not by learning from the positive and negative examples in them (1 Cor. 10:11)?

But here believers may identify with John in his weakness: We are all utterly dependent on a Savior (Rev. 5:4–5). Identifying with biblical characters becomes easier when we remember that they had weaknesses, too. James reminds us that Elijah was a person who experienced the same struggles as we, yet at God's command he could stop the rain (James 5:17). Discouraged that even fire from heaven left Jezebel as his mortal enemy, Elijah wanted to give up and die (1 Kings 19:4). Not content with deep sorrow, Job and Jeremiah actually wished that they had never been born (Job 3:3; Jer. 20:14–15)! Struggling with doubt, John the Baptist questioned whether Jesus really fit his proclamation about the Messiah (Matt. 11:3). Joseph seems to have kept his faith in his dreams while in prison (Gen. 40:8), but forgot at least part of their message in his prosperity (41:51). And we needn't even start talking about Peter! God has chosen people just like us—not so we can boast how great we are, but so

---

29. Cf. 3 Enoch 17:2; 35:1; Apoc. Zeph. 4:2; 8:2. From Dan. 7:10 later rabbis deduced that God regularly created fresh angels for worship out of a fiery stream from his throne (b. Hag. 14a; Gen. Rab. 78:1). Angelic cries with "a loud voice" are not unexpected (2 Bar. 6:8), but for such a multitude "loud voice" is restrained language.

30. For creatures "under the earth" (5:3, 13), John may mean the sea (10:6; 14:7; 21:1), but "sea" and "under the earth" cannot interchange in 5:13, and he more likely means the chthonic realm (Phil. 2:10; Prayer of Joseph 11; ARN 2A), which Greeks might identify with Hades (Homer, Il. 3.276–78; Hesiod, W.D. 141; Virgil, Aen. 12.199; Dionysius of Halicarnassus, 11.37.6; Livy, 31.31.3; Chariton, Chaer. 5.7.10; PGM, 1.264, 315–16; 17a.2–3), as Jews would recognize (Josephus, Apion 2.240).

he can show what he can make out of clay jars filled with his glory, "to show that this all-surpassing power is from God and not from us" (2 Cor. 4:7).

Because his role as the first receiver of this revelation is positive and prefigures our role as its recipients (1:1), John is not only the implied author but functions as a model for the ideal reader as well. Thus his weeping at the despair of the world without a heavenly advocate (5:4) implies the tone with which we are expected to approach this devastating potential situation.[31] And we with John also experience relief at the appearance of Jesus. Like John, we already know that Jesus is our champion, but Revelation unfolds its message not in traditional theological propositions but in graphic images that confront us with the familiar message of the gospel in an ever-fresh way. This may suggest that we should seek God's help to find creative ways to communicate his message in ever-fresh ways to our generation as well.

Jesus' conquest through his self-sacrifice (5:5–6) provides a model for believers, for Revelation also portrays martyrs as sharers in Jesus' sacrifice (see comment on 6:9). Thus, "'conquering' in both cases, that of Christ and that of Christians, means no more or less than dying."[32] We must read each passage in light of the whole book of Revelation (wherever possible, as a prism refracting its various themes), and then be ready to reapply that message to today. The way we offer ourselves in sacrifice may differ in different situations, but the call of the gospel to count the cost remains the same.

Social location. Discussions in biblical studies today often focus on social location: Readers from different backgrounds approach the text with different questions and tend to pick up on different themes. In its radical form, this approach can constitute part of a larger agenda that makes all interpretations relative. As a descriptive discipline, however, it can prove relevant in challenging the biases of our own culture and tradition each of us brings to the text, thereby helping us to hear more clearly the inspired message of Scripture.[33]

One valuable insight this approach has yielded is that those who are suffering or marginalized may identify most quickly with a suffering Savior (5:5–6).[34] Those who are parts of minority cultures or cultures where

---

31. Michaels, *Revelation*, 18.

32. Boring, *Revelation*, 111.

33. Reader-response criticism (on which see Jane P. Tompkins, ed., *Reader-Response Criticism: From Formalism to Post-Structuralism* [Baltimore: Johns Hopkins, 1980]) has been used prescriptively, but we adopt here only its descriptive use. Since our own goal in hearing Scripture is to hear the message God inspired its authors to communicate, we still seek the authors' intention (see E. D. Hirsch Jr., *Validity in Interpretation* [New Haven: Yale, 1967]).

34. For some examples of how slaves and abolitionists, as opposed to slaveholders, read biblical texts about justice and deliverance, see Glenn J. Usry and Craig S. Keener, *Black Man's Religion: Can Christianity be Afrocentric?* (Downers Grove, Ill.: InterVarsity, 1996), 98–109.

Christians are small minorities may find special encouragement in this passage, as Gentile believers probably did at the end of the first century. God's concern for all peoples (5:9–10) may prove especially encouraging to groups that feel marginalized in society or in the church. Of course, the groups that feel this may vary from one era to another. The cultures of the Bible were mainly Middle Eastern, North and somewhat East African, and (in the New Testament) southern European.[35] Although northern Europeans were well-known in the Roman empire, it was usually as primitive savages, and they appear nowhere in the Bible except in these sorts of summary statements.[36]

The East African empire of Axum converted to Christianity around A.D. 333, close to the time of the Roman empire's conversion.[37] Other missionaries quickly spread eastward.[38] But many of us white and Western Christians have grown accustomed to thinking of Christianity as the heritage of the Western world, while Muslims exploit prospective African and other converts with the lie that Christianity is a "white man's religion." Meanwhile, the birthplace region of Christianity is one of the places where it now struggles the hardest to regain a foothold. If the apostles needed to remind their early audiences that the church is not for Israel alone, we must also remember that no culture or region has a permanent claim on the gospel. Thus we must seek to contextualize the gospel message for all cultures and encourage Christians in all cultures to take the lead in effectively evangelizing their peoples.[39]

---

35. For some indication of north and east African as well as western Asiatic presence in the Old Testament, see Usry and Keener, *Black Man's Religion*, 60–82; in the ancient Mediterranean, see especially Frank M. Snowden, *Blacks in Antiquity* (Cambridge, Mass.: Harvard Univ. Press, 1970); idem, *Before Color Prejudice* (Cambridge, Mass.: Harvard Univ. Press, 1983).

36. Herodian, 3.14.6–7, remarks on Britons who run around naked so as not to cover their animal tattoos.

37. For early African Christian history, see Keener and Usry, *Defending Black Faith*, 13–19; Elizabeth Isichei, *A History of Christianity in Africa from Antiquity to the Present* (Lawrenceville, N.J.: Africa World; Grand Rapids: Eerdmans, 1995), 13–44.

38. Ruth A. Tucker, *From Jerusalem to Irian Jaya* (Grand Rapids: Zondervan, 1983), 45; Stephen Neill, *A History of Christian Missions* (Baltimore: Penguin, 1964), 95–97.

39. See Roland Allen, *Missionary Methods: St. Paul's or Ours?* (Chicago: Moody, 1956); Melvin L. Hodges, *The Indigenous Church* (Springfield, Mo.: Gospel, 1976); David Tai-Woong Lee, "Missionary Training by Nationals," *Training for Cross-Cultural Ministries* (April 1998), 1–3 (in *Mission Frontiers Bulletin* [May 1998]). On contextualization, see the essays in D. A. Carson, ed., *Biblical Interpretation and the Church: The Problem of Contextualization* (Nashville: Nelson, 1985); William A. Dyrness, *Emerging Voices in Global Christian Theology* (Grand Rapids: Zondervan, 1994); Craig Blomberg, "The Globalization of Hermeneutics," *JETS* 38 (Dec. 1995): 581–93.

THE SIGNIFICANCE OF **God's judgments.** If the seals attest the veracity of believers' future inheritance in the kingdom (as we have suggested, albeit tentatively), then God's judgments on the world around us should invite us not to fear but to hope. Judgments testify that God, not our oppressors, remains sovereign. Suffering Christians like those in Smyrna and Philadelphia need not feel as if God will ignore their sufferings until the final day; judgments on the society that hates them constitute their vindication. Meanwhile, more prosperous Christians in places like Sardis or Laodicea may fear the judgments because their well-being flows from the well-being of their society—one reason believers are often called out of such dependence (13:17; 18:4). If we feel uncomfortable with the idea of judgment, perhaps it is because we have grown more comfortable with the world than with suffering among Jesus' witnesses.

The angel asks who is worthy to open the book (5:2), and this time no unworthy Isaiah is purified by coals from the altar (Isa. 6:5–7). Jesus alone proves worthy. Keeping Jesus in his rightful place, as our only possible Savior, keeps the rest of us from the arrogance of assuming our own indispensability. Indeed, when we wish to identify with other characters in the Bible, we find people like ourselves with great flaws whenever they are described much. David nearly killed much of Nabal's household in anger (1 Sam. 25:21–22); Sarah chose Hagar to help out God's plan and then mistreated her (Gen. 16:2–6); Joshua acted without God's wisdom toward the Gibeonites (Josh. 9:14–18); Moses protested God's will so much that it nearly cost him his life at the beginning of his call (Ex. 4:13–14, 24–26); Gideon doubted his ability to carry out God's call (Judg. 6:15–17). Israel's judges were often flawed people, some who had minor dysfunctionalities that did not stop them from doing God's will (1 Sam. 8:1–3); others never surmounted their dysfunctionalities and ended in tragedy despite God's blessing (Judg. 11:34–40; 16:30; see also comment on 1:3). The only perfect hero we may honor unconditionally is Jesus; if we start placing others on pedestals and try to pretend to climb on one ourselves, we invite inevitable failure.

Most noteworthy is the fact that none of subsequent history, including God's judgments, may take place until the Lamb himself opens the seals. As F. F. Bruce notes, it is the arrival of the newly slaughtered Lamb that brings to fulfillment God's purposes: "This is the central message of Revelation: The crucial event of all time is the sacrifice of Calvary; that was the decisive victory which has ensured the final triumph of God's cause and God's people over all the forces opposed to them."[40] Revelation is part of our New

---

40. F. F. Bruce, *The Message of the New Testament* (Grand Rapids: Eerdmans, 1981), 84.

Testament precisely because it preaches the same gospel as the rest of the New Testament preaches. All of history depends on the cross, the central event in God's plan of salvation (1 Cor. 1:18–2:16; Col. 1:18–23).

Overcoming through dying. That Jesus overcomes through dying challenges our ways of doing things. We like to gain political or social power and dictate God's terms from the top down.[41] By contrast, Jesus shows us that the true victory comes in sacrifice and weakness, which force us to depend on God's vindication. Jesus' army of followers must imitate his example (see comment on 7:4–9).

One might think of the nine physically or mentally disabled competitors running the hundred-yard dash at a recent Seattle Special Olympics. When one boy stumbled and began to cry, the other eight children all stopped and returned to comfort him. A girl with Down's syndrome gave him a kiss, and then all of them proceeded to the finish line arm in arm. The crowd offered a standing ovation for ten minutes; by relinquishing personal victory, each of the children had achieved a far greater triumph.[42]

Philip Yancey notes that the Christian message brought the world empathy for victims, because for the first time a victim (Jesus) was the hero; the oppressed hold "the moral high ground" in the Western conscience because of Christian teachings.[43] Yancey recounts his amazement at how Henri Nouwen devoted his precious time to serving a mentally challenged man for whom most busy people would have not taken time. Henri Nouwen saw this man as a gift to him, to remind him what we humans are, what matters most, and that our character counts more before God than our accomplishments.[44] In our fast-paced and hectic schedules to accomplish much (I am preaching to myself most of all), we need to be reminded that the victory lies with God and is accomplished as often through our apparent defeat as through our public triumph. Jesus' death also shows the depth of his love for us (1:5), which provides us an assurance—and a model for our demonstrations of Christian love.

---

41. Chuck Colson notes that he "found fulfillment not in power, but in prison" ("My Journey from Watergate," *CT* [Sept. 13, 1993], 96).

42. This true story was forwarded to me by Dr. Jeremiah Wright, pastor of Trinity United Church of Christ in Chicago.

43. Philip Yancey, "Why I Can Feel Your Pain," *CT* (Feb. 8, 1999), 136.

44. See esp. the account of Henri Nouwen's regular service to a severely disabled person, in Philip Yancey, "The Holy Inefficiency of Henri Nouwen," *CT* (Dec. 9, 1996), 80; cf. also the service of Nancy, a disabled woman, to lonely people in her community in Tony Campolo, *Wake Up America* (Grand Rapids: Zondervan, 1991), 87–88. Sometimes we are more like the first disciples, who were so intent on getting Jesus quickly to Jerusalem to set up the kingdom that they missed what the kingdom was all about: blessing some children and healing a blind beggar (Mark 10:13–16, 48).

The dangers of ethnocentrism. That Jesus redeemed for himself a people from among all nations (5:9) warns us against the dangers of ethnocentrism. Multiculturalism is not just a fad or an invention of theological liberals (though like most good things, it can become a tool of evil as well as good; see 13:7–8); God desired a multicultural body of Christ from the very start (Matt. 28:19; Acts 1:8). Indeed, early Christians networked across the Mediterranean world, apparently the only religion in the early Roman empire that developed transregional organization.[45] This implies that God is no respecter of persons; he cares for all peoples. That acknowledgment in turn demands that we love fellow believers across racial and cultural lines enough to hear their perspectives, especially when the issues on which we comment often impinge more directly on their lives.[46]

Billy Graham notes that he grew up on a small southern farm where he rarely considered the situation of African-Americans; but once he realized the implications the gospel had for race relations, he took down the ropes separating blacks and whites in a southern crusade in 1952. From then on, he refused ever to preach at a segregated crusade.[47] In different parts of the United States different racial dynamics come to the fore; but if current trends continue in our nation as a whole, every ethnic group, including whites, will eventually constitute an ethnic minority, and those who cannot adjust will be culturally disadvantaged.[48]

I recall some of my first days as a white Christian living in a predominantly black housing project, where the children knew everything about my culture from television and elsewhere, but I did not even know how they prepared their hair. I was working on my doctorate, but I grew so ashamed of my ignorance that day, and felt cheated by an educational system that had left me ill-prepared to work among any ethnic group other than my own—the one ethnic group that did not think that it was one. Again, different barriers are relevant to people in different locations, but the basic point is that we must transcend all these barriers if the world is to receive a foretaste of heaven through watching Christ's body united among all peoples.

---

45. So Robert Louis Wilken, "Roman Redux," *Christian History* 57 (1998): 42–44 (p. 43).

46. On Acts 10:34 (a text used by African-American Christians for abolitionism—James Melvin Washington, *Frustrated Fellowship* [Macon, Ga.: Mercer, 1986], 27), see esp. J. Julius Scott Jr., "Acts 10:34, a Text for Racial and Cultural Reconciliation Among Christians," pp. 131–39 in *The Gospel in Black and White*, ed. D. L. Ockholm (Downers Grove, Ill.: InterVarsity, 1997). For the centrality of ethnic reconciliation in Paul's message, see Craig S. Keener, "The Gospel and Racial Reconciliation," 117–30 in *Gospel in Black and White*.

47. Graham, *Approaching Hoofbeats*, 144–45; Edward Gilbreath, "Billy Graham Had a Dream," *Christian History* 14 (Aug. 1995): 44–46; on Graham, see further William Curtis Martin, *A Prophet with Honor* (New York: Quill, William Morrow, 1991).

48. Russell Chandler, *Racing Towards 2001* (Grand Rapids: Zondervan, 1992), 28.

Worship pleasing to God. God receives our worship and our prayers as incense, an aroma pleasing to him (5:8).[49] Various activities typically surround worship in Revelation and elsewhere in Scripture, such as singing, hence the psalms (e.g., 1 Chron. 15:22, 27; 25:7; 2 Chron. 23:18; 29:30; Ezra 2:65; Neh. 12:46). It was often instrumental as well (e.g., 1 Chron. 13:8; 15:16, 28; 16:5; 25:1), as here (5:8), although I will concede that the noninstrumental churches today have produced some beautiful acappella harmonies. In the Bible, worship was often joyous celebration (expressions of joy over a hundred times in Psalms), often including shouting (over twenty times in Psalms).

If this seems too celebrative for some of our more solemn churches, many of the fastest growing movements around the world find it much more amenable to human nature than our solemnity. They have discovered that at least some forms of worship can be fun! (We should also note, however, that the psalms also do include prayers of mourning and sorrow, covering the whole gamut of human emotion.) Worship can also be contextualized; when some people tried to prevent the music minister from securing drums in a church where I was on staff, I preached from Psalm 150, including the diversity of instruments in 150:3–6. I noted that they used all the instruments available in their culture (including those used by their pagan neighbors), because God is worthy of the most splendid praise we can give him.

At the same time, joy, shouting, instruments, and celebration do not by themselves constitute worship; otherwise some college frat parties would qualify! The heart of worship is declaring to God (whether in the second person or sometimes in the third person but with God in mind, as in some psalms) how majestic he is and how great his works are, which in short means articulating the truth about him. Theology can thus be worshipful, though biblical worship is generally not simply rational but affective as well, devoting one's whole being in attention to God. (When conjoined with dancing, often a sign of rejoicing in Israel's culture, it can be physical as well; e.g., Ps. 149:3; 150:4.) Theologians often must speak the language of their guild, but all believers, when they have a proper understanding of God, can participate by articulating biblical themes that glorify God in the artistic, metaphoric language of poetry and song. As C. S. Lewis also recognized, given the limitations of human language, musical metaphors and apocalyptic images may communicate God's glory to most people better than our dry treatises would.

---

49. In later tradition self-sacrificial devotion to God provided a favorable aroma to him (*Gen. Rab.* 34:9; 47:7; *Song Rab.* 4:6, §1), as sacrifices did (Gen. 8:21; 1QM 2.5; Jub. 3:27; 6:3–4; 21:14); incense was also useful in triumphs (Josephus, *War* 7.72), though the temple image fits better here. On spiritual sacrifices, see Ps. 50:14; 51:16–19; 69:30–31; 141:2; Isa. 1:11–17; 58:6–7; Hos. 6:6; Amos 5:21–24; Mic. 6:6–8; 1QS 9.4–5.

Many biblical "worship" phrases have become virtually meaningless in our different culture (what does it mean for God to lift up our head?).[50] I think of many biblical worship choruses today which, taken from their original context, are used completely differently from the way the Bible used the biblical phrases they use.[51] At the same time, we should, as John did, continue to celebrate biblical, redemptive history, as well as God's rule over the cosmos and in our lives and contemporary events. Biblically saturated hymns like those of Charles Wesley are ideally suited to such worship. But even when our lips utter the right words or our emotions celebrate a joyful rhythm, the worship for which God longs most of all is our heart and lives as living sacrifices (cf. Rev. 6:9–11; also Rom. 12:1).

A transformed life. That Jesus made us a kingdom and priests (5:10) fills out some of our popular twentieth-century notions of conversion. It indicates that God has called us to pray and worship as priests and to rule (5:10), not simply to "go to heaven" someday (crucial as that destination is). The redemption the heavenly chorus describes here is thus not merely personal piety; it is entrance into an intercessory community of faith destined to rule the world.

In the early nineteenth century many churchgoers in the United States believed that salvation was an event they could hope for at the end of their lives; the emphasis on conversion in the evangelical revival shifted the focus from salvation as a goal to salvation as the beginning of a new, transformed life that enabled one to make an impact on the world.[52] Thus as Finney witnessed tens of thousands making professions of faith in Christ, he immediately enrolled their new commitment in the service of the abolitionist movement.[53] Jesus did not redeem us for irrelevance, but to become his agents in this world.

The worship of all creation in 5:13 probably suggests more than that nature testifies to its Creator by what one sees there (Ps. 8:3; 19:1–6; Rom.

---

50. For a sampling of how much Israel's worship language reflected its culture, see Mitchell Dahood, *Psalms 1: Psalms 1–50*, AB 16 (Garden City, N.Y.: Doubleday, 1966), though he probably depended too heavily on Ugaritic parallels. Worship styles change; the Anglican church did not sanction hymn-singing (cf. 1 Cor. 14:26; Eph. 5:19; Col. 3:16) until 1820 ("Did You Know?" *Christian History*, 31 [1991]: front inside cover.)

51. For example, "This is the day the LORD has made" refers not to every day but to the momentous day when the stone rejected by the builders became the chief cornerstone (Ps. 118:22–24).

52. Gilbert Hobbs Barnes, *The Antislavery Impulse, 1830–1844* (New York: Harcourt, Brace & World, 1964), 3–11.

53. Timothy L. Smith, *Revivalism and Social Reform: American Protestantism on the Eve of the Civil War* (Baltimore: Johns Hopkins, 1980), 180; Usry and Keener, *Black Man's Religion*, 106–7.

1:20); the image seems closer to the active celebration envisioned in Psalm 96:11–13; Isaiah 44:23; 55:12. To be sure, animals and inanimate creation are less intelligent than people made in God's image; yet we have so debased our wisdom that sometimes animals are smarter than we are (Isa. 1:3; Rom. 1:21–23; 2 Peter 2:16).

Revelation 6:1–8

I WATCHED AS the Lamb opened the first of the seven seals.
Then I heard one of the four living creatures say in a voice
like thunder, "Come!" ²I looked, and there before me was a
white horse! Its rider held a bow, and he was given a crown,
and he rode out as a conqueror bent on conquest.

³When the Lamb opened the second seal, I heard the second living creature say, "Come!" ⁴Then another horse came
out, a fiery red one. Its rider was given power to take peace
from the earth and to make men slay each other. To him was
given a large sword.

⁵When the Lamb opened the third seal, I heard the third
living creature say, "Come!" I looked, and there before me was
a black horse! Its rider was holding a pair of scales in his hand.
⁶Then I heard what sounded like a voice among the four living
creatures, saying, "A quart of wheat for a day's wages, and
three quarts of barley for a day's wages, and do not damage
the oil and the wine!"

⁷When the Lamb opened the fourth seal, I heard the voice
of the fourth living creature say, "Come!" ⁸I looked, and there
before me was a pale horse! Its rider was named Death, and
Hades was following close behind him. They were given
power over a fourth of the earth to kill by sword, famine and
plague, and by the wild beasts of the earth.

THIS PASSAGE PRESENTS the notorious four horsemen of the Apocalypse as fierce images of terrifying judgment. A little historical consideration
will help us understand how these images would
have threatened the worldly security of a first-century audience, thereby inviting us to sense the same dread these images would have originally evoked.

It is doubtful that we should read the four riders or other judgments as a
chronological map of history before the end; rather, they are probably images
of the kinds of judgments that characterized that time, arranged in the
sequence in which John saw them.¹ Some regard the seals as past, a prelude

---

1. See González, *Revelation*, 53. Apocalyptic visions schematized the Tribulation in various ways (e.g., the 12-part tribulation in 2 Bar. 27), but some of these judgments would overlap rather than yielding a clear sequence (2 Bar. 27:14–15).

to present or future judgments elsewhere in the book.[2] More likely, the seals cover the same span of time covered by the trumpets and bowls, because all three sets of judgments climax in the end of the age (6:12–14; 11:15, 18; 16:17, 20; on the timing of Revelation, see comment on 12:5–6).

The judgments threatened by the four horsemen are judgments that Jesus said would characterize the present age (Mark 13:7–8).[3] Many ancient prophecy teachers catalogued special sufferings they expected in the degenerate time of the end. Jesus took some of these and (in contrast to some modern prophecy teachers, who have failed to read him closely), explicitly said that such events did not signal the end; rather, "the end is still to come," for these are merely "the beginning of birth pangs" (Mark 13:7–8; cf. Matt. 24:6, 8).Both Jesus and Revelation omit some signs mentioned by ancient prophecy teachers, however, such as mutant babies.[4]

John's depiction of judgment here reflects both literary artistry and immersion in Scripture. The list of four plagues resembles some from the Old Testament (Deut. 32:24; 2 Chron. 20:9; Jer. 15:2; Ezek. 5:17; 14:21), but such a fourfold formula recurs specifically in Revelation 6:8 and may not stand behind the horsemen as a whole (since that summary substitutes "wild beasts" for conquest).[5] A more compact list of three judgments (combining war and conquest, but retaining pestilence and famine) is far more common, suggesting that Revelation makes the image of war and conquest emphatic.[6]

The four riders appear to be angels of judgment, though their identity should not be pressed too much, given their symbolic literary function.[7] They most directly recall Zechariah 1:8, where many riders on four different colors of horses represent the Lord's patrol that report back to him about quiet on the earth (Zech. 1:8–11). Later God sends out four chariots, each drawn by horses of a different color, as his patrol (6:1–8), more impressive

---

2. Wesley, *Commentary on the Bible*, 597 (viewing chs. 6–9 as past; chs.10–14 as current; and chs. 15–19 as imminent).

3. Some even think Rev. 6 reflects Mark 13 (Beasley-Murray, *Revelation*, 129–30).

4. Judaism probably derived this from paganism: e.g., Hesiod, *W.D.* 180–81; among regular portents, see, e.g., Livy, 36.37.2; Appian, *C.W.* 1.9.83; Lucan, *C.W.* 1.526–27. In Judaism, see 4 Ezra 5:8, 6:21.

5. See also the fourfold formulas in Ps-Philo 3:9; T. Jud. 23:3; and war, famine, pestilence, and invasion in Sib. Or. 3.331.

6. The threefold list of sword (war), pestilence, and famine (e.g., Jer. 14:12; 21:7–10; 27:8; 29:17–18; 32:24, 36; 34:17; 38:2; 42:17, 22; 44:13; Ezek. 5:12; 6:11–12; 7:15; 12:16). Cf. sword, famine, and death in Sib. Or. 3.335; the fivefold adaptation in *Sifre Deut.* 43.9.1; but longer lists are also common (e.g., Sib. Or. 3.601–3).

7. Cf. four angels of judgment in 1 Enoch 87:2–89:1; but other numbers of angels appear elsewhere. Aune, *Revelation*, 2:390, cites the various colored four heavenly horses of Greek gods, though the parallel may simply reflect the ideal number of chariot horses.

than the Persian patrols from which the image may derive. Here he has assigned some angels a more active role; some Jewish texts picture God's routing of mortal enemies by means of mounted angels (2 Macc. 3:24–30).

The description of the rider on the white horse (6:2) has occasioned various explanations, including an allusion to the antichrist figure Gog (Ezek. 39:3) and the archer and prophecy deity Apollo.[8] The evidence is not clear enough to support a connection with Gog. Readers would find in the white horse an imitation of Christ's horse (hence to be associated with an antichrist figure) only if they had already read 19:11 (no "white horse" appears in the prophets except in Zech. 1:8). Although Revelation's audience would undoubtedly hear the book read more than once, white horses are common enough to weaken the significance of the proposed link. Likewise, the link with Apollo, though brilliantly argued, is probably too subtle; other allusions to Apollo are missing here, and Apollo was not the only deity who carried a bow (cf. Artemis, Eros). Others parallel this white horse with Christ's and see the first rider as preaching the gospel before the end (cf. Matt. 24:14).[9] Others find in the call to "Come" (Rev. 6:1, 3, 5, 7) an allusion to the call to Christ to "come" (22:20), so that all four horsemen are epiphanies of Christ coming in judgment in history.[10] But though the Lord does ultimately stand behind these angels, the symbols that follow are negative and cast their negative light over this one as well.

A more general allusion is possible; one might also reduce the significance of starting with the white horse by noting that such horses might be prized.[11] The biblical prophets also used the "bow" as a metaphor for conquest no less than the "sword" for war, though the image is associated most frequently with particular peoples known for such skills (e.g., Isa. 21:15;

---

8. For the antichrist from Gog, see Mathias Rissi, "The Rider on the White Horse: A Study of Revelation 6:1–8," *Interpretation* 18 (1964): 407–18; idem, *Time and History*, 72–73; Walvoord, *Prophecy Knowledge Handbook*, 553; Daniel K. K. Wong, "The First Horseman of Revelation 6," *BibSac* 153 (1996): 212–26. For Apollo, see the careful work of Allen Kerkeslager, "Apollo, Greco-Roman Prophecy, and the Rider on the White Horse in Rev 6:2," *JBL* 112 (Spring 1993): 116–21; he finds Apollo allusions in 9:11 and 12:1–5 (pp. 119–20); but in neither case are the Apollo allusions primary.

9. Oscar Cullmann, *Christ and Time*, tr. F. V. Filson (Philadelphia: Westminster, 1950), 161; idem, "Eschatology and Missions in the New Testament," 409–21 in *The Background of the New Testament and Its Eschatology*, ed. W. D. Davies and D. Daube (Cambridge: Cambridge Univ. Press, 194), 416; Ladd, *Theology*, 623.

10. Greeks spoke of interventions of deities as their "epiphanies" (Martin Persson Nilsson, *Greek Piety*, tr. H. J. Rose [Oxford: Clarendon, 1948], 106). More likely here is the Jewish conception of a heavenly voice (Josephus, *Ant.* 13.282–83; *b. Ab.* 6:2; *Sifre Deut.* 357.10.3) decreeing God's purposes.

11. See Homer, *Il.* 10.437; Livy, 5.28.1; *b. Sanh.* 93a.

22:3; 41:2; Jer. 6:23; 46:9; 49:35; 50:14, 29, 42; 51:3; Hos. 1:5, 7; 2:18). But given other allusions to the Parthians in Revelation (Rev. 9:14; 16:12)—allusions that would probably be evident to an audience in Asia Minor—an allusion to the Parthians seems most likely here.[12]

Parthians were famous, like Scythians, for their horses. They were known as mounted warriors, and their cavalry were especially known for their formidable archery.[13] Whereas in Roman armies only auxiliaries used the bow and made up the cavalry, the Parthians were all mounted archers; they were the only group of mounted archers known in the ancient Mediterranean world.[14] White was the sacred color of the Parthians, and every Parthian army included some sacred white horses.[15] (In their triumphs, Roman generals also had white horses, which were the best; but they were used to draw chariots.)

Furthermore, many Jewish people in the eastern Mediterranean expected Parthians to play a role in an eschatological war (1 En. 56:5–7; Sib. Or. 5.438).[16] Even in 19:11–16, where the rider on the white horse is clearly the Lord Jesus, the book may strike terror into Roman loyalists' hearts with an allusion to the Parthian threat; the title "King of kings" may allude to the Parthian ruler (see comment on 19:16). But Revelation uses this image merely to underscore the point of hostile invaders, not to predict a specifically Parthian invasion. The point is that Roman rule will someday collapse—not to yield an eternal rule by Parthia, but ultimately by God (11:15–19).[17]

The threat of war and conquest challenged the deceptive claim of a *pax Romana*, the Roman peace. Rome kept peace within the boundaries of its empire—though it was less genuinely peace than pacification and subjugation—but its propaganda of "peace" did not terminate attempts to expand its borders. More powerful invaders would now reveal the emptiness of the Roman peace.[18]

---

12. See William M. Ramsay, *The Cities of St. Paul: Their Influence on His Life and Thought* (London: Hodder & Stoughton, 1907; reprint: Grand Rapids: Baker, 1979), 430; González, *Revelation*, 47.

13. On horses, see Tacitus, *Ann.* 15.17; 1 Enoch 56:7; Horace, *Sat.* 2.1.15. For famed Parthian archery, see Virgil, *Aen.* 12.857–58; *Georg.* 4.290, 313–14; Plutarch, *Pompey* 70.3; Tacitus, *Ann.* 15.4, 7, 9; Seneca, *Ep. Lucil.* 35.7; Jewish sources also associate archery with the east (Sib. Or. 5.116–17).

14. Ramsay, *Letters to the Seven Churches*, 58; Caird, *Commentary on Revelation*, 80.

15. Ramsay, *Letters to the Seven Churches*, 58–60, also noting that Parthian rulers regularly carried bows as their authority symbol.

16. Roman texts are full of allusions to the Parthian menace (e.g., Lucian, *How to Write History*), and many Palestinian Jews also had reason to fear them (cf. Josephus, *War* 1.248–273). For eschatological wars, see 1QpHab 3–4; but cf. also the final battle in 1QM.

17. With Boring, *Revelation*, 122.

18. See Kraybill, *Imperial Cult and Commerce*, 147.

"Conquest" (6:2) would be followed by bloodshed (6:4), and in their wake would follow famine because of economic destabilization (6:5–6) and widespread death (6:8), as is frequent in wars. Bloodshed, the second rider, presents a grisly image. Readers would likely catch an allusion to blood in the "red" horse; later rabbis understood Zechariah's "man riding a red horse" (Zech. 1:8; cf. 6:2) as the Lord's bringing judgment, wishing to turn the world into blood (*b. Sanh.* 93a). The "sword" represents the judgment of warfare and violent death, an idiom that occurs well over one hundred times in the Old Testament alone (e.g., Lev. 26:33; Num. 14:43; Deut. 32:25; Isa. 31:8; 65:12; Jer. 4:10; 19:7).[19] No specific mention is made of different nations here, so making people "slay each other" might (though need not) involve civil war, as some commentators suggest.[20] Certainly the most memorable battles of the previous generation were wars within the empire itself, especially the Judean revolt (A.D. 66–73) and the violent power struggles in Rome during A.D. 68. Because it involved bloodshed of one's own citizens, civil war often appeared the most horrible.[21]

Famine (the third horse) likewise constitutes a terrifying specter. The image of the balance (6:5), normally used in the marketplace to weigh out the amount of food one could buy for one's money, suggests God's sovereignty over the food supply. Both famine (Sib. Or. 3.236) and pestilence (Sib. Or. 3.538) often accompanied war. Pestilence could follow, for example, from rotting corpses in the water supply; famine could follow pestilence when many farmers grew ill.[22] Both pagans and Jews also understood that such hardships often represented divine judgments, and they called for repentance (Lev. 26:26; Jer. 11:22; 21:6; Ezek. 4:16; 33:27).[23]

The famine affects many of the basic staples of the Mediterranean diet, which consisted of such foods as barley, wheat, and perhaps cheese and olives, plus fish for those near bodies of water. A "quart of wheat" is not much; those limited to half this amount of barley a day quickly became

---

19. In other early Jewish literature, see 1 Enoch 14:6; 88:2; 90:19; 91:11–12; Jub. 5:9; 9:15; 20:6; 22:8; 23:22–23; CD 1.4, 17; 1QM 11.11–12; 12.11–12; 15.3; 16.1; 1QpHab 6.10; 4QpNah 2.5; 2 Bar. 27:3–5; Sib. Or. 3.316, 689; T. Abr. 18 A; tos. B.K. 7:6; Suk. 2:6.

20. Mounce, *Revelation*, 154–55, also arguing (155 n. 12) that the term for killing is not the usual kind of death in battle. Usually, in fact, it is a ritual term, sometimes used for slaying prisoners, but it occasionally does apply to killing in battle (Judg. 12:6; Jer. 19:7).

21. E.g., Appian, *C.W.* 1.intro. 5; Lucan, *C.W.* 2.148–51; 4 Ezra 6:24. The current Flavian dynasty of which Domitian was a part had seized power during a sort of civil war in Rome.

22. See Dionysius of Halicarnassus, 10.53; Livy, 4.25.4–6.

23. Hierocles, *How to Conduct Oneself Toward the Gods* 1.3.53–54; Ps. Sol. 17:18–19; 2 Bar. 27:6; b. Ber. 55a. For pestilence as a divine judgment, see Diodorus Siculus, 14.69.4–14.71.4; Pes. Rab. 15:14/15.

undernourished and proved susceptible to deadly diseases.[24] Still, subsistence wages for peasants were not uncommon; hired laborers on a farm could be paid as little as two loaves of bread a day (about half a kilogram), just enough food for themselves and their family.[25]

A denarius was roughly a day's wage in this period; a quart of wheat would feed a single worker for a day, but if he had a family to support he would buy instead three times as much barley, which was cheaper. One could eat, but the grain here costs at least five times and as much as fifteen times what it might in better times.[26] Given the average size household in poorer regions like Egypt, many younger children would die or become stunted from malnutrition.

Why does the text mention the sparing of oil and wine (6:6), less necessary to life than the grain?[27] Some suggest that it indicates that the wealthy will still have the luxury items (cf. 18:13; Job 24:11; Prov. 21:17).[28] Whether or not this proposal is accepted, this disparity probably points to inequities inherent in the Roman economy. Although the stark reality of famine would have been felt by most people in antiquity, especially in cities dependent on the countryside, this image may have particularly grabbed the attention of an audience in Roman Asia in the 90s of the first century. Because the wine trade was more profitable than grain, Roman owners of provincial estates grew more vines than grain, leading to a wine surplus but grain shortage. Around the time Revelation was written, the emperor Domitian was trying to restrict vine production in places like Asia, but his attempts proved unpopular and unsuccessful.[29] If enforced, his policy would have struck Philadelphia (Rev. 3:7–13) particularly hard, because it was especially dependent on vine production.[30]

So much of Asia's land was dedicated to producing olive oil and wine for profitable export that its own cities often needed to import grain from Egypt

---

24. See Plutarch, *Nicias* 29.1; for the staples, see Plutarch, *Love of Wealth* 2, *Mor.* 523F.

25. Naphtali Lewis, *Life in Egypt Under Roman Rule* (Oxford: Clarendon, 1983), 69.

26. Eight times the price of wheat and five and one-third that of barley (see Aune, *Revelation*, 2:397); the higher figure is in Beasley-Murray, *Revelation*, 132–33.

27. Many tried to exploit astrology to predict the prices of various commodities, sometimes even in ancient Judaism (Tr. Shem 1.11; 2.5, 8; 5.1–4; 6.7–11; 7.4–7, 14; 8.6–7; 11.8–9; 12.9).

28. Caird, *Commentary on Revelation*, 81; Beasley-Murray, *Revelation*, 133. The expense of wine if the vines were unhurt may reflect widespread drunkenness (*m. Sot.* 9:15; *Pes. Rab.* 15:14/15; cf. Joel 1:5). Wine and oil could be counted, however, as staples (Deut. 7:13; 11:14; 12:17; 14:23; 18:4; Neh. 5:11; Ps. 104:15; Mic. 6:15).

29. Suetonius, *Dom.* 7.2; 14.2.

30. Hemer, *Letters to the Seven Churches*, 158–59; though note the cautions in Aune, *Revelation*, 2:398–400. The economic difficulties of Domitian's reign particularly impacted Roman Asia (Helmut Koester, *Introduction to the New Testament* [Philadelphia: Fortress, 1982], 2:251).

or the Black Sea. Thus while owners and shippers profited, most people in Asia often had to pay higher prices for their food.[31] Even well-to-do congregations in Sardis, Thyatira, and Laodicea would understand how near to them such a judgment might be, and might recognize the complicity of empire-wide economic practices in bringing about such hardship, which would prove most difficult for the poor.[32] Inflation was already heavy at the end of the first century; famine, however, always drove inflation out of control (2 Kings 6:25).[33]

But the sparing of oil and wine also reveals God's mercy in the midst of judgment ("do not damage" in 6:6 is the same Greek expression as "do not harm" in 7:3). Ancient Mediterranean warfare included destroying the standing crops in the fields but not the vines and olive trees; destruction of vines and olive trees would produce a long-range devastation of the local economies (and so negate the entire point of conquering the land). Destroying wheat and barley meant hardship for a year until the new harvest would come, but destroying olive trees (which took about seventeen years to grow) and vines spelled enduring disaster.[34] In ancient Mediterranean thought, only the most savage of barbarians would destroy all means of food production; the wars of 6:2–4 were not total wars, but they would lead up to more powerful threats (16:12–16).

The "pale horse" (6:8) could be literally a "green" one, but the term when applied to complexions means simply "pale," as the NIV correctly translates it.[35] The coming of "Death" may sum up the result of the previous horsemen or may refer particularly to plague and pestilence (cf. 2:23).[36] Death often appears personified in Jewish sources, typically as an angel subservient to God's design or sometimes as the equivalent of Satan, who also, however, cannot strike God's people apart from God's will.[37] Personified Death and Hades

---

31. Kraybill, *Imperial Cult and Commerce*, 66–67.

32. Wesley, *Commentary on the Bible*, 599, thinks the prophecy was fulfilled in the famine during the reign of Trajan (early second century).

33. See also Josephus, *War* 6.198. For inflation at the end of the first century, see William White Jr., "Finances," 218–36 in *The Catacombs and the Colosseum*, ed. S. Benko and J. J. O'Rourke (Valley Forge, Pa.: Judson, 1971), 234.

34. See Ramsay, *Cities*, 431–32; idem, *Pauline and Other Studies in Early Church History* (New York: A. C. Armstrong & Son, 1906; Grand Rapids: Baker, 1979), 241.

35. Longus, 1.17; Aune, *Revelation*, 2:400, cites texts in which this pallor relates to sickness, which may evoke pestilence (6:8).

36. Cf. Black, "Greek Words," 136.

37. E.g., 2 Bar. 21:23; T. Abr. 8, 16A; 9B; Syr. Men. Sent. 444–46; Sib. Or. 3.393, 692; *Sifre Deut.* 305.3.3; ARN 12A; *Pes. Rab Kah. Sup.* 1:14. Death may be personified in Rev. 9:6; cf. 8:11; 20:14; Sir. 41:1–2; Ps. Sol. 7:4; Horace, *Sat.* 2.1.58. For famine personified, see Sib. Or. 3.331–32.

appear together in some biblical poetry (2 Sam. 22:6; Ps. 49:14; 116:3; Isa. 28:15; 38:18; Hos. 13:14; Hab. 2:5).

The four riders together slay with sword (violent death, as perhaps in the first two riders), famine (the third rider), pestilence (perhaps the fourth), and wild animals (6:8), perhaps added because it elsewhere appears in biblical lists of four plagues (Ezek. 5:17; 14:21). It also appears elsewhere as a judgment (2 Kings 2:24; Wisd. Sol. 11:15–18; 12:9).

EQUIVALENT IMAGES. To apply these images we should translate them into images that would evoke an equivalent impact today. Wars, famines, and plagues remain terrifying matters today. To evoke afresh the message of 6:1–8, we should embrace the full horror of the vision, then contemplate that God is sovereign in these judgments. By revealing his anger against the world's sin he both serves notice on oppressors and mercifully prevents us from becoming too comfortable with a world system destined to pass away (1 John 2:15–17). God is sovereign in history, even over sufferings; they are the seals, the marks of divine witness to the veracity of his promises.

Prophecy teachers have interpreted these images in various ways, not always with attention to their original historical context. Hal Lindsey, for example, says the rider on a white horse is a European Antichrist who rules from Rome (who secures the help of a Jewish Antichrist ruling from Israel).[38] But the probable allusion to the Parthians means that the text would have likely scared Romans, not affirmed their sense of imperial pride! This figure would be ruling from Rome only if he first conquered it.

If the first rider bears the image of a Parthian conqueror, we must ask how to translate that image beyond the first-century Roman world. Rome ultimately succumbed to invaders from beyond the empire, but the fiercest and most successful proved to be from the north rather than from the east; was Revelation's warning mistaken? Such a question forces us to grapple with the nature of Revelation's images. The point is not that the Parthians alone could overthrow Rome, but that the vision portrays the most frightening image of war to the Roman world of its day to communicate the point that war was coming.

Likewise, we should not think that the fall of Rome exhausts the significance of Revelation's image of terrifying judgment. The point applies not only

---

38. Lindsey, *New World Coming*, 103.

to Rome, but to all empires in history; Rome was the mightiest in its day, but with the other empires of history now lies buried in the dust, succeeded by other kingdoms no more eternal than Rome proved to be.

If those of us for whom famine and pestilence seem distant realities are to hear the dread the text conveys, we must consider analogies closer to home. Many people in most of our churches are but a paycheck or two away from missing house or rent payments, so images like Revelation's are more relevant than we may want to think. With downsizing, shifting markets, and so forth, few jobs are fully secure even in corporate America.[39] In ministering in an urban context I have more than once encountered a former college professor who through some crisis lost work and ended up on the street. Widespread cholera or yellow fever may be far from American minds, but AIDS and cancer are not. The whole world stands under the curse of suffering and death, hence this text invites us to grapple with its horrifying images and their meaning. Not every suffering is the result of personal sin, but sufferings do result from the fallen state of the world in general, reminding us that God does judge the world order and summons its attention.

The four riders. What do we make of the four riders? As noted above, Judaism spoke of angels of death, usually in a terrifying manner. Even among Greeks and Romans, the deity that stirred war was considered a horrible, repulsive one.[40] Yet all these horsemen act at God's bidding and as his agents (also 8:5–6; 14:19); even a renegade spirit like the devil must submit to God's bidding (20:1–3), as Luther's song puts it: "One little word shall fell him." In the midst of this world's suffering—suffering that inevitably touches the lives of all mortal beings, including ourselves—we must remember that God does have everything under control and is bringing to completion his purposes in history. This does not mean that we should not work against the evil nor that God does not offer selective protection to his own (7:3), but that even in the suffering we can discern a long-range, redemptive purpose that is bigger than we are, as well as a reward for faithful endurance (21:4).

Sometimes interpreters have applied the images of the four riders only to a future time of tribulation. For a number of reasons, this view is unlikely (see esp. comment on 12:5–6). But on the level of application, the point is the same: God is sovereign in his judgments, summoning the world's attention. We dare not grow comfortable with this world, which is not our home.

---

39. E.g., "How Safe Is Your Job?" *NW* (Nov. 5, 1990), 44–47; "Young, Gifted and Jobless," *NW* (Nov. 5, 1990), 48–55; Marc Levinson, "Thanks. You're Fired," *NW* (May 23, 1994), 48–49.

40. E.g., Virgil, *Aen.* 7.323–40.

GOD'S SOVEREIGNTY OVER HISTORY. This passage underlines the recognition that God is sovereign over history; terrible things may happen that seem beyond explanation, but on the larger scale God is using such forces to bring history to its climax. This text presents us not the God of Deism promoted by Jefferson, Franklin, and many other disciples of the "Age of Reason"; it declares the true and living God.[41] The modern experiment to overcome the need for "superstition" and religion has failed. The modern world's values have proved inadequate to confront the threats our world experiences; continuing wars, weapons of massive destruction, and other plagues have hurled modern humanity "into an apocalyptic age, without a faith in Christian eschatology."[42] Terror with teleology can only remind us of our mortality, our need to depend on someone greater than ourselves. Terror without teleology produces despair.

Ellul regards the four horsemen as "the four chief components of history"; history is characterized by their hideous imprint.[43] If John received his vision today, the terrifying symbols might be different, but they would convey the same message as they did then. We can cling to nothing other than trust in the sovereign God who rules history, for nothing else remains certain.

Contemporary judgments. Judgments can come in a variety of ways, one of which is suffering caused by *war and terrorism*. The image of war may be glorified by generations that have never known it firsthand (cf. Judg. 3:2), but it is viewed more realistically by those who have suffered its ravages. My heart aches for friends in nations currently at war, but the threat is somewhat vivid even here. Needless to say, conquest and war remain terrifying specters for our generation. Expounding at great length on the red horse, Billy Graham several decades ago warned about "stockpiles of 60,000 hydrogen bombs" that could destroy human life on earth "seventeen times over."[44] At the time of this book's writing fear of nuclear catastrophe has faded, but nuclear and chemical arsenals have actually proliferated, so that some may be found in the hands of terrorists with less fear of retaliation than nuclear states once had.[45]

41. For Christian conflicts with early American Deism, see Mark A. Noll, *A History of Christianity in the United States and Canada* (Grand Rapids: Eerdmans, 1992), 135–36, 166; Steven J. Keillor, *This Rebellious House: American History and the Truth of Christianity* (Downers Grove, Ill.: InterVarsity, 1996), 100–101; Philip Yancey, "The Last Deist," *CT* (April 5, 1999), 88.

42. Keillor, *Rebellious House*, 254.

43. Ellul, *Apocalypse*, 150.

44. Graham, *Approaching Hoofbeats*, 123.

45. On nuclear proliferation, see Carrol Bogert, "Selling Off Big Red," *NW* (March 1, 1993), 50–51; Dorinda Elliott, "Psst! Wanna Buy a Missile?" *NW* (Sept. 6, 1993), 28; Tom

By some estimates, the world "still has about fifty thousand nuclear weapons," more than enough to end modern civilization.[46] Terrorists without bombs make do with what they have to make their political statements; thus radical Islamic terrorists have murdered thousands of politically uninvolved peasants in Algeria, including one "eight-year-old boy . . . nearly decapitated while having his throat slit."[47]

International terrorism such as embassy bombings is on the rise, but domestic terrorism also poses a genuine threat. Timothy McVeigh, whose truck bomb killed 168 people in Oklahoma City, was not an isolated activist. He took the script for this bombing directly from William Pierce's Neo-Nazi novel, *The Turner Diaries*. He had peddled the book, which has sold over 200,000 copies, as he traveled on the gun circuit. The novel not only prescribes the sort of truck, explosives, and time of day for McVeigh's bombing; it also describes plans for what violent white supremacists hope to do after they have destabilized the federal government, for instance the lynching of tens of thousands of "race-mixers" from lamp posts in Los Angeles.[48] Active terrorists in this mold are few, but they are propagating their views at an alarming rate; one music company promoting violent white power lyrics sells 50,000 compact disks a year.[49]

War is brutal and does not choose its victims fairly.[50] Whether because we know more about it or because killing machines and ideologies have become more efficient, the twentieth century we have just left has been one of the most savage in human history. Most readers are familiar with the Nazi holocaust against Jews and the genocides in Cambodia and Rwanda. Less often discussed is the rape of Nanking, where—after the Chinese city's surrender—

Masland, "For Sale," *NW* (Aug. 29, 1994), 30–31; Sharon Begley, "Chain Reaction," *NW* (July 12, 1993), 50–51; "Nuclear Challenges," *WPR* (Oct. 1995), 4. On chemical and bacteriological weapons, see "The New Face of War," *WPR* (March 1989), 11–21; "The 'Winds of Death,'" *NW* (Jan. 16, 1989), 22–25; John Barry, "Planning a Plague?" *NW* (Feb. 1, 1993), 40–41; Sharon Begley, "The Germ Warfare Alert," *NW* (Jan. 7, 1997), 25; Geoffrey Cowley and Adam Rogers, "The Terrors of Toxins," *NW* (Nov. 24, 1997), 36–37.

46. See the secular doomsday scenario in Richard Kyle, *The Last Days Are Here Again: A History of the End Times* (Grand Rapids: Baker, 1998), 172.

47. Gary Haugen, *Good News About Injustice* (Downers Grove, Ill.: InterVarsity, 1999), 111–12.

48. "Neo-Nazi Novel a Blueprint for Hate," *SPLC [Southern Poverty Law Center] Report* 25 (Sept. 1995): 1, 5. Terrorism is hardly new; anarchists bombed Wall Street in Sept. 1919, killing thirty-three people (Steven J. Keillor, *This Rebellious House: American History and the Truth of Christianity* [Downers Grove, Ill.: InterVarsity, 1996], 231).

49. *SPLC Intelligence Report* 28 (Winter 1998): 2.

50. Ancients also recognized the danger to noncombatant bystanders (e.g., Phaedrus, 1.30). For dealing with children traumatized by war, see Phyllis Kilbourn, ed., *Healing the Children of War* (Monrovia, Calif.: MARC, 1995).

women were gang-raped and killed and men were butchered for bayonet practice.[51]

One may also remember the sufferings of Korea in the twentieth century. Violating their treaty of 1882, the United States in 1905 approved Japan's annexation of Korea in return for Japan's allowing the United States to occupy the Philippines; this was viewed as Korea's first recorded subjugation in 5,000 years. Between 1941 and 1945, about 200,000 Korean women were abducted for daily rape by the occupying soldiers; after virgins became rare married women were taken. The Japanese army used these "comfort women" for "an average of twenty to thirty and up to seventy soldiers a day." Some had their breasts cut off; many committed suicide; most were slaves. At the end of the war most were "left behind to die in isolated areas or were exterminated to conceal evidence of these atrocious crimes. The soldiers had comfort women stand in open graves and then opened fire on them." About two hundred were reportedly forced into a submarine, which was then torpedoed.[52]

I have some very close, zealous Christian friends in other nations whose lives are in danger not only because of their Christian faith, but because they may belong to the "wrong" tribe or because of food or health-care shortages. Those of us who do not face such tests would be facing them if we were born in such countries; we should make good use of the blessings God has given us for his kingdom, and honor and pray for our brothers and sisters. Part of Revelation's message is the warning that all Christians must be ready to suffer. Suffering is unpleasant, but it is nearly universal, and we must be prepared for it. It is also our opportunity to prove what we are made of. How many of us are ready to cling to God's grace the way our brothers and sisters in many nations must cling? But the sufferings of Revelation 6 are in principle God's judgment call on the world, meant to vindicate rather than to crush God's true remnant.

Wars thus remind us that our "modern civilization," which so often regards with disgust the "barbarism" of ancient civilizations (and ancient writings like the Bible), remains captive to the same sinful human nature as past eras. Indeed, one could describe the twentieth century, at its beginning predicted as an apex of civilization, as one

> open-mouthed grave: an entire generation of European youth composting the World War I battlefields of Verdun and the Somme, Hitler's

---

51. See Iris Chang, *The Rape of Nanking: The Forgotten Holocaust of World War II* (Baltimore: Penguin, 1997); idem, "Exposing the Rape of Nanking," *NW* (Dec. 1, 1997), 55–57; Ralph Kinney Bennett, "The Woman Who Wouldn't Forget," *Reader's Digest* (Sept. 1998), 102–9.

52. Andrew Sung Park, *Racial Conflict and Healing: An Asian-American Theological Perspective* (Maryknoll, N.Y.: Orbis, 1996), 12–15.

six million Jews, Stalin's twenty million Soviet citizens, Mao's tens of millions of political enemies and peasant famine victims, Pol Pot's two million Cambodians, the Interhamwe's million Tutsi Rwandans, and the millions of lives wasted away during apartheid's forty-year reign.[53]

Rather than evolving morally, humanity has simply developed more effective means of killings its fellow humans than were available in the past.

Famine (6:5–6) is also one of God's frequent acts in history that serves as a wake-up call to the world. If famine and disease are less horrifying for many Western readers than they might be, it is only for lack of exposure to suffering that is a standard part of history and the present experience of tens of millions. Commenting on the black horse, Billy Graham likewise expounds at length on the terrors of famine in the modern world, noting, for instance, that "one child in three of those who survive birth in the poor countries is unhealthy because of inadequate nutrition."[54] Ron Sider retells the plaintive account of a child begging her parents to sell her to rich neighbors so she could eat.[55] At the time of this book's writing, the specter of famine is returning to the Sudan, where our Christian brothers and sisters in the south have already suffered so much.[56]

We do not have to wait for famine to strike on a large scale to imagine the effects of poverty at the present, which often go beyond food deprivation to other kinds of vulnerability. Such images remind us that our world is already a place of suffering for many people. We may think, for example, of millions of children in the world forced to live on the streets or in garbage heaps, sometimes treated as dangerous to the fabric of society.[57] Take Nahamán Carmona López, a thirteen-year-old street boy in Guatemala who, on March 4, 1990, was beaten by police. He arrived at the hospital in a coma, with "a ruptured liver, six broken ribs and bruises over 70 percent of his body. He died 10 days later."[58]

Then there was fourteen-year-old Wellington Barbosa, gunned down by an ex-cop in a busy Brazilian street; his sister, who witnessed the murder, pleaded

53. Haugen, *Injustice*, 47.

54. Graham, *Approaching Hoofbeats*, 159.

55. Sider, *Rich Christians*, 11.

56. Bruce W. Nelan, "Sudan: Why Is This Happening Again?" *Time* (July 27, 1998), 29–32. For previous famines, exacerbated by the civil war, see Bruce Bander, "Sudan's Civil War: Silent Cries to a Deaf World," *World Vision* (June 1996), 2–7.

57. For street children in India, see R. Shane Clark, *When I Grow Up: Street Children of India* (Columbus, Ga.: Positive Press, 1997). Some estimate 200 million street children around the world and suggest that at the current rate that number will be 800 million by 2020 (*Asia's Little Ones Update* 8 (Jan. 1999): 1).

58. Ron Lajoie, "Shelter from the Storm," *Amnesty Action* (Summer 1998), 6–8 (p. 6); see also *Amnesty Action* (Sept. 1991), 6.

with the reporter to take her away because she was also slated to die.[59] Death squads, roughly 70 percent of their members police officers, have sought to "clean up" the streets; in one eighteen-month period, Brazilian press reports documented at least 130 street children in Brazil murdered by police death squads, and some human rights activists there estimate such a murder every day.[60] About 200,000 children live on the streets in Brazil; sixty out of every thousand there die before their first birthday, and 7.4 million never finish elementary school. At age eleven, Derivan Ferreira Lima has worked in the sisal industry since he was five; he works twelve hours a day for the same wage as other children there—$2.50 a week. A neighbor of his lost one eye at work and then his second eye in another work accident, blind at age eight.[61] Of Brazil's work force 11.6 percent consists of 7.5 million workers below age eighteen.[62]

Likewise, missionaries in Manila noticed street girls with whom they had been working, mainly orphans and runaways, being abducted into brothels where "they would be raped several times a day." The local police would not help, because they were on the brothel's payroll; happily International Justice Mission was able to intervene on the children's behalf.[63]

Even in the United States, for that matter, there are tens of thousands of homeless children and teenagers. When I worked in a street mission in the early 1980s, I witnessed a transition from mainly men to also women and children living on the streets.[64] We also observed that many were on the streets due to mental illness, especially after federal funding for the mentally ill was cut.[65] Many children end up selling their bodies on the street to survive; mere ser-

---

59. Brook Larmer, "Dead End Kids," NW (May 25, 1992), 38–40 (p. 38).

60. Larmer, "Kids," 38; "Children of the Streets: Life and Death Among Brazil's Disposable Youth," Amnesty Action (Sept. 1990), 1, 3, including a photo of a five-year-old street girl receiving a police "mug shot." Cf. also "Armed and Dangerous," WPR (Aug. 1995), 41. For homelessness in Europe, see Pascal Privat, "Down and Out in Europe," NW (June 29, 1992), 32; "Down and Out in London," WPR (March 1994), 46–47; Peter Dammann, "St. Petersburg's Street Kids," WPR (Aug. 1992), 50.

61. "Tragedy, Success and Precocity: Brazil's 7.5 Million Young Workers," WPR (Jan. 1996), 10–12 (pp. 10–11).

62. Larmer, "Kids," 38–39. For conditions, cf. also "Wage Slaves of Brazil," WPR (Aug. 1993), 46.

63. Haugen, Injustice, 42.

64. See William L. Chaze, "Behind Swelling Ranks of America's Street People," USNWR (Jan. 30, 1984), 57–58; idem, "Helping the Homeless: A Fight Against Despair," USNWR (Jan. 14, 1985), 54–55; Muriel Dobbin, "The Coming of the 'Couch People,'" USNWR (Aug. 3, 1987), 19–21; "Hard Times," NW (March 21, 1988), 46–58; Beth Spring, "Home, Street Home," CT (April 21, 1989), 15–20; David Gelman, "Some Really Good Scouts" (on homeless girls), NW (Jan. 14, 1991), 58.

65. For the strains producing and produced by homelessness, see Donald Baumann and Charles Grigsby, Understanding the Homeless (Austin: Hogg Foundation for Mental Health, Uni-

mons against prostitution cannot prove effective if they come from churches uninvolved with the needs of the poor in their communities.[66] Christians can, however, work for justice, as when they secured the arrest of two New Orleans police officers who had raped a teenage runaway, or, over a century ago, Christian activist Katherine Bushnell's successful fight against police-protected, forced child prostitution in northern Michigan and Wisconsin mining towns.[67]

Plagues are also a continuing part of life in the 1990s, though in the West we have tried to sanitize them away. We need not hark back to the fourteenth century, when the "Black Death" (bubonic plague) killed 30 percent of Europe's population, carried by a type of flea infesting the black rats that were then everywhere.[68] God was working during this time, but the Black Death whipped up an apocalyptic frenzy.[69] We may think in our own society of the million or more people who are currently HIV-positive and who will ultimately die of AIDS unless God heals them or they die of something else first.[70] In Japan a cult released deadly nerve poison in a subway; intelligence officials have intercepted people who wished to release deadly plagues such as anthrax here.[71]

---

versity of Texas, 1988); for the lifestyle of the mentally ill on the streets, see Pamela Diamond and Steven Schnee, *Lives in the Shadows* (Austin: Hogg Foundation for Mental Health, University of Texas, 1991); for an account of how a person could become homeless, see further Marie James and Jane Hertenstein, *Orphan Girl: The Memoir of a Chicago Bag Lady* (Chicago: Cornerstone, 1997).

66. See moving accounts in Mary Rose McGeady, *God's Lost Children* (New York: Covenant House, 1991); idem, *Does God Still Love Me? Letters from the Street* (New York: Covenant House, 1995); idem, *Please Help Me, God* (New York: Covenant House, 1997); Bruce Ritter, *Sometimes God Has a Kid's Face* (New York: Covenant House, 1988). For some further solutions, see Larry Wilson and Alice Shabecoff, "Three Ways Your Church Can Help the Homeless," *World Vision* (Oct. 1994), 17–19; Ronald J. Sider, "Homelessness and Public Policy," *World Christian* (Jan. 1990), 28–33.

67. Haugen, *Injustice*, 40–41, 53–55; cf. also an Alabama minister's opposition to the exploitation of child laborers in the early twentieth century (55–57).

68. See Vicki Arnold, "Black Death Was Unparalleled for Panic and Fear," *Duke Dialogue* (Dec. 11, 1987), 1, 5, summarizing the course taught by Duke University historian Tom Robisheaux; Mark Galli, "When a Third of the World Died," *Christian History* 49 (1996): 36–39.

69. On God's work, see "Wycliffe's England: A Time of Turmoil," *Christian History* 2/2 (1983): 6–9, 8; on the apocalyptic frenzy, Kyle, *The Last Days*, 51.

70. At the current rate of increase, AIDS will be the country's leading killer of young men (*NW* [July 19, 1993], 8; cf. "AIDS: At the Dawn of Fear," *USNWR* [Jan. 12, 1987], 60–70; "Surviving the Second Wave," *NW* [Sept. 19, 1994], 50–51). It has become a major threat to heterosexual women as well (Muriel Whetstone, "The Increasing Threat to Black Women," *Ebony* [April 1994], 118–20; "Danger Signs," *NW* [March 21, 1994], 70).

71. On the sarin attack in Japan, see "A Cloud of Terror—and Suspicion," *NW* (April 3, 1995), 36–41. For arrests in the U.S., see *NW* (May 29, 1995), 4; in the event of foreign terrorism, see "Fears of Bio-Warfare," *NW* (Aug. 27, 1990), 4; Barry, "Planning a Plague?" *NW* (Feb. 1, 1993), 40; Begley, "Germ Warfare Alert," *NW* (Jan. 7, 1997), 25.

God does use plagues to get our attention. One Sunday I felt led to preach about sexual sin, and many people repented of sexual sin that day. Not current on the news, I later learned why the Lord had led me to preach that message on that particular Sunday: Magic Johnson had just announced that he was HIV-positive, and many of the people who came forward that day were particularly receptive.

Those of us who share these texts with others have a moral responsibility to do our best to avoid being misinterpreted. Such plagues are wake-up calls to humanity, but we must remember that they are judgments against societies, not necessarily against individuals. Because innocent sufferers often hear our blanket statements about judgment as personal condemnations, we should always make clear what we already know, that not everyone who suffers is experiencing personal judgment.[72]

For example, many have contracted HIV through blood transfusions, often because of hemophilia. This includes one of the first widely publicized AIDS cases, Ryan White, a fourteen-year-old Christian. Mention can also be made of Steve Sawyer, who now spends his final years in Campus Crusade proclaiming the gospel to thousands of college students; or the daughter-in-law of a former president of the Southern Baptist Convention, whose two children also died with her.[73] Some Christian women in Uganda have died of AIDS precisely because they remained sexually faithful to sexually unfaithful husbands, and that nation faces tens of thousands of new orphans through AIDS.[74] We must hear in the world's suffering not condemnation of suffering individuals but, on a larger scale, God's calling for the world's attention.

Christian response. What should be our response to such suffering? (1) In the light of Revelation, we recognize that famine is a corporate judgment (on societies, not individuals), one of God's methods for waking up an unrepen-

---

72. Churches should be taking the lead in ministering to AIDS victims; see "Churches Urged to Lead the Way in AIDS Care," *CT* (June 17, 1988), 58; "The Church's Response to AIDS," *CT* (Nov. 22, 1985), 50–51; Andrés Tapia, "High-risk Ministry," *CT* (Aug. 7, 1987), 15–19; "Joining the AIDS Fight," *NW* (April 17, 1989), 26–27; Doug Murren, "What the Church Should Do About AIDS," *Ministries Today* (May 1992), 53–55, and other articles in that issue.

73. Edward Gilbreath, "Insider Turned Out," *CT* (Feb. 5, 1996), 35–36; Erik Segalini, "Dying to Tell You," *Worldwide Challenge* (July 1998), 22–25. Ryan attended St. Luke's United Methodist Church in Kokomo, Indiana, where he found acceptance (*Pentecostal Evangel* [March 22, 1987], 27).

74. See "AIDS in Africa," *CT* (April 8, 1988), 36–40; "Of Orphans and AIDS," *WPR* (March 1991), 34; "Scared Celibate," *WPR* (Sept. 1993), 46; Ken Sidey, "AIDS Reshapes Africa's Future," *CT* (Oct. 22, 1990), 47–49; Ginni Freshour, "AIDS in Uganda," *InterVarsity* (Fall 1994), 16–17; "Making Men Listen," *NW* (Sept. 25, 1995), 52; esp. "The War Against HIV," *CT* (April 4, 1994), 70–73.

tant world. But believers in wealthier countries dare not stop with this observation: The text provides no exemption for any nations, and all peoples are in principle susceptible to this judgment, especially those so arrogant as to suppose that it cannot happen to them (18:7–8). Even God's people were subject to such judgments (e.g., 2 Sam. 21:1; 24:13); how much more a nation whose official public religion has become secularism. Those who denied that such sufferings would come on God's people regularly appear in the Bible as false prophets (Jer. 5:12; 14:13–16). God often warned of famine in advance so people could prepare for it (Gen. 41:28–36; Acts 11:28–30).

(2) We must do our best to serve and empower those who are truly impoverished through circumstances beyond their control. Some skeptics of Christianity have asked whether Christians can work against plagues and famines when they believe these hardships to be judgments sent by their God.[75] But John the Baptist and James the Lord's brother, both prophets of judgment, define true repentance before God by our commitment to care for others' needs (Luke 3:11; James 2:14–17). Jesus spoke of giving up possessions as much as proves necessary to care for others' needs, because our brothers and sisters matter more than possessions do (Luke 12:33; 14:33). Unlike the rich man who was judged for letting Lazarus starve at his doorstep, however (16:25), few of us could be judged for letting a poor person starve at our doorstep—but only because in our society we would not let someone that poor get near our doorstep.

We remain responsible, once we know their need, to supply whatever necessary for believers in famine-stricken areas of the world, trusting that if possible, they will also help us in our hour of need (2 Cor. 8:13–15). To be sure, some American congregations will not want to hear such a message any more than John's or Jesus' hearers did, but to deny our personal responsibility for the poor is to deny Scripture.[76] Selective theological liberalism is no less liberalism because it picks and chooses which Scriptures it will obey; it is simply more hypocritical because it pretends to affirm Scripture when in fact it believes only those portions it finds convenient. Such selective piety gives occasion to the Lord's enemies to blaspheme (cf. 2 Sam. 12:14).

In his comments on this passage Billy Graham warns that if we do not heed, our own lifestyles one day "will be spread before us in judgment."[77]

---

75. Philosopher Albert Camus posed a moral dilemma: Should a Christian combat a plague God had sent? But the Bible answers with the character of Jesus, who sacrificially provided healing (Matt. 8:16–17) and resources (Mark 6:38–42).

76. See also the radical demands of leaders in earlier revivals, such as John Wesley (Theodore W. Jennings Jr., *Good News to the Poor: John Wesley's Evangelical Economics* [Nashville: Abingdon, 1990]) and Charles Finney (*Lectures on Revivals of Religion* [New York: Revell, 1869], 53, 127).

77. Graham, *Approaching Hoofbeats*, 159.

Russell Chandler comments on the inequitable distribution of resources even in our own country, where 1 percent of the households "hold one-third of all our country's personal wealth." Although there is much truth in the dictum that diligence pays off (cf. Prov. 10:4), one might be tempted to entertain some skepticism that this 1 percent has worked harder than most of the rest of the country put together.[78] Evangelical organizations like World Vision, Food for the Hungry, and the Salvation Army can make excellent use of development funds donated to them. Chandler suggests that if all church members tithed, we would be able to "eliminate the worst of world poverty," have seventeen billion dollars for domestic need, and enough left over to maintain "church activities at current levels."[79]

Yet one wonders if, apart from a true revival, churches will use God's funds in such productive ways. Currently, 99.9 percent of our budgets are spent on ourselves or other churches; of eight billion dollars allotted for missions worldwide, less than one tenth of 1 percent is directed toward reaching the non-Christian world.[80] How would Jesus, who focused on the unevangelized and outcasts of his day and fed the hungry crowds, evaluate our priorities?

Even when we do our best, however, Revelation reminds us that in this age suffering is often God's calling for the world's attention, even when we do not choose to listen (9:20–21).

---

78. Chandler, *Racing Towards 2001*, 30.
79. Ibid., 220.
80. Ibid., 223.

Revelation 6:9-17

WHEN HE OPENED the fifth seal, I saw under the altar the souls of those who had been slain because of the word of God and the testimony they had maintained. ¹⁰They called out in a loud voice, "How long, Sovereign Lord, holy and true, until you judge the inhabitants of the earth and avenge our blood?" ¹¹Then each of them was given a white robe, and they were told to wait a little longer, until the number of their fellow servants and brothers who were to be killed as they had been was completed.

¹²I watched as he opened the sixth seal. There was a great earthquake. The sun turned black like sackcloth made of goat hair, the whole moon turned blood red, ¹³and the stars in the sky fell to earth, as late figs drop from a fig tree when shaken by a strong wind. ¹⁴The sky receded like a scroll, rolling up, and every mountain and island was removed from its place.

¹⁵Then the kings of the earth, the princes, the generals, the rich, the mighty, and every slave and every free man hid in caves and among the rocks of the mountains. ¹⁶They called to the mountains and the rocks, "Fall on us and hide us from the face of him who sits on the throne and from the wrath of the Lamb! ¹⁷For the great day of their wrath has come, and who can stand?"

Original Meaning

WITHIN THE SEVEN seals, the four horsemen (6:1–8) form a unit and the seventh (8:1) is separated from its predecessors by a lengthy digression (7:1–17); this leaves us the fifth and sixth seals to treat together in the present chapter. The fifth seal presents the martyrs who have suffered at the hands of a hostile world for their message about Jesus Christ, crying out for vindication; the sixth seal portrays the fate of the world at the hands of the Lord, whose agents they martyred. Together these testimonies provide a strong encouragement to believers that we should stand as witnesses regardless of what opposition we may face.[1]

---

1. Similarly, sinners assume that the death of the righteous is their end in 1 En. 102:6–8, but God encourages the righteous (102:4) and in the end destroys sinners (103).

The Fifth Seal (6:9–11)

JOHN SEES SOULS under the altar, martyrs for their testimony.[2] The martyrs cry out for vindication: "How long?"[3] Because they had been condemned to death in human courts, they now awaited vindication from God's own court; in ancient law, a plaintiff normally pleaded his own case, so if the judge— earthly or heavenly—failed to vindicate the plaintiff, this silence functioned as a de facto approval of the defendant.[4] As current plaintiffs, the martyrs sought vindication from the heavenly judge.

"How long?" is a typical plea for God's swift intervention in biblical prayers (e.g., Ps. 79:5; Isa. 6:11; Jer. 47:6; Hab. 1:2; Zech. 1:12). Thus in 4 Ezra the righteous ask, "How long?" and the archangel Jeremiel responds, "When the number is complete" (4 Ezra 4:33–37). Like them, the storehouses that keep them are eager for the end, waiting to hand them over for resurrection (4 Ezra 4:41–42).[5] An earlier tradition assures the righteous dead to continue crying out for judgment, for God will avenge them and give them great reward (1 Enoch 104:3–4).

That the full number of martyrs had to be completed before the end was probably a familiar apocalyptic theme to the churches in Asia (1 Enoch 47:2– 4; 4 Ezra 4:35–37).[6] More than this, it reflects biblical sensibilities about justice and the cost of the gospel. God did not allow the Israelites to slaughter the Canaanites until the sin of the latter had become so perverse that the slaughter would function as a corporate capital punishment (Gen. 15:16); full judgment did not fall on Jerusalem until descendants of those who had killed the prophets had climaxed this heritage by killing God's own Son (Matt. 23:31–32; Mark 12:4–8).[7] Further, while Jesus paid the price for the world's

---

2. Many apocalyptic visions also allowed the seers to view disembodied "souls," e.g., Apoc. Mos. 13:6; 32:4; T. Job 52:9/4; Apoc. Paul 13. Aune, *Revelation*, 2:404 cites Greek traditions about the visibility of the soul. Cf. a celestial altar in Aratus, *Phaen.* 403.

3. As the only prayer for supplication in Revelation, 6:9–11 is significant for the entire book; cf. J. P. Heil, "The Fifth Seal (Rev 6,9–11) as a Key to the Book of Revelation," *Biblica* 74 (1993): 220–43.

4. Caird, *Commentary on Revelation*, 85.

5. In Revelation as opposed to 4 Ezra, the storehouses are above rather than below; but 4 Ezra compares eagerness for the consummation with a woman in travail (4 Ezra 4:41–42), as Paul had much earlier (Rom. 8:22–23, 26). In 3 Enoch 44:7–8 the righteous dead cry out "How long?" and learn that the evil of the wicked delays the kingdom.

6. Cf. also 1 Enoch 89:68–69; 2 Bar. 23:3–5. The suffering of the righteous often characterizes the end time in Jewish texts (e.g., T. Moses 8:4; *m. Sot.* 9:15; *b. Ket.* 112b).

7. The metaphoric image of "filling up a measure" (also 1 Thess. 2:16) is an old one in Greek literature (Homer, *Il.* 8.354; 11.263; Apollonius Rhodius, 1.1035, 1323); Jews also spoke of the appointed period of one's life being "filled" (cf. 1 Chron. 17:11; T. Abr. 1 B). Both emphasize the sovereignty of God or (in the pagan view) fate.

sins, his messengers share in his sufferings in the sense that they bring that message to a still hostile world (Col. 1:24).

Earlier biblical prophets had predicted the witness of God's people to the nations (e.g., Isa. 42:1, 6; 43:10–12; 44:8; 49:6), the conversion of the nations (Isa. 19:19–25; Jer. 3:17; Zech. 2:11; 8:22–23), and the suffering of God's people in the end time (Dan. 7:21). The vision in Revelation 6:9–11, however, connects these three themes (as in Mark 13:9–10); the suffering witness of believers is a necessary prerequisite for the fullness of the Gentiles to come in from among the nations, the event followed by the final turning of Jewish people to faith in Jesus (cf. Rom. 11:25–27).[8] All peoples must be evangelized before the end (Matt. 24:14; 2 Peter 3:9–12; cf. Rev. 7:9). Bauckham declares this to be the heart of Revelation and the climax of biblical prophecy:

> Whereas the prophets had predicted the conversion of all the nations
> . . . and obscurely foreseen the oppression of God's people by pagan
> power in the last days, John's prophecy reveals that the former is to be
> the consequence of the latter, and that the key to both is the task of
> faithful witness in the face of opposition . . .[9]

The position of these martyrs "under the altar" undoubtedly recalls the place where priests poured the blood (hence the "life"—Lev. 17:11) of their sacrifices (e.g., Lev. 4:7, 18, 25, 34; 5:9; 8:15; 9:9).[10] Pagan tradition sometimes metaphorically compared violent deaths with sacrifices, but Jewish tradition especially developed the image, arguing that martyrs could help expiate God's anger against the people as a whole (4 Macc. 9:24).[11] Jewish tradition recognized that the martyrs were with God and at peace (Wisd. 3:1–3) and were sacrifices accepted by God (3:6). Here in Revelation the sacrifices are not vicarious per se, but the martyrs do share in Christ's sacrificial suffering; they are allies of the sacrificed Lamb of 5:6, 9 and will also share his exaltation (3:21; 20:4). They are "sacrifices offered to God. In fact, they were slain on earth . . . but in Christian faith the sacrifice was really made in heaven, where their souls—their lives—were offered at the heavenly altar."[12]

---

8. David Wenham, *The Rediscovery of Jesus' Eschatological Discourse*, vol. 4 of *Gospel Perspectives* (Sheffield: JSOT, 1984), 208, finds in Rev. 6:11 an allusion to the tradition in Luke 21:24, the fulfilling of the times of the Gentiles.

9. Bauckham, *Climax of Prophecy*, xvi.

10. Caird, *Commentary on Revelation*, 84. The later rabbinic tradition linking burial in the land with burial under the altar (e.g., Ford, *Revelation*, 110) merely illustrates rabbinic emphasis on the holiness of the land; more tellingly, all souls were under the throne of glory (*ARN* 12A; 25, §51B), in God's treasuries (2 Bar. 30:2).

11. Sallust, *Letter to Caesar* 4.2; Livy, 10.38.11; Phaedrus, 4.6.9; Josephus, *Ant.* 17.237. Cf. likewise Phil. 2:17; 2 Tim. 4:6; Ignatius, *Rom.* 4.2; possibly T. Moses 9.

12. Ladd, *The Last Things*, 39.

Although they are told to wait, they receive divine assurance (6:11). The passive voice in "was given" suggests that God himself rewards them with white robes (see comment on 4:4), and that he himself responds to their plea.[13] They should "rest" until that time (cf. 14:13). "A little longer" is indeterminate by human time, measured only by God's standards (cf. 10:6; 12:12; 17:10; 20:3), but nevertheless functions as an assurance that the time is finite, hence it will not prove too long for them to bear.

The Sixth Seal (6:12–17)

THE SIXTH SEAL portrays the end of the cosmos as humanity knows it. Far from merely a repeatable judgment within history, like the four riders (6:1–8), this judgment includes the dissolution of the heavens (6:12–14) and the world finally recognizing that it stands under its Creator's wrath (6:16–17).

This graphic portrayal of destruction opens with an earthquake (6:12), which is part of the moving of the mountains (6:14) beneath which the wicked seek to flee (6:15–16). Ancient writers sometimes depicted earthquakes in exaggerated language, declaring, for example, that they could "make mountains collapse."[14] Jewish writers also used similar poetic language for cataclysmic events other than the end of the age (Jer. 4:24; 8:16; Mic. 1:4).[15] But this earthquake seems to be no exaggeration: It is the climactic, eschatological earthquake that truly removes mountains (Rev. 11:13; 16:18; cf. Ps. 97:5; Ezek. 38:19–20; Zech. 14:5), which often appears in Jewish scenes of the end (1 Enoch 1:6–7; 53:7; 4 Ezra 6:13–16; T. Moses 10:4).[16] Yet God's faithfulness to his elect (7:17) overshadows any terror of earthquakes (Isa. 54:10). Because some of the cities whose churches are addressed in Revelation had been devastated by earthquakes only a few decades earlier, this image probably proved particularly graphic and terrifying for them (as in Sib. Or. 5.291).[17]

13. The "white" may reflect those purified by tribulation (Dan. 11:35; see Beale, *Revelation*, 394, 437).

14. See Livy, 22.5.8. The earthquakes in Isa. 5:25 and Sib. Or. 5.438–39 may represent war; cf. the locust armies in Joel 2:10.

15. It also resembles the Sinai theophany (Ex. 19:16–18; Hab. 3:6, 10; Ps-Philo 11:5; 23:10); earthquakes were often judgments within history (Sib. Or. 1.187; 3.449–59). Cf. the apparently eschatological language for a past event in Sib. Or. 3.286–92.

16. On the eschatological earthquake, see further Richard Bauckham, "The Eschatological Earthquake in the Apocalypse of John," *NovT* 19 (1977): 224–33. The collapse of creation to its original formlessness (Gen. 1:2) is a sign of judgment (cf. Jer. 4:23; 1QM 17.4); the end-time earthquake in 1 Enoch 1:6–7 recalls the quaking at Sinai (1:4–5).

17. See Bauckham, *Climax of Prophecy*, 206–7. Pagans also generally regarded earthquakes as portents of judgment (Ovid, *Metam.* 15.798; Pausanias, 7.24.6), though some explained them as purely natural phenomena (Diodorus Siculus, 15.48.3–4; Diogenes Laertius, 7.1.154; 10.105).

Discoloration or eclipsing of the sun or moon symbolized terrifying judgments both among Jews and pagans.[18] Ancient texts occasionally employ
the disappearing of stars, formation of islands, and so forth, as metaphoric
images for traumas in past history (Sib. Or. 4.58–60); Revelation (Rev. 12:7)
or Jewish texts (Sib. Or. 5.512–31) sometimes speak of celestial disruptions
in terms of spiritual conflict in the heavens.[19] But that is not the usual significance of this imagery, and the image here is worse than a mere eclipse;
especially in this kind of literature, the conjunction of various celestial signs
normally points to the end of the age, when the sun and moon will be darkened (Isa. 13:9–11; 24:21–23; 1 En. 102:2–3).[20]

The rolling up of the heavens "like a scroll" (6:14) comes from day of the
Lord images in Isaiah 34:4, referring to the cosmic judgment when God punishes the wicked nations, a text in which heaven's hosts also wither like a leaf
on a fig tree (cf. Rev. 6:13).[21] For most of Revelation's audience, the picture
likely evoked the mundane image of reading a scroll, which one would typically unroll with the right hand while with the left one rolled up what one
had just finished reading.[22] But the mundane image here translates into one
of terror for humanity! Earlier texts had used this image of the heavens being
rolled up like a scroll (Sib. Or. 3.82) to emphasize God's sovereignty over the
heavens (3.81) and that the entire dome of heaven would collapse on the
earth (3.83), as the entire universe unraveled at its seams (3.80).[23]

---

18. E.g., Livy, 37.4.3; Diodorus Siculus, 20.5.5; Dio Cassius, 57.4.4; *tos. Suk.* 2:6. Some,
however, gave them purely naturalistic explanations as generally today (Livy, 44.37.6–7;
Pliny, *N.H.* 2.6.47; Diogenes Laertius, 10.114–15).

19. Even if angels are in view here (cf. 12:4), it is presumably because they are linked
with the stars (Isa. 24:21); for astral battles, cf. Judg. 5:20; Sib. Or. 5.211–13, 512–31.
Islands would include those with exiles (1:9). Beale, *Revelation*, 397, notes that many of the
Old Testament allusions reflect temporal judgment on a sinful nation; but we regard the con-
fluence of images as finally eschatological for most first-century readers. Aune, *Revelation*,
2:415, cites ancient texts in which falling stars were simply signs of impending temporal
judgment; but most of these are either poetic, refer to only some stars, or would be understood differently by the first century.

20. Cf. Isa. 50:3; Joel 2:10, 31; see further 4 Ezra 7:38–42; Sib. Or. 1.200–202; 3.800–
804; 5.476–84; 8.190–93, 204; T. Mos. 10:5; analogous irregularities in 4 Ezra 5:4–5 may
reflect the Roman tradition of portents (cf. Livy, 29.14.3).

21. The looseness of unripe, green figs would have been an image with which most
people in the Mediterranean world would have been familiar. See Mounce, *Revelation*, 161
n. 35; F. F. Bruce, *The New Testament Documents: Are They Reliable?* 5th ed. (Grand Rapids: Eerdmans, 1980), 73–74.

22. Milligan, *Thessalonians*, 124. Ford suggests the clatter of metal scrolls like Qumran's
copper scroll (Ford, *Revelation*, 100).

23. For geographical upheavals in the eschatological time, see also Sib. Or. 3.680–86;
5.447–83.

The passage also indicates that it is ultimately loyalty to Jesus Christ, not social status, that determines one's fate. Ancients sometimes summarized humankind by simply contrasting opposites, for example, "slave and free";[24] death would annul such distinctions (Job 3:19). But John lists the entire social order in verse 15, emphasizing that no marks of distinction will exempt anyone from judgment—from the "divine" Caesar on down.[25]

In 6:15–17 Revelation recalls an image of inescapable judgment from Hosea 10:8 (where fugitives from God's wrath plead for hills and mountains to cover them; cf. Luke 23:30) and Isaiah 2:19 (where people flee to caves and holes in the ground in the day of God's wrath; cf. 2:10).[26] Caves and mountain clefts (6:15) were useful for hiding from human enemies, and Christians in Sardis could have thought of the cave-tombs of the mountain facing their acropolis.[27] But such sites would prove utterly futile in obstructing the One who moved whole mountains in his wrath (6:14).[28]

The flight of these people from God's wrath in the heavens may reflect the destruction of the heavens (6:12–14), but it also suggests some sort of image that reveals the coming of God and the Lamb in the sky (cf. Matt. 24:30).[29] Lambs were considered among the most docile creatures (Isa. 11:6; Sir. 13:17); hence "wrath of the Lamb" is a striking and terrifying image. Note that those who have not yet repented, who seek refuge from caves and mountains, do not cry out to God or the Lamb for mercy; it is now too late for that (cf. 1 En. 50:2–5; 63:1–12).

The final image of the sixth seal, in which the disobedient to God's will cry out, "Who can stand [in the day of wrath]?" (6:17, adapting the language of Joel 2:11, which follows the cosmic judgment image of Joel 2:10; cf. also

---

24. See Demosthenes, *Against Phormio* 31; Cornelius Nepos, 2.6.5.

25. Many texts list similar distinctions (e.g., Plato, *Theaetetus* 175A; T. Abr. 19A). God's judgment against the powerful (e.g., 1 Enoch 48:8; 54:2; 62:3–12; Sib. Or. 5.380) emphasizes his power and the pretentiousness of their arrogance.

26. Other texts speak of the wicked unsuccessfully desiring to hide at the judgment (Sir. 16:17–19; 1 Enoch 104:5; Sib. Or. 5.273), some making allusion to Isa. 2:18–20 (Sib. Or. 3.606–7). Universal fear would characterize this time (cf. Isa. 2:19–21; 1 Enoch 1:5; Sib. Or. 3.679).

27. On the caves in Sardis' Necropolis, see Hemer, *Letters to the Seven Churches*, 140. One might hide beneath a hollow rock (Ovid, *Metam.* 9.211). Although it is probably not John's own focus, former pagans in his audience may have seen in 6:15 judgment on their deities as in Ex. 12:12; mountains, for instance, were reputed dwellings of Pan (Dionysius of Halicarnassus, 1.38.1).

28. One might hide in caves even from human aggressors, yet die by other means (Ezek. 33:27).

29. In some Jewish traditions, God's face might appear at the judgment (Sib. Or. 3.556–61); an image in the sky functioned as a terrible portent of doom (Herodian, 8.3.8–9).

Mal. 3:2), prepares the reader for the answer that comes in the following vision: The servants of God can stand in that day (7:1–17).[30] They can stand during the plagues within history (7:3), which in turn provides an assurance that God will be with them at the close of the age.

SPEEDING THE END. When we say that the good news of God's kingdom must be proclaimed among all nations before the kingdom actually comes (Matt. 24:14), how do we quantify the completion of such a task? Some have classified unreached people groups (a project helpful for missionary activity), but the New Testament does not expend much energy defining the size or parameters of a "people group." Perhaps only Jesus' return will verify that we have sufficiently completed the job of evangelizing the world; the fact that he has not yet come indicates that we have not yet completed the task. If we genuinely "look forward to the day of God," we can "speed its coming" (2 Peter 3:12) by attending to God's agendas; that day is delayed because God wants "everyone to come to repentance" (3:9). Revelation warns us, however, that our task will be finished only at a great price to ourselves. The fifth seal warns, however, that we cannot value our lives or possessions and yet complete the task; we cannot have one foot in Babylon with the other in the heavenly city.

The nature of the martyrs' prayers. The martyrs in this passage, like some righteous sufferers in the Old Testament (1 Sam. 24:12; 2 Chron. 24:22; Ps. 79:10; Jer. 18:21), cry out for vengeance.[31] Jesus, however, teaches us to pray for those who persecute us (Matt. 5:44; Acts 7:60), and contrary to what sometimes constitutes our natural tendencies, he probably did not intend us to pray, "Lord, please strike them dead!" How can we as responsible interpreters harmonize both biblical teachings? Jesus also spoke of the blood of martyrs crying out, from the blood of Abel (Gen. 4:10) to that of Zechariah (2 Chron. 24:20–22; Matt. 23:35); a tradition about the latter complains that God especially judged the temple because Zechariah's killers failed to treat his blood as respectfully as they would have treated

---

30. Various texts emphasize God's incomparable greatness in contrast to human mortality by asking who may stand in God's presence (Ps. 76:7; 130:3; Jer. 49:19; 50:44), some with reference to his day of wrath (Nah. 1:6; Mal. 3:2; 2 Bar. 48:17; Apoc. Zeph. 12:7).

31. Cf. also prayers for corporate judgment in early Judaism, e.g., 1 Enoch 9:10; 84:6; 95:2; 99:3; 1QM 12.11–12; CIJ, 1:524, §725; also Deissmann, *Light From the Ancient Past,* 413–24. Greeks readily prayed for others' destruction (Walter Burkert, *Greek Religion,* tr. J. Raffan [Cambridge, Mass.: Harvard Univ. Press, 1985], 75; Aune, *Revelation,* 2:409).

sacrifices.[32] And Jesus' own blood would also demand vindication (Matt. 23:30–32; 27:25); such sentiments appear elsewhere in the New Testament as well (Luke 18:7; 2 Tim. 4:14).

The very suffering of the righteous cries out for vengeance (cf. 1 En. 47:1), and the cry of the martyrs here is ultimately a cry for justice, a plea for vindication, answered in God's judgments on a sinful world (Rev. 8:4–6; 16:6) and ultimately by his final judgment (6:12–17; 18:21, 24; 19:2). Releasing the debts of our individual enemies does not mean that we need to quit hoping for vindication, *provided that* we are hoping more for that vindication by their personal repentance rather than their deaths, for God himself prefers their repentance (Ezek. 18:23). In contrast to the one-sided ethics of many Christians today, this is a cry for justice and the overthrow of evil, a New Testament as well as Old Testament concept.[33]

Earthquakes, stars, and cosmic collapse. The way we apply the principles in the text will depend on the culture for which we are contextualizing it. In traditional Shona culture, for instance, earthquakes are caused by God walking in the earth, and some other tribes traditionally attribute earthquakes to special deities.[34] In such a context, announcing God's sovereignty over the earth (6:12) may be paramount. Such a message of God's control over earthquakes may likewise prove encouraging to Christians living near the San Andreas fault in California. "God just clapped his hands," announced one witness of the Bay area earthquake of 1989 that claimed fifty-five lives and billions of dollars in property damage.[35] Because John's ancient Asian audience knew and feared earthquakes, such an image of judgment, though expected in any case from the Old Testament prophets, would prove particularly unnerving.

Relating the image to analogous modern images of fear (especially geographically relevant ones) will help translate the image for today's

---

32. See *Pes. Rab Kah.* 15:7. See in more detail Keener, *Matthew* (Downers Grove, Ill.: InterVarsity, 1997), 341.

33. See here Michaels, *Revelation*, 108. For judgment as liberation, see Stephen Hre Kio, "The Exodus Symbol of Liberation in the Apocalypse and Its Relevance for Some Aspects of Translation," *BibTrans* 40 (Jan. 1989): 120–35; for Revelation's value for the oppressed, see Christopher Rowland, "Keeping Alive the Dangerous Vision of a World of Peace and Justice," *Concilium* 200 (1988): 75–86.

34. John S. Mbiti, *African Religions and Philosophies* (Garden City, N.Y.: Doubleday, 1970), 70. Greeks typically attributed earthquakes to Poseidon (Pausanias, 7.24.6), the "Earth-Shaker" (hundreds of times in ancient literature [e.g., Homer, *Il.* 7.445; 20.13; *Od.* 1.74]); sometimes to Zeus (*Orphic Hymn* 15.8); but some attributed them to natural causes (Diodorus Siculus, 15.48.3–4; Diogenes Laertius, 7.1.154; 10.105).

35. "After the Shock," *NW* (Oct. 30, 1989), 22–27, 22. One fifty-seven-year-old survivor's rescue after ninety hours of being buried alive elicited his ex-wife's praise to God ("Out of the Ruins, a Miracle," *NW* [Oct. 30, 1989], 32).

audience.[36] But ultimately Revelation portrays the final earthquake and the terror that awaits the unrepentant world just before the coming of Christ. Thus, the most central application is to take courage that God will vindicate his suffering saints (6:9–11) and make the world recognize the Creator they have spurned (6:12–17).

One need not be an astronomer to understand that the ancient images of stars falling to earth (6:13) are physically impossible. All stars would have to become black holes to fit on earth, and then trillions of them would have to hurl, at millions of times the speed of light, into the earth's surface; no one could live long enough to lament their misery as in 6:16–17.

Yet in merely beginning to imagine such a scenario we have experienced some of the terror that may have seized ancient hearers; the evocative effect is roughly equivalent. As in other ancient texts (which occasionally reapplied such images for local judgments within history, as noted above), the specific images contributed to the overall picture of the dissolution of the cosmos as we know it, the reversal of creation. The impact on the reader is to be complete: There is no security, no firm ground to stand on, nothing in the universe to depend on except God himself. The rest of creation will collapse.

AVAILABLE AS SACRIFICES. The invitation to be available as sacrifices to God by martyrdom takes exhortations such as the call to be "living sacrifices" (Rom. 12:1) to their logical conclusion. Although the world persecutes Christ's witnesses (as the fifth seal testifies), God will vindicate them (as the sixth seal confirms); therefore we should witness boldly. Yet in the United States, it is often my experience that Christians are complacent, satisfied with their own conversion and personal "growth." As I witness to members of various cults like Mormons, I often find a greater commitment to spreading their message—though it is a false gospel—than I find among most evangelical churchgoers.[37]

Cultists' biblical arguments are usually easy to refute, but how does one respond to the complaints of cult members who are former evangelicals (like the Jehovah's Witness I shared Christ with today) who for the first time

---

36. See, e.g., "Bracing for the Big One," *NW* (Oct. 30, 1989), 28–32; "Coping with Quake Fear," *NW* (Oct. 30, 1989), 42–47; "The Quake's Fearful Wake," *NW* (Jan. 8, 1990), 54. Many areas of the U.S. are currently vulnerable to quakes; see the charts and data in "'Any Old Day Now . . . ,'" *NW* (Jan. 30, 1995), 28.

37. For that matter, those who market secular products like Coca-Cola often work more strategically than Christians seeking to propagate the gospel (see Paul Eshleman with Carolyn E. Phillips, *I Just Saw Jesus* [Laguna Niguel, Calif.: The Jesus Project, 1985], 173–74).

learned a form of "discipleship" in a cult? While I was a graduate student, I helped some students out of the extremist International Churches of Christ movement. But I could offer only a little consolation as they afterward struggled to find sound churches with the same degree of fervor and fellowship they found in their ICC church. The fellowship at the sectarian church may have been insincere (immediately terminated upon their withdrawal) and much of the discipleship based on selective use of proof texts; but their zeal bore more resemblance to early Christianity (at least outwardly) than most complacent churches I know.[38]

On several occasions in street ministry I have been beaten or had my life threatened. On one occasion on Flatbush Avenue in Brooklyn I was urging a man that Jesus was the only way to be reconciled to God when finally, in anger, he announced that he had a gun and was going to kill me. "You talk about heaven," he charged. "We'll see how ready you are to die." I responded that I knew where I was going, but I would prefer to stay alive longer to keep witnessing to people like him. After a few more threats he walked away, and the next night even returned to apologize and say that he and his wife wanted to visit the church I was working with. But the danger had been a real one, and that summer of witnessing in 1986 could have been my last. When some in my Revelation class were getting nervous about the possibilities of martyrdom, Emmanuel Itapson, a minister from northern Nigeria, explained that martyrdom looks small when you actually face it. If we have proved our faithfulness in most of the tests we face today, we will have practiced for bigger tests if they come.

In the late nineteenth century, Hudson Taylor, in seeking more recruits for his mission to raise up culturally sensitive indigenous Chinese churches, claimed that those he needed were "men and women . . . such as will put Jesus, China, souls, first and foremost in everything and at every time—even life itself must be secondary."[39] Such a commitment was bound to be tested in time. The Boxer Rebellion of 1900, responding to the insensitivity of Westerners in general, slaughtered 188 Protestant missionaries and 30,000 Chinese Christians. Yet this slaughter led to "threefold church growth in the next decade."[40] Cross-cultural missionaries sometimes face martyrdom today as well.[41]

---

38. On the International Churches of Christ (not to be confused with the mainstream Churches of Christ), see Randy Frame, "The Cost of Discipleship?" *CT* (Sept. 1, 1997), 64–88. Despite my opposition to the group's extreme tactics and doctrine, I believe that it contains many genuine Christians.

39. Roger Steer, "Pushing Inward," *Christian History* 52 (1996), 10–18 (p. 18). Taylor was so passionate that he could not bear to remain in one church service in England where he saw over 1,000 Christians rejoicing while millions perished unreached (ibid., 14).

40. Mark Galli, "Fury Unleashed," *Christian History* 52 (1996), 31–33 (p. 33).

41. See "Burning Shame," *India Today* (Feb. 8, 1999), 10–16 (an Indian magazine strongly condemning the killing of a missionary and his sons).

The good news will not be fully proclaimed to all nations (Matt. 24:14) until a generation of Christians rises who is radical enough to literally die for the sake of reaching the unreached. It currently appears that some hard Islamic and Hindu strongholds will be reached only the way Europe and that most other mission fields were originally pried open—through the blood of martyrs.[42] In many nations, such as the Sudan, Iran, and Pakistan, the ground has already been receiving the blood of many of our brothers and sisters. Yet with some important individual exceptions, the current generation of North American Christians shows little inclination to sacrifice for the gospel, much less to die for it. As musician John Fischer put it:

> Point a gun at each of the 60 million people who, according to Mr. Gallup's poll, are born-again Christians. Tell them to renounce Christ or have their heads blown off, and then take a recount. I think George, like Gideon, would find his troops dwindling. Actually, the price probably wouldn't have to be so extreme today. Threatening to confiscate their TV sets might just produce the same results. When faith is cheap, it is easily pawned.[43]

Those of us with a vision to reach the world for Christ must begin investing in a younger, increasingly multicultural generation, equipping them for sacrificial leadership. The younger leaders must begin preaching a biblical gospel from which some (with notable exceptions) in the present generation have shrunk from preaching: The gospel is worth our lives and all we have, and no cost is too great to reach the world for Jesus Christ our Lord. In his comments on Revelation, Billy Graham struggles with whether over the years he had "made the Christian faith look too easy," with whether he had preached what Bonhoeffer called "cheap grace." He asks: "In my eagerness to give away God's great gift, have I been honest about the price He paid in His war with evil? And have I adequately explained the price we must pay in our own war against the evil at work in and around our lives?"[44] It is a question that challenges most of us.

The coming vindication. As the martyrs cry for vindication, so do suffering believers today. That God grants the martyrs' request but it does not come right away should encourage us to persevere. Many generations of

---

42. On past fields, see Ruth A. Tucker, *From Jerusalem to Irian Jaya* (Grand Rapids: Zondervan, 1983), 35, 49, 57, 222, 294, 419–36. For some twentieth-century martyrs, including many missionaries, see James and Marti Hefley, *By Their Blood: Christian Martyrs of the 20th Century* (Milford, Mich.: Mott Media, 1979); cf. more recently Paul A. Marshall, *Their Blood Cries Out: The Worldwide Tragedy of Modern Christians Who Are Dying for Their Faith* (Dallas: Word, 1997).
43. John Fischer, "When Christianity Pays," *Contemporary Christian Magazine* (Dec. 1985), 46.
44. Graham, *Approaching Hoofbeats*, 26.

American slaves cried to God for freedom (cf. also Ex. 2:23–25) before the liberation from slavery came; many South Africans died fighting apartheid before it was finally abolished. Prophets and apostles like Jeremiah (Jer. 43:4–7) and Paul (2 Tim. 1:15) never lived to see the full impact of their ministries, but we recognize them in retrospect; the generation immediately following Jeremiah embraced his message (2 Chron. 36:21–22; Ezra 1:1; Dan. 9:2). God showed Habakkuk impending judgment on Israel's oppressors and encouraged him to trust in the vision: "Though it linger, wait for it; it will certainly come and will not delay" (Hab. 2:3). In time the promised judgment fell on John's Babylon, and it will come on the final Babylon no less decisively.

God's time is not always our time, but even if we do not live to see the fulfillment of all our prayers, we can die in hope that God will bring about the things he has promised. After the saints' cries, God judges the world (6:12–17); despite the arrogant fantasies of God's enemies (Prov. 18:11), human power will provide no refuge in that day when the true King executes justice on the entire social order from Caesar on down (6:15).

Revelation 7:1-8

AFTER THIS I SAW four angels standing at the four corners
of the earth, holding back the four winds of the earth
to prevent any wind from blowing on the land or on
the sea or on any tree. ²Then I saw another angel coming up
from the east, having the seal of the living God. He called out
in a loud voice to the four angels who had been given power
to harm the land and the sea: ³"Do not harm the land or the
sea or the trees until we put a seal on the foreheads of the servants of our God." ⁴Then I heard the number of those who
were sealed: 144,000 from all the tribes of Israel.

⁵ From the tribe of Judah 12,000 were sealed,
    from the tribe of Reuben 12,000,
    from the tribe of Gad 12,000,
⁶ from the tribe of Asher 12,000,
    from the tribe of Naphtali 12,000,
    from the tribe of Manasseh 12,000,
⁷ from the tribe of Simeon 12,000,
    from the tribe of Levi 12,000,
    from the tribe of Issachar 12,000,
⁸ from the tribe of Zebulun 12,000,
    from the tribe of Joseph 12,000,
    from the tribe of Benjamin 12,000.

**Original
Meaning**

ONE MIGHT THINK further judgments incongruent
with the end of the age already depicted in 6:12–
17. But that John saw "after this" (7:1) a vision of
the 144,000 (7:1–8) does not mean that the
events of 7:1–8 occur after the sixth seal, any more than that "after this" in
7:9 means that the innumerable multitude there chronologically follows the
144,000. Rather, the verb that follows "after this" is "saw": John receives his
next vision, and this one appears to report the state of Christ's "servants" during the entire period of Tribulation. The earth, sea, and trees suffer during
the Tribulation (8:7–8; 11:6). Clearly the command to seal God's servants
before harming the earth, sea, or trees (7:2) cannot follow the destruction of
the earth and sky at the Tribulation's end (6:12–16)! The point is simply that

those who can withstand the day of God's wrath (6:17) are those whom God has empowered to withstand the previous plagues (7:2–3).

Thus, many scholars rightly take chapter 7 as a parenthetical intermission located between the sixth and seventh seals for literary purposes; such interludes occur at similar points in the trumpets and bowls series.[1] Such a parenthesis serves the literary function of building suspense. Many parenthetical interludes in Revelation (e.g., 14:1–5; 15:2–4; 20:4–6), especially hymns (12:10; 19:1–8), also concern the protection or salvation of the righteous, placing the judgment scenes in an encouraging context. Judgment serves a redemptive purpose, not only to invite repentance from the disobedient (9:20–21) but to vindicate the righteous oppressed (6:10).

The Identity of the 144,000 (7:4–8)

BUT WHO ARE the 144,000? The matter is open to question, but the form of the text may suggest a census, usually used in the Hebrew Bible to assess military preparation (Num. 1:3, 18, 20; 26:2, 4; 1 Chron. 27:23); this also explains the specification of adult males in 14:4. It further makes sense of why a given number is listed from each tribe (cf. Num. 1:20–47); in a real war one might draft twelve equal contingents from different tribes or regions (Num. 31:4–6; 1 Chron. 27:1–15).[2] Battalions of one thousand were also fairly standard units, suggesting "that each tribe supplies twelve battalions of a thousand men each."[3]

This vision may thus represent an end-time army, prepared for a spiritual battle (cf. 12:7–9). If so, it may be the army that returns with Jesus in 19:14, clothed with the righteous acts of the saints. The only other time in Revelation where John hears a "number," it is the number of the world's army, two hundred million strong (9:16). God's earthly army may be overwhelmingly outnumbered by the world's army (9:16; cf. 20:8; but cf. 5:11), but they will surely overcome.

Yet this fact does not solve the question: Who constitutes this army? One view takes them literally as Jewish Christians from each of the twelve tribes,

---

1. E.g., Tenney, *Revelation*, 73. Ford, *Revelation*, 120, provides other examples in Jewish judgment texts.

2. Bauckham, *Climax of Prophecy*, 216–18; Caird, *Commentary on Revelation*, 178; Michaels, *Revelation*, 170–71. Cf. 1QM 2.1–3.

3. Bauckham, *Climax of Prophecy*, 218 (see 1 Macc. 3:55; Josephus, *War* 2.578; 1QM 4.2, 16; 5.3). The actual numbers in Jewish units, as in Roman units, may have often been less than their paper strength. John's vision may adapt the Jewish image of twelve tribes participating in the final war (1QM 2.2–3, 7; 3.13–14; 14.16; Bauckham, *Climax of Prophecy*, 219). The absence of clearer military imagery makes Aune seem skeptical at one place (*Revelation*, 2:436), though he elsewhere seems to accept the end-time army view (pp. 444, 463).

although not usually taking the people all as recruits for the messianic army.[4] This view is far more plausible than most of its opponents are willing to grant and has some factors in its favor, most notably the fact that if one speaks of the end-time Jewish remnant, it is difficult to think of a more explicit way to make this clear than to enumerate the tribes. Other images in Revelation may be consonant with this one, especially if the woman in Revelation 12 represents Israel (see 12:6, 17). There is also sufficient biblical precedent for speaking of a massive turning of Jewish people to faith in Christ in the end time (e.g., Rom. 11:25–27; probably Matt. 23:39; cf. Isa. 61:1–9; Jer. 31:15–40; Ezek. 36:8–38; Hos. 2:14–23; 11:8–11; 14:4–7; Amos 9:11–12), and there is no reason to doubt that John as a Jewish Christian would emphasize this view (cf. Rev. 11:8, 13).

Nevertheless, other factors in the text of Revelation itself suggest that John is probably adapting this pattern of a Jewish end-time remnant to portray instead all believers.[5] Although he undoubtedly expects an end-time turning of Jewish people as many other early Christian writers did, that need not be his point here; for John all believers have become part of the "lampstands" (see comment on 1:20), part of the "kingdom and priests" (1:6), in contrast to those who falsely claim to be Jews (2:9; 3:9). For John, faith in Jesus and obedience to God's commandments stand together (cf. 12:17; 14:12); nothing is more in keeping with his Jewish, biblical heritage than affirming Jesus, and nothing more incompatible with that heritage than denying him. Hence for John, Gentiles who believe in Jesus become part of the Jewish movement of faith in Jesus. Two thousand years later, a history of Gentile "Christian" anti-Semitism has made it harder for us to hear about Gentiles being grafted into Israel and about Gentile Christians recognizing the Jewishness of their faith; but John wrote before all those tragic events.

What are the cues in the text that incline us toward the view, shared by most contemporary commentators, that the 144,000 represent all believers? (1) Most important, those to be protected from God's judgments are his "servants" without qualification (7:3), who everywhere else in Revelation represent all believers or witnesses (1:1; 2:20; 6:11; 10:7; 11:18; 19:2, 5, 10; 22:3, 6, 9). If one takes their ethnicity literally, then one should also take the numbers and other details literally. But if we do that, and if "servants" represents all believers, then the total number of the genuinely saved through history

---

4. See González, *Revelation*, 55; Tenney, *Revelation*, 78; Ryrie, *Revelation*, 51; Walvoord, *Revelation*, 143. See esp. the insightful arguments of A. Geyser, "The Twelve Tribes in Revelation: Judean and Judeo-Christian Apocalypticism," *NTS* 28 (July 1982): 388–99.

5. Aune, *Revelation*, 2:443, makes a forceful argument that the 144,000 represent those believers who would survive the end-time Tribulation, but makes too much of a distinction of "from" in 7:4–8 and the contrast with the multitude of 7:9–17.

(or, on other readings, through the Tribulation) are limited to 12,000 male Jewish virgins from each tribe (though the passage that specifies 144,000 male virgins does not specify their ethnicity [14:1–5]). If one takes "servants" here in a narrower sense than it usually appears in Revelation (by identifying "prophets" with a special group of believers in 10:7; 22:9), then God affords his special protection only to a group within the church based on their ethnicity, gender, and marital status; all Gentile, female, and married believers must suffer from the plagues (9:4).

(2) The seal on their foreheads (7:3; 14:1) also connects them with all believers (3:12; 22:4; cf. 2 Cor. 1:22; Eph. 1:13; 4:30) and contrasts them with all followers of the beast (Rev. 13:16–17; 14:9, 11; 16:2; 19:20; 20:4).

(3) The 144,000 do not fit the description of literal Israel. Already by John's day most tribes were "missing," and while many Jews expected them to be restored, it has since become impossible to genuinely reconstruct from which tribes most Jewish people are descended.[6] More important, one of the tribes is missing—in fact, the first who was supposed to receive his inheritance, Dan (7:4–8; cf. Ezek. 48:1).

(4) Revelation emphasizes the Jewishness of all believers (cf. comments on 1:20; 2:9).

(5) The rest of Revelation leads us to expect that the numbers are probably symbolic (twelve, the number of God's people, squared, times ten cubed). The numbers 12,000 and 144 elsewhere appear for the holy community (21:16–17); the new Jerusalem is laid out as a square and shaped as a cube (21:16). Thus, the 144,000 represent all those destined for the new Jerusalem. Even cumulatively, while these arguments might not prove absolutely decisive, they do weight the case significantly in favor of the 144,000 standing for all true believers in Jesus.[7]

Given these arguments, it seems simplest to read the second vision here (7:9–17) as another interpretation of the first (7:1–8), as second visions sometimes were (Gen. 41:17–32; Dan. 7:9–22; 4 Ezra 9:38–10:28; 10:38–59). The second vision (see comments on 7:9–17) involves a decisive reinterpretation of a standard Jewish end-time image about the remnant of God's people, and this resembles the way Revelation teaches elsewhere. John *hears*

---

6. On the restoration of the "lost" ten tribes, see Joachim Jeremias, *New Testament Theology* (New York: Charles Scribner's, 1971), 235; E. P. Sanders, *Jesus and Judaism* (Philadelphia: Fortress, 1985), 96–97.

7. Most modern commentators acknowledge this. See Heinrich Schlier, *Principalities and Powers* (New York: Herder and Herder, 1961), 70; Caird, *Commentary on Revelation*, 94–95; Rissi, *Time and History*, 89, 110; Mounce, *Revelation*, 168–70; Beasley-Murray, *Revelation*, 140; Bauckham, *Climax of Prophecy*, 399; Johnson, *Revelation*, 85; Michaels, *Revelation*, 113; Beale, *Revelation*, 412–23.

about a conquering Lion from the tribe of Judah (5:5), but turns to *see* instead a slaughtered Lamb (5:6); here John "hears" the number of God's servants (7:4) but "sees" a countless multitude (7:9). As the conquering Lion turns out to be a slaughtered Lamb, the end-time army of Israel turns out to be the host of martyrs from among the nations.[8] Our "holy war" is our faithful, nonviolent witness to the death.[9]

Sealing the Tribes (7:1–3)

GOD'S SOVEREIGNTY OVER the winds (7:1) is a standard feature of Jewish apocalyptic and astronomical lore; whereas pagans worshiped a variety of deities and even had deities (like Boreas) over specific winds, God controls the winds and delegates them to angels who perform only his bidding.[10] God could send some winds for blessing and some for judgment (1 En. 36:2–3; 76:4). Some believed that the winds supported the dome of heaven (1 En. 18:2–5); other ancients noted that if unchecked, the winds would blow away earth, sea, and heaven (Virgil, *Aen.* 1.56–59). In one tradition, God checked the rampaging winds after the Flood of Noah's day, signaling the dawn of another era (Sib. Or. 1.195; cf. Gen. 8:1).

The four winds correspond to the "four corners of the earth" (also a judgment image in Jer. 49:36), a common phrase that simply means the four directions.[11] Here they serve to show God's sovereignty over the furthest reaches of the earth, like Zechariah's four horsemen, who were the four spirits of heaven going patrolling in four directions (Zech. 6:1–5). The Greek version of Zechariah acceptably renders the prophet's Hebrew as "four winds" (6:5). The blowing of four winds could also serve as the harbinger of the evil world empire (Dan. 7:2–3). Here God prevents the winds from blowing in judgment (Rev. 7:1; cf. 6:13) until he has provided protection for his servants (7:3).

---

8. Bauckham, *Climax of Prophecy*, 215–16; Michaels, *Revelation*, 113.

9. Richard Bauckham, "The Book of Revelation as a Christian War Scroll," *Neot* 22 (1988): 17–40.

10. See 1 Enoch 18:1; 35:1–36:2; some manuscripts of Jos. and Asen. 12:2/3; God restrains them for the world's survival in *Gen. Rab.* 24:4; *Lev. Rab.* 15:1. They prove especially useful for navigating heavenly chariots (1 En. 72:5; 73:2; Apoc. Moses 38:3; cf. Ps. 18:10; 104:3), which chariots also appear regularly as an image in Gentile sources. In Virgil, *Aen.* 1.56–59, Aeolus keeps the winds in check.

11. Although most ancients believed that the earth was relatively flat, they viewed it as a circle, not a square. For four winds meaning all directions, see Ezek. 37:9; Dan. 7:2; 8:8; Zech. 2:6; Mark 13:27. For four corners, see Rev. 20:8; also Isa. 11:12; 2 Bar. 6:4–5; Test. Asher 7:3. For heaven's spherical (dome) shape, see Aristotle, *Heavens* 2.4, 286b10; a few astronomers also had recognized the earth as a sphere by this period (cf. Diogenes Laertius, 9.9.57). The harmful winds were from NE, NW, SE and SW (Mounce, *Revelation*, 166).

The angel rising "from the east" (7:2) may recall God's glory returning to his house (Ezek. 43:2) or the eastern orientation of the eschatological temple (46:1, 12; 47:1), or it may imply God's judgment from the east (Rev. 16:12). But most likely the image points to the rising of the sun (which the Greek here literally says, though it was a common way of saying, "from the east").[12] Greeks and Romans worshiped the sun god, and their myths warned of the scorching or freezing of the earth if he veered from his appointed course; Jews regarded him as merely a powerful angel.[13] An angel "from the rising of the sun" might be as powerful as the sun angel, but here his task is simply to pass on a message from God (cf. 19:17). God is sovereign over the sun (cf. 6:12; 7:16; 8:12; 9:2; 16:8; 21:23) as he is over the winds (7:1).

The angel's "seal" probably implies a signet ring, by which a king could authorize an agent to carry out an activity on his behalf. In this context, it may imply that the angel was one of God's agents of judgment who initially attested the plagues just mentioned (6:1–7; on those seals, see comment on 5:1–2). Scholars have proposed a variety of interpretations for the image of the sealing of the righteous here. Some cite the marking of soldiers or others on the hand, forehead, or neck; this could relate to the probable image of the 144,000 as God's army in 14:1–5. The hand and forehead were also the location for the phylacteries, by which God's servants showed their fidelity to his law.[14] Many relate the sealing here to the branding of animals and slaves (cf. Ex. 21:6); this would explain their identity as God's "servants" (Rev. 7:3; cf. 22:3–4) and the contrast with servants of the world (13:16–18). This view has much to commend it, though only a minority of slaves were branded.[15] Because Christians are a kingdom and priests (1:6), John may have thought also of the engraving "like a seal" on the high priest's forehead, "HOLY TO THE LORD" (Ex. 28:36–38), a fitting contrast to Babylon, whose forehead identifies her as a prostitute (Rev. 17:5), or to servants of the beast (13:16).

---

12. This is a far more common image (e.g., Homer, *Od.* 3.1; 19.434) than any other for the east and is, as here, part of a common idiom for "east."

13. See Sophocles, *Oedipus Tyrannus* 660–61; *Orph. Hymns* introduction 3–4; Josephus, *Apion* 2.265; for naturalistic views, Diogenes Laertius, 7.1.144; 8.2.77; Plutarch, *Oracles at Delphi* 12, *Mor.* 400BC. For the Jewish views, see 1QS 10.1–5; CD 10.15–16; 1 Enoch 72:2–37; 75:4; 4 Bar. 4:4; T. Sol. 6:10; 2 Enoch 11:4; 14:3; 3 Enoch 17:4; tos. Ber. 6:6.

14. Phylacteries in Ex. 13:8–9; Deut. 6:8; 11:18 may have been intended figuratively. For a fuller list of views and supporting sources, see Ford, *Revelation*, 116–17.

15. See Martial, *Epig.* 3.21; Plutarch, *Nicias* 29.1; Ps-Phocylides, 225; for a slave collar, see *CIL*, 15.7194; slave tattooing may be implied in the oppression of Jews in 3 Macc. 2:28–29. For slave branding in an earlier period, see I. Mendelsohn, "Slavery in the Ancient Near East," *BA* 9 (Sept. 1946): 78–88 (pp. 80–82). Some peoples tattooed their children (Artemidorus, *Oneir.* 1.8; Sextus Empiricus, *Outlines of Pyrr.* 1.148; 3.202), but not in Asia. On branding, tattooing, and other marking, see more fully Aune, *Revelation*, 2:456–59.

The word "seal" (*sphragizo*) itself can imply a special stamp of ownership or approval, as 4 Ezra declares for the righteous (4 Ezra 6:5) and for Zion (10:23).[16] Some use Jewish traditions concerning the *tav* mark mentioned in Ezekiel 9:4 to suggest the mark of the cross here, but surely John would have been more explicit had he been able to cite this; rather, John envisions the mark as the name of God and the Lamb (Rev. 14:1), the opposite of the name of the beast (13:17–18).[17]

In any case, the seal does function to attest ownership (Isa. 44:5), and its title contrasts with what is merely a "mark" (Rev. 13:16–17). The most important source for the image is Ezekiel 9, where God marks the righteous remnant to protect them from his judgments.[18] God will also set a sign among the surviving remnant of his people and make them witnesses for his glory among the nations (Isa. 66:19). Early Jewish texts also envisioned God's placing a "sign" on the righteous to protect them from harm in famine and war, whereas the wicked were marked with a "sign" for destruction (Ps. Sol. 15:6–9). As in the plagues of Exodus, to which many of Revelation's plagues allude, God draws a line of demarcation between his people and the world (Ex. 8:28; 9:4; 11:7).[19]

Judah may be listed first (7:5–8) as the military leader (cf. 5:5), with most of the others following birth order or pairing with the appropriate brothers.[20] Scholars debate why Dan in particular is chosen for omission, since it clearly

---

16. Sealing seems to function as divine consecration for a task in T. Job 5:2; and impressing for service in T. Sol. 2:5. Aune, *Revelation*, 2:758, cites Pindar, *Olymp.* 3.29–30 as evidence that bearing a deity's name can indicate divine ownership; cf. 3 Macc. 2:28–29.

17. For the cross here, see David Daube, *The New Testament and Rabbinic Judaism* (Peabody, Mass.: Hendrickson, n.d.; London: University of London, 1956), 401–2; see data in *b. Shab.* 55a; Ford, *Revelation*, 123; perhaps cf. *m. Men.* 6:3.

18. Cf. also the protective sign in Gen. 4:15; Ex. 12:23. The "sign" of circumcision (Gen. 17:11), appropriate to the image of Israelites, would spare Israel from end-time destruction (Jub. 15:26). For delaying judgment until the righteous can be preserved or informed, see 1 En. 66:1–67:2; 4 Bar. 3:5. God protects his people while judging the wicked in 1 Enoch 100:5; Talbert compares also the protection of God's people during the final trial in 2 Bar. 29:2; 71:1 (*Apocalypse*, 36).

19. Josephus, *Ant.* 2.294–95; 3.17. Cf. also the principle in Gen. 18:23–25.

20. See Bauckham, *Climax of Prophecy*, 221, although what he suspects as unsuccessful memory of the birth order I suspect may simply represent mixed criteria; the Old Testament arranges the tribes list nearly twenty different ways! Christopher R. Smith, "The Portrayal of the Church as the New Israel in the Names and Order of the Tribes in Revelation 7.5–8," *JSNT* 39 (1990): 111–18, suggests the handmaids' sons are promoted to signify Gentile inclusion (Bauckham disagrees in "The List of the Tribes in Revelation 7 Again," *JSNT* 42 [1991]: 99–115). R. E. Winkle, "Another Look at the List of Tribes in Revelation 7," *AUSS* 27 (1989): 53–67, suggests a counterclockwise reversal of the list of Ezek. 48:31–34 (cf. Rev. 21:12), while keeping Judah first; but this scheme is not obvious.

was not omitted in the biblical prophets (Ezek. 48:1–2). Many point out its associations with idolatry (Judg. 18:30; 1 Kings 12:29), further negative rabbinic traditions about Dan, Dan's association with Satan in Testament of Dan 5:6, and Irenaeus' suspicion (possibly based on this passage in Revelation) that the Antichrist would come from Dan.[21]

But these explanations do not fully satisfy; texts say hard things about Dan, but also about many of the other tribes (e.g., Gen. 49:3–7); Jewish thought normally expected Dan's repentance (Test. Dan 5:9). Others suggest that the omission was random; one tribe had to be omitted in order to include Levi, Manasseh, and Ephraim separately, yet end up with twelve.[22] Perhaps if some tribe had to be omitted, one with more negative associations (see above) than others would be chosen first. The informed reader might think of Dan's association with a serpent (Gen. 49:16–17; cf. Jer. 8:16–17), which he or she might then link with the serpent of Eden (Gen. 3:1–15), who represents the devil in Revelation 12:9.

READING THE COSMOLOGY of Revelation. How do we read the cosmology of Revelation? Some take parts of it literally (although they cannot maintain this same pattern of interpretation consistently throughout the book). Hal Lindsey, for example, relates God's stopping the wind in 7:1 to global weather changes now occurring.[23] While weather changes do seem to be occurring, it is tenuous to relate such changes to this verse.[24] If the winds literally stopped, we would face immediate, ter-

---

21. Beasley-Murray, *Revelation*, 143–44; Caird, *Commentary on Revelation*, 99; Ford, *Revelation*, 118; Talbert, *Apocalypse*, 35. For idolatry, see e.g., *tos. Shab.* 7:3; *Gen. Rab.* 43:2; *Pes. Rab.* 12:13; for the Antichrist tradition, Irenaeus, *Her.* 5.30.2; see Hippolytus, *On the Antichrist* 14; earlier but less clear, see *Jub.* 44:28–33. Dan is one of the few tribes appearing almost exclusively in a negative light in Judges.

22. Bauckham, *Climax of Prophecy*, 222–23. The title "Ephraim" may have connoted Pharisees in some Qumran texts (see Stephen Goranson, "The Exclusion of Ephraim in Rev. 7:4–8 and Essene Polemic Against Pharisees," *Dead Sea Discoveries* 2 [1995]: 80–85), but it seems doubtful that John's audience would know that specifically Essene polemic.

23. Lindsey, *New World Coming*, 116–17.

24. On threats of environmental catastrophe, see "Ravage in the Rain Forests," *USNWR* (March 31, 1986), 61–62; "Facing Life in a Greenhouse," *USNWR* (Sept. 29, 1986), 73–74; several articles in *NW* (July 11, 1988), 16–24; "More Bad News in the Air," *NW* (Feb. 17, 1992), 26; Gregg Easterbrook, "Return of the Glaciers," *NW* (Nov. 23, 1992), 62. For more cautious views, see "Is It All Just Hot Air?" *NW* (Nov. 20, 1989), 64–66; "Feuding Over Global Warming," *WPR* (July 1995), 6–11; Sharon Begley, "Odds on the Greenhouse," *NW* (Dec. 1, 1997), 72.

---

rible environmental consequences, not least of which would presumably be the rapid settling of tons of toxic waste now held in the upper atmosphere, which would suffocate human life from the planet.

One could therefore argue that those who do not expect to be raptured before the Tribulation ought to either start an atmospheric purification program or buy gas masks, but such an approach misses the text's point. Just as John wrote in the language we call Koine Greek, he communicated in images familiar in his day. Because we speak a different language or use different images today does not change the point his graphic images sought to depict: God rules the cosmos and can protect his people from the consequences of judgments he sends to get the world's attention.

The 144,000. What is the point of the 144,000 today? Jehovah's Witnesses, of course, supply one well-known answer, but their method of interpretation here is astonishingly arbitrary. They take the number literally, but the other details (e.g., male Jewish virgins [14:4]) symbolically.[25] Given the plethora of symbolic numbers in this book, if any element is more symbolic than the others, it must be the number (cf. comment on 21:16–17)![26]

But Jehovah's Witnesses are not alone in reading their theology into the text. For example, one modern writer contends that the 144,000 cannot represent "the church" because the church is not God's "servants" (citing John 15:15).[27] Yet one wonders what he does with other uses of "servant" in Revelation that plainly refer to Christians (e.g., 1:1; 22:3). Lindsey argues that these are Jewish evangelists converted after the Rapture of the church.[28] His view that they are evangelists could be both right and wrong: wrong in that he reads into the text a calling not specified there, but right in that all true believers in Revelation are God's servants invested with the spirit of prophecy to witness for Christ (19:10).

Some have challenged the view that the 144,000 represent all believers by pointing out that the literal interpretation is not impossible.[29] This objection,

25. *Revelation: Grand Climax*, 115–18. They then take the great crowd of 7:9–17 as those sealed from 1935 forward, after J. F. Rutherford's new revelation when the literal number was nearly complete (ibid., 119–29). Hans Hut, an effective sixteenth-century evangelist, also tried to prepare a literal 144,000 (Gentile Christians) for Christ's return ("A Gallery of Factions, Friends & Foes," *Christian History* 4 [1985]: 13–16 [p. 14]).

26. Though numerical improbabilities were commonly accepted (e.g., Jos. and Asen. 2:6/11, where all Aseneth's seven servant women were born the same night as she), symbolic numbers were standard fare in apocalyptic texts (Leon Morris, *Apocalyptic* [Grand Rapids: Eerdmans, 1972], 39).

27. Strombeck, *Rapture*, 145. Contending that they represent Israel, he claims this proves that Israel must be on earth during the Tribulation (ibid., 119)—a point that no one actually disputes, but which he believes implies the church cannot be on earth (a classic non sequitur).

28. Lindsey, *New World Coming*, 112–16.

29. Ibid., 120–21.

to be sure, is true, but it does not establish the likelihood of one position over another. The symbolic interpretation is also not impossible, and on the whole probably better fits the nature of Revelation, which revels in insightful symbolism and reinterpreting traditional Jewish end-time symbols.

The probable identity of the 144,000 calls us as believers in Jesus to remember our heritage in God's dealings with the patriarchs and prophets, our spiritual ancestors, and to recognize our destiny as heirs of the promises given through the prophets to God's people. It also reminds us of something John probably would have been amazed to discover that the church has since forgotten: the church's Jewish heritage. Technically, Gentile Christians have not "replaced" Israel or made Israel obsolete (a common sentiment among those who take the 144,000 as symbolic for all Christians), but have been grafted into Israel's heritage alongside Jewish Christians (cf. Rom. 11).

SEVERAL PRINCIPLES ARE most conspicuous when we read this passage in its context. (1) God views us as his army, yet we triumph through sharing the Lamb's suffering (Rom. 8:17; 2 Tim. 2:11–13). (2) Nevertheless, we have nothing to fear; God, who is sovereign over his creation, can protect us from plagues. Certainly he shields us from experiencing any troubles as acts of his anger. (3) Finally, God also views us as his people. Ethnic Gentiles, once considered outsiders, are now welcomed (along with Jewish believers) as full converts to Israel's true faith, hence part of Israel's promised inheritance (Isa. 56:3–7; Eph. 2:11–13). In sealing us, God proudly marks us as his own.

God as sovereign over history. In this passage we also learn that God is sovereign over the events of history in two ways. (1) He is sovereign in sending his judgments on nature, including the earth, the sea, and the trees (7:1). Traditional religions usually personify trees, rivers, and so forth as containing spirits; this leaves people seeking to propitiate such spirits, fearing offending them.[30] Modern secularism, by contrast, denies any power greater and more directed than nature and thus leaves people fearing the random destruction of West Coast earthquakes, Midwest tornadoes, Gulf Coast hurricanes, and so forth. But the Bible assures us that God rules nature.

(2) God can exempt people selectively from his judgments (7:2–3). He did not, as the Deists thought, merely wind up the universe like a clock and let it tick down. He is intimately concerned for his own servants and arranges

---

30. See John S. Mbiti, *African Religions and Philosophies* (Garden City, N.Y.: Doubleday, 1970), 71.

their protection. One missionary told me of heavy shelling in Brazzaville that ruined most of the large stores and hotels. Many of the Christians and their church's neighbors crowded into the large church building, and though everything around the church was destroyed, the church remained undamaged.[31] Others can tell stories of tornadoes that unexpectedly ripped through their rooms, destroying everything but leaving the Christian family inside unharmed.[32]

On the level of application, however, this raises the question: What happens when the righteous are not protected?[33] For example, a pregnant woman in the Philippines and the child she carried both miraculously survived several shots in her torso from a high-powered weapon at close range—but the other seventeen victims gunned down with her died.[34] Emma Moss, daughter of Salvation Army founders William and Catherine Booth, was serving with her husband in the United States when, at a relatively young age, she was the only person to die in a train accident.[35] Many of us lamented the loss of Christian musician Keith Green, his pilot, and a missionary family in what appeared to be a senseless plane crash.[36] Likewise, three days after I assured Spencer Perkins that I believed God would keep him around for a long time because of his strategic role in the U.S. racial reconciliation movement, he died of a heart attack at the age of forty-three; many of us felt devastated.[37] Revelation leads us to expect that many Christians must die martyrs' deaths, but what about train accidents, plane crashes, and heart attacks?

Sometimes we may face death because we have ignored a proper warning (2 Chron. 35:21–24), sometimes because we failed to discern true from false warnings (1 Kings 13:21–22), sometimes because we disrespect other believers (1 Cor. 11:29–30), but sometimes also because God simply wills to take us home (Deut. 34:4; 1 Kings 2:1). God is also at work in ways we only understand much later. William Wilberforce lost his father at age nine, and his aunt and uncle were childless; but through the combination of these two tragic events, Wilberforce was exposed to the evangelical preaching of

---

31. Eugene Thomas, personal correspondence (Aug. 15, 1998).

32. Dawn Sundstrom, "Twister?" *Worldwide Challenge* (July 1998), 38–41.

33. Crowding into a church, as in the above account of divine protection, does not necessarily bring safety; cf. horror stories from Rwanda (e.g., Gary Haugen, "Rwanda's Carnage," *CT* [Feb. 6, 1995], 52–53; Richard Nyberg, "Bloodletting Sweeps Rwanda," *CT* [May 16, 1994], 54; Joshua Hammer, "Inside a War Zone: 'The Situation Is Desperate,'" *NW* [June 20, 1994], 44–46).

34. Gary Haugen, *Good News About Injustice* (Downers Grove, Ill.: InterVarsity, 1999), 30.

35. Norman H. Murdoch, "The Booths' Children," *Christian History* 26 (1990): 26.

36. Melody Green and David Hazard, *No Compromise: The Life Story of Keith Green* (Chatsworth, Calif.: Sparrow, 1989), 265–85; *Last Days Newsletter* 5 (Sept. 1982).

37. See the articles in *Reconcilers* (Spring 1998).

abolitionist John Newton.[38] Wilberforce ultimately became the leading champion of abolitionism in England until, on his deathbed, slavery was abolished in the British empire. What is most important for us to remember is that not a hair of our head falls to the ground without our Father's knowledge (Matt. 10:29–31).[39] Often in Scripture God healed the infirm; but even when he did not (e.g., 1 Kings 1:1; 14:4; 2 Kings 13:14; Gal. 4:13; 1 Tim. 5:23; 2 Tim. 4:20), believers could trust that he was always faithful and loving.

Victory by proper defense and offense. The picture of the 144,000 as God's martyr army also challenges us deeply. We usually want to achieve power and overcome by power; God summons us to overcome by weakness. Aleksandr Solzhenitsyn had long been trying to resist his captors in the Soviet gulag, trying to achieve some semblance of control over his schedule, his food, or other matters. When he became a Christian, he relinquished such attempts at control, hence "became free of even his captors' power."[40] Likewise, a Hezbollah leader was shocked when Brother Andrew offered his life in exchange for that of a prisoner; the Muslim leader became Brother Andrew's friend. But observing the lack of commitment among most Christians, he later protested, "Andrew, you Christians ... are not following the life of Jesus anymore.... You must go back to the book, the New Testament." Brother Andrew adds that the teaching of Jesus we must reclaim includes loving our enemies.[41] What a radical witness to much of the Islamic world nonviolent martyr Christians could be!

Contemporary North American sermons, Christian music, and personal exhortations regularly encourage Christians to "stand firm" when facing personal needs and trials. While that is a legitimate emphasis, our balance is often wrong. We are God's army, and this war is not merely a personal matter. A purely defensive strategy can never win a battle or a game; it can at best delay the inevitable. Jesus Christ has not called us merely to stand our ground (Eph. 6:11–14), but also to advance with our feet shod with the gospel (Eph. 6:15). Although Roman soldiers carried two offensive weapons, the *pilum* or lance and the short sword, Paul lists only one offensive weapon, the one used for close combat: the "word of God" (Eph. 6:17; cf. 1:13). In Paul's writings this phrase usually means the gospel.

---

38. Christopher D. Hancock, "The 'Shrimp' Who Stopped Slavery," *Christian History* 53 (1997): 12–19 (p. 12).

39. In context, texts like Matt. 10:29–31 and 1 Peter 4:19 esp. address persecution by God's enemies, the circumstances where we would be least likely to acknowledge God's hand.

40. Charles Colson, *Kingdoms in Conflict* (Grand Rapids: Zondervan, 1987), 273.

41. Wendy Murray Zoba, "Brother Andrew's Boldest Mission Yet: 'Smuggling' Jesus into Muslim Hearts," *CT* (Oct. 5, 1998), 50–56.

Thus, Christ has called us not to simply preach in our churches, waiting for the lost to come in or the fruits of past revivals to finish dying off; he has challenged us to take the news of our King outside the walls of our churches, to strike offensively as well as stand defensively. "Who wants to enroll in the King's army?" we proclaim. "Who is prepared to die in hope of eternal life?"

Our spiritual heritage. If our interpretation of the 144,000 is correct, then all God's servants, Jewish or Gentile, are also viewed through the prism of Israel. That is, Gentile Christians as well as Jewish Christians should recognize their spiritual heritage in the patriarchs and prophets of ancient Israel. This does not mean that God "replaced" Israel with Gentile Christianity; it means that Gentile Christians have been grafted into the heritage of Israel and can speak of Abraham as "our father." They recognize a spiritual heritage in the history of God's people that runs deeper than any ethnic heritage to which we might otherwise claim allegiance (Rom. 2:26–29; Gal. 3:29; see also comments on Rev. 20). The omission of Dan may be incidental; but if not, it provides a warning that even those who seem certain to be saved may not appear in the final number if they fail to persevere (Mark 13:22; John 6:70–71).[42]

---

42. Cf. here also Christopher R. Smith, "The Tribes of Revelation 7 and the Literary Competence of John the Seer," *JETS* 38 (June 1995): 213–18 (p. 217).

Revelation 7:9–17

FTER THIS I looked and there before me was a great multitude that no one could count, from every nation, tribe, people and language, standing before the throne and in front of the Lamb. They were wearing white robes and were holding palm branches in their hands. ¹⁰And they cried out in a loud voice:

> "Salvation belongs to our God,
> who sits on the throne,
> and to the Lamb."

¹¹All the angels were standing around the throne and around the elders and the four living creatures. They fell down on their faces before the throne and worshiped God, ¹²saying:

> "Amen!
> Praise and glory
> and wisdom and thanks and honor
> and power and strength
> be to our God for ever and ever.
> Amen!"

¹³Then one of the elders asked me, "These in white robes—who are they, and where did they come from?"

¹⁴I answered, "Sir, you know."

And he said, "These are they who have come out of the great tribulation; they have washed their robes and made them white in the blood of the Lamb. ¹⁵Therefore,

> "they are before the throne of God
>   and serve him day and night in his temple;
> and he who sits on the throne will spread his tent
>   over them.
> ¹⁶Never again will they hunger;
>   never again will they thirst.
> The sun will not beat upon them,
>   nor any scorching heat.
> ¹⁷For the Lamb at the center of the throne will be
>   their shepherd;
> he will lead them to springs of living water.
> And God will wipe away every tear from their eyes."

Original Meaning

REVELATION EXPLICITLY CONTRASTS the second multitude (7:9–17) with the first one (7:1–8). John "heard" the first number and "saw" the second group (7:4, 9); the first was numbered (7:4) and the second "no one could count" (7:9); the first was Jewish (7:4–8) and the second "from every nation" (7:9).[1] The image probably draws from the Jewish expectation of an end-time pilgrimage of Israel's survivors along with survivors from the Gentiles (cf. also 21:24–26).[2]

But does John's vision simply borrow the traditional Jewish image unmodified, or does it adapt and transform the image? If, as we argued above, the first vision portrays symbolically God's end-time spiritual army, then this second vision is a more literal interpretation of the first.[3] All of us as God's people are his end-time army, and we vanquish our foes not by killing them but by martyrdom at their hands (11:7; 12:11; 13:7; 15:2; 21:7). In this, we are like our Lord (5:5–6).

That the multitude is countless probably echoes the promise to the patriarchs (Gen. 13:16; 15:5; 32:12). But here the promised multitude is gathered from all nations; the hope of the gospel has touched all peoples.[4] It is striking that Christians appear here as a group "no one could count" (numbering at minimum in the millions; cf. 5:11), "since the number of Christians, both Jews and Gentiles, living toward the end of the first century A.D. cannot have been very large."[5] This vision would encourage John of the success of Christian witness.

"White robes" are appropriate for worship (see comment on 4:4) but also may reflect their victors' attire and may well connect them with the martyrs of 6:11 and other overcomers of 3:4–5, 18. That they are washed in the Lamb's blood (7:14) may also suggest that they overcame by martyrdom, just as he did (12:11), though the focus of the image is sharing the effects of Christ's expiatory sacrifice on their behalf (cf. 1:5; 1 John 1:7).

"Palm branches" (7:9) sometimes recall the Feast of Tabernacles, which in turn recalls deliverance from slavery in Egypt and God's presence with his

---

1. In some texts a "countless multitude" could stand for Gentile oppressors (20:8), building suspense (Jdt. 2:20), but texts also apply it to Jewish people (3 Macc. 4:17). Though most scholars today identify the two groups in Rev. 7, most scholars at the turn of the twentieth century distinguished them (Aune, *Revelation*, 2:447).

2. Cf. Jonathan A. Draper, "The Heavenly Feast of Tabernacles: Revelation 7.1–17," *JSNT* 19 (Oct. 1983): 133–47, who associates it (probably too specifically) with the end-time pilgrimage for Tabernacles in Zech. 14:16–19 (note the palm branches in 7:9). Ford, *Revelation*, 126, suggests 7:9–17 may portray the Jewish Diaspora remnant.

3. E.g., Ladd, *The Last Things*, 71–72.

4. Bauckham, *Climax of Prophecy*, 223–24.

5. Aune, *Revelation*, 2:466–67.

people in the desert until he brought them into their final inheritance.[6] But most often they reflect any military triumph, as with Maccabean princes and probably with expectations during Jesus' Triumphal Entry in John (John 12:13).[7] The end-time army John has heard about (7:1–8) actually hails the ultimate Victor, Jesus, who has led them to triumph. Like the Lamb, they "conquer" through their own deaths (5:5–6; cf. 6:9–11). Heaven functions like an antiphonal chorus (cf. Ex. 15:21), with the martyrs hailing God and the Lamb, who have led them to their victory (Rev. 7:10), and all of heaven responds with further praises.[8]

When the elder deliberately asks John a question that must provoke him to admit his need of the elder's answer (7:13), he does not expect a knowledgeable answer. Instead, he follows an accepted pedagogic technique of John's culture. Such promptings appear in apocalyptic texts, as do unsolicited questions and consequent responses; questions and answers were part of the standard rhetoric of the genre.[9] When the Lord asked Ezekiel a rhetorical question, the latter responded, "LORD, you alone know" (Ezek. 37:3; cf. Rev. 7:13–14 here). Identifying the saints in white robes as those "who have come out of the great tribulation" (7:14) undoubtedly refers to the superlative tribulation of Daniel 12:1 (cf. also Dan. 9:25; cf. Jer. 30:7), which Matthew (Matt. 24:21) also calls a great tribulation ("great distress"; on the duration of this Tribulation, see comment on 12:6).[10] They have endured the dramatic end-time Tribulation and proved faithful to death.

---

6. See Jub. 16:31. Some see Tabernacles allusions here (Draper, "Feast"; T. F. Glasson, *Moses in the Fourth Gospel* [Naperville, Ill.: Alec R. Allenson, 1963], 107–8); but cf. Aune, *Revelation*, 2:449. For a worship background in general, see G. Adolf Deissmann, *Bible Studies*, tr. A. Grieve (Edinburgh: T. & T. Clark, 1923), 370.

7. See thorough documentation in Aune, *Revelation*, 2:468. Even Tabernacles' palm branches are interpreted with reference to victory (before God's court) in *Pes. Rab Kah.* 27:2.

8. Revelation often employs sevenfold praises; multiple praises appear elsewhere as well (Ford, *Revelation*, 119, identifies seven in 4QS 1.37–40). For "standing" (7:11), Aune, *Revelation*, 2:471, cites the Jewish tradition that no one was permitted to sit in God's presence (4Q405), though the elders are an exception (Rev. 4:4).

9. With promptings, as here, see Zech. 4:2, 5, 13; 5:2; Apoc. Paul 19; without promptings, see Dan. 8:13–16; 12:8; Zech. 1:9, 19, 21; 4:4, 12; 5:6; 6:4; 4 Ezra 10:29–37; 2 Bar. 38:3; T. Abr. 10 A; Apoc. Zeph. 6:16–17. Aune, *Revelation*, 2:472, parallels questions used to identify visitors or visions in the underworld.

10. That Matthew applies it at least partly to the period surrounding A.D. 66–70 is difficult to deny in view of Matt. 24:34 (cf. 23:36–38); see Craig Keener, *Matthew* (Downers Grove, Ill.: InterVarsity, 1997), 347–49 and other commentators. More general "tribulation" is possible (2 Enoch 9:1; 2 Bar. 51:13–14) but unlikely here; the eschatological test fits better (e.g., 1QM 1.11–12), though (with Beale, *Revelation*, 433–35) it may be understood as present.

If triumph in martyrdom sounds like an oxymoron, so does washing one's robes white in blood (7:14).[11] But such vivid contrasts with human expectations prepare the hearer for the graphic picture of blessedness for those who have suffered this world's hostility. These people refused to deify the enthroned emperor; now they are before God's throne (7:15). They resisted the temples of Caesar and other false gods; now they serve continually in God's temple (7:15). They suffered economic deprivation for refusing to serve the world system (13:17); now they are freed from suffering and sorrow, and all their needs are provided (7:16–17).[12]

That this throng serves God day and night (7:15; cf. 4:8) reminds us that the saints are a kingdom of priests (1:6; 5:10), doing what priests and Levites did in the temple courts (1 Chron. 9:33; Ps. 134:1). Ironically, these priests are probably intended as identical with the sacrifices they have offered (see comment on 6:9; also 5:5–6). God's spreading his tabernacle over his people (7:15; cf. 13:6; 21:3) probably alludes to Isaiah 4:5–6, where God promised to restore his people Israel and cover them with his glory as a protective shelter. That text in turn promised a new exodus (cf. Rev. 12:14) by alluding to God's dwelling with his people in the desert, subsequently evoked annually at the Feast of Tabernacles.[13]

Revelation 7:16–17 especially recalls Isaiah 49:10. In that passage God had already promised that in the time of Israel's restoration, his people would no longer hunger or thirst, nor would heat or the sun beat down on them (Isa. 49:10; cf. Rev. 21:23).[14] Further, God as the One with compassion on his people (cf. Isa. 49:10–15) would "guide them and lead them beside springs of water" (49:10; cf. Jer. 31:9).[15] God himself also promised to wipe away the tears of his people (Isa. 25:8).

---

11. Blood notoriously stains what is white (cf. Isa. 1:15, 18), and bathing in blood can function as a metaphor for dying (Sib. Or. 3.696). Though some Asian readers could have wondered if John has adapted the image from the Cybele cult's use of blood baptisms (cf. e.g., Walter Burkert, *Ancient Mystery Cults* [Cambridge, Mass.: Harvard Univ. Press, 1987], 6; Gasparro, *Soteriology*, 107–18; Duthoy, *Taurobolium*, 126–27), a better background is ritual cleansing with blood (Lev. 14:14–28, 52; 16:19; Ezek. 43:20; Heb. 9:14, 22).

12. Kraybill, *Imperial Cult and Commerce*, 222, contrasts God's supply with the imperial dole of food to Rome.

13. The Targum on Isa. 4:2–6 mentions the Messiah (Ford, *Revelation*, 119), though this may be too late for consideration here. Cf. somewhat similar pictures, without the Isaiah allusion, in 1 Enoch 62:14; T. Abr. 20 A; for God as a present shelter from heat and sun, see Ps. 121:5–6; Sir. 34:19.

14. The background of "scorching heat" may well be the Palestinian sirocco (Ford, *Revelation*, 121); but the sense of the identical LXX term is usually more neutral (Gen. 8:22; 31:40; 2 Sam. 4:5; cf. Isa. 4:6).

15. For eschatological springs, see (representing wisdom) 1 Enoch 48:1; 49:1; in the afterlife, *p. Hag.* 2:2, §5; *Sanh.* 6:6, §2 (depicting paradise conditions; cf. the luxury in Jos. and Asen. 2:12/20).

"The Lamb" in 7:17 clearly fulfills a role Isaiah assigned to Yahweh; John is assuredly claiming Jesus' deity. The image is striking for another reason: God's compassionately leading his people to water presents him as a shepherd (Ps. 23:1–2; Isa. 40:11); yet in Revelation, the Lamb is the shepherd (7:17).[16] Lambs were the weakest members of the flock (Isa. 40:11), but Jesus is the Shepherd precisely because he was the slaughtered Lamb, the one slain for his people (John 10:11; cf. Isa. 53:7) and whose mortal weakness became the conduit for God's power (2 Cor. 13:4).[17]

God promised an end to sorrow when he restored his people (Isa. 35:10; 51:11); but here eschatological rest from pain for the righteous is available immediately upon death (cf. Rev. 21:4; cf. Isa. 57:1–2).[18] Most notably a biblical promise to Israel becomes the hope of believers from all nations grafted into Israel's heritage of obedience to the true God (Rev. 7:9).

THE GOSPEL FOR ALL. The international focus of Revelation goes far beyond its contemporaries' expectations and proves central to New Testament teaching because it is so radical: Gentile Christians can be grafted into God's people. In contrast to the early church, no one today is surprised to discover that many Gentiles are Christians, but we can still learn from the principle that God embraces those whom we do not expect. Sometimes we harbor our suspicions about various groups' receptivity to the gospel (e.g., Hindus or Muslims). Some peoples may be more open to the gospel because they have experienced more positive exposure to it; ironically, Jewish people, from whom the gospel spread to the Gentiles, have often been turned off to the gospel by centuries of "Christian" hostility, including being tortured during the Inquisition, burned on crosses, and forcibly drowned in the name of baptism.

Yet the gospel challenges our prejudices. I and my multicultural teammates had the opportunity to lead many African-Americans, many Puerto

---

16. This is also the image of a new exodus (Isa. 35:7–10; 48:21); see also "shepherding" (literally) with the rod of iron in Rev. 2:27; 12:5, and leading the 144,000 in 14:4.

17. To be sure, we know of sheep leading other sheep (Beasley-Murray, *Revelation*, 149); but this remains distinct from calling a lamb the "shepherd." Metaphorical uses of "shepherd" exist (Sib. Or. 3.642), but it was an ancient image for leadership (see C. S. Keener, "Shepherd, Flock," 1090–93 in *Dictionary of the Later New Testament and Its Developments*, ed. R. P. Martin and P. H. Davids [Downers Grove, Ill.: InterVarsity, 1997]).

18. For eschatological rest from suffering for the righteous, see 2 Thess. 1:7; 1 Enoch 25:6; 2 Enoch 65:9; T. Moses 10:1; Ex. Rab. 23:11; for peace in heaven now, cf. Sifre Num. 42.2.3. This is more than simply the cessation of sorrow (as in Euripides, Alc. 935–38).

Ricans, and a few Anglos to Christ doing personal evangelism in New York City; during the same time I was unsuccessful in leading to Christ any of the Russian Jews among whom I also ministered. But many did begin to listen to us, and a harvest came later. We have no right to decide who will receive God's good news, and we may be grateful that those who witnessed to us or to our spiritual predecessors did not prejudge its proper recipients. But if we claim any loyalty to Christ's gospel, this requires us to transcend our cultural prejudices both to witness to and to lovingly embrace believers from all cultures (cf. Rom. 1:14–16; 1 Cor. 12:13; Gal. 3:28).

Interpreting positive images. We should also be careful to interpret the accumulation of positive images positively. A literal lack of all heat (pressing 7:16 as far as it can be pressed) would spell death to every human long before the temperature dropped to absolute zero. Yet the image is a positive, not a negative, one: Just as shepherds guard their flock from excessive heat, removing them from direct sunlight during the hottest time of day, so Jesus will protect us from uncomfortable exposure (Ps. 121:6).[19]

Some believers wonder how there can be joy in heaven unless God erases any memory of loved ones who have perished without Christ, and appeal to the lack of tears in 7:17. But the text says nothing about erasure of memory; God may just put events in a magnificently broader context. But one wonders whether in the hereafter we will ever contemplate the fate of the damned. Contrast the lack of tears with traditions such as those found in the first-century Similitudes of Enoch, in which those in the heavens could observe what was occurring on earth (1 En. 57:2); in that work, the wicked might remain as a spectacle for the righteous after the judgment (62:12) but then be banished forever from their sight (62:13).

TRUE HEROES. Our society is full of celebrities, and the church often trots out its own celebrity cult as well (cf. 1 Cor. 1:12; 3:4).[20] But the biblical conception of heroes differs markedly from our culture's conception. The great end-time army of God (Rev. 7:1–8) turns out not to be powerful warriors who slay the wicked for God, but an army of martyrs who die for proclaiming God's message (7:9–17). They hail the

---

19. On herders protecting animals from the sun, see Virgil, *Georg.* 3.331–34; Longus, 1.8, 25.

20. For warnings against Christian celebrity cultism, see 1 Cor. 3:4–7; Chuck Colson, "The Celebrity Illusion," *CT* (Dec. 11, 1987), 72; idem, "The Pedestal Complex," *CT* (Feb. 5, 1990), 96. In secular society, few explicitly Christian heroes except the Pope and the late Mother Teresa have ranked high in polls ("Heroes Are Back," *USNWR* (Apr. 22, 1985), 44–48).

ultimate hero, their leader Jesus (7:9). The world's temporary favor allows us to get some work done (Matt. 21:8–11; Acts 2:47; cf. 1 Sam. 18:7–8, 16, 30), but is always fleeting (Matt. 27:22–25; Acts 12:3; cf. 1 Sam 25:10). May we aspire not to be great heroes according to the world's values, but according to God's.

This text reminds us who the true hero is. Almost every hero in the Bible exhibits some flaws, whether major flaws like Samson and Jephthah or minor ones like Abraham and Samuel. The one exception is Jesus, the only true hero in the ultimate sense. That the martyr army holds palm branches to praise their conquering general reminds us of our dependence on Jesus and summons us to worship. Referring to the Second World War, Colson notes that "many soldiers died to bring about the victory in Europe. But in the Kingdom of God, it was the death of the King that assured the victory."[21] The text reminds us most of all that our triumph rests on the finished work of Christ (7:14), and our future hope is in fellowship with him (7:15–17).

The nature of triumph. That these believers overcome by suffering and the victory of the Lamb rather than by armed resistance redefines for us the nature of triumph for the present age. Christ reveals his power more clearly through the broken than the powerful, more through the Mother Teresas than through the Stalins, more through the cross than through the sword. One Jewish writer observes her respect for one sort of Christianity: "When Christianity speaks of God's strength being revealed in weakness, I understand it best through the deeds of evangelicals who do not overlook those who are weak and apparently powerless."[22]

Examples of such grace evident in weakness often move even hard hearts. Some homeless teenagers who grew up on Philadelphia's streets beat to death a Korean honors graduate from Eastern College doing graduate studies in medicine at the University of Pennsylvania. The victim had been mailing a letter to his family at home in Korea. The parents sat silently through his murderers' entire trial, asking merely for an opportunity to speak at the end. After the guilty verdict they knelt before the judge, and

> before a stunned audience these parents begged . . . the judge to release their son's murderers to them so that they could give the boys the home and care they had never had. They were Christians, they explained to the judge, and they wanted to show something of the

---

21. Colson, *Kingdoms in Conflict,* 85.
22. Blu Greenberg, "Mission, Witness and Proselytism," 226–39 in *Evangelicals and Jews in an Age of Pluralism,* ed. Marc H. Tanenbaum, Marvin R. Wilson, and A. James Rudin (Grand Rapids: Baker, 1984), 237.

grace they had received from God to those who had done them such grievous evil. The judge, who newspaper reporters claimed had a reputation for being hard and unemotional, had tears in his eyes as he explained, "That is not the way our system of justice works!"[23]

By their forgiveness, the parents testified of a kingdom utterly different from the kingdoms of this world, a kingdom for which all long who dare to believe its existence.

John does not explicitly tell us that all who leave the Tribulation (7:14) die martyrs' deaths, but this is the only particular exit from the Tribulation he elsewhere specifies for believers.[24] Not every individual Christian has the privilege of martyrdom, but we are a martyr church, fueled by passion to evangelize the world no matter what the cost. As Tertullian put it, thinking of the martyrs of his day (late second and early third centuries A.D.), "So we have conquered, when we are killed; we escape when we are condemned." When we are surrounded by firewood and burned alive, "this is our garb of victory, the robe embroidered with the palm; this our triumphal chariot."[25]

Most of us today, at least those in comfortable lifestyles and with families, do not think of martyrdom as a privilege. Yet if we must die in some manner if the Lord tarries, should we not wish our deaths, as well as our lives, to bring God as much glory as possible? Here the martyrs, like suffering apostles before them (Acts 5:41), joyfully praise their eternal commander for leading them to this victory through their refusal to compromise his honor (7:10).[26] If we take this vision seriously, it may invite some dissonance for those of us who are too comfortable with this world. Just how much does the honor of our Lord Jesus Christ matter to us?

From all nations. How should we envision Revelation's multicultural throng? Both archaeology and writings from John's day show us that his audience knew of not only the Mediterranean world, but also of kingdoms and traders from west and east Africa, India, China, and the British Isles, all peoples so remote from the first Christians that the image of "every tribe" may

---

23. Tony Campolo, *Wake Up America* (Grand Rapids: Zondervan, 1991), 47–48.

24. Most commentators do accept them as martyrs, including Walvoord, *Revelation*, 144; idem, *Prophecy Knowledge Handbook*, 560 (so also Lindsey, *New World Coming*, 123, though he views them as converts of the 144,000). Aune, *Revelation*, 2:474, regards it as "a reasonable inference" that at least some of them are (he applies it to all Christians who die before the end, 2:447).

25. Tertullian, *Apol.* 50.3 (LCL, p. 223).

26. Because of the Lamb's victory, "death is no longer a horror for the church, but only a passing out of great tribulation (7:14)" (Rissi, *Time and History*, 110; cf. 2 Cor. 5:8).

have demanded considerable faith. Our geographical knowledge today is richer, and the gospel entrenched in far more cultures.[27] Imagine the multicultural chorus of saints from all ages—ancient Israel's Levite psalmists, clapping African saints with joyful praises, European Reformers with their majestic hymns, monks with their Gregorian and Ethiopian Coptic chants, Latin American Pentecostals with shouts of triumph, messianic Jews dancing the *horah,* and a generation of North American street evangelists doing gospel rap!

Many Christians today think that the gospel obliterates cultural distinctions (and sometimes expect Christians from other cultures to simply join their churches and assimilate into their "normal" cultural style of worship). But this text suggests that, far from obliterating culture, God takes what is useful in each culture and transforms it into an instrument of praise for his glory.[28] One of my professors in my missions concentration during my seminary career was Morris Williams, for the previous decade the U.S. missions director for a Pentecostal denomination in Africa.[29] It was he who first opened my eyes to the fact that this text suggests not the obliteration of cultures in the world to come, but the celebration of the gifts God has given each people and culture (and mixture of cultures) offered for his glory.

As Charles Wesley cried, "O for a thousand tongues to sing my great Redeemer's praise!" Worship in the Spirit (see comment on 1:10) transcends cultural prejudices, but often brings forth God-given elements in various cultures, because God is too big to be limited to a single culture's worship style, even if it is a dominant culture that thinks it has the only normative way of offering praise! This is not to suggest that we can or should try to blend or represent all these expressions in one local congregation, which must prove relevant first to its own community. But it offers a hope for the future as well as an ideal for the present. God has sown into thousands of cultures through history aspects of his image in humanity; just as human immune systems are stronger the more genetically distinct their parents, so the body of Christ is strongest when it incorporates the perspectives of all its members.[30]

---

27. For where the gospel is growing most rapidly (Latin America, Africa, and much of Asia), see Sharon E. Mumper, "Where in the World Is the Church Growing?" *CT* (July 11, 1986), 17–21.

28. Often recognized, e.g., Steve Hawthorne, "Laying a Firm Foundation for Mission in the Next Millennium," *Missions Frontiers Bulletin* (March 1998), 9–14 (p. 11). For the biblical mandate of reaching people groups, not just individuals, see John Piper, *Let the Nations be Glad! The Supremacy of God in Missions* (Grand Rapids: Baker, 1993), 169–81.

29. For his emphasis on the indigenous church and partnering with national churches, see Morris O. Williams, *Partnership in Mission,* rev. ed. (Springfield, Mo.: Morris Williams, 1986).

30. For God's work in many cultures even before the message of salvation, see Don Richardson, *Peace Child* (Ventura, Calif.: Regal, 1974).

William Seymour, the African-American leader of the Azusa Street revival that birthed the hundreds of millions of Pentecostals and charismatics in the world today, concluded that the greatest sign of the Spirit's work was love, especially and necessarily as expressed across racial and ethnic lines.[31] We should not be too surprised to think that biblical writers shared a similar emphasis (Acts 1:8; 2:5–11; Eph. 2:18, 22).[32]

---

31. Cecil M. Robeck Jr., "William J. Seymour and 'the Bible Evidence,'" in *Initial Evidence: Historical and Biblical Perspectives on the Pentecostal Doctrine of Spirit Baptism*, ed. Gary B. McGee (Peabody, Mass.: Hendrickson, 1991), 79–81; cf. H. V. Synan, "Seymour, William Joseph," 779–81 in *Dictionary of Pentecostal and Charismatic Movements*, ed. Stanley Burgess, Gary McGee, and Patrick Alexander (Grand Rapids: Zondervan, 1988), 781.

32. Many fine books exist on reconciliation, including Spencer Perkins and Chris Rice, *More Than Equals* (Downers Grove, Ill.: InterVarsity, 1993); Raleigh Washington and Glenn Kehrein, *Breaking Down Walls* (Chicago: Moody, 1993); John Dawson, *Healing America's Wounds* (Ventura, Calif.: Regal, 1994). For biblical and theological approaches, see the essays in *The Gospel in Black and White: Theological Resources for Racial Reconciliation*, ed. Dennis L. Ockholm (Downers Grove, Ill.: InterVarsity, 1997), including my essay on its centrality in New Testament thought ("The Gospel and Racial Reconciliation," 117–30).

Revelation 8:1–13

WHEN HE OPENED the seventh seal, there was silence in heaven for about half an hour.

²And I saw the seven angels who stand before God, and to them were given seven trumpets.

³Another angel, who had a golden censer, came and stood at the altar. He was given much incense to offer, with the prayers of all the saints, on the golden altar before the throne. ⁴The smoke of the incense, together with the prayers of the saints, went up before God from the angel's hand. ⁵Then the angel took the censer, filled it with fire from the altar, and hurled it on the earth; and there came peals of thunder, rumblings, flashes of lightning and an earthquake.

⁶Then the seven angels who had the seven trumpets prepared to sound them.

⁷The first angel sounded his trumpet, and there came hail and fire mixed with blood, and it was hurled down upon the earth. A third of the earth was burned up, a third of the trees were burned up, and all the green grass was burned up.

⁸The second angel sounded his trumpet, and something like a huge mountain, all ablaze, was thrown into the sea. A third of the sea turned into blood, ⁹a third of the living creatures in the sea died, and a third of the ships were destroyed.

¹⁰The third angel sounded his trumpet, and a great star, blazing like a torch, fell from the sky on a third of the rivers and on the springs of water—¹¹the name of the star is Wormwood. A third of the waters turned bitter, and many people died from the waters that had become bitter.

¹²The fourth angel sounded his trumpet, and a third of the sun was struck, a third of the moon, and a third of the stars, so that a third of them turned dark. A third of the day was without light, and also a third of the night.

¹³As I watched, I heard an eagle that was flying in midair call out in a loud voice: "Woe! Woe! Woe to the inhabitants of the earth, because of the trumpet blasts about to be sounded by the other three angels!"

THE FIRST SIX TRUMPETS (8:1–9:21), like the first six seals, form a literary unit partitioned from the seventh in the series by an interlude (10:1–11:14). Of these, the first four form one unit (8:7–12), like the four horsemen (6:1–8); the final three form another, summarized in 8:13 as the three "woes." Like the bowls of God's anger that follow (ch. 16), most of the judgments associated with these trumpets recall the plagues of Exodus. That the number is reduced from ten to seven does not diminish the resemblance; Revelation is full of sevens, and other Jewish writers sometimes omitted or rearranged the plagues.[1]

The Seventh Seal (8:1)

AFTER SIX THUNDEROUS seals of judgment (6:1–17) and a dramatic interlude in 7:1–17, the reader may be pardoned for a sense of anticlimax when reaching the final seal and hearing—silence. Yet this very anticlimax is part of the narrative's dramatic jarring technique, shocking us into attention with its ironies. Scholars debate the meaning of the silence in 8:1. An assembly may experience silence because no one will volunteer for a difficult task, such as leading a battle; perhaps the time signals the inadequacy of those waiting until God's appointed agent comes (cf. 5:3).[2] Then again, it may recall the sort of silence appropriate to the completion of speech (1 Esd. 4:41), because matters have been settled; or the sort that characterizes a break in conversation before a new topic emerges.[3]

A better interpretation (although not the one we most prefer) is that all of heaven is silenced to allow the prayers of the saints to be heard.[4] This interpretation has much in its favor. Most important is the evidence that incense and sacrifice were supposed to be offered in silence in the Jerusalem temple.[5] One could even silence others' prayers so that a leader's prayer could be heard (3 Macc. 6:1). Commentators especially cite a Jewish tradition for the

---

1. See Ps-Philo 10; also Artapanus in Eusebius, *P.E.* 9.27.28–33. The plagues also appeared as God's "war" on Egypt (*Pes. Rab Kah.* 7:11). For a thorough treatment of a seven-plague tradition in early Judaism, see Aune, *Revelation*, 2:502–4.

2. Appian, *R.H.* 6.4.18. Silence may also stem from grief (Achilles Tatius, 1.13.1).

3. Plutarch, *T.T.* 8.2.1, *Mor.* 718B.

4. Michaels, *Revelation*, 117; Beasley-Murray, *Revelation*, 150; Caird, *Commentary on Revelation*, 106–7.

5. See Israel Knohl, "Between Voice and Silence: The Relationship Between Prayer and Temple Cult," *JBL* 115 (1996): 17–30 (pp. 20–23); Peter Wick, "There Was Silence in Heaven (Revelation 8:1): An Annotation to Israel Knohl's 'Between Voice and Silence,'" *JBL* 117 (Fall 1998): 512–14. But given the bleating of sacrificial sheep, etc., the sanctuary itself would not really have been quiet.

silencing of angels so Israel's prayers may be heard (e.g., *b. Hag.* 12b), though this is of uncertain date.[6] Against this interpretation one can protest that it allows some interpreters to think that the trumpets follow the seventh seal rather than coinciding with the earlier seals (8:2–5); but this objection will work only if John's visionary time is identical with real time, which it is not.[7] The schematic arrangement of the trumpets after the seals reflects the progression of John's visions, not a chronological sequence of history.

A specifically eschatological interpretation to the silence, however, seems most likely. In some ancient texts, silence characterizes respectful listening to another's speech.[8] There is no speech mentioned here, but silence may similarly come from awe (Job 40:4).[9] Texts refer to the world's silence before God at the Day of Judgment (Zeph. 1:17; Zech. 2:13; Rom. 3:19; cf. Rev. 18:22–23; 20:12).[10] The silence may be a signal of return to the primeval creation, characterized by such silence and followed by the resurrection (see 4 Ezra 7:30; 2 Bar. 3:7).[11]

The Power of Prayer (8:2–6)

THESE VERSES ADDRESS the efficacy of the saints' prayers. The seven angels "who stand before God" (8:2) probably struck most of John's audience as the seven archangels of Jewish tradition (e.g., Tob. 12:15; 1 En. 20:1–8)—powerful angels authorized to act directly by God himself. Many possible sources exist for the image of trumpets given to these angels, for people employed

---

6. Bauckham, *Climax of Prophecy*, 73, seeks earlier evidence in 4QShir Shabb (4Q405 20–22), but most of his early evidence (74–83) is ambiguous. He estimates reasonably that the approximate duration of the morning incense offering (which immediately follows in this vision, 8:3–4) was half an hour (ibid., 83); but was this period standard enough knowledge for Revelation's first audience to have grasped it?

7. For the seventh seal and trumpet each giving way to the following series of judgment visions, see Ellul, *Apocalypse*, 44.

8. For silence while listening to another, see Homer, *Il.* 19.255–56; Apollonus Rhodius, 1.513–15; Virgil, *Aen.* 10.100–103; 11.241, 300. For opening a court, see Chariton, *Chaer.* 5.4.9; for silencing a proud interlocutor, see Matt. 22:34; Aulus Gellius, 1.2.13; Demosthenes, *On the Crown* §112; for not knowing what to say, see Chariton, *Chaer.* 8.2.12.

9. In reverent worship, Diogenes Laertius, 8.1.33; in awe, Chariton, *Chaer.* 5.5.9; in shame (Arrian, *Alex.* 7.8.3; 7.11.2); in mourning (Arrian, *Alex.* 7.14.8).

10. See further judgment images in Beale, *Revelation*, 446–52. Ford, *Revelation*, 134, also notes that 1QpHab 13.2–4 in this way applies Hab 2:20.

11. Cf. also the pause of waters for three hours before the end in 4 Ezra 6:24. The new creation image is the one preferred here by Joachim Jeremias, *The Central Message of the New Testament* (New York: Charles Scribner's Sons, 1965), 89; Rissi, *Time and History*, 4. Though one could parallel the seventh trumpet with the seventh day of creation, the idea of eschatological rest (cf. 14:13; T. Jud. 22:2) is probably not present here.

---

trumpets in a variety of ways.[12] Given the other temple imagery in heaven (e.g., Rev. 4:6; 6:9; 15:5), however, the trumpets (8:2) likely recall those used in the temple for worship.[13]

Yet these instruments of worship also signal imminent judgments (cf. 15:6–8), playing on another common usage of trumpets as calls to war.[14] The altar of incense and censer are temple instruments implying impending judgment (8:3–5). The idea of a heavenly temple was an ancient one, probably even implied in the symbolism of the original tabernacle in the desert (Heb. 8:5).[15]

Most important, however, the incense explicitly represents "the prayers of all the saints" offered before the heavenly temple (8:3–4), an idea those steeped in the Old Testament would easily understand (Ps. 141:2; Luke 1:10; cf. Jub. 2:22). That judgment immediately follows this offering of prayers makes sense when we consider the prayers of saints offered so far: They have been crying out for vindication (6:10), and though the final judgment is not yet (6:11), some of their vindication occurs within history.[16] They may wonder why the answer to their prayers has been delayed (6:10); this passage may also provide an explanation, or at least a comparison that makes sense. Just as the full amount of proclamation and attendant suffering must be fulfilled (6:11), perhaps the prayers of the saints must also come to a particular level before the intervention takes place.

Thus, it is as fresh prayers for vindication are added to other prayers (8:3) that judgment is sent into motion. The sufferings of God's people invite his

---

12. Caird, *Commentary on Revelation*, 108–10, focuses on trumpets for the day of judgment (cf. also Apoc. Zeph. 9:1), comparing the New Year's festival; but this comparison is most apt for the final trumpet (10:7; cf. 4 Ezra 6:23–25); Beasley-Murray, *Revelation*, 154, notes Sinai imagery (Ex. 19:16, 19; 20:18). Cf. heavenly trumpets blown by angels also in Apoc. Moses 37:1–2; T. Abr. 12 A. For a description of the narrow, short silver trumpet, see Josephus, *Ant.* 3.291.

13. See 2 Chron. 7:6; 29:26; Ezra 3:10; *m. Arak.* 2:5; *R.H.* 3:2–4:2; *Suk.* 5:4; *Tam.* 7:3. Cf. trumpets at the Sabbath offerings in J. M. Baumgarten, "The Sabbath Trumpets in 4Q493 Mc," *RevQ* 12 (1987): 555–59.

14. For trumpets as battle calls, see Num. 10:9; 31:6; Judg. 3:27; 6:34; 1 Sam. 13:3; 1 Macc. 5:31–33; Josephus, *War* 3.89–91, 265; Livy, 24.46.3; Appian, *R.H.* 6.9.52; Lucan, *C.W.* 4.750; Arrian, *Alex.* 6.3.3. For trumpets at a battle John's contemporaries would understand as the final one, see Zeph. 1:16; see further Aune, *Revelation*, 2:519.

15. See Umberto Cassuto, *A Commentary on the Book of Exodus*, tr. I. Abrahams (Jerusalem: Magnes, 1967), 322; Richard J. Clifford, "Tent of El and Israelite Tent of Meeting," *CBQ* 33 (April 1971): 221–27 (p. 226); Keener and Usry, *Defending Black Faith*, 143, and other sources cited there.

16. Others concur that 8:4 alludes to 6:9–11 (Bowman, *First Christian Drama*, 61). Roloff, *Revelation*, 107, objects that most prayer in the book is praise; but John does not use these terms interchangeably. "Smoke" can be positive (15:8) or refer to judgment (9:2–3, 17–18; 14:11; 18:9, 18; 19:3).

---

intervention, even if his time is not always our time (Ex. 2:23–25; Luke 18:7).[17] What takes place in heaven clearly affects what occurs on earth (Rev. 8:5), and though we cannot always see the processes, many judgments come in response to human prayers.[18]

Punishment by Plagues (8:7–12)

IN 8:7–12, JOHN reports the first four trumpets, a group set off to correspond numerically with the first four seals (6:1–8), to be followed by still more dramatic plagues (8:13). These plagues resemble those in Exodus: God sent hail mixed with fire both in Egypt and in Revelation (Ex. 9:23–24; Rev. 8:7); he turned Egypt's water supply to blood (Ex. 7:20–21), so God turns much of the world's water into blood (Rev. 8:8–9) and otherwise makes it undrinkable (8:10–11); he sent the plague of darkness on Egypt of old (Ex. 10:22) and on the world in Revelation (8:12). The righteous, however, are protected (7:1–8), just as Israel was (Ex. 8:22; 9:26); in the end both are preserved by the blood of the paschal Lamb (Ex. 12:13; Rev. 5:5–6).

John's audience will readily recognize the allusion to the biblical plague of hail in 8:7, but the theme of judgment would not have been lost even on their pagan contemporaries. Dangerous hail or hail mixed with other things appeared as a prodigy, a warning of divine judgment in the ancient Mediterranean world.[19] Jewish sources also recognized both hail and the raining of fire (probably lightning) as God's judgments on the world, especially in the end time.[20] The destruction of one-third of the trees (8:7) means shortages of fruit, including essential staples like olives, figs, and presumably grapes for wine (if vines are included as trees, as in Columella, *Trees* 11.1–2). The destruction of all the green grass means the impending death of sheep, goats, and cattle—hence the end of the world's supply of meat, milk and cheese.[21]

---

17. Talbert, *Apocalypse*, 40, compares the delivery by angels of saints' cries for vengeance as a catalyst for God's intervention in 1 Enoch.

18. For portals in the heavens, see Gen. 7:11; *Baal Epic* 2.6.25–35. Those in heaven could observe earth in 1 En. 57:2.

19. Including bloody rain (Homer, *Il.* 16.459; Livy, 24.10.7; 40.19.2; 43.13.5; Appian, *C.W.* 2.5.36) or stones raining down (Livy, 25.7.7; 26.23.5; 27.37.1, 4; 42.2.4; 43.13.4; 45.16.5; Appian, *C.W.* 4.1.4). Hail also seems to have functioned as a metaphor for war when so qualified by the context (Virgil, *Aen.* 9.669–71; Sib. Or. 5.93), though that sense is unlikely here.

20. For eschatological hail, see Sib. Or. 3.691; *Ex. Rab.* 12:2; for fire, Sib. Or. 5.337–79; 2 Bar. 27:10.

21. On the use of sheep's and goat's milk for cheeses, see Longus, 1.23; Epictetus, *Disc.* 1.16.8; in more detail C. S. Keener, "Milk," in *Dictionary of New Testament Background*, ed. Craig Evans and Stanley Porter (Downers Grove, Ill.: InterVarsity, forthcoming).

The blood and fire in the hail may portend the following plagues of bloody water (8:8) and the fiery stars or mountains falling into the seas (8:8–10). The transformation of water into blood (8:8) recalls the first judgment on Egypt for refusing to release God's people from captivity (Ex. 7:17). Although only one-third of the sea is affected here, allowing human life to continue on earth, the plague is severe. Egypt, which was totally dependent on the Nile not only for drinking water but also both for fish and irrigation for its fertile soil, was economically devastated even by the first plague (7:18); Rome, which profited from its sea trade with other peoples, would suffer likewise (cf. Rev. 13:1; 17:1; 18:17–18).[22] Most people ate more fish than meat, so this plague might prove more devastating to the food supply than its predecessor (8:7). Even had anyone missed the allusion to the first plague in Egypt, everyone would recognize the turning of any water to blood as a sign of divine displeasure.[23] Such a plague could come either directly in response to the saints' cries for vindication (8:4–5), as here, or in response to prophetic announcements (11:6).

The mountain's burning with fire (8:8) may recall Sinai and God's law (Ex. 24:17; Deut. 4:11; 5:23; 9:15; Heb. 12:18), but may also simply be another apocalyptic symbol of judgment. Heavenly stars (often symbolizing angels; cf. Rev. 9:1; 12:4) can appear like burning mountains (1 En. 18:13; 21:3), and a burning star falls into the sea in Sibylline Oracles 5.158–61 and burns not only the sea but Babylon and Italy, as judgment for the suffering of righteous Jews. Both the Sibylline Oracles and Revelation may depend on the less obvious image in Jer. 51:25, 42.[24]

The third plague (8:10–11) resembles the turning of water into blood in 8:8–9 in that it also addresses the destruction of the water supply on which humanity depends. Thus it recalls the plagues, but adds to them an allusion to the bitter, polluted waters of Marah, which God had purified (Ex. 15:23); now pure water becomes poisoned. All ancients recognize this as a terrible divine judgment (Jer. 8:14).[25] "Wormwood" was known for its bitterness (Prov. 5:4; Lam. 3:15, 19) and sometimes was thought to be poisonous (Deut.

---

22. Blood is the first of the plagues listed also in Jub. 48:5; later rabbis said that even the Egyptians' spittle became blood, and when Israelites gave real water to Egyptians, it became blood in their hands (Ex. Rab. 9:10; Num. Rab. 9:14).

23. Cicero, *De Divinatione* 1.43.98; Virgil, *Aen.* 4.453–63; *Lives of Prophets* 4.20 (§27 in Schermann). Judgment by water appears in Sib. Or. 3.461–62; with reference to the Flood in 1 En. 66:1; 89:5–6; bloody waters serve as a battle metaphor in Isa. 15:9.

24. Cf. here Caird, *Commentary on Revelation*, 114–15; Ford, *Revelation*, 133. "Blazing like a torch" (8:10) uses the same wording as 4:5, but unless the "spirits" are angels (cf. comment on 1:4), this is probably simply common imagery. On falling stars as omens of disaster, see Aune, *Revelation*, 2:520. There may also be an allusion to burning debris affecting bodies of water at the eruption of Vesuvius in A.D. 79, at which over 10,000 people died (ibid.).

25. Lucan, *C.W.* 1.648; as an end-time omen of disaster, see 4 Ezra 5:9.

29:18; Jer. 9:15; 23:15); it also appears as a metaphor for sin (Deut. 29:18; Amos 5:7; 6:12).[26]

The smiting of the celestial lights (8:12) may refer to shortening of the times as in some other end-time predictions (2 Bar. 20:1), but more likely focuses on the darkness itself.[27] The darkness surely recalls the penultimate plague on Egypt (Ex. 10:21–22; cf. Wisd. Sol. 17), probably representing judgment against Egypt's highly esteemed sun god (Ex. 12:12).[28] Pagans also feared darkness over the land, which represented a catastrophic judgment.[29] This sort of judgment (also Rev. 9:2) foreshadows the ultimate smiting of sun and moon (6:12–13) and their absence in the new world (21:23).

The narrative sets the three remaining plagues off from the first four as particularly traumatic; they receive the title "woes" (8:13). John's Jewish-Christian audience would understand the harsh nature of these judgments readily; they were probably familiar with a similar use of "woe" found in early Jewish texts like 1 Enoch.[30] Overhearing a message not specifically directed toward the hearer is also a standard rhetorical device in prophetic and apocalyptic literature (Dan. 8:13, 16; Zech. 6:7; 1 En. 67:12), though it was often for the hearer's benefit (Dan. 8:14, 17; Zech. 6:8).

The significance of "an eagle" declaring this message is more difficult. Perhaps it simply stands for a heavenly creature (4:7; 12:14; Apoc. Moses 33:2), but this leaves unexplained why an eagle is chosen here rather than another creature (cf. Mark 1:10). Eagles were used to carry messages, like some other birds (2 Bar. 77:19; 4 Bar. 6:15–16; 7:4, 6), but they were not known for literally speaking the words (as here)! It could also represent simply a heavenly throne angel (Rev. 4:7).

---

26. Where wormwood in the technical sense is meant, it is bitter but not poisonous, and may have narcotic uses (F. Nigel Hepper, *Baker Encylcopedia of Bible Plants* [Grand Rapids: Baker, 1992], 152).

27. Apocalyptic interpreters' hermeneutics may have allowed the ceasing of day in Gen. 8:22 to indicate the end of earth. Mark 13:20 refers only to the shortening of the elect's suffering.

28. Some later rabbis felt this plague of darkness would now focus on Rome (*Lev. Rab.* 6:6; *Pes. Rab.* 17:7), though they also claimed the darkness slew the wicked of Israel (*Pes. Rab Kah.* 5:9; *Ex. Rab.* 14:3; *Num. Rab.* 15:12; *Song Rab.* 2:13, § 1).

29. Ovid. *Metam.* 2.394–96; 4.200–201; Livy, 40.45.2. Sometimes it would be withdrawn in response to petitions (Homer, *Il.* 17.644–50). Early Judaism continued to acknowledge darkness as a judgment (Sib. Or. 4.56–58), including eschatologically (*Pes. Rab Kah.* 9:1; *Ex. Rab.* 14:3), though sometimes it functioned as a more general metaphor of judgment (Sib. Or. 11.45). Aune, *Revelation*, 2:523, suggests this fourth plague reverses the creation of celestial lights on the fourth day (Gen. 1:14–19).

30. See 1 En. 91–105 in R. A. Coughenour, "The Woe-Oracles in Ethiopic Enoch," *JSJ* 9 (1978): 192–97. "Woes" and laments regularly appear in early Jewish prophetic texts as in the Old Testament (Matt. 11:21; 1 En. 94:6–8; 100:7–9; Sib. Or. 3.319, 480, 483, 492, 504, 508, 512; 11.138; *ARN* 24 A); cf. Rev. 18:19.

Undoubtedly the eagle functions as a symbol of judgment, but the specific association remains elusive. The primary emblem of a Roman legion was a silver or gold eagle (*aquila*) carried on a pole; thus, perhaps the image is one of Rome's legions judged by legions superior to them (9:7–10, 14–17).[31] Because eagles were predators, believed to carry off even a live lamb to feed their young (Babrius, 137.1–2), an eagle could stand for judgment (Deut. 28:49; Jer. 48:40; Hos. 8:1); certainly they so function in depictions of birds (probably vultures) that devour carcasses of the slain (Matt. 24:28; Luke 17:37; cf. Ezek. 39:17; Hab. 1:8; Rev. 19:17–18).

But while its message is judgment, this eagle is the messenger, not necessarily a symbol of its content (cf. 19:17). Thus, the symbolic interpretation is plausible, but uncertain. Yet Greeks viewed eagles as omens (whether of good or evil) from Zeus, and Romans, who sought to predict the future by the flight of birds, may especially see a symbol of a divine messenger here.[32] In any case the eagle ascends to "midair," to the sun's zenith, "so that the entire world may hear his cry."[33]

GOD'S ACTS IN THE PAST. By reusing the plagues of Exodus (and God's protection of his own people there) Revelation alludes to God's acts in the past, reminding us that his work in history is our firmest assurance for the future. (It is no wonder, then, that theological liberalism, shaped as it was by Enlightenment antisupernaturalism, has been inspired to doubt the historicity of anything supernatural in Scripture. But it is difficult to deny some historical miracles that Revelation itself predicts, such as the fall of the Roman empire, in contrast to the perseverance of Christianity and the Jewish people.)[34] If God judged the oppressors of our spiritual predecessors, he will also overturn in due time the powers that seek to crush his people now.

---

31. On the eagle as a legionary emblem, see Everett Ferguson, *Backgrounds of Early Christianity* (Grand Rapids: Eerdmans, 1987), 40; cf. Josephus, *Ant.* 17.151. The eagle of 4 Ezra 11:1–12:39 is Rome.

32. Homer, *Il.* 8.247; 24.315; *Od.* 2.146; 15.161; 19.543; 20.243; Callimachus, *Hymn* 1.67–68. Eagles also functioned as divine metaphors in Jewish tradition (Ex. 19:4; see Ben Zion Wacholder and Steven Bowman, "Ezechielus the Dramatist and Ezekiel the Prophet: Is the Mysterious *zōon* in the *Exagōgé* a Phoenix?" *HTR* 78 [July 1985]: 253–77).

33. Beasley-Murray, *Revelation*, 159. This seems more likely (cf. 19:17) than assuming the middle of various layers of heaven (2 En. 17:1).

34. Other events in this category include the destruction of Jerusalem one generation after Jesus' crucifixion (Matt. 23:36–24:2, 15, 34) or the restoration of Judah from Babylon (also foretold in preexilic works, e.g., Deut. 4:29–30; 32:36; Jer. 16:15; 27:22; 29:14).

The point of alluding to the plagues in Exodus is probably not that all water will literally turn to blood again, but to indicate that God is sovereign over these natural elements and sends judgments on such matters throughout history. (Today we might terrify some Westerners analogously by talking about a pervasively destructive computer virus.) Even if one applies these judgments literally and only to a future tribulation, the application principle for today is the same: God seeks people's attention through judgment. Hail (8:7–8) shows us that God can use atmospheric weather conditions for judgments. We may think not only of hail, but of floods, hurricanes, and tornadoes.[35] Likewise, we can find judgments against water (8:8–11) in the pollution of water and the shrinking supply of drinkable water for some cities and regions.[36]

Darkness (8:12) makes work more difficult, but also speaks to those terrified by forces of nature. The eagle indicates that matters will grow much worse. Our secular contemporaries prefer to explain such events by purely naturalistic causes; but while God works through natural forces, as also in the plagues of Exodus, he has his ways of getting our attention through them.[37] When confronted with destructive judgments from which their reductionistic naturalism offers no protection, some secularists prove open-minded enough to become more religious![38]

---

35. E.g., "Hugo Is a Killer," *NW* (Oct. 2, 1989), 18–19; "Andrew's Wrath," *NW* (Sept. 7, 1992), 16–21; "Was Andrew a Freak—Or a Preview of Things to Come?" *NW* (Sept. 7, 1992), 30; "Come Hell or High Water," *NW* (July 18, 1994), 26–31; "The 'Billion-Dollar Flood' Keeps on Rolling Along," *NW* (July 19, 1993), 22–23; "A Deadly Spree for Georges," *NW* (Oct. 5, 1998), 38–39. But churches can also be devastated by such storms (e.g., "Andrew Goes to Church," *CT* [Oct. 5, 1992], 60; Owen Wilkie, "When Disaster Strikes," *Pentecostal Evangel* [March 29, 1987], 13). Note, however, that in God's sovereignty, some of these same phenomena in other ways contribute to sustaining optimum conditions for life on the planet; see Hugh Ross, "Design Update: Hurricanes Bring More Than Destruction," *Facts & Faith* 12/4 (1998): 4–5.

36. For pollution, see "Alaska After Exxon," *NW* (Sept. 18, 1989), 50–62; "More Oil on the Waters," *NW* (June 25, 1990), 60–61. For shortages, see "How to Make Sure There's Enough Good Water," *USNWR* (March 18, 1985), 65–68; "Mideast Water Wars," *WPR* (Jan. 1995), 37–39; "Next, Wars Over Water?" *WPR* (Nov. 1995), 8–13; "The New Politics of Thirst," *WPR* (Nov. 1992), 18–20. For relief work in supplying wells for drinkable water, see *World Vision Partners* (Spring 1994); *World Vision Report* (Fall 1995).

37. See H. M. Duncan Hoyte, "The Plagues of Egypt: What Killed the Animals and the Firstborn?" *The Medical Journal of Australia* 158 (1993): 706–8; Terence E. Fretheim, "The Plagues As Ecological Signs of Historical Disaster," *JBL* 110 (1991): 385–96.

38. Their secular framework seems not to predispose them to understand any larger framework for catastrophe than their personal state of grief (see A. J. Conyers, "After the Hurricane," *CT* [Nov. 9, 1992], 34–36); but cf. also the opportunities to demonstrate God's love ("Massive Rebuilding Effort Continues After Andrew," *CT* [June 21, 1993], 52).

SILENCE BEFORE GOD. That the world will one day be silenced before God (8:1) offers encouragement to those of us who hear its people loudly now. The arrogance of the political, academic, and other elites who ridicule or ignore God will be silenced. The text also has a word for those who declare, "When I get to heaven, I will tell God a thing or two," a line I have heard more than once from those determined to blame God for the world's injustices while trivializing the effects of human sin. Because of God's mercy their tongues can spew invective now, but on the day of his justice they will be silenced along with all other perpetrators of injustice.

Prayer that shapes history. God is sovereign, but in his sovereign plan he has chosen to make the prayers of his people part of the exercise of his will. As Beasley-Murray puts it, it appears "that God has willed that the prayers of his people should be part of the process by which the kingdom comes."[39] Or as Eugene Peterson notes:

> While conflicts raged between good and evil, prayers went up from devout bands of first century Christians all over the Roman empire. Massive engines of persecution and scorn were ranged against them. They had neither weapons nor votes. They had little money and no prestige.[40]

But they did have prayer. That prayer had the power to shape the course of human history! One may compare Daniel, whose prayer becomes the battleground for angelic powers greater than the earthly rulers affected by them (Dan. 10:13; 10:20–11:1); while the leaders of empires rise and fall as little more than pawns in the hands of a sovereign God (11:2–12:3), Daniel himself is greeted as one highly esteemed by God himself (10:11).[41] We often fail to see the effects of our seemingly insignificant lives; in Hannah's day, who would have thought that the future of Israel lay in her humble prayer rather than in the spiritual legacy of Israel's high priest Eli (1 Sam. 1:10–20)? Details for which we pray are sometimes answered "No," but in the big picture, the entire course of human history, God's plan is secure and is advanced in his sovereign will through the prayers of his people.

We should therefore encourage fellow believers to continue banding together for strategic prayer on matters of long-range concern for God's

---

39. Beasley-Murray, *Revelation*, 151.

40. Peterson, *Reversed Thunder*, 87.

41. My words are not intended to challenge the doctrine of individual free will (cf. Rev. 3:19) but to suggest that God is so sovereign (1:8) that he can grant, foreknow, and work through such will, and the broad scope of history reveals his sovereignty.

kingdom. Many Christians now band together on Fridays, the Muslim prayer day, to pray for outreach to the Islamic world, what has appeared the most impenetrable fortress against the gospel in our day; and reports abound of Muslims in "closed countries" being converted even through dreams and visions.[42] One of the most useful prayer tools, which should be acquired and used by as many Christians as possible, is Patrick Johnstone's *Operation World*.[43] Though it is difficult to keep such works up-to-date and accurate on every detail for all nations, they provide one of our most strategic tools for relevant prayer for the nations.

God's wrath and judgment. That judgment comes in response to prayer may not seem high on our priority list of prayer requests. But for suffering, persecuted people, judgment on the world that represses them is a sign of hope, a signal that God will not wait only until the Second Coming to begin vindicating them. God will consummate history on that Day; but he is Lord of history even now.[44]

God's wrath has important moral implications. While people suffer in much of the world, others frequently profit from their sufferings through political or religious repression. Yet as much as relativistic Western culture has forgotten it, God is a God of justice, who does acknowledge that one side can be right and another wrong in a situation. He is a God of wrath, who provides us the necessary "moral clarity" to take sides when clear examples of oppression are taking place.[45] H. Richard Niebuhr rightly challenged the liberal social gospel movement of watering down the offense of the cross: "A God without wrath brought me without sin into a kingdom without judgment through the ministrations of a Christ without the cross." Yet while we evan-

---

42. E.g., Del Kingswriter, "Miracles in the Muslim World," *Mountain Movers* (May 1992), 12–13; Mohammad, "I Saw Jesus," *Mountain Movers* (Nov. 1990), 16–17; Marilyn Ford, "Hadijah," *Mountain Movers* (Aug. 1991), 5; "We Met in a Dream," *Arab World Ministries Update* (4, 1993): 4.

43. Patrick Johnstone, *Operation World: The Day-by-Day Guide to Praying for the World*, 5th ed. (Grand Rapids: Zondervan, 1993); these are often available at a discount at InterVarsity's triennial Urbana missions conventions. On the importance of missions prayer, see David Bryant, *In the Gap: What It Means to be a World Christian* (Ventura, Calif.: Regal, 1984), 78–80, 221–24.

44. Jehovah's Witnesses wrongly interpret 8:1–9:21 as "Jehovah's Plagues on Christendom" (*Revelation: Grand Climax*, 129–41), when in fact the plagues are against the "world"; but when the church is worldly, we should remember that God's discipline starts first with his own house (Ezek. 9:6; 1 Peter 4:17).

45. See Gary A. Haugen, *Good News About Injustice* (Downers Grove, Ill.: InterVarsity, 1999), 84–91, "Hope in the God of Moral Clarity." This is not to deny that some situations involve varying degrees of innocence and guilt, but to acknowledge with Scripture that some involve innocent victims (Deut. 19:13; 1 Kings 21:19; 2 Kings 21:16; 24:4; Ps. 10:8; 106:38; Isa. 59:7; Jer. 2:34; 7:6; 19:4; 22:3, 17).

gelicals denounce such old-school liberalism, is our silence about impending judgment against sinful nations not a form of ignoring God's wrath? And "once we have given up wrath, can sin, judgment, or the Cross be far behind?"[46]

Despite the protests of some marginal popular teachers like Charles Capps, the text also reminds us that God controls the events of nature (e.g., Ps. 65:6–12; 89:8–13; 93:3–4; 104:2–8; 107:23–30; 135:6–7; 147:15–18; 148:8) and often uses them as judgments (e.g., Isa. 5:10, 13; Amos 4:6–13; Hag. 2:16–19). In contrast to our modern worldview, natural catastrophes are not simply random events, nor is our ability to predict many of them the same as ability to harness and control them.

Too often we have viewed disasters as happening only in other parts of the world—floods in Bangladesh, an earthquake in Japan or Mexico, famine in East Africa—or at least in other parts of the country. Thus Midwesterners fear California earthquakes, Californians marvel that anyone would live in the Midwest's tornado alley, rural people recognize that cities provide more vulnerable targets for missiles or terrorists, and so forth.[47] But our assumptions are common to the ways we humans try to pacify our anxieties with dubious assurances (1 Sam. 23:7; 2 Sam. 18:25–27). The West's relative prosperity at the moment of this writing does not guarantee God's blessing; Babylon exercised far more military and economic power than Judah, yet Babylon's empire has been no more than memories for over two millennia.

The history of parts of the West as mission-sending nations probably provided much of the divine favor under which we now live, but far more born-again Christians now live in the developing nations of Latin America, Africa, and Asia. Meanwhile, the secular revolt against God and its accompanying moral apostasy are certainly inviting judgment. American Christians dare not now reecho Abraham Lincoln's claim that its nation's people are "the almost chosen people."[48] The tokens of Christian commitment that remain in the public square are surely no greater than Judah's temple, but contrary to the assurances of Jeremiah's contemporaries, even God's house could not stay his wrath against a disobedient people (Jer. 7:4–15).

Indeed, the vestiges of Christian heritage and the remnant of Christian proclamation in our own day make us, like the biblical prophets' contemporaries, all the more accountable (e.g., Amos 3:2). Thus, as evangelical Old Testament scholar Walter Kaiser, now president at Gordon-Conwell

46. William D. Eisenhower, "Sleepers in the Hands of an Angry God," *CT* (March 20, 1987), 26–28 (p. 26).

47. Sometimes we even deny that disasters will recur in disaster-prone areas where we live; see Eloise Salholz, "Disaster and Denial," *NW* (July 26, 1993), 27.

48. See Mark Noll, "Is This Land God's Land?" *CT* (July 11, 1986), 14–15.

Theological Seminary, put it a couple decades ago: "North American society is headed for destruction and judgment. And we had better believe it's coming, because there is no sign that repentance is near. It is coming, or else God is a liar and His word is not true. The prophet's message must be preached again today."[49]

Judgments have already come to seize our attention; but surely greater judgments lie in store. Those who study both Scripture and the moral state of secular society can hardly think otherwise, though in our day, as in Jeremiah's, there will surely remain false prophets of peace merely telling people what they wish to hear (Jer. 6:14; 8:11; 14:13; 23:17; see Ezek. 13:16; Mic. 3:5; 2 Tim. 4:3–4).

---

49. See Walter C. Kaiser Jr., *The Old Testament in Contemporary Preaching* (Grand Rapids: Baker, 1973), 97–99 (p. 99).

Revelation 9:1–21

THE FIFTH ANGEL sounded his trumpet, and I saw a star that had fallen from the sky to the earth. The star was given the key to the shaft of the Abyss. ²When he opened the Abyss, smoke rose from it like the smoke from a gigantic furnace. The sun and sky were darkened by the smoke from the Abyss. ³And out of the smoke locusts came down upon the earth and were given power like that of scorpions of the earth. ⁴They were told not to harm the grass of the earth or any plant or tree, but only those people who did not have the seal of God on their foreheads. ⁵They were not given power to kill them, but only to torture them for five months. And the agony they suffered was like that of the sting of a scorpion when it strikes a man. ⁶During those days men will seek death, but will not find it; they will long to die, but death will elude them.

⁷The locusts looked like horses prepared for battle. On their heads they wore something like crowns of gold, and their faces resembled human faces. ⁸Their hair was like women's hair, and their teeth were like lions' teeth. ⁹They had breastplates like breastplates of iron, and the sound of their wings was like the thundering of many horses and chariots rushing into battle. ¹⁰They had tails and stings like scorpions, and in their tails they had power to torment people for five months. ¹¹They had as king over them the angel of the Abyss, whose name in Hebrew is Abaddon, and in Greek, Apollyon.

¹²The first woe is past; two other woes are yet to come.

¹³The sixth angel sounded his trumpet, and I heard a voice coming from the horns of the golden altar that is before God. ¹⁴It said to the sixth angel who had the trumpet, "Release the four angels who are bound at the great river Euphrates." ¹⁵And the four angels who had been kept ready for this very hour and day and month and year were released to kill a third of mankind. ¹⁶The number of the mounted troops was two hundred million. I heard their number.

¹⁷The horses and riders I saw in my vision looked like this: Their breastplates were fiery red, dark blue, and yellow as sulfur. The heads of the horses resembled the heads of lions, and

out of their mouths came fire, smoke and sulfur. [18]A third of mankind was killed by the three plagues of fire, smoke and sulfur that came out of their mouths. [19]The power of the horses was in their mouths and in their tails; for their tails were like snakes, having heads with which they inflict injury.

[20]The rest of mankind that were not killed by these plagues still did not repent of the work of their hands; they did not stop worshiping demons, and idols of gold, silver, bronze, stone and wood—idols that cannot see or hear or walk. [21]Nor did they repent of their murders, their magic arts, their sexual immorality or their thefts.

THIS PASSAGE INCLUDES the fifth and sixth trumpets, both of which deal with invasions. Whether the invaders are human or demonic, however, is debatable; most important is the repentance that such horrifying judgments should evoke—but do not (9:20–21).

Invasion, the Fifth Trumpet (9:1–11)

THE FALLING STAR (9:1) may represent an angel's *moral* fall (cf. 12:4; the angel of the Abyss in 9:11), which then underlines God's sovereign ability to use even those who are evil to accomplish his ultimate purposes. But more likely the image simply represents a geographical descent (cf. 20:1).

Knowing ancient traditions can help us better understand how John's contemporaries would have heard his words about the Abyss (9:1–2). Many in John's day assumed a real location on earth called the Abyss (1 Enoch 83:4); apocalypses sometimes indulged in exotic "geography" (1 Enoch 17–18; 21:7).[1] Later texts also described guardians of the keys of hell (2 Enoch 42:1), described a great angel with charge over the Abyss and Hades and all the wicked souls imprisoned there (Apoc. Zeph. 6:15), or spoke of an antichrist figure ascending from Tartarus (Gr. Ezra 3:15). Some believed the wicked were "children" or "men of the 'pit,'" i.e., those destined for damnation there (1QS 9.16, 22; CD 6.15; 13.14).

In Revelation (in contrast to the LXX) the Abyss is a place of evil (11:7; 17:8) and a place where evil entities are imprisoned (20:1, 3; cf. Luke 8:31). That creatures from there oppose the evil forces of the empire (Rev. 9:1–11)

---

1. Compare Erebus in Greek and Roman myth (though various regions below were mixed; cf. Virgil, *Aen.* 7.140).

thus only emphasizes again God's sovereignty: He employs even evil agents to destroy other evil agents (cf. 17:17).[2]

The fifth trumpet judgment may refer to a human invasion. "Locusts" undoubtedly appear because, in keeping with most of the other trumpet judgments, this one recalls a plague against Egypt (Ex. 10:13–14). Locusts cloud the sky when they come (Joel 2:2, 10; cf. Livy, 42.2.5). Most hearers in urban Asia, no less than in the countryside, would have recognized that scorpions strike with their tails. Emphasizing God's sovereignty, Jewish people would recognize that God could use scorpions to execute his judgment (9:3, 10).[3] Some existing creatures were considered composite,[4] but such mixtures were more often considered frightening, sometimes supernatural. The centaurs of Greek myth mixed horses and humans; Babylonians portrayed mixtures of humans with scorpions or horses.[5] Commentators point out that a locust's head resembles that of a horse, sometimes also citing an Arabian proverb that makes this explicit.[6]

The specific description of these locusts, however, stems from the book of Joel (1:6; 2:4), where the locusts are described as an invading army (2:11, 20, 25; cf. 1:4), but an invading eschatological army also seems to be prefigured by the locusts (3:9–12). Clearly John does not envision normal locusts; locusts target the very sorts of vegetation that these locusts do not harm (9:4), but these locusts harm people. The human faces (9:7) may indicate the composite design of an angelic creature (Ezek. 1:10), but may also suggest that it is symbolic of a human army. That the locusts' wings sound like chariots (9:9) may also suggest a human army, though that too comes directly from Joel (Joel 2:5).[7]

The "breastplates of iron" may compare locusts' scaled bodies with the scales of eastern soldiers, as in some Jewish texts.[8] "Crowns of gold" (9:7) usually designate royalty or high office (cf. Ex. 39:30; 2 Sam. 12:30; 1 Chron. 20:2; Ps. 21:3); hence they may suggest that each locust commands others,

---

2. See in further detail on this point Beasley-Murray, *Revelation*, 160–61.

3. *Gen. Rab.* 10:5; *Ex. Rab.* 10:1; *Koh. Rab.* 5:8–9, §§2, 4. Later rabbis recounted a popular story how a frog carried a scorpion on his back across a river so it could kill someone, then transported it back (*b. Ned.* 41a; *Gen. Rab.* 10:7).

4. Philo, *Mos.* 1.130–32.

5. Ford, *Revelation*, 145, noting also the use of locusts for the scorpion in zodiacs and the long hair on centaurs and Sagittarius; she suggests an army of centaurs. Cf. Apollodorus, 2.4.2.

6. Mounce, *Revelation*, 196, also noting the German and Italian names for locusts (hay-horse and little horse respectively), and suggesting (n. 21) that the golden crowns may be related to the yellow on their breasts. The proverb compares their antennae with maidens' hair.

7. For eschatological chariots, see 1 En. 57:1–3.

8. See Robert P. Gordon, "Loricate Locusts in the Targum to Nahum iii 17 and Revelation ix 9," *VetT* 33 (July 1983): 338–39.

suggesting in turn an army far more vast than John can portray. Others argue that the crowns parody the bronze burnish on Roman soldiers' bronze helmets.[9]

If Revelation has a particular army in view here, it is probably that of the Parthians. Some features that might recall the Parthians, such as the horses (9:7; cf. comment on 6:2), simply stem from Joel (Joel 2:4; cf. Jer. 51:27). But other details missing from Joel's locusts but present here may point to the Parthians, especially their long hair (9:8; in the Roman empire, women's hair was usually longer than men's, cf. 1 Cor. 11:14–15).[10]

Ultimately, however, specifically Parthian connections are few, and whatever genuine connections are here may simply be borrowed from Roman fears about Parthia in order to intensify the composite picture of horror. Long hair may simply be part of a terrifying vision of monstrous or superhuman images.[11] The "lions' teeth" (Rev. 9:8) reflect Joel's locusts (Joel 1:6), as does the appearance "like the thundering of many horses," noted above (Rev. 9:9; Joel 2:4), and the sound of "chariots rushing into battle" (Joel 2:5; cf. Jer. 8:16).[12] By contrast, the case for a Parthian background in the sixth trumpet is much stronger.

The monstrosities from the Abyss may represent angels of judgment, as some scholars suggest.[13] This suggests a purely supernatural judgment; elsewhere God accomplished such judgment through his angels (Ezek. 9:1–7), but here apparently he unleashes evil forces to wreak their havoc. That God sets limits on their destructiveness, both in intensity (Rev. 9:6) and duration (9:10), may suggest his mercy and again underlines his sovereignty. Five months is approximately a normal locust's life span, and God does not choose to extend it.[14] Scorpion stings usually bring terrible pain but not death to humans, although these are not purely literal scorpions.[15] By preventing their

9. Ford, *Revelation,* 151.

10. On Parthians' long hair, see Suetonius, *Vesp.* 10.23. This also characterized northern barbarians (Dionysius of Halicarnassus, 14.9.4), as well as heroes and divine images of an earlier period (Homer, *Il.* 2.51; 3.43; Virgil, *Aen.* 9.638). The Persian army that absorbed Parthia included all males and some women (Herodian, 6.5.3).

11. E.g., Demeter in Pausanias, 8.42.4; terrifying angels in Apoc. Zeph. 4:4; 6:8. Mounce, *Revelation,* 196, rejects the comparison with locusts' antennae (made in an Arabian proverb), but admits a possible connection with hair on the locusts' legs or bodies.

12. Vigorous animal teeth or tusks contributed to visions of terror (Dan. 7:5, 7, 19; Apoc. Zeph. 4:3; 6:8).

13. So Talbert, *Apocalypse,* 42, citing 1 Enoch 66:1; 2 Enoch 10:3; T. Levi 3:2–3.

14. Herschel H. Hobbs in George, ed., *Revelation: Three Viewpoints,* 103. Aune, *Revelation,* 2:530, notes this datum but prefers "five" as a round figure for a small number (1 Cor. 14:19).

15. For the pain of scorpions, see 1 Kings 12:11, 14; 2 Chron. 10:11, 14; Plutarch, *Divine Vengeance* 20, *Mor.* 562C. If this is a demonic army, cf. perhaps Luke 10:19, though Luke 10 draws on Ezek. 2:6; scorpions are associated with witchcraft in *Sifre Deut.* 172.1.1.

death God augments the pain of those who would rather be out of it (9:6), so one can read this limitation as an increase in the judgment's intensity, which fits the context of fierce judgment. Other writers spoke of troubles so intense that sufferers simply wished to die.[16]

But the purpose of such judgments is to turn people to repentance, so even this limitation may also serve to allow repentance (9:20–21).[17] Five months' of torment (9:5), like 1,260 days of torment (cf. 11:10), thus contrasts with eternal torment (14:10–11; 20:10). That the locusts harm no vegetation but only people without God's seal (9:4) also turns the attentive listener back to 7:3, where vegetation should not be harmed until God had sealed his servants. This connection reinforces the point: God specifically exempts his servants from this judgment, perhaps emphasized especially if this is a demonic army.

"Abaddon" was a subterranean place of the dead in the Old Testament (Job 31:12), which is regularly linked with death and the realm of the dead (Job 26:6; 28:22; Ps. 88:11; Prov. 15:11; 27:20). It is linked with the Pit in the Dead Sea Scrolls.[18] It is thus equivalent to Hades, the sometimes-personified realm of the dead (Rev. 6:8), over which God (20:13–14) and Christ (1:18) have ultimate control. But here the control is delegated temporarily to an evil angel, who appears to have been imprisoned with the other spirits of the pit.

"Apollyon" is related to *apollymi*, the Greek verb meaning "to destroy" (cf. 17:8), but John may be adapting the title slightly to make his point. Thus, many suggest that this title is also intended to ridicule Apollo, the archer god, one of whose emblems (alongside mouse and lizard) was the locust (see Aeschylus, *Agamemnon* 1080–86.) More significantly, Domitian had sometimes portrayed himself as the god Apollo—which may imply here that the emperor himself or his patron deity will lead the demonic host in destroying Rome.[19] The precise referents of these images may be less critical than their intended evocative impact: Judgment will be horrifying, and those who do not embrace God's protection (9:4) may as well prepare for such horrors.

---

16. See Jer. 8:3; Euripides, *Medea* 96–97, 144–47; cf. perhaps Rev. 6:16.

17. The exclusion of death was sometimes positive (Job 2:6; T. Job 4:4), though it could also represent extended torture (Lucan, *C.W.* 2.177–80); it did indicate God's sovereignty (cf. Jos. and Asen. 16:18/13).

18. See 4Q286.10.2.7. See Paul J. Kobelski, "Melchizedek and Melchiresa: The Heavenly Prince of Light and the Prince of Darkness in the Qumran Literature" (Ph.D. diss., Fordham University, 1978), 97. The linking of "destruction" and "abyss" in Gr. Ezra 4:21 might depend on Christian tradition stemming from 9:11. More helpfully, Beale, *Revelation*, 504, cites Hos. 13:14, which combines Hades, "plagues," and "destruction" (cf. 9:10).

19. Caird, *Commentary on Revelation*, 120; Ford, *Revelation*, 152; esp. Beasley-Murray, *Revelation*, 162.

A Parthian Invasion (9:12–21)

WHEN THE SIXTH angel sounds, a voice from the golden altar addresses him (9:13). The golden altar represents the incense altar (Ex. 30:1–3; Heb. 9:4) rather than the sacrificial altar (Ex. 35:16), hence implying that this judgment represents a further response to the prayers of the saints (8:4–6). By reminding the audience that the final three trumpets are "woes" (cf. 8:13), 9:12 reinforces the dramatic nature of this sixth trumpet, equivalent to the sixth bowl of God's anger, that of Armageddon (16:12–16). That bowl also involves "kings from the East" from across the Euphrates; as here, an audience in the eastern Mediterranean would think especially of the Parthians.[20]

The mention of "the great river Euphrates" leaves no doubt that Parthians are in view, for the Euphrates repeatedly appeared as the traditional boundary between Roman and Parthian territories throughout Mediterranean literature.[21] Pompey had established this boundary in the first century B.C., and it remained in John's day.[22] When Parthians crossed the Euphrates, it was to fight Romans. A later writer observes that these two most powerful empires in the world were separated only by a river.[23]

Parthians were the archrivals of the Roman empire, far more feared than the Germanic barbarians on the northern frontier. Early imperial propaganda celebrated Augustus's defeat of Parthia, but not every generation since had met with equal success.[24] Though Rome claimed to subject the north, west, and south, they admitted that they could not defeat the Parthians to the east. Parthians were known for boldness in battle and could not be trusted; they were considered the appropriate enemies of Rome. Parthian kings were known for their power and authority.[25]

Earlier, pagan prophecies of an Asian invasion of Rome had terrified the Romans, but nothing had come of it.[26] Now God was speaking and they had

---

20. Commentators routinely recognize the Parthians here, e.g., Tenney, *Revelation*, 76; Ford, *Revelation*, 146; Beasley-Murray, *Revelation*, 164.

21. Virgil, *Georg.* 4.561; Appian, *R.H.* pref. 9; Tacitus, *Ann.* 12.11; 15.7, 16–17; Suetonius, *Calig.* 14; Chariton, *Chaer.* 5.1.3; Josephus, *War* 1.179–80; 2.388–89; 7.105; *Ant.* 18.101; Sib. Or. 4.120, 124.

22. For Pompey's involvement, see Appian, *R.H.* 12.15.105; 12.17.116. Parthians were Rome's enemies in that period (Sallust, *Mithridates* 1–23) and long after the first century (Herodian, 6.3.2).

23. Herodian, 4.10.2. Parthians would cross the Euphrates to fight Rome (Lucan, *C.W.* 8.354–58).

24. For Augustan propaganda, see Horace, *Epistle* 2.1.256; *Ode* 1.12.53; 1.21.13–16; 3.5.3–4; 3.8.19–20; 4.25–27; *Epode* 7.9–10. For later struggles, see Tacitus, *Ann.* 13.34–41; 15.1–18, 24–31; Suetonius, *Tib.* 41.

25. For the information in this paragraph, see Horace, *Epistle* 2.1.112; *Ode* 1.19.12; 4.15.23; Lucan, *C.W.* 2.552; 10.48–51; Martial, *Epig.* 2.53.10.

26. See Meeks, *Moral World*, 29.

real reason to fear! Some Jewish speculation believed that Nero, whom Christians saw as a precursor of the Antichrist, would cross the Euphrates into Parthia, betraying Rome (Sib. Or. 4.119–24). Palestine was close to the eastern frontier of the Roman empire, making it, with the rest of the Roman province of Syria, a natural place for them to strike.[27] Thus some first-century Jewish traditions also suggested that God's angels would call together a Parthian invasion of the holy land (1 En. 56:5–6).[28]

Evil angels were thought to be bound in various places (9:14; 20:2, 7), including subterranean chasms (1 En. 10:4–6, 12–13; 88:1–3; Jub. 5:6) and bodies of deep water (Test. Sol. 6:3–6; 25:7).[29] Jewish people also understood about angels stirring the eastern kings of the Parthians and Medes to war, invading Palestine (1 En. 56:5–6). The four angels bound in the Euphrates River (Rev. 9:14–15) are thus likely evil angels whom God will use as agents of judgment on a wicked world, undoubtedly by their stirring of the Parthians.

These angels have stings in tails (9:19), as in the previous plague (9:10). Parthian archers had perfected the art of riding forward while shooting backward. They often retreated up hills, and when the Romans followed, the mounted archers devastated them with a volley of arrows. They destroyed a couple legions before the Romans learned not to pursue Parthians up hills! Romans had long remembered and feared them for this technique.[30]

But are these "mounted troops" actually the Parthians (9:16)? Some suggest that the symbolic images of the Parthians blend with horrific imagery for a demonic army, hence producing "a nightmare version of a familiar first-century fear."[31] John heard their number, just as he had the godly army of the 144,000 (7:4); but as when he "saw" the 144,000 they turned out to be literally something different (7:9), perhaps this army will also turn out to be something other than mere Parthians (9:17). Smoke-belching fiery creatures (9:17) may symbolize the ultimate form of God's judgments on humanity, an intensification of the plagues against Egypt (Wisd. 11:18). The closest approximation to these creatures in Greek literature was the horrifying monster called the Chimaera, which had "the head of a lion, the tail of a dragon

---

27. Aulus Gellius, 15.4.4.

28. Later rabbis claimed Rome was wealthier but Persia mightier (*ARN* 28A), and debated whether Rome or Persia would emerge victorious (*b. Yoma* 10a).

29. Or in Hades (Apoc. Zeph. 6:15); or Tartarus or Gehenna (Sib. Or. 1.101–3; Ps-Philo 60:3; T. Sol. 6:3); some texts even place their prison in the second heaven (2 Enoch 7). Some Jewish traditions circulating in John's day spoke of "angels that bring punishment," releasing the subterranean waters to bring a flood (1 Enoch 66:1).

30. This was especially emphasized a century before John (Virgil, *Georg.* 3.31; Horace, *Ode* 2.13.18; Propertius, *Elegies* 2.10.13–14). See Aune, *Revelation*, 2:533, for ancient depictions of the Parthians' "armored cavalry."

31. Caird, *Commentary on Revelation*, 122.

or serpent, and the body of a goat and belching fire"; in ancient pictures, it could have a lion body with a goat head.[32] In contrast to their predecessors (Rev. 9:5), these invaders kill (9:18). In short, Revelation portrays an invasion of terrifying monsters. That fire comes from their mouths indicates that like God's true prophets (11:5), this demonic army also exhibits supernatural power to execute judgment on the world.

The specific images do transcend a mere army of Parthians from across the Euphrates. In contrast to the mere iron breastplates of their predecessors (9:9), these warriors bore breastplates of (literally) "fire and brimstone" (9:17). Although the NIV is probably partly right to render this description in terms of color (red, blue, and yellow)—sulfur is yellow and burns with a blue flame—the literal rendering cannot be ignored here, for "fire, smoke and sulfur" also "[came] out of their mouths" (9:17; probably also symbolic in 11:5; cf. 12:15–16).[33] That the horses' heads are like those of lions recalls the earlier army in 9:8 and appeals to the standard ancient image of the lion as a fierce and dangerous predator (cf. 1 Chron. 12:8; see comment on 5:5). The serpent-like tails may evoke hideous pictures in Greek mythology, like the Medusa or various demons with snake hair;[34] they may also allude to the strong-tailed dragon of 12:3–4, although a first-time reader would not yet catch this comparison.

Then again, John explicitly says that what he saw was a "vision" (9:17), which probably allows for considerable symbolic elements and enables us to hold that he is describing in horrific terms a literal human army. Whether the vision focuses on a demonic army portrayed with features of Parthians, or Parthians portrayed as a hideous symbolic army alters the final effect only slightly: in either case, the images evoke terror.

The killing of one-third of the world's population (9:15, 18) is unparalleled catastrophe. At the same time, it is less than many other apocalyptic traditions—for instance, the Jewish tradition that a revived Nero would attack the west and kill two-thirds of the people (Sib. Or. 5.102–3), or that God's judgments would destroy two-thirds of humanity (3.540–44), or a prophetic warning that two-thirds of God's people Israel would be slaughtered (Zech. 13:7–8). Often in Revelation God's judgments strike only one-third (Rev. 8:7–12; cf. 12:4) or even a tenth (11:13), indicating that he strikes a remnant rather than the majority, hoping that others will come to repentance (9:20–21). The death of one-third of the world is judgment, but it is also mercy.[35]

---

32. Aune, *Revelation*, 2:539, documenting thoroughly.

33. Sulfur appears in various judgments (e.g., Sib. Or. 3.462).

34. See Homer, *Od.* 11.634–35; cf. Apuleius, *Metam.* 11.3.

35. The pattern of judgment on one-third (8:7–12; 9:13–19) does not appear in other Jewish end-time works, but may loosely recall Ezek. 5:2, 12 (see Aune, *Revelation*, 2:500, 519).

That the angels of judgment are prepared (NIV, "kept ready") for a designated time (9:15; cf. perhaps 9:7; 12:6; 16:12) reinforces Revelation's emphasis that God controls all judgments on earth; believers need not fear the world's sufferings as if God is not in control.[36] Some commentators think that the number of the army, two hundred million, reflects computations based on God's own host in Psalm 68:17; Daniel 7:10, arguing that though this is a demonic army, it also must serve the commands of God.[37] This number may offer a contrast to the much smaller number of the 144,000 (Rev. 7:4–8), who will not need to take up arms against Rome; God, who hears their cries, will raise up evil ones to fight other evil ones. In any case, the number will be terrifying: These troops probably outnumbered the entire population of the Mediterranean world.

The climax of the account comes in 9:20–21. God allows one-third of humanity to die and spares the remaining two-thirds to invite their repentance. Like Pharaoh during the plagues on Egypt, however, the world refuses to repent (Ex. 7:22–23). They worship and probably seek help from false gods rather than the true God, frustrating his powerful designs to offer them repentance and explaining why God's patience with them will ultimately justly run out (cf. Rom. 2:4; 9:22).

Many philosophers believed that the gods sent punishment to produce repentance.[38] Most people in the Roman world attributed plagues to the anger of their deities, but some objected that such events merely occurred by chance.[39] Jewish teachers also recognized that God often sent signs or judgments to seek repentance before bringing harsher judgment; some later teachers even declared that those addicted to their sin would not repent even at the gates of hell.[40] Jewish writers sometimes complained about those who refused to repent despite seeing God's works (Ex. 7:23; 2 Chron. 28:22; Ps-Philo 7:1), or noted that because of the wicked plagues afflicted the world, causing everyone to suffer (ARN 9A). They recognized that God sent plagues on Egypt to invite repentance.[41] He continues to seek repentance through judgments (Amos 4:6–11; Hag. 2:17).

Most important, it signifies God's mercy and distinguishes these judgments intended to invite repentance from the final judgment to come.

36. For angels of judgment in Jewish texts (including Enoch's Similitudes), see Aune, *Revelation*, 2:538.

37. Beasley-Murray, *Revelation*, 165.

38. Abraham J. Malherbe, *Moral Exhortation: A Greco-Roman Sourcebook*, LEC 4 (Philadelphia: Westminster, 1986), 86, on Hierocles. On suffering as divine education in ancient thought, see Talbert, *Apocalypse*, 43.

39. Dionysius of Halicarnassus, 7.68.2.

40. See ARN, 32A; *b. Erub.* 19a.

41. Beale, *Revelation*, 466, notes that Jewish interpreters understood that they invited repentance for Egypt (citing Philo) and indeed for all humanity (citing Josephus).

Jewish texts condemn those who worship gods of wood, stone, and precious metals (Isa. 37:19; 44:19; 1 Enoch 99:7; Sib. Or. 3.586–90; 5.82–83). Both early Christians (1 Cor. 10:20) and many Jews (Bar. 4:7; 1 En. 19:1; 99:7; Jub. 1:11; 22:17) would have shared Revelation's view that pagans worshiped demons (Rev. 9:20).[42] That Revelation connects mistreatment of people made in God's image with rejection of the true image of God by idolatry (9:20–21) also should not surprise us (Rom. 1:23–27).[43]

Bridging Contexts

DERIVING LESSONS FROM **the Bible.** Each part of the Bible is useful for teaching (2 Tim. 3:16), but different passages are useful for different circumstances. Passages like the fifth and sixth trumpets in this chapter usually will not comfort the bereaved or lonely, but they are useful for shaking us from our complacency. They provide a reality check, denouncing our fantasies that life will always continue as normal and summoning us to recognize the terrible suffering of the world around us.

Understanding the locusts and other prophetic symbols. Modern prophecy teachers differ in their specific approach to the locusts. Some view them as "demons who take the form of these unique locusts";[44] others allow that they may be literal, demon-possessed mutant locusts but seem to prefer the view that they are symbolic, perhaps for the sort of Cobra helicopters with nerve gas in the tail used in Vietnam.[45]

The Cobra helicopter analogy is something of a stretch, the sort of suggestion that can grow rapidly out of date. Yet it has more value than most of us scholars are inclined to appreciate. If Revelation employs one of the most graphic, fierce images of invasion in its day, perhaps images of attacking helicopters with nerve gas provides a rough modern equivalent in our day— provided we can recognize in such dramatic images judgments from the God who directs human history (1:8). That is, we should seek analogies that convey in modern images the same terror the first images would have conveyed:

---

42. Also Test. Job 3:3; Test. Sol. 5:5; 6:4; *Sifre Deut.* 318.2.1–2; Athenagoras, 26. This view may have been shared by Zoroastrians (A. T. Olmstead, *History of the Persian Empire* [Chicago: Phoenix Books, Univ. of Chicago Press, 1959], 96, 195).

43. "Magic arts" literally includes potions (and poisons), normally used against other people (or to seduce them). Judaism officially rejected this practice (Sib. Or. 3.225), but it must have been common in Roman Asia (Acts 19:19; cf. Rev. 18:23).

44. Ryrie, *Revelation*, 61.

45. Lindsey, *New World Coming*, 138–39. Sorcerers are reputed to send literal animals to attack their enemies (John S. Mbiti, *African Religions and Philosophies* [Garden City, N.Y.: Doubleday, 1970], 261–62).

---

a devastating invasion. Restricting the terrifying images to the Parthians—
though they plainly filled the role for John's contemporaries and supplied
some of the imagery—is inadequate, "reducing the book's dramatic metaphor
to the level of shallow prose."[46] That is not how much of the Bible's prophetic
symbolism functions.

Some interpreters may be troubled by this way of approaching biblical
prophecy. Surely if John envisions a devastating Parthian invasion that has
not yet materialized, we should expect a literal revival of Parthia so they can
invade again (the way some expect a revived Roman empire).[47] But if the
point of John's vision is sought in the message it conveys rather than in the
details of the image, it may simply warn that God will use the empire's fiercest
enemies to judge it, wicked as they also may be. Persecuted Christians need
fear no evil empire; Satan's kingdom is divided, and God uses one evil empire
to destroy another, while the church of Jesus Christ remains and grows.

That Revelation can borrow Joel's locusts for a plague different from Joel's
literal locusts does not invite us to freely recycle biblical images without attention to their meaning. Rather, it reminds us that God, whose character never
changes, generally acts in history according to consistent patterns. The judgments he has sent in past eras thus provide warnings of analogous judgments
he will continue to send for different societies until the end (1 Cor. 10:6–
12). Our own life spans are too short to learn everything by experiencing it,
but if we are wise we may learn from history. But history must be interpreted
according to overarching perspectives, so the most useful history for moral
instruction is in the Bible, which provides God's perspective on history.

In bridging contexts, we should also be careful about how we apply the
message of the texts. For Romans, Parthians were a feared menace, but their location to the "East" (16:12) was purely a matter of geography.[48] Some American
prophecy teachers in the late twentieth century appeal to contemporary fears
about Communist China or Japanese economic competition. Hal Lindsey,
remarking that China's standing army is over two hundred million (9:16), regards
the "kings from the East" (16:12) as an "Oriental" invasion of the Middle East.[49]

---

46. Bowman, *First Christian Drama*, 67.

47. Less than twenty years after Revelation was written the Romans defeated Parthia in
another major war; see sources in Robert K. Sherk, ed., *The Roman Empire: Augustus to Hadrian*,
TDGR 6 (New York: Cambridge Univ. Press, 1988), 168–77. Prophecy teachers often
envision a revival of the Roman empire to fulfill—or perhaps, re-fulfill?—Dan. 7:23–24,
but this interpretation of that empire's revival started, not surprisingly, before the demise
of the Holy Roman Empire and has continued by tradition since then.

48. Much earlier the Euphrates divided Jacob from Laban (Gen. 31:21) and David's territory to the north (Gen. 15:18; 2 Sam. 8:3; 1 Chron. 18:3), but many Jews now lived across
the Euphrates (Josephus, *War.* 1.5, 179; b. *B.M.* 28a).

49. Lindsey, *New World Coming*, 140–41.

Without diminishing the importance of concerns about justice in recent Chinese history, an approach that equates the modern world's "east" (as east Asia) with John's "east" (as Parthia) misses the point and runs the risk of bolstering unjust prejudice against Asians (see comment on 16:12). In applying the text, it remains perfectly legitimate to compare modern fears of our contemporaries with those of the Romans, and thus to explain and evoke the same kind of emotional impact John's contemporaries experienced when hearing his vision. It is not, however, legitimate or consistent to take the Parthian images symbolically but "east" literally and fixate on one group of people.[50] For that matter, this Parthian invasion is meant not to terrify obedient believers so much as to provide them vindication against their Roman oppressors.

Reading of the fiery cavalry with lions' heads in 9:17, Lindsey prosaically suggests, "My opinion is that he is describing some kind of mobilized ballistic missile launcher."[51] But there is no clear reason to prefer this interpretation when fire-belching creatures were standard fare in first-century images. Lindsey misses the point, for apocalyptic texts are not meant to be read the way we read straightforward narratives; they are more like the poetry of many biblical psalmists and prophets. The visionary imagery is intended to evoke images of terror more than to convey an exact, literal portrait of the threats' appearance.

Yet at the same time, Lindsey's reading of the text does catch its basic significance, insofar as he translates the horrifying images of John's day into images that evoke analogous horror in our own.[52] In so doing, he allows the text to speak with its intended impact more freely than some scholars who merely bury it in an analysis of ancient parallels. When we convey the text's meaning for today, we should offer comparisons with graphic images that have the same effect on today's audiences.

GOD'S INVOLVEMENT IN HISTORY. Some older Christians in my church circles used to talk about "holding their peace" and "letting the Lord fight their battles." That may be a primary moral of the

---

50. Michaels, *Revelation*, 130, after noting some regimes that have made Americans nervous, adds contemporary fears about space aliens. Though I am inclined to see little positive value in contemporary horror movies (even of the science fiction variety), they may provide some helpful illustrations for communicating Revelation's emotional impact here.

51. Lindsey, *New World Coming*, 141.

52. Lindsey's one-for-one correspondence of some details (like fire coming forth), while ignoring other details that cannot fit his modern equivalents, is admittedly too prosaic. Some other images of horror less bound to specific features of John's images may communicate the equivalent impact more easily.

present passage. We as the end-time army of God (7:1–8) will not slay others with physical weapons; we may even prove a host of martyrs (7:9–17). But God has other armies to overthrow worldly empires, whether he uses supernatural or human armies. God raised up Babylon to judge Judah, then judged Babylon for its own sins. Sometimes today evil acts of terrorism even turn public opinion against the terrorists, producing at least a temporary diminution of bloodletting.[53]

The militia movements that seek to arm themselves to survive the end-time battles misunderstand Revelation.[54] The Lord does not depend on our carnal means to accomplish the purposes of his kingdom (Matt. 26:52; Luke 22:51).

A message for Christians. The intended impact of Revelation's images on those who deliberately reject its truth is harsh: John is not like some refined modern preachers unwilling to "scare" someone into repentance. But few who reject Revelation's message will read this far; its main audience is Christians, and its main message at this point may therefore be twofold. (1) Christians flirting with compromise with the world should think twice, because the entire social order will be destroyed in the awful catastrophes of war; Christ alone is an adequate security.

(2) Christians suffering at the hand of the world should never envy the position of their persecutors. Their persecutors will suffer too; invasions by other ungodly persons or spirits function as God's judgments on a wicked society, hence active vindication of his persecuted people. Of course, Christians often die in wars, such as during the genocide in Rwanda in the 1990s. John does not promise specific, total immunity for God's servants from all the ravages of war, but the demonic predators, at least, can not touch them (9:4).[55]

---

53. See, e.g., *The Ku Klux Klan: A History of Racism and Violence*, 4th ed., ed. Sara Bullard (Montgomery, Ala.: Klanwatch, Southern Poverty Law Center, 1991), 22; the account of a friend in YWAM about the effects of the murder of three Catholic children in Northern Ireland in summer 1998. Right-wing terrorists in the Oklahoma City bombing and Muslim extremists in the Nairobi embassy bombing both weakened their causes at least in the short run.

54. On these movements, most of whose members are conservative Protestants, see Richard Abanes, *American Militias: Rebellion, Racism and Religion* (Downers Grove, Ill.: InterVarsity, 1996), 87–97. More specifically on Elizabeth Clare Prophet and her Church Universal and Triumphant, see Joe Szimhart, "Lambs to Slaughter—An Insider's Report of Cultic Bondage," *SCP Newsletter* 19/3 (Winter 1995): 1, 9, 13–14.

55. Cf. the ancient images of (usually) demonic psychopomps assigned to escort the wicked to hell (T. Asher 6:4–5; 3 Enoch 44:2; Apoc. Zeph. 4:2–4; Questions of Ezra 15 A; *Sifre Deut.* 357.11.2; probably adapted from paganism—*Egyptian Book of Dead Spell* 1, S5; Diogenes Laertius, 8.1.31; cf. further Erwin R. Goodenough, *Jewish Symbols in the Greco-Roman Period*, 13 vols. [New York: Pantheon for Bollingen Foundation, 1953–68], 12:149–52), though omitted in the biblical picture (Luke 16:22–23).

Furthermore, John provides one perspective on troubles in the world that complements other biblical perspectives: God is not absent in times of the world's hardship, but remains in control. Christians must also recognize another biblical perspective that summons us to work to heal the pain around us: The cross testifies that God loves a world hostile to him and even shared our pain to ultimately liberate us from it. Yet we also need Revelation's perspective, which addresses the stark division between God's martyrs and their persecutors: God does not merely wait until Christ's return to act in history on behalf of justice.

Finally, the message of repentance (9:20–21) is not only for the world, but for professing Christians who have grown too comfortable with the world's values (2:5, 16, 21–22; 3:3, 19; cf. 18:4).

Revelation 10:1-11

THEN I SAW another mighty angel coming down from heaven. He was robed in a cloud, with a rainbow above his head; his face was like the sun, and his legs were like fiery pillars. ²He was holding a little scroll, which lay open in his hand. He planted his right foot on the sea and his left foot on the land, ³and he gave a loud shout like the roar of a lion. When he shouted, the voices of the seven thunders spoke. ⁴And when the seven thunders spoke, I was about to write; but I heard a voice from heaven say, "Seal up what the seven thunders have said and do not write it down."

⁵Then the angel I had seen standing on the sea and on the land raised his right hand to heaven. ⁶And he swore by him who lives for ever and ever, who created the heavens and all that is in them, the earth and all that is in it, and the sea and all that is in it, and said, "There will be no more delay! ⁷But in the days when the seventh angel is about to sound his trumpet, the mystery of God will be accomplished, just as he announced to his servants the prophets."

⁸Then the voice that I had heard from heaven spoke to me once more: "Go, take the scroll that lies open in the hand of the angel who is standing on the sea and on the land."

⁹So I went to the angel and asked him to give me the little scroll. He said to me, "Take it and eat it. It will turn your stomach sour, but in your mouth it will be as sweet as honey." ¹⁰I took the little scroll from the angel's hand and ate it. It tasted as sweet as honey in my mouth, but when I had eaten it, my stomach turned sour. ¹¹Then I was told, "You must prophesy again about many peoples, nations, languages and kings."

Original Meaning

BETWEEN THE SIXTH and seventh seals (6:12; 8:1), Revelation has provided a picture of the state of the saints during the period of the seals (7:1-17); the book provides a similar interlude between the sixth and seventh trumpets (9:13; 11:15).[1] Revelation 12-14 then functions

---

1. Aune, *Revelation*, 2:499, suggests a parallel with the discussion of Passover in Ex. 12:1-18, placed between the ninth and tenth plagues.

as the heart of the book, sandwiched between the trumpets and bowls of God's anger.

In 10:1, John sees a magnificent angel. Pictures of shining angels (10:1) are common in Jewish literature (see especially Dan. 10:6).[2] The rainbow on this angel's head probably functions like a brilliant crown (cf. 12:1; 14:14), which some traditions attribute to high angels (3 En. 22:5; 26:7); the rainbow may represent the divine glory (Rev. 4:3). Being "robed in a cloud" (cf. 11:12; 14:14–16) simply emphasizes his heavenly stature.

Jewish tradition emphasized many giant angels, some as high as the heavens.[3] That this angel's feet are "like fiery pillars" may recall the ancient tradition in which the world was supported by pillars; that his feet straddle sea and land support this image of magnitude (10:2).[4] But appearing right after comparisons with the rainbow and the sun, his luminosity is probably emphasized more, alluding to the Jewish tradition of God's glory manifest to Israel as a pillar of fire in the desert, apparently extending to heaven (Ex. 13:21–22; 14:24; Num. 14:14; Neh. 9:12, 19). The magnitude of such angels helped ancient readers of such accounts, including Revelation, to stand in awe of the God who was infinitely greater than such angels.

Scholars diverge widely in their views of the "little scroll" the angel holds (10:2).[5] Some regard it as a prophetic commission (see Ezek. 3:1–4).[6] But because it becomes the content of John's prophecy (Rev. 10:10–11), it seems more likely that this scroll represents the substance of the book of Revelation (1:11; 22:7–10, 18–19). It is possible that this is the book whose seals are broken in 6:1–8:1, but whose contents constitute the entire message of

---

2. See Dan. 10:6; 2 Enoch 14:3; 19:1; 3 Enoch 14:5; 22:4; 26:2–7; 35:2; T. Abr. 12 A; see also comment on Rev. 1:14–16. This glory appears widely enough (cf. Ford, *Revelation*, 158) so that no identity between this angel and Jesus in 1:13–16 is necessary (Beale, *Revelation*, 524–25, takes this as Christ as the Old Testament "angel of the LORD"); the "lion's voice" in 10:3 also need not allude to Jesus in 5:5 (cf. 4:7).

3. Both evil angels (1 Enoch 7:2; T. Reub. 5:6) and good ones (3 Enoch 9:2; 22:3; 33:3; 35:2; b. Hag. 13b). This resembled Greek portraits of massive deities (Apollonus Rhodius, 2.679–82; Babrius, 68; Callimachus, *Hymn* 6.57–58; Apollodorus, 1.6.3) and demons (Homer, *Il.* 4.440–43; Longinus, *Sublime* 9.4) as well as semidivine giants.

4. On the supporting pillars, see Homer, *Od.* 1.52–53. For the "pillars of Heracles," cf. e.g., Appian, *R.H.* 6.1.1; 12.14.93; for Atlas see Aeschylus, *Prometh. Bound* 350–52. Comparing legs with pillars emphasized their strength (Song 5:15). Aune, *Revelation*, 2:556, points out multiple parallels with the Colossos of Rhodes in Asia, a 105-foot tall bronze statue of the sun god; although not standing in this period, it was widely known.

5. Though one normally held an open book in both hands, ancient art often portrayed it in one hand, especially if reading had been interrupted (Aune, *Revelation*, 2:558); also, the book may be quite "little" by comparison with this massive angel.

6. Beasley-Murray, *Revelation*, 171–72.

Revelation—the book opened by the Lamb (5:1–9), which may in some sense include the book of life (3:5; 13:8; 17:8; 20:12, 15; 21:27).

The image of thunder is appropriate. Ancients widely understood that the supreme God ruled thunder (see comment on 4:5), and in some traditions thunder could sound like God's voice (cf. John 12:29). The content of the seven thunders, however, is deliberately mysterious (Rev. 10:4). Some think John uses these thunders to explain why he has omitted one series of judgments revealed to him. One could also regard them as an ironic parallel to the Ten Commandments that followed the ten plagues of Exodus, except that this revelation remains secret (though why they remain secret makes little sense on such a view). Others argue that the thunders remain mysterious as a literary technique, to build suspense.[7]

If the content of the seven thunders is related to the little book in the angel's hand (10:1–3), it may not be written in John's book (10:4), yet may be revealed in the prophesying of the one who ate the little book (10:8–11). Thus one can argue that the passage implies that God will reveal further details through John and through the two witnesses (11:3), that is, through the testimony of God's people facing a hostile world. Such an interpretation does not violate the theology of the book. Although one dare not add to the book of Revelation itself (22:18), the book does not imply that God stopped speaking with the close of Revelation or even the close of the canon. Rather, anywhere that people testify about Christ God will continue speaking (19:10). Appealing as this interpretation is, however, it seems more likely that the seven thunders will be revealed only at the time of the end, when God's "mystery" is finished (10:7).

Most likely the seven thunders remain mysterious in order to teach that the hidden things belong to God (Deut. 29:29; cf. 2 Cor. 12:4; Rev. 2:17; 19:12).[8] Revelation, unlike Daniel, does not seal up most of its contents (Rev. 22:10; cf. Dan. 12:9), but some things must remain sealed. The concealment of the meaning of the seven thunders reminds us that God knows far more about the future than he tells us.

The angel lifts his hand to swear (10:5), hence emphasizing the certainty of his claim that the end will finally come. Lifting one hand was a standard practice for swearing an oath in ancient Israel (Deut. 32:40) and later Jewish custom (Jub. 13:29), and Greeks could affirm the sincerity of an oath by

---

7. For this last view see Michaels, *Revelation*, 134. Against the view that the thunders represent a distinct source taken over by Revelation, see Friedrich W. Horn, "Die sieben Donner, Erwägungen zu Offb 10," *SNTU* 17 (1992): 215–29.

8. For parallels in ancient revelatory literature to one thing remaining hidden, see especially Aune, *Revelation*, 2:562–63.

proposing to touch Zeus in heaven while swearing, were it possible.[9] The specific description of the oath here recalls Daniel 12:7, where a revealing angel raises his hands toward heaven and swears by the one who lives forever (cf. Rev. 1:18; 4:9) that only three and a half years remain before the end. Here, however, the Tribulation period is already finished, and at the seventh angel's voice there remains no further interval before the end. (Note that because the angel who speaks in 10:1–3 appears to announce the seventh angel in the series of trumpeters, it is unlikely that he himself is the seventh angel; Revelation contains many angels.)

That "there will be no more delay" (10:6) can be translated "there will be no more time." This may suggest a shortening of time periods as the end drew near, as in some apocalyptic traditions (2 Enoch 65:6–7). But the NIV more accurately translates "delay" here. The Greek term *chronos* can mean "delay" (as in Hab. 2:3; Heb. 10:37; cf. Rev. 2:21; 6:11; 20:3); no further interval of time remains before the end. John's point is probably that the prayers of the saints for final vindication await no further delay (6:9–11); judgment has come (11:18; 14:7).[10]

The completion of "the mystery" (10:7) probably indicates that the seven thunders will no longer remain secret (10:4); all will be revealed at the consummation (cf. 1 Cor. 13:8–12).[11] Although in Revelation anything symbolic may have been a "mystery" until explained (1:20; 17:5–7), the divine "mystery" here seems to involve God's kingdom (Dan. 2:44, 47; Mark 4:11). God's purposes will be "accomplished" (Rev. 10:7; cf. 11:7; 15:1; 16:17; 17:17), as promised to "his servants the prophets" (10:7; 11:18; cf. Acts 3:21–24).

At the command of a heavenly voice John takes the small book from the angel's hand, similar to what Ezekiel did (Ezek. 2:9; Rev. 10:8–9). The voice from heaven (Rev. 10:4, 8), distinguished from that of the seventh angel (10:7), is probably that of Jesus (1:10; 4:1). The angel instructs John to eat the book (10:9), just as God instructed Ezekiel (Ezek. 2:8; 3:1); and as in Ezekiel, the book proves sweet as honey in his mouth (Ezek. 3:3; Rev. 10:9–10).[12]

---

9. Chariton, *Chaer.* 3.2.5. "Raising the hand" actually means "swearing" in Hebrew idiom (cf. Ex. 6:8; Num. 14:30; Ezek. 20:5–6).

10. See Oscar Cullmann, *Christ and Time*, tr. F. V. Filson (Philadelphia: Westminster, 1950), 49; Rissi, *Time and History*, 24. Aune, *Revelation*, 2:568, prefers the nuancing of "the time will be up."

11. For such language describing the fulfillment of prophecy, cf. Sib. Or. 3.698–700.

12. Eating the book, like measuring the temple in 11:1–2, probably occurs only in the visionary realm. The author of 4 Ezra 14:38–41, 45 also applies Ezekiel's image to the Spirit's empowerment. Later teachers applied Ezekiel's experience to the study of the law (William Barclay, *Train Up a Child* [Philadelphia: Westminster, 1959], 12–13). Angels often provide explanations (e.g., 3 Bar. 9:5), and what tastes good but proves bitter may have been proverbial (Prov. 5:3–4; cf. Diogenes Laertius, 6.2.61). Cf. Num. 5:23.

That it proves bitter in John's stomach (10:9–10; albeit not poisonous, as in 8:11) probably points to the message's content: sorrow and mourning (Ezek. 2:10); God's words and wisdom are often compared with honey (Ps. 19:10; 119:103; Prov. 24:13–14).[13] Eating the book symbolizes internalizing its contents, because the eater can then prophesy (Ezek. 3:1; Rev. 10:11). But whereas Ezekiel was to deliver the message only to the house of Israel (Ezek. 3:1), John will prophesy to "many peoples, nations, languages and kings" (Rev. 10:11), like Jeremiah (Jer. 1:10)—and the two witnesses (Rev. 11:3).[14]

MOST CONTEMPORARY GENRES of discourse do not emphasize angels. Most people do, of course, believe in angels, and the interest in angels, even among those who hold distorted and anti-Christian views (for further elaboration on this problem, see comments in Contemporary Significance section of 19:10), has been remarkable.[15] But few think in terms of giant beings related not merely to us as individuals but to the ordering of the cosmos, though the Bible may imply the involvement of angels in the latter (cf. Ps. 148:2–10; Gal. 4:8–10).

To achieve the same effect that the original narrative evoked from its first audience, we must understand something about first-century Jewish conceptions of angels. Then we can appreciate more fully the graphic way this narrative emphasizes God's sovereignty. This angel is portrayed as mightier than most Greeks portrayed their gods; yet this angel is simply an obedient servant of the true God, who is infinitely greater than such a portrait could visualize.

By examining the points and associations that Revelation's images conveyed to the original audience, we can articulate analogous points for our contemporary contexts. Such points include the angel's awesomeness (inviting us to contemplate and articulate God's greater majesty), the paradoxical (to

---

13. Cf. also Aune, *Revelation*, 2:572, for the Greek idiom of "sweet" speech.

14. Ezekiel also gave oracles to the nations (Ezek. 25–32), as did other prophets (Isa. 13–23; Jer. 25:15–38; 46:1–51:64); but the particular scroll in Ezek. 3:1 addresses Israel. Though John technically prophesies here only to seven urban church communities, his message will be spread by others (see David Hill, "Prophecy and Prophets in the Revelation of St John," *NTS* 18 [July 1972]: 401–18 [pp. 417–18]). For prophetic inspiration concerning all peoples, see Sib. Or. 3.162–64, 297–99, 518–19.

15. Cf. Geoffrey Hodson, *Clairvoyant Investigations* (Wheaton, Ill.: Theosophical Publishing House, 1984); R. Gustav Niebuhr, "Long unemployed, angels now have their work to do: as guardians, especially, they are popular with people, religious and otherwise," *Wall Street Journal* 73 (May 12, 1992): 1, 6.

us) silence of the thunders, the certainty that the end will come in its time, and John's model of obedience and experience as a Spirit-empowered witness.

THIS PASSAGE PROVIDES us several lessons, each of which can be contextualized in turn for a particular audience or particular circumstances in our own lives. (1) The awesomeness of the angel obedient to God implies that God rules all suprahuman and supernatural forces. Whatever crises we as individuals or God's people as a whole must confront, we can take courage in the Bible's continual reminders that God has everything under control.

(2) The thunders reveal that some matters are not yet ours to know (10:4). The hidden things belong to God alone (Deut. 29:29); until Jesus returns, we know in part only (1 Cor. 13:9). This does not mean that we should not seek knowledge (Prov. 18:15; 23:12; 25:2); it does mean that God has set boundaries to what is best for us to know, and we should acknowledge those boundaries (Rom. 16:19). In other words, we should avoid undue speculation about matters on which we cannot be certain and should avoid speaking dogmatically about them (1 Tim. 1:4; 2 Tim. 2:23). God rules the future, but we do not need to know the details. He has not guaranteed us such knowledge, especially about the final details before the "delay" is over. The seven thunders may constitute one of the most important words to prophecy teachers in the entire book.

In contrast to this principle, some prophecy teachers fill in too many details on which the text does not comment. Prognosticators may satisfy our curiosity about the future, but the biblical expositor's job is to help us hear and obey (1:3) the message of Scripture, not to add to it (22:18). We are more than ready to refute cults when they prognosticate. I talked with a Jehovah's Witness who defended the Watchtower view of a progressive resurrection in Revelation 20 by saying that it was only logical that God would not resurrect everyone from different times and cultures simultaneously. My problem with this line of argument is that such "logic" contradicts the explicit statement of the narrative, and it stems from the same belief system that insists on taking literally the number (but not the ethnicity or gender) of the 144,000.

I used that inconsistency to point out that for all their claims to rely only on Scripture, Jehovah's Witnesses must buy into the entire Watchtower scheme of thought to come up with many of their views; and any theological or philosophical system looks consistent from inside the system. These Witnesses admitted at that point that their beliefs depended not only on

Scripture but also on their group's special claim to be right—a claim made by many other groups as well.

Many years ago my witness to people in cults forced me to recognize that sometimes orthodox Christians work with the same sort of interpretive fallacies that cults do. For example, although the "oil" of Deuteronomy 33:24 is undoubtedly olive oil, evangelical oilmen more committed to excellence in drilling than to excellence in interpreting Scripture wasted over $13,000,000 that might have better been contributed to missions, based on an interpretation of that verse.[16] As a young Christian, I listened with interest as a prophecy teacher in September 1981 promised on the basis of Scripture that Iran would fall into the hands of the Soviet Union in the next twelve months; I wrote the prediction down, set it aside, and checked it for accuracy a few years later. Nearly two decades later this solemn assurance remains unfulfilled, especially since the Soviet Union no longer exists (I understand too that the prophecy teacher has invested in a different line of work). We must investigate some matters of speculation for apologetic reasons (e.g., many non-Christians ask, "Where did Cain get his wife?"), but we must always be humble about our response (e.g., "This approach may or may not be correct, but shows how your question might be answered").

(3) The promise of "no more delay" (10:6) reminds us that though we must wait now, delay will not last forever. A time is coming when God will fulfill all his promises made throughout history (Acts 3:21). As an earlier A. M. E. Zion minister, Joseph Charles Price, put it, "No matter how dark the night, I believe in the coming of the dawn."[17]

(4) We should follow John's example, obeying even when the message we are called to proclaim proves bitter or does not make sense to us. Some circles, especially those that emphasize prosperity, condition audiences to expect only pleasant things from God; but his message is not always pleasant, though he always provides the obedient grace to endure it (cf. Jer. 39:18; 45:5).

(5) The message of Revelation concerns "many peoples" (10:11). No one is exempt from its warnings, and those most inclined to comfort themselves with the current ease of their society should take special heed. The cup of judgment will come to all people (Jer. 25:15–17), as will the suffering of believers (Matt. 24:9).

---

16. See "Are There Treasures Hid in the Sand'?" *Pentecostal Evangel* (Jan. 5, 1986), 13.
17. Inscribed on Heritage Hall at Livingstone College, Salisbury, N.C. (cf. Ps 30:5).

Revelation 11:1–14

I WAS GIVEN a reed like a measuring rod and was told, "Go and measure the temple of God and the altar, and count the worshipers there. ²But exclude the outer court; do not measure it, because it has been given to the Gentiles. They will trample on the holy city for 42 months. ³And I will give power to my two witnesses, and they will prophesy for 1,260 days, clothed in sackcloth." ⁴These are the two olive trees and the two lampstands that stand before the Lord of the earth. ⁵If anyone tries to harm them, fire comes from their mouths and devours their enemies. This is how anyone who wants to harm them must die. ⁶These men have power to shut up the sky so that it will not rain during the time they are prophesying; and they have power to turn the waters into blood and to strike the earth with every kind of plague as often as they want.

⁷Now when they have finished their testimony, the beast that comes up from the Abyss will attack them, and overpower and kill them. ⁸Their bodies will lie in the street of the great city, which is figuratively called Sodom and Egypt, where also their Lord was crucified. ⁹For three and a half days men from every people, tribe, language and nation will gaze on their bodies and refuse them burial. ¹⁰The inhabitants of the earth will gloat over them and will celebrate by sending each other gifts, because these two prophets had tormented those who live on the earth.

¹¹But after the three and a half days a breath of life from God entered them, and they stood on their feet, and terror struck those who saw them. ¹²Then they heard a loud voice from heaven saying to them, "Come up here." And they went up to heaven in a cloud, while their enemies looked on.

¹³At that very hour there was a severe earthquake and a tenth of the city collapsed. Seven thousand people were killed in the earthquake, and the survivors were terrified and gave glory to the God of heaven.

¹⁴The second woe has passed; the third woe is coming soon.

THIS SECTION IS perhaps the most difficult passage to interpret in the entire book of Revelation. Like John (10:11), the two witnesses prophesy (11:3); but who are these two witnesses? We will return to this question, central to the interpretation of this section, after examining the question that presents itself first: What is the temple in 11:1–2?

The Temple (11:1–2)

REVELATION REGULARLY BORROWS end-time portraits from its contemporaries, but reapplies them with a new and surprising meaning; the picture of the desecrated temple may fall into this category. John may be referring to a literal temple if he is writing before the temple's destruction in A.D. 70, during a period of great distress for Jerusalem in A.D. 66–70; but most scholars date Revelation in the 90s. Some regard the oracle about the threat to the temple as an oracle originally directed to the literal temple in Jerusalem before A.D. 70, which John has now reapplied to the spiritual situation in the tribulation of his own day.[1] Whatever the merit of this proposal, it is possible that Revelation is reapplying the literal three and a half year period of Daniel's tribulation figuratively to the entire period between Christ's first and second coming (see comment on 12:5–6).

Some believe that 11:1–2 demands the rebuilding of the literal temple.[2] Given beliefs among John's contemporaries that the temple would be rebuilt, such a view makes sense; but some factors incline us to favor a more symbolic reading of the passage. (1) The time period described (1,260 days) is probably symbolic for a period most of which lacked a literal temple (see comment on 12:5–6). (2) The witnesses are probably symbolic (see comment below on 11:3–14). (3) Since John is writing after the temple's demise, he probably expects his audience to understand that he refers to a spiritual temple, because no temple stands in his day and he provides no explicit indication that the physical temple will be rebuilt. (4) Most important is the fact that the temple is symbolic elsewhere in Revelation (3:12; 13:6).

---

1. Beasley-Murray, *Revelation*, 37–38, 176–77; cf. Helmut Seng, "Apk 11,1–14 im Zusammenhang der Johannesapokalypse: Aufschluss aus Lactantius und Hippolytus," *Vetera Christianorum* 27 (1990): 111–21. Similar language (including "trampling") would suit a literal Gentile desecration of the temple (1 Macc. 3:45; 4:60; 2 Macc. 8:2; 3 Macc. 2:18; Judith 9:8; Ps. Sol. 2:2; CD 1.3–4; T. Jud. 23:3; Luke 21:24), which might stem from judgment (2 Bar. 8:1). If there was an oracle, it may have been a Jewish-Christian one, stemming from the time of Caligula (cf. 2 Thess. 2:4) or the late 60s (cf. Mark 13:14).

2. So Lindsey, *New World Coming*, 156 (who suggests that it may be rebuilt after the Rapture, 160).

But if the temple is symbolic, what does it mean? John's term for "temple" here is *naos*, the word that in the Greek translation of ancient Israel's Scriptures generally designates the most sacred parts of the temple, not the entire building complex. Some suggest that the temple represents Israel and its altar the faithful remnant who refuse to assimilate with the world.[3] This interpretation accords with ancient biblical prophecies about Israel; it possibly refers to the suffering of the literal Jewish people during the present age, surrounding a remnant of Jewish Christians who genuinely hold faithful to God in Christ. Surely the book of Revelation remains interested in the Jewish foundation and character of the believing community (1:20; 2:9; 3:9; 7:1–17).

In early Christian literature, however, the temple regularly symbolizes Christians, both Jewish and Gentile (1 Cor. 3:16; 2 Cor. 6:16; Eph. 2:18–22; 1 Peter 2:5). This is also what the temple symbolizes elsewhere in Revelation (Rev. 3:12; 13:6); not surprisingly, this is the more common scholarly interpretation of this temple today.[4] Some thus suggest that the "outer courts" represent Christians who compromise with the world's values (like some Christians in Thyatira), arguing that only they, not faithful Christians, will fall away under the world's oppression.[5] Others similarly argue that the enemies of God trample "the outward and visible church" in this age but that the invisible church hidden in Christ will not be crushed but will ultimately persevere.[6] Still others maintain that the protection this passage refers to is physical rather than spiritual, hence that the inner part of the temple refers to those brought safely through the Tribulation, who survive to the end—the outer court being Christians who suffer death.[7]

Given the whole context of this passage, however, it is possible to adopt a more specifically Jewish Christian reading. In this case, the *naos* represents the church as the faithful remnant of Israel (including grafted-in Gentile Christians). The trampling of the outer courts then depicts the rule of the evil one, who misleads the rest of the Jewish people, the end-time remnant who

3. Rissi, *Time and History*, 99.

4. Caird, *Commentary on Revelation*, 132; Metzger, *Breaking the Code*, 70; Talbert, *Apocalypse*, 44. The Dead Sea Scrolls also sometimes portrayed their community as a house or temple (see Bertril Gärtner, *The Temple and the Community in Qumran and the New Testament* [Cambridge: Cambridge Univ. Press, 1965], 16–46), regarding the literal temple in Jerusalem as spiritually defiled (e.g., CD 4.18; 5.6–7; 1QpHab 9.4–10.1).

5. Talbert, *Apocalypse*, 45.

6. Caird, *Commentary on Revelation*, 152; Beale, *Revelation*, 557–65. Michael Bachmann, "Himmlisch: der 'Tempel Gottes' von Apk 11.1," *NTS* 40 (July 1994): 474–80, applies 11:1 to a heavenly temple.

7. Aune, *Revelation*, 2:598, identifying the survivors with his interpretation of the 144,000.

eventually understands and repents (11:8, 13).[8] This fits the description of unrighteous Jerusalem below (11:8). If we are correct here, the use of the outer courts is profoundly ironic, for it was Gentiles who were restricted to the outer court in the most recent temple that John's contemporaries remembered.[9] But while this proposal seems plausible to me, it is hardly certain; the exact meaning of the outer court remains open to debate.

What is the point of John's "measuring rod" (11:1)? In the early 1500s Francis Lambert argued that the temple was the church and that the measuring rod was God's Word.[10] He may have at least been right that the first readers would have understood the act of measuring symbolically; a first-century Jewish work used the measuring of Paradise to signify the resurrection of the dead (1 En. 61:1–5). One might "measure" the righteous (1 En. 70:3–4), just as one might seal them to preserve them from judgment (Rev. 7:3).

The most likely symbolic interpretation of the act of measuring here is a promise of preservation, as in the measuring of Jerusalem (Ps. 48:12–13; Zech. 2:1–2) or the temple (Ezek. 40–42, esp. 40:3).[11] It may also indicate the spiritual unpreparedness of Israel, if the outer courts relate to the Jewish people not yet turned to the Messiah (Amos 7:7–9). Most important, however, no measurements are given here; this defers the mention of the measuring rod until 21:16, when John begins to measure the gloriously massive new Jerusalem, which is shaped like the Most Holy Place.[12] The small, persecuted remnant oppressed during this age constitutes the glorious Holy City of the age to come (cf. Mark 4:31–32).

The Identity of the Witnesses (11:3−6)

INTERPRETERS HAVE DIVERGED widely on the identity of the two witnesses.[13] We may begin our own quest with the most obvious allusion, the two olive

---

8. Heinrich Schlier, *Principalities and Powers in the New Testament* (New York: Herder & Herder, 1961), 72, seems to view the outer court as the earthly Jerusalem as opposed to the heavenly.

9. Beasley-Murray, *Revelation*, 182, thinks that it symbolizes the unbelieving world. If the courts symbolize assimilated Christians, lesser purity may constitute the primary focus.

10. Petersen, *Preaching in the Last Days*, 151. On the physical nature of such a rod when used literally, see Ford, *Revelation*, 168.

11. With Talbert, *Apocalypse*, 44; see the frequent use of the measuring rod in Ezek. 40:3–42:20 (LXX). The suggested parallel in Lev. 16 (Kenneth A. Strand, "An Overlooked Old Testament Background to Revelation 11:1," *AUSS* 22 [1984]: 317–25) lacks the measuring rod.

12. Cf. the expectation of a new (literal) temple in early Judaism (see E. P. Sanders, *Jesus and Judaism* [Philadelphia: Fortress, 1985], 77–90), an image that may be reinterpreted here.

13. See Petersen, *Preaching in the Last Days*, passim; for the Reformers, who saw a revival of prophecy in their own day, see ibid., 59–87.

trees and the two lampstands (11:4). The olive trees recall the anointed king and priest who will truly lead God's people in Zechariah 4:11–14. In the immediate context in Zechariah, these were Joshua and Zerubbabel, who worked for the good of a city trampled by Gentiles (Zech. 3–4; cf. Rev. 11:2).[14] The lampstand in Zechariah 4:2 may refer to the source of the Spirit (cf. 4:6); presumably it burned by the same olive oil by which the two anointed ones were anointed. But Revelation regularly reapplies earlier symbols in strikingly new ways. This book, which elsewhere uses lampstands to symbolize the church, also would not present the Spirit himself as a martyred witness, and it hardly proposes the *literal* return of Joshua and Zerubbabel![15]

While we may debate a present or future identity for the witnesses, the past figures to which they allude (even more plainly than Joshua and Zerubbabel) are easier to determine. Calling down fire recalls Elijah, who also was taken into heaven and who brought drought for three and a half years (cf. James 5:17). Turning water into blood and sending other plagues recall especially Moses, who some Jewish traditions also claimed ascended.[16] Revelation may also conflate a few other allusions to provide a fuller symbolic picture, such as fire from the mouth (hence alluding to Jeremiah in Jer. 5:14) and a Jewish tradition that Isaiah was martyred for calling Jerusalem Sodom.[17]

Some suggest that John envisions the literal return of Elijah and Moses.[18] Such a view is not impossible; Hippolytus, Tertullian, and Jerome, for example, believed that Enoch and Elijah remained alive and would return as witnesses.[19]

---

14. Moses also appears as a lampstand in some Jewish texts (*Sifre Num.* 93.1.3), and later as one of the anointed ones of Zech. 4:14 (*Ex. Rab.* 15:3).

15. Scholars have long noted that Revelation sometimes reapplies old prophecies in new ways (e.g., Wesley, *Commentary on the Bible*, 594).

16. Bauckham, *Climax of Prophecy*, 169, cites Josephus, *Ant.* 4.326; Clement of Alexandria, *Strom.* 6.15.2–3. Josephus tones down Elijah's ascent, however (*Ant.* 9.28).

17. See Asc. Isa. 3:10. See here esp. Bauckham, *Climax of Prophecy*, 169–70. Although rooted in Elijah's ministry (1 Kings 18:38; 2 Kings 1:10–14; *Lives of Prophets* 21:2), fire from heaven became a standard means of judgment attributed to the pious (T. Abr. 10A; 12B; Jos. and Asen. 25:6/7); some rabbis also reportedly disintegrated the disrespectful with their gaze (b. B.B. 75a; Shab. 34a; Pes. Rab Kah. 11:16; 18:5; Gen. Rab. 79:6). Unsolicited fire or lightning from heaven appears as confirmation in Ex. 40:38; Plutarch, *Aemilius Paulus* 24.1; p. Hag. 2:1, §§4, 9; Song Rab. 1:10, §2; as judgment in Diodorus Siculus, 4.67.2; 16.83.2; Dionysius of Halicarnassus, 3.35.2; 9.6.5; Pausanias, 9.25.10; cf. Lev. 10:2; Num. 16:35; 1QM 17.2–3; Josephus, *Ant.* 4.55–56.

18. Lindsey, *New World Coming*, 162–63; Frost, *Matthew Twenty-Four*, 212. Daniel K. K. Wong, "The Two Witnesses in Revelation 11," *BibSac* 154 (July 1997): 344–54, prefers two literal end-time witnesses but whose identity is yet unknown, coming with Elijah's and Moses' power.

19. For summaries of views, see Ford, *Revelation*, 177–78; Petersen, *Preaching in the Last Days*, 13. Elijah's return appears pervasive in early Judaism (Mal. 4:5–6; Sir. 48:10; Sifre Deut. 41.4.3; 342.5.2; Mark 9:11).

In John's day other Jewish writers expected the return and preaching of those who had never died, presumably Elijah and Enoch (4 Ezra 6:26); other traditions also suggested that Moses had not died.[20] But while this passage does model the two witnesses after Moses and Elijah, it also deliberately modifies the connections. Thus, for example, fire comes from the witnesses' mouths (11:5) rather than from heaven, as with Elijah; this is figurative language for the harsh power of God's word, as in Jeremiah's ministry (Jer. 5:14). Is it not therefore more likely, given John's consistent reinterpretation of traditional Jewish symbols elsewhere, that he transforms this traditional Jewish expectation of returning prophets, reapplying it symbolically?

Suggesting that the two witnesses are symbolic is, however, not helpful unless we can determine what they symbolize—one of the more difficult interpretative tasks in this book. Some view them as symbolic for the Law and the Prophets.[21] Others suggest that the witnesses are Peter and Paul, both probably executed roughly the same time under Nero.[22] (They were not, however, raised, as in 11:11.) Still others point to olive tree symbolism for Israel (Jer. 11:16; Hos. 14:6; Rom. 11:17) and argue that the two witnesses represent Israel and the church.[23]

While such proposals are as reasonable for guesses as any guesses may be, another view draws more directly from the evidence of the text. The most common view is that the two witnesses represent the prophetic witness of the church.[24] Various factors support this interpretation.

(1) They are "lampstands" (11:4), which Revelation elsewhere explicitly identifies as churches (1:20).[25]

---

20. For Moses, see *Sifre Deut.* 357.10.5; ARN, 12A; cf. T. Moses 11:8; contrast 1 Enoch 89:38. Probably Enoch's and Elijah's martyrdom in Apoc. Elij. 4:7–19 reflects a later Jewish-Christian interpretation of the tradition in Rev. 11:3–7; others cite the eschatological appearance of Moses and Elijah in later rabbis (T. Francis Glasson, *Moses in the Fourth Gospel* [Naperville, Ill.: Alec R. Allenson, 1963], 27, 69).

21. Corsini, *Apocalypse*, 193–98; cf. similar interpretations some have offered concerning Moses and Elijah in Mark 9:4.

22. John Randall, *The Book of Revelation: What Does It Really Say?* (Locust Valley, N.Y.: Living Flame, 1976), 71.

23. González, *Revelation*, 72.

24. Bowman, *First Christian Drama*, 71; Hill, *New Testament Prophecy*, 89; Bauckham, *Climax of Prophecy*, 166, 273–75; Michaels, *Revelation*, 138–39; Talbert, *Apocalypse*, 45–46; Aune, *Revelation*, 2:631; Beale, *Revelation*, 572–75; cf. Newton, *Observations*, 286. Mounce, *Revelation*, 218, thinks they represent the end-time church.

25. As seven lampstands together signify the entire church, so here the two (Beasley-Murray, *Revelation*, 184), underlining the church's role as witnesses (Num. 35:30; Deut. 17:6; Bauckham, *Climax of Prophecy*, 274).

(2) Joshua and Zerubbabel were the high priest and king seeking the restoration of their holy city; what could better symbolize the saints as a kingdom and priests (1:6; 5:10) seeking their new Jerusalem?[26]

(3) Like John in this context, they prophesy (10:11; 11:3, 6), fulfilling the standard Christian mission of testifying for Christ (cf. 19:10).

(4) If the time period is symbolic for the entire Christian era, which may well be the case (see comment on 12:5−6), the witnesses would need to be symbolic for something of equally long duration (or to conceal their supernatural longevity with something more effective than merely Grecian formula).

(5) The cumulative adaptation of diverse Old Testament prophetic motifs, such as fire coming from the witnesses' mouths rather than from heaven, suggests a broader symbolic interpretation.

The case for the two witnesses being the church is debatable, but it seems the best of available options. Those who object to the witnesses being the church do so especially on grounds that the literal details, such as lying in the street for three days, do not fit the church.[27] Such objections are not unreasonable, but they presuppose that details in Revelation's narratives must be read literally, a premise that contradicts much of what we find in the rest of the book. Likewise, some insist that a serious reading of Scripture requires us to take the figure of two witnesses as two literal individuals; but in Revelation, unlike many genres in Scripture, it is difficult to apply that interpretive method with consistency: few would insist, for example, that the women in chapters 12 or 17 must represent literal individuals.

If the witnesses represent the church, one can view the 1,260 days in one of two ways. (1) One can see here the church's successful end-time witness (as opposed to its witness in most of church history). (2) One can instead take 1,260 as a symbolic number (fitting the symbolism in much of the book), in which case Revelation reinterprets this Jewish symbol as it does many others (see comments on 12:5−6). In this case Revelation is borrowing Daniel's figure not to tell us the length of time but to inform us of the kind of time, that the era of the church is characterized by great suffering, as in Daniel's tribulation.

John uses 1,260 days for the church's time and the equivalent figure of 42 months to describe the beast's time. The 1,260 days represent 42 months or

---

26. That some of the Qumran scrolls emphasize an anointed priest as well as prophet in the end-time (e.g., 1QS 9.11; 4Q540) reinforces the probability that John reapplies a widespread end-time image in a new way here. The royal and priestly components of Zech. 4:3−14 were obvious enough (*Pes. Rab.* 8:4).

27. E.g., Strombeck, *Rapture*, 185.

three and a half 360-day years; this is likely intended as a symbolic number (see comments on 12:5–6). Revelation prefers this to a sum of 364 days for a year (1 Enoch 74:12–13), or Daniel's 1,290 (Dan. 12:11) and 1,335 days (12:12), probably for reasons obvious to ancient geometers, who found great significance in numerical patterns.[28]

If indeed Revelation presents the two witnesses as the church, the biblical allusions provide a pattern for the church's prophetic mission: "for those whose witness is a greater thing even than Moses' or Elijah's and against whom the beast musters greater forces. . . ."[29]

The witnesses are probably two in number for several reasons. (1) Biblical rules of evidence required a minimum of two witnesses for valid testimony (Deut. 17:6; 19:15). (2) Early Christian witnesses were sent in pairs whenever possible (Mark 6:7; Acts 13:2–4).[30] (3) More important, the allusion to Zerubbabel and Joshua in Zechariah 4 demands two representatives. (4) Finally, the dual nature of the witnesses provides a literary contrast with the two evil leaders in 13:11–12, one of whom also produces fire (13:13). The anointed king and priest of chapter 11 contrast starkly with the wicked ruler and his priest in chapter 13. This portrait reinforces John's contrast between the church and the world system; the latter holds power to kill God's witnesses, but the witnesses will triumph nevertheless, even through their sacrifice.

The two witnesses also present a different aspect of the church than we would see if we had only the following chapter. To be sure, God will provide for his people in the desert (12:6, 14), protecting them from the plagues (7:3). Here, however, they boldly challenge the evil rulers, who embody the spirit of Antichrist. Like the original apostles, the church confirms its message about Jesus with signs—and by suffering. They die at the Antichrist's hand (11:7; 13:7), but in their very martyrdom they overcome him (12:11). Cutting-edge witness always demands the threat of suffering, and Christian witness and suffering together must precede the end (6:9–11).

---

28. 1,260 is the sum of even numbers up to 70, and 42 of even numbers up to 12. Further, 1,260 is the thirty-fifth rectangular number (corresponding to the square 1,225), and 42 the sixth rectangular number (corresponding to the square 36, which is the triangular root of 666); after 1, the first and second numbers that are both squares and triangular numbers are 36 and 1,225, respectively. The rectangular number after 1,260 is 1,332 (used for the Tribulation in Asc. Isa. 4:12, 14), the corresponding triangle of which is 666 (Bauckham, *Climax of Prophecy*, 401–3).

29. Bauckham, *Climax of Prophecy*, 170.

30. This remained the pattern in John's day (e.g., 11QTemple 61:6–7; 64:8; CD 9.3–4, 17–23; Josephus, *Life* 256; *Ant.* 4.219; *b. Sanh.* 37b, *baraita*), including among Christians (Matt. 18:16; 2 Cor. 13:1; 1 Tim. 5:19).

The History of the Two Witnesses (11:7–14)

THE WITNESSES ARE authorized to prophesy, that is, to speak God's message by his Spirit and on his behalf, like ancient Israel's prophets. They wear sackcloth (11:3), a sign of mourning and self-humiliation, often specifically the mourning of repentance.[31] This contrasts starkly with the gaiety that follows after their deaths (11:10), suggesting that the world would rather enjoy deception than hear unpleasant truth.

That the beast who rises from the Abyss (9:11, described in greater detail in 13:1–3) will "war" with the two witnesses (11:7, lit. trans.; NIV "attack them") borrows the holy war language often adapted in Revelation.[32] But the true Christian warriors (see comment on 7:1–8) are martyrs (7:9–17), and the ultimate battles will prove spiritual (in the heavens, where Satan loses without dispute; see 12:7) and eschatological (when Jesus destroys his challengers; see 17:14; 19:11; cf. the foretaste in 2:16). Worshipers of the beast ask who can make war with him (13:4); the answer is the slain Lamb, who also happens to be the supreme king (17:14). That the beast "overpowers" or "conquers" the saints (11:7; 13:7) indicates merely the temporal, human perspective. In the final analysis, the saints overcome the world by accepting martyrdom without compromise (2:10–11; 3:9, 12; 12:11; 15:2).

John's images seem deliberately polyvalent (as in 17:9–10, where the same image represents two things).[33] "The great city" (11:8) may refer to the ungodly world as a whole (i.e., Babylon), envisioned in John's day as Rome; after all, representatives of all peoples (11:9–10) suggests the empire. But the reference to the place of Jesus' crucifixion (11:8) presumably specifies Jerusalem (Mark 10:33; Luke 13:33–34; Heb. 13:12).[34] The holy city that was trampled by pagans during the period of the witnesses' testimony (11:2) was Jerusalem; Jesus' witnesses thus suffer where he did. John's insight regarding the names of the city is not "figuratively ... Sodom and Egypt" (so NIV), but literally, "Spiritually"—that is, by the Spirit, who inspires prophets to understand God's

---

31. In the Old Testament, see Isa. 20:2; Jer. 6:26; Lam. 2:10; Joel 1:13; later, 1 Macc. 2:14; Jos. and Asen. 10:14/16; 13:2. It remained appropriate for prophets living apart from a wicked society (Asc. Isa. 2:10).

32. In early Judaism, see 1QM 1.4. This language also applies to the Messiah's warring against Beliar (T. Dan 5:10), or the wicked trying to war against God (*Gen. Rab.* 38:6).

33. Cf. this possible understanding in Qumran's pesher interpretation (e.g., 1QpHab passim). Pagan oracles also freely recycled images (H. W. Parke, *Sibyls and Sibylline Prophecy in Classical Antiquity*, ed. B. C. McGing [New York: Routledge, 1988], 15).

34. See Ford, *Revelation*, 180; Rissi, *Future of the World*, 55–56. A population of 70,000 (11:13) also fits Jerusalem better than Rome (Beasley-Murray, *Revelation*, 177; Aune, *Revelation*, 2:628).

revelations (as in 17:3–5).[35] "Sodom" was a prophetic title for Jerusalem that implied its judgment (Isa. 1:9–10; Jer. 23:14; Lam. 4:6)—not surprising in a book that calls Rome "Babylon" and false prophets "Balaam" and "Jezebel."

Yet by John's "spiritual" insight, this city also stands for the broader world in some sense, for representatives from all nations witness the bodies (11:9).[36] The "great city" (11:8) may be Jerusalem in some sense here (perhaps the "holy city" of 11:2), but usually in this book it is explicitly Babylon (17:18; 18:10, 16, 18–21).[37] As Babylon it contrasts with the new Jerusalem, the "Holy City" (21:2, 10, 19), whose dimensions prove incomparably greater than the "great city" (cf. 21:16). The Antichrist's world system of John's day would have been epitomized in Rome, but not limited to it. Unbelieving Jerusalem blends into the imperial world system of which it is a part, just as Jewish accusers of Christians to local officials have their synagogues linked with Satan in 2:9 and 3:9. "Egypt" (11:8) is an appropriate title for a world that has oppressed God's servants but stands under plagues like those of the Exodus (chs. 8–9; 16); "Sodom" also fits a world system destined for destruction by fire (20:9; cf. 11:5).

That the witnesses lie in the street (11:8) indicates that they remain unburied, receiving what was considered the most shameful treatment in the ancient world, normally reserved for the most vile of criminals.[38] The world's celebration and mockery of the martyrs is deeply ironic: In earlier biblical tradition God's servants escaped genocide, hence killed their enemies and celebrated with gifts (Esther 9:19). Here, by contrast, the enemies of God's servants exchange gifts after slaughtering them, yet many are ultimately converted (11:11–13). But as in the biblical tradition of holy war, God's side will enjoy the final exultation; heaven will rejoice over this city's collapse (19:1–7).[39]

---

35. See also Bruce, "Spirit," 339; Bauckham, *Climax of Prophecy*, 168–69; Roloff, *Revelation*, 133. See Fee's understanding of "spiritual" in Paul as "of the Spirit" (Gordon D. Fee, *God's Empowering Presence: The Holy Spirit in the Letters of Paul* [Peabody: Hendrickson, 1994], 28–31).

36. Some interpreters view this city as a symbol of the world rather than simply Jerusalem in particular (e.g., Bowman, *First Christian Drama*, 71; Caird, *Commentary on Revelation*, 138; Beale, *Revelation*, 591–92). In this case Aune, *Revelation*, 2:619–20 (cf. also 587), may well be right that an earlier end-time tradition about Jerusalem has been here reapplied. Rome boasted a large international population (11:9; Aune, *Revelation*, 2:621).

37. Rome also fancied itself "greatest of cities" (see references in Aune, *Revelation*, 3:959).

38. See Isa. 5:25; Sophocles, *Antig.* 21–30, 697; Virgil, *Aen.* 9.485; Tacitus, *Ann.* 6.29; Petronius, *Sat.* 112. That they lie in the public "street" (11:8) underlines the shame and contrasts with the glorious street of the end-time city (21:21; 22:2).

39. See in greater detail Bauckham, *Climax of Prophecy*, 281–82. Because Jewish people annually celebrated Purim, the allusion to Esther 9 would not be obscure. Aune, *Revelation*, 2:623, details the regular Greco-Roman practices surrounding gift exchanges, especially prominent on the Roman festivals of Saturnalia and Kalends.

The three and a half days of the bodies' defilement indicates that their corpses will be rotting, but probably also alludes to the three-and-a-half years of their ministry (11:9, 11). The text cannot function as a coherent narrative if John claims that they were continuously martyred during their ministry, but he may imply as much, indicating that while death cannot silence the church's witness (cf. Matt. 16:18), martyrdom frequently accompanies its prophetic ministry.[40]

The witnesses are protected for the duration of their ministry (11:5) but die at the end (11:7). This may provide a way to show that God will preserve his church throughout the age for the sake of their witness, but that as the universal proclamation of the gospel is fulfilled, the world finally appears to crush the church through massive martyrdoms. (In John's day, believers probably expected such events to follow immediately in the Roman empire, but they are no less believable in today's volatile world.)

Thus the church will follow in the steps of its Lord: Christians will die but should look for the hope of the resurrection (11:11; cf. 1:5; 2:8–10; Heb. 11:35–12:4). The "breath of life" (Rev. 11:11), which can also be translated "Spirit of life" (cf. Rom. 8:2), alludes to God's care in Genesis 2:7 (as in John 20:22) and contrasts with the false life imparted in Revelation 13:15.[41] Like Jesus at the beginning of the era of hardship (cf. 12:5), these witnesses are caught up to heaven at its end (11:12), a sign of vindication and ultimate deliverance (12:5). In contrast to the "come up here" cited in 4:1, this instance of the phrase is a "rapture"; but in contrast with some popular North American eschatological schemes, it occurs immediately preceding the end of the age, not several years before (11:15).[42]

Given the world's persistent refusal to repent in the face of God's plagues (9:20–21; 16:9–11, toward the end of the trumpets and bowls), the repentance of the city in 11:11–13 is heartening. "And gave glory to the God of

---

40. Some take the three and a half days as "a limited time, but shorter than three and a half years" (Talbert, *Apocalypse*, 46). Coptic Apoc. Elij. 4:7–15 probably borrows its story (Enoch and Elijah lie three and a half days in the marketplace and are raised up) from this passage. Both "7000" (11:13) and a resurrecting spirit of life (11:11) appear in T. Abr. 17–18A.

41. "Spirit of life" may also relate to raising the dead in 1 Enoch 61:7; T. Abr. 18A; to life in general in T. Reub. 2:4. "Standing on one's feet" was sometimes an initial confirmation of resuscitation (2 Kings 13:21; Ezek. 37:10; Mark 5:42; cf. Luke 7:15; John 11:44).

42. The ascent may allude again to the image of Elijah (2 Kings 2:11; Rev. 11:6), though ascent traditions apply also to Enoch and Moses in early Jewish texts (1 Enoch 39:3; Josephus, *Ant.* 4.326), or to divinized mortals in pagan myth (Ovid, *Metam.* 14.824–28; Diogenes Laertius, 8.2.68; Phaedrus, 4.12.3); Aune, *Revelation*, 2:626–27, also mentions witnesses and atmospheric or seismic phenomena in Greco-Roman rapture accounts. The voice and cloud may allude to traditions about the church's rapture (1 Thess. 4:16–17) as well as Jesus' exaltation (Acts 1:9; cf. Rissi, *Time and History*, 103).

heaven" (11:13) plainly involves worship (4:9; 19:7), but for the unrighteous, also repentance (16:9; cf. 14:7). Their newfound fear of God (11:11, 13) also suggests an appropriate response to his judgments (Deut. 21:21; Acts 5:11; for the end-time earthquake, see also 6:12; 16:18–19). In this case the symbol's significance seems limited to the image's narrower meaning of Jerusalem or ethnic Jewry rather than to the world system as a whole. If 11:8 and the inverted allusion to Purim in the book of Esther suggests that the enemies here include unbelieving Jerusalemites, this text may imply the eschatological conversion of the bulk of the Jewish people in Jerusalem not previously converted. Such a prediction fits early Christian expectations (Matt. 23:39; Rom. 11:25–27), whereas the nonrepentance of most surviving Gentiles at the end seems assumed (Rev. 6:16–17).[43]

In this case Revelation includes a hopeful irony. Biblical prophets sometimes limited the surviving remnant after judgment to a tenth who would ultimately follow the Lord (Isa. 6:13; Amos 5:3). Here, however, the tenth dies (7000 suited well the image of a remnant, 1 Kings 19:18; Rom. 11:4), while the majority come to faith.[44]

PARADIGMATIC WITNESSES. Those who view the two witnesses as future literal witnesses can view them as paradigmatic for the church, because we are also witnesses (19:10) in a time of hardship (1:9). Those who view the witnesses as symbolic for the church in this age will naturally view them as even more paradigmatic. Others have offered various historical explanations, but even in this case often have allowed the witnesses to function as models for their own experience.

Many throughout history have applied the sufferings of the two witnesses to their own experiences as a martyr church. For example, Pareus in the late 1500s to the early 1600s linked the two witnesses with the sufferings of Wycliffe and Hus and the Inquisition. Similarly, Jonathan Edwards (1703–1758) understood the suffering of the Protestant Reformers under the

---

43. Esp. from Rom. 11, belief in an end-time conversion of Jewish people persisted in some circles through most of church history: e.g., the Dominican Humbert of Romans in a 1272 treatise (Humbert of Romans, "Objections to the Crusades Answered," *Christian History* 40 [1993]: 20–21); nineteenth-century premillennialist Lord Shaftesbury (John Wolffe, "Dismantling Discrimination," *Christian History* 53 [1997]: 37–39 [38]).

44. See most fully Bauckham, *Climax of Prophecy*, 282–83, who believes it is the suffering of the remnant that brings the others to repentance (others, e.g., Caird, *Commentary on Revelation*, 140, see the 7000 as killed in retribution for the death of the remnant). A tenth remnant appears in Jub. 10:9, though for fallen angels.

Antichrist.[45] While it may be illegitimate to suggest that John's focus was on a range of events as narrow as this, such sufferings surely fall within the range of acceptable *application*.

When called on to suffer for our Christian witness, we should identify with the two witnesses, because like them and like our Lord, we will be raised beyond death when Christ comes to avenge us. The problem arises when we assume that a specific application of the principle of the suffering witnesses is the text's only proper interpretation. Hans Hut, for example, one of the most effective and devoted Anabaptist evangelists of the 1500s, thought the two witnesses were the martyred Thomas Müntzer and his coworker. Thus he expected Christ's return in 1528; he died too soon to see his prediction disconfirmed.[46]

Three and a half years. Modern popular understanding of Revelation focuses on a literal seven-year Tribulation. One problem with this view is that it assumes that the entirety of Daniel's seventieth seven-year week is the period of which Revelation speaks, when in fact Revelation speaks of only half that time, three and a half years. One might add two of the three-and-a-half year periods together (11:2–3; 12:6, 14; 13:5) to get seven years, but what does one do with the other ones? Why combine some but not all of these time references?[47]

Another problem is that Revelation regularly reapplies earlier Jewish images, including those from the biblical prophets, in fresh symbolic ways; did the literal three and a half years begin immediately after Jesus' exaltation (for more detail, see comment on 12:5–6)? Taking into account Revelation's genre forces us to at least grapple with the question as to whether even the stated time frame of 1260 days is symbolic or literal.

Divine vengeance. A doctrine of divine vengeance may sound socially "primitive" to many unbelievers (who assume their ever-changing cultural values a moral standard superior to divine revelation!), hence embarrassing to some Christians. But the oppressed can resonate with such promises. Those who are not oppressed should not hear in such texts a call to hate those who are not really oppressing them, but rather a summons to value the kingdom above worldly favor, lest we find our hearts ever drawn to Babylon more than to the new Jerusalem.

Mission to Jewish people. Those who see in our text or in other texts (especially Rom. 11:26) a report of Jerusalem's final turning to faith in the

---

45. Petersen, *Preaching in the Last Days*, 168, 231. Sectarian groups experience the same temptation; Jehovah's Witnesses applied the 1260 days literally to their testing during World War I (Oct. 1914–1918) (*Revelation: Grand Climax*, 162, 164); they view the city of 11:8 as Christendom (ibid., 168).

46. "A Gallery of Factions, Friends & Foes," *Christian History* 4 (1985): 13–16 (p. 14).

47. See this critique in Michaels, *Interpreting Revelation*, 141.

Messiah Jesus are sometimes tempted to misapply this assurance. Some neglect bringing the message about Jesus to the Jewish people because "they will be converted anyway."[48] This approach is both illogical and misses the point of the text. Scripture mentions only the conversion of the surviving remnant of the final generation, not the majority of Jewish people in history until that point. Moreover, both Revelation (Rev. 11:3) and Paul (Rom. 1:16–17; 11:14, 25, 31) presuppose that believers must continue to proclaim the message to ethnic Israel as well as to Gentiles.

That church history reflects more of the tragedy of anti-Semitism (including Jewish people burned on "crosses" and drowned in mock baptisms) than a culturally sensitive witness to the people who gave the world the gospel reinforces all the more the need for believers to emulate the sacrificial, martyr witness depicted here (cf. 11:7). Nor dare we rest content with the current "remnant" of messianic Jews, sizeable though it may be.[49] When Paul spoke of Jewish believers as a remnant (Rom. 11:5), he contrasted that with Israel as a whole (11:26). The percentage of Jewish believers in Jesus was much higher in his day than in ours, and this reflects the history of Christendom's anti-Semitism, which we must now surmount.[50]

THE APPLICATION IS difficult unless we can agree on the original meaning of the text, which on many points remains debatable. But we may offer some suggestions. The trampling of the outer courts probably signifies the suffering of God's people (maybe Jewish, maybe Christian) in this age; more clearly, however, the measuring is deferred until

---

48. On evangelism including Jewish people, see Vernon C. Grounds, "The Problem of Proselytization," 199–225 in *Evangelicals and Jews in an Age of Pluralism*, ed. M. H. Tanenbaum, M. R. Wilson, and A. J. Rudin (Grand Rapids: Baker, 1984); from nonmessianic Jewish perspectives, see in the same book Blu Greenberg, "Mission, Witness, and Proselytism," 226–39; and Sanford Seltzer, "Mission, Witness, and Proselytization: A Jewish View," 240–54.

49. On the mushrooming size of the movement, see information in Gary Thomas, "The Return of the Jewish Church," *CT* (Sept. 7, 1998), 62–69; being in Philadelphia, I have many friends at Beth Yeshua, where the photographs were taken.

50. On this history, see Edward H. Flannery, *The Anguish of the Jews: Twenty-three Centuries of Anti-Semitism* (New York: Macmillan, 1965); James Parkes, *The Conflict of the Church and the Synagogue: A Study in the Origins of Antisemitism* (New York: Atheneum, Temple Books, 1979); Adriaan H. Bredero, *Christendom and Christianity in the Middle Ages*, tr. R. Bruinsma (Grand Rapids: Eerdmans, 1994), 274–318. Christian anti-Judaism originated in pre-Christian Roman paganism, often imported into the church along with other pagan aspects of the converts' cultures; see J. N. Sevenster, *The Roots of Pagan Anti-Semitism in the Ancient World*, NovTSup 41 [Leiden: E. J. Brill, 1975]).

the new Jerusalem of 21:16. Those who serve God may be a minority, often a persecuted minority, but the future is ultimately ours. God often works through what is small, broken, and despised in this age, but he will ultimately vindicate his remnant.

The two witnesses as symbols for today. If the two witnesses are the church, they provide a direct model for us. Those who interpret them as two literal individuals can also recognize that they nevertheless provide role models for us, just as other men and women of God in Scripture do (cf. 1 Cor. 10:11). We must therefore be Spirit-empowered witnesses to the world, ready to pay any cost and utterly dependent on God's power to accomplish his purposes.

Various reasons exist for the dual number of the witnesses, but one may be the principle of shared witness (Deut. 17:6): We do not testify only by ourselves. Our own witness may not always bring a person or culture to Christ by itself, but our witness contributes to the broader witness of the entire prophetic remnant of the church. To whatever extent the witnesses represent the kingly and priestly aspects of the church's mission, the text may also imply the importance of the church's various functions. But again, such applications may be disputed, especially if the interpretations on which they are based remain disputed.

More clearly, like prophetic voices in the Bible, we must sometimes stand virtually alone, if need be, to challenge the wrongs of our day.[51] Most often we stand as voices for the truth of God's message in Christ. By reaching people for Christ and discipling them into mature witnesses (Matt. 28:19–20), we can multiply our impact many times over.[52]

In 1870 a Hindu convert to Christ led to Christ Ditt, a lame man from the untouchable Chuhra caste. He faced considerable persecution as he carried the message of Jesus Christ with him from village to village, but within eleven years over 500 Chuhras became Christians. "By 1900, more than half of these lowly people ... had been converted, and by 1915 all but a few hundred members of the caste professed the Christian faith."[53] As some committed to evangelism have put it, "Today, in a world where three out of four persons have yet to believe in Jesus Christ and at least two out of every four

---

51. See Vernon C. Grounds, "Dare to Be a Micaiah," *CT* (March 18, 1988), 24–25.

52. See Robert E. Coleman, *The Master Plan of Evangelism* (Huntingdon Valley, Pa.: Christian Outreach, 1963).

53. George G. Hunter, III, "The Key Strategy: Finding the Bridges of God," 28–40 in *Church Growth: Strategies That Work*, by Donald McGavran and George Hunter III (Nashville: Abingdon, 1980), 29–30, following J. Waskom Pickett, *Christian Mass Movements in India* (New York: Abingdon, 1933), 45.

have yet to hear of Jesus Christ, if a congregation is not reproducing, it is not a New Testament church, no matter what it calls itself!"[54]

We may rejoice in statistics that suggest large numbers of born-again Christians in our own and many other parts of the world. But even in apparently saturated regions like the United States, most younger unchurched people (and many church people) have never really understood the claims of the gospel. On the streets in some parts of the country, among some cultural groups, and among university students, I find that Christian experience is often largely partitioned off in the church; this is probably because most Christians share their faith primarily with fellow-Christians lest they face rejection from non-Christian peers.

If two fundamental Baptists had not witnessed to me on the street in 1975, I may never have heard the gospel, because I was at that time an atheist who would never have set foot in an evangelical church. Most amazingly, even in churches some people do not understand the gospel unless it is explained to them one on one. I have served in churches where attenders had heard salvation carefully and frequently explained from the pulpit but who never really understood how to be saved until it was explained to them personally. We dare not take too much for granted, and we must be ready to pay whatever price to spread God's message, just as the two witnesses of Revelation were.

Signs and wonders. God empowered his church with prophetic anointing at Pentecost (Acts 2:17–18); although this includes prophecy in the narrower sense (21:9–10), that anointing's focus is the power to witness (1:8).[55] That these two witnesses performed signs and wonders suits the witness of the apostolic leaders of the church and other evangelists in Acts (2:43; 5:12, 16; 6:8; 14:3); signs and wonders constitute one of the most frequent methods of drawing the world's attention to the gospel there (3:6–12; 8:6–7, 13; 9:34–35, 40–42; 19:10–20; 28:8–9). When I noticed this in Acts, I began praying for healing for people with whom I shared Christ; some were dramatically healed and responded quickly to the gospel message that God was confirming.

Yet the Western church today rarely experiences miracles. Indeed, even those parts of the Western church most triumphalistic about miracles rarely can testify of miracles on the scale on which they appear in the biblical

---

54. Donald A. McGavran and Winfield C. Arn, *Ten Steps to Church Growth* (San Francisco: Harper & Row, 1977), 96.

55. See more fully Craig Keener, *3 Crucial Questions About the Holy Spirit* (Grand Rapids: Baker, 1996), 35–37; idem, *The Spirit in the Gospels and Acts: Divine Purity and Power* (Peabody, Mass.: Hendrickson, 1997), 200–201. On the association of prophecy and the Spirit in early Judaism, see Keener, *Spirit in the Gospels*, 10–13.

ministries of Moses, Elijah, Elisha, Jesus, or Paul. Some respond to this dearth of miracles and interpret Scripture in light of their experience to suppose that God stopped the flow of miracles after the completion of the canon. This explanation denies too much, however; the Bible assumes the continuance of supernatural gifts until the end of the age (1 Cor. 13:8–12; Eph. 4:11–13; Rev. 11:5–6), and both church history and recent revivals in some parts of the world attest that God still sovereignly graces his church with miracles.[56]

God's sovereignty and Western rationalism may both account for some of the rareness of miracles in Western Christianity. Even more than that, however, we have on the whole too much in common with the compromised Christianity of cities like Laodicea, Thyatira, and Sardis, which were too comfortable with the world, or with the lovelessness of Ephesus.[57] Miracles in the Bible appear most frequently on the cutting edge of God's activity, especially spreading the good news of the kingdom (Acts 6:8; 14:3; 19:11–12). I have witnessed them far more when believers have been breaking new ground with the gospel than when we have become self-absorbed with our own comfort this side of paradise. Only when the church becomes prepared to challenge the idols of society with the claims of Christ, as the two witnesses do in our text, will we witness God's power in biblical fullness.

On martyrdom. That no one can harm the witnesses until God allows their martyrdom (11:5) recalls how God's judgments on the world will also not harm his servants (7:3). This reminds us that God is sovereign not only over nature but even over our enemies' attempts to destroy us; truly not a hair of our heads will fall apart from our Father's will (Matt. 10:29–30).

But the text also reveals that God's servants who proclaim his Word in the world cannot always expect deliverance; Revelation calls us to prepare ourselves as a martyr church. The moment we become Christ's followers, we forfeit our lives for the work of the kingdom (Mark 8:34–38); yet for the most part we have failed to prepare ourselves and our fellow servants for this calling. Our culture insulates us better than most from most confrontations with "natural" death; it certainly does not prepare us for martyrdom. Yet if we believe our Lord's teaching, we must work to get the church ready for suffering, even martyrdom, if that becomes the necessary price of our witness to those who do not wish to hear (Rev. 2:10; cf. John 12:25–26; 15:18–21).

Divine vindication. In the end God vindicates his servants in the sight of the very ones who ridiculed them; such vindication is also a frequent bibli-

---

56. See Jack Deere, *Surprised by the Power of the Spirit* (Grand Rapids: Zondervan, 1993), esp. 45–56; Keener, *3 Questions,* 81–127. On power encounters, see Contemporary Significance section on 13:13.

57. See also this observation in Jack Deere, *Surprised by the Voice of God* (Grand Rapids: Zondervan, 1996), 88.

cal pattern (Ps. 23:5), though we do not always live to see it individually. Some of those who ridicule our message now may repent later. One drug addict I testified to during my high school days seemed as closed against the gospel as I had been as an atheist, and I frankly doubted he would ever be converted; on my return from my first year of college, guess who I found in church?

But sometimes it takes more than our preaching to make people's hearts receptive. Two of us new converts witnessed boldly in high school, but the turning point in many people's receptivity was after a two-month period when six individuals who had rejected and mostly mocked our message died in various ways. What preaching and witness may not accomplish for our land, God's judgment may yet accomplish for those who survive it. In this age his judgment is always an act of love; he normally leaves a remnant who can learn from the judgment.

God's vindication of the martyrs immediately prior to the end leads to the equivalent of a deathbed conversion of the city where Jesus was crucified: The bulk of survivors are converted (11:11–13). But while judgments get people's attention, we cannot depend on them always happening immediately (6:10). Most people through history will not be alive at the time of Jesus' return, nor will most people in the world who are alive genuinely repent (6:16–17; cf. 1:7). The appropriate time for repentance is therefore always "now" (cf. 2 Cor. 6:2). But we may note that while judgment often gets people's attention for the truth, in Revelation acts of judgment apart from witness failed to do so (Rev. 9:20–21).

Revelation 11:15-19

T HE SEVENTH ANGEL sounded his trumpet, and there were loud voices in heaven, which said:

"The kingdom of the world has become the kingdom
 of our Lord and of his Christ,
 and he will reign for ever and ever."

¹⁶And the twenty-four elders, who were seated on their thrones before God, fell on their faces and worshiped God, ¹⁷saying:

"We give thanks to you, Lord God Almighty,
 the One who is and who was,
because you have taken your great power
 and have begun to reign.
¹⁸The nations were angry;
 and your wrath has come.
The time has come for judging the dead,
 and for rewarding your servants the prophets
and your saints and those who reverence your name,
 both small and great—
and for destroying those who destroy the earth."

¹⁹Then God's temple in heaven was opened, and within his temple was seen the ark of his covenant. And there came flashes of lightning, rumblings, peals of thunder, an earthquake and a great hailstorm.

Original Meaning THE CLOSING VERSES of chapter 11 address the seventh trumpet. Although the final trumpet concludes the series of seven (11:15), it also fits the occasion here; trumpets were normally blown at the accession of a king to his throne (1 Kings 1:34–41; 2 Kings 9:13; 11:14). The Bible had promised that the Davidic Messiah would "reign for ever" (Rev. 11:15; cf. Isa. 9:7; 1 Macc. 2:57); naturally Jewish people recognized that God would reign forever (Ps. 10:16; 146:10; 1 En. 84:2).[1] Daniel had

---

1. This promise drew on the earlier promise of David's eternal throne (Ps. 89:29, 36; 132:12) and fits the Son of Man prophecy (Dan. 7:14). C. F. D. Moule, *The Birth of the New*

emphasized the final triumph of God's kingdom over the successive world empires (Dan. 2:44; cf. 7:17–18), a hope celebrated by many of John's contemporaries.[2] Jewish people also emphasized that whereas the nations ruled now, God and his people would reign in the world to come (cf. also comment on 19:6).[3] The kingdom "of our Lord and of his Christ" (11:15) probably recalls the language of Psalm 2:2, where the nations challenge them but will ultimately be crushed (see comment below on 11:18).

God's people often have praised him in response to his deliverance of his people (Ex. 15:18; Rev. 11:17–18; 15:3–4; on God's omnipotence and eternality expressed in 11:17, see comment on 1:8). The wrath of the nations in 11:18 recalls the raging of the nations against God and his anointed king in Psalm 2:1–2, which in turn is met by God's wrath (Ps. 2:12). Here their wrath (NIV: "were angry"; cf. the devil's being "enraged" in Rev. 12:17) is met by God's "wrath" on the Day of Judgment (11:18; cf. 6:16).

Jewish tradition also emphasized the rewards God would give his people at the time of the end (11:18; cf. 22:12).[4] Contrary to some Christian attempts to denigrate Jewish tradition, reward is no less a Christian concept, though the works it rewards are impossible apart from the grace experienced in Christ (Matt. 5:11, 46; 6:1; Mark 9:41; 1 Cor. 3:8, 14; 9:17–18; 2 John 8). Everyone, both righteous and wicked, receive their rewards at this time (Rev. 11:18).

God's "servants the prophets" (11:18) is a regular idiom in the Hebrew Bible (close to twenty times), but for John the expression may be identified with "saints" and with "those who reverence" God's name (11:18). All believers are meant to be "prophets" in the general sense of Spirit-empowered witnesses for Christ (19:10; cf. 11:3), contrary to the arguments of some commentators. "Small and great" (11:18; cf. 6:15; 13:16; 19:5, 18; 20:12), like "least" and "greatest," is a common idiom meaning "everyone" (close to forty times in the Old Testament; e.g., 2 Kings 23:2).[5]

Testament (New York: Harper & Row, 1962), 23, finds here and in 19:6–8 Christian enthronement psalms.

2. E.g., 1QM 1.5–6; T. Moses 10:1.

3. See *Gen. Rab.* 95 (MSV); on the two ages, see 4 Ezra 7:50; *tos. Taan.* 3:14; *Sifre Num.* 115.5.7; *Sifre Deut.* 29.2.3; cf. A. J. Ferch, "The Two Aeons and the Messiah in Pseudo-Philo, 4 Ezra, and 2 Baruch," AUSS 15 (1977): 135–51; John J. Collins, *The Sibylline Oracles of Egyptian Judaism*, SBLDS 13 (Missoula, Mont.: Society of Biblical Literature, 1972), 320, 358–59.

4. E.g., Wisd. 5:15; 4 Ezra 7:98; *m. Ab.* 2:2; *Sifra A.M.* par. 8.193.1.11; *Sifra Behuq. pq.* 2.262.1.9; see most fully Morton Smith, *Tannaitic Parallels to the Gospels* (Philadelphia: Society of Biblical Literature, 1951), 163–84. Jewish teachers often emphasized doing good for its own sake rather than the reward (*Sifre Deut.* 48.6–7; see M. Brocke, "Tun und Lohn im nachbiblischen Judentum: Ein Diskussionsbeitrag," *Bibel und Leben* 8 [1967]: 166–78).

5. This continued in early Jewish usage (see Bar. 1:4).

The reference to "those who destroy the earth" (11:18) and so merit judgment is more difficult. Perhaps it refers to the devastation that ravages the land in response to sinners' disobedience (7:3; cf. Jub. 9:15), but "destroying" may suggest more active involvement. It may refer to aggressors against God's people, invaders who seek to devastate the holy land (2 Kings 18:25). That nothing in the context narrows the image specifically to the holy land, however, generalizes the image: The evil empire, like Babylon of old, devastates the whole earth (the Greek translation of Jer. 51:25 uses the same Greek words as here and is probably the source for the image in our text). That those who harmed others will suffer an identical fate was a commonplace of biblical and broader ancient wisdom (e.g., Matt. 26:52).[6]

Verse 19 is pivotal in that it introduces the following section (12:1–6; both involve visions in the heavens), but we will discuss this verse here to avoid confusion. Jewish people generally believed that God had hidden the ark, but that it would be restored in the end time (see comment on 2:17). Thus, once the time for the final judgment has come (11:15–18), God unveils his heavenly temple, indicating the end (11:19). Furthermore, regulations had previously prevented people on earth from viewing the ark when it was in the temple, for it remained shrouded in the Most Holy Place (Ex. 40:21; Lev. 16:2); the present revelation thus indicates an extraordinary change of affairs.

The picture of the ark suggests a variety of associations, especially involving the Sinai covenant, by which God demanded an accounting from a disobedient world. In the ancient Near East a nation usually deposited a covenant with another people before the deity in the temple, thereby inviting the avenging curses mentioned in the covenant if it were broken. It may also be relevant that edicts were displayed in public places, such as temples. Further, just as Israelites had taken the ark before them to war (1 Sam. 4:3–9), so the Romans believed the numen of their state would go forth from its temple to war and return afterward.[7] The meteorological phenomena (Rev. 11:19) probably signify a new revelation from heaven comparable to the revelation of God's word at Mount Sinai (cf. 4:5; Ex. 19:16).[8]

---

6. E.g., Demosthenes, *Against Zenothemis* 6; Aulius Gellius, 7.4.4; Sir 27:25–27; Jub. 4:32; 1QpHab 12.5–6; m. Ab. 2:7; see further Aune, *Revelation*, 2:646.

7. See more fully on such points Meredith G. Kline, *Treaty of the Great King: The Covenant Structure of Deuteronomy* (Grand Rapids: Eerdmans, 1963), 24; John Pairman Brown, "The Ark of the Covenant and the Temple of Janus. The Magico-Military Numen of the State in Jerusalem and Rome," *BZ* 30 (1986): 20–35. Torah arks would have been in public view in most synagogues (see Rachel Hachlili, "The Niche and the Ark in Ancient Synagogues," *BASOR* 223 [Oct. 1976]: 43–53 [p. 53]).

8. The opening of heaven often symbolizes revelations (1 Enoch 34:2; 2 Bar. 22:1; see comment on 4:1).

SYMBOLIC IMAGERY IN 11:15–19, such as the ark in heaven, originally elicited a particular evocative impact, but what it evoked for its original audience would have more substance than what it evokes for us today. Because modern readers are typically unfamiliar with the many traditions and associations linked with these images, we need to explain the texts (focusing more attention on the Original Meaning section than may be necessary, say, with Philippians).

Often we focus simply on the lexical meaning of words in our interpretations. But moving from exegesis to biblical theology requires sensitivity to the "rhetoric" or nature of writing in our documents, without which we will find many "contradictions," often even within the same book of the Bible. This passage provides an example of one such "contradiction" that is best resolved by understanding the nature of the language Revelation uses. That both the righteous and the wicked receive rewards at the same time (11:18) suggests either that the chronological distinction between the two resurrections in 20:4–6 is symbolic, or that such statements as the present ones are summaries not intended for chronological precision. In any case the author views both passages as complementary presentations of the end.

Further, if God's "servants the prophets" refers to the saints, coextensive with those who fear God's name (11:18), this means that all believers are empowered for prophetic witness in some way (19:10). But in what ways are witnesses like biblical prophets? How can we learn from the biblical prophets and encourage other Christians to do the same? Scripture sometimes speaks of a specific gift of prophecy (1 Cor. 14), but when Revelation refers to the prophetic witness of the entire church, it probably focuses on the need for us to depend on the power of God's Spirit to understand and announce his message.[9]

NO RESPECTER OF PERSONS. Those who face grief or any hardship in the world will find comfort in the message of these verses. They announce that this world ultimately belongs to God (11:15) and that God will right all the wrongs of history in the Day of Judgment, shattering all opposition (11:18); they also invite worship as we contemplate

---

9. Most ancient readers would have recognized the association, even where implicit, between prophecy and the Spirit (see Craig Keener, *The Spirit in the Gospels and Acts* [Peabody, Mass.: Hendrickson, 1997], 10–13).

God's coming intervention to rule (11:16–17). Moreover, they remind us that God will reward both small and great (11:18) just as he will punish both great and small (6:15); God is no respecter of persons.

Traditionally in the Black church tradition that I know best firsthand, especially in the hardships of the past, many who were oppressed in society looked forward to coming to church, where janitors could be deacons, just as in early Christianity those who were slaves and freedpersons in society could rise to the office of bishop. Today we often transfer worldly status (not just experience) into church offices; one wonders if we have not lost sight of something (1 Cor. 6:4).

Environmental concerns. The earth is the Lord's (Ps. 24:1), and the kingdom will be his (Rev. 11:15); hence those who devastate the earth challenge God's rule. Far from being merely a modern reading, this reflects an apocalyptic theology in which those who corrupt or abuse God's creation warrant judgment (4 Ezra 9:19–22; 2 Bar. 13:11).[10] This devastation thus may imply corrupting the earth, a reversal of the original creation mandate in Genesis 1:26; conquerors usually destroyed natural resources (Deut. 20:19; Isa. 14:8). This text thus may have significance for Christian environmentalists today who want believers to become more responsible stewards of the resources God has provided the world.[11]

Environmental degradation ultimately harms not only the rest of creation but also people, starting with the poor, even in the short run.[12] While many environmentalists focus on the problem of global warming, a far more immediate threat is water-born diseases in unsafe drinking water, which kills over three million children each year.[13] International toxic waste is regularly dumped in the Third World.[14]

---

10. For some ecological issues (to use modern terms) in rabbinic texts, see Gerhard Langer, "Pflanzen, Schützen und Bewahren—eine ökologische Ethik der Rabbinen," *Bibel und Liturgie* 64 (1991): 86–92.

11. For Christian environmentalist perspectives, see *World Christian* (April 1990), whole issue; William Dyrness, "Are We Our Planet's Keeper?" *CT* (April 8, 1991), 40–42; "Eco-Myths" and other articles in *CT* (April 4, 1994), 16–33; Lionel Basney, *An Earth-Careful Way of Life* (Downers Grove, Ill.: InterVarsity, 1994); and most regularly, *Creation Care* magazine (Wynnewood, Pa.; formerly *Green Cross* magazine). To make such statements is not to affirm the agendas of neopagan religion associated with some extreme environmentalists; on this see *SCP [Spiritual Counterfeits Project] Journal* 16/1 (1991) and 17/3 (1992); Tod Connor, "Is the Earth Alive?" *CT* (Jan. 11, 1993), 22–25.

12. See several articles in *NW* (June 1, 1992).

13. Gregg Easterbrook, "A House of Cards," *NW* (June 1, 1992), 24–33 (p. 33); he expects Western nations to attend to this issue far less because it affects "only the abstract legions of the brown, distant poor."

14. "The Global Poison Trade," *NW* (Nov. 7, 1988), 66–68; Franz Schurmann, "Third World Becomes Garbage Dump for the West," *National College Newspaper* (Oct. 1988), 9.

Likewise, over several decades Nigeria's northern powerbrokers stripped Ogoniland of its resources and contaminated its countryside to the extent that Ogonis faced increasing health risks from the black smoke hanging over their land, the poisoning of their water, and the ruining of their farms.[15] The oil companies paid the government, taking land but providing for the locals in return less than one-half of one-thousandth of their revenues in development. When one village demanded guarantees of better environmental protection from Shell Oil, the company refused to talk, but the police showed up, burning to death the village elder and his sons and gunning down many other people.[16]

Widely respected Nigerian writer Ken Saro-Wiwa protested the massive environmental degradation of his native Ogoniland as a "slow genocide."[17] But eventually Saro-Wiwa and some other nonviolent activists, falsely accused of murders they could have had nothing to do with, were summarily executed by the corrupt military dictatorship that profited from the oil revenues. A Christian, Saro-Wiwa led his fellow prisoners in prayer before their executions.[18] Shell Oil, which did business with Sani Abacha's dictatorship and had made as much as $35.5 billion from Nigerian oil over the past three decades, failed to publicly condemn Abacha for the murders. "We do not get involved in politics," they claimed.[19]

The allusion to Jeremiah 51 in this text focuses especially on the harm conquest does to human lives; though the word "earth" (ge) can refer to the planet (Rev. 7:1–3), it usually refers to humanity in Revelation (13:12, 14). Significantly, the wicked earth-dwellers may destroy earth, but not cannot harm "heaven," with which it is coupled over ten times (e.g., 5:3, 13; 12:12). Thus the passage condemns not only environmental destruction (though that would be included because of its effects on people) but any unjust exploitation of power that destroys others. God will judge evil empires who oppress others; the modern proverb "what goes around comes around" is appropriate for the wicked empire that passes its cup to all other nations (14:8) and finally must drink itself (14:10).

---

15. "A State's Well-Oiled Injustice," *WPR* (Jan. 1996), 14–15 (data taken from a British weekly).

16. Detlef Pypke, "Partners in Crime?" *WPR* (Jan. 1996), 16 (data taken from a German newsmagazine).

17. Tim Ledwith, "Nigeria's Year of Shame," *Amnesty Action* (Winter 1997), 3.

18. "The Making of a Legend," *NW* (Dec. 18, 1995), 47. See his own account of detention in "Notes From a Gulag," *WPR* (Oct. 1995), 40–41.

19. Pypke, "Partners"; "Nigeria Defies the World," *Amnesty Action* (Winter 1996), 5. Note that Royal Dutch/Shell includes the U.S. Shell Oil Company, but the latter had no operations of its own in Nigeria (letter to the author from G. C. Goodier, Shell Oil Company [May 1, 1996]).

Symbolism of the ark's unveiling. The unveiling of the heavenly ark means that the hidden things (10:4) will all come to light in the end. But the fact that it is recorded in Revelation indicates that, concerning the "hidden" things that really matter in this age, we Christians already have an "inside scoop." We know enough about heaven's perspective that we should choose to live accordingly.

Revelation 12:1–17

GREAT AND wondrous sign appeared in heaven: a woman clothed with the sun, with the moon under her feet and a crown of twelve stars on her head. ²She was pregnant and cried out in pain as she was about to give birth. ³Then another sign appeared in heaven: an enormous red dragon with seven heads and ten horns and seven crowns on his heads. ⁴His tail swept a third of the stars out of the sky and flung them to the earth. The dragon stood in front of the woman who was about to give birth, so that he might devour her child the moment it was born. ⁵She gave birth to a son, a male child, who will rule all the nations with an iron scepter. And her child was snatched up to God and to his throne. ⁶The woman fled into the desert to a place prepared for her by God, where she might be taken care of for 1,260 days.

⁷And there was war in heaven. Michael and his angels fought against the dragon, and the dragon and his angels fought back. ⁸But he was not strong enough, and they lost their place in heaven. ⁹The great dragon was hurled down—that ancient serpent called the devil, or Satan, who leads the whole world astray. He was hurled to the earth, and his angels with him.

¹⁰Then I heard a loud voice in heaven say:

"Now have come the salvation and the power and
the kingdom of our God,
and the authority of his Christ.
For the accuser of our brothers,
who accuses them before our God day and night,
has been hurled down.
¹¹They overcame him
by the blood of the Lamb
and by the word of their testimony;
they did not love their lives so much
as to shrink from death.
¹²Therefore rejoice, you heavens
and you who dwell in them!
But woe to the earth and the sea,
because the devil has gone down to you!
He is filled with fury,
because he knows that his time is short."

¹³When the dragon saw that he had been hurled to the earth, he pursued the woman who had given birth to the male child. ¹⁴The woman was given the two wings of a great eagle, so that she might fly to the place prepared for her in the desert, where she would be taken care of for a time, times and half a time, out of the serpent's reach. ¹⁵Then from his mouth the serpent spewed water like a river, to overtake the woman and sweep her away with the torrent. ¹⁶But the earth helped the woman by opening its mouth and swallowing the river that the dragon had spewed out of his mouth. ¹⁷Then the dragon was enraged at the woman and went off to make war against the rest of her offspring—those who obey God's commandments and hold to the testimony of Jesus.

THIS CENTRAL SECTION of the book (Rev. 12–14), lodged between the trumpets and bowls, not only reinterprets traditional images that it recounts, but provides a key to interpreting other symbols throughout Revelation. This seems especially likely with regard to the duration of the Tribulation in Revelation, if we have correctly understood 12:5–6 (see below). Ancient writers sometimes employed mythical images in digressions, and Revelation seems to enclose three substantial digressions in this section: the woman and her seed (11:19–12:17, including its own digression for a heavenly perspective in 12:7–12); the beasts of chapter 13; and miscellaneous visions about coming judgments (ch. 14). David Aune suggests that these digressions portray the past, present, and future respectively.[1]

John is explicit that he is dealing in symbolism here; he calls both the woman and the dragon "signs" (12:1, 3; cf. 15:1).[2] Greeks sometimes applied the term used here (*semeion*) to constellations in the heavens, so some Greeks may have considered the woman as the constellation Virgo and the dragon as Draco or the serpent; but differences in their portrayal here from Greek mythology will quickly alert them that these signs do not denote constellations, but a combination of traditional symbols reapplied to communicate a unique point.

But what do the symbols mean? Interpreting them in light of our modern world apart from their ancient context will not do. Thus a few centuries

---

1. Aune, *The New Testament in Its Literary Environment*, 242. Some find seven signs in this central section, but John explicitly refrains from numbering them here (Caird, *Commentary on Revelation*, 105–6); Ford prefers six (*Revelation*, 47).

2. "Signs" are typically the symbolic language of prophetic assurances (e.g., Isa. 8:18; 20:3; 37:30; Jer. 44:29; Ezek. 4:3; 12:6, 11; 24:24, 27), though cf. Aratus, *Phaen.* 46.

ago interpreters viewed the sun as the Christian world, the moon as the Islamic world, and the war with the saints (12:7) as the Pope's assaults on the Waldenses and Albigenses.[3] Few interpreters today would regard this view as an adequate contemporary application of the text. Serpents are an object of disgust in many circles, but many traditional cultures also venerate them, so even this image is not transculturally intelligible.[4] For those of us who read the Bible as God's message to us, the normative *basis* for how we apply these texts today is what the text communicated to the original audience addressed (1:4). We must thus examine each of the characters to determine what they symbolize in Revelation and how they would have been understood in the first century.

The Mother (12:1)

THE FIRST CHARACTER to appear in the text is the "woman," a frequent symbolic character in ancient vision reports.[5] This woman is a mother, somehow the antecedent of the faithful bride of Christ, the new Jerusalem (21:2), and a contrast to the harlot, Babylon (17:5). Scholars have proposed various backgrounds for the woman, many of them compatible with other proposals.[6] One source is the Greek and Egyptian myth of the mother in childbirth who confronts a hostile dragon; we will treat this myth in further detail below. But if John uses symbolism from this myth (as he probably does), he also reinterprets it to communicate a different meaning, so our quest cannot stop here. Some have suggested that the woman is God's creation through whom he brings the Messiah, but this reading is too general.[7]

---

3. Wesley, *Commentary on the Bible*, 604–5.

4. See Balaji Mundkur, "The Roots of Ophidian Symbolism," *Ethos* 6 (Fall 1978): 125–58; idem et al., "The Cult of the Serpent in the Americas: Its Asian Background," *Current Anthropology* 17 (Sept. 1976): 429–41.

5. See Plutarch, *Divine Vengeance* 33, *Mor.* 568A; 3 Bar. 9:3; Herm. *Vis.* 1.1.1–9; 2.8.1. The use in Shepherd of Hermas is unusual, apparently developing the image in a more sexually conscious direction (see comments in C. S. Keener, "Marriage, Divorce and Adultery," 712–17 in *Dictionary of the Later New Testament and Its Developments* [Downers Grove, Ill.: InterVarsity, 1997], 713–14).

6. On the woman here, see in further detail C. S. Keener, "Woman and Man," 1205–15 in *Dictionary of the Later New Testament and its Developments*, 1209–10. For divine Wisdom, see G. H. Dix, "The Heavenly Wisdom and the Divine Logos in Jewish Apocalyptic," *JTS* 26 (Oct. 1924): 1–12 (p. 2).

7. Ellul, *Apocalypse*, 85. Earth does appear as "mother" not only in Greco-Roman paganism (*Homeric Hymn* 30.1; Apollonius Rhodius, 3.716; Virgil, *Aen.* 6.595; Ovid, *Metam.* 1.393; *Gr. Anth.* 7.461) but also in 4 Ezra 5:50; 10:9–14 and Philo, *Creation* 133, but 4 Ezra more often emphasizes Zion as mother (9:41–10:24). Her twelve-star headdress may symbolize cosmic rule or significance by way of the zodiac (a common symbol even among ancient Jews), but this spells identity with the cosmos only to a pantheist; she is no more the cosmos than Joseph is Helios, the sun-god, in Jos. and Asen. 5:5/6.

More to the point, the woman represents Israel or the faithful remnant of Israel. The theological source most widely available to early Christians would have been the Old Testament, though they would have also shared the common experience of the life and thought in the Greco-Roman world. The prophets portrayed righteous Israel as the mother of the restored future remnant of Israel (Isa. 54:1; 66:7–10; Mic. 4:9–10; 5:3; cf. Isa. 7:14; 9:6; 26:18–19), an image they mixed with that of Israel as a bride (Isa. 62:5). In Jewish tradition Zion or Jerusalem often appeared as a mother.[8] Here, as often in the Bible, images become conflated; the offspring of Jerusalem may be the restored or new Jerusalem (4 Ezra 10:44–46).

The sun, moon, and twelve stars on the woman confirm this vision as symbolizing Israel or its faithful remnant (Gen. 37:9).[9] If she symbolizes the Old Testament righteous remnant before Christ's exaltation (12:1–5)—that is, righteous Israelites and Gentile converts—she probably continues to symbolize the righteous remnant of Jewish and Gentile followers of Jesus after his exaltation (12:6–17), although this interpretation is debated.

Because the woman is Jesus' mother, many scholars naturally link her with Mary (usually in connection with, rather than instead of, Israel).[10] Yet Revelation nowhere provides explicit teaching about Mary, and we cannot extrapolate from this passage about her without further comment in the text. One may also doubt that Mary was specifically persecuted after Christ's enthronement, requiring protection for 1,260 days (12:6, 13–16).[11] More helpful, sometimes in conjunction with Mary, scholars have found here hints of the story of Eve.[12] God had promised that this woman's "seed" would ultimately crush the

---

8. See Tobit 13:9; 4 Ezra 9:38–10:59 (esp. 10:7); 2 Bar. 3:1–3; Gal. 4:26. "Mother-cities" were those that founded others, hence capitals of empires (Dionysius of Halicarnassus, 3.11.1–2; 3.23.19), and Philo applied this to Jerusalem (*Embassy* 281; cf. Isa. 1:26 LXX, though the LXX uses the title more loosely). Mother images also apply to Sarah (Isa. 51:2; Philo, *Cong.* 6) and Wisdom (Sir. 15:2). For Jerusalem's personification, see also Ps. Sol. 1.

9. Such cosmological imagery appears elsewhere for the patriarchs (T. Abr. 7A; 7B; T. Naph. 5:3–5).

10. Peter Paul James, "Mary and the Great Sign," *American Ecclesiastical Review* 142 (May 1960): 321–29; N.-D. O'Donoghue, "A Woman Clothed with the Sun," *Furrow* 11 (1960): 445–56; J. Edgar Bruns, "The Contrasted Women of Apocalypse 12 and 17," *CBQ* 26 (Oct. 1964): 459–63. Some hold this view by way of secondary application: Feuillet, *Apocalypse,* 115; idem, "Le chapitre XII de l'Apocalypse: Son caractère synthétique et sa richesse doctrinale," *Esprit et Vie* 88 (1978): 674–83.

11. Among those who reject the Marian exegesis here are Ford, *Revelation,* 207; Caird, *Commentary on Revelation,* 149; L. Stefaniak, "Mulier amicta sole (Apok 12,1–17)," *Ruch Biblijny i Liturgiczny* 9 (1956): 244–61. The Marian interpretation does not appear to predate the sixth century A.D. (Beale, *Revelation,* 629 n. 29).

12. Charles Hauret, "Ève transfigurée de la Genèse à l'Apocalypse," *RHPR* 59 (1979): 327–39; including connections with Mary, see Elio Peretto, "María Donna in Gv 2,3–4;

---

serpent (Gen. 3:15), a promise surely echoed in Revelation 12:9, 17. This association supplements but does not overpower the image of God's people here.

Labor Pains and the Dragon (12:2–3)

AS NOTED ABOVE, the prophets portrayed righteous Israel as the mother of the restored future remnant of Israel. The Dead Sea Scrolls depict a period of great tribulation as childbirth, probably with reference to the bringing forth of the new community (1QH 3.7–12).[13] In one passage God promises the suffering, pregnant Israel that she will truly bear new life in the time of the resurrection (Isa. 26:17–19), the day of God's wrath in which he will slay the serpent (26:20–27:1).[14]

Biblical tradition announced that the serpent Leviathan had many heads (Ps. 74:14), identified in Canaanite tradition as seven.[15] Many in the ancient world believed giant serpents or dragons existed literally in other parts of the world, but John again tells us that he speaks symbolically, of a "sign" (12:3).[16] Serpents (sometimes called "dragons") proved significant in pagan religion, especially the cult of Asclepius, who was worshiped in some of the cities to whom the book of Revelation was addressed.[17] But for John the dragon is

19,26–27; Ap 12,1–6: Ipotesi di lettura continuativa in prospettiva ecclesiale," *Ephemerides Mariologicae* 39 (1989): 427–42.

13. See Matthew Black, *The Scrolls and Christian Origins* (London: Thomas Nelson & Sons, 1961), 149; John Pryke, "Eschatology in the Dead Sea Scrolls," 45–57 in *The Scrolls and Christianity*, ed. Matthew Black (London: SPCK, 1969), 50–51; Schuyler Brown, "Deliverance From the Crucible: Some Further reflexions on 1QH iii.1–18," *NTS* 14 (1968): 247–59. Various sources refer to pain in childbirth (e.g., Ovid, *Metam.* 9.292–304; Life of Adam 19:1–20:3), including Old Testament judgment oracles (e.g., Ps. 48:6; Isa. 13:6–8; 21:3; 26:17–19; 42:14; Jer. 4:31; 6:24; 13:21; 22:23; 30:6; 31:8; 48:41; 49:22, 24; 50:43; Hos. 13:13). Some think 1QH 3.7–12 more specifically refers to the birth of a Messiah; see the debate between Lou H. Silberman, "Language and Structure in the Hodayot (1QH 3)," *JBL* 75 (June 1956): 96–106; William H. Brownlee, "Messianic Motifs of Qumran and the NT, II," *NTS* 3 (1956–1957): 195–210.

14. Cf. also 1QH 3.28 for God's wrath against Belial, in the context of the new community (3.7–12) and Belial's torrents (3.29, 32; cf. Rev. 12:15).

15. *Baal Epic* 67.1.1–3 in *ANET*, 138; J. Philip Hyatt, "Canaanite Ugarit" *BA* 2 (Feb. 1939): 1–8 (p. 8); Walter C. Kaiser, "The Ugaritic Pantheon" (Ph.D. diss., Brandeis University, 1973), 112, 132–33, 214. The dragon's seven heads are the seven ages in which Death devastates the world in T. Abr. 19A.

16. On giant serpents or dragons, see e.g., Philostratus, *V.A.* 3.6–8; p. Ned. 3:2, §1.

17. Lucian, *Alexander the False Prophet* 12–14; Pausanias, 2.27.2. Serpents are connected with Hera in Diodorus Siculus, 4.10.1; Zeus in Homer, *Il.* 12.208–9; Ares in Ovid, *Metam.* 3.31–32; the Furies in Virgil, *Aen.* 7.346–55; Ovid. *Metam.* 4.454, 475, 491–99; Medusa, in Ovid, *Metam.* 4.617–20; and especially Athena in Plutarch, *Isis* 71, *Mor.* 379D. Egyptians revered crocodiles (Plutarch, *Isis* 75, *Mor.* 381B), though Greeks regarded them negatively (Artemidorus, *Oneir.* 3.11). For snake cults in the East see Ramsay MacMullen, *Enemies of the Roman Order* (Cambridge, Mass.: Harvard Univ. Press, 1966), 118.

especially the "ancient serpent" (12:9), the one in Genesis who led Adam and Eve to death by enticing them to disobey God (Gen. 3:1–15; Jub. 2:17–23), just as Balaam later did with the Israelites (cf. Rev. 2:14). Jewish tradition sometimes identified the serpent with the devil or linked him with the devil in other ways.[18]

Yet these associations do not exhaust the dragon's significance for John. Like some other apocalyptic writers, Revelation adapts widely used themes of ancient myths to communicate its point more graphically. The Old Testament emphasized God's conquest of the primeval dragon Leviathan (Ps. 74:14; Isa. 27:1); this seems to symbolize especially God's conquest of Egypt (nicknamed "Rahab") in the Red Sea (Ps. 89:10; Isa. 30:7; 51:9), which is fitting in a tale of a new exodus (Rev. 12:6).[19] Jewish tradition developed various stories about Leviathan as a literal beast whom God would destroy at the end.[20]

A similar story line was widely repeated among pagans by the late first century, when John wrote, and his audience would have recognized the irony in the way he retells the story with different characters. In Egyptian mythology, Isis (Hathor), portrayed with the sun on her head, birthed Horus, and the red dragon Typhon sought to slay her, but she escaped to an island and her son Horus overthrew the dragon.[21] In the Greek version of the story, the great dragon Python, warned that he would be killed by Leto's son, pursued the pregnant Leto, who was hidden by Poseidon on an island, which he then temporarily submerged. After Python had left, Leto birthed the god Apollo, who in four days was strong enough to slay the dragon.[22]

---

18. Satan in Wisd. Sol. 2:24; 3 Bar. 9:7; as Sammael in Targum Ps-Jon. Gen. 3:6 (Martin McNamara, *Targum and Testament* [Grand Rapids: Eerdmans, 1972], 121); the devil used the serpent in Apoc. Mos. 16:1, 5. For the association of serpents or dragons with demons, see 1 En. 69:12; 2 Bar. 10:8; Luke 10:19; with witchcraft in Horace, *Sat.* 1.8.33–35; *PGM*, 4.662–64, 2426–428, 2614.

19. Early Christians applied the same image of conquest to Christ's victory (Ode Sol. 22:5), as they also viewed him as the sacred child conqueror (Sib. Or. 8.196–97).

20. See 1 Enoch 60:7–8; 2 Bar. 29:4; *Pes. Rab Kah. Sup.* 2:4 (though cf. plural leviathans in Apoc. Abr. 10:10; *b. B.B.* 74b). Leviathan takes on demonic connotations in Aramaic incantation texts 2.3–4; 6.8. Virgil, *Ecl.* 4.24 expected serpents to perish in the future era.

21. See Roland Bergmeier, "Altes und Neues zur 'Sonnenfrau am Himmel (Apk 12)': Religionsgeschichtliche und quellenkritische Beobachtungen zu Apk 12:1–17," *ZNW* 73 (1982): 97–109; Koester, *Introduction*, 1:188. Dragons also appear in Babylon tradition (as Jews recognized, e.g., Bel and the Dragon 23–27). For divine mothers, see Gail Paterson Corrington, "The Milk of Salvation: Redemption by the Mother in Late Antiquity and Early Christianity," *HTR* 82 (Oct. 1989): 393–420.

22. For the dragon's significance for a variety of ancient cultures, see Ivan M. Benson, "Revelation 12 and the Dragon of Antiquity," *Restoration Quarterly* 29 (1987): 97–102. The theme in Greek myth is as early as the Titan Kronos's swallowing his children to prevent his overthrow (Hesiod, *Theog.* 459–64).

Most commentators do not stop with such general pagan background for the image. In the first century, coins reveal that some emperors linked themselves with the sun-god, Apollo. In Roman propaganda in Asia Minor the goddess Roma was the new mother goddess and the Roman emperor her child, the world's savior. In John's vision it is the Lord Christ who will ultimately slay the dragon and its related beast; the emperor in reality is simply one of the dragon's puppets! Most commentators understand such a conflict with the imperial cult as part of the background here.[23]

The meaning of the stars also deserves comment. One can take their fall as a description of cosmic catastrophe (6:13), but 12:4 probably implies more than that. In Jewish symbolism, stars could represent the righteous, as even in this context (12:1; cf. Gen. 26:4; Dan. 12:3); hence this passage may be describing apostasy (cf. perhaps Dan. 8:10).[24] One can also describe a fall from greatness into shame as a fall from heaven to earth (Isa. 14:12, 15; Lam. 2:1; Sib. Or. 3.359–62). But in Revelation the stars usually symbolize angels (1:20; 9:1), which is also a frequent application of the image in Jewish literature.[25] Pagans often viewed stars as divine beings, whereas many Jewish people viewed them as angels.[26] Jewish people recognized that Satan's revolt had long ago led to the fall of many angels (often associated with Gen. 6:2), a view apparently supported in 1 Peter 3:19–22; 2 Peter 2:4.

But John provides a Christocentric reapplication of this fall story: The greatest revolt of Satan and the ultimate goal of angelic apostasy was

---

23. Ray Summers, "Revelation 20: An Interpretation," *RevExp* 57 (1960): 176–83; Caird, *Commentary on Revelation*, 148; Beasley-Murray, *Revelation*, 191; Elisabeth Schüssler Fiorenza, "The Revelation to John," 99–100 in *Hebrew-James–1 & 2 Peter-Jude-Revelation*, ed. G. Krodel (Philadelphia: Fortress, 1977), 111. The dragon may be Rome in Ps. Sol. 2:25–26, as successor of Babylon and Egypt (Beale, *Revelation*, 632–33). A divinely chosen boy's birth characterizes propaganda from Augustus's reign (cf. Virgil, *Ecl.* 4; Wilfred L. Knox, *St. Paul and the Church of the Gentiles* [Cambridge: Cambridge Univ. Press, 1939], 18–19).

24. For the righteous becoming stars in the afterlife or future era, see Dan. 12:3; 1 En. 104:2; 4 Macc. 17:5; 2 Bar. 51:10; Ps-Philo 33:5; for comparisons in the present, see 1 En. 43:1–4; *Sifre Deut.* 47.2.5, 8; *b. Ber.* 56b; cf. Jos. and Asen. 2:6/11.

25. See 1 Enoch 6:7 (Aramaic); 8:3; 18:14–16; 20:4; 21:3, 6; 80:6–8; 86:1–4; 88:3; 2 Enoch 7:3; 29:4–5 rec. J; 31 rec. J; 2 Bar. 51:10; T. Sol. 20:16–17. Isa. 24:21 was understood to refer to end-time judgment of celestial powers that stand behind earthly kings. Beale, *Revelation*, 636–37, plausibly proposes that the stars are both people(s) and the angels who represent them in heaven (cf. Rev. 1:20).

26. As gods, Cicero, *De Nat. Deor.* 2.15.39–40; *De Re Publica* 6.15.15; Seneca, *Benef.* 4.23.4; 1 Enoch 80:7–8; as souls in Plato, *Timaeus* 41E; Philo, *Giants* 7–8; 4 Macc. 17:5; as angels, 1QM 10.11–12; 2 Enoch 4:1; 29:3A; 3 Enoch 46:1; 2 Bar. 51:10; Philo, *Plant.* 12–14; *Pes. Rab Kah.* 1:3; associated with demons, T. Sol. 2:2; 4:6; 5:4; 6:7; 7:6; ch. 18. Some preferred naturalistic explanations (Varro, 5.10.59; Diogenes Laertius, 7.1.152–53). Stars participate in the final battle and fall to earth in Sib. Or. 5.512–31 (perhaps written close to John's time).

opposition to Jesus' mission on earth (12:4). But Satan and his angels failed, and precisely at Jesus' exaltation Satan's kingdom received its complete notice of defeat (12:7–9)!

The Final Exodus (12:5–6)

IN THE COMMON myth, the child born to the woman was a god or the emperor worshiped without controversy by the world system; John reinterprets the myth so that the child is the Lord Jesus, the crucified leader of the persecuted sect of Christians. That Jesus and not his church is in view here is clear not only from his ruling with a rod of iron (cf. 19:15)—his servants will rule but only with him (2:27)[27]—but also after Jesus is caught up, the woman has other offspring who follow Jesus (12:17).[28] This story is the centerpiece of Revelation and the centerpiece of its review of history; no one other than our Lord Jesus Christ may fill that role.

Further, whereas the common myth focused on the birth of a divine child, Revelation focuses not on Jesus' birth but on his exaltation (12:5). Jesus was "begotten" as king at his resurrection and enthronement (Ps. 2:7; Acts 13:33; Heb. 1:3–5). If read together with John's Gospel, Revelation may even depict Jesus' enthronement as beginning with the cross, where he was crowned "king of the Jews" (John 19:19–21; cf. 16:21); it was at the cross that Satan was "cast out" of heaven (12:31; 14:30; 16:11; cf. Rev. 12:9, 13); it was by the cross that Jesus "prepared a place" for his followers (John 14:2–3; cf. Rev. 12:6).[29]

Time is also different in Revelation than in the apocalyptic tradition. The "1,260 days" likely adapts Daniel's Great Tribulation (cf. Dan. 12:11); working from a 360-day year, 1,260 days would be three and a half years (7:25; 9:27; 12:7).[30] Revelation here reinterprets the traditional Jewish symbol of end-time tribulation in light of Christian beliefs about Jesus. Following Daniel, writers could envision a final three-and-a-half-year Tribulation (Dan. 9:24–27; 12:1, 11). Various Jewish traditions adapted the duration of the final

---

27. Most commentators hold that Christ is in view here, including dispensational writers like Walvoord, *Revelation*, 189–90.

28. In early Christian texts, when the word *harpazo* (trans. "snatched up" here) applies to divine activity, it typically means lifting (Acts 8:39), even to heaven (2 Cor. 12:2, 4; 1 Thess. 4:17).

29. Others (e.g., Caird, *Commentary on Revelation*, 149–50) also find the cross here. Beale, *Revelation*, 648–49, finds a spiritual sanctuary in this "place" (cf. Dan. 8:11; Matt. 24:15, but the word *topos* is used far more broadly; the parallel in John, however, may support this sense (cf. the "Father's house" in 14:2).

30. Perhaps 1,260 days is preferable to Daniel's 1,290 because the days are shortened (Mark 13:20), perhaps because of a Jewish tradition (*Ruth Rab.* 5:6), or perhaps for numerical reasons. Three and a half years was a historic period of Israel's oppression (e.g., Josephus, *War* 1.19) reapplied to other, analogous periods (*Lam. Rab.* 2:2, §4).

Tribulation at various lengths (most commonly forty years). But Revelation seems to employ this figure to tell us about the kind of time rather than the length of time, emphasizing primarily that it is tribulation. If Jesus is king and Christ, and if Jesus has come and yet will come again, then Christians are already living in the final era, regardless of that era's length (e.g., Acts 2:17; 1 Tim. 4:1; 2 Tim. 3:1; 2 Peter 3:3). Likewise, John's Jewish contemporaries anticipated Satan's future defeat, but John, for whom the Messiah has already invaded history and staked his claims, declares Satan's defeat in the past.[31]

For several reasons, John's adaptation of his contemporaries' prophecy charts should not surprise us. (1) Revelation rarely takes over Jewish symbols of the end, even those from the divinely inspired Old Testament, without reapplying them in light of what Christians know about Jesus. Revelation is full of symbolic numbers (see comment on 7:1–8). (2) The book of Daniel itself, under God's direction, reapplies Jeremiah's seventy years prophecy to a much longer period, which leads to the length of Tribulation stated there (Dan. 9:2, 24; cf. Test. Moses 3:14). (3) Jesus regarded Daniel's Tribulation as at least partly literally fulfilled in the events of A.D. 66–70, when the Temple was desecrated and destroyed, and became a site for sacrifices to Caesar.[32] (4) Some of John's contemporaries had also symbolically reapplied Daniel's figure for the Tribulation.[33]

Such arguments support only the possibility that John reapplies the figure, but it is the text of Revelation itself that takes us further, for the narrative reads as if Jesus' exaltation is immediately followed by the Tribulation (12:5–6). Moreover, Satan's expulsion from heaven cannot be a future event here; rather, it accompanies the arrival of "salvation" and God's "kingdom," and such language suits only two moments. One is Christ's return in glory (19:1; cf. 11:15), but this cannot be in view here, for that would hardly leave Satan even a "short" time (12:12). The other is Jesus' triumph through his death, resurrection, and enthronement (1:9; 2:27; 7:10), which therefore

---

31. With Rissi, *Time and History*, 38, 117; Bowman, *First Christian Drama*, 78; Beale, *Revelation*, 646–47; cf. A. Kassing, "Das Weib das den Mann gebar (Apk 12,13)," *Benediktinische Monatschrift* 34 (1958): 427–33; for the figure in 12:14, see Rissi, *Time and History*, 112. Bauckham, *Climax of Prophecy*, 185, calls this transformation of Jewish expectation "unprecedented."

32. See Craig Keener, *Matthew* (Downers Grove, Ill.: InterVarsity, 1997), 348–49, and sources cited there.

33. The Qumran texts reapply Daniel's language in quite different ways (cf., e.g., 1QM 1.4 in Yigael Yadin, *The Scroll of the War of the Sons of Light Against the Sons of Darkness*, tr. B. and C. Rabin [Oxford: Oxford Univ. Press, 1962], 180). Cf. F. F. Bruce, "Qumran and Early Christianity," *NTS* 2 (Feb. 1956): 176–90 (p. 177); D. S. Russell, *The Method and Message of Jewish Apocalyptic* (Philadelphia: Westminster, 1964), 198–201. For three and a half years elsewhere, see Josephus, *War* 1.19; p. Taan. 4:5, §10; *Ruth Rab.* 5:6; *Lam. Rab.* Proem 25, 30; *Lam. Rab.* 2:2, §4.

must be in view here.[34] As John's audience are already aware, believers will face tribulation in the world, but Jesus promises that his finished victory matters much more than such tribulation (John 16:33).[35]

In the Isis and Leto myths, the woman escaped to an island; John offers a distinctly different image here, deliberately recalling Israel's exodus into the desert (12:6). Because the prophets had promised a new exodus into the desert at the time of Israel's future redemption (Isa. 40:3; Hos. 2:14), some Jewish people literally withdrew into the desert to await its arrival (1QS 8.14–15; 9.19–20).[36] Others anticipated messianic figures in the desert (Matt. 24:26; Acts 21:38; Josephus, *Ant.* 20.189; *War* 2.259, 261–62); in addition, even apart from engaging insurgencies and guerilla warfare, the desert was the natural place to seek refuge (Ps. Sol. 17:17). But John uses the desert symbolically to refer back to the first Exodus, as in his Gospel (John 3:14; 6:31, 49), announcing a spiritual new exodus (1:23).

Revelation then shifts, like a good apocalypse, to a heavenly perspective on the events just described. Christ's triumph over the dragon on earth is envisioned in terms of a heavenly combat between God's and Satan's forces, with Satan's forces inevitably losing.[37] As noted above (see comment on 12:4), Jewish people often talked about the fall of angels in the distant past; now John relates this event specifically to Christ's triumph (12:7–11). Satan's fall here clearly refers to a past event; "salvation" and God's "kingdom" (12:10) are completed at Christ's return, but were begun at his death, resurrection, and enthronement.

Celestial Combat (12:7–12)

THE CELESTIAL COMBAT portrayed here reapplies many traditional Jewish images. The end-time theme of holy war, as in Qumran's war scroll (cf. comment on Rev. 7:1–8), is reapplied to a heavenly conflict whose outcome was

---

34. The accumulation of such terms suited the day of judgment (1 Enoch 60:6), but commentators normally agree that the cross and resurrection are in view (Schlier, *Principalities*, 49).

35. Though I do not currently think it the most natural way to construe the narrative, it is possible to read it as if it refers to a literal future three and a half years that are merely stated next because they carry out the logical conclusions of Jesus' victory (Walvoord, *Revelation*, 191). But even in this case, we could probably all agree that the practical implications would remain the same: that the Tribulation would so impinge on the present that it would function as if potentially present.

36. For further detail, see, e.g., F. F. Bruce, "Qumrân and Early Christianity," *NTS* 2 (1956): 176–90 (p. 177). For the new exodus in Rev. 12, see especially Beale, *Revelation*, 643–45.

37. That the celestial combat corresponds to the earthly work of Christ is often observed (see Ellul, *Apocalypse*, 87; Caird, *Commentary on Revelation*, 153; idem, *Apostolic Age*, 98 n. 5). For the popular ancient image of expulsions from heaven (including Greek legends about the Titans), see Aune, *Revelation*, 2:699.

fully established at the cross.[38] Based on Daniel (Dan. 10:13, 21; 12:1), Jewish people recognized that Michael was their guardian prince, who would defend them from the angels of the other nations who sought to oppress them.[39] Michael could single-handedly ward off angels of other nations (Dan. 10:13, 21).

Yet there were limits to Michael's power. He could not overstep his own authority, hence could not act against Satan himself without God's permission (Jude 9); moreover, he would be ordered to stand out of the way so Israel could experience the final Tribulation (Dan. 12:1; perhaps 2 Thess. 2:7). Here, however, Michael and his forces cast down Satan's forces, because Michael and his allies represent the heavenly victory won by Christ on earth. God not only rules the world through events in the heavens; he also fits these events to his acts on earth. John perceives not only the fallen angels but even the activity of Michael through his focus on our Lord's triumph.

Satan's being hurled to the earth ends his position of privilege in God's court.[40] Ironically, Satan's loss of "place" (*topos*, 12:8) contrasts starkly with the "place" (*topos*) of refuge God provides his own people persecuted by Satan (12:6, 14). The Bible already declared that Satan functioned as an accuser (Zech. 3:1), including directly before God's throne (Job 1:6; 2:1). Jewish tradition amplified this idea, so that in later texts he was said to accuse Israel day and night, except on the Day of Atonement.[41] Here, however, his accusations against the saints have been silenced, for Christ's victory is sufficient to silence all objections of the once-heavenly prosecutor (12:10). The opposite of a prosecutor was an advocate, and John's audience is probably already familiar with the idea that Jesus is our sufficient advocate (1 John 2:1; also John 14:16, where "Counselor" translates "advocate"). Satan's activity here is

---

38. But Qumran also viewed all human existence as a spiritual conflict between the princes of light and darkness (1QS 3.20–21). Beale, *Revelation*, 653, suggests that the heavenly army in Josephus, *War* 6.297–99, may correspond to the Romans on earth.

39. See 1QM 17.6; *b. Yoma* 77a; more fully see Otto Betz, *Der Paraklet Fürsprecher im Häretischen Spätjudentum, im Johannes-Evangelium und in neu Gefundenen Gnosticischen Schriften*, AGJU 2 (Leiden: Brill, 1963), 149–58. Guardian angels also protected individuals from demons (*Sifre Num.* 40.1.5; cf. 1 En. 40:7, 9). In Revelation, however, Michael is not connected solely with ethnic Israel, as in some Jewish views (3 Enoch 44:10; 1QM 17:6–7; T. Moses 10:2).

40. The Greek expression for "lost their place" in 12:8 is the same dramatic expression found in 20:11.

41. See *b. Yoma* 20a; *Lev. Rab.* 21:4; *Num. Rab.* 18:21; *Pes. Rab.* 45:2, 47:4; for Satan as accuser, see *Jub.* 48:15–16; 3 Enoch 14:2; 26:12; *Gen. Rab.* 38:7; 84:2; *Ex. Rab.* 31:2; *Lev. Rab.* 21:10; *Koh. Rab.* 3:2, §2; for other accusing angels, 1 Enoch 40:7; 3 Enoch 4:6–7; 28:8; *Apoc. Zeph.* 3:8–9; 6:17; *Pes. Rab Kah.* 24:11. "Satan" originally meant "accuser," but even in the Old Testament and Jewish tradition, Satan's position depended on God's permission (Job 1:12; 2:6; T. Job 8:1–3; 16:4/2; 20:3).

"day and night"; like the torment of his followers (14:11; 20:10), this contrasts with the unceasing role of God's worshipers in 4:8; 7:15.

Satan's defeat in heaven does not mean an end to physical suffering on earth. The saints here continue to overcome the devil as they overcome the world—by faithfully testifying of Christ's victory even to the point of death (12:11). This is a sacrifice to which Jesus long ago called anyone who would be his follower (John 12:25), but in the context of "overcoming" (translated "overpower" and "conquer" in Rev. 11:7; 13:7), may recall especially the image of military martyrs (see comment on 7:1–17).[42] The victory is past, won by Christ's "blood" (12:11; cf. 1:5; 7:14); the conquering Lion was a slain Lamb (5:5–6). The saints implement that victory by faith (cf. 1 John 4:4; 5:4–5), boldly proclaiming Christ regardless of the cost to themselves (Rev. 12:11; 20:4), thus hastening the coming of the end and the fulfillment of God's purposes in human history (6:9–11).

Satan oppresses Jesus' followers (12:10–12) and pursues the woman into the desert, just as Pharaoh pursued Israel in the Exodus. In Jewish tradition, Belial (Satan) would be unleashed in special fury against Israel in the end time (CD 4.12–13). Here that time of suffering for God's people corresponds to their deliverance before God; Satan's only activities remain earthly deception and repression. The devil's "short" time (12:12), like the "little while" between the cross and resurrection (John 16:16–19), is an interim period that involves both suspense and hardship—but whose outcome is predetermined. The devil's "time" (*kairos*, 12:12) will run out when the "delay" (*chronos*, 10:6) ends—that is, when God's purposes are complete (10:7) and the kingdom becomes his at the time (*kairos*) of his judgment (11:15–18). This is the same span of time (*chronos*) for the saints' remaining sufferings (6:11).[43]

The woman fled to the desert for an extended period. The period "times, time and half a time" (12:14) refers to three and a half years, the period of Great Tribulation (as in Dan. 7:25; 12:7; for the symbolic significance of this number, see comment on 12:6). The psalmist prayed for bird's wings to flee into the desert (Ps. 55:6–7), but the eagle's wings that God provides her

---

42. Loving not life even to death was appropriate for war heroes (Judg. 5:18). Death in battle was viewed as noble (e.g., Demosthenes, *Or.* 60, *Funeral Speech* 19) and one might promise to be ready to die for a leader like Caesar (*IGRR* 3.137), but the conquerors in our text triumph precisely by martyrdom. On the Greek motif of dying for a cause, see Aune, *Revelation*, 2:703.

43. Cf. Rissi, *Time and History*, 25; pace some commentators, Revelation appears to use these two words roughly synonymously. Jewish hopes longed for the devil's final defeat (T. Moses 10:1); the summons for the heavens to rejoice is a literary form for a promise of triumph (Rev. 19:7; 1 Enoch 105:2; T. Moses 10:8).

(Rev. 12:14) probably allude to God's own help. The Exodus tradition spoke of God's bearing his people on eagle's wings (Ex. 19:4; Deut. 32:11), an image also applicable to the new exodus (Isa. 40:31; 1 En. 96:2; Test. Moses 10:8).[44] The miraculous provision in the desert here echoes the manna God gave his people at the first exodus; he provides "daily bread" (cf. Matt. 6:11).

In Greek stories river deities could send floods against their enemies (Homer, *Il.* 21.248–327); in Scripture, the serpent God overthrew in the first exodus lived in the waters (Ps. 74:13; Ezek. 29:3; 32:2). That "water like a river" comes from the serpent's mouth (Rev. 12:15; cf. 16:13) may be a symbol for slander, as with Satan's agents of accusation in 2:9 and 3:9; Satan, who can no longer accuse the saints to God, accuses them to the world instead. In prophetic language, a "flood" could represent any sufferings (cf. Ps. 32:6), including divine judgment (Isa. 28:2; Jer. 47:2), but also including unjust opposition (Ps. 18:3–4; 69:1–4, 14–15; 124:2–5).[45]

Mouths in Revelation typically function as symbols for speech, especially for God's Word (1:16; 2:16; 10:9–10; 19:15, 21), even when they adapt another image (11:5). In the next chapter, the mouth of the wicked is used for arrogant words and blasphemies (13:2–6) against God, but affecting the saints (cf. Dan. 7:8, 20, 25); by contrast, the saints have no lie in their mouths (Rev. 14:5). What supports the slander interpretation more clearly is that serpents' mouths appear for slander in Psalm 140:1–5. Whatever the trial of waters, God promised to bring his people through them (Isa. 43:2); it also appears as a significant irony that the earth's "mouth" counters the dragon's "mouth" in Revelation 12:16.

In the most common form of the Greek myth, the serpent Python was a Titan son of Earth, but here the earth, obeying God, helps the woman (12:16). The image would be a familiar one. Other Jewish texts portray the earth protesting lawlessness (1 Enoch 7:6; Apoc. Moses 40:5; cf. Isa. 26:21). At God's command, the earth might swallow something to protect it (2 Bar. 6:9; 4 Bar. 3:10, 19), or swallow Israel's oppressors (1 Enoch 90:18) or other sinners (Num. 16:32; 26:10; Deut. 11:6; Ps. 106:17; T. Abr. 10A; 12B); or Sheol might open its mouth to swallow the end-time invaders of the holy land

---

44. Cf. Jewish expressions about God's patronage as the sheltering "wings of the Presence" (e.g., Ruth 2:12; Ps. 17:8; 36:7; 63:7; 91:4; 1 Enoch 39:7; 2 Bar. 41:4; ARN, 12A; *Sifre Num.* 80.1.1). The eagle here is not likely Rome (4 Ezra 11:1–12:39; see comment on Rev. 8:13), nor are the wings likely God's commandments (b. Ber. 53b) or his enmity (Jer. 48:40; 49:22). Jer. 48:9 uses wings figuratively for flight, though from judgment. Greeks might envision metamorphosis stories as in their mythology (cf. Aune, *Revelation*, 2:704–6).

45. 1QH 3.29, 32, applies figuratively the image of Belial's torrents (see other sources in Beale, *Revelation*, 672); he would attack Israel in the time just before the end (CD 4.12–13).

(1 Enoch 56:8).[46] Perhaps most important, the defeat of Israel's enemies at the first exodus in the Red Sea is described as the earth swallowing them (Ex 15:10, 12).

That the woman before Jesus' coming in 12:1–5 is the faithful remnant of Israel is fairly clear; her precise identity through the rest of the chapter is more debatable. Does she refer to the church, to ethnic Jewry, or specifically to Jewish Christians? John would likely hold that all these groups survive through the end time, and modern interpreters usually answer these questions according to their broader theological frameworks. After the coming of Jesus, the faithful remnant is comprised only of Jewish Christians or (as more interpreters hold, with some good reason) of all Christians, or could one give either answer depending on the context? What is clear in any case is that, regardless of the woman's corporate survival, individual believers can still suffer death from the serpent's mouth.

The dragon's rage against the woman (12:17) carries forward his "fury" (12:12) and that of his agents (11:18), but now he focuses his activity against her seed.[47] That he "went off to make war" may suggest that individual saints are not all shielded in the desert; they may be portrayed more like the witnesses, confronting the world with the gospel (11:8). The woman's "offspring" or "seed" here (12:17) echoes the language of Genesis 3:15; they may suffer the serpent's bite but will emerge victorious (cf. Rom. 16:20).[48] These other offspring represent those who keep God's commandments, that is, true disciples of Jesus (Rev. 3:10; 14:12; cf. John 14:21; 1 John 3:22); they hold the testimony of Jesus (cf. Rev. 1:2, 9; 19:10; 20:4).

Some doubt that the woman's seed refers to believers in Jesus throughout history, protesting that "the church" is mentioned in Revelation 1–3 but never in chapters 4–19.[49] This protest is hardly consistent: The church is not mentioned on earth in these chapters, but neither is it mentioned in heaven. In 19:8, the bride of Christ also consists of the "saints," not the "church." Furthermore, chapters 1–3 mentions "churches," not the "church" as a whole;

---

46. Other objects, whether trees (p. Sanh. 10:2, §6) or the deep (Ps-Philo 26:4), also "swallowed" things at God's command; in Ovid, Metam. 5.639–41, the earth opens to allow water to escape its pursuer. It is possibly relevant that Cain as the serpent's seed struck Abel, but the earth, which "opened its mouth" to Abel's blood, helped Abel's case (Gen. 4:10–11; cf. Sib. Or. 3.696–97). In one form of the Leto myth the earth helps the women (Beasley-Murray, *Revelation*, 192); earth also helps a divine savior in Hesiod, *Theog.* 459–64.

47. Greek stories likewise recognized the principle that the removal of a defender, even by ascension, rendered more vulnerable this patron's dependents (Apollodorus, 2.8.1 in Aune, *Revelation*, 2:708).

48. R. A. Martin, "The Earliest Messianic Interpretation of Genesis 3:15," *JBL* 84 (1965): 425–27, argues that the Septuagint may preserve a messianic interpretation of Gen. 3:15.

49. Lindsey, *New World Coming*, 78.

given the rest of the book, there is simply no reason to doubt that those to hold to the "testimony of Jesus" (12:17) are all believers (1:2, 9; 2:13; 19:10). The "saints" or "holy ones" are the righteous, which Jewish tradition applied to the righteous remnant of Israel (e.g., 1 En. 100:5), but which early Christian sources apply, in every case where the context makes the sense clear, to believers in Jesus (e.g., Rom. 1:7; 8:27; 1 Cor. 1:2; 6:1–2; Phil. 4:22).[50] The price they must be prepared to pay for this testimony is death (Rev. 12:11).[51]

Precisely how does the devil make war with the rest of the woman's seed (12:17)? The answer is the theme of the following chapter, describing the world's repression.

MARY AND CHURCH TRADITION. Some regard the woman in this passage as Mary and use it to support later Catholic traditions about an exalted Mary (not all Catholic exegetes, however, hold this view). Protestant and Catholic commentators often differ here less in their interpretation of what is explicitly in this text than in their decisions about acceptable interpretive methods. If one begins with the premise of *sola scriptura* and cannot read later traditions into this text, it provides little if any direct teaching about Mary. By contrast, if later tradition can interpret Scripture, then one may find clues about Mary's exalted status implicit in the text.[52]

This raises a legitimate interpretive issue. I have sometimes talked with Catholic friends disgusted with liberal Protestant conclusions about matters such as the Trinity or Jesus' deity, who felt that the best way to prevent heresy was to appeal to the continuity of the orthodox faith in Catholic

---

50. The Christian view requires faith in Jesus as a prerequisite for true holiness, whether a person is Jewish or Gentile.

51. Most commentators do accept them as believers in general (e.g., Hill, *New Testament Prophecy*, 81; George E. Ladd, *The Blessed Hope* [Grand Rapids: Eerdmans, 1956], 98–99). Early Christian tradition expected the Antichrist figure to persecute the saints (Apoc. Elij. 4:20–29).

52. For various views about the development of doctrine in the church, see Peter Toon, *The Development of Doctrine in the Church* (Grand Rapids: Eerdmans, 1979). Divided between minimalists and maximalists concerning Mary's mediatorial role, the Second Vatican Council avoided a firm stance (G. C. Berkouwer, *The Second Vatican Council and the New Catholicism* [Grand Rapids: Eerdmans, 1965], 226–38; Walter M. Abbott, ed., *The Documents of Vatican II* [New York: Guild, 1966], 86–93, articles 53–63). *Catechism of the Catholic Church* (Mahwah, N.J.: Paulist, 1994), 122–28, affirms Mary's sinlessness but does not mention her mediation; for one survey of various views about Mary in diverse cultures, cf. George H. Tavard, *The Thousand Faces of the Virgin Mary* (Collegeville, Minn.: Liturgical, 1996).

history. I respond that I agree with the essentials of their orthodox faith but insist that we share the same view because it grew from the apostolic witness preserved for us in Scripture. They reasonably counter that Scripture must be interpreted, and who better to interpret it than the orthodox tradition? I then argue that Scripture is best understood in light of its original context, which provides the meaning at the foundation of the original orthodox tradition. They in turn maintain, in a tradition going back to second-century apologists, that the Bible is the church's book, authored by and for the church.

Although I agree that God gave the Bible for the church (Rom. 15:4), I hold that the church is meant to be the Bible's community and that the Bible stems not from the whole people of God but from God's inspiration of apostles and prophets, often challenging the errors of God's people. The church must always stand under Scripture's teaching, reapplying it only after we have understood its original meaning as the authors were inspired to address their audiences.

Lately, more evangelicals have adopted this traditional Catholic line of argument, and for reasons that are understandable. Longstanding historical tradition provides a helpful line of defense against faddish critical theories about the Bible and theology and surely merits a voice in critiquing ideas that would never have occurred to anyone outside the artificial culture of academia. At the same time, its value in determining details of the faith remains debatable. If the Bible is the "church's" book, who defines the church? The Roman Catholic Church cannot historically claim to be older than the Eastern Orthodox churches; the earliest claims to primacy for the bishop of Rome are over a century after the rise of monarchial bishops in the East.[53]

Nor does early Catholic tradition guarantee unanimity on all details, though it provides a broad consensus for the faith (which I and other orthodox Christians embrace). And Protestants who appeal to church tradition will certainly have a worse time of it than Catholics, for we do not offer even a pretense of unanimity! One also wonders how Luther, Calvin, Wesley, or others would feel about some who in their name privilege theological traditions above firsthand study of Scripture itself.

I believe that, as valuable a corrective as church tradition is, it must always stand under the judgment of God's Word in Scripture (Mark 7:6–9). The collective mind of later Christians is helpful, but it is not the same as the inspiration experienced by holy apostles and prophets and hence cannot serve as

---

53. See Geoffrey Barraclough, *The Medieval Papacy* (New York: W. W. Norton, 1968), 13–37. If Damasus (366–84) was the first bishop of Rome to claim "papal" authority (cf. Henry Chadwick, *The Early Church* [Baltimore: Penguin, 1967], 160–64), this was long after the bishops of different patriarchal sees had risen (ibid., 51, 131).

a "canon" or measuring stick to the same degree. Moreover, its corrective value must be free to cut both ways. Recognizing our traditions may help us evaluate the source of our presuppositions so that we can try to read Scripture in a way that is free to challenge rather than merely rehearse our presuppositions. Only in this way can Christians raised in diverse traditions surmount those barriers in honest dialogue.

Much of the symbolism surrounding the woman evokes Israel. How modern interpreters apply that connection diverges, based on their interpretation of the text; but even if her "seed" includes both Jewish and Gentile believers (whoever holds to Jesus' testimony and keeps God's commandments, 12:17), this symbol suggests continuity in salvation history. Such continuity has implications for how we read Scripture in general; some tend to read only discontinuity between the Testaments, but there are numerous points (including here) that suggest a substantial measure of continuity as well.

Dealing with tribulation. If, as we have argued above, Revelation's "tribulation" differs from that predicted by Daniel and Jesus (which was already fulfilled by Revelation's day), does that mean that there is no future tribulation? To the contrary, suffering is inseparable from the preaching of the gospel (see comment on 6:9–11), and the end will come only after Jesus' followers have carried out the Great Commission (Matt. 24:14). When we see a generation of believers radical enough to endure martyrdom to evangelize the most resistant areas, we will also see intensified tribulation. But while such tribulation may be part of the backdrop of Revelation's portrait of tribulation, its direct point in 12:6 is probably that our experience between Jesus' first and second comings includes the devil's enmity. Yet in the midst of such tribulation, we should be of good courage: Jesus has overcome the world (John 16:33).

On spiritual warfare. Revelation 12:7–9 portrays spiritual warfare in the heavens corresponding to Christ's triumph on the earth (12:5, 10). Clearly this indicates that our battle is spiritual, a reality recognized even as early as Jacob's preparation to face his brother Esau (Gen. 32:26) and Elisha's awareness of heaven's armies on his side (2 Kings 6:17).[54]

Some contemporary interpreters have misapplied biblical teaching about spiritual warfare, however. Once I visited a "prayer meeting" where the entire meeting was spent addressing and rebuking the devil; God was rarely if ever addressed. The Bible gives plenty of precedent for expelling a demon if it is present (e.g., Mark 1:25–26; Acts 16:18), but not a single text supports addressing the devil, as if he were omnipresent, during prayer. Texts that are often cited in support are frequently misapplied by well-meaning believers;

---

54. On OT roots for spiritual warfare, see Gregory Boyd, *God at War: The Bible and Spiritual Conflict* (Downers Grove, Ill.: InterVarsity, 1997), 73–167.

they refer to resisting the devil, not rebuking him.[55] That no text supports addressing the devil as present during prayer at the very least should suggest that some contemporary spiritual warfare practices are overdone. The practice of ridiculing the devil, popular in some peripheral charismatic circles today, is explicitly unbiblical (Jude 8–10).[56]

Today some spiritual "warriors" seek spiritual shortcuts to changing reality by "casting down" forces in the heavens. Perhaps they think Daniel had to wait twenty-one days (Dan. 10:2–3) only because he did not know any better; but it seems more likely that our culture's emphasis on instant gratification has made them too impatient with traditional methods of prayer.[57] Although angels of nations, "territorial spirits," appear to be a reality (Dan. 10:13, 20; Eph. 1:21; 6:12), Scripture remains silent on many details about them, presumably because there are some issues into which we are not supposed to delve (Deut. 29:29; Rom. 16:19; 2 Peter 2:10–11).

This is not to deny that God may indeed respond to such believers' faith despite their method, but to suggest that their method is not, strictly speaking, biblical. Revelation 12 portrays angelic war in the heavens, but the outcome here has already been decided by Christ's exaltation, and the rest of the battle is carried out by ground forces (12:10–11). God can provide us plenty of "air cover" in response to our prayers to him for his work, but genuine spiritual warfare requires the advance of ground forces. Jesus appears to have bound the strong man (Mark 3:27) by resisting his temptation (1:13), and (if we rightly understand the passage) the god of this age retreated from his position of authority as Jesus' disciples preached God's reign and cast demons from those possessed by them (Luke 10:17–19).[58]

---

55. In context, James 4:7 and Eph. 4:27 apply to resisting the devil by standing against the world's moral values; 1 Peter 5:9 applies to withstanding persecution, as in Rev. 12:11. Against this, see Kenneth Hagin, *I Believe in Visions* (Old Tappan, N.J.: Revell, 1972), 83–84; idem, *Authority of the Believer* (Tulsa, Okla.: Kenneth E. Hagin Evangelistic Association, 1978), 19–20; idem, *Demons and How to Deal with Them* (Tulsa, Okla.: Kenneth E. Hagin Evangelistic Association, 1977), 25—works that have influenced hundreds of thousands of Christians. Mal. 3:11, sometimes cited (Kenneth Copeland, *The Laws of Prosperity* [Fort Worth, Tex.: Kenneth Copeland Publications, 1974], 81), simply refers to God withholding locusts from one's crops!

56. The practice of cursing Satan that Jude opposes seems to have been widely known (1QM 13.1–2; 4Q280–87; Life of Adam 39:1), and some others also opposed it (Sir. 21:27; *b. Kid.* 81ab).

57. Believers are not called to "cast down territorial spirits"; see Clinton E. Arnold, *3 Crucial Questions About Spiritual Warfare* (Grand Rapids: Baker, 1997), 143–98.

58. On Luke 10, see the interpretation in George E. Ladd, *The Gospel of the Kingdom* (Grand Rapids: Eerdmans, 1959), 49–50; idem, *A Theology of the New Testament* (Grand Rapids: Eerdmans, 1974), 67, 625–26. For Mark 3, see Craig S. Keener, *The Spirit in the Gospels and Acts* (Peabody, Mass.: Hendrickson, 1997), 106.

Based on such texts and on Paul's discussion of God's armor (Eph. 6:10–18), it appears as if Christians deal with the devil by delivering the oppressed and proclaiming the gospel, waging a "ground war"; in response to our ground war and prayers, God removes the heavenly rulers. The one offensive weapon in the spiritual armor God has provided us is his "word" (Eph. 6:17), which in the context of Paul's usage means the gospel (e.g., Eph. 1:13). We read the same principle in this passage: The woman's offspring overcame the devil "by the word of their testimony," that is, by their verbal witness for Christ (what "testimony" means elsewhere in Revelation). If we are teaching people spiritual shortcuts that neglect actually evangelizing the world, we may be undercutting rather than serving God's purposes in the world.

The whole and its parts. I usually prefer to preach from a paragraph (an expository sermon) rather than a textual sermon on one verse. But each book of the Bible, including Revelation, was meant to be taken as a whole—possibly excepting Psalms and Proverbs. Thus, whether we preach an entire paragraph or even a verse, we should use the specific unit as a sort of prism to refract the themes of the book.

Once in Africa I preached from 12:11, but used that verse merely to provide structure for touching on three themes of the book as a whole. Starting with the theme of "overcoming," I traced the immediate context of the passage, hence what it meant for these believers to overcome. Then I turned to how that overcoming might look different to believers in different situations, following the theme of overcoming in the letters to the churches (and applying the lessons to some of the sorts of situations my audience faced). Focusing next on "the word of their testimony," I traced the theme of witness through the book. I concluded by detailing what Revelation taught about giving our lives for the gospel and how those who suffer for the gospel are truly God's triumphant army (6:9–11; 7:1–17; 14:1–5). The better our understanding of any unit in Revelation is informed by the whole, the more we will understand and communicate it the way God inspired it to be understood.

Reading Revelation's symbols in light of modern Western ideas instead of their ancient significance is a popular temptation. Hal Lindsey, for example, made the eagle a symbol of the United States (fortunately for both Lindsey and other Americans, Ben Franklin failed in his attempt to make the national bird a turkey). Thus, Lindsey suggests that 12:14 may refer to an airlift from U.S. aircraft, such as the U.S. Sixth Fleet in the Mediterranean; not wishing to speculate unduly, he suggests merely that they might be removed to Petra.[59] But no one in the rest of history could have understood the symbol

---

59. Lindsey, *New World Coming*, 179.

as the United States, and the text itself provides us no reason to understand the symbol in such terms.

INTERPRETING BIBLICAL IMAGES **for today.** Christ is the dragon-slayer and Caesar, who may have claimed to be dragon-slayer, was merely a puppet of the dragon. Shortly before Roman officials in Carthage ordered Perpetua's execution as a Christian, the young woman had a vision of a ladder leading to heaven with a dragon at its foot. "'He will not harm me,' I said, 'in the name of Christ Jesus.'" Then she stepped on his head and climbed up the ladder; she understood this vision as the Lord's assurance that she would triumph through her martyrdom.[60]

There is a place for reappropriating the world's stories, songs, dramatic themes, and so forth for the gospel. When our culture emphasizes personal sexual gratification, we can respond by speaking of the truest love found in Christ, who will never betray you. When the world packages its violent action heroes, we can speak of the truest hero, who courageously received our violence and shamed what is wrong in our values.

The image of conflict here also reminds us that God's people must always be ready to confront the world's hostility; the contrast between the mother in chapter 12 and the prostitute in chapter 17 reminds us that the city of God and Babylon never coexist naturally in this world. Especially in view of the use of the image of labor pains in the Hebrew Bible, this image here further reminds us that God's purposes are often accomplished only through suffering (cf. John 16:21–22; Rom. 8:22–23). The devil's hostility, probably expressed as slander (see comments on 12:15), also warns us to expect false accusations, though we should do our best to prevent them (1 Tim. 3:7; 5:14–15).

That Revelation recycles the ancient serpent of Genesis for its own day further underlines the continuity of the same enemy throughout history. It should not surprise us that many of Satan's devices (e.g., sexual temptation, political oppression, unforgiveness) remain the same today as they have been. Unlike Satan, however, his agents (e.g., the Roman emperor identifying with Apollo) repeat the arrogance of all their evil predecessors, while remaining seemingly oblivious to the fate of those who perished before them. Each generation has its own crop of antichrists (cf. 1 John 2:18), but the character of supernatural evil behind them remains unchanged until the

---

60. Trans. by Herbert Musurillo, "The Martyrdom of Perpetua," *Christian History* 17 (1988): 32–33 (p. 33).

Lord's return. Both the earthly pursuit of the woman and the image of heavenly warfare warn us not to grow content with any truce we have with the world in secular, materialistic America or elsewhere. Comfort is a goal of our society, but given the right conditions our bold witness ("the testimony of Jesus," 12:17) will invite opposition.

That Revelation reapplies Christologically both the fall of the stars and the period of Tribulation reminds us of Christ's centrality in everything; as Christians, we must view both past and future through the lens of God's purposes in Christ. As the angels learned, the greatest rebellion is rebellion against Christ's Lordship, acting as if our own lives belong to us.

Retreat or engagement? The desert theme is important. Some survivalist groups in the United States have withdrawn into the wilderness in order to survive coming troubles.[61] Such behavior may prolong life in the event of a nuclear or perhaps biochemical holocaust, but it misses the point of Revelation. The rest of this book teaches that our goal as Christians is not to escape suffering or death but to announce Jesus to the world (6:9–11; 11:3–7; 19:10). We must not withdraw from sinners (though we must withdraw spiritually from the world's corruption, cf. 18:4), but invade the world with the message and example of God's redeeming love.

The real point of the desert in this passage (see Original Meaning section) is not a call to universal monasticism but a picture of the present era as a time between our first and final redemption. After Israel sighed on account of its bondage and God redeemed his people from slavery in Egypt, they experienced an interim period, led by God in the desert, until they entered their "inheritance." Early Christians used such language to depict the interim period between the first and second comings, to explain why God brought salvation in two stages (e.g., Rom. 8:14, 17, 23; Eph. 1:14).[62]

In other words, Christians live in what some scholars call the "already/not yet": We have begun to experience the life of the coming world even though we have yet to enter it fully. Our bodies remain mortal, but God has empowered us to live our lives in obedience to the ways of the future kingdom. The desert theme is thus one of present suffering and detachment from material wealth (like the redefinition of the Tribulation), not a retreat from engaging our culture when we are able to engage it.

---

61. On some right-wing movements' misapplications of biblical texts, see Richard Abanes, *American Militias* (Downers Grove, Ill.: InterVarsity, 1996), 87–97; for their infiltration of some conservative evangelical circles, see ibid., 191–221. Many are preparing to fight in Armageddon (e.g., Kyle, *The Last Days*, 161).

62. The two comings of Christ seem to have provided an apologetic problem for second-century Christians in dialogue with Judaism (see Justin, *1 Apol.* 52, 111; Ep. Barn. 7; Tertullian, *Apol.* 21.15; *adv. Jud.* 14).

Cosmic spiritual warfare. Although Jesus' side has won the victory, much of the world does not know this and remains in deception. Thus what we call spiritual warfare continues today on a cosmic level; for example, the worldview shift in the United States toward New Age and Eastern mystic thought. Roughly half of the country believes in extrasensory perception, a quarter in ghosts, a quarter in astrology, and ten percent in channeling.[63]

The Bible provides essential insights for our warfare in this age. The battle is a spiritual one, and God is sovereign; the devil's time is limited and continues only by God's permission. The angel greeted Daniel, a man of prayer, as highly esteemed before God, then went on to recount how the kings who seemed to move the nations were merely pawns in the larger plan of God for history. The future belongs to God!

Witnessing and suffering in our day. Many Christians in the United States are afraid that their witness may offend someone, but this passage emphasizes that our witness for Jesus is worth even our lives (12:11). As noted above, when I preach on this passage, I sometimes use 12:11 as a prism to refract themes that run through Revelation. After dealing with the immediate context, I deal with overcoming (especially in the letters to the seven churches) and with suffering for our testimony as the Lamb did (5:6; 6:9–11). In many parts of the world, in fact, believers have been laying down their lives; and, given the truth of Christ's message, that is a cost well worth paying. As F. F. Bruce notes on this passage:

> Their only means of resisting the enemy's attack ... is patient endurance and faithful confession. This may mean suffering and death; but it was precisely by suffering and death that their Leader had conquered. It is to Jesus, not to Caesar, that world dominion belongs; it is Jesus, not to Caesar, who is Lord of history, and those who confess him faithfully before Caesar and Caesar's representatives participate in his victory and kingly power.[64]

Experts estimate tens of thousands (some estimate hundreds of thousands) of martyrs for Christ annually around the world. Thus, individual examples of suffering for Christ can easily be multiplied. For instance, the Cuban government imprisoned Noble Alexander, an Adventist youth pastor, for twenty-two years. For refusing to renounce Christ,

---

63. Arnold, *Questions About Spiritual Warfare*, 28–29. In the United States, two novels especially popularized a renewal of interest in spiritual warfare and the importance of prayer as part of it; see Frank E. Peretti, *This Present Darkness* (Westchester, Ill.: Crossway, 1986); idem, *Piercing the Darkness* (Westchester, Ill.: Crossway, 1989).

64. F. F. Bruce, *The Message of the New Testament* (Grand Rapids: Eerdmans, 1981), 85.

he suffered food poisoning for eating maggot-ridden gruel. He lost consciousness being dunked in an icy lake while bound. He passed out three times from the pain of being whipped with electrical cables. He sustained gunshot wounds in his hand, leg, and thigh.

He spent ninety days "inside a coffinlike box where he could barely move" for having a Bible; for refusing to work on the Sabbath he was "dunked into a cesspool of rotting debris and putrid excrement for three hours." His hardest suffering was that his Christian wife divorced him while he was in prison; this brought him so much despair that he did not remarry until twenty-eight years later. "No one can be truly certain of his faith and endurance until he is forced to test them," Alexander warns.[65]

One encouragement in any of our testings is that Satan's time is limited (12:12); we must endure for only a limited duration of time. I know a celibate, single thirty-nine-year-old who would like to be married but happily reasons that if it does not happen, he has less than half his life left to wait. If we have already endured some tests successfully, we know from experience that God can give us the strength to finish the race. Further, the devil can no longer accuse us before God (12:10), so the most important issue is settled. We also know that the remnant of the church will triumph in the end (15:2; 21:7). If the eagle's wings allude to Exodus 19, they indicate God's intimate care for us.

The book of Revelation helps us by preparing us for hardship. Billy Graham notes that his wife grew up in a missionary family in China and saw "how God prepared His church there during times of trouble to withstand the even greater troubled times ahead." He notes that the hardships actually have strengthened the church and that God's warnings provide help.[66] By portraying the time between Jesus' comings as a Great Tribulation, like the one Daniel spoke about, Revelation reminds us that Jesus' followers share his cross; hence, it warns us to prepare. Suffering belongs to us in this world, but our Lord Jesus is victorious anyway (John 16:33).

---

65. John W. Kennedy, "Bittersweet Cuban Memories," *CT* (Jan. 12, 1998), 24.
66. Graham, *Approaching Hoofbeats*, 39.

Revelation 13:1–10

AND THE DRAGON stood on the shore of the sea. And I saw a beast coming out of the sea. He had ten horns and seven heads, with ten crowns on his horns, and on each head a blasphemous name. ²The beast I saw resembled a leopard, but had feet like those of a bear and a mouth like that of a lion. The dragon gave the beast his power and his throne and great authority. ³One of the heads of the beast seemed to have had a fatal wound, but the fatal wound had been healed. The whole world was astonished and followed the beast. ⁴Men worshiped the dragon because he had given authority to the beast, and they also worshiped the beast and asked, "Who is like the beast? Who can make war against him?"

⁵The beast was given a mouth to utter proud words and blasphemies and to exercise his authority for forty-two months. ⁶He opened his mouth to blaspheme God, and to slander his name and his dwelling place and those who live in heaven. ⁷He was given power to make war against the saints and to conquer them. And he was given authority over every tribe, people, language and nation. ⁸All inhabitants of the earth will worship the beast—all whose names have not been written in the book of life belonging to the Lamb that was slain from the creation of the world.

⁹He who has an ear, let him hear.

¹⁰If anyone is to go into captivity,
  into captivity he will go.
If anyone is to be killed with the sword,
  with the sword he will be killed.

This calls for patient endurance and faithfulness on the part of the saints.

Original Meaning

IN CHAPTER 12, the woman, after giving birth to a son, flees into the desert. This woman also has other offspring, who most likely represent the church, the righteous remnant of Jewish and Gentile followers of Jesus. There in the desert, the dragon, who represents the devil, makes war against these believers. The precise manner in which he does so is the theme of this chapter.

The Sea Beast (13:1–2)

THE BEAST IN 13:1–10 recalls Daniel 7:3–8, where four beasts arise from the "sea" (Dan. 7:2), as here; the sea may also be significant as the location of the mythical serpent God overthrew in the Exodus (Ps. 74:13–14; 89:9–10; Isa. 27:1; 51:9–10).[1] Daniel's four beasts are a winged lion (a griffin?) that becomes somewhat human, a devouring bear, a winged leopard, and finally a ten-horned beast fiercer than its predecessors (Dan. 7:3–8), apparently immediately preceding the Son of Man's coming (7:9–14). The dominant ruler of the final beast will persecute the saints for three and a half years (7:21, 25; cf. 9:25–27). Jewish tradition understood the fourth beast as Rome, which most Jews believed would be the fourth world empire to subdue Israel (4 Ezra 12:10–11; 2 Bar. 39:7).[2] Judeans (as well as an exile on Patmos or citizens of Ephesus) would perceive Rome as coming from "the sea" even geographically, and the sand of the seashore may represent "the nations" over whom the beast claims to rule (Rev. 20:8).[3]

Yet the beast in Revelation differs from the fourth beast of Daniel, being a composite of different beasts: Besides ten horns (13:1; cf. Dan 7:7, 24) it is in some respects like a leopard, in others like a bear, and in others like a lion (Rev. 13:2). Composite descriptions can amplify the glory of a creature (Ezek. 1:10), but here they amplify its hideousness. Thus, though John makes

---

1. For Leviathan in the sea, see 4 Ezra 6:52. Rome rises from the sea in 4 Ezra 11:1; for the messianic figure from the sea in 4 Ezra 13:1, 52, see Gregory K. Beale, "The Problem of the Man From the Sea in IV Ezra 13 and Its Relation to the Messianic Concept in John's Apocalypse," *NovT* 25 (1983): 182–88. Some associate the sea with evil (Caird, *Commentary on Revelation*, 161), but it probably refers to Rome's location across the sea (Ramsay, *Letters to the Seven Churches*, 103–4; cf. Caird, *Commentary on Revelation*, 162).

2. See also *Sifre Deut.* 317.4.2; 320.2.3; p. *Taan.* 2:5, §1; *Pes. Rab Kah.* 12:25; *Midr. on Ps* 40, §4; cf. similar Greek typologies of world empires (E. C. Lucas, "The Origin of Daniel's Four Empires Scheme Re-Examined," *TynBul* 40 [1989]: 185–202; D. Mendels, "The Five Empires: A Note on a Propagandistic Topos," *American Journal of Philology* 102 [1981]: 330–37. If the fourth beast was Greece, as some think (cf. Sib. Or. 8.6–11), the application to Rome is nevertheless understandable (Chrys C. Caragounis, "Greek Culture and Jewish Piety: The Clash and the Fourth Beast of Daniel 7," *ETL* 65 [1989]: 280–308, attributes it to Rome's absorption of Hellenistic culture). Christian interpreters, including Jerome, have viewed the fourth empire as Rome, though many modern critical scholars insist on the Seleucids because they date Daniel late and deny predictive prophecy (Lewis, *Questions*, 106).

3. Sand appears as a metaphor for God's people in Gen. 22:17; Isa. 10:22; 48:19; cf. 2 Chron. 1:9; T. Abr. 1.15–16; 4; 8A. But it is also a natural image by the "sea" (13:1).

his allusion by way of Rome, the point goes beyond Rome to the general threat of an "evil empire."[4]

The "ten horns" and "seven heads" (13:1) connect this beast with its suprahuman mentor, another beast, namely, the serpent (12:3); this image in Revelation fits the Bible's use of images from the ancient myth of the superhuman enemy (Ps. 74:14).[5] The "blasphemous name" (Rev. 13:1) probably evokes the arrogant boasts of Daniel 7:8, 20, as do his blasphemies or slanders against God and the saints in Revelation 13:6.[6] These would prove especially relevant to John's audience: Roman coins in the eastern Mediterranean announced that the emperor was "son of God" and "God"; Domitian even demanded the title "Lord and God."[7] We will comment further on this beast in 17:1–11.

Revelation 13:1–7 adapts many images from Daniel 7, but the paragraph in Revelation 13 that follows reflects new information and images directly relevant to John's audience. Bauckham lists parallels with Daniel 7:

Revelation	*Daniel*
13:1	7:2–3, 7
13:2	7:3–6
13:4	7:6, 12
13:5a	7:8, 25
13:5b	7:25 (cf. 12:7, 11–12)
13:6	7:25 (cf. 8:10–11; 11:36)
13:7a	7:21
13:7b	cf. 7:14

---

4. See George E. Ladd, *A Theology of the New Testament* (Grand Rapids: Eerdmans, 1974), 626; Feuillet, *Apocalypse*, 55; Michaels, *Revelation*, 158; Tremper Longman III, *Daniel*, NIVAC (Grand Rapids: Zondervan, 1999), 190; cf. Beale, *Revelation*, 685. In rabbinic parables "dangerous beasts represent the enemies of Israel, or the sufferings they cause" (Robert M. Johnston, "Parabolic Interpretations Attributed to Tannaim" [Ph.D. diss., Hartford Seminary Foundation, 1977], 595).

5. The Canaanite myth of Lotan, on which the biblical imagery draws, mentions seven heads (Baal 67.1.AB 1 in *ANET*, 138; J. Philip Hyatt, "Canaanite Ugarit," *BA* 2 [Feb. 1939]: 1–8 [p. 8]; Walter C. Kaiser, "The Ugaritic Pantheon" [Ph.D. diss., Brandeis, 1973], 132–33, 212–13). In 4 Ezra 11:1, Rome has three heads. For comments on Leviathan and the beast here, see Howard Wallace, "Leviathan and the Beast in Revelation," *BA* 11 (Sept. 1948): 61–68.

6. This language of boasting or arrogance is applied to early antichrist figures like Antiochus Epiphanes and Pompey (1 Macc. 1:24; Ps. Sol. 17:13). The same term for "blasphemy" applies to "slander" against the saints in Rev. 2:9; see comment on 13:6.

7. See Caird, *Commentary on Revelation*, 163; Beasley-Murray, *Revelation*, 209; Ramsay, *Letters to the Seven Churches*, 94; Aune, *Revelation*, 2:734.

Bauckham notes that the parallels run out after 13:7 and argues that the section after 13:7 refers to a new Nero tradition, also attested in Ascension of Isaiah 4:2–14.[8]

Nero Strikes Again (13:3)

ALLUSIONS TO NERO, however, probably begin as early as 13:3. Revelation goes beyond earlier biblical and apocalyptic traditions in its portrayal of the Antichrist, using not only biblical images but also symbols borrowed from contemporary events that Christians in the churches of Asia would have recognized. Most New Testament scholars, liberal and evangelical alike, recognize the image of a new Nero here.[9] Nero was the first emperor to declare an official state persecution against Christians (though probably limited to Rome), and he burned hundreds of Christians alive to light his imperial gardens at night and butchered others in various ways.[10]

Nero died June 9, A.D. 68, but even at the end of the first century, many believed that he remained alive.[11] Even if he is exaggerating, it illustrates the point when Dio Chrysostom suggests that "most people" believed Nero was still alive, despite the impostors who had risen in his name (*Or.* 21, *On Beauty* 9–10). A false Nero arose shortly after Nero's death (Tacitus, *Hist.* 2.8–9), and another during the brief time Titus was emperor, about a decade and a half before Revelation was written (Dio Cassius, 66.19.3). Finally, around A.D. 88—during Domitian's reign and less than a decade before Revelation was written—another false Nero arose, and this one proved a terrifying threat to the empire, garnering the support of the feared Parthians

8. Bauckham, *Climax of Prophecy*, 424–27.

9. Kraybill, *Imperial Cult and Commerce*, 161–65; Bauckham, *Climax of Prophecy*, 423–31, 441–44; C. H. Dodd, *The Apostolic Preaching and Its Developments* (London: Hodder & Stoughton, 1936), 39; Eduard Lohse, *The New Testament Environment*, tr. J. E. Steely (Nashville: Abingdon, 1976), 206; William Barclay, "Great Themes of the New Testament: V. Revelation xiii," *ExpTim* 70 (1959): 260–64, 292–96; Bowman, *First Christian Drama*, 87; Caird, *Commentary on Revelation*, 164–65; Bo Reicke, *The New Testament Era*, tr. D. E. Green (Philadelphia: Fortress, 1974), 243; F. F. Bruce, *1 & 2 Thessalonians*, WBC 45 (Waco, Tex.: Word, 1982), 182; idem, *New Testament History* (Garden City, N.Y.: Doubleday, 1972), 402; Aune, *Revelation*, 2:737–40; but contrast Beale, *Revelation*, 690–92.

10. Tacitus, *Ann.* 15.44; Tertullian, *Apol.* 5.3–4; see Harold Mattingly, *Christianity in the Roman Empire* (New York: W. W. Norton, 1967), 31–32; Murray J. Harris, "References to Jesus in Early Classical Authors," 343–68 in *The Jesus Tradition Outside the Gospels*, ed. D. Wenham, vol. 5 of Gospel Perspectives (Sheffield: JSOT, 1984), 5:348–50. Nero was widely known for evil deeds (e.g., Dio Cassius, 61.2.1–63.4).

11. This belief has long been noted, e.g., F. Crawford Burkitt, *The Church and Gnosis: A Study of Christian Thought and Speculation in the Second Century* (Cambridge: Cambridge Univ. Press, 1932), 21.

(Suetonius, *Nero* 57).[12] This fits Revelation's warning about a Parthian invasion (9:14–16; 16:12).

Some Jewish people also believed Nero would return (Sib. Or. 5.33–34, 137–54, 361–85). Shortly before Revelation was written they even predicted that Nero, "the fugitive from Rome," would return at the head of the Parthians (4.119–20, 124, 137–39) and conquer all lands (5.365, 368–69). Some even expected that he had died yet would return (5.367). Christians expected a new Nero (8.68–72), who would be called "a great beast" (8.139–59).[13] The myth of the new Nero continued to develop in the decades following Revelation.[14] The tradition that Nero would come back as the final Antichrist became so pervasive that in the Armenian language "Nero" actually became the equivalent for Antichrist.[15]

Here in Revelation we read of a head that is wounded, then restored (13:3)—an account that presumably points to the Roman ruler (17:10). Although the image of multiple heads on a beast may come from the four heads of one of the beasts in Daniel 7:6 in addition to the seven heads of the dragon (Rev. 12:3), a Roman tradition may also be of interest. Early Romans found a human head buried in the earth and understood it as a prophecy of Rome's future rule.[16] What would retroactively clinch the allusion to Nero for informed members of John's audience is the riddle of 13:18 (or, if they failed to catch it, the riddle of 17:9–11).

None of this is to say that Revelation predicts a literal return of Nero from the dead—at least not before the resurrection of the damned (Rev. 20:6, 14). Rather, the final Antichrist or the tradition of antichrist figures would be like Nero, just as John the Baptist was another Elijah (Matt. 17:12–13; Luke 1:17).[17] Romans could speak of emperors this way; Claudius was

---

12. The date depends on Suetonius's estimate. Paul Trudinger, "The 'Nero Redivivus' Rumour and the Date of the Apocalypse of John," *St Mark's Review* 131 (1987): 43–44, dates Revelation to A.D. 68–69 to accommodate the expectation (Martin Bodinger, "Le myth de Néron. De l'Apocalypse de saint Jean au Talmud de babylone," *RHR* 206 [1989]: 21–40, dates an original Jewish Revelation to this period and suggests it was retained in the later edition), but it remained just as alive two and three decades later.

13. One oracle predicts that Beliar (Satan) will come from the imperial line (Sib. Or. 3.63). False rumors of a wounded ruler's death sometimes circulated (Livy, 42.16.1–9).

14. See Larry Kreitzer, "Hadrian and the Nero Redivivus Myth," *ZNW* 79 (1988): 92–115.

15. Beasley-Murray, *Revelation*, 211. Cf. explicitly Victorinus in the third century; on the Nero Antichrist tradition in early Christian texts (including Tertullian, *Apol.* 5; Augustine, *Civitas Dei* 20.19; Jerome, *Dialogue* 21.4), see Miriam T. Griffin, *Nero: The End of a Dynasty* (New Haven: Yale Univ. Press, 1984), 15.

16. Dionysius of Halicarnassus, 4.59.2; 4.61.2; Dio Cassius, frag. in Zonaras, 7.11.

17. So also others, e.g., Caird, *Commentary on Revelation*, 165.

another "Germanicus," Tiberius another "Augustus."[18] Thus the imperial power of Domitian and emperors to come were a sort of new Nero "in the same sense as the church ... is Moses and Elijah" (cf. Rev. 11:3–6).[19]

Some doubt that John is alluding to the Nero story here. One scholar rejects it on the dubious premise that John lacks interest in the political situation of his day.[20] Another rejects it because the first-time reader would not recognize the new Nero until Revelation 17 (where he does see the theme).[21] But both passages imply a return of a ruler to life (13:3; 17:11), and John often clarifies earlier visions by later ones (e.g., 7:1–17). Further, one wonders whether a book with such complex numerical patterns as Revelation was intended to be read to the churches only once; ancient works were often meant to be reread (Quintilian, 10.1.20–21).

After Nero's death, chaos ensued as rival candidates for emperor successively seized control of Rome; the peace of the empire had apparently died with Nero. The original imperial line was dead, and some may have hoped for the restoration of the Republic. But with the accession of Vespasian, Domitian's father, the empire regained a semblance of stability and power. The empire had for all practical purposes returned from the brink of death—but Revelation declares that this evil empire would yet die (18:2–8).[22]

The Dragon, the Beast, and the Lamb (13:4–10)

MORE IMPORTANT IN this passage than the allusion to Nero is the contrast between the beast and the Lamb. While the story of Nero's return provides a backdrop for the plot, the real plot action is a more deliberate picture of resurrection and its public consequences. The return from death is a parody on Jesus; likewise, the ten-horned beast contrasts starkly with the seven-horned Lamb (5:6; cf. perhaps 13:2 with 5:5). The earth's first question, "Who is like the beast?" (13:4), parodies worship properly due God alone (Ex. 15:11).[23] But in contrast to imperial Rome, Jesus had defeated death and now ruled its domain (Rev. 1:18); thus the implicit answer to the earth's second

---

18. Cf. the Roman leader in 390 B.C. hailed as "a Romulus," a second founder of Rome (Livy, 5.49.7); or the spirit of Pompey settling in Brutus and Cato to slay Caesar (Lucan, *C.W.* 9.15–18). Some wrongly feared Titus would prove a new Nero (Suetonius, *Titus* 7).

19. Bauckham, *Climax of Prophecy*, 449.

20. Corsini, *Apocalypse*, 15–16, 231.

21. Michaels, *Revelation*, 157.

22. See Caird, *Commentary on Revelation*, 164; Bauckham, *Climax of Prophecy*, 452.

23. Cf. the similar parody in Judith 6:2–3; Sir. 33:5, 10. For various parodies of Christ in the Antichrist, see Bauckham, *Climax of Prophecy*, 431–41; Cullmann, *The State in the New Testament* (New York: Charles Scribner's Sons, 1956), 75. Cf. implications of imitation in Gr. Ezra 4:35; Sib. Or. 3.66.

question, "Who can make war against him?" (13:4), is, "the King of kings" (17:14; 19:16).

Likewise, more horrifying than the image of a new Nero is the fact that those impressed by the "resurrection" recorded in verse 3 worship not only the emperor but the dragon who stands behind him. In A.D. 89/90, maybe five or six years before the book of Revelation arrived in the churches of Asia, Ephesus issued a coin that conformed Domitian to the image of the chief deity, Zeus.[24] Although the imperial cult offered sacrifices to the emperor, even more often it offered sacrifices "for the emperor to the gods"; for John any compromise with pagan religion is worship of Satan himself (2:13, 24).[25] The beast "blasphemes" or "slanders" both God's name and that of his tabernacle (13:6; cf. 2 Thess. 2:4; some mss. of 1 Enoch 45:1).

The image of desecrating the temple was not unfamiliar to John's audience; within the previous half-century one emperor who thought he was a god had tried to set up his image in the temple, and Titus, the older brother of Domitian, had presided over the burning and desecration of the temple.[26] But John means the heavenly temple, and he means it symbolically, as he explicitly notes (Rev. 13:6): God's tabernacle or temple is his saints (cf. 3:12), and whoever harms it will be judged (cf. 1 Cor. 3:17; cf. Dan. 7:25, adapted here). Emperors portrayed themselves in military form and at least claimed to perform a significant military role; but here instead of making war on external threats to the empire's security, the ruler makes war on the saints, hated by the dragon (13:7).[27]

That the beast "was given . . . authority" and "power" (13:5, 7, presumably from God), however, reminds John's audience that even the Antichrist is a pawn in God's greater design on behalf of his people. To be sure, the devil is the immediate source of the beast's authority (13:2, 4), just as other evil partners share their authority (13:12; 17:13). But in the end only God can authorize the devil or the beast to rule the nations (13:7; 17:12, 17; see Dan. 4:32); he authorizes other agents of judgment as well (Rev. 6:2, 8; 9:3).[28] That the authority is limited to "forty-two months" (13:5; cf. 11:2) emphasizes that the beast's opportunity to do evil is for a limited season; its day of reckoning will come (19:20).

The unity of the beast's kingdom (13:7–8)—even if only temporary (17:15–17)—reflects the understanding that God has permitted the world

24. Kraybill, *Imperial Cult and Commerce*, 28.

25. See Bauckham, *Climax of Prophecy*, 445.

26. On such desecrations and earlier ones, see 1 Macc. 3:45; 3 Macc. 1:29; 2:14; 2 Bar. 5:1; T. Asher 7:2; tos. *Suk.* 4:28; CD 4.17–18; Keener, *Matthew*, 348–49.

27. On emperors in military form, see Griffin, *Nero*, 221–34.

28. With Caird, *Commentary on Revelation*, 167; Beasley-Murray, *Revelation*, 213.

to stand together under a single evil empire to test his saints. Jewish tradition had long recognized the tendency of evil empires to try to force conformity on subject peoples, hence getting them to forsake the uniqueness of the God of Israel (e.g., Dan. 3:4–6; 1 Macc. 1:41–43).[29] By contrast, the saints had their own multicultural unity (7:9–10), of which the world's was but a pale parody.

Nor is the beast's claim to rule the whole world to be taken completely at face value. That the kings of the east (9:14–16; 16:12) do not appear to belong to his dominion suggests limits to his rule. The emperor Augustus had claimed to rule the entire inhabited world, having subdued even the Parthians; but in fact this was purely Roman propaganda to impress the empire's subjects.[30] The Babylonian king likewise claimed authority over all humanity (Dan. 3:4, 7; 4:1; 5:19), but this claim was hyperbolic. The beast "conquers" the saints (Rev. 13:7; cf. Dan. 7:21), but their apparent defeat, like the cross, really spells their victory (Rev. 12:11; cf. 5:5–6; NIV's "overcame" in 12:11 [nikao] is the same Greek word translated "conquer" in 13:7).

Jewish teachers often commented on the predestination of the righteous in God's book (cf. also 17:8). Here, however, the book belongs to the Lamb (13:8), again underlining the critical difference between John and most other Jewish apocalyptists.[31] But like most forms of Jewish thought, John's idea of predestination does not negate human responsibility.[32] In fact, the summons

---

29. For subduing "all the earth" see Jer. 27:6–8; Dan. 4:22; 7:23; Jdt. 2:7, 19; 6:4; 11:1, 7; 3 Macc. 6:5. Alexander had tried to fuse all cultures into one (Michael Avi-Yonah, *Hellenism and the East* [Jerusalem: Hebrew Univ. Press, 1978], 20–21).

30. James M. Scott, "Luke's Geographical Horizon," 483–544 in *The Book of Acts in Its Graeco-Roman Setting*, ed. D. W. J. Gill and C. Gempf (Grand Rapids: Eerdmans, 1994), 491, citing the *Res Gestae Divi Augusti* 29.2; 32.2. Likewise, the Greek historian Polybius (1.1–2, 64) claimed that the Romans controlled "nearly" the whole world after the fall of Carthage, obviously excluding the Parthians and others outside the Mediterranean. Cf. similar language in Sallust, *Catil.* 36.4; Appian, *R.H.* Preface 7; Cornelius Nepos, 18.3.3–4; 23.8.3.

31. Commentators cite somewhat analogous language in 1 Enoch 62; Assumption of Moses 1:14. "From the creation" in v. 8 is closer in the sentence to "slain," but some prefer to link it with "written" (Vincent Taylor, *The Atonement in New Testament Teaching* [London: Epworth, 1945], 41).

32. E.g., Ps. Sol. 9:4; *Sifre Deut.* 319.3.1; cf. Sirach in Gabriele Boccaccini, *Middle Judaism: Jewish Thought 300 B.C.E. to 200 C.E.* (Minneapolis: Fortress, 1991), 105–9; see also David Winston, "Freedom and Determinism in Greek Philosophy and Jewish Hellenistic Wisdom," *Studia Philonica* 2 (1973): 40–50; idem, "Freedom and Determinism in Philo of Alexandria," *Studia Philonica* 3 (1974–1975): 47–70. Even Essenes, who were heavily predestinarian (e.g., 1QS 10.1ff.; cf. 1 Enoch 1:1–3, 8; 5:7–8; 25:5; 38:4; 48:1, 9; 50:1; 58:1; 61:4, 12; 93:2; Jub. 11:17) did not deny free will (F. Nötscher, "Schicksalsglaube in Qumrân und Umwelt (2. Teil)," *BZ* 4 [1960]: 98–121; E. P. Sanders, *Judaism: Practice and Belief, 63 BCE–66 CE* [Philadelphia: Trinity Press International, 1992], 251), pace Josephus, *Ant.* 18.18.

to heed in 13:9 (see comment on 2:7) performs the opposite rhetorical function: In view of the blindness—hence lostness—of those not predestined, anyone who proves able ought to respond to God's call immediately and find strength to persevere.

One can read 13:10 as a summary of the way saints will be executed (13:7), hence inviting "patient endurance" from the saints (13:10).[33] But a similar invitation to "patient endurance" (14:12) promises the destruction of the beast's worshipers (14:9–11). Thus this passage probably claims that those not destined for eternal life (13:8) are destined to die in various ways, a promise meant to encourage the faith of the suffering saints (13:10). This is the language of God's judgment, recalling Jeremiah 15:2; 43:11.[34] In either case, the words invite endurance from the saints and warn "against armed resistance of any kind."[35]

Bridging
Contexts

MANY ANTICHRISTS. If John envisioned the Antichrist as a new Nero, this does not imply that his vision was relevant only in his century. He speaks of an oppressor after the current one (17:8), one that embodies evil, as Nero did. Because he is recycling older images like Nero and biblical traditions about Antiochus IV Epiphanes and others, the issue is more the pattern than the person—the "secret power of lawlessness" rather than a "man of lawlessness" (2 Thess 2:3, 7). The ultimate incarnation of evil simply epitomizes and carries forward the character of his predecessors, so we may find many evil rulers whose behavior provides analogies.

We know enough about Nero to translate his image readily into that of our contemporaries, perhaps by saying something like: "You thought Hitler was bad. Wait till you see what's coming." Perhaps in our generation some will find other names (such as those of some contemporary terrorists) even more terrifying to hearers of our era than Hitler's. In any event, until Jesus returns, the world has not seen its end of antichrists.[36] Because Satan does not know the time of Jesus' return (Mark 13:32), he must always have antichrists in waiting, so that we will know which is the final one only by when Jesus comes and

---

33. The textual variant, referring in the active voice to those who "kill with the sword," would definitely not refer to the saints, but the textual evidence is not clear.

34. For similar language applicable to judgments, cf. Jub. 24:32.

35. Michaels, *Revelation*, 160–61; see Oscar Cullmann, *The State*, 84.

36. Cf. George Eldon Ladd, *The Gospel of the Kingdom* (Grand Rapids: Eerdmans, 1978), 37: "The Beast of Revelation 13 is both actual historical Rome and the future eschatological Antichrist."

wipes him out. Until then, the spirit of lawlessness continues in the world (2 Thess. 2:7), and we continue to experience many antichrists (1 John 2:18).

Some, however, use this passage to pinpoint a contemporary particular antichrist figure. The favorite candidate of early Protestants (not popular today) was the Papacy; thus even the early Swiss exegete Theodorus Bibliander (1504–64), who viewed the wound in Revelation 13 as Nero's death, believed the Roman imperial line continued in his day in the Papacy, located in Rome.[37] Other interpreters preferred Napoleon in his time or other conquerors of their own eras.[38] Yet most modern speculations as to details about the final Antichrist are unfounded. Revelation fortunately omits the sort of speculation about the Antichrist's awful features (e.g., fingers like scythes) found in later apocalypses (Gr. Ezra 4:29–31; Apoc. Elij. 3:13–18).

Some modern interpreters take the unity of the kingdom under the beast as demanding a new Roman empire, which they understand as the European Common Market.[39] But just because Rome performed the function of the world system in John's day does not require us to locate contemporary Babylon in or near Rome today (so those who find it in the Vatican). If "Babylon" today is not an empire with Rome as its head, then neither need it be an empire in which Rome and Italy merely play a role. Next to Antarctica, Europe may be the least evangelized continent today, and one of the least evangelized regions next to much of the Middle East. But antichrists and evil empires have risen in many parts of the world, and if Europe (or specifically literal Rome) produces the final one, it will be only as a crowning touch of divine irony and not because the text of Revelation demands it.[40]

Is armed resistance permissible? If 13:10 warns against armed resistance, what kind of contexts does it address? To be sure, a persecuted minority taking up arms against Rome may have proved suicidal and pointless, but is violent resistance ever commendable when there is a better chance of winning? Does John here urge a mere fatalism? Since he envisions a God who cares for the persecuted, fatalism is too strong a term; but what of the accusation that Christianity is "pie-in-the-sky," not radical enough to fight injustice in ways that terrify the unjust?

---

37. See F. F. Bruce, "The History of New Testament Study," 21–59 in *New Testament Interpretation: Essays on Principles and Methods*, ed. I. Howard Marshall (Grand Rapids: Eerdmans, 1977), 34.

38. Kyle, *The Last Days*, 71.

39. Lindsey, *New World Coming*, 186–88.

40. The modern division of Asia from Europe and Africa stems from ancient Greek tradition but is not based on clear geographical boundaries or enduring cultural continuums; see Glenn Usry and Craig Keener, *Black Man's Religion* (Downers Grove: InterVarsity, 1996), 41–44.

John's point seems to prohibit Christians *persecuted as Christians* from retaliation, but does not address participation in revolutionary movements that are not specifically Christian, yet work against tyranny or genocide. Given John's commitment to waiting on God's action, he may have preferred that Christians would avoid violence altogether.[41] Yet even if this is not the case, those who insist that violence is sometimes necessary must at least prove consistent. Many white Americans think the American Revolution—which involved taxes and representation—a just war against colonial exploitation, yet condemn Nat Turner's slaughter of civilian whites to protest slavery. That the latter nevertheless addresses a harsher degree of injustice than the former should warn us to screen as much bias as possible from our criteria for just violence.

History provides many examples of believers prepared for martyrdom without resistance. In the tradition of Jesus (Luke 23:34) and Stephen (Acts 7:60), Protestant Michael Sattler, as he was being tortured and executed, "prayed for his persecutors" and called on them to be converted.[42] Anabaptist Dirck Willems escaped across a frozen lake, but when the ice cracked and his pursuer fell into the water, Willems rescued the man who had sought his death. This delay allowed his capture, and his enemies burned him at the stake in 1569.[43] Protestant leader George Wishart (1513–1546), seeing his impending martyrdom, sent away his friends, noting that "one is sufficient for a sacrifice."[44] He peacefully surrendered and was quickly executed. Whereas such martyrs died in the spirit that appears in Revelation, however, much of church history and much of today's church leads me to wonder if we are prepared to be like the saints described in Revelation.

WORLDLY POWER VERSUS **courageous faith.** Satan has signs, including even a false resurrection; how does this impact Christian apologetics? To put the matter differently, what proof of the truth can believers offer in the public arena (i.e., apart from our subjective experience) that trumps this? Satan's kingdom acts from worldly power, but God's peo-

---

41. Views like Tertullian's, disallowing military service, prevailed for the first three centuries, but provided less guidance for the sort of relationship between church and state that existed after Constantine (Robert A. Krupp, "Risky Lifestyles," *Christian History* 51 [1996]: 40–41 [p. 41]).

42. Leonard Gross, "Showing Them How to Die, How to Live," *Christian History* 4 (1985): 22–25 (p. 23).

43. "Did You Know?" *Christian History* 4 (1985): 6.

44. J. Stephen Lang, "Martyrs and Architects," *Christian History* 46 (1995): 33–35 (p. 34).

ple act from courageous faith. Islamic regimes repress Christians and other Muslim sects and anything else that challenges their hegemony; true Christians multiply through martyrdom. History shows that every kingdom based on power has ultimately collapsed; yet God's people have persevered and now leaven the nations. Thus, Christ's power is greater even in this world (though hidden like a mystery; see Matt. 13:31–33); those with the eyes of faith can look ahead to ultimate victory![45]

Today when charismatics and social justice activists commonly belong to different streams of biblical Christian piety, we rarely think of contemporary prophecy in terms of pronouncing judgment on ungodly political structures. The biblical prophets repeatedly denounced social injustices, however. Greek and Hellenistic Jewish oracles also were often political prophecies, sometimes resembling biblical oracles against the nations (e.g., Sib. Or. 4).[46]

The passage warns us about the demonization of the state: We must render to Caesar what is Caesar's (including taxes—Mark 12:17; Rom. 13:6), but when a state begins to claim the worship due God alone, it has usurped a divine prerogative and succumbed to the spirit of the Antichrist.[47] Genuine Christians differ over where to draw the line between the state's legitimate authority and idolatry, but they cannot deny that such a line exists. Some grounds exist for civil disobedience, whether that disobedience is resisting the worship of Caesar or refusing to serve in the military enforcing South African apartheid.[48]

By refusing to support Hitler's war, for example, German Christians faced death.[49] When Pastor Martin Niemoller, one of a few hundred German pastors to publicly stand against Hitler from the pulpit, was imprisoned, a shocked chaplain asked what he was doing in prison. "'And, brother, why are you not in prison?' Niemoller replied."[50] Many German and Swiss Christians resisting Nazi totalitarianism made abundant use of Revelation 13.

45. This has implications for those who try to enforce Christ's values merely through the world's power; see Charles Colson, *Kingdoms in Conflict* (Grand Rapids: Zondervan, 1987), 265–75.

46. See further John J. Collins, *The Sibylline Oracles of Egyptian Judaism*, SBLDS 13 (Missoula, Mont.: SBL, 1972), ch. 1.

47. Cf. Cullmann, *The State*, 75; Ellul, *Apocalypse*, 93–94; Corsini, *Apocalypse*, 231.

48. For imprisonment of Christians refusing to serve in the military under apartheid, see *ESA Advocate* (Nov. 1989), 11–12; (May 1991), 11–12. For other Christian antiapartheid protests, see articles in *World Christian* (July 1986); "Church Leaders Condemn Apartheid," *CT* (Dec. 17, 1990), 54; *ESA Advocate* (May 1990), 11–12; (June 1990), 11–13; an African nun detained for months without trial in *ESA Advocate* (March 1991), 11.

49. See John Dear, "The Solitary Witness of Franz Jagerstatter," *Sojourners* (Aug. 1993), 7; on Bonhoeffer, see *Christian History* 32 (1991), passim.

50. Charles Colson, *Kingdoms in Conflict* (Grand Rapids: Zondervan, 1987), 152.

Only by eyes of faith or in the retrospect of eternity can we see how the rewards of faithfulness outweigh its cost. Boris Kornfeld, a Jewish doctor who had just become a believer in Jesus, refused to cooperate in the deaths of prisoners in the Soviet Gulag, hence lived long enough to witness to only one patient before he was brutally murdered. The patient, however, soon became a Christian and multiplied the influence of that conversion many times over; his name was Alexandr Solzhenitsyn.[51]

How the devil works. This passage reveals just how hideous evil is. Anthropological studies attest the pervasiveness of spirit-possession in various cultures, and the concrete existence of personal evil is one of the most empirically verifiable doctrines of the Christian faith.[52] The frequent denial of the devil in the Western world is less rational than it pretends to be and plays into the devil's hands.[53]

Yet what is truly horrific in this passage is that here, as in most of the Bible, the devil works not independently but through people. This passage testifies to the awfulness to which humans can descend in following the devil's ways (Eph. 2:1–3)—the Neros, Hitlers, Stalins, Maos, and Pol Pots; the Arab and Western slave trade; the genocide in Rwanda; and so forth—these all testify to the reality of demonic power amplifying human sin and crushing its usual restraints. Who could have believed the mass gang rapes, followed by murder, of surrendered Chinese women at Nanking?[54] If witnesses and documentation did not remain, how could we believe the raping and execution of young Korean women, including new brides, as "comfort women" by imperial Japanese soldiers?[55]

Nearly all of us today recognize slavery as unconscionable, but many continue to tolerate the racial prejudice or neglect that permits it. As the 1837 women's antislavery convention declared—the morning after their meeting hall was burned to the ground by an angry Philadelphia mob for daring to allow blacks and whites to meet together—"Prejudice against color is the very spirit of slavery."[56] Human rights investigator Gary Haugen discovered in Rwanda that mass murder does not require "pathological" killers:

---

51. Charles Colson, *Loving God* (Grand Rapids: Zondervan, 1987), 27–34.

52. For depictions of spirit-possession in anthropological literature, see Felicitas D. Goodman, *How About Demons? Possession and Exorcism in the Modern World* (Bloomington, Ind.: Indiana Univ. Press, 1988); Ari Kiev, ed., *Magic, Faith, and Healing: Studies in Primitive Psychiatry Today* (New York: Free Press, Macmillan, 1964), passim.

53. Cf. C. S. Lewis, *The Screwtape Letters*, rev. ed. (New York: Macmillan, 1982).

54. See Iris Chang, "Exposing the Rape of Nanking," *NW* (Dec. 1, 1997), 55–57.

55. Andrew Sung Park, *Racial Conflict and Healing: An Asian-American Theological Perspective* (Maryknoll, N.Y.: Orbis, 1996), 12–15.

56. Dorothy Sterling, ed., *We Are Your Sisters: Black Women in the Nineteenth Century* (New York: Norton, 1984), 115.

"When all restraints are released, farmers, clerks, school principals, mothers, doctors, mayors, and carpenters can pick up machetes and hack to death defenseless women and children." Haugen concludes, "The person without God . . . is a very scary creature."[57]

We object to evil when it gets quantitatively out of hand, but what we do not want to admit is that qualitatively the evil that brutally crushes families and lives on a large scale is the very depravity that also surfaces in daily human relationships. This passage not only reminds us that the devil plays without rules; it testifies to the unimaginable horror of our human sin that most of us would refuse to believe possible if not confronted with its more dramatic evidences.

That the world worships not merely the gods they think they worship but also the dragon that stands behind them (13:4) is also a wakeup call for us. Some Christians in Asia Minor merely wanted to accommodate food offered to idols, but in so doing, they were involved in the worship of Satan himself (2:24; cf. 1 Cor. 10:20). Indeed, there are only two sides, and Christians lulled into complacency by worldly acceptance or pursuits should take note. As the church was to be a multicultural chorus of worship to the Lamb (Rev. 7:9–10), so the world becomes a multicultural chorus of worship to the beast (13:6–7).[58] If we do not worship God alone, we participate in the worship of what the world values.

Multiculturalism and the Christian. Further, the world's multiculturalism (13:7–8) is a parody on that of God's church (7:9–10). God created all cultures and delights to bring them together in Christ, but the world tries to bring cultures together around different centers. Whereas the world often imposes conformity by force, economic necessity, or simply peer pressure, the church must provide an alternative multicultural unity linked by love for one another and by the same heavenly Lord rather than by his earthly counterfeits.

On many college campuses, it has become "politically correct" to tolerate anything that can be associated with any cultural view.[59] But a moment's reflection will show the shallowness of unity possible if based only on

---

57. Gary Haugen, *Good News About Injustice* (Downers Grove, Ill.: InterVarsity, 1999), 111.

58. Rissi, *Time and History*, 72, speaks of "making the world into the church of the Antichrist (13:3f.; 12, 15)."

59. See, e.g., Tim Stafford, "Campus Christians and the New Thought Police," *CT* (Feb. 10, 1992), 15–20; John G. Stackhouse Jr., "PC: Almost Correct?" *CT* (Nov. 23, 1992), 17; Lynda Hurst, "Censorship for the Kindergarten Set," *WPR* (June 1993), 46–47; R. Judson Carlberg, "Culture of Disrespect," *CT* (June 20, 1994), 18–19; Ginni Freshour, "When It's Wrong to Be Right," *InterVarsity Summer* (1994), 4–6; David Gates, "It's Naughty," *NW* (Oct. 10, 1994), 73–75; S. D. Gaede, *When Tolerance Is No Virtue* (Downers Grove, Ill.: InterVarsity, 1993).

tolerance, because tolerance, if taken too far, eradicates justice. Tolerance is good, but social tolerance is not identical with moral relativism. As one social commentator observes, "Tolerance is only a virtue when it is difficult—when it involves keeping strong beliefs on a short leash. Tolerance that reflects the absence of strong beliefs is a symptom of a distinctively contemporary form of decadence."[60]

When some traditional societies want to practice female circumcision (genital mutilation) as a cultural practice, Western women's rights organizations rightly protest that this is an injustice to the girls so mutilated.[61] But the moment anyone appeals to a standard of right and wrong that applies to all cultures, we have limited how far we push multiculturalism, as many more responsible multicultural advocates point out.[62] In many parts of today's church, however, the reverse problem is probably more common: We do not work hard enough to understand or embrace our brothers and sisters who are culturally different (see comment on 7:9–10).

Moral relativism can be a deadly scourge for modern secular multiculturalism. Once when a New Age friend of mine was explaining why right and wrong were merely illusions, a Greek Orthodox friend of mine asked what the New Ager thought of Hitler. "Maybe Hitler had a reason for what he did," my New Age friend responded with chilling "tolerance." Without a sense of right and wrong, there is little basis for justice, and anything goes—leading to the suicide of civilization as we know it.

The beast's multiculturalism in this passage is based on just such a limited kind of tolerance. The Roman empire was polytheistic, always able to accommodate new deities. The only religions it found intolerable were those it felt subverted public order—or those who insisted that others should renounce polytheism to serve one true God (cf. Acts 14:15; 1 Thess. 1:9). Is it possible that by completely accommodating postmodernity and simply offering Christ as one help to people among others rather than the only true Lord, many American Christians have embraced the mark of the beast?

At the same time, this passage offers hope to those who dare grasp it here: God is the One who gives the beast authority for forty-two months, and he does so to execute his purposes of judging the world by handing it over to its own evil ways (cf. 17:17; Rom. 1:18, 24, 26, 28). Thus "one has

---

60. George F. Will, "Intolerable Tolerance," *NW* (May 11, 1998), 94.

61. David Kaplan, "Is It Torture or Tradition?" *NW* (Dec. 20, 1993), 124.

62. Appreciation of cultural diversity need not obscure moral absolutes; see Ricardo L. García, "Educating for Human Rights: A Curricular Blueprint," *Multicultural Education for the Twenty-first Century*, ed. Carlos Díaz (Washington, D.C.: National Education Association, 1992), 167–68; Stephen A. Grunlan and Marvin K. Mayers, *Cultural Anthropology: A Christian Perspective* (Grand Rapids: Zondervan, 1979), 12–13.

to say with Luther that even when the Devil works his worst he remains God's Devil. At no time in history does this appear with such clarity as in the hour when the Son of God died on the cross" by the hands of his enemies.[63] The promise of judgment is also given to encourage the saints (13:10); it reminds us that God is just, that there are some moral certainties and issues of justice in the world, and that God will vindicate justice in the end.

---

63. Beasley-Murray, *Revelation*, 213.

Revelation 13:11-18

THEN I SAW another beast, coming out of the earth. He had two horns like a lamb, but he spoke like a dragon. ¹²He exercised all the authority of the first beast on his behalf, and made the earth and its inhabitants worship the first beast, whose fatal wound had been healed. ¹³And he performed great and miraculous signs, even causing fire to come down from heaven to earth in full view of men. ¹⁴Because of the signs he was given power to do on behalf of the first beast, he deceived the inhabitants of the earth. He ordered them to set up an image in honor of the beast who was wounded by the sword and yet lived. ¹⁵He was given power to give breath to the image of the first beast, so that it could speak and cause all who refused to worship the image to be killed. ¹⁶He also forced everyone, small and great, rich and poor, free and slave, to receive a mark on his right hand or on his forehead, ¹⁷so that no one could buy or sell unless he had the mark, which is the name of the beast or the number of his name.

¹⁸This calls for wisdom. If anyone has insight, let him calculate the number of the beast, for it is man's number. His number is 666.

MANY INTERPRET THIS second beast as the imperial priesthood, dedicated to promoting the worship of the first beast.[1] Some argue that its derivation from "the earth" (13:11) as opposed to "the sea" (13:1) refers to native, provincial authority, hence local priests of the imperial cult.[2] Others view it as the personification of all pagan cults that participated in emperor worship (see comment on 13:4).[3]

That the beast had two horns "like a lamb" (13:11) reflects its imitation of the seven-horned Lamb of God (5:6), though the two horns may come

---

1. E.g., Bowman, *First Christian Drama*, 87; Beasley-Murray, *Revelation*, 216–17.

2. Ramsay, *Letters to the Seven Churches*, 97, 103–4; Caird, *Commentary on Revelation*, 171. Others think it refers to the imperial priesthood through the empire (e.g., Bauckham, *Climax of Prophecy*, 446). For two beasts in some mythic schemes, see Beasley-Murray, *Revelation*, 215.

3. Feuillet, *Apocalypse*, 55.

from the ram of Daniel 8:3. But this "lamb" speaks like the dragon; "whereas the Lamb of God is and speaks the Word of God (19:13 . . .), the beast from the land is the 'Lamb' of Satan, and it is and speaks the word of Satan."[4] Its message gives it away. The real Lamb died in weakness, raised by God's power; the fake lamb promotes one who pretends to have recovered no less significantly (Rev. 13:12). Some take the parody so far that they view the second beast as part of a "satanic trinity" of the two beasts and the dragon (cf. 1:4; 16:13), though John never makes this point explicitly.[5]

The act of worshiping an image (13:14–15) would be familiar to John's audience. Not many years after Revelation was written, we have evidence of a legal tradition of executing Christians for refusing to worship the emperor's statue (Pliny, *Ep.* 10.96). Revelation was written perhaps five years after Domitian dedicated an imperial statue nearly eight meters high in the imperial temple in Ephesus.[6] But John's audience would also think of Nebuchadnezzar's image, which was to be worshiped by all peoples. The heroes of ancient Jewish piety had determined to resist such worship even if it ultimately cost their lives (Dan. 3:12–18). Yet whereas Daniel's friends were divinely rescued (3:23–27), Revelation warns that many faithful Christians of the current time will die (Rev. 13:7, 15). This text indicates power and intention to kill, not that literally no Christians would survive (cf. 1 Cor. 15:51; 1 Thess. 4:15; cf. Mark 13:20). But certainly no Christian may count on surviving![7]

Sorcerers and magical practices in pagan religion were pervasive in the Mediterranean world. The association of signs and sorcery with the imperial cult may have been less obvious to John's audience, though some can be adduced. Various sources confirm the claim that priests of some cults staged wonders like moving or speaking statues and thunder or fire, often using machines. For example, Lucian explains how the false prophet Alexander made a fake god speak (*Alexander* 26), while some church fathers commented that demons could make statues appear to speak (Athenagoras, 26–27). Some emperors also reportedly employed machines like

---

4. Beasley-Murray, *Revelation*, 216; cf. Bowman, *First Christian Drama*, 87. Peterson, *Reversed Thunder*, 123, describes it as "a clumsy counterfeit" of the true Lamb. Dragons were thought to make hissing sounds, but speaking "like a dragon" simply connects him with Satan (Aune, *Revelation*, 2:757).

5. Rissi, *Time and History*, 62, 69, 84. Roloff, *Revelation*, 161, traces this view back to Johann Heinrich Jung-Stilling (1740–1817).

6. Kraybill, *Imperial Cult and Commerce*, 28. Romans feared to offend images in temples; see e.g., Livy, 36.20.3.

7. Cf. Caird, *Commentary on Revelation*, 177; as well as demands for apostasy or death in Dan. 3:13–20; 6:10–13; 1 Macc. 1:50–51.

these to achieve such effects and link themselves with Zeus as hurlers of thunder.[8]

Babylonian and Greco-Roman magic included rituals to seek to animate images; an entire branch of magic, called theurgy, specialized in animating statues so they could give oracles.[9] The most important function of these signs is that they continued the parody on God and his agents (cf. 13:13 with 11:5). As Christ died and lived again (2:8), so the second beast claimed for the first beast (13:14); the coming of the breath of life to the sea beast's image (13:15) parodies the breath of life experienced by resurrected saints (11:11). No image of Christ needs to be revived, however; the worship of images was a purely pagan practice.

Such activities do not surprise Jesus' followers. Jesus warned that false prophets would perform signs in the end time (Matt. 24:24), and Paul recognized that the man of lawlessness (whether as an individual or a composite line) would perform such signs (2 Thess. 2:9). Even ancient Israelite law recognized that false prophets could exercise wonders (Ex. 7:11) or predict signs (Deut. 13:1–2).[10]

The beast enforces a unity that cuts across all social lines (Rev. 13:16), though the attentive reader will remember that God's judgment also cuts across just such distinctions (6:15; 11:18). The use of a mark to enforce national or empire-wide unity already had a long history known to John's audience. Ptolemy IV Philopator, ruler of Egypt, required Jewish people in his realm to be enrolled in a census and to be branded with an ivy leaf, the symbol of Dionysus (3 Macc. 2:28–29).[11] Deissmann cites the imperial seal or mark (*charagma*, same word as used in Rev. 13:16–17) stamped on commercial documents.[12] One could do little in commerce (13:17) without handling such a "mark," because allusions to the emperor's divinity appeared on many coins and even shipping bills and other documents.[13]

---

8. See Steven J. Scherrer, "Signs and Wonders in the Imperial Cult: A New Look at a Roman Religious Institution in the Light of Rev 13:13–15," *JBL* 103 (1984): 599–610; Roloff, *Revelation*, 163; Talbert, *Apocalypse*, 56–57. Weaker suggestions appear in Ramsay, *Letters to the Seven Churches*, 100–103; Ford, *Revelation*, 224. For emperors, see Dio Cassius, 59.28.6; Dionysius of Halicarnassus, 1.71.3.

9. See especially Aune, *Revelation*, 2:762–64. Cf. statues weeping in Livy, 40.19.2, and speaking in Dionysius of Halicarnassus, 8.56.2–3.

10. The Antichrist performs signs and raises the dead in Sib. Or. 3.66–67 (possibly a Christian interpolation, but in a pre-Christian context). Caird, *Commentary on Revelation*, 172, cites other sources and suggests here a "false Elijah," an apt forerunner of the "false Messiah."

11. Kraybill, *Imperial Cult and Commerce*, 137, finds this the primary allusion.

12. G. Adolf Deissmann, *Bible Studies*, tr. A. Grieve (Edinburgh: T. & T. Clark, 1923), 242–46. Followed also by Caird, *Commentary on Revelation*, 173; Collins, *Crisis and Catharsis*, 125.

13. Kraybill, *Imperial Cult and Commerce*, 137–39. Though it tells us little about John's day, in the middle third century A.D. the imperial government went so far as to require certificates

This mark stands in direct contrast to the seal of 7:3–4, which alludes to a "mark" on the righteous in Ezekiel 9:4–6. Whereas the mark on the righteous was to protect them in Ezekiel (cf. also Gen. 4:15; Ps. Sol. 15:6–7), the idea of a mark of destruction on the forehead of the wicked also predates Revelation (Ps. Sol. 15:8–9, where the mark is literally a "sign"). Both Ezekiel's mark on the righteous and the mark on the wicked in the Psalms of Solomon are symbolic marks visible only to God and his angels, not to people.

Whereas the symbolic mark of protection or judgment was normally on the forehead (Ezek. 9:4; Ps. Sol. 15:9), John adds here the "right hand." This may imply a pagan parody on the Jewish practice of wearing boxes of Scripture (called *tefillin* or phylacteries) on the forehead and left hand as a sign of loyalty to God's covenant.[14] Perhaps more important is the idea of a slave brand, though branding on the forehead was a sign of disgrace rather than loyalty; similar is the idea of branding soldiers on the hands as a sign of loyalty.[15] Enslavement to the system of the beast cuts across all class distinctions (Rev. 13:16), as will judgment (6:15).

A mid-third-century emperor demanded certificates of sacrifice to the emperor to participate in commerce and escape prosecution; he likely sought to eradicate Christians. Many Christians compromised by bribing officials or by using other practices; some preferred death and were accordingly executed.[16] Even in John's day, however, one could not handle money without involvement in the imperial system.[17] To withdraw from an economic system permeated with imperial worship—even to withdraw from trade guilds, whose meetings included meat offered to idols—was in many cities economic suicide. Well-to-do Jewish communities in cities like Sardis had much to lose by boycotting the system, and Christian merchants as a smaller minority would lose even more.[18] Under other circumstances, a blockade preventing some from buying and selling could lead to their starvation (1 Macc. 13:49).

---

proving that people had offered pagan sacrifices (*P. Oxy.* 1464; *P. Ryl.* 12); see also Ramsay, *Letters to the Seven Churches*, 106; Kenneth Scott Latourette, *A History of the Expansion of Christianity*, 5 vols.; vol. 1: *The First Five Centuries* (Grand Rapids: Zondervan, 1970), 148–49.

14. E.g., Ford, *Revelation*, 225; Collins, *Crisis and Catharsis*, 125.

15. Caird, *Commentary on Revelation*, 173; Ford, *Revelation*, 215. Soldiers normally served at least two decades. Cf. also the custom of branding devotees in some eastern cults (Cullmann, *The State*, 77).

16. A. M. H. Jones, *A History of Rome Through the Fifth Century*; vol. 2: *The Empire* (New York: Walker, 1970), 327.

17. In Hermas, *Vis.* 3.6.5–7, some would deny Christ to maintain their businesses; for idolatry's relation to money, see Richard, *Apocalypse*, 116.

18. See Kraybill, *Imperial Cult and Commerce*, 197.

But God would supply his people's needs, miraculously if need be (Rev. 12:6, 14). Meanwhile, whereas many accept the mark to be able to engage in commerce (13:17), every following mention of the "mark" in Revelation implies the judgments its recipients merit (14:9–11; 16:2; 19:20; 20:4). Those with faith to believe God's warnings recognize that despite the world's perspective, the saints are really better off in the long run.

What is the number of the beast's name? Some scholars understandably think that the meaning made sense to the first audience but is now forever lost.[19] Enigmatic riddles were common in prophecies (e.g., Sib. Or. 3.812; Mark 13:14), and the meanings of some riddles clear to the original audience are now lost (e.g., Phaedrus, 3.1.7). But in most cases we should not give up so quickly. That 13:18 invites the hearer to interpret the riddle implies that the answer was not inaccessible at least to believers in the seven churches, even if the answer proves somewhat less obvious than in the parallel invitation of 17:9.[20]

Ancients were adept at the use of symbolic numbers, of which Revelation includes several (e.g., 7:4–8). The number 666 is a triangular number, with the root 36; 36 is also a triangular number with the root 8. Since the root of triangular numbers provide their significance, "8" may prepare the reader for the eighth ruler of 17:11, generally agreed to be a new Nero.[21] The number 666 is one of only four doubly triangular numbers between 100 and 1000; perhaps less relevant, numbers that are both squares and triangles (as is 36) are also rare (the first three are 1, 36, and 1225). Those interested in ancient numeric speculation would be familiar with 666.[22]

Probably more important, six could also function as a parody of seven, hence 666 could imply evil (Irenaeus, *Her.* 5.28.2; 5.29.2).[23] Interestingly, John's audience may know that "Jesus," the true Christ, yields 888.

---

19. So Guthrie, *Relevance*, 106. Riddles were common (e.g., Josephus, *Apion* 1.111, 114–15; Matt. 24:15).

20. The eschatologically discerning may be an apocalyptic motif; see 2 Bar. 27:15; 28:1–2; 48:33; Mark 13:14; esp. Gregory K. Beale, "The Danielic Background for Revelation 13:18 and 17:9," *TynBul* 31 (1980): 163–70. Such riddles appear in other Jewish prophetic traditions (Sib. Or. 1.141, 145–46), whose meaning has been lost.

21. Rissi, *Time and History*, 76. But "8" also can symbolize a new creation (Gr. Ezra 4:39).

22. See Bauckham, *Climax of Prophecy*, 390–94. The number 666 is also about two-thirds of 1000 (technically two-thirds of one should also be added to it), and Revelation sometimes calculates judgments in thirds (8:7–12; 9:15, 18).

23. Walvoord, *Revelation*, 210, develops this view in part by noting that Nebuchadnezzar's image was 60 by 6 cubits (Dan. 3:1); this proposal fits the context (Rev. 13:15), but given the other proposals there is not sufficient reason for us to appeal to that source for the 6's here. (It could almost as easily constitute an allusion to Solomon's wealth in 1 Kings 10:14; 2 Chron. 9:13; or an Adonikamite, as in Ezra 2:13—neither of which is likely.)

Although the coincidence would not have been as obvious in ancient Mediterranean numeric systems as it is today, ancients using base ten would not miss the significance of the threefold repetition of sixes (13:18 spells it out).[24]

But it is also possible that John wants us to look for a particular name; his invitation to the reader to "calculate" the name looks like a technical invitation to *gematria*.[25] In this period many Jews and some early Christians practiced *gematria*, interpreting words according to the numerical value of their constituent Hebrew letters.[26] At first glance, narrowing the list to a particular name seems impossible without knowing the key to the riddle; even in the late second century many names could fit 666 (Irenaeus, *Her.* 5.30), and suggestions have multiplied since then.[27]

But one need develop no special methods to arrive at the figure of 666; Greek and Hebrew both used letters as numerals, and that numeric system was well-established. Names often appear as numbers in graffiti recovered from the Roman empire, and it is said that a macabre play on the number of "Nero Caesar" in Greek letters circulated throughout the empire (Suetonius, *Nero* 39).[28] Calculating names of rulers as numbers (based on first initials) was standard practice in one Jewish prophecy tradition (Sib. Or. 5.14–42; 11.29–30, 91–92, 114, 141–42, 190, 208, 256; Bk. 12 passim), which in this manner also surveyed all the emperors from Julius to Hadrian.[29]

---

24. Only 1 percent of the numbers between 100 and 1000 fit this pattern. In Roman numerals 666 includes all the characters to 500 once (DCLXVI). A deity's secret name may be calculated at 9999 (*PGM*, 2.129). It is possible the name would be calculated on the market abacus used for buying and selling (cf. E. M. Bruins, "The Number of the Beast," *Nederlands Theologisch Tijdschrift* 23 [1969]: 401–7; *NTA* 14:206), but not necessary.

25. So Cullmann, *The State*, 80.

26. E.g., Sib. Or. 1.141–46; 3.24–26; 5:14–42; 11:29–30, 91–92, 114, 141–42, 190, 208, 256, 274; book 12 passim; Tr. Shem 3:1–2; *b. Ned.* 32a; *Pes. Rab Kah.* 2:8; Irenaeus, *Her.* 1.3.2; 1.14–15; Ep. Barn. 9.8. Numbers are used to spell person's names in Lucian, *Alexander the False Prophet* 11.

27. See the listing in Caird, *Commentary on Revelation*, 174–76. Among more recent suggestions: the abbreviations on Vespasian's coins transliterated into Hebrew (W. G. Baines, "The Number of the Beast in Revelation 13:18," *Heythrop Journal* 16 [1975]: 195–96); "Nikolaitēs" in Hebrew, recalling the Nicolaitans (Michael Topham, "Hanniqola'itēs," *ExpTim* 98 [Nov. 1986]: 44–45); "you should destroy" in Hebrew (Michael Oberweis, "Die Bedeutung der neutestamentlichen 'Rätselzahlen' 666 (Apk 13:18) und 153 (Joh 21:11)," *ZNW* 77 [1986]: 226–41). "Babylon" unfortunately comes to only 1285 in Greek.

28. For examples of graffiti, see G. Adolf Deissmann, *Light From the Ancient East* (Grand Rapids: Baker, 1978), 276–78.

29. See Bauckham, *Climax of Prophecy*, 385, citing Sib. Or. 5.12–51. Jewish astrologers found significance in any letters used in a person's name (Tr. Shem 3:1–2; 6:1; 7:13; 8:11; 9:1; 10:1; 11:1; 12:1).

The majority of commentators find an allusion to Nero Caesar's name as written in Hebrew characters here.[30] Other commentators object that John writes in Greek rather than in Hebrew; but this is not the only place where John employs a wordplay requiring some knowledge of Hebrew (9:11; 16:16). Further, some other documents calculate the numbers of Greek words in Hebrew letters (3 Bar. 4:3–7, 10, including "dragon").[31] Some commentators also doubt that the spelling of "Nero Caesar," which comes out to "666," was the most natural way to spell the name in Hebrew; but John had other reasons (noted above) to spell it so as to come up with "666," and archaeologists have uncovered a document from the Judean desert that spells the name precisely this way.[32] Interestingly, some copyists preferred for "666" the questionable reading "616," which is another way that one could count "Nero Caesar" (omitting a debatable letter). This change suggests that the scribes knew the tradition of the name that the number should spell, and respelled it accordingly![33]

When the people of the empire played on Nero's name in Greek, they calculated not only the number of his name but linked his name with an appropriate phrase that yielded the same number ("he killed his mother"—Nero was a matricide). "Beast" (*therion*) can be transliterated into Hebrew as "*TRYVN*," which also comes out to 666; the number "of the beast" is not surprisingly literally the "beast"! (Note again that the less original reading "616"—written in Hebrew letters as "*TRYV*"—can transliterate the Greek "*theriou*," that is, the possessive form "of the beast.")[34] Many Jewish Christians moved to Asia after the fall of Judea in the war of A.D. 66–70, and many of them would have known some Hebrew. But undoubtedly John writes in a riddle the answer to which many would already have known.[35]

---

30. E.g., Bowman, *First Christian Drama*, 87; Beasley-Murray, *Revelation*, 219–20; John A. T. Robinson, *Can We Trust the New Testament?* (Grand Rapids: Eerdmans, 1977), 70–71; Koester, *Introduction*, 2:255; Boring, *Revelation*, 163.

31. See further Gideon Bohak, "Greek-Hebrew Gematrias in 3 Baruch and in Revelation," *Journal for the Study of the Pseudepigrapha* 7 (1990): 119–21.

32. Thus newer commentators (Bauckham, *Climax of Prophecy*, 388–89; Boring, *Revelation*, 163) cite DJD 2:101, plate 29 line 1. For the objection about Greek see Tenney, *Revelation*, 19; about the spelling (which he regards as unclear even in the wilderness document), see Beale, *Revelation*, 719–20.

33. Metzger, *Breaking the Code*, 76–77.

34. See Bauckham, *Climax of Prophecy*, 388–90; Roloff, *Revelation*, 166; Oberweis, "Bedeutung." ("Caesar is God" also comes out to 616; see Deissmann, *Light*, 278 n. 3; Schlier, *Principalities*, 89.) This would be more than an interesting wordplay; Jews and Greeks both used plays on words as arguments. Because the founder of Rome was raised by beasts, Sib. Or. 11.274 calls him "the son of the beast."

35. Bauckham, *Climax of Prophecy*, 403–4, makes a strong case from Asc. Isa. 4:12–14 that the numeric tradition behind Rev. 13:18 was already circulating among early Christians.

Bridging Contexts

FREQUENT ERRORS IN **understanding this pas-sage.** One error in applying the text to today's world is to ignore its broader message for the sake of a particular prophetic reading that requires one to read many apocalyptic-prophetic texts literally. Thus, for example, to harmonize his interpretations of various texts, Lindsey suggests two Antichrists in the end time: a European who rules from Rome and a Jewish religious prophet ruling in Israel.[36]

Another danger is to fixate on this text apart from its context in the rest of Revelation. Thus, some who rightly warn of end-time deception unfortunately issue a blanket condemnation of all signs and wonders. But this is an inconsistent application of the text; if we take seriously the false signs of the devil's agents (13:13), we should also take seriously the true signs of Christ's agents (11:5–6). Signs by themselves can be positive or negative; what enables us to discern true prophets from false ones is not to discard prophets altogether, but to evaluate them by their moral character. The point is that we know them by their message and their fruit, not by their gifts (Deut. 13:1–5; Matt. 7:15–23).

Some have associated restraint from buying and selling with a sophisticated banking system.[37] Unfortunately as a young Bible college student I asked about these matters at my local bank, where the poor tellers not only knew nothing about it, but grew anxious that perhaps I knew something they didn't! (They need not have worried.) Many prophecy teachers have speculated on how the Antichrist will install a literal mark, noting (correctly) that computer technology exists that can do so.[38] That some future Antichrist may seek to use a mark is possible, especially if he or she acts in direct defiance of the book of Revelation. Thus, for example, members of a white supremacist group that planned to bomb every state capital and poison the water supplies of several American cities with fifty gallons of cyanide showed their loyalty to that group with a mark (an old Klan tattoo of an "N" with a drop of blood on it).[39]

---

36. Lindsey, *New World Coming*, 103. A form of the double Antichrist view seems to originate with a thirteenth-century monk (Kyle, *The Last Days*, 50).

37. The idea of sophisticated banking was not, however, beyond ancient readers; Roman banks could settle debts by transferring credits in their own books, and devised some basic ways to do the same with other banks (M. Cary and T. J. Haarhoff, *Life and Thought in the Greek and Roman World*, 4th ed. [London: Methuen & Company, 1946], 126).

38. For views among conspiracy theorists associated with right-wing militias, such as 666 as supermarket bar codes or the current favorite, computer microchips implanted beneath the skin, see Richard Abanes, *American Militias* (Downers Grove, Ill.: InterVarsity, 1996), 92.

39. "Plot Against SPLC Alleged," *Southern Poverty Law Center Intelligence Report* (Spring 1998), 4.

But speculating on what some antichrist figure may do, especially in light of this text, is not the same as interpreting the meaning of this text. Such interpretations fail to interpret this passage in the context of the rest of Revelation, or Revelation in the context of symbolism that already existed in its day. Taken by itself, 13:16 can refer to a literal mark, a possibility that may have seemed plausible in John's day no less than in our own.[40] But the context of the rest of the book qualifies the likelihood of this reading. Note that we take the other names written on people in Revelation symbolically (3:12; 17:5; 19:16; 22:4), probably even with reference to the 144,000 (7:3–4; 14:1; for their symbolism, see comment on 7:1–8). If every other mark in Revelation is symbolic, should we take this one literally simply because that is the longstanding tradition of many prophecy teachers?

In translating the principles of the text as lessons for our own situations, we need to remember how concretely the text would have spoken in John's day. The demand that inhabitants of the empire worship the emperor's image (and other statues of deities) was a dramatic insult to the honor due God alone. Today the world often offers more subtle opportunities for allegiance to God's competitors or ways to deny God's supremacy in our lives. The early Christians were not called to tear down physical idols and insult their neighbors' beliefs (which would have proved an ineffective witness in any case), but they could not share in their idolatry. If Christ is Lord of our lives, we must graciously part company with much of what our contemporaries value, not only morally but recreationally and in other respects—misfits in our culture though we may appear.

The number 666. Prophecy teachers have forced many names to come to 666. Naturally some sixteenth-century interpreters came up with either the Pope or Martin Luther, depending on which side of the Reformation debate they stood on.[41] An academic commentator divides 2520 (which is double 1260) into four (for Daniel's four empires), then adds 36 as the square of 6 to achieve 666.[42] Of course Hitler could be made to arrive at 666.[43] Among the more creative suggestions of the late twentieth century was the view that Ronald Reagan's name implied this number (having six letters in his first, middle, and last names)![44]

---

40. On the possibility of a literal ink mark used for market control in the Roman Empire, see E. A. Judge, "The Mark of the Beast, Revelation 13:16," *TynBul* 42 (1991): 158–60.

41. Morrice, "John the Seer," 44. Most Catholics, however, viewed the Antichrist as a future individual (Kyle, *The Last Days*, 62).

42. Corsini, *Apocalypse*, 239. Simply halving 1260 and adding 36 would be simpler.

43. Kyle, *The Last Days*, 111.

44. He later moved to a home in Los Angeles, the address of which had to be changed from 666 to 668 St. Cloud Drive (*CT* [Feb. 3, 1989], 40); yet he seems an unlikely candidate for the final Antichrist today.

One current favorite is the allegation of 666 on some international product codes, which relates to buying and selling (though not yet on the hand and forehead).[45] Others have suggested the nine-digit Social Security number or an eighteen-digit figure; thus one California resident fought in court to prevent his daughter receiving a Social Security number.[46] But the Greek text does not allow us to read six plus six plus six (still less half that number), but six hundred sixty-six.

If we adapt the rules to make names conform (say, multiply by seven, add four, then divide by three) we can eventually make any name fit 666.[47] Indeed, everything from biblical scholars (of course!), scientists, and labor unions to Teenage Mutant Ninja Turtles has surfaced as candidates for the Antichrist.[48] A friend downloaded from the Internet fresh speculation about Barney, the oft-loved dinosaur of children's television. If one adds up the potential Roman numerals in "Cute Purple Dinosaur" (counting "U" as "V," hence as 5), one ends up with 100 + 5 + 5 + 50 + 500 + 1 + 5, for a total of 666. We think that one was a joke.

But on a more serious note, Christians who have suffered intense persecution and martyrdom have often supposed that they were suffering the final Tribulation before Christ's return.[49] And why not? They may have been wrong that Christ would return in their generation, but each generation had a right to expect him. Many who now deny that the Lord's coming could have been imminent before Israel's return to the land taught differently before 1948; previously many held that Jesus would return Israel to the land only after his "secret" coming for the saints (i.e., the Rapture).[50]

---

45. Collins, *Crisis and Catharsis*, 13, cites allegations of 666 on some international product codes (referring to Mary Stewart Relfe, *The New Money System "666"* [Montgomery: Ministries, 1982], advertised by Relfe as sequel to her 1981 "#1 International Bestseller" *When Your Money Fails*). In dreams Relfe realized that the Tribulation would begin in 1990 and that Christ would return after Armageddon in 1997 (Relfe, *Economic Advisor* [newsletter; Feb. 28, 1983], as cited in Kyle, *The Last Days*, 120, 224).

46. "Social Security: The 666 Challenge?" *Contemporary Christian* (June 1984), 19. Lindsey, *New World Coming*, 194–95, suggests the literal imprinting of social security numbers on hand or forehead.

47. On mathematical manipulations, see also the critiques of alleged "Bible codes" in John Winston Moore, "Bible Codes, or Matrix of Deception?" *SCP Newsletter* 22 (Fall 1997): 1–2, 8, 14, 16; Hugh Ross, "Cracking the Codes," *Facts and Faith* 11/3 (1997): 10–11; Ben Witherington, "A Cracked Code," *CT* (July 12, 1999), 60). Even accepting the need for elementary text criticism, even for spelling variations, undermines most such "codes" completely.

48. See Robert C. Fuller, *Naming the Antichrist: The History of an American Obsession* (New York: Oxford Univ. Press, 1996); for a briefer survey and comments, see Michael W. Holmes, *1 & 2 Thessalonians*, NIVAC (Grand Rapids: Zondervan, 1998), 241–42, 244.

49. E.g., the Anabaptists; see Kyle, *The Last Days*, 58.

50. See ibid., 108.

From the standpoint of their own experience of martyrdom, many Christians have been engaged in their own final struggle with the forces of Antichrist (see Luke 12:4; 1 John 2:18). When Stalin, for instance, murdered ten to thirty million people in seventeen years, we would have undoubtedly thought him the final Antichrist had we lived in the Ukraine—and we could have been right, God willing. In a future holocaust we will probably think its perpetrator the final Antichrist—and we may be right. But if history surprises us once more, we will be reminded of how the mystery of lawlessness continues its hideous incarnations until the end (2 Thess. 2:7). Because neither we nor Satan know the time of the end, all such antichrists are experienced as antichrists, but what will finally indicate that we have witnessed the final Antichrist will be Jesus' return to wipe him out.

THE SUBTLE PRESENCE of the Antichrist. Billy Graham imagines a situation in which a Christian in the ancient world is offered freedom if he or she will simply engage in a ritual act of offering incense to Caesar. Who would be so stubborn as to choose suffering over such a simple act? But the act constituted "a symbol of a wider disobedience," and Christ summons his true disciples to refuse the compromise as unacceptable.[51]

We do not need an emperor like Domitian to confront this sort of conflict. Some Christians who opposed Hitler and looked for transcultural significance in this text found in the second beast a clear symbol of the totalitarian state's ministry of propaganda.[52] And why not? Satan does not know when Jesus will return (Mark 13:30) and must always have an antichrist in waiting.[53] In a broader sense, this temptation merely mirrors all temptations to assimilate the world's values that deny the kingdom of God. Would the early Christians adopt their society's values (Rev. 2:14, 20; 3:16-18)? Or would they "come out" (18:4)? It is a question that continues to challenge today's church.

By the time Revelation was written, many arrogant rulers had already offered themselves for a portrait of the Antichrist by exalting themselves as gods, such as kings of Babylon (Isa. 14:12-14; Dan. 3:5), Tyre (Ezek. 28:2, 9), Pharaoh (29:3), Antiochus IV Epiphanes (perhaps Dan. 11:36-37), and other pagan rulers (Ps. 82:1, 6-7). In Rome itself, before Domitian came, Gaius Caligula and Nero had exalted themselves as gods. The spirit of the evil empire that exalts

---

51. Graham, *Approaching Hoofbeats*, 33.

52. Cullmann, *The State*, 76.

53. Some Jewish sources also recognized that any generation could prove the final one (e.g., *b. Sanh.* 94a).

itself as god exists in oppressive, totalitarian regimes today. The predictions of George Orwell's dystopian novel, *1984*, failed to take hold in our society by its scheduled date, but other societies have experienced such horrors, and it is not impossible that some of us may confront similar horrors (Matt. 24:9).

But what should frighten us even more is that the same spirit of the self-deifying empire remains in every human heart that seeks to make itself the center of life while burying thoughts of its own mortality. From openings pried for it by earlier transcendentalism to the modern New Age movement, our consumer culture has democratized self-idolatry to include everyone's divinity and freedom to seek self-fulfillment instead of answering to a higher authority.[54]

The real Lamb died in weakness and was raised by God's power; the fake lamb promotes one who pretends to have recovered no less significantly (13:12). Satan's counterfeits derive their false legitimacy from imitating God, so those who do not embrace the hard message of the cross and its suffering are susceptible to succumbing to counterfeits. This happened, for instance, in Germany in the 1930s; Hitler feigned friendliness to church leaders whose position in society had somewhat eroded, and when he came to power "few were more jubilant than Protestant church leaders."[55] But Bonhoeffer's lectures on Christology daringly included "reflections on false messiahs ... a direct challenge to Hitler," who contrasted with "the humiliated and crucified Messiah." Such challenges inevitably drew the ire of the Nazi state.[56] Religion has become increasingly acceptable in recent years in many circles in secular America—but the necessity of the Lamb's cross remains a scandal.

Because Satan's counterfeits imitate God's works, it is not surprising that false signs continue to lead many people astray today; some are fake, whereas others are demonic.[57] One thinks, for example, of psychic healers and perhaps of some modern mind-science techniques.[58] One Catholic scholar

---

54. See "Best-Selling Spirituality," *Mars Hill Audio Report* (Charlottesville, Va.: Berea Publications; 1999).

55. Richard V. Pierard, "Radical Resistance," *Christian History* 32 (1991), 30–33 (p. 30).

56. Clifford Green, "Exploring Bonhoeffer's Writings," *Christian History* 32 (1991): 34–36 (p. 35).

57. For fake signs, see Danny Korem, "Pychic Confession" (video; Korem Productions; promoted through Spiritual Counterfeits Project); Robert Burrows, "Firewalking: The Ultimate Burn," *SCP Newsletter* 14/4 (1989): 5–6.

58. See John Weldon and Zola Levitt, *Psychic Healing* (Chicago: Moody, 1982). Many therapeutic methods associated with New Age concepts remain controversial; see Joe Maxwell, "Nursing's New Age?" *CT* (Feb. 5, 1996), 96–99; *SCP Journal* (Aug. 1978); *SCP Newsletter* 8 (Oct. 1982); *SCP Newsletter* 9 (Sept. 1983). That a PBS special series on Healing and the Mind in Feb. 1993 could report more on meditation techniques from other cultures than on any Christian healing may represent the intense secularism (and Enlightenment hangover) of our culture and the ability of other movements to repackage their practices as merely "cultural" agendas acceptable to secularists.

warns against false apparitions of Christ and Mary that exhibit signs, yet teach what is false.[59] Although God can do anything, it should also be noted that statues that are purported to weep or sweat are not a specifically Christian phenomenon.[60] But missiologists comment on power encounters, noting that, as in the Bible (Ex. 7:11–12; Acts 13:11), God's power is stronger than Satan's.[61] The two witnesses prevailed with their signs until the appointed time of their martyrdom (11:7), and today's church should be able to demonstrate God's power more effectively than occult sources demonstrate theirs.[62]

Persecution for Christ today. We must pray for our brothers and sisters suffering persecution; where possible, we should also work for their protection.[63] Some experts claim that over one hundred thousand people are martyred for Christ each year.[64] Even if that statistic seems inflated in most

59. John Randall, *The Book of Revelation: What Does It Really Say?* (Locust Valley, N.Y.: Living Flame, 1976), 79. On apparitions of Mary, see discussion in *SCP Newsletter* 19 (July 1995); *SCP Newsletter* 20 (Jan. 1995); Elliot Miller and Kenneth Samples, *The Cult of the Virgin: Catholic Mariology and the Apparitions of Mary* (Grand Rapids: Baker, 1992); for a more positive appraisal, see René Laurentin, *Apparitions of the Blessed Virgin Mary Today* (San Francisco: Veritas, Ignatius Press, 1990); Pierre-Marie Théas, *The Faith of Bernadette*, tr. M. Roch (Hamilton, Ont.: Image, 1982).

60. Characteristics associated with some modern sacred statues like weeping (see Livy, 40.19.2; 43.13.4), sweating (see Livy, 27.4.14; Appian, *C.W.* 2.5.36; 4.1.4) or even speaking (Dionysius of Halicarnassus, 8.56.2–3; cf. Euripides, *Iphig. Taur.* 1165–67) are attested in pre-Christian paganism, as are visions of goddesses (Dionysius of Halicarnassus, 8.56.1; Chariton, *Chaer.* 2.2.5; Eric Wolf, "The Virgin of Guadalupe: A Mexican National Symbol," *Journal of American Folklore* 71 [1958]: 34–39); by contrast, almost always only God and angels, but never deceased persons, appear in biblical visions.

61. See David A. Powlison, *Power Encounters: Reclaiming Spiritual Warfare* (Grand Rapids: Baker, 1994); Stan Guthrie, "Muslim Mission Breakthrough," *CT* (Dec. 13, 1993), 20–26 (p. 26); essays on "Signs and Wonders," *Mountain Movers* (April 1988); Judy Graner, "Appointment with a Piachi," *MM* (Sept. 1993), 16; Robert Cobb, "To Battle With Hoes and Machetes," *MM* (April 1993), 14–15; Mel Tari, *Like a Mighty Wind*, 2d ed. (Carol Stream, Ill.: Creation House, 1972), passim.

62. Compare the *bhaghat* (witch doctor) in Mandala, India, who asked the true God to answer his request by fire, and Jesus was the only one to respond (Paul Eshleman with Carolyn E. Phillips, *I Just Saw Jesus* [Laguna Niguel, Calif.: The Jesus Project, 1985], 114–15).

63. *International Christian Concern* in Washington, D.C., provides regular reports on persecution around the world (cf. the "Top-Ten Priority Watch List of Countries Where Christians Are Persecuted," *ICC Concern* (Aug. 1998); Christian Solidarity International in Corona del Mar, Calif., also provides information and help. International "Days of Prayer" for persecuted churches have drawn an estimated 200,000 churches to prayer (*CT* [Oct. 5, 1998], 17).

64. David Barrett estimates that over 160,000 Christians were martyred in 1996 ("Annual Statistical Table on Global Mission: 1997," *International Bulletin of Missionary Research* [Jan. 1997], 25). On persecution in the modern era, see Paul A. Marshall, *Their Blood Cries Out: The Worldwide Tragedy of Modern Christians Who Are Dying for Their Faith* (Dallas: Word, 1997).

regions of the world, many are dying for their faith; I have personally talked with some of the survivors, who saw colleagues murdered.

Examples of severe persecution today are numerous.[65] Some have to do with the group from which the believer is converted, which responds with hostility to the conversion. In a small Asian country an assassin named Ranjit, who had gunned down many officers, was converted through the witness of a pastor. Through this new believer's preaching and changed life many other people were converted, but the terrorist group of which he had been a part demanded that he continue to work with them. When he refused, they came to the pastor's home and demanded that he come out. The pastor hid him and was about to be killed in his place, but rather than allow his pastor to die, he came out and handed himself over. Ranjit was beaten to death, his final message being, "Tell my pastor I died a believer."[66]

More often, Christians are executed or tortured for their witness. Taken to prison for the fifth time, one witness who had been preaching Christ for twenty years was placed in a hot, eighteen-by-twenty-four-foot room, with no windows and twenty-five other prisoners, each fed two bowls of rice a day. Once his nine-hour daily interrogations began, he preached to his interrogators for half a year; meanwhile many of his cellmates were being converted after interrogation hours. His next prison station also brought many converts, so he was moved to a labor camp where 120 men shared two toilets in a cell one hundred meters square. Yet he was eventually released.

A man this witness led to Christ in prison was released shortly after his conversion and went back to evangelize his unreached tribal group, in one month winning five villages with over 750 people.[67] Christians who are committed to suffer for their faith make bold witnesses! An American missionary was taken aback by the vibrant witness of an Iranian Christian who remarked to him, "It is a shame for a believer to die of natural causes."[68] The courage of our brothers and sisters should summon our attention to endure joyfully the much smaller opposition most of us currently face.

In some places believers are slaughtered simply because they are Christians. Reports abound of Christians crucified and enslaved in the Sudan; someone I know witnessed sales receipts openly marked, "Christian slaves."

---

65. See accounts in *Mountain Movers* (April 1995); (May 1995). Recently, in Peru, see John Maust, *Peace and Hope in the Corner of the Dead* (Miami: Latin America Mission, 1987); "Sauñe Brothers Murdered in Peru," *Mountain Movers* (Feb. 1993), 11. Under the old Soviet regime, believers could be confined to psychiatric hospitals (Lori Cydilo, "The Insanity of Russian Psychiatry," *WPR* [Aug. 1993], 44).

66. Ronald Q. Tuttle, "Tell My Pastor I Died a Believer," *Mountain Movers* (Feb. 1992), 4.

67. "The Harvest God Is Bringing About," *Mountain Movers* (March 1995), 16–17, 26.

68. Jerry Parsley, "Acts Revisited," *Mountain Movers* (Dec. 1993), 26.

Such suffering abounded throughout the past century; when the Japanese conquered Korea (1937–1940), they "ordered Christians to worship at their Shinto shrines. Many Christians refused and were imprisoned and tortured."[69]

The church in China offers many examples of suffering. George Chen was forced to work all day deep in a cesspool filled with human waste, but he rejoiced because the odor kept others away, allowing him to pray and sing as he worked all day. While he was in prison, the churches he had planted grew from 300 to 5,000.[70] "While the underground church does not want persecution, they are not afraid. It is a way of life for them."[71] One American observer, commenting on the bold and joyful witness of suffering Chinese Christians, remarked, "I have sat at the feet of believers in China who are being fitted even now for those white robes that will adorn the saints. Compared to their finery, I feel spiritually naked."[72]

As a zealous young Christian sometimes beaten or threatened with weapons for my witness, I looked forward to a martyr's crown by 1980. In his great mercy, God has spared my life for other work for the moment. But I dare never forget that as Christians, our lives in this world remain forfeit because we belong to another world (Mark 8:34–38). One of my gravest concerns is that, despite biblical teachings, most Western Christians remain unprepared to face martyrdom relatively joyfully—and perhaps to face it at all.

The temptation to compromise. The economic temptation in this passage (13:17) also remains relevant. Christians in Thyatira already could identify with the economic conspiracy between imperial religion and commerce (see comment on 2:18).[73] Christians after Constantine still faced such pressures for compromise. For example, John Chrysostom regularly criticized wasteful use of wealth and scandalously continued to live simply even as bishop of Constantinople; he finally alienated some other powerful bishops and the sociopolitical elite, ultimately leading to his banishment and death.[74] Likewise, the wealthy heir Olympias freely gave her money to the poor

---

69. Johnson, *Revelation*, 41, citing Han Woo Keun, *History of Korea*, ed. G. K. Muntz, tr. Lee Kyen-Shik (Seoul: Eul-Woo, 1970), 496. For Christian suffering in Japanese prison camps, see Rodney Clapp, "Laboratories of the Soul," *CT* (March 7, 1986), 23–26.

70. Timothy C. Morgan, "A Tale of China's Two Churches," *CT* (July 13, 1998), 30–39 (p. 38).

71. David Neff, interview with Don Argue, "China Mission: More Than 'Ping-Pong Diplomacy,'" *CT* (July 13, 1998), 34–38 (p. 37).

72. Karen M. Feaver, "Chinese Lessons: What Chinese Christians Taught a U.S. Congressional Delegation," *CT* (May 16, 1994), 33–34.

73. Hemer, *Letters to the Seven Churches*, 126–27.

74. See Robert A. Krupp, "Golden Tongue and Iron Will," *Christian History* 44 (1994): 6–11 (pp. 7, 9–11); Carl A. Volz, "The Genius of Chrysostom's Preaching," *Christian History* 44 (1994): 24–26 (p. 25).

despite opposition; her continuing support of her bishop, John Chrysostom, finally led to her banishment and the seizure of the remainder of her wealth.[75]

Insightful Christians today might likewise recognize the links that appear in many professions (notably in the entertainment industry, politics, and education) between economic success and reflecting the values of the broader society. Economic compromises like those some of the churches in Asia Minor made (to "buy and sell") are common in our society. One *Christianity Today* interview suggests that even though bankruptcy rates are 18.6 percent higher in counties with casinos than in other counties, and suicide rates average four times higher in heavy gambling areas, the government gets benefits "and the gambling industry even gives money to churches and charities. Their goal is to silence you by compromising you."[76]

But is this different from any of us who tell people what they want to hear about themselves rather than telling them God's message? Some ministers have been afraid of alienating their economic support base. One Baptist I led to Christ asked his pastor why he had never explained genuine conversion from the pulpit; the pastor expressed his happiness that the young man had found his way to Christ but noted that he had to be careful what he preached lest he offend the deacons. To be sure, we want to communicate truth in the most strategic and sensitive ways possible. But when we are more concerned about what people think about us, whether they continue supporting our church, and so forth, than whether we are helping them, we engage in the same kinds of compromise as some of our spiritual predecessors.

Even in our religious subculture we often confront the temptation to tell people what they want to hear rather than what we genuinely believe God is saying. Many ministers during the Civil Rights Movement failed to protest racial segregation because they might lose their job;[77] many ministers today feel forced by other "politically correct" constraints on the right or the left. Job security has often mattered more than justice (John 19:12–16), and even religious professionals have made decisions based on professional advancement (Judg. 18:18–20). If status and materialism so entice us, how would we fare under persecution?[78]

Indeed, every time we buy something we don't need because our neighbors have one, we compromise with the world system's values. Can we be

---

75. Mary L. Hammack et al., "Other Women of the Early Church," *Christian History* 17 (1988): 12–18 (p. 18).

76. Thomas Grey and Kevin Miller, "How to Fight Gambling," *CT* (May 18, 1998), 39.

77. See Douglas Hudgins in Charles Marsh, *God's Long Summer* (Princeton: Princeton Univ. Press, 1997), 82–115.

78. Graham, *Approaching Hoofbeats*, 106–8, also notes that today many worship not false religions in the traditional sense but materialism; an idol is whatever apart from God dominates our lives.

frivolous when we know that 40,000 people die every day of starvation, that fifty cents could provide food for a child for one day in some famine-stricken areas, that the extra hours worked for that squandered money could have been spent with our children or in witnessing to our neighbors?

If, as suggested above, the mark on the wicked (13:16–18) is symbolic like all the other marks in Revelation (3:12; 7:3; 14:1; 17:5; 19:16; 22:4), then John is telling us about it less to satisfy our end-time curiosity than to warn us about compromise. This mark may function like a slave brand, possibly like the seal in 7:3–4; whereas the 144,000 "servants of God" belong to God and Christ, those who take the mark of the beast are its servants. The beast settles for nothing less than a slave brand, "an imitation of the invisible seal of baptism recognizable only by faith."[79]

Revelation allows for no divided allegiance: We must decide between God and the world and between what each side values. Yet we cannot read this passage's warning properly without also grasping the rest of the book: Every Babylon of the past has fallen, and so will every empire that oppresses us (18:2; 19:2). The future belongs not to Babylon but to the faithful, whose home is the Jerusalem to come (21:2–8).

---

79. Schlier, *Principalities,* 88.

Revelation 14:1–20

THEN I LOOKED, and there before me was the Lamb, standing on Mount Zion, and with him 144,000 who had his name and his Father's name written on their foreheads. ²And I heard a sound from heaven like the roar of rushing waters and like a loud peal of thunder. The sound I heard was like that of harpists playing their harps. ³And they sang a new song before the throne and before the four living creatures and the elders. No one could learn the song except the 144,000 who had been redeemed from the earth. ⁴These are those who did not defile themselves with women, for they kept themselves pure. They follow the Lamb wherever he goes. They were purchased from among men and offered as firstfruits to God and the Lamb. ⁵No lie was found in their mouths; they are blameless.

⁶Then I saw another angel flying in midair, and he had the eternal gospel to proclaim to those who live on the earth—to every nation, tribe, language and people. ⁷He said in a loud voice, "Fear God and give him glory, because the hour of his judgment has come. Worship him who made the heavens, the earth, the sea and the springs of water."

⁸A second angel followed and said, "Fallen! Fallen is Babylon the Great, which made all the nations drink the maddening wine of her adulteries."

⁹A third angel followed them and said in a loud voice: "If anyone worships the beast and his image and receives his mark on the forehead or on the hand, ¹⁰he, too, will drink of the wine of God's fury, which has been poured full strength into the cup of his wrath. He will be tormented with burning sulfur in the presence of the holy angels and of the Lamb. ¹¹And the smoke of their torment rises for ever and ever. There is no rest day or night for those who worship the beast and his image, or for anyone who receives the mark of his name." ¹²This calls for patient endurance on the part of the saints who obey God's commandments and remain faithful to Jesus.

¹³Then I heard a voice from heaven say, "Write: Blessed are the dead who die in the Lord from now on."

"Yes," says the Spirit, "they will rest from their labor, for their deeds will follow them."

¹⁴ I looked, and there before me was a white cloud, and seated on the cloud was one "like a son of man" with a crown of gold on his head and a sharp sickle in his hand. ¹⁵Then another angel came out of the temple and called in a loud voice to him who was sitting on the cloud, "Take your sickle and reap, because the time to reap has come, for the harvest of the earth is ripe." ¹⁶So he who was seated on the cloud swung his sickle over the earth, and the earth was harvested.

¹⁷Another angel came out of the temple in heaven, and he too had a sharp sickle. ¹⁸Still another angel, who had charge of the fire, came from the altar and called in a loud voice to him who had the sharp sickle, "Take your sharp sickle and gather the clusters of grapes from the earth's vine, because its grapes are ripe." ¹⁹The angel swung his sickle on the earth, gathered its grapes and threw them into the great winepress of God's wrath. ²⁰They were trampled in the winepress outside the city, and blood flowed out of the press, rising as high as the horses' bridles for a distance of 1,600 stadia.

THE SCENE IN Revelation 14 suddenly shifts to a new vision, a stark contrast to what preceded it. After the horrific vision of the beast requiring his name on the foreheads of his followers (13:16–18), we see again the 144,000 followers of the Lamb (cf. 7:1–8), with the name of God and of the Lamb on their foreheads (14:1).

The Army on Mount Zion (14:1–5)

ONE CAN THINK of a number of Jesus' name, contrasted with that of the beast just mentioned; whatever name comes to "666," there is no dispute that the name "Jesus" comes to "888." Nevertheless, Revelation mentions the name rather than a number, saving the import of symbolic numbers for the army of 144,000.[1] The glorious fate of these martyrs contrasts starkly with the fate of those who took the beast's mark and thereby opted to be damned (14:9–11). The warning against compromise is clear.

The action of judgments, finished with the seventh trumpet (11:15), is resumed with angelic proclamations of judgment in 14:6–12. Framed between these sections is a picture of the woman and her offspring persecuted by the

---

1. For the significance of the contrast between 144 (as in 144,000) and 666, see comment on 21:17.

dragon and his offspring. The dragon makes war on the woman's seed (12:17), a war depicted in more thorough detail in 13:5–7, in the context of the world's idolatry (13:1–18). Now the narration returns to the woman's offspring, who preferred bearing the Lamb's name to the beast's (13:17–14:1) and who preferred obeying God's commands (12:17) to the fake phylacteries of the worshipers of the beast (13:16). The 144,000 portray the woman's seed not as persecuted saints but as a conquering army—now that they have overcome (15:2) by martyrdom.[2] Like their Lord the Lamb, they have crushed the serpent's head precisely by letting it strike their heel (Gen. 3:15; cf. Rom. 16:20).

Perhaps most significant for our observation here is the location of the 144,000. They are with the Lamb on Mount Zion, God's dwelling in the present (Ps. 74:2; 76:2) and the future (Zech. 2:10; 8:3), a place of Israel's hopes for salvation (Ps. 53:6; 69:35; 87:5; 102:13) and triumph (Ps. 110:2; Obad. 21; 2 Bar. 40:1). Although Jerusalem after A.D. 70 lay mostly in shambles and the nations were now trampling God's sanctuary even in a symbolic sense (Rev. 11:2), John's audience knew that the prophets had promised Zion's restoration (Isa. 1:27; 4:5; 46:13; 51:3; 62:11; Mic. 4:2, 7). God would dwell in the midst of Zion as the triumphant warrior who delivered them (Zeph. 3:15–19). He would make war from Mount Zion (Isa. 31:4; cf. Zech. 14:4); Jewish apocalyptic tradition added that the Messiah would stand atop Mount Zion when preparing to make war (4 Ezra 13:35).

Other apocalyptists may seek perspective by standing on Mount Zion (2 Bar. 13:1), but in Revelation Zion is also the new Jerusalem, the holy city (Rev. 3:12; 21:2–22:2), the antithesis of Babylon, whose demise is about to be introduced (14:8).[3] The Jews remembered Babylon of old for its destruction of Jerusalem and expected God's judgment on her (Ps. 137; Jer. 50:28; 51:10, 24, 35); so with the new Babylon, oppressor of the spiritual children of Jerusalem (cf. Rev. 12:17; 18:24).[4] Thus begins Revelation's "Tale of Two Cities"—a contrast between the city of God and the city of the world.

---

2. The message of 14:1–20 is synthetically recapitulated in 15:1–16:21, with the triumph of the saints (14:1–5) in the conquerors of 15:2 (cf. Talbert, *Apocalypse*, 59).

3. Early Judaism, like its Bible, applied "Mount Zion" both to the temple mount specifically (1 Macc. 4:37; 5:54; 7:33; 14:27; Judith 9:13) and to Jerusalem in general (Bar. 4:14; 4 Ezra 13:27, 44). Emblematic use for Israel as a whole was relatively rare (cf. 1QM 12.13; *p. Meg.* 3:6, §2; *Taan.* 4:2, §13). Early Christians recognized that Mount Zion would be a new Jerusalem (Heb. 12:22).

4. They should also flee Babylon before its judgment, as in Zech. 2:7–8; see comment on Rev. 18:4. The promise of God's judgment on Zion's oppressors appears before the Exile (Mic. 4:11–13); the original Babylon was one in a succession of evil empires, as in Dan. 7:3–27 (1 En. 90:1; 2 Bar. 39:3–8; 67:7–8; Sib. Or. 3.158–61); it would be destroyed for destroying God's temple (Sib. Or. 3.302–3).

After John sees the 144,000 on Mount Zion, he hears a voice from heaven (14:2). As his vision of the redeemed martyrs in 7:9–17 constitutes the interpretation of what he heard about God's army of 144,000 in 7:1–8, so here his hearing helps to interpret his vision of the 144,000. The "sound from heaven" is the song of 144,000 taken from the earth and now in heaven (14:3). "The roar of rushing waters," which may represent God's voice (1:15; cf. Ezek. 43:2), in this context undoubtedly represents the sound of the innumerable heavenly multitude (Rev. 19:6; cf. the voice like a tumult in Dan. 10:6, or the cherubim's wings like God's hosts in Ezek. 1:24). The "loud peal of thunder" can also represent God's voice (Job 37:5; Ps. 29:3), perhaps alluding to the Sinai revelation or to judgment (cf. Rev. 4:5; 8:5; 11:19; also Ex. 19:16; Isa. 29:6), but here it surely represents the voice of an innumerable multitude (Rev. 19:6). "The sound . . . of harpists playing their harps" pictures the heavenly chorus of worshipers (5:8; 15:2), a priesthood that offers praise to God (e.g., 1 Chron. 25:1–6; Ps. 81:2).[5]

That the 144,000 are those "redeemed" (14:3) and "purchased" (14:4; both forms of the same Greek word, *agorazo*) from the earth and from among humanity reminds us that they stand for all believers (5:9). That the Lamb bought them more than makes up for the fact that, a few verses earlier, they could neither buy nor sell (13:17). That they are the ones who "follow the Lamb" (14:4) supports the position that they represent all believer's (7:17); in this life they are the people led by the Spirit (John 16:13; Rom. 8:14). John's audience will also understand that following the Lamb may mean following him to his sacrificial death (John 13:36–37; 21:19–22; Rev. 6:9). "Firstfruits" (14:4) is also sacrificial language, for Israel was to offer the first of their harvest to the Lord (Ex. 23:19; 34:26; Lev. 2:12; 23:10; Num. 28:26; Neh. 10:35). Greek business documents speak specifically of *people* as "firstfruits" when they were offered to a deity (e.g., as temple servants); these spiritual warriors are thus devoted to the Lamb.[6]

Why do the 144,000 sing this "new song"? They are probably portrayed as God's end-time army (see comment on 7:4–8) and have just overcome the world (see 15:2–4, where this song is spelled out in more detail). It was customary for victors to celebrate after holy war (2 Chron. 20:27–28; 1 Macc. 13:51; 1QM 19.1–3).[7] Here, however, the saints praise God for the victory

---

5. Gershom G. Scholem, *Jewish Gnosticism, Merkabah Mysticism, and Talmudic Tradition* (New York: Jewish Theological Seminary of America, 1965), 23, interestingly compares Hekhaloth hymns in Jewish mysticism, but most shared features derive from a common source in the OT.

6. See Aune, *Revelation*, 2:814–17. Perhaps the 144,000 are all priests (1:6), with a specific contrast intended with a role once limited to Levi (7:7).

7. See Bauckham, *Climax of Prophecy*, 230, who also notes that the "new song" applied to holy war in Ps. 98:1–3; 144:9; Isa. 42:10–13; Jdt. 16:2–3 (Aune, *Revelation*, 2:808, thinks the "new song" is military only in Ps. 144:9 and prefers the Greco-Roman motif of heavenly songs).

of the Lamb (as in Rev. 5:6–14; 7:9–12), just as the Israelites praised God when he overthrew their enemies in the Red Sea (Ex. 15:1–21; cf. comment on Rev. 15:2–4). This new song is their unique experience shared by no one else in creation (14:3), just as believers have a new name known to no one else (2:17; 3:12).

Why are the 144,000 celibate? This passage does not emphasize their Jewishness as 7:4–8 did; it emphasizes instead that they have kept themselves from women.[8] This may be part of Revelation's portrait of God's end-time army, because in ancient Israel's armies only men could normally participate in holy war, and they were apparently required to stay away from women (Deut. 23:10; 1 Sam. 21:5; 2 Sam. 11:11).[9] Just as biblical prophets often portrayed Israel as either an unfaithful prostitute or as a pure virgin or bride for God, so Revelation portrays unrepentant humanity as a prostitute (Rev. 17:1–5) and those faithful to Christ as his pure spouse (19:7; 21:2, 9). These 144,000 have refused to commit immorality with Babylon, the prostitute (cf. 18:3).[10] The symbolism thus makes a strong point: Christians must be pure and faithful to Christ if they wish to be prepared for and engage in the Lamb's holy war. Unlike the world (13:17), believers cannot indulge in divided interests.[11]

That "no lie [is] found in their mouths" (14:5) probably recalls the promise that among the remnant of Israel there would be no lie (Zeph. 3:13).[12] This picture contrasts God's faithful with the world's liars, who slander believers (Rev. 3:9), who praise the false divine ruler (13:4), who embrace the lies from the spirit of antichrist that denies Jesus' unique role (1 John 2:22), and whose fate is damnation (Rev. 21:8). Whereas the world issues false propaganda (Rev. 13:5–6, 11, 15), God's saints speak the truth of the gospel and renounce idols regardless of the cost (6:9–11; 11:3; 12:11); this is part of what it means for them to be pure (14:4). That "they are blameless" (14:5) may reflect the image of holy warriors who, like priests, must lack all blemish

---

8. Though rare, the image of male "virgins" appears (1 Cor. 7:25; Jos. and Asen. 4:7/9; 8:1; cf. celibate males in the Qumran scrolls); but we argue that the image here is symbolic, not referring to lifelong celibacy. On celibacy in antiquity, see Aune, *Revelation*, 2:818–22; C. S. Keener, ... *And Marries Another* (Peabody, Mass.: Hendrickson, 1991), 68–78.

9. Some Jewish people believed that women would not be allowed in the camp of God's end-time army (1QM 7:3–6).

10. Michaels, *Interpreting Revelation*, 138, thus argues (probably rightly) that "defilement" with women does not involve marriage (which appears favorably in 19:7; 21:2).

11. Caird, *Commentary on Revelation*, 179; Bauckham, *Climax of Prophecy*, 231; Talbert, *Apocalypse*, 60–61; Meeks, *Moral World*, 146. An alternative view contrasts them with fallen angels in 1 Enoch (Daniel C. Olson, "'Those Who Have Not Defiled Themselves With Women': Revelation 14:4 and the Book of Enoch," CBQ 59 [July 1997]: 492–510).

12. See also Fekkes, *Isaiah*, 191. Later rabbis associated Rome (cf. 14:8) so much with lying that they claimed even dogs in Rome knew how to deceive (Gen. *Rab.* 22:6).

(1QM 7.4); or it may simply continue a more literal explanation of the purity symbolized in 14:4.[13]

Four Heavenly Announcements (14:6–13)

JOHN OFTEN COMMENTS that he saw "another angel" (7:2; 8:3; 10:1), but 14:6 reports his first vision of an angel since the sounding of the seventh trumpet in 11:15. The heavenly proclamations in 11:15 and 14:6 frame the intervening section about the saints and the beast (12:1–14:5), with emphasis on the sufferings (12:17; 13:7) and triumph (14:1–5) of the saints. In 14:7–11 we have three announcements of judgment: general (14:7), on Babylon (14:8), and on the beast's worshipers (14:9–11). Such announcements assure the saints of vindication (14:12) and are followed by an announcement of peace for the righteous martyrs (14:13).[14]

The "eternal gospel" proclaimed by the angel to all peoples (14:6) probably does not imply an angel literally spreading the saving gospel to all the nations before the end, which is the work of the church (Matt. 24:14; Rev. 6:9–11). Because angels in Revelation often correspond to earthly realities (12:5–7), the angel's flight may correspond to the spread of the gospel through martyrs.[15] Another sense of "gospel" is perhaps more likely here, however. In the prophetic tradition, "good news" is not just the announcement that God is restoring his people (Isa. 40:9; 41:27; 52:7; 61:1) but also the announcement of judgment on their enemies (Nah. 1:15); in context, this angel announces impending judgment (14:7).[16]

To be sure, the angel calls the world to fear and glorify God—a sign of praise (19:5) that may imply a future hope for the nations (15:4) and a call to repentance (11:13; 16:9). Yet given the evocative imagery of apocalypses and the other announcements in the context (14:8–13), the angel's announcement is probably intended more for Revelation's audience than envisioned as a voice heard by the unrepentant world in the end time.

---

13. The word *amomos* usually designates moral purity in early Christian texts (Eph. 1:4; 5:27; Phil. 2:15; Col. 1:22; Jude 24). Bauckham, *Climax of Prophecy*, 232, opts for either holy warriors or unblemished sacrifices (cf. Ex. 29:38; Lev. 1:3; Heb. 9:14; 1 Peter 1:19; cf. different sacrificial imagery in the "firstfruits" of 14:4).

14. Fekkes, *Isaiah*, 286–87, compares the oracles of chs. 14–19 with Old Testament prophets' oracles against the nations. For an early Jewish example of oracles of doom against nations, see Sib. Or. 4.88–101.

15. Caird, *Commentary on Revelation*, 182.

16. Cf. Talbert, *Apocalypse*, 64; for the significance of the "hour," cf. Rissi, *Time and History*, 5. Cf. also Bauckham, *Climax of Prophecy*, 286–89, who finds an allusion to Ps. 96:2, though the LXX obscures rather than clarifies the allusion. Similar language appears in 1 Chron. 16:8–36 (Willem Altink, "1 Chronicles 16:8–36 As Literary Source for Revelation 14:6–7," *AUSS* 22 [1984]: 187–96), but it is common biblical praise language.

The double "fallen" in the description of Babylon (14:8; 18:2) is emphatic and alludes to idolatrous Babylon's prophesied fall in Isaiah 21:9, perhaps viewed as fulfilled in Revelation 11:13; 16:19.[17] The Romans applied "Babylon" poetically to their archenemy Parthia (which ruled old Babylonia); but there can be no question that this text implies especially Rome.[18] Early Jews often used Babylon as a code name for Rome, as did early Christians (1 Peter 5:13).[19] Such allusions made sense; as Israel once experienced exile under the evil empire Babylon, now they are experiencing the captivity of a new evil empire in Rome. Both Babylon and Rome destroyed the temple. Other Jewish prophets, rooted in biblical perspective of divine vindication, also expected Rome's impending destruction.[20]

Babylon is judged because she has made nations drink from "the maddening wine of her adulteries" (14:8). The word "maddening" here and in 18:3 (*thymos*) can refer to passion (hence her "passionate" adulteries), but normally in Revelation it refers to anger (God's in 15:1, 7; 16:1; the devil's in 12:12), including when it is specifically connected with wine (16:19; 19:15), as in the immediate context (14:10, 19). This verse may therefore either contrast Babylon's own cup of "passionate" wine with the passionate wine of God's anger against Babylon, or it may simply introduce that cup of God's wine as anger *against* Babylon's "adulteries," which Babylon brought on all the nations with whom she committed such immoralities. Since she drinks double from the same cup she mixed for other nations (18:6), the latter interpretation is more likely. All the final plagues are poured from the wine bowls of God's anger (15:7; 16:1), though Babylon is finally toasted and forced to drink the consequences of her sins most fully at the end (16:19), when God's winepress is also overflowing (14:18–20).

Worshipers of the beast who have received his mark will face judgment (14:9–10). Idolatry had some temporal advantages in a world where idolatry was sophisticated and powerful whereas monotheists were a despised

---

17. The rabbis applied Isa. 21:9 to historic Babylon but at the same time could condemn Roman "Edom" in their own day (e.g., *Gen. Rab.* 44:17); Edom was another nickname for Rome (4 Ezra 6:9; *p. A.Z.* 1:2, §4; *Taan.* 4:5, §10; *Pes. Rab Kah.* 23:2). For parallels between Rome and some biblical oracles against Babylon, see Kraybill, *Imperial Cult and Commerce,* 149–50.

18. For "Babylon" as Parthia, see Lucan, *C.W.* 1.10. Many Jews lived in literal Babylonia (though cf. Josephus, *Ant.* 18.371–79), which could also appear in early Jewish texts (Sib. Or. 5.434–46). Some modern teachers expect a rebuilt, end-time Babylon on the Euphrates (Charles H. Dyer, "The Identity of Babylon in Revelation 17–18. Part 2," *BibSac* 144 [1987]: 433–49).

19. See Sib. Or. 5.143, 159–61; 4 Ezra 3:1–2, 28; 2 Bar. 11:1–2; 67:7; cf. 4QHab on Hab. 1:6.

20. See Sib. Or. 3.52. For further comments on Babylon's identity and "adulteries," see 17:2, 9–11; 18:3, 12–13.

minority (13:17), but it promised only eternal death. Receiving that mark is, however, a symbolic act that does not make one incapable of repentance. The world (9:20–21; 16:9–11) and even false prophets (2:16, 21–22) are invited to repent, and many of those who ridiculed the witnesses will repent (11:13).[21] The "burning sulfur" refers to the torment of those burned eternally in the lake of fire (19:20; 20:10; 21:8), but also spells a suitable judgment for the denizens of spiritual "Sodom" (11:8; Gen. 19:24; Deut. 29:23; Luke 17:29).[22]

Ancients normally diluted wine with two parts water to every part wine, except when they wished to get drunk.[23] But God will administer this wine of his anger "full strength" (14:10). The "cup" is a standard symbol for God's anger, both temporarily against his people (Isa. 51:17, 22; Ezek. 23:31–33) and against the wicked nations (Ps. 75:8; Jer. 25:15–17, 28; 49:12; Lam. 4:21; Hab. 2:16; Zech. 12:2).[24] The primary allusion here is to Jeremiah 51:7, where Babylon was a cup in God's hand, making the nations of the earth mad with drunkenness from her wine. The context is God's warning of Babylon's fall (Jer. 51:8) and his notice to those who will heed him to flee from Babylon, lest they partake of its judgment (Jer. 51:6, 9; see Rev. 18:4).

Those tormented will be able to look on the Lamb and the holy angels they despised (14:10), now unable to evade the reality they once ignored (1 En. 108:15; 4 Ezra 7:37). Some Jewish writers also envisioned the saints witnessing the torment of the damned (1 En. 27:3; 48:9; 108:14), but no such entertainment is in view here. The emphasis here is "the inescapability and finality of judgment, not the satisfaction it could afford to those who witness it."[25] That the smoke of their torture rises "for ever and ever" (Rev. 14:11; 19:3; cf. Isa. 34:10) must mean eternal torment rather than annihilation; this same phrase applies to God's and Christ's eternality (Rev. 1:18; 4:10; 10:6; 11:15; 15:7), to the reign of the saints (22:5), and to the eternal suffering of the beast (20:10).[26] Whereas angelic worshipers in the heavenly temple never cease to

---

21. With Caird, *Commentary on Revelation*, 185–86.

22. Ancients knew that sulfur was often spewed forth from within the earth in volcanoes. They also knew it as a terrifying weapon, since besieged citizens could pour burning sulfur on attackers below, and it proved "horribly effective because it stuck to the body" (Aune, *Revelation*, 2:835).

23. See Apollonius Rhodius, 1.473; Plutarch, *Bride* 20, *Mor.* 140F; *T.T.* 1.4.3; *Mor.* 621CD; *Sifra Sh.* par. 1.100.1.3.

24. For early Jewish allusions, see for Israel 1QpHab 11.14–15; 4QpNah 4.5–6; Ps. Sol. 8:14; for the nations, *Gen. Rab.* 16:4.

25. Beasley-Murray, *Revelation*, 226; also Caird, *Commentary on Revelation*, 187. The visibility of the damned appears also in other strands of tradition (e.g., *Koh. Rab.* 7:14, §3).

26. Talbert, *Apocalypse*, 66; Beale, *Revelation*, 761–62. One could argue that Isa. 34:10 symbolizes annihilation, but John's contemporaries would probably read it in light of Isa. 66:24 (cf. the interpretation in Mark 9:48)

worship God day or night (4:8), the damned never cease to suffer (14:11). Even more directly relevant in the context, the damned have "no rest" (14:11), but the righteous martyrs enter into rest (14:13).[27]

While the saints are not explicitly granted a vision of the torment of the damned, they are encouraged to stand firm in view of it (14:12). Either they should be encouraged because this judgment is their vindication (cf. 1 En. 104:3–4), or they should be exhorted to fill their role as martyr-witnesses so that more people may be spared from the agonies of eternal torment for worshiping the beast.[28]

Finally, a heavenly voice promises peace for the martyr-witnesses of Jesus; the Spirit then confirms this with a prophetic assurance (14:13).[29] Jewish texts often speak of the righteous receiving rest from their sufferings (cf. 2 Thess. 1:7). Some texts promise a voice from heaven announcing end-time rest from suffering, as here (1 En. 96:3). Others promise peace or rest for the righteous when they are martyred (Wisd. Sol. 3:3; 4:7). Most significant is the standard Jewish tradition that also stands behind our traditional "Rest in Peace (R.I.P.)": Jewish texts regularly promised rest for the righteous after death.[30] "From now on" may refer to "from the time of the cross," or it may be better read as "assuredly."[31] Everyone is judged according to "works" (Rev. 2:23; 20:12–13; 22:12; cf. 1 Enoch 41:1), but the righteous can be satisfied in theirs (Rev. 14:13). The key phrase is that these dead are "in the Lord" (14:13; cf. 1 Thess. 4:16).

---

27. In the end-time judgment the wicked will have no "rest" or peace (1 En. 99:13–14).

28. See Caird, *Commentary on Revelation*, 188, on the Greek construction.

29. Heavenly voices often appear in Jewish texts as a form of divine communication, often a substitute for the prophetic Spirit (Craig S. Keener, *The Spirit in the Gospels and Acts* [Peabody, Mass.: Hendrickson, 1997], 55); the Spirit often involved prophecy in early Judaism (ibid., 10–13). In Revelation see 10:4, 8; 11:12; 12:10; 18:4; the voice may refer to Jesus (1:10; 4:1), though not necessarily always (14:2; 19:1). Some think 14:13 includes an independent oracle (Aune, *Prophecy in Early Christianity*, 283); on the Spirit's "Amen," see Bruce, "The Spirit in the Apocalypse," 342. This is one of seven beatitudes in Revelation (see discussion in Bauckham, *Climax of Prophecy*, 29).

30. For funerary inscriptions, see Harry J. Leon, *The Jews of Ancient Rome* (Philadelphia: Jewish Publication Society of America, 1960), 123; *CIJ* 1:198–99, §283; 1:230, §292; 1:233, §296 and passim (I counted well over 50 in *CIJ* alone); in Greco-Roman letters of consolation, see Stowers, *Letter Writing*, 145. Cf. 1 Enoch 103:3; Syriac Menander, *Sent.* 470–73; Gr. Ezra 1:12. In times of tribulation one may also lament that the dead are more blessed than the living (2 Bar. 11:6–7).

31. For the former, see Rissi, *Time and History*, 29; for the latter, see Beasley-Murray, *Revelation*, 227, reading *ap' arti* as *aparti* (note that the earliest manuscripts included no breaks between words).

The Harvests Have Come (14:14–20)

IN 14:14–20 THE action shifts from heavenly announcements (14:6–13) to visions of symbolic actions. Commentators debate whether the figure "like a son of man" in 14:14 represents Jesus, as the language may well suggest (1:13; Dan. 7:13), or simply an angel that appears human (Rev. 4:7; cf. 21:17). In favor of the former (the majority view), when Jesus appears in 19:12–13 his garments are spattered from treading out the winepress of human blood; in favor of the latter, one would not expect Jesus to act in conjunction with an angel's command (14:15) or to parallel a mere angel (14:17). True, Jesus comes in the clouds (1:7), but clouds are not limited to him (10:1; 11:12); Jesus has diadems (19:12), but the term for "crown" here always applies to others (2:10; 3:11; 4:4; 6:2; 9:7; 12:1). Yet the clouds fit very well the image in Daniel that also provides for Jesus the "son of man" title, so Jesus is perhaps in the background here.[32]

The primary exegetical problem in this text, however, is whether to identify the grain harvest of the first vision with the grape vintage of the second harvest (a typical feature of Revelation is to have a second vision interpret the first), or to interpret them differently. Undoubtedly, the entire passage develops an image from Joel's prophecy about judgment on the nations in the day of the Lord. God calls for the sickle to gather the ripe harvest and for the grapes of the nations' wickedness to be trampled to fill his winepress (Joel 3:13; against Babylon, cf. Jer. 51:33; Jerusalem in Lam. 1:15).[33] Whereas both harvests are likely parallel images for judgment in Joel, some commentators suggest that Revelation uses only the second image for judgment (14:17–20). The grain harvest, by contrast, includes the evangelism and gathering of God's people, as the grain harvest is used in many early Christian texts (Mark 4:20, 29). Note too that the martyrs in 14:4 were the "firstfruits" from a godly grain harvest, that is, a sacrifice that foreshadowed the rest of the harvest like them (Lev. 23:9–14).[34]

This passage, in other words, may be continuing the contrast between the fate of the righteous and the wicked found in 14:6–13. But one convinced

---

32. Gregory M. Stevenson, "Conceptual Background to Golden Crown Imagery in the Apocalypse of John (4:4, 10; 14:14)," *JBL* 114 (1995): 257–72 (pp. 271–72), notes some Jewish texts in which the leader of the angelic host wears a golden wreath, but concludes that it fits better Daniel's son of man as a ruler-judge. Jesus appears to be "Lord of the harvest" (cf. Matt. 9:38; Luke 10:2).

33. Later rabbis could depict Rome's destruction by the winepress image of Isa. 63 (*Lev. Rab.* 13:5).

34. Bauckham, *Climax of Prophecy*, 290–94; cf. Caird, *Commentary on Revelation*, 193. For the view that both harvests refer to judgment, see Aune, *Revelation*, 2:801–3; Beale, *Revelation*, 775–79.

by John's frequent repetition of parallel images can respond that in this apocalyptic image the 144,000 as the "firstfruits" may simply portend a harvest in general, and that even in images of the harvesting of the righteous the wicked are judged (Matt. 3:12; 13:40–42). In Revelation a second vision often reinterprets the first (Rev. 7:1–17). The matter is not easily settled, but it seems more likely on the whole that both visions involve judgment, as in Joel.

Whatever the point of the first vision, the meaning of the second vision is relatively plain. It portrays the wicked as gathered grapes now crushed into wine in God's winepress, responding to the cup of the wine of God's anger poured out on them.[35] Wine was sometimes called "the blood of grapes" (Gen. 49:11; cf. Deut. 32:14); and as the red wine of Passover provided a useful symbol for Jesus' blood at the last supper, wine here deliberately evokes the gruesome image of human blood crushed out of maimed flesh. Some time around August or September workers collected ripe grapes in baskets and deposited them in long wooden or stone troughs. There, often to the rhythm of a flutist, workers trampled the grapes into juice with their feet.[36] God had already promised that he would go out and trample the blood of the wicked like wine in a winepress until his garments were stained with their blood (Isa. 63:1–6); in Revelation Jesus assumes this divine role (Rev. 19:13, 15). John recycles images; the wicked must drink the wine of God's wrath (14:10), which is ultimately their own blood (14:20; 16:6).

The angel "who had charge of the fire" (14:18) may allude to the Jewish conception of angels over various elements of nature (cf. 16:5).[37] But since this angel comes from the altar, it is almost certainly the angel who keeps the fire of the incense altar (8:5). This image suggests that God again sends judgment in response to the cries of his oppressed saints (6:9–11; 8:3–5).

The blood flows high "outside the city," vividly portraying a horrible end for Babylon (14:20).[38] The image of blood flowing in terrible streams became standard in ancient descriptions of wars, both historical and

---

35. Ford, *Revelation*, 250, thinks the vine is Israel (in favor of this, cf. esp. the vine of Sodom in Deut. 32:32; cf. Rev. 11:8); Caird, *Commentary on Revelation*, 192, compares martyrs here. Probably this vine supplies a contrast with God's people as portrayed in John 15:1–7. Early Jewish writers applied the image of treading the winepress in various ways, but one is judgment (see Joshua Schwartz, "Treading the Grapes of Wrath: The Wine Press in Ancient Jewish and Christian Tradition," *Theologische Zeitschrift* 49 (1993): 215–18.

36. See Naphtali Lewis, *Life in Egypt Under Roman Rule* (Oxford: Clarendon, 1983), 125.

37. E.g., Jub. 2:2; 1 En. 20:2; 60:12–22; 66:1–2; 2 En. 5:1–2; 1QM 10.11–12; *b. Pes.* 118ab; perhaps Ps 148:2–3. For the angel of fire, see Ps-Philo 38:3; for pagan deities of fire, see e.g., Virgil, *Aen.* 12.90; Diogenes Laertius, 7.1.147.

38. See Joel 3:12–14, which supplies the vintage and harvest images, places the judgment in the Valley of Jehoshaphat (Joel 3:2, 12), which tradition placed outside Jerusalem (cf. also Zech. 14:1–4; Mounce, *Revelation*, 282); but Babylon is in view in 14:8.

fictitious.[39] Others complained of rivers flowing with blood when people were slain in them.[40] Some spoke of so many bloodstained birds feeding on a field of corpses that the trees dripped with dew and pieces of flesh dropped from the sky when satiated birds grew weary of carrying them.[41]

Naturally, apocalypses with their figurative license freely amplified such descriptions. Thus while blood flowed in streams (1 Enoch 100:1), horses would walk up to their chests in sinners' blood and chariots would be covered (1 Enoch 100:3; 4 Ezra 15:35). Another source warns that corpses will fill deep ravines in high mountains and blood will sweep through the plains (Sib. Or. 3.682–84).[42] Later rabbis, amplifying the slaughter of their people by the Romans at Bethar in A.D. 135, described horses drowning in blood and blood rolling huge boulders forty miles out to the sea; the blood filled the sea as far away as Cyprus.[43] Sometimes the more extreme descriptions were merely figurative ways of expressing the horrific bloodshed (e.g., Ezek. 32:5–6; Jdt. 6:4).

The "1,600 stadia" (14:20) may be a rounded number with figurative significance, just like many others in Revelation. As 1000 is ten cubed, as 144,000 is twelve squared times ten cubed (a cube being the shape of the new Jerusalem—21:16), and as 666 is a double triangular number as well as the triangle of a square number, 1,600 is the square of the familiar biblical number forty.[44] But while John rounds to a square number, its primary significance is to

---

39. E.g., Homer, *Il.* 4.451; 17.360–61; 20.494; *Od.* 11.420; Apollonius Rhodius, 3.1391–92; Virgil, *Aen.* 11.382; Ovid, *Metam.* 12.110; Livy, 25.12.6; Lucan, *C.W.* 7.728–29; Herodian, 3.4.5; 4.9.8. Romans counted an unexplained river of blood as a dangerous omen (Livy, 26.23.5; 27.37.3).

40. Homer, *Il.* 21.21; Virgil, *Aen.* 11.393–94; 12.35–36; Ovid, *Metam.* 12.71, 111; Lucan, *C.W.* 2.214–20; Longinus, *Sublime* 38.3 (citing Thucydides, 7.84); Sib. Or. 4.61; 5.200–204. In a few accounts (like Lucan's), the blood allegedly even obstructed ships until most of the blood flowed out to sea.

41. Lucan, *C.W.* 7.831–40. Other texts speak of people slipping in the gore or falling over piles of corpses (Ovid, *Metam.* 12.113–14; Polybius, 15.14; Dionysius of Halicarnassus, 9.21.21; 14.114.5). Lucan characteristically claims that corpses were piled as high as the wall (*C.W.* 6.180).

42. See further Sib. Or. 3.453–54, 695–97 (second century B.C.). In apocalyptic texts the image is typically eschatological (see Bauckham, *Climax of Prophecy*, 40–44).

43. E.g., *b. Git.* 57a; *p. Suk.* 5:1, §7; *Taan.* 4:5, §10; *Lam. Rab.* 2:2, §4. Rabbis also told of Israelite women who menstruated so much they filled the Babylonians' chariots (e.g., *Pes. Rab Kah.* 17:6). Most ancient readers recognized the reality to which exaggerations typically pointed (Livy, 3.8.10).

44. Beasley-Murray, *Revelation*, 230, suggests forty as the number for punishment in the Old Testament (e.g., Num. 14:33; Deut. 25:3). He also notes evidence (though he ultimately does not accept it) that some thought the boundaries of the Holy Land to be about 1,600 to 1,700 stadia.

compound the grotesqueness of the image: None of the army gathered against God—none of the beast-worshipers committed to the world's values—will survive. Some commentators also suggest a contrast here: Whereas the river of paradise flows from God's throne (22:2) to a significant height (Ezek. 47:4–5), the wicked will drown in a river of their own blood (Rev. 14:20).

BABYLONS. BABYLON MAY be Rome, but it is also the city of the "world" system; it thus encompasses the city of Sodom and Egypt and unrepentant Jerusalem in 11:2, 8. The world as we know it did not come to an end with Rome's fall sixteen centuries ago, but for John's audience Rome constituted the world system, the typical evil empire. Revelation uses the symbols of that day to send a message to the seven churches of Asia. Evil empires are those that abuse their power, multiplying the evil of personal sin and selfishness on a corporate scale.[45] John's oracles recycle the language of judgment against literal Babylon in earlier prophecies (Jer. 51:7); but if Rome is a revived Babylon, later empires can also be a revived Rome. The connection is not geographical location but the fact that an empire oppresses God's servants.

The spirit of the Roman empire remains alive and well in today's world—an empire that both claimed tolerance of many gods but suppressed dissent from those who preached the truth of the one God and his Son Jesus Christ. "It is all one by whatever name she be called—she is also Rome, Calcutta, London, New York—anywhere and everywhere that men worship something other than the true and living God."[46] Thus in Revelation, both the holy city and the prostitute Babylon share in wicked Jerusalem (11:8); the battleground is neither topographical Rome nor Judea, but the churches of Asia—and the world and churches of today—wherever the new Jerusalem and Babylon wage war.[47]

Specific details. We must determine how literally or symbolically to apply some details, and then determine how to apply these details. Does the text praise literal and lifelong celibacy in 14:4 (cf. 1 Cor. 7:8), or does it, as we have argued, apply symbolically the image of temporary abstinence? If we apply it as a symbol of disentanglement from the world, who determines

---

45. On the nature of injustice, see especially Gary Haugen, *Good News About Injustice* (Downers Grove, Ill.: InterVarsity, 1999), 119–41.

46. Bowman, *First Christian Drama*, 91; cf. Tenney, *Revelation*, 82.

47. Paul S. Minear, *Images of the Church in the New Testament* (Philadelphia: Westminster, 1960), 95.

which aspects of the society are really "worldly"? Some aspects of our culture, relatively distinctive against the background of history as a whole (such as respect for human rights), are compatible with Christian teachings and somewhat derived from them. But a basic distinction is that Christians should value what matters most to God (e.g., evangelizing the world, helping people made in God's image) rather than what matters to the world but not to God (e.g., acquiring wealth and status for oneself). A spiritual celibate set aside for God cannot sleep with the world "on the side" and remain qualified for God's triumphant army.

That "no lie" was in the mouths of God's servants (14:5) also invites consideration. Sometimes the Bible presents a general principle with the understanding that it must be qualified in particular situations. In general, lying is bad, but what if the deception is to save a human life? In that instance, the Bible portrays godly people lying for a godly reason (Ex. 1:18–21; Josh. 2:4–6; 2 Sam. 17:20; Jer. 38:24–27) and never condemns it; sometimes it is even done at a divine command (1 Sam. 16:2–4; cf. 2 Kings 8:10). In this context the truthfulness of God's agents (14:5) contrasts starkly with the deception and blasphemy of Satan's agents (13:5–6, 11–15).

Understanding the rhetorical function of each text in its context is essential to apply correctly the vivid images of Revelation. Some may ask if we can really rejoice in heaven if we know the eternal fate of the damned (14:10–11). But the purpose of recording this announcement is to assure oppressed Christians of their coming vindication (14:12). For those of us who generally face a much lesser level of oppression, the image may not strike us as cause for celebration. To fully capture the spirit of the text, we need to enter into the sufferings of our oppressed brothers and sisters elsewhere in the world. If God chooses an angel by the altar as an agent of judgment (14:18) because of the prayers of the saints (6:9–11; 8:3–5), this text may remind us that judgment often comes as vindication of those who have been wronged.

John's image of God's winepress (14:19–20) is from the Old Testament, but he does not tone it down. He is not afraid of scaring away mildly interested inquirers concerning the Christian faith; he intends to scare anyone sitting on the fence of indecision into radical obedience to Christ. The lines are drawn; the wicked will be destroyed, and those who are wise must make their choice for Christ now. Such images function more effectively in a community experiencing persecution and increasingly alienated from a society that represses them, but should we bother to translate images of terror for a more civil society, as we think our own is? In answer, note that Revelation was written not only for persecuted churches like Smyrna and Philadelphia; it was also written for compromising churches like Sardis, Thyatira, and Laodicea, and for some experiencing both like Pergamum. All of us need to be reminded that there are only two sides and that our actions will contribute to one side or the other.

ON THE ROAD to victory. This passage offers numerous principles for application. For example, in 14:1–5 the text highlights the contrast between worshipers of the beast and of the Lamb, emphasizing the latter's conquest by brave martyrdom; "following" the Lamb involves a cost for us. The glorious fate of the martyrs (14:1–5) contrasts strikingly with the fate of those who took the mark of the beast (13:16–18) and so were damned (14:9–11). This warns us to avoid the present world's concepts of value and status: Rather than acquiring status symbols or other means to be comfortable in society, we should sacrifice ourselves and our resources to extend the kingdom. In the process, we may actually be witnesses to some of our neighbors as to why kingdom values are different from and more important than those of the world.

Following the Lamb promises us a glorious future as the people of the new Jerusalem if we persevere. The contrast between Zion (14:1), with its glorious future in the new Jerusalem (21:2–22:5), and Babylon (14:8), with its impending demise (18:2–19:3), warns us to invest in the future city rather than the present one (cf. Matt. 6:19–20). The new Jerusalem is visible only by faith now (cf. Heb. 11:10, 16; 13:14), but God will vindicate that faith just as he has vindicated the faith of the generations who waited before us.

The harps (14:2) remind us that heaven will be like a new temple, a place of worship (see comment on 4:8–11; 5:9–14). Though the world seemed to triumph over God's people (13:7, 15–17), the saints who had overcome by failing to compromise with the world's values praised God for victory (14:3). By faith we can celebrate that victory now, because it is rooted in the past victory in which the Lamb redeemed us (14:3; 15:2–4).

The text also invites us to sexual and spiritual purity (14:4); as God's army we dare not compromise with the world or harbor divided interests. The spiritual chastity of believers contrasts with Babylon, full of adulteries (14:8); God is justly angry when we prefer other matters to him, the fountain of life. We could comment here on divided interests of many Christians today, but we have commented on these topics at other points in the commentary (especially on the letters to Pergamum and Thyatira).

Judgment on the world and its system. Revelation 14:6–20 also invites numerous application principles, most of them already familiar to the reader who has worked through the book to this point. Verses 6–13 underline the certainty of vindication for the saints, portrayed most graphically in the judgment of their oppressor Babylon, the world system. Babylon's judgment likewise reminds us of the principle of judgment recurrent throughout the book: Babylon crushed others, but what goes around comes around.

The passage also summons us to an eternal perspective that guards against compromise with the evil system that oppresses the saints; the short-term advantages of the mark are not worth eternal damnation. That the tormented wicked view the Lamb and angels (14:10) warns us that everyone will have to face reality ultimately, later if not now. While the wicked have no rest, the righteous will experience eternal rest. The images of terror and bloodshed in the final paragraph (14:14–20) should evoke repentance; the passage offers no hope that any beast-worshipers will survive the final battle.

The idea of eternal torment (14:9–11; cf. 20:10) is so naturally revolting to most of us that modern readers have found a number of ways to circumvent it. Some teach annihilation, which seems to contradict a number of texts about eternal torment (Matt. 3:12; 25:46; Mark 9:43, 47–48; Luke 3:17), but which is not a pleasant alternative in itself.[48] This view is not heretical, and it does not lessen the need for people to embrace Christ; but it is not likely correct.

Many today avoid trying to "scare" people into the kingdom. In a culture in revolt against authority and skeptical of threats, emphasizing God's loving invitation may be a more strategic approach. But John had no such scruples against "scaring" people, and as long as we speak the truth and are able to reason with people (Acts 19:9; 24:25), there remain occasions when this approach is appropriate. A young atheist chose to consider the claims of Christ immediately rather than deferring the decision because the doctrine of hell made the stakes too high to ignore. Twenty-four years later that former atheist remains a committed Christian—and is writing this commentary.

---

48. For representatives of an annihilationist position from an evangelical perspective, see "John's Stott's Response to Chapter 6," 306–31 in David L. Edwards and John Stott, *Evangelical Essentials: A Liberal-Evangelical Dialogue* (Downers Grove, Ill.: InterVarsity, 1988), 313–20; also most Adventist evangelicals.

Revelation 15:1-8

I SAW IN HEAVEN another great and marvelous sign: seven angels with the seven last plagues—last, because with them God's wrath is completed. ²And I saw what looked like a sea of glass mixed with fire and, standing beside the sea, those who had been victorious over the beast and his image and over the number of his name. They held harps given them by God ³and sang the song of Moses the servant of God and the song of the Lamb:

> "Great and marvelous are your deeds,
>   Lord God Almighty.
> Just and true are your ways,
>   King of the ages.
> ⁴Who will not fear you, O Lord,
>   and bring glory to your name?
> For you alone are holy.
> All nations will come
>   and worship before you,
> for your righteous acts have been revealed."

⁵After this I looked and in heaven the temple, that is, the tabernacle of the Testimony, was opened. ⁶Out of the temple came the seven angels with the seven plagues. They were dressed in clean, shining linen and wore golden sashes around their chests. ⁷Then one of the four living creatures gave to the seven angels seven golden bowls filled with the wrath of God, who lives for ever and ever. ⁸And the temple was filled with smoke from the glory of God and from his power, and no one could enter the temple until the seven plagues of the seven angels were completed.

Original Meaning

THE BOWLS, like the seals and the trumpets, are administered by angels. But John makes it clear that what he sees is a symbolic portrayal of judgments; like the woman and the dragon, this scene of angels preparing to pour out bowls is a "sign" in the heavens (12:1, 3; 15:1).[1]

---

1. For similar language of apocalyptic signs, see 1 En. 34:1.

Thus when he declares that these seven plagues are the "last plagues," completing God's anger, he probably does not imply that Revelation arranges all judgments in literal chronological sequence (though this book does emphasize completion of God's purposes; 10:7; 11:7). Rather, "last" implies that these bowls begin John's final sequence of judgments. They are the last in terms of John's narrative—based on the sequence of his visions rather than on the sequence of history. Note that in 15:1, 8, the completion of these plagues forms an inclusio around the entire scene of heaven in 15:1–8, thereby framing this section with an emphasis on the plagues.

The word used for the "bowls" of divine anger (*phiale*, 15:7; 16:1–17:1; 21:9) is also used for the bowls that contained the prayers of the saints (5:8), suggesting a connection between the saints' intercession and their vindication through the world's judgments, as with the trumpet plagues (8:3–5).[2] Probably these bowls, like those in 5:8, contain incense representing the prayers of the saints; it is also possible that the image here implies cups of judgment leading up to the final judgment of the wine cup of God's anger (14:10, 19–20). That the judgments in this passage issue from God's presence and follow worship by the conquering martyrs (15:2–4) probably implies that God has chosen to release his acts in history in response to the worship of faithful saints.[3]

Those who have "been victorious over the beast" (15:2) are the saints who overcame by way of the cross, that is, by being defeated on a purely earthly level by refusing to compromise with the agendas of the tyrannical beast (12:11; 13:7). This is the same group already portrayed as God's conquering army in 14:1–5, who conquered by martyrdom (see also comment on 7:4–8). The location of the overcomers is significant. The "sea of glass" (15:2) recalls the heavenly temple (see comment on 4:6); perhaps the mixture "with fire" indicates that these saints have overcome the "lake of fire," although it has not yet been mentioned (19:20; 20:10, 14–15; 21:8).

The song in 15:2–4 drives home the point. The harpists explicitly recall 14:2, and this passage spells out the "new song" of the 144,000 in 14:3; it declares how they have been victorious. Their song is the "song of Moses . . . and the song of the Lamb," recalling the Exodus both in terms of Moses' leading out of Egypt (cf. 11:8) and deliverance from God's plagues by the

2. For temple bowls, see Ex. 25:29; 37:16; Num. 4:7; 7:84; for "bowls" of water and wine used at the altar for the Feast of Tabernacles ritual, cf. *m. Suk.* 4:9; *tos. Suk.* 3:14. Ford, *Revelation*, 254, notes that *phiale* applies to "a broad, flat bowl often used for drinking or pouring libations" (cf. Josephus, *Ant.* 3.150), but she also suggests the possibility of incense bowls (cf. Josephus, *Ant.* 3.143).

3. See Talbert, *Apocalypse*, 69–70. "Overcome from the beast" (lit.) may reflect Latin grammar (David Aune, "A Latinism in Revelation 15:2," *JBL* 110 [1991]: 691–92).

blood of the Passover lamb.[4] Some compare the song with Moses' song in Deuteronomy 31:30–32:43, which may in fact originate some of the imagery employed by later prophets and Revelation (esp. the themes of divine vengeance, the vine of Sodom, and their deadly wine, 32:32–35).[5] But the primary allusion is surely the song of the Exodus in Exodus 15:1–18, which evokes more of the Exodus themes alluded to here.[6] This song continued to generate much attention in early Jewish circles.[7]

Israel sang this song, led by Moses and summarized antiphonally by Miriam (Ex. 15:21), when God brought his people through the Red Sea and destroyed their enemies, the Egyptians. As God conquered Egypt in the sea, there figuratively slaying the primeval dragon (Ps. 74:13–14; Isa. 51:9), so here the 144,000 are the people of the new exodus, delivered and standing as conquerors on the sea of glass and fire. This song proved a fitting climax for the plagues on Egypt of old or Revelation's equivalent (11:8), from which the righteous were shielded (7:1–8).

The song in verses 3–4 praises God in language developed from Israel's ancient worship, especially Psalm 86:8–10.[8] The saints address God as either "King of the ages" or "King of the nations" (Rev. 15:3); both readings have significant support and we cannot tell conclusively which is more likely the original reading. "King of the ages" means "eternal King,"[9] which certainly fits the context: God is the Alpha and the Omega (1:8) and will reign forever (11:15). On the other hand, "King of the nations" also makes sense; God has triumphed over the nations as he triumphed over Egypt in the Exodus, and now the nations will come to worship him

---

4. Glasson, *Moses*, 96, cites as background a single reference to a dream that compares Moses to a lamb (*Jerusalem Targ.* to Ex. 1:15); but it is best to distinguish Moses from the Lamb in Rev. 15:3 (the Greek does not link them by a hendiadys).

5. For the use of Deut. 32 in early Christian literature, see Richard N. Longenecker, *Biblical Exegesis in the Apostolic Period* (Grand Rapids: Eerdmans, 1975), 179.

6. See Bauckham, *Climax of Prophecy*, 296–307; Roland Meynet, "Le cantique de Moïse et le cantique de l'Agneau (Ap 15 et Ex 15)," *Gregorianum* 73 (1992): 19–55. Markus Barth, *The People of God*, JSNTSup 5 (Sheffield: JSOT, 1983), 14, sees the church portrayed in Rev. 15 as the community of the Exodus.

7. Cf. Philo, *Contemp. Life* 85–87; *Husbandry* 80–82; 4Q365, fr. 6a in George J. Brooke, "Power to the Powerless—Long-Lost Song of Miriam," *BAR* 20 (May 1994): 62–65. Roloff, *Revelation*, 183, cites a Tannaitic tradition that Moses and the resurrected would sing Ex. 15 again at the resurrection.

8. Mounce, *Revelation*, 287, finds LXX language (in sequence) from Ps. 11:2; 139:14 (God's marvelous deeds); Amos 4:13; Deut. 32:4; Ps. 86:9; Mal. 1:11; Ps. 144:17; 98:2. For God alone being holy, see 1 Sam. 2:2, and the idea of Ex. 15:11.

9. With Rissi, *Time and History*, 31. "God of the ages" is not unknown (e.g., Jub. 31:13; Gen. Apoc. 2.7; 21.2; some manuscripts of Jos. and Asen. 12:1/2).

(15:4).[10] Further, "King of the nations" (15:3) is linked with the prayer, "Who should not revere you?" in Jeremiah 10:7 (the addition of "glorify" is from the base text, Ps. 86:9). Both expressions probably reflect a Semitic understanding of the original *melek haʿolam*, which can be rendered either "King of the ages" or "King of the world."[11] God is also "Almighty," as Revelation declares eight other times, usually in praises (see comment on 1:8).

God's greatness and his "marvelous . . . deeds" (15:3) recall Psalm 86:10 (cf. Job 9:10), since verse 4 explicitly quotes Psalm 86:9. Yet the "great and marvelous . . . deeds" in Revelation's own context especially refer to the "great and marvelous" plagues of Revelation 15:1, that is, God's judgments.[12] Likewise, after God drowned the Egyptian army in the Red Sea, the Israelites recognized God as One "working wonders" (Ex. 15:11); Psalm 86 probably alludes back to that proclamation in Exodus, because 86:8 and 10 recall its language.[13] God is both "just and true" in his judgments (Rev. 15:3; 16:7; 19:2; cf. 6:10)—"just" or "righteous" in executing appropriate judgment (16:5–6), and "true" in his faithfulness to the saints, whose blood he now vindicates (3:7, 14; 19:9, 11; 21:5; 22:6).[14]

Yet whereas in the Exodus God overthrew Egypt for oppressing Israel, here he welcomes those from all nations who have joined God's servants in resisting the world. The nations now come to God in worship (15:4), as in 21:24. Judgment brings representatives of all peoples to repentance (for more on this, see Bridging Contexts section, below).

As with the judgments of the seals (5:1–2) and the trumpets (8:2), the plagues from the bowls (16:1–17) are introduced with a scene in heaven (15:5–8), reminding us that earthly disasters are not merely accidents, but methodically arranged events determined by God's sovereign vindication of his saints. These angels of judgment, in contrast to destroying angels in some

---

10. This reading may have slightly more in its favor, but not much (cf. Bruce M. Metzger, *A Textual Commentary on the Greek New Testament*, 2d ed. [New York: United Bible Societies, 1975], 753–54). Phrases like "Lord of the world" were common (1 Enoch 84:2; 2 Macc. 7:9; Ps. Sol. 2:32; T. Moses 1:11; *Sifre Deut.* 306.3.1; 306.5.1; *p. Sanh.* 6:3, §1). Rhetoricians might extol deities on the ground of widespread worship of them (Robert M. Grant, *Gods and the One God*, LEC 1 [Philadelphia: Westminster, 1986], 56).

11. Thus, e.g., Knibb's and Isaac's variant translations of 1 Enoch 81:10.

12. Cf. God as "just and true" in T. Job 4:11/9; of his ways in Neh. 9:13; Dan. 4:37. God displays his "wonderful" strength at the final battle in 1QM 15.13 (probably also in 1QM 12.7).

13. Jewish tradition sometimes applied God's "deeds" specifically to his plagues on Egypt and judgment of them at the Red Sea (*Sifre Deut.* 27.5.1; 27.7.1). God's "works" could refer to his mighty acts (CD 13.7–8) and could invite praise (1QS 1.21; 11.20; 1QM 10.1–2, 8–9). For God's "righteous" and "true" judgments, see T. Job 43:13.

14. The language also may counter imperial propaganda that praised the emperor as "just," among other virtues (Aune, *Revelation*, 2:874, citing Augustus, *Res Gestae* 34.2).

strands of Jewish tradition, are willingly obedient servants of God (cf. 17:1; 21:9); it is a throne angel that hands them the judgments to pour out on humankind (15:7).[15]

That this scene takes place in the heavenly temple is significant.[16] The angels' linen clothing (15:6) may simply reflect the tradition that angels normally wore white or linen (1 En. 71:1; Ps-Philo 9:10; John 20:12), but alongside the mention of golden breastplates (cf. Ex. 39:8; probably Rev. 1:13) undoubtedly reminds the reader that these angels fulfill priestly acts in the heavenly temple (15:5–6). Worshipers in temples normally wore linen or white,[17] and this was required for service in the Most Holy Place (Lev. 16:4). The prerequisite for such service was righteousness (Rev. 19:8). Priests in the heavenly temple respond to the earthly priests (1:6) of the oppressed earthly temple (11:1–2), whose prayers (6:9–11; 8:3–6) have invited the judgments about to begin.

That "smoke" filled the heavenly temple (15:8, note contrast with the smoke of the world's torment in 14:11) alludes to God's glory filling his house in some Old Testament theophanies (Isa. 6:4; Ezek. 10:3–4). Under these circumstances the priests could not minister in the temple (1 Kings 8:10–12; 2 Chron. 7:2), nor could even Moses enter the tabernacle (Ex. 40:35); the glory exceeded human ability to withstand. God had filled the earthly tabernacle with his glory at its dedication and a time of celebration (Ex. 40; cf. 1 Kings 8); now he fills the temple with glory in response to the worship of his martyred conquerors through history, and responds with systematic judgments (probably also poured out throughout history). Judgment, as well as mercy, reveals God's great glory.

THE NATIONS. The nations come to God in worship in 15:4. Revelation blends various portrayals of the future in the biblical prophets, including judgment on the nations (19:18–21; 20:8–9; cf. Joel 3:12; Mic. 4:13), the nations' turning to God (Rev. 21:24, 26; cf. Isa. 19:25; Zech. 2:11; 8:22–23), and the nations' becoming servants to God's people (Rev. 21:24–26; cf. Isa. 45:14; 49:23; Dan. 7:14).

To harmonize such portrayals on the theological level, we must understand at least some of them on a symbolic level. Since other early Christian

---

15. On "angels of destruction," see 1QS 4.12.

16. Aune, *Revelation*, 2:878, parallels the opening of this temple to the temple of Janus, opened whenever war was declared. Most important, "opened" heavens relate to divine revelation (4:1; 11:19; 19:11; cf. John 1:51).

17. Pausanias, 2.35.5; 6.20.3; Josephus, *Ant.* 11.327; see comment on 4:4.

literature is unanimous that there is no Christian conversion apart from faith in Christ, and since Revelation also portrays the destruction of the nations, it is likely that the turning of the nations refers to the repentant remnant among the nations. Some take this as the majority who are not killed, hence predict the conversion of much of the world (cf. 11:13, if it refers to the world rather than to Jewish people). But perhaps it simply reminds us that as the beast has its kingdom from all peoples, so also does Christ, and the remnant of all nations will worship him. The praise of the nations indicates that in the end the world will recognize the falsehood of idols and the truth of God, the Lamb, and their people.

The wrath. Some interpret the bowls of God's anger as the "wrath" from which Paul promised believers deliverance through sharing Christ's resurrection (1 Thess. 1:10; 5:9). But the syllogism that (1) the Tribulation is God's wrath, (2) the saints will not go through God's wrath, (3) hence the saints will escape the Tribulation is logically vulnerable. To identify the "wrath" in (1) with the "wrath" in (2) is no more straightforward than saying saints are appointed to tribulation (1 Thess 3:3), hence must endure the Great Tribulation.

Is the sense of "wrath" equivalent in both contexts? In Paul's writings, "wrath" (*orge*) sometimes refers to God's present anger, which is not against us, but neither are we removed from the world that endures it (Rom. 1:18; Eph. 5:6; 1 Thess. 2:16). Usually, however, Paul means future wrath at the Second Coming, the Day of Judgment (Rom. 2:5, 8; 9:22); he nowhere unambiguously applies it to the Tribulation period. When Paul speaks of salvation from wrath, he refers to a promise for all believers, not only the final generation (Rom. 5:9).

To read Revelation into Paul, as if Paul's first readers could simply flip over to Revelation (not yet written) to understand his meaning, is historically naive. But even if we jump from Paul's use to Revelation, Revelation always applies the same Greek term for wrath (*orge*) to the judgment at Christ's coming, not during the Tribulation (6:16–17; 11:18; 14:10; 16:19; 19:15). The synonymous Greek word *thymos* sometimes applies to the Tribulation period (15:1, 7; 16:1), but even that usually refers to the Second Coming wrath (14:10, 19; 16:19; 19:15).[18]

Whatever else may be said about Tribulation saints, it must be said that they do not stand under God's anger, since Christ died for them (7:14). If they will not suffer God's wrath during the Tribulation, we have no reason to argue that the church must be raptured out before it to escape God's wrath;

---

18. For the function of God's wrath in apocalyptic literature in general, see Talbert, *Apocalypse*, 65.

if they will be protected during wrath, the same might be said of the church. In any case, this provides no logical argument here for a Rapture before the Tribulation.[19]

 SPIRITUAL WARFARE AND **overcoming**. This text, like the rest of Revelation, provides a graphic model of spiritual warfare for us: We overcome by being physically defeated, by enduring the world's suffering (see comment on 5:5–6; 7:9–17). The conquerors provide us a model of unwavering faithfulness to God and to his purposes. "The Beast has conquered them in martyrdom but in that same martyrdom *they had conquered the Beast,* for he had been utterly unable to make them deny Christ. This is their victory: loyalty to Christ in tribulation."[20]

For Christians struggling against the imperial cult in John's day or subsequent forces of the Antichrist in history, "this song affords great encouragement. The last word of history is not with Satan and his Antichrist, but with the Lord and his Christ."[21] The Church has nothing to fear, in this age as well as the age to come, for God reigns forever (or, over all peoples, depending on which variant reading one prefers). As Ladd puts it, "Even when evil is strongest on the earth, when God's people are most violently attacked by Satan, God is still the 'King of the ages' (Rev. 15:3)."[22]

Like Israel in the Exodus, God's people will again triumph; the certainty of the new redemption is rooted in our confidence in the old one.[23] For John, the songs of Moses and the Lamb were not two separate songs, as if Old Testament redemption and New Testament redemption were discontinuous and incompatible ideas. Jesus as the Lamb has provided the climactic act of redemption, akin to the paschal lamb of the first Exodus, so the song of Moses is also the song of the Lamb. That the overcomers stand on the sea (15:2) may indicate afresh the triumph of the Exodus that subdued even the sea (Ex. 15:8; Ps. 78:13; 89:9–10).

Praising God. The song reminds us that we must praise God for his deliverance and acknowledge his greatness (15:3–4; for more on the former, see

---

19. Gundry, *Church and Tribulation,* 44–45.

20. Ladd, *The Last Things,* 70, italics his. Cf. Ladd, *Theology,* 625: "In the day when the eternal destiny of men is at stake, martyrdom will itself be a victory."

21. Beasley-Murray, *Revelation,* 236–37.

22. Ladd, *Gospel of the Kingdom,* 31.

23. On the historical certainty of the first one, see, e.g., comments in Kevin D. Miller, "Did the Exodus Never Happen?" *CT* (Sept. 7, 1998), 44–51; Craig Keener and Glenn Usry, *Defending Black Faith* (Downers Grove, Ill.: InterVarsity, 1997), 147–65.

comment on 5:9–10; on the latter, see comment on 4:8). The text also invites us to praise God for his judgments on the world (15:1, 3; cf. 19:1–6), though we must qualify what we mean by this praise. It is praise not for the suffering of our fellow human beings, for whose well-being we should work and pray (Luke 6:28; 1 Tim. 2:1–2). Rather, we see in these judgments, as in the plagues of the first Exodus, acts of deliverance for God's people; the sufferings of this age are birth pangs for a better one. Nor does God look on such activity merely passively (Zeph. 3:17). That God's heavenly temple is filled with glory (15:8) indicates that he celebrates the triumph with us.

The bowls. That "bowls" are used both for God's anger (15:7) and the saints' prayers (5:8) probably emphasizes, as noted earlier, the importance of prayer in the way God moves history and brings about his purposes. This may suggest that God seeks not only a generation of radical witnesses before the end (6:9–11; cf. Matt. 24:14) but a people of prayer. God often uses prayer, itself moved by God's Spirit, to prepare for the fulfillment of many of his purposes in history (e.g., Ex. 2:23–24; Matt. 9:37–38).

That the judgments (16:1–17) are prefaced with a scene of heaven (15:5–8; cf. 5:1–2; 8:2) reminds us that God is sovereign. The world's catastrophes, while not directed against each individual who suffers them, often function as wake-up calls to the world, vindicating God's message and the prayers of his people that he will reveal himself in the world. Such judgments thus serve as a foretaste of the final Day of Judgment, to warn people to get ready for it before it is too late (9:20–21; 16:9).

Revelation 16:1–21

THEN I HEARD a loud voice from the temple saying to the seven angels, "Go, pour out the seven bowls of God's wrath on the earth."

²The first angel went and poured out his bowl on the land, and ugly and painful sores broke out on the people who had the mark of the beast and worshiped his image.

³The second angel poured out his bowl on the sea, and it turned into blood like that of a dead man, and every living thing in the sea died.

⁴The third angel poured out his bowl on the rivers and springs of water, and they became blood. ⁵Then I heard the angel in charge of the waters say:

> "You are just in these judgments,
>> you who are and who were, the Holy One,
>> because you have so judged;
> ⁶for they have shed the blood of your saints and prophets,
>> and you have given them blood to drink
>>> as they deserve."

⁷And I heard the altar respond:

> "Yes, Lord God Almighty,
>> true and just are your judgments."

⁸The fourth angel poured out his bowl on the sun, and the sun was given power to scorch people with fire. ⁹They were seared by the intense heat and they cursed the name of God, who had control over these plagues, but they refused to repent and glorify him.

¹⁰The fifth angel poured out his bowl on the throne of the beast, and his kingdom was plunged into darkness. Men gnawed their tongues in agony ¹¹and cursed the God of heaven because of their pains and their sores, but they refused to repent of what they had done.

¹²The sixth angel poured out his bowl on the great river Euphrates, and its water was dried up to prepare the way for the kings from the East. ¹³Then I saw three evil spirits that looked like frogs; they came out of the mouth of the dragon,

out of the mouth of the beast and out of the mouth of the false prophet. ¹⁴They are spirits of demons performing miraculous signs, and they go out to the kings of the whole world, to gather them for the battle on the great day of God Almighty.

¹⁵"Behold, I come like a thief! Blessed is he who stays awake and keeps his clothes with him, so that he may not go naked and be shamefully exposed."

¹⁶Then they gathered the kings together to the place that in Hebrew is called Armageddon.

¹⁷The seventh angel poured out his bowl into the air, and out of the temple came a loud voice from the throne, saying, "It is done!" ¹⁸Then there came flashes of lightning, rumblings, peals of thunder and a severe earthquake. No earthquake like it has ever occurred since man has been on earth, so tremendous was the quake. ¹⁹The great city split into three parts, and the cities of the nations collapsed. God remembered Babylon the Great and gave her the cup filled with the wine of the fury of his wrath. ²⁰Every island fled away and the mountains could not be found. ²¹From the sky huge hailstones of about a hundred pounds each fell upon men. And they cursed God on account of the plague of hail, because the plague was so terrible.

IN RESPONSE TO the worship of martyrs (15:3–4), seven angels bring out the seven bowls of God's anger as a further rite of worship (15:5–7). Here the bowls, reminiscent of the plagues in Exodus, are poured out on the unrepentant world.

More Plagues (16:1–11)

A VOICE COMES from "from the temple" (16:1), the heavenly temple that has just been mentioned (15:5–8). Jewish people would think most naturally of a heavenly voice from God, known to speak sometimes in the temple. Heavenly voices abound in Revelation (10:4, 8; 11:12; 12:10; 19:5; 21:3), at least sometimes representing Christ (1:12–13; 4:1), though not always (14:2). The wicked have trampled the earthly temple (11:2), so judgment goes forth from the heavenly temple (11:19; 14:15, 17; 15:5–16:1; 16:17). The "seven bowls of God's wrath" represent urns in the temple, perhaps for libations of incense (see comment on 15:7).[1] The bowls are much like the trumpets, even

---

1. The "pouring" of God's wrath is a familiar Old Testament expression (I have randomly counted nearly thirty examples: e.g., 2 Chron. 12:7; 34:21, 25; Jer. 6:11; 7:20; 10:25; 42:18;

in sequence, the differences being "but variations on common themes," though the bowls emphasize humanity's rebellion and extend the areas judged under the trumpets.[2]

Most of the bowls, like the trumpets, recall the plagues of the Exodus: sores (16:2), water into blood (16:3–4), and darkness (16:10, and in this case its antithesis, 16:9). By recalling the plagues, this series of judgments also reminds believers that as God protected his own people in Goshen during the plagues, so he will protect them from his judgments (7:1–8; 12:6, 16). The final two bowls represent the promised end-time battle and the completion of God's promises.

The water into blood plague is repeated for emphasis (16:3–4), to demonstrate the appropriateness of God's judgment (16:5–7).[3] Jewish people believed God assigned various angels to superintend various features of nature (which Greeks attributed to gods or other spirits); here "the angel in charge of the waters," whose domain was turned to blood, praises God's justice (16:5–6).[4]

The angel's and altar's praise provides the most striking feature of these judgments that adds to what the hearer already experienced in the trumpet judgments (16:5–7). The recitation of God's justice (or righteousness) and holiness (16:5) develop the song of Moses in 15:3–4, which also comments on God's judgments. The basis for recognizing God's holiness and justice here is "because you have so judged" (16:5; again in 19:2).

Most Jewish people knew the story of Tobit, including Tobit's cry, "Righteous are you, O Lord ... and you judge true and righteous judgment forever" (Tob. 3:2). But whereas Tobit's mention of God's righteousness emphasizes his forgiving his people (3:3–4), our passage emphasizes the justness of his punishing the wicked (16:5–6).[5] As God's enemies "have shed" ("poured out")

44:6; Ezek. 20:8, 13, 21, 33–34; 30:15; Dan. 9:11, 27; Hos. 5:10; Nah. 1:6). One of these is specifically in the context of God's protecting his own (Ezek. 9:8), and one specifically for the shedding of innocent blood (36:18).

2. Beasley-Murray, *Revelation*, 238–39; cf. also Beale, *Revelation*, 809–10.

3. For Jewish traditions emphasizing the cry for vindication implicit in the blood of righteous martyrs, sometimes by actual fountains of blood, see sources in Craig S. Keener, *Matthew* (Downers Grove, Ill.: InterVarsity, 1997), 341; idem, *A Commentary on the Gospel of Matthew* (Grand Rapids: Eerdmans, 1999), 956–57.

4. For angels of nature, see Jub. 2:2; 1 Enoch 20:2; and other references under Rev 14:18. The plural "rivers" probably reflects Ex. 7:19 or Ps. 78:44.

5. Some suggest that John here omits "who is to come" from 16:5 (from "who is and who was"—1:4, 8; 4:8) because the Lord is no longer the "coming one" since he now acts in judgment (cf. Gerhard Delling, "Zum Gottesdienstlichen Stil her Johannes-Apokalypse," *NovT* 3 [1959]: 107–37); but this is not the final judgment, nor would he cease to be Lord of the future; thus, the omission may be coincidental.

---

blood (16:6), so he "poured out" judgments (16:1–17), including blood (16:3–4); he avenges the world's repression of his servants, fulfilling his martyrs' anticipation (6:9–11; 14:20; 17:6; 18:24). The appropriateness of blood for those who shed blood also fits the Jewish tradition that God turned the Nile bloody to avenge the earlier Egyptian murder of Israelite infants (Wisd. 11:6–7).[6]

"The altar" confirms God's justice (16:7), undoubtedly because it harbors the prayers of the saints (either the altar of sacrifice [6:9] or the altar of incense [8:3, 5]); hence it participates in the judgment (9:13; 14:18). It echoes Moses' song in 15:3: God is powerful enough ("Lord God Almighty") to execute his "true and just" judgments.

The plagues of scorching sun and darkness (16:8–10) recall the Old Testament plague of darkness, a judgment on Egypt's sun-deity, Amon-Re; they may also recall other events of the Exodus.[7] That the darkness actually causes pain (16:10) may reflect the darkness of Moses' day, which could be "felt" (Ex. 10:21; cf. Ps. 107:10).[8] But instead of understanding God's justice and responding with repentance, the objects of his wrath grow harder against God and blaspheme him all the more (16:9, 11; cf. 9:20–21; 16:21; on blaspheming, see comment on 13:1, 6).

Racing Toward Judgment (16:12–21)

THE "GREAT RIVER Euphrates" (16:12) recalls the terrifying image of 9:14, just as "prepare" recalls the same passage's emphasis that God will bring judgments at the appropriate hour ("kept ready" [9:15] is the same Greek verb as here). Although many rivers in the Near East occasionally dried up, the massive Euphrates was never known to do so under natural circumstances. This fact augments the terror of the image and is evidence of divine judgment (Isa. 50:2; Hos. 13:15; Nah. 1:4).[9]

---

6. On "deserving" such punishments, see also Wisd. Sol. 16:1, 9; 18:4; 19:4; cf. also *Ex. Rab.* 9:10; contrast Rev. 3:4. On similar appropriate judgments involving flesh or blood, see Isa. 49:26; Josephus, *War* 6.216; *Lev. Rab.* 33:6; Homer, *Il.* 16.459. On devouring people, cf. 1 Enoch 103:11, 15; on God pouring out people's blood in judgment, cf. 1 En. 94:9; on drinking blood as a metaphor for murder, see Suetonius, *Tib.* 59.

7. J. Massyngberde Ford, "The Structure and Meaning of Revelation 16," *ExpTim* 98 (1987): 327–30, finds in the fourth and fifth bowls the contrast between the pillar of fire and cloud, in the sixth (more likely) an allusion to the drying of the Red Sea, and in the seventh an allusion to the theophany at Sinai. Aune, *Revelation*, 2:889, mentions the Greek myth in which Phaethon accidentally scorched the earth with the sun chariot.

8. Some later rabbis said the darkness killed the wicked, even in Israel (*Pes. Rab Kah.* 5:9; *Song Rab.* 13, §1). The beast's "throne" (16:10; cf. 2:13) contrasts with God's (4:2); his "kingdom" (16:10) will become God's (11:15; the singular may reflect the beast's pretension that he controls the entire world).

9. Aune, *Revelation*, 2:890–91.

Ancient Jewish hearers would have readily grasped the image of the drying of a river to invite invasion; one Jewish tradition announced that a river was to be frozen to allow the invasion of Asia (Sib. Or. 4.464–67), and some Jewish people expected God to part the Euphrates for the ten "lost" tribes to return to their land (4 Ezra 13:43–47; cf. Isa. 11:15–16).[10] Indeed, the parting of the Jordan for Israel invited the conquest of Canaan (Josh. 3:14–17; 4:23–5:1).[11] Yet as noted earlier (9:14), people in the ancient Mediterranean remembered the Euphrates especially as the boundary between the Roman and Parthian empires. People expected Nero to bring the kings of the East across the Euphrates to wreak his vengeance on Rome (see comment on 9:14–16; 13:1–4).[12]

The text may be suggesting the dragon, beast, and false prophet as a sort of a satanic trinity (see comment on 13:11–12). That it speaks of frogs coming out of their mouths may recall another Egyptian plague (Ex. 8:2–13; Ps. 78:45; 105:30), but like the plague of locusts (Ex. 10:13–14; Rev. 9:3) it is transformed into something different in Revelation's symbolism. Presumably there are three frogs because they issue from three mouths; because they issue from mouths, they probably represent propaganda (13:2, 5–6; contrast 14:5). In the end, however, the frogs prove no match for God's truth as a sword from the mouth of the Word made flesh (1:16; 19:15).

The image is grotesque; ancients usually viewed frogs as unclean, ugly, and vicious.[13] They could function as a terrible omen, especially if they leaped from another creature's mouth.[14] One writer close to John's day remarked tongue-in-cheek that Nero nearly was reincarnated as a viper, but mercifully was allowed to become a frog so he could continue his singing.[15] Some Jewish people also expected the release of more demons in the end time (16:14; 2 Bar. 27:9). These "spirits of demons" perform persuasive "miraculous signs" (Rev. 16:14), like the beast they serve (13:13–14).

---

10. Beale, *Revelation*, 827, also notes Cyrus's diversion of the Euphrates to allow the unexpected capture of Babylon (Herodotus, 1.190–91; Xenophon, *Cyropedia* 7.5.1–36; prophesied in Jer. 50:38; 51:36).

11. Cf. Fekkes, *Isaiah*, 201–2. Some of these Jewish traditions may reflect more the promise that the Euphrates would constitute a boundary for Israel's empire (Gen. 15:18; Ex. 23:31; Deut. 11:24).

12. See also Talbert, *Apocalypse*, 74; Kraybill, *Imperial Cult and Commerce*, 162–64.

13. Ovid. *Metam.* 6.370–81. For their swampy habitat, see Ps-Hesiod, *Battle of Frogs and Mice* 56–64; Babrius 120. For spirits issuing from the mouth or nose, see Aune, *Revelation*, 2:894.

14. Apuleius, *Metam.* 9.34. In dreams they could be held to symbolize cheaters and beggars (Artemidorus, *Oneir.* 2.15). They are linked with evil in Persian religion (Beasley-Murray, *Revelation*, 244) and in some other cultures (Catherine Berndt, "The Role of Native Doctors in Aboriginal Australia," 264–82 in *Magic, Faith, and Healing*, ed. Ari Kiev [New York: Free Press, 1964], 227).

15. Plutarch, *Divine Vengeance* 32, Mor. 567F–68A.

The devil and his agents then gather the nations together in order to battle the true God, though in reality they were being gathered simply for God's great day, that is, for their destruction (16:14; cf. 19:11–18; 20:8–9). The gathering of the wicked for their own destruction is a common end-time image (Joel 3:10–16; Mic. 4:11–13; Zeph. 3:8; Zech. 12:3–4; 14:2–3).[16]

Such an announcement proves an appropriate point for John to remind his hearers that Jesus will come like a thief (16:15), as he stated earlier (3:3) and as most early Christians seem to have been warned (Matt. 24:43; Luke 12:39; 1 Thess. 5:2, 4; 2 Peter 3:10). Alluding back to this earlier warning (esp. harsh toward the sleeping church of Sardis), John insists that those found unprepared will be stripped instead of walking with Jesus in robes of white (cf. Rev. 3:4–5, 17–18); nakedness was a great shame to Jewish people.[17] The righteous must remain righteous without compromise, for terrible times are coming; but Jesus will come when the world does not expect him.

The meaning of "Armageddon"—most likely Hebrew for "Mount Megiddo"—is obscure. Megiddo lay on a plain (2 Chron. 35:22; Zech. 12:11) rather than on a mountain (though it was above sea level and near hill country), but apocalyptic geography allowed considerable symbolic flexibility. The valley of Megiddo was the site of some significant battles in history (Judg. 5:19; 2 Kings 23:29) and was strategically located for further ones. Although a valley would have worked well as an image of end-time judgment (Joel 3:12, 14), Megiddo may appear here as a mountain to symbolize its stature or as a contrast with Mount Zion (21:10), where in some traditions the Messiah would do battle with the gathered nations (4 Ezra 13:34; cf. Rev. 14:1).[18]

---

16. Cf. likewise 1QM 15.3; 4 Ezra 13:33–34; for nations gathered against Babylon or other enemies of Israel, see Jer. 49:14; 50:29. In 1 En. 56:5–7, angels stir the Parthians in the East and a spirit drives them into the holy land until the Parthians are defeated. For other gatherings of the wicked, see Isa. 43:9; 66:18; 1 Enoch 100:4; Matt. 3:12; 13:41; 24:39–41; 25:32.

17. See Jub. 3:21–22, 30–31; 7:8–10, 20; 1QS 7.12; tos. Ber. 2:14; Sifre Deut. 320.5.2. There is a Jewish tradition that sleeping guards will be beaten and on the second offense will have their clothes burned (Ford, *Revelation*, 263). Note God's threat that Babylon will be stripped naked as a consequence of her infidelity (cf. Isa. 20:4; 47:1–3; Rev. 17:16) and that Judah's lovers will expose her nakedness before them (Ezek. 16:37). Nakedness appears to have been a punishment for infidelity in the Old Testament period (see Jer. 13:22, 26–27; Lam. 1:8; Ezek. 23:26–29; Hos. 2:3; Cyrus H. Gordon, *The Ancient Near East* [New York: W. W. Norton, 1965], 229–30), fitting for those in league with Revelation's "prostitute."

18. Others have identified the mountain with Mount Carmel, where Elijah confronted Baal's prophets (William H. Shea, "The Location and Significance of Armageddon in Rev 16:16," *AUSS* 18 [1980]: 157–62); connected it with the LXX rendering "cut down" in Zech. 12:11 (Hans K. LaRondelle, "The Etymology of Har-Magedon [Rev 16:16]," *AUSS* 27 [1989]: 69–73, likely unavailable to John's audience); linked it with the *har mo'ed*, "mount of assem-

The seventh bowl "poured out . . . into the air" (16:17) refers to judgment either over the air (cf. winds in 7:1) or over the entire world in the "air realm" (the lowest of the heavens in Greco-Roman thought).[19] In either case it reminds the reader of God's continuing sovereignty over the cosmos. With this judgment, the judgments are "done" (16:17), as at the final trumpet (10:7) and the consummation of God's plan for history implied in the new creation (21:6).

The thunder, lightning, and earthquake (16:18) suggest a revelation of God's glory as at Sinai (Ex. 19:16; see comment on 4:5; cf. 8:5; 11:19); but the earthquake also signals the end of the age (6:12; 11:13).[20] The "great city" that divided into three parts (16:19) may refer to Jerusalem (if that is the "great city" of 11:8, 13), but there only one tenth of the city is destroyed by an earthquake (if we press the details literally). The other "great city" is Babylon, called both "Babylon the Great" (14:8; 17:5; 18:2) and "the great city" (17:18; 18:10, 16, 18–21); because Babylon is called "the Great" immediately after this (16:19), Babylon (Rome) is certainly in view here.[21] The city now drinks the cup of God's wrath (cf. 14:8–10), a fitting image for one portrayed as sexually unfaithful (Num. 5:23–24).

Some allegorize the disappearance of mountains (16:20), connecting them with idol worship in ancient Israel (Ezek. 6:3, 13–14), but then find themselves hard-pressed to explain the islands (Rev. 16:20).[22] But the moving of islands and mountains, as in 6:14, is merely part of the image of dramatic, cosmic judgment (Isa. 42:15; 64:1–3; Nah. 1:5–6), especially appropriate to the end time (Ezek. 38:19–20; Mic. 1:3–4; Zech. 14:5; 1 En. 1:6–7).

As in 8:7, the "hail" (16:21) recalls the plague against Egypt's crops (Ex. 9:18–34), severe enough to kill those caught out in it (9:19). But this is a

---

bly" in Isa. 14:13 (Rissi, *Time and History*, 84; but see Fekkes, *Isaiah*, 202–3), which can symbolize Mount Zion (Roland E. Loasby, "'Har-Magedon' According to the Hebrew in the Setting of the Seven Last Plagues of Revelation 16," *AUSS* 27 [1989]: 129–32; Meredith G. Kline, "Har Magedon: The End of the Millennium," *JETS* 39 [June 1996]: 207–22; logical, though this requires connections that much of John's audience might not catch); or see it as the end-time location of slaughter (Magog in Ezek. 38:8–39:16).

19. For "air" as the lowest realm of the heavens, see Cicero, *De Nat. Deor.* 2.26.66; 2.36.91; *PGM*, 1.179–82; 4.3043–44; 12.67; Philo, *Giants* 9; *Som.* 1.135.

20. Amos Nur and Hagai Ron, "Earthquake! Inspiration for Armageddon," *BAR* 23 (July 1997): 48–55, observe that Megiddo, probably just alluded to in 16:16, was known for many earthquakes. But could John have expected most of his audience to know this?

21. For Babylon's fall by an earthquake and Parthians, see Sib. Or. 5.34–44.

22. Caird, *Commentary on Revelation*, 209, who can only suggest the islands as a reference to detention (1:9). His connection of a mountain with Babylon in 17:9 ignores the parallel with the new Jerusalem in 21:10.

judgment at the end of the age, and one does not need training in modern physics to recognize that hailstones weighing "about a hundred pounds each" will easily kill whomever they strike.[23] Yet in contrast with the repentant of Jerusalem (11:13), Babylon's inhabitants become harder and curse God all the more when judged (16:21), having learned nothing from their unrepentance during earlier plagues (16:11).[24] The world dies in its sin, unwilling to repent.

Bridging Contexts

ON IDENTIFYING THE judgments. Those tempted to apply the judgments one at a time may find trouble differentiating some of them from others; trying to link them with specific past events is even more difficult. This is not to deny that such correlations have often been attempted. Jonathan Edwards recognized the parallels between the plagues on Egypt and those on the Antichrist, but believed that the first bowl was "poured out in the days of Wyclif, Hus, and Jerome of Prague, the second in the Reformation."[25]

But we should not read too much into the sequence of individual judgments; they are meant to be read as a series. They presumably do not convey a time line or history written in advance, but summarize the sorts of judgments God inflicts on humanity; that is, the God who acted powerfully in the Exodus is the God who still acts in history. He still has his Moses to speak for him (11:5–7), but sends his judgments as long as the world, like Pharaoh, hardens its heart and refuses to stop oppressing people.[26]

In the nineteenth century most Protestants identified the kings of the East either with the Turks or with the lost tribes of Israel. After the collapse of the Turkish Ottoman Empire, Japan became the new favorite of the prophecy movement until and during the Second World War. After Japan's defeat and the ascent of Communist China, this "yellow peril" has become the new backdrop for modern Western interpretations of the "kings from the East."[27] On this view, the invasion from Communist China and the rest of Asia will require the rest of the world's army to mobilize to fight them.[28]

---

23. Ford, *Revelation*, 265, compares the destructiveness of catapult stones of nearly this weight in Josephus, *War* 5.270–73.

24. Rissi, *Time and History*, 11, also emphasizes this contrast.

25. Petersen, *Preaching in the Last Days*, 232.

26. Later rabbis also recognized that God struck Pharaoh for what he had done to Israel (*Num. Rab.* 10:2).

27. See Kyle, *The Last Days*, 111; on the Reformers' views of the Turks (identifying them with Gog, allies of the Antichrist), see ibid., 61.

28. Lindsey, *New World Coming*, 225; Jack T. Chick, *Kings of the East* (Chino, Calif.: Chick Publications, 1975).

This perspective reflects a total lack of understanding of what the Euphrates River represented to ancient hearers in the Mediterranean world. To be sure, the Parthians were no longer a kingdom; but a geographical equivalent would be closer to Iran and Iraq than to China. China's military might is certainly formidable, and its role in future battles cannot be ruled out. My point, however, is that there is nothing in this text to indicate east or south Asia's role in general or China's role in particular; this reading of "kings from the East" is a wholesale guess based on the assumption that the current lineup of world powers is the final one, and it is uninformed by the most basic knowledge of how the expression was used in the ancient world.

Reducing prejudice. Many in our culture harbor anti-Asian prejudice, so we need to be careful how we articulate and apply the biblical texts lest we encourage such prejudice. As an example of such prejudice, we may take Chinese-American Vincent Chin, who at age twenty-seven was getting married in nine days. Some former Detroit Chrysler workers, wrongly assuming that Chin was Japanese and blaming Japan for their own unemployment, beat Chin to death with a baseball bat. As he passed out, he truly pleaded, "It isn't fair." Although they later received harsher sentences, at their first trial the murderers were given merely three years probation and a fine of $3,780 each.[29]

At the same time, a specific application to Iran or Iraq, though geographically more appropriate, is also questionable; it certainly would not have made sense to all generations of history. Whether it might apply at some point depends on whether John simply uses the Parthians to symbolize a terrifying invasion in general or more specifically an invasion literally from across the Euphrates. Certainly the "Parthians" of 9:14–19 were symbolic composite judgments, but a more specific invasion is possible here; the geography of the holy land certainly permits an invasion from the East. While the principle of invasion is clear, the way many biblical prophecies will be fulfilled is unclear until after the fulfillment. In any event, as Christians we need to be careful not to promote hatred of any people for whom Christ died, turning John's images of terror for Rome into invitations for prejudice.

A conservative Baptist writer notes that the war with Iraq in 1991 challenged him to remember that we have a heavenly citizenship that is higher than earthly loyalties; one of his friends was a U.S. army chaplain and another an Iraqi-born Christian worker in Baghdad when the fighting started. He had friends from both countries to pray for.[30] In any case, Scripture suggests

---

29. Andrew Sung Park, *Racial Conflict and Healing* (Maryknoll, N.Y.: Orbis, 1996), 16–17.

30. A. Charles Ware, *Prejudice and the People of God* (Indianapolis: Baptist Bible College of Indianapolis, 1998), 77.

that God will gather all nations for this judgment, not just the "kings from the East" (16:14; cf. Joel 3:10–16).

DIVINE JUDGMENT AND its purpose. This passage announces that God's judgments are just; the world oppresses God's children and then wonders why it must suffer so much. Many people today do not like to talk about divine judgment; in their view, that is not what a god is for. But Santa Claus theology "cannot cope with the reality of evil" or seemingly senseless sufferings. To make God kind but never firm (as many liberals have done) is "to deny his omnipotence and lordship over" a world full of sufferings; facing such hardships without assurance that God has a purpose in them leads to fatalism.[31] A God who never inflicts corporate judgments on the world is not the God of Scripture, but an idol of our own making. As A. W. Tozer observed, "when God acts justly He is not doing so to conform to an independent criterion, but simply acting like Himself in a given situation."[32]

This is not to say that each of those sufferings on an individual level constitutes a judgment; one person may experience a particular kind of suffering as judgment whereas another experiences the same kind of suffering as a test of faith. The sufferings themselves do not reveal their purpose, but they do summon our attention to the God who can give us understanding of their purposes (see Contemporary Significance of 6:1–8).

God sends judgments not only to vindicate his oppressed people (6:9–11; 8:3–6), but also to get the world's attention and offer them the opportunity for repentance (16:9, 11, 21). That many people do not repent when they face judgment is not too surprising (16:9). One survivor of a plane crash recounts that he always expected people who were dying to cry out to God for mercy in their final moments, but noted that he heard many respond with cursing, following the habits they had spent their lives developing. Whether God acts with justice or mercy, some refuse to believe (16:9). They are like the wicked who took Lot's admonitions about impending judgment as jesting (Gen. 19:14), and when Lot tried to prevent homosexual rape, he was accused of being judgmental (19:9).

That the world dies unrepentant in the face of God's judgments (16:9, 11, 21) reveals their obduracy and the depth of human rebellion against God.

---

31. J. I. Packer, *Knowing God* (Downers Grove, Ill.: InterVarsity, 1993), 160.
32. A. W. Tozer, *The Knowledge of the Holy* (New York: Harper & Row, 1961), 93. For more on judgments, see Contemporary Significance section of 8:7–12.

Seeking to illustrate the same sort of point, C. S. Lewis hypothesized that those committed to sin throughout their life might not choose life even after they have been banished to eternal alienation from God.[33] While this perspective does not match literally what we read about hell in Scripture, it does illustrate the point about those who seek to be alienated from God in this life.

Propaganda and truth. That the beasts issue evil propaganda to gather the nations for a final battle against God and his people (16:13; cf. 13:1, 6) also fits our experience as Christians in the present world, whether in the professions, in the academy, or even in slander-filled churches. Horrible crimes like abuse of family members are a grim reality, but the sin is merely compounded when false accusations smear the reputation of godly leaders, as in a couple cases with which I am familiar. The horror of these crimes is so great that the accused have sometimes been judged guilty before the evidence has been evaluated, sometimes on the basis of "recovered memories."[34] If false accusations can devastate on a smaller level, that they occur on a larger level should not surprise us.

More often deception is used by oppressors (wife or child abusers, rapists, robbers, dictators, terrorists) to cover up their injustices or to get the rest of the world to think there may be "truth on both sides." Both because there sometimes is truth on various sides and because relativistic culture has grown increasingly skeptical of truth claims, oppressors can generate the perception of moral ambiguity, leading avengers of injustice to equivocate. Christians must work to expose deceptions (Eph. 5:11–13) and not equivocate in the face of deception and injustice.[35]

At the height of the cold war American leaders portrayed the Soviet Union as a deadly evil empire; after its collapse Russia became a place for U.S. business investment, and various expansionist Middle Eastern regimes and Islamic

---

33. C. S. Lewis, *The Great Divorce* (New York: Macmillan, 1946), esp. 6–9.

34. See "Anatomy of an Abuse Case," *NW* (July 26, 1993), 52–53; "Was It Real or Memories?" *NW* (March 14, 1994), 54–55; "Misty, Watercolored Memories," *NW* (Dec. 13, 1993), 68–69; Jon Meacham, "Trials and Troubles in Happy Valley," *NW* (May 8, 1995), 58–60; and the 1990s story of the Menendez brothers. Cf. also Reinder Van Til, *Lost Daughters: Recovered Memory Therapy and the People It Hurts* (Grand Rapids: Eerdmans, 1997), and sources he cites. Again, we are not minimizing the terrible impact of genuine abuse, which is common.

35. For solutions against oppression by dictators and others in power, see Gary Haugen, *Good News About Injustice* (Downers Grove, Ill.: InterVarsity, 1999), 142–53; for oppressors' use of deception to generate equivocation, see ibid., 129–41. One Nigerian colonel was tortured until he falsely denounced a former head of state, leading to the latter's imprisonment under the dictator Abacha (see Olusegun Obasanjo, *Guides to Effective Prayer* [Abeokuta: Olusegun Obasanjo, 1998], 7–8).

terrorists have become the featured enemy. Although true evils exist in these places, they can be caricatured to make all Soviets or all Muslims appear alike. Even with the free press in the United States, truth can be manipulated to galvanize people to act with one mind, especially in times of war.

But these are people we Christians are called to love! Can we really settle for knowledge about political blocs while remaining ignorant of the people held in them? Muslims often grow up hearing falsehood about Christianity; one Saudi businessman quickly ran out of objections to Christianity after I answered the false propaganda he had heard about Christians as he was growing up. Races and tribes are often set against each other by atrocity stories which, true or false, cannot condemn every individual with one stroke, but often lead to countermassacres.[36] Deception is a deadly game in this world, and Christians must work diligently to reveal truth.[37]

We are nothing before God. The "great city "(16:19) encounters judgment. That city stands for the world in its pomp; the might of empires like Egypt, Assyria, Timbuktu, and others are now but memories, and the glories of the old British empire and Soviet Union are quickly fading. The most magnificent of human power remains at best pretentious, nothing before God. We do well, then, to remember that we are nothing before him (1 Cor. 8:2; 2 Cor. 12:11; Gal. 6:3), and accordingly we should depend solely on his power (2 Cor. 12:9–10; 13:4).

---

36. Take, for example, long memories in Serbia and Bosnia (for volatile religious propaganda there, see Michael Sells, "Bosnia: Some Religious Dimensions of Genocide," *Religious Studies News & Notes* (May 1994), 4–5); or white supremacist ideologies that fostered colonialism in Africa (see Glenn Usry and Craig Keener, *Black Man's Religion* [Downers Grove, Ill.: InterVarsity, 1996], 25–26).

37. Christians must also engage in ethical forms of persuasion; cf. discussions in Em Griffin, "Winning Over: How to Change People's Minds," *Eternity* (May 1976), 29–34; Duane Litfin, "The Perils of Persuasive Preaching," *CT* (Feb. 4, 1977), 14–17; Raymond W. McLaughlin, *The Ethics of Persuasive Preaching* (Grand Rapids: Baker, 1979).

Revelation 17:1–18

ONE OF THE seven angels who had the seven bowls came and said to me, "Come, I will show you the punishment of the great prostitute, who sits on many waters. ²With her the kings of the earth committed adultery and the inhabitants of the earth were intoxicated with the wine of her adulteries."

³Then the angel carried me away in the Spirit into a desert. There I saw a woman sitting on a scarlet beast that was covered with blasphemous names and had seven heads and ten horns. ⁴The woman was dressed in purple and scarlet, and was glittering with gold, precious stones and pearls. She held a golden cup in her hand, filled with abominable things and the filth of her adulteries. ⁵This title was written on her forehead:

MYSTERY

BABYLON THE GREAT

THE MOTHER OF PROSTITUTES

AND OF THE ABOMINATIONS OF THE EARTH.

⁶I saw that the woman was drunk with the blood of the saints, the blood of those who bore testimony to Jesus.

When I saw her, I was greatly astonished. ⁷Then the angel said to me: "Why are you astonished? I will explain to you the mystery of the woman and of the beast she rides, which has the seven heads and ten horns. ⁸The beast, which you saw, once was, now is not, and will come up out of the Abyss and go to his destruction. The inhabitants of the earth whose names have not been written in the book of life from the creation of the world will be astonished when they see the beast, because he once was, now is not, and yet will come.

⁹"This calls for a mind with wisdom. The seven heads are seven hills on which the woman sits. ¹⁰They are also seven kings. Five have fallen, one is, the other has not yet come; but when he does come, he must remain for a little while. ¹¹The beast who once was, and now is not, is an eighth king. He belongs to the seven and is going to his destruction.

¹²"The ten horns you saw are ten kings who have not yet received a kingdom, but who for one hour will receive

authority as kings along with the beast. ¹³They have one purpose and will give their power and authority to the beast. ¹⁴They will make war against the Lamb, but the Lamb will overcome them because he is Lord of lords and King of kings—and with him will be his called, chosen and faithful followers."

¹⁵Then the angel said to me, "The waters you saw, where the prostitute sits, are peoples, multitudes, nations and languages. ¹⁶The beast and the ten horns you saw will hate the prostitute. They will bring her to ruin and leave her naked; they will eat her flesh and burn her with fire. ¹⁷For God has put it into their hearts to accomplish his purpose by agreeing to give the beast their power to rule, until God's words are fulfilled. ¹⁸The woman you saw is the great city that rules over the kings of the earth."

JOHN NOW MOVES from the topic of general judgments of God, typified in the bowls of his wrath (ch. 16), to the specific judgment on "Babylon the Great" (16:19), pictured here as "the great prostitute, who sits on many waters" (17:1).

The Mother of Prostitutes (17:1–5)

AN ANGEL BIDS John to "come" so that he may "show" him the judgment of the prostitute (17:1). He then carries him "away in the Spirit" (17:3; cf. Ezek. 8:3; 11:1, 24), just as an angel will later show him the bride, the prostitute's antithesis (21:9), and carries him "away in the Spirit" (21:10).[1] Here he sees a high-class prostitute who has intoxicated the nations with her immorality (17:2), but is herself drunk with the blood of the saints (17:6). The image is calculated to put the evil empire's true hideousness in perspective; the ancient horror of cannibalism was great, and imaginary creatures like Cyclops, thought to eat humans, were revolting even to pagans.[2] The heads, horns, and blasphemous names link the beast with the dragon and an earlier vision of the beast (17:3; cf. 12:3; 13:1).

The Old Testament prophets often portrayed Israel as a woman, either God's faithful bride when pure (e.g., Isa. 54:5–6; 62:5; Hos. 2:19–20) or an

---

1. For angels taking visionaries up, see also 1 Enoch 17:1; 2 Bar. 6:3–4; T. Abr. 10B; Apoc. Zeph. 2:1; cf. perhaps Ezek. 8:2–3. For "showing," cf. Rev 1:1; 4:1; 21:9–10; 22:1, 6.

2. For disgust with cannibalism, see Herodotus, *Hist.* 1.123, 129; Diodorus Siculus, 34/35.12.1; Achilles Tatius, 5.5.

adulteress when unfaithful to him (e.g., Lev. 17:7; Isa. 1:21; Jer. 3:1; Ezek. 16:20).[3] Revelation contrasts two cities, Jerusalem and Babylon, as a bride and prostitute respectively (17:5; 21:2). In two Old Testament instances, the "prostitute" is not Israel, Judah, or Jerusalem, but an evil world empire: Nineveh or Tyre. Nineveh will seduce the nations with her prostitution and witchcraft (Nah. 3:4; see comment on Rev. 18:23); Tyre will play the prostitute "with all the kingdoms on the face of the earth" (Isa. 23:17), yet her wealth will ultimately be laid up for the righteous (23:18).

Some background for the image of the queen here may be found in Jezebel's pagan repression of God's prophets; she is condemned for "immorality" in 2:20–22. But Babylon sits as queen in Isaiah 47:5–7. Literal Babylon also lived by "many waters" (Jer. 51:13), though most prosperous ancient cities (including Rome on the Tiber) had water; the "waters" representing the nations here probably imply Rome's international power.[4]

Likewise, Gentile rhetoric often imagined one's ancestors or homeland personified as a woman.[5] Coins and other artwork typically depicted a city as a wealthy goddess enthroned beside a river.[6] Thus, for example, a bronze coin from the rule of Domitian's father included the goddess Roma (who personified Rome's power) sitting on seven hills (cf. 17:9).[7] Official state worship included not only worship of the emperor but also worship of the goddess Roma. Some scholars have proposed that Babylon here partly symbolizes Jerusalem.[8] Others suggest it predicts a revived role for literal Babylon.[9] But

3. For later contrasts between Israel as faithful or unfaithful wife, see *Pes. Rab Kah.* 19:4.

4. Jewish interpreters could also identify waters with "many nations," based on Isa. 17:12–13 (T. W. Manson, *On Paul and John: Some Selected Theological Themes*, SBT 38 [London: SCM, 1963], 102, citing *Song Rab.* 8:6–7). It is uncertain how widespread was Babylon's reputation for immorality (Herodotus, 1.99). Sib. Or. 8.194 probably borrows Revelation's image.

5. Demetrius, *On Style* 5.265.

6. Ford, *Revelation*, 277; most fully, Aune, *Revelation*, 3:920–22, also tracing components of the *ekphrasis* genre here on pp. 923–27. Cf. Rome as a mother of beasts in Sib. Or. 3.469.

7. Robert Beauvery, "L'Apocalypse au risque de la numismatique. Babylone, la grande Prostituée et le sixième roi Vespasien et la déesse Rome," *RevBib* 90 (April 1983): 243–60, though his linkage of the image of the she-wolf (*lupa*) who nursed Romulus with its other Latin sense of an immoral woman (also in Aune, *Revelation*, 3:929) probably would have occurred to John's audience only with prior instruction.

8. See Corsini, *Apocalypse*, 200. Iain Provan, "Foul Spirits, Fornication and Finance: Revelation 18 From an Old Testament Perspective," *JSNT* 64 (1996): 81–100, sees Jerusalem in the Old Testament images of Rev. 18; but Revelation clearly reapplies many of its images to metaphoric heirs (e.g., descriptions of Tyre to end-time Babylon); Christians may have also reapplied some earlier sentiments against religious persecutors in Jerusalem to Rome. By contrast, S. G. F. Brandon, *Jesus and the Zealots* (New York: Charles Scribner's Sons, 1967), 60 n. 3, suggests that it reflects a Jewish source seething with anti-Roman hatred.

9. For a literal Babylon, see Dyer, "Identity."

especially in view of its place on seven hills (17:9), most commentators recognize that Rome is in view, whether or not they believe the text also looks beyond Rome. As commentators often also recognize, Babylon the prostitute is a deliberate contrast with new Jerusalem as the bride.[10] Others also contrasted Zion and Babylon, lamenting Babylon's prosperity but anticipating its judgment (2 Bar. 11:1–3; 4 Ezra 3:29, 31).

The "kings of the earth" who have "committed adultery" with the prostitute (17:2) will suffer along with her. Some ancient writers used the term *kings* for any of the wealthy, but the expression was even more suitable for the client-rulers who ruled their people as local agents of Roman authority (cf. also 17:12, 16, 18).[11] Thus Babylon is Rome here, but especially "as a *corrupting influence* on the peoples of the empire"; its economic and political power made Rome a vehicle of propagating international idolatry and immorality.[12] This portrait of Rome would have been familiar to much of John's audience; thus some Jewish Sibylline Oracles complain about Rome's drunken weddings with her many suitors, probably the kings of the East she was seducing (Sib. Or. 3.356–59).

That the woman sits "on a scarlet beast" with "seven heads and ten horns" (17:3) identifies the beast with the seven-headed, ten-horned red dragon (12:3) as well as with Rome (13:1); this identification is something like calling Rome "Satan incarnate." It also identifies this beast with the final evil empire destined to be destroyed by God himself (Dan. 7:7, 20, 24).[13]

In more ways than one, Babylon is "dressed to kill." Her clothing in purple and scarlet (17:4) indicates her wealth, for purple dye was expensive, and entirely purple garments were associated especially with high-class prostitutes.[14] Her gold, precious stones, and pearls (17:4) further contribute to this picture of wealth (18:12, 16), but also help underpin the impending contrast with the city of God, which was built of gold, had streets of gold and

---

10. For Rome here, see F. F. Bruce, *The Message of the New Testament* (Grand Rapids: Eerdmans, 1981), 86; Michaels, *Revelation*, 196; for the contrast, Paul S. Minear, "The Cosmology of the Apocalypse," 23–37 in *Current Issues in New Testament Interpretation*, ed. W. Klassen and G. F. Snyder (New York: Harper & Row, 1962), 30.

11. See Ramsay, *Letters to the Seven Churches*, 94.

12. Bauckham, *Climax of Prophecy*, 343.

13. Sib. Or. 3.396–400 apparently applies Daniel's image to Hellenistic kings after Alexander. Some have compared the scarlet beast to the scapegoat (Lev. 16:8–26; Ford, *Revelation*, 277), perhaps coalesced with the red heifer (Num. 19:2).

14. For its association with wealth, see e.g., Lucretius, *Nat.* 5.1423; Horace, *Ode* 1.35.12; 2.18.7–8; 1 Macc. 10:20, 62, 64; 14:43–44; Sib. Or. 8.74; some writers complained about its extravagance (Seneca, *Dial.* 12.11.2; Plutarch, *T.T.* 3.1.2, *Mor.* 646B; some manuscripts of 1 Enoch 98:2). For prostitutes' purple, see Ps-Melissa, *Letter to Kleareta* (in Malherbe, *Moral Exhortation*, 83).

gates of pearls, and had precious stones on its foundations (21:18–21). The true and ultimate wealth comes not from trade with Babylon, not from buying and selling with the beast (13:17; cf. Ps. 73:6), but from relinquishing worldly wealth for the promises of Jesus (3:17–18).

No scarlet or gold adornments will protect this sexually unfaithful figure from ultimate rejection and murder by her own lovers (17:16 with Jer. 4:30). The name written on her forehead contrasts with the name written on Jesus in Revelation 19:12–13; presumably the name is on her forehead both to link her with the mark of 13:16 and (if the texts are correctly understood) to draw a parallel with Roman prostitutes wearing their names on their headbands.[15] It is possible (though by no means certain) that John and his readers were aware of the ancient tradition that Rome had a "secret" name used by the priesthood, which at least some thought was *Amor* (Roma spelled backwards), "Love"—which Revelation could parody in the image of a prostitute.[16] In any case, as the "mother of prostitutes" (17:5), she is the prototype for prostitutes, the prostitute par excellence after whom the entire profession is modeled—a world in rebellion against God.

Seven Heads As Mountains and Kings (17:6–11)

As ROME MADE others drunk with her immorality (17:2), she also became drunk herself with the blood of the saints (17:6; cf. 18:20–24). Ancient writers sometimes portrayed prostitutes as drinkers, but "drunk with ... blood" transforms this from a merely troublesome image into a horrifying one.[17] The image of drinking blood was a hideous one for Jews (Lev. 17:14; Deut. 12:23), but not unprecedented in deliberately terrifying oracles (Deut. 32:42; Isa. 49:26; Ezek. 39:19).[18] By John's day many saints had been martyred under Nero but probably not many under Domitian (2:13); yet in the centuries that follow, many more will die martyrs' deaths, especially to entertain Roman

---

15. Bauckham, *Climax of Prophecy*, 344; Mounce, *Revelation*, 310; but the supporting references are questionable. Some later Christians may have taken the name written too literally (Gr. Ezra 4:31). For the significance of a prostitute's forehead (perhaps signifying brazenness; cf. Isa. 48:4; Ezek. 3:8–9), see Jer. 3:3; Hos. 2:2; in this period some Jews may have applied it to an uncovered head, which could signify sexual availability (see C. S. Keener, "Head Coverings," in *Dictionary of New Testament Background*, ed. C. Evans and S. Porter [Downers Grove, Ill.: InterVarsity, forthcoming]).

16. Aune, *Revelation*, 3:926–27, with documentation. The tradition fits the Roman claim to be descended from Venus, goddess of love, through Aeneas.

17. See sources in Aune, *Revelation*, 3:937.

18. Cf. 1 Enoch 62:12. Mounce, *Revelation*, 310, cites also Roman writers who used this figure (Suetonius, *Tib.* 59; Pliny, *N.H.* 14.28; Josephus, *War* 5.344).

audiences.[19] Visionaries sometimes asked angels or others to explain what they were seeing (e.g., Dan. 12:8; 2 Bar. 38:3), but John simply is astonished, inviting the angelic response (Rev. 17:6–7). The expression could suggest an appreciative marveling that requires correction (13:3; 15:1; 17:8); but given John's knowledge of what she is drunk with, it is doubtful that his appreciation is positive.

As the angel explains the mystery of the woman and the beast (17:7–18), only the purest semblance of subtlety remains; in several different ways, the beast is identified with Rome (on "mystery," see comment on 1:20).[20] (1) The woman sits on seven mountains (17:9); Rome was regularly portrayed in this manner. (2) The leader of Babylon is apparently the new Nero (17:8–11); although Nero was associated also with the Parthians, as a ruler in the series of the seven he will rule Rome. (3) This empire rules over the other kings of the earth (17:18), who rules the nations gathered around the sea as a maritime power (17:15). (4) "Babylon" was a standard Jewish title for Rome by this period (see comment on 14:8; both empires destroyed the temple).

Rome regularly appears as a city on seven hills or mountains, as Caird points out:

> From the time of her sixth king, Servius Tullius, Rome had been known as *urbs Septicollis*, and the festival of Septimontium was celebrated every year in December to commemorate the enclosure of the seven hills within her walls (Suetonius, *Dom.* 4). Latin literature is full of references to this well-known feature of Roman topography.[21]

Revelation's symbolism is so transparent that non-Christian Romans would have immediately understood its import and regarded the document as subversive; "All the seers who announced the impending doom of Roman sov-

---

19. Ramsay, *Letters to the Seven Churches*, 94–95; see also Eusebius, *Book of Martyrs* 6 (Agapius); William H. C. Frend, *Martyrdom and Persecution in the Early Church* (Garden City, N.Y.: Anchor, 1967); idem, "Evangelists to the Death," *Christian History* 57 (1998): 31–33; Paul Keresztes, *Imperial Rome and the Christians* (Lanham, Md.: Univ. Press of America, 1989). From Tacitus (*Ann.* 15.44) I suspect that hundreds were martyred under Nero alone, so I think many current historians underestimate the number of martyrs in later centuries.

20. See Talbert, *Apocalypse*, 80; Beasley-Murray, *Revelation*, 256; Mounce, *Revelation*, 314; Martin Hengel, *Property and Riches in the Early Church* (Philadelphia: Fortress, 1974), 48. Note also Sib. Or. 2.18; 11.113, 116, which describe Rome as a city on seven hills.

21. Caird, *Commentary on Revelation*, 216 (see sources cited there, such as Virgil, *Geor.* 2.535; *Aen.* 6.782–83). We can add Dionysius of Halicarnassus, 4.13.2–3; Varro, 5.7.41. The hills were Palatine, Capitol, Aventine, Caelian, Esquiline, Viminal, and Quirinal (Andrew D. Clarke, "Rome and Italy," 455–81 in *The Book of Acts in Its Graeco-Roman Setting*, ed. D. W. J. Gill and C. Gempf [Grand Rapids: Eerdmans, 1994], 457). For Jewish use of seven mountains for paradise (1 Enoch 24:2; 32:10), see comment on 21:1.

---

ereignty were understandably viewed as enemies of the state."[22] But in addition to seeing Rome, many commentators also view the great prostitute as the evil world system that in principle continues beyond Rome's fall.[23]

Most commentators also find an allusion to Nero in 17:8–11.[24] The invitation to discern wisdom in 17:9 recalls the same formula in 13:18; while that does not necessarily imply a connection between the identities of the two mysterious kings, it draws attention to the connection between two passages that on other grounds seem to address the same revived ruler.[25] That the seven heads can represent both seven mountains and seven kings suggests that Revelation freely reapplies as polyvalent its imagery. Perhaps John even expects hearers to smile at his application of seven heads to the "seven hills" of Rome.

Who are the seven kings (17:10)? Daniel's beast had ten horns and another one that cast down three horns, which leaves seven (Dan. 7:20, 24); but even if this is part of John's reason for numbering seven kings, Revelation probably wants seven of them anyway. Its scheme may be somewhat forced, because John has to maintain the "seven" scheme for his own literary patterns (the "ten" kings of 17:12, 16, are borrowed from Daniel); "To limit Satan's messianic dynasty to seven Roman emperors is to impose upon John's poetic imagery a literalism which it will not bear."[26] Or, as another commentator puts it, seven is one of John's symbolic numbers, "and they would remain seven no matter how long the actual list happened to be."[27]

Nevertheless, John can make his point fit into his seven schema; it is not at all difficult to find a pattern of rulers that accommodates the revived Nero image that John seems to employ here.[28] The king who "is" (17:10) must be Domitian, if early church tradition correctly dates the book; five kings back from Domitian easily includes Nero if we skip the three interim usurpers

---

22. Howard Clark Kee, *Christian Origins in Sociological Perspective: Methods and Resources* (Philadelphia: Westminster, 1980), 71 (on Rev. 13).

23. E.g., Tenney, *Revelation*, 82; Desmond Ford, *The Abomination of Desolation in Biblical Eschatology* (Washington, D.C.: Univ. Press of America, 1979), 269.

24. E.g., Talbert, *Apocalypse*, 79.

25. Bauckham, *Climax of Prophecy*, 394–96, suggests a detailed mathematical parallel: 666 is the "double triangle" of 8, and is the eighth doubly triangular number; one of the first seven doubly triangular numbers is 6, allowing the eighth to be one of the seven.

26. Bowman, *First Christian Drama*, 115. These kings are the "kings of the earth" in 17:18 (Beale, *Revelation*, 878).

27. Caird, *Commentary on Revelation*, 218–19. Cf. the seven kings promised in Sib. Or. 3.191–94, 318, 608–10, probably in pre-Roman Egypt.

28. Roman literature often speaks of its first seven kings as a special group (e.g., Appian, *R.H.* 1.2), the sixth of whom (cf. 17:10) established the seven hills; but if this number has any significance, it may simply contrast with John's listing of seven kings toward the end of Rome's history (cf. twelve kings ending in Domitian in 4 Ezra 11:1–35).

who reigned for only a few months between Nero and Vespasian before their violent deaths (otherwise Nero misses the count by two emperors).[29]

The "eighth king" is one of the rulers from the first seven who returns, undoubtedly the head earlier mentioned as wounded as if to death but recovered (13:3). This constitutes a parody of Jesus' resurrection—just as the phrase "[who] once was, now is not, and will come" (17:8) parodies the Lord "who is, and who was, and who is to come" (1:4, 8; cf. 4:8).[30] Because some forms of the Nero myth expected his return to destroy Rome at the head of the Parthians, Bauckham argues that the return of Nero in 17:10–11 may refer not to his parody resurrection (as in 13:3) but to his parody parousia—the final king of Rome leading the Parthians to overthrow it.[31] On this view, one could thus think of a "pagan messiah," Satan's last attempt to establish a kingdom, which would ultimately undermine his Roman power and show the futility of any universal human or satanic government opposed to God's kingdom. The Parthian menace is not clear in this passage, so this proposal remains speculative. In any case, the thought of Nero's return would be no less terrifying to the current Roman regime that had supplanted it than to the Christians, who had suffered under Nero's purges before.

Ten Horns (17:12–18)

THE "TEN HORNS" as "ten kings" (17:12) comes from Daniel 7:7, 20, 24, and in Revelation may simply refer to the continuing imperial system.[32] Others

---

29. Cf. Roloff, *Revelation*, 198–99. A. Strobel starts with Tiberius (from Christ's exaltation) and skips the interim emperors ("Abfassung und Geschichtstheologie der Apokalypse nach Kap. xvii.9–12," *NTS* 10 [1964]: 433–45); Jarl H. Ulrichsen interestingly counts Domitian as both sixth and tenth, using seven heads for emperors from Caligula without the three interregnum emperors and ten horns including them ("Die sieben Häupter und die zehn Hörner. Zur Datierung der Offenbarung des Johannes," *ST* 39 [1985]: 1–20). Many scholars start with Julius (cf. Josephus, *Ant.* 18.225) and count Nero as the sixth (current) emperor (E. Lipinski, "L'apocalypse et le martyre de Jean à Jérusalem," *NovT* 11 [1969]: 225–32; Sproul, *Last Days*, 147), or with Augustus and count the sixth as Vespasian (Rissi, *Time and History*, 81). Some texts count the three interregnum emperors as rulers (Josephus, *War* 4.494, 498; Sib. Or. 5.35), but others recognize them as usurpers (cf. Suetonius, *Vesp.* 1), which probably represents the dominant Roman view under Domitian, who belonged to the dynasty that supplanted them (cf. Mounce, *Revelation*, 314–15).

30. Bauckham, *Climax of Prophecy*, 396–97, suggests a possible parody of Christ also in the number eight, given early Christian emphasis on the "eighth day" and Jesus as 888.

31. Ibid., 438–40. Cf. the parody of the Parousia suggestion earlier in Bowman, *First Christian Drama*, 115.

32. See Ramsay, *Letters to the Seven Churches*, 95, 113; Bowman, *First Christian Drama*, 117. For similar uses of animal body parts to symbolize kings, see 4 Ezra 12:19–20; for the idea that judgment will come after just one more king, see *Gen. Rab.* 83:4. Daniel's ten kingdoms probably appear in *Pes. Rab.* 1:7.

have suggested that they are the "kings from the East," temporarily joining forces with Rome to crush God's church, only to turn and become Rome's enemies (17:16).[33] Most likely they are viewed as Rome's client kingdoms; in the end, Rome's empire will collapse and turn on the one with whom they have committed prostitution.[34] The number of client kingdoms Rome ruled varied from one period to another, as some became provinces at various times;[35] but "ten" seems to provide a round figure that fits Daniel 7. They have a common purpose with the beast (17:13; cf. Ps. 83:5), but they will prove as unfaithful as the prostitute with whom they have had intercourse (Rev. 17:16). They will reign with the beast briefly, "for one hour" (17:12), to wage war against the Lamb (17:13–14); that their time is brief is emphasized by the repetition of "one hour" in the depiction of how instantly Babylon will be destroyed (18:10, 17, 19).[36]

Whoever the kings are, they will inevitably fall after their "hour." "King of kings" (17:14) was the title of the Babylonian king long before (Ezek. 26:7) and remained the title of the Parthian ruler in John's day.[37] But the king here is not the Parthian ruler; it is Jesus (see comment on 19:16), and the kingdoms of the world will soon be his (11:15). The Roman king thought himself ruler of all the other kings of the earth (17:18), but this role ultimately belongs to Jesus (1:5), who is "Lord of lords and King of kings" (17:14).

Jesus is the mighty conquering king, and he does not come alone. Rather than being described at this point as fierce or heavily armed, his army is described as "called, chosen, and faithful" (17:14). The first two terms designate the certainty of their victory, for the eternal outcome is already determined in God's sovereign foreknowledge ("called" is translated "invited" in 19:9). "Faithful" may involve their perseverance to the death (2:10, 13); it contrasts sharply with the disloyalty of the earthly kings (17:16).[38]

---

33. Beasley-Murray, *Revelation*, 258, citing as possibly relevant the fourteen satraps of Parthia; John is limited to Daniel's "ten."

34. Cf. Caird, *Commentary on Revelation*, 219–20; the myth of Nero's ten satraps in Rissi, *Time and History*, 80. They can represent the seven kings with the addition of the three usurpers (Ulrichsen, "Haüpter"), but both John's "seven" (by his numerical patterns and the beast's heads) and his "ten" (from Daniel) have been predetermined, allowing him less flexibility in producing clear applications.

35. Aune, *Revelation*, 3:951. Less relevantly, Aune (ibid.) mentions the Roman board of *decemviri*, "ten men" who codified Roman law.

36. For similar language in other oracular literature, see Sib. Or. 12.26. "In one hour" can mean "instantly" (T. Job 7:12/11).

37. Plutarch, *Pompey* 38.2; it can apply to any superlative ruler (T. Jud. 3:7). Aune, *Revelation*, 3:954–55, provides a detailed summary of usage in the East.

38. Such a triple designation is not unusual (e.g., God is "holy," "faithful," and "righteous" in Jub. 21:4).

The imperial system and the rulers of allied nations will eventually devastate Rome herself (17:16); the world's allegiances are self-interested, hence temporary. Revelation will develop some of these images further: They will "bring her to ruin" (cf. 18:17); they will "eat her flesh" (cf. the carrion birds in 19:18); she will be burned (cf. 18:8). The prostitute's stripping may allude to the way one may disgrace oneself after having drunk too much (Lam. 4:21), especially if she were an evil empire who had made others drink (Hab. 2:15–16). Stripping was also standard practice before scourging or execution;[39] most relevant here, it signifies a standard ancient penalty for sexual unfaithfulness (Ezek. 16:37–38; Hos. 2:3; see comments on Rev. 16:15). Burning was the normal fate of conquered cities (e.g., Josh. 6:24; 8:28) and the promised fate of the final Antichrist figure (Dan. 7:10–11), but it was also the penalty for the most serious acts of promiscuity (Gen. 38:24; Lev. 20:14; 21:9). God had long before used betrayal by unfaithful lovers to punish Israel's unfaithfulness (Jer. 4:30; Lam. 1:2; Ezek. 23:9; Hos. 2:7). Thus the diabolic system will meet a fitting end.

Perhaps the most striking statement about God's great rule is the fact that he is sovereign even in their evil, using it for his own long-range purposes (17:17).[40] He can use evil powers to judge other evil people (e.g., Isa. 10:5–15; Jer. 51:11, 29; Joel 2:11). To be sure, Rome ruled the kings of the earth (17:18).[41] But in a far more important way, God ruled Rome and its enemies (17:17). The "kingdom of the world" will one day be God's unchallenged (11:15), but his judgments in human history are meant to remind us that even now, behind the scenes, God remains the Lord of history and his purposes will be accomplished.

Bridging Contexts

THE SYMBOLISM OF ROME. Given that Rome long ago fell, how do we apply a prophecy whose primary short-range target was Rome? That Revelation itself describes this destruction by borrowing familiar images first offered in Old Testament prophecies against earlier evil empires provides the clue: Human sinfulness and God's consistent justice

---

39. Before execution, see Dionysius of Halicarnassus, 7.69.2; Josephus, *Apion* 1.191; 2.53; *m. Sanh.* 6:3; *b. Sanh.* 45a, bar.; before public beatings, see Longus, 2.14; Aulus Gellius, 10.3.3.

40. Early Judaism understood this principle (e.g., 1QS 3.23; 1QM 1.8; *b. Yoma* 10a; *Lam. Rab.* Proem 23; 4:19, §22). Even if Satan claimed to rule the kingdoms of the world (Luke 4:6), that role truly belongs only to God (Dan. 4:32; Wisd. Sol. 6:3). Dio Chrysostom can praise Alexandria no more highly than to call her the second city under the sun (32nd *Discourse* §35), because Rome was known to be first.

41. Dionysius of Halicarnassus (1.9.1) called her the "lady who rules the earth and sea," and Diodorus Siculus (1.4.3) claimed that Rome was so powerful it rules "as far as the ends of the inhabited world."

---

yield familiar patterns in his dealings over the long haul of history. Jacques Ellul states the matter as well as any: The great prostitute was "Rome, to be sure, for the given historical moment; but not she alone: in reality the summation of all that which is prostitution, as Babylon in her time, who became the symbol of it." Rather than sexual prostitution per se, this prostitution involves unfaithfulness to God's covenant, "being in communication (by sacred prostitution) with the religious and spiritual powers, with the satanic sources, and esotericism."[42] The spirit of Babylon and Rome (which John calls a new "Babylon") outlasts both individual empires to represent evil empires as the world in its most tyrannical form.[43]

The issue in Revelation 17–18 is not simply that Rome is an evil empire; the issue is that its privileged position in international trade made it a prime exporter of immorality. Thus while we rightly might want to denounce evil empires that oppress their peoples by force, this passage allows us to apply Babylon's model closer to home (see Contemporary Significance, below).

In seeking to apply this text, however, interpreters have handled it in strange ways. For many years it was customary for Protestants to associate Roman Catholicism with the beast by way of the Pope's geographical proximity to Rome.[44] After the rise of an ecumenical movement, some of whose representatives compromised historic Christian beliefs, one strain of conservative Protestant piety expected an apostate worldwide church including both Catholics and mainline Protestants.[45] Those who needed to find an apostate end-time church after the Rapture of the true, Philadelphia church often located it here.[46]

Some of this unlikely thesis is related to the idea of "Babylonian" mystery religions purportedly mixed in with Roman Catholic practices.[47] Yet whereas the church may have adapted some pagan Roman practices, most of the evidence for "Babylonian mystery religions" is a creation of recent centuries of

42. Ellul, *Apocalypse*, 190. Cf. Mounce, *Revelation*, 303.

43. Jewish sources regularly spoke of the "four kingdoms" (Babylon, Persia, Greece and Rome, based on their understanding of Daniel's beasts) that oppressed Israel, viewing Rome as the last (2 Bar. 39:4–5).

44. This view has not completely died down in Protestantism; see Tim LaHaye, *Revelation Unveiled* (Grand Rapids: Zondervan, 1999), esp. 65–71, 260–77.

45. Cf. James DeForest Murch, *The Coming World Church* (Lincoln, Neb.: Good News Broadcasting Association, 1971), 22; R. W. DeHaan, "The Coming World Church," *Radio Bible Class* (March 1969).

46. For a similar view, see John F. Walvoord, "Revival of Rome," *BibSac* 126 (1969): 317–28; idem, *Revelation*, 243–44; *Prophecy Knowledge Handbook*, 604–8. Lindsey, *New World Coming*, 242–43, predicts a rebuilding of literal Babylon.

47. Walvoord, *Revelation*, 247–48.

speculation, not rooted in the hard data of history.[48] More significantly, what in the text supports the view that the prostitute in chapter 17 is "ecclesiastical Babylon," a false religion, in contrast to the "political" Babylon such interpreters find in chapter 18? John had in mind Rome, but if we are going to apply John's principles today, we should not limit the application to all other groups besides ourselves. There are lessons for everyone seduced by the grandeur of the world, whether theologically or in our lifestyles.[49] From my observations, this includes a warning for many modern North American evangelicals as well as other people.

Problems with John's language. Some modern critical commentators have complained that John's portrayal of Babylon or the world as a prostitute and new Jerusalem as a bride represents sexist stereotypes. To be sure, these are stereotypical roles, but Revelation is merely using images already current in its day (see Original Meaning section). He identifies all believers, male and female, with the faithful bride of 19:7–8 and 21:2 (cf. also 12:1–2). This revelation originally communicated the message effectively for a culture that readily grasped the import of these images. It is therefore appropriate to explain this background for those parts of Western culture today uncomfortable with the language; but to evaluate and condemn John for using such images of his day is culturally insensitive and anachronistic.[50]

Another problem may arise when we share the message of this text with new believers. Even though our strongest words usually target those with the hardest hearts, those who respond most sensitively are the softer hearts more prone to guilt. Even though the passage does not directly address physical immorality, one person I know bristled at the language of this passage and wondered if her past sins were forgivable. Just as when we preach against physical immorality, it is important to preach with such grace that those who have long since repented of immoral lifestyles are forgiven and welcome among God's people (cf. Matt. 21:31).

Interpretations of John's symbols. Many symbols have lent themselves to diverse interpretations through history. Granville Sharp (1735–1813),

---

48. The mysteries were primarily a Greek phenomenon with influence from Asia Minor (Walter Burkert, *Ancient Mystery Cults* [Cambridge, Mass.: Harvard Univ. Press, 1987], 2–6, 37; idem, *Greek Religion* [Cambridge, Mass.: Harvard Univ. Press, 1985], 166, 177; Giulia Sfameni Gasparro, *Soteriology and Mystic Aspects in the Cult of Cybele and Attis*, ÉPROER 103 [Leiden: Brill, 1985], 49). See a more thorough response to older views about the mysteries in C. S. Keener and Glenn Usry, *Defending Black Faith*, 50, and notes.

49. Walvoord, *Revelation*, 245, thinks the purple and other ornaments fit Roman Catholic and Greek Orthodox officials better than pagan Rome (but see comments on 18:12–13).

50. See C. S. Keener, "Woman and Man," *Dictionary of the Later New Testament and Its Development*, 1205–215 (pp. 1209–211).

prominent Greek scholar and antislavery activist, "once gained an interview with the prominent statesman Charles Fox and proceeded to explain to him why Napoleon should be identified with the 'little horn in Daniel 7.'"[51] Such historical missteps may have warned subsequent generations to exercise greater caution, but alas, most of us rarely study history, and we quickly forget the lessons of the past. Our own lives are too brief to learn by experience all the lessons we need to know; it is a faithful saying that warns that those who do not learn from history are destined to repeat its mistakes.

Modern "pop" interpreters have had a field day reinterpreting the symbols in Revelation, many without much understanding of the original context or consistency in their interpretive methods. For instance, from the time of the Holy Roman Empire, many expected a literal revived Roman empire. When the European states agreed on a Common Market, prophecy buffs took this as the ten horns of Daniel and Revelation (although they do not correspond geographically to the broader Mediterranean empire of Rome). In the 1960s and 1970s the Common Market had fewer than ten member nations, but many prophecy teachers heralded the triumph of their interpretive tradition when the count reached ten in January 1981. Unfortunately, "by the 1990s the Common Market had fifteen members, which caused another problem."[52]

As noted in our introduction, we should examine the Bible on its own terms and not read modern events into it. We should apply it to the events of our day, but—unless we have clear biblical indication that our time is somehow special (which usually comes only in retrospect)—we should apply it as we would to the events of every generation and to our own lives.

THE HARD WORK of relevant application. John employs images of his day, which reminds us to contextualize and apply the biblical message for those with whom we share his message today. Normally, we have not done the work of application if we can only point the finger to figures in the distance, and in this case we have plenty of application potential close to home. Even from secular corners, some have called for repentance in our society. The editor of a widely read secular magazine remarked in the context of a readers' poll on religious values:

> When our federal government buys claw hammers for $250 each from defense contractors while cutting welfare payments to people who

---

51. Bruce Hindmarsh, "Aristocratic Activists," *Christian History* 53 (1997): 23–27, 25.
52. Kyle, *The Last Days*, 129.

get blankets from charity and when a Wall Street crook can get a standing ovation from students at a prestigious business school by telling them that they have a right to be selfish, a return to basic moral values is long overdue.[53]

American immorality as one application of Revelation. An application of the image of the prostitute solely to military imperialism (which we usually apply to totalitarian societies rather than to ourselves) misses the connection in the text. Rome no longer needed to control the entire empire by troops since economic imperialism had rendered most of its empire dependent on it.

One writer epitomizes Babylon as "the essential version of the demonic in triumph in a nation," whether in Nazi Germany or in the United States of America.[54] The United States today is not an evil empire in the sense of totalitarian or politically repressive states like the Assyrians or Nazi Germany, or (at the time of this book's writing) Iran, the Sudan, or Milosevic's short-lived genocidal agendas in Serbia—all of which invite judgment unless they repent. But we can still apply the text's principles in ways relevant to our society; we have become one of the world's primary exporters of immorality. Is it any wonder some Muslim nations—who try to guard against public exposure at least for one gender—have regarded the United States as the "Great Satan" when the most widely watched television program in the world is *Baywatch?*[55]

At least we can gather that U.S. government priorities are clear; when the Saudi government demanded that the U.S. embassy close down both worship services and nightclubs for American citizens, the embassy "compromised: If they could keep the nightclubs open, they would close the worship services."[56] Sex scandals in the highest reaches of U.S. government are, not surprisingly, a cause of ridicule in the Muslim world, with major consequences for American foreign policy and American lives—hardly simply a "private" matter as some have insisted.[57]

The export of American democracy to some postcommunist countries has accompanied a dramatic rise in black market economies and Mafia-type

---

53. David Jordan, in *Better Homes and Gardens* (Jan. 1988), 15.

54. William Stringfellow, *An Ethic for Christians and Other Aliens in a Strange Land,* 3d ed. (Waco, Tex.: Word, 1979), 33; this work was brought to my attention by John Herzog of Bethel College.

55. On the dangers of U.S. pornography, see Tom Minnery, "Pornography: The Human Tragedy," *CT* (March 7, 1986), 17–22; idem, ed., *Pornography: A Human Tragedy* (Wheaton, Ill.: Christianity Today, Inc., and Tyndale, 1986); for cyberporn, John Zipperer, "The Naked City," *CT* (Sept. 12, 1994), 42–49.

56. Chuck Colson, "Save the Christians," *Jubilee* (Spring 1996), 15.

57. See Howard Fineman, "Collateral Damage," *NW* (Aug. 31, 1998), 18–23, 21.

crime, and popular songs in some of those countries glorify drugs or rape, courtesy of our nation's entertainment industry.[58] "Alarmed by divorce rates approaching 25 percent, what they see as rampant infidelity and a younger generation that gleans its values from Hollywood and MTV," Chinese officials understandably have sought stricter laws governing public morality.[59]

Although the medium can also be used for good, the U.S. entertainment media has become largely an agent for propagating destructive values.[60] Many children and some adults have copied crimes witnessed in a movie.[61] Thus, for example, a nineteen-year-old man stabbed to death an eighteen-year-old college woman, then killed himself; police found in his room ninety horror movies, plus a machete and goalie mask modeled after those used in the *Friday the Thirteenth* movies.[62] Thirty-one percent of teenagers say they have copied what they see; "according to the California Justice Department, 21% of teenage crime is directly copied after what the teenagers see in movies and on television right down to the minute gory details."[63]

By the age of sixteen the average child raised in the United States has witnessed "26,000 overt sex acts and as many as 400,000 sexual references and innuendos, as well as 200,000 portrayals of violence, including 33,000 murders, on television and in movies."[64] One horror filmmaker admits that "often the murders are filmed from the point of view of the murderer," but then amazingly protests that this does not lead horror fans to identify "with the psychopathic killers"![65] Statistical evidence is now clear that such entertainment media violence desensitizes us to real violence, helping to produce violence among a generation raised on it.[66]

---

58. Note the rise in promiscuity, hence in AIDS, in Russia (Matthew Kaminski and Kim Palchikoff, "The Crisis to Come," *NW* [April 14, 1997], 44–45).

59. "China's New Family Values," *NW* (Aug. 24, 1998), 36.

60. For protests, see Bruno Bettelheim, "TV Stereotypes 'Devastating' to Young Minds," *USNWR* (Oct. 28, 1985), 55; Susan Baker and Tipper Gore, "Some Reasons for 'Wilding,'" *NW* (May 29, 1989), 6–7; Kevin Perrotta, "Television's Mind-Boggling Danger," *CT* (May 7, 1982), 20–22. On trash television, see Harry F. Waters et al., "Trash TV," *NW* (Nov. 14, 1988), 72–78.

61. For copycat crimes based on entertainment media, see data in John Leland, "Violence, Reel to Real," *NW* (Dec. 11, 1995), 46–48.

62. Mary Rose McGeady, *Covenant House Newsletter* (Aug. 1993), 1.

63. Ted Baehr, "Redefining Culture Through Media," *SCP Journal* 18/1–2 (1993): 36–43 (p. 39). A survey in England concluded that teenagers who watched much violence committed "49% more violent and anti-social behavior" than those who did not (Baehr, "Culture," 40).

64. Baehr, "Culture," 40.

65. John Russo, "'Reel' Vs. Real Violence," *NW* (Feb. 19, 1990), 10.

66. See David Gelman, "The Violence in Our Heads," *NW* (Aug. 2, 1993), 48; David Neff, "Shootout at the Not-So-OK Corral," *CT* (Nov. 9, 1992), 12–13; esp. violence psychologist David Grossman, "Trained to Kill," *CT* (Aug. 10, 1998), 30–39.

One may object that the American church is not responsible for the behavior of its culture, but when buying and television viewing habits of Christians differ little from that of our secular neighbors, can we deny responsibility for supporting an industry that is killing the world?[67] Early Christians refused to go into theaters to be "entertained" by watching other people suffer.[68] It is said that in the fourth century an Asian monk named Telemachus visited Rome and was horrified by a gladiatorial fight in the Colosseum. Hurling himself between the gladiators he sought to prevent either of them from being killed, until he was killed instead. As he lay still on the ground, one spectator got up in disgust, followed by others, until everyone had gone. This marked the end of gladiatorial contests in Rome's Coliseum.[69] Unfortunately, what early Christians avoided in public, modern Christians invite into their living rooms.

Judgment on the nations of the world. Those who participate in others' sin and allow themselves to be deluded by it must share their judgment, though the seducers will face harsher judgment than the seduced (17:2; 18:9). That the ten kings turn on the prostitute in the end (17:16) shows us something about the world's loyalties. Even in Roman politics, it was understood that alliances were often a temporary measure to gain what one wanted, and one might shift loyalties if it proved in one's own interests to do so. God often uses the wicked to destroy themselves (cf. Judg. 7:22; 2 Chron. 20:23). Such a "falling out," a dividing of Satan against Satan, "is inevitable in 'a moral universe.' And the end for every evil power is internal strife, self-destruction, death."[70]

Every empire in history, from the Assyrians to the Soviet Union, has collapsed, usually strangled by its own internal contradictions before being finished off by invaders. We need fear no empire and no repression, because history guarantees that every mere human or demonic empire will fall. God's saints suffer for now, but God's purposes in history will prevail. This truth encourages believers to stand firm, for the future lies with God, not with the mightiest empires on today's horizon.

Evil rulers have their "hour" (17:12)—then they and ultimately their empires fade. From the short vantage point of our individual lives, justice seems delayed; from the long perspective of history, however, the power of oppressors is always brought to an end. This is certain because, as this pas-

---

67. Partly for lack of time, partly to protest the glorification of violence, I have never owned a television.

68. See Tertullian, *On Spectacles.*

69. The story is told in Charles Colson, *Loving God* (Grand Rapids: Zondervan, 1987), 243.

70. Bowman, *First Christian Drama,* 117.

sage also illustrates unambiguously (17:17), God remains sovereign even over choices made by evil empires. One might think of Hitler's fateful decision to turn against Stalin and send troops to the Russian front. In terms of years of war preparation and strategy, Germany was ahead of the Allies; but toward the end Hitler made some severe strategic blunders, was forced to execute some brilliant tacticians like Rommel, and ultimately destroyed his own cause.

Revelation 18:1–24

A FTER THIS I saw another angel coming down from heaven. He had great authority, and the earth was illuminated by his splendor. [2]With a mighty voice he shouted:

"Fallen! Fallen is Babylon the Great!
     She has become a home for demons
and a haunt for every evil spirit,
     a haunt for every unclean and detestable bird.
[3]For all the nations have drunk
     the maddening wine of her adulteries.
The kings of the earth committed adultery with her,
     and the merchants of the earth grew rich from
          her excessive luxuries."

[4]Then I heard another voice from heaven say:

"Come out of her, my people,
     so that you will not share in her sins,
     so that you will not receive any of
          her plagues;
[5]for her sins are piled up to heaven,
     and God has remembered her crimes.
[6]Give back to her as she has given;
     pay her back double for what she has done.
     Mix her a double portion from her own cup.
[7]Give her as much torture and grief
     as the glory and luxury she gave herself.
In her heart she boasts,
     'I sit as queen; I am not a widow,
     and I will never mourn.'
[8]Therefore in one day her plagues will overtake her:
     death, mourning and famine.
She will be consumed by fire,
     for mighty is the Lord God who judges her.

[9]"When the kings of the earth who committed adultery with her and shared her luxury see the smoke of her burning, they will weep and mourn over her. [10]Terrified at her torment, they will stand far off and cry:

> ¹⁰"Woe! Woe, O great city,
> > O Babylon, city of power!
> In one hour your doom has come!'

¹¹"The merchants of the earth will weep and mourn over her because no one buys their cargoes any more—¹²cargoes of gold, silver, precious stones and pearls; fine linen, purple, silk and scarlet cloth; every sort of citron wood, and articles of every kind made of ivory, costly wood, bronze, iron and marble; ¹³cargoes of cinnamon and spice, of incense, myrrh and frankincense, of wine and olive oil, of fine flour and wheat; cattle and sheep; horses and carriages; and bodies and souls of men.

¹⁴"They will say, 'The fruit you longed for is gone from you. All your riches and splendor have vanished, never to be recovered.' ¹⁵The merchants who sold these things and gained their wealth from her will stand far off, terrified at her torment. They will weep and mourn ¹⁶and cry out:

> "'Woe! Woe, O great city,
> > dressed in fine linen, purple and scarlet,
> > and glittering with gold, precious stones and pearls!
> ¹⁷In one hour such great wealth has been brought to ruin!'

"Every sea captain, and all who travel by ship, the sailors, and all who earn their living from the sea, will stand far off. ¹⁸When they see the smoke of her burning, they will exclaim, 'Was there ever a city like this great city?' ¹⁹They will throw dust on their heads, and with weeping and mourning cry out:

> "'Woe! Woe, O great city,
> > where all who had ships on the sea
> > became rich through her wealth!
> In one hour she has been brought to ruin!
> ²⁰Rejoice over her, O heaven!
> > Rejoice, saints and apostles and prophets!
> God has judged her for the way she treated you.'"

²¹Then a mighty angel picked up a boulder the size of a large millstone and threw it into the sea, and said:

> "With such violence
> > the great city of Babylon will be thrown down,
> > never to be found again.

²²The music of harpists and musicians, flute players
and trumpeters,
will never be heard in you again.
No workman of any trade
will ever be found in you again.
The sound of a millstone
will never be heard in you again.
²³The light of a lamp
will never shine in you again.
The voice of bridegroom and bride
will never be heard in you again.
Your merchants were the world's great men.
By your magic spell all the nations were led astray.
²⁴In her was found the blood of prophets and of the saints,
and of all who have been killed on the earth."

REVELATION CONTINUES ITS depiction of Babylon described in 17:1–18, now developing in great detail the warning of its destruction (17:16–18). Chapter 18 contains a series of laments. John opens this section with the mourning of a funeral dirge over Babylon (18:2) and concludes with rejoicing over its fall, which paves the way for the joy of a wedding (19:1–9).

The Death of Babylon (18:1–8)

THE LAMENT JOHN writes down, however, is more like a curse! The Old Testament prophets sometimes used funeral dirges, the language of mourning, as a creative way of announcing judgment, which could prove a cause of exulting (e.g., Isa. 16:7–11). They similarly reported the mourning of others as a creative way to communicate impending judgment (Isa. 3:26; 19:8; Jer. 48:17; Mic. 1:10).¹ Laments over destroyed cities became a recognized

---

1. Mourning could also be genuine (e.g., Jer. 6:26; 8:21). Laments over the dead were standard throughout Mediterranean antiquity (e.g., Achilles Tatius, 1.14; Emanuel Feldman, "The Rabbinic Lament," *JQR* 63 [1972]: 51–75), and often addressed them (e.g., Tobit 10:5). Greek forms for mourning and eulogies often affected Jewish forms (J. C. H. Lebram, "Die literarische Form des vierten Makkabäerbuches," *Vigiliae Christianae* 28 [June 1974]: 81–96), but a Qumran lament over Jerusalem emphasizes Old Testament language (Maurya P. Horgan, "A Lament Over Jerusalem (4Q179)," *JSS* 18 [Autumn 1973]: 222–34).

literary form in antiquity.[2] The announcement of an oppressor's fall was good news (Nah. 1:15), just as the restoration of Zion was (Isa. 40:9; 41:27; 52:7).

"Fallen! Fallen is Babylon the Great" recapitulates 14:8, both of which recall the dirge over Babylon in Isaiah 21:9 (cf. Jer. 51:8). The lament is especially joined by those who committed immorality with the prostitute—the client-kings whose rule depended on Rome (18:9–10) and the merchants whose prosperity likewise depended on it (18:11–19). By contrast, the dwellers in heaven rejoice (18:20; 19:1–3).[3] One can compare merchant kingdoms' laments over Tyre, the economic prostitute of old (Isa. 23:5–7, 15–17).

Mention that Babylon will become a dwelling place of unclean birds (18:2; cf. 19:17) is a creative way of announcing judgment. When cities were depopulated, no one could prevent animals from taking over. Thus Rome's population decreased from as much as a million in John's day to some 30,000 after its fall a few centuries later.[4] The prophets had announced such a fate for many powerful cities (Isa. 34:11–15; Jer. 49:33), including Babylon (Isa. 13:20–22; Jer. 50:13; 51:29, 37) and Jerusalem (Jer. 9:11; 10:22), though God promised that Jerusalem would be restored (Isa. 35:7).

Some of these prophetic descriptions include creatures that the LXX calls "demons" (Isa. 34:14; cf. Bar. 4:35), among which descriptions are judgment oracles against Babylon (Isa. 13:21). Becoming a dwelling place of demons is a suitable judgment for a power once mobilized by demons (Rev. 16:14; cf. 9:20). That such spirits are "imprisoned" there (18:2, but not the Old Testament texts) may be a figurative way of suggesting their appropriate judgment (20:7; in contrast to believers' sufferings, 2:10).[5] Babylon faced such judgment (Jer. 51:37) precisely because they had crushed God's people (51:33–36; cf. Rev. 18:24; 19:2).

In Rome's propaganda, circulated by local elites (whose own rank depended on Rome's patronage), Rome brought good to many peoples; but

---

2. E.g., "Lamentation over Ur" in *ANET*, 455–63; Lam. 1:1–5:22; 1 Macc. 2:6–13; *Greek Anthology*, 9.151. For prophetic lamentation over a city's future destruction, see also Sib. Or. 5.98–99.

3. The structure here alternates between an angel (18:1–3, 21–24) and a voice from heaven (God or a high agent, 18:4–8, 20; 19:5; the saints in 19:1–3, 6–7); the heavenly voice also narrates the nations' lament (18:9–19).

4. González, *Revelation*, 116. Recent estimates place Rome's early population lower (Richard L. Rohrbaugh, "The Pre-Industrial City in Luke-Acts: Urban Social Relations," 125–49 in *The Social World of Luke-Acts: Models for Interpretation*, ed. J. H. Neyrey [Peabody, Mass.: Hendrickson, 1991], 133), but traditional estimates are based on Roman records of the grain dole reported in Roman historians (Clarke, "Rome and Italy," 464–66). Even earlier in the Republic the number cannot be below half a million, because the Roman census usually showed about 100,000 citizens, not including women, children, foreigners, and menial workers or slaves (e.g., Dionysius of Halicarnassus, 5.20.1; 5.75.3; 6.96.4; 9.15.2; 9.36.3).

5. The LXX most often associates "demons" with idolatry (Deut. 32:17; Ps. 96:5; 106:37; Isa. 65:3; Bar. 4:7), which fits Babylon/Rome (Rev. 9:20). Early Jewish literature often comments on the imprisonment of fallen angels in various locales (see commentaries on 2 Peter 2:4).

---

in a scathing critique, the prophet here announces that Rome relates to other peoples only for her own personal gain. Three times the text zeroes in on Babylon's "luxury" (18:3, 7, 9).[6] That the nations will mourn her destruction only reveals the extent to which they have been intoxicated and bewitched by her exploitive seduction (14:8; 17:2; 18:3, 23).[7] But John's audience will not lose sight of God's sovereignty, for the language here echoes Jeremiah: God has made Babylon a wine cup to intoxicate the nations and drive them insane (Jer. 51:7; cf. Zech. 12:2), inviting mourning over Babylon (Jer. 51:8) and the flight of God's people (Jer. 51:6, 45; cf. Zech. 2:7).

Those who mourn for Babylon include both "kings" and "merchants," Rome's political and mercantile allies (18:3); John focuses more on the latter group (18:11–19) than the former (18:9–10). His oracles against Babylon (18:1–19:8) are full of allusions to the Old Testament prophets, including not only prophecies against Babylon but also the oracle against Tyre in Ezekiel 26–28. Revelation borrows heavily from Old Testament images concerning Tyre because Tyre (also a prostitute—see Isa. 23:15–17) was an economic power like Rome: "If Rome was the heir of Babylon in political and religious activity, she was also the heir of Tyre in economic activity."[8] Tyre, which many considered invincible despite Ezekiel's prophecy, ultimately met a terrible end at the hands of Alexander the Great.

Not all John's audience is persecuted by the beast at this point; some of them in Laodicea and Sardis, in fact, are prospering as part of the same system that elsewhere is killing the saints. The summons to "come out" (18:4) may thus include withdrawal from the economic arenas that required compromise with emperor worship or other forms of idolatry.[9] John's prophecy counters "Balaam" and "Jezebel," prophets of compromise who supported immorality, perhaps figuratively with the beast (2:14, 20; cf. 18:3). Other Jewish texts used similar language against compromise with the world's evil.[10]

Those who remain in Babylon will share Babylon's judgment, so Jeremiah had long ago prophesied to his people to flee (Jer. 51:6), though he meant

---

6. Aune, *Revelation*, 3:990, connects Babylon's luxury or wealth in 18:3, 9, 16–17, 19 with the four mentions of Tyre's wealth in Ezek. 27:12, 18, 27, 33.

7. Bauckham, *Climax of Prophecy*, 347.

8. Ibid., 346; cf. Kraybill, *Imperial Cult and Commerce*, 152–61.

9. See Bauckham, *Climax of Prophecy*, 376–77; Kraybill, *Imperial Cult and Commerce*, 29. Collins, *Crisis and Catharsis*, 127, associates this with social rather than physical removal (12:6, 14).

10. Cf. Jeremiah's warnings to stay far from Babylonian sins (4 Bar. 7:37); Enoch's warnings to stay far from sinners whose "secret" deeds are known to God (1 Enoch 104:6–8); warnings that those who heed the world will share its destruction (T. Job 33:4); Tobit's warning to depart from Nineveh before its destruction (Tobit 14:8); the summons to separate from "those destined for the Pit" (CD 6.14–15); and the belief that the eschatological remnant will flee from the apostates to the true Israel (4QpNah 3.5).

these words as a prophecy of future judgment rather than a present warning (29:7). This warning to flee comes in the same context as the mention that Babylon was an intoxicating cup for the nations and would be mourned (51:7–8). That people are still invited to escape just before the judgment reveals the greatness of God's mercy. God invites his people to leave Babylon because they have a better city (Rev. 21:2–3).

The judgment comes when Babylon's sins are piled as high as heaven (18:5); sometimes God delays judgment only to wait until the measure for judgment over several generations is full (cf. Gen. 15:16; Matt. 23:36; Luke 11:50). Such prophecies indicate that those who profit from the sins of their ancestors will also share the judgment due their ancestors as well as that due their own sin.[11] Eventually the cup of Babylon's sins, as well as the incense cup of the saints' cries for vindication, becomes full and rises before God (Rev. 6:10; 8:4). Those who destroy Babylon will be repaying her double for her sins (18:6), as literal Babylon had once been God's agent in judging God's people double for their sins (Isa. 40:2); this was the sort of recompense exacted from a thief (Ex. 22:4, 7, 9).[12] Babylon will drink from its own cup (Rev. 14:8–10; cf. Isa. 51:22–23; Jer. 50:15, 29; Obad. 15).

The message of judgment against Babylon's arrogance in 18:7 reflects the language of an ancient oracle against Babylon. Babylon claimed to be an eternal queen (18:7; cf. Isa. 47:7), living luxuriously (or sensuously—Rev. 18:7; cf. Isa. 47:8) and denying that she would be widowed or lose her children (18:7; cf. Isa. 47:8).[13] Thus plagues will come on her all in one day (Rev. 18:8; cf. Isa. 47:9); she will no longer deceive by her sorcery (Rev. 18:23; cf. Isa. 47:9). Isaiah's prophecy is well-suited to Rome, which claimed to be an eternal city.[14] Other Jewish writers also saw the relevance of applying this oracle against Rome (Sib. Or. 5.169–74).[15]

---

11. This principle was also recognized by Jewish interpreters (*Sifre Deut.* 332.2.1). For the reparation of 18:20, 24, as in Luke 11:50–51, see also F. F. Bruce, *The Time Is Fulfilled* (Grand Rapids: Eerdmans, 1978), 106.

12. On drinking a cup of judgment to the dregs, see Ps. 75:8. On double payment, cf. 1 Tim. 5:17; Sherk, *Empire*, 92, 159–60; other Greek references in Aune, *Revelation*, 3:992–93.

13. Cf. Jerusalem's fate in Lam. 1:1. A cognate of this word for arrogance appears in an oracle against Assyria in 2 Kings 19:28; the loss of children was judgment on the immoral woman of Rev. 2:23; famine and death (18:8) come on the world in 6:8. Famine and pestilence frequently accompanied a city's demise (Aune, *Revelation*, 3:996).

14. Kraybill, *Imperial Cult and Commerce*, 57, cites *I. Eph.* 599; Josephus, *War* 5.367. Cf. the addition to Gen. 11:4 in Ps-Philo, 7:1.

15. God would also avenge the sufferings of Asia on Rome the conqueror (Sib. Or. 3.350–55) and judge Rome's arrogance (3.466–68; 8.75–76). Egypt (and/or Cleopatra) is a widow (11.279; cf. 3.75–92) but even worse will marry Rome (11.290). Such reapplication of language was not meant to cancel Isaiah's literal meaning; Sib. Or. 5.444–45 applies Isa. 47 against literal Babylon.

The extent to which Rome glorified itself (Rev. 18:7) may be illustrated by the spread of the worship of the emperor and the goddess Roma, personification of Rome. As a means of propaganda and social control, Rome expected worship of what it stood for. Babylon's giving "glory" to itself in 18:7 contrasts starkly with the new Jerusalem, which has God's glory (21:11, 23) and the gathering of the glory of the nations into the latter (21:24, 26). A day is coming in which honor will be taken from the arrogant (cf. 13:5) and belong to God and his people alone. Babylon will be burned (see comment on 17:16); the punishment will come, because the Lord God who judges is mighty (18:8; cf. Deut. 3:24; 9:26; Ps. 89:8; Ezek. 20:33; Joel 2:11).

Die Hard: Crying Kings, Mourning Merchants (18:9–20)

IN THIS DYSTOPIAN prophecy, the kings mourn the destruction of the evil empire (18:9–10); by contrast, the righteous remnant of all peoples will participate in the new Jerusalem, and their kings will bring their glory into it (21:24). The worldly rulers in the provinces have reason to lament here, for they profited personally from Roman rule (cf. 18:3), some rising to power and status because of the emperor's patronage; Rome "provided security and prosperity for its friends."[16] Asia, where John's audience was located, was the richest of the provinces.[17] Thus these leaders mourn not only for Babylon (Rome) but for themselves! Both kings and merchants who profited from Babylon's rule will mourn over her demise, but at a safe distance because they fear her torment (18:10, 15; cf. Ezek. 26:18); the world's love is self-interested, not self-sacrificing (Rev. 17:16–17).

"Kings of the earth" refers to Rome's client-kings (17:2, 18; 18:3), though the language is adapted to the Old Testament. It is a common Old Testament expression (used at least fifteen times), but this text recalls a few passages in particular: The Messiah would rule the kings (Ps. 89:27; Rev. 1:5); they would gather against God's Son and be shattered (Ps. 2:2; Acts 4:26; Rev. 19:19); and they became wealthy through Tyre's trade (Ezek. 27:33). Their cry of "Woe! Woe!" is repeated by the merchants in Revelation 18:10, 16, 19.

The longest laments come from the merchants, who profited from Rome's trade.[18] Aristocrats and the many people who shared their perspective remained dazzled with Rome's grandeur and all the wealth of the empire

---

16. Kraybill, *Imperial Cult and Commerce*, 57, 59–82.

17. Ibid., 65–66.

18. Other writers expected great wealth to perish when God judged Rome (Sib. Or. 2.18), as well as when he judged Phoenicia's maritime cities (3.492–94) and prosperous Alexandria (5.98). By contrast, those who portrayed a utopian future expected mercantile ships to cease because every land would bear all fruits (Virgil, *Ecl.* 4.37–39).

brought into it.[19] Rome was the mightiest empire next to that of the gods, some claimed.[20] Yet Rome lived luxuriously on the basis of inequitable trade policies toward its provinces. In less than one year the usurper Vitellius wasted the equivalent of more than twenty million dollars, mainly on extravagant foods, "delicacies like peacocks' brains and nightingales' tongues."[21] Commenting on merchants and shippers, Kraybill notes:

> From Egypt, North Africa and the Black Sea region they ferried some 400,000 tons of grain annually for the capital city. While provincials paid high prices for grain and sometimes had none, 200,000 families in Rome received from the government a regular "dole" of free grain.[22]

Rome's insatiable appetites and seductive wealth lured provincials with money to invest in what they could export to Rome rather than the needs of their people. Landowners in Asia used so much land for export items like wine that Asia's cities had to import grain from Egypt to the south or from the Black Sea area to the north; consequently, the landowners profited, but everyone else paid higher prices for basic food needs.[23]

Rome's commercial interests also propagated its pagan religion, and most people were more committed to buying and selling than to resisting Rome's demands (13:17). The merchant's lament that no one now buys their cargoes (18:11) is ironic retribution for those who worshiped the beast that they might buy and sell (13:17)! Pagan symbols were prominent at major Mediterranean ports, and activities of the shipping lines and merchant guilds involved aspects of the imperial cult.[24] Jews were exempt from participation in the imperial cult, but Christians kicked out of the synagogues presumably had to participate or lose income.[25] In this passage John identifies with the provincial poor "because he believed Christians no longer could participate in an unjust commercial network thoroughly saturated with idolatrous patriotism."[26]

---

19. Bauckham, *Climax of Prophecy*, 375–76, citing Aelius Aristides, Or. 26.7, 11–13. Bauckham is surely right that John himself is denouncing rather than mourning Rome's wealth (ibid., 338–83).

20. Livy, 1.4.1. Later rabbis claimed that Rome's wealth was incomparable (ARN, 28A) and that there were 133,225 palaces in Rome, each with 365 stories—each story with enough food to feed the world (*b. Pes.* 118b).

21. Mounce, *Revelation*, 329.

22. Kraybill, *Imperial Cult and Commerce*, 107, citing *Res Gestae* 15. Emperors used grain to maintain stability in their capital (Pliny, *Panegyricus* 29.1–5); when they withheld it, riots ensued (Appian, *C.W.* 5.8.67; Tacitus, *Ann.* 6.13; 12.43).

23. Kraybill, *Imperial Cult and Commerce*, 66–67.

24. Ibid., 29, 123–41; for pagan symbols at ports, see 125–27; cf. Acts 28:11.

25. Ibid., 197.

26. Ibid., 23.

Rome's port, Ostia, built by Claudius roughly half a century before Revelation was written, held a large colonnaded square full of offices for the *navicularii*, the merchants.[27] Lists of goods destroyed were appropriate to a detailed lament or oracle of judgment (2 Bar. 10:19), but many of the specific items in this list reveal Revelation's critique of luxury goods (18:12–13).[28] We review these briefly as follows.

Rome's new rich in this period typically flaunted their "gold" and "silver." The city imported most of these metals from Spain, where it owned a number of mines, some confiscated from their owners; the slaves who worked such mines rarely lived more than a few years.[29] They imported "precious stones," worn in men's rings but especially by women, mainly from India; many of John's contemporaries regarded "pearls" as the epitome of luxury. They secured some pearls from the Red Sea, better ones from the Persian Gulf, and the most abundant source was India; by John's day this may have become the largest part of Rome's trade with the East.[30]

Rome imported "fine linen" from Spain, Asia Minor, and especially Egypt; it had begun to replace wool in Rome by this period. "Purple" had long been a symbol of affluence, imported especially from Tyre; "scarlet cloth" was also a symbol of luxury, derived mainly from kermes oaks in Asia Minor. Romans, who thought silk grew on trees, imported it from China especially through northwest Indian ports and some overland through Parthia. Given the distance traveled, it is hardly surprising that it was a symbol of conspicuous consumption limited to the wealthy.[31]

"Citron wood" (or citrus wood) originally came from the north African coast from Cyrene westward, but the supply was by this period so depleted that most such wood was imported from Morocco; tables made of citron wood were "one of the most expensive fashions in early imperial Rome." Thus one table was sold for the price of a large estate.[32] The "ivory" trade had nearly

---

27. Caird, *Commentary on Revelation*, 226.

28. Most of what follows is especially from Bauckham, *Climax of Prophecy*, 352–66, who documents elaborately. Others provide valuable details (e.g., Caird, *Commentary on Revelation*, 228; Ford, *Revelation*, 298–99; Aune, *Revelation*, 3:998–1002), but Bauckham provides the most to date.

29. On mine slaves, see Naphtali Lewis, *Life in Egypt Under Roman Rule* (Oxford: Clarendon, 1983), 137–38. After the first century, Rome turned more to the Balkans for gold (Aune, *Revelation*, 3:998).

30. Not directly familiar with gathering oysters, ancients sometimes had interesting views of how they were harvested (e.g., Arrian, *Indica* 8.11–12).

31. In addition to Bauckham, see on silk production and trade through history Richard N. Frye, *The Heritage of Central Asia: From Antiquity to the Turkish Expansion* (Princeton, N.J.: Markus Wiener, 1996), 153–57. Rome traded with China especially A.D. 90–130, probably nearly 45 million sesterces a year (and 55 million with India; Aune, *Revelation*, 3:999).

32. See Pliny, *N.H.* 13.95, as cited in Bauckham, *Climax of Prophecy*, 356–57.

driven the Syrian elephant to extinction and few elephants remained in north Africa; those who wished to flaunt wealth used it in table legs and idols. Other "costly wood" (18:12) probably refers to maple, cedar, and cypress, all of which were used as expensive luxury items (ebony was rare in Rome). The most famous "bronze" in the empire was Corinthian bronze; the best "iron" was imported from the East, though available elsewhere; Romans imported "marble" from Africa, Egypt, and Greece, especially for use in palaces.

"Cinnamon" probably came especially from Somalia in East Africa and could include both cassia (most trade specialized in this wood of the cinnamon plant) and "cinnamon proper (the tender shoots and the delicate bark), which was extremely expensive."[33] Ships involved in the east African trade went as far south as Zanzibar off the Tanzanian coast, in a two-year round trip voyage.[34] The term for "spice" designates an aromatic spice from southern India; "incense" was used not only for religious rituals but to perfume wealthy homes. "Myrrh" was imported from Yemen and Somalia; "frankincense," known as a luxury good (e.g., T. Job 32:10/11), was from South Arabia. Some Romans in this period were complaining that other Romans were spending too much on luxury goods from the east.

Rome procured its best "wine" from Sicily and Spain, though it was available from elsewhere. In John's day the empire experienced a grain shortage along with a wine surplus (cf. comment on 6:6); because the wine trade was more profitable than grain, wealthy Roman owners of *latifundia* (large estates) in the provinces cultivated vines more than grain. Italy produced some of its own "olive oil" but imported more in this period from Africa and Spain. "Fine flour" (in contrast to wine, oil, and wheat) was a luxury good, the best being imported from Africa.

Africa and Egypt supplied most of Rome's "wheat" via the imperial grain fleet, which consisted of thousands of ships run by merchants but supervised by the state. Much of this wheat came from taxes on the provinces, but it was distributed free to Rome's inhabitants, so not just the rich but the whole populace of Rome "survived only at the expense of the rest of the empire." This was one sense in which the prostitute Rome rode on the beast of imperial power.[35]

Even the rich rarely ate beef; "cattle" were used especially as work animals, and in the first century the rich procured as ranches large estates in Italy and (generally by confiscation or conquest) in the provinces. Some "sheep" were used for mutton, but Italy mainly imported sheep for rich estates that produced

---

33. Bauckham, *Climax of Prophecy*, 360. The cheapest cinnamon cost 50 times as much as the same weight in wheat, and rose to 300 times that much during a shortage (Kraybill, *Imperial Cult and Commerce*, 105, citing Pliny, *N.H.* 12.93, 97).

34. Ibid., 104.

35. Bauckham, *Climax of Prophecy*, 363.

wool. Italy lacked sufficient pasture for "horses" but imported them from Africa, Spain, and elsewhere to use for chariot races in public entertainment. Horses also pulled the four-wheeled chariots from Gaul, sometimes plated with silver, in which the rich traveled "in Rome and to their country estates."[36]

John concludes climactically with "bodies and souls of men." Because this period did not produce sufficient wars to supply Rome slaves directly, Rome had to locate other sources to maintain its needs. Many poor people in the empire discarded babies they felt unable to raise; while many of these were eaten by birds and dogs, many were also rescued for slavery; Asia exported a large number to Rome, probably through the port of Ephesus.[37] Human "souls" or (as the word used can also be translated) "lives" may derive from the Greek version of Ezek. 27:13, where "human lives" (lit. trans.)—part of Tyre's vicious trade—means "slaves" (cf. NIV).[38] Biblical law condemned stealing another's "life"—that is, kidnapping for slave-trading—as a capital offense (Deut. 24:7). "Riches and splendor" (Rev. 18:14) summarizes the list, in Greek containing the sort of play on words (lipara and lampra) sometimes used by Greek rhetoricians and Israelite prophets.

This is the longest extant list of products from the Roman period. John adapts Ezekiel's list of forty products in which Tyre traded (Ezek. 27:2–24), but updates it accurately for the trade realities of first-century Rome. Whereas Ezekiel's list is arranged geographically, John's is arranged topically, by type of cargo.[39] Although he includes some items that were not expensive (oil, though imported in massive quantities), John focuses mostly on expensive imports, overlapping substantially with another writer's list of twenty-nine expensive items.[40]

A few sources in John's day acknowledged that Rome's rich indulged themselves at the expense of the rest of the empire, but most sources that criticized luxury did so merely because it corrupted aristocrats and made them dependent. While perhaps sharing some of this critique, Revelation explicitly condemns Rome for profiting at the expense of the empire; the prosti-

---

36. Ibid., 365.

37. Abandoned babies were common (e.g., Diodorus Siculus, 4.64.1; 8.4.1; 19.2.3–5; Juvenal, Sat. 6.602–9; Longus, 1.2, 5; 4.24, 36; Pausanias, 2.26.4) and often were raised as slaves (Justin, Apol. 1.27; Lewis, Life in Egypt, 54, 58). Like Jews (Josephus, Apion 2.202; Diodorus Siculus, 40.3.8), Egyptians opposed child abandonment (Diodorus Siculus, 1.80.3).

38. Bauckham, Climax of Prophecy, 370; Ford, Revelation, 299. For references on human "bodies" signifying slaves, see G. Adolf Deissmann, Bible Studies, tr. A. Grieve (Edinburgh: T. & T. Clark, 1923), 160.

39. Bauckham, Climax of Prophecy, 350–51.

40. Ibid., 366 (Pliny, N.H. 37.204 includes thirteen of Revelation's twenty-eight, and Revelation includes eighteen of Pliny's items).

tute is decked with her imports (17:4; 18:16).[41] Although much of the chapter condemns Rome's luxury itself, partly for its arrogance (18:7), oppression is also in view (18:24).

Those who mourn in 18:17 include those who work on ships, but this probably implies the sorrow of ship owners as well. The merchants were the "great" people of the earth (18:23), which ranked them directly below kings in Revelation's scheme of worldly status (6:15; 18:23). But Revelation reveals the ultimate emptiness of the status for anyone "of the earth" (1:5, 7; 17:2, 18; 18:3, 9, 11).[42] Because transport was cheaper by sea, Rome imported most of the goods listed in 18:12–13 through its port of Ostia. Shipwrecks could ruin ship owners, but some grew wealthy enough to own many ships, reducing the risk.[43] With the fall of Rome, however, both ship owners and their employees would be out of business, little better off than the agrarian peasants Rome cruelly exploited with high taxes.[44]

For a city that had burned less than half a century earlier (blamed by the first Nero on Christians), the threat of such burning as 18:18 describes would be a vivid one (see Tacitus, *Ann.* 15.38–44). Casting dust on one's head (18:19) was a traditional act of mourning (Josh. 7:6; 1 Sam. 4:12; 2 Sam. 1:2; 15:32; Lam. 2:10; Ezek. 27:30).

Vengeance for the Saints (18:20–24)

A "MIGHTY ANGEL" announces a message in 18:21–24, but the thought of the narrative continues from what precedes. Verses 20 and 24 bracket this

---

41. Ibid., 368–69. On a parallel denunciation of Rome's exploitation of Asia in the Sibylline Oracles, see pp. 378–83. Aune, *Revelation*, 3:990, argues that the passage denounces luxury (as do some contemporary Roman critiques of Roman society) rather than exploitation (though cf. 3:1010 and the ancient link between seafaring and greed, 3:989), since provinces (especially Asia) also profited from Rome's trade. But a provincial shut out of the merchant class (13:17–18; 18:3) may recognize that Rome acquired its wealth from the provinces in unjust trade patterns that helped only those welcome to participate.

42. The phrase "great of earth" (lit.) may stem from Isa. 23:8 (against Tyre) but fits merchants of the Roman empire; though not of high social rank, they were often wealthy (Bauckham, *Climax of Prophecy*, 373).

43. See ibid., 373–74; cf. Hesiod, *Works and Days* 689–91; Brian M. Rapske, "Acts, Travel and Shipwreck," 1–47 in *The Book of Acts in Its Graeco-Roman Setting*, ed. D. W. J. Gill and C. Gempf (Grand Rapids: Eerdmans, 1994), 25–28. For captains' safe delivery contracts, see *P. Oxy.* 3250.

44. To be sure, the tribute inflow (probably about 10 percent of the empire's Gross National Product) stimulated trade and the outflow of cash, benefiting the overall economy of the urban empire (Aune, *Revelation*, 3:989); but most rural peasants—the bulk of the empire's people—experienced taxation as oppressive (see C. S. Keener, *Matthew* [Grand Rapids: Eerdmans, 1999], 292–93).

---

paragraph with the theme of vengeance for the blood of the saints, a biblical theme that appears elsewhere (Deut. 32:43; 2 Kings 9:7; Ps. 79:10; Joel 3:21).[45]

In contrast to the earth dwellers' mourning, heaven rejoices over Babylon's fall (18:20; cf. the dragon's fall in 12:12).[46] That God will pronounce sentence on Babylon on behalf of the martyred saints, apostles, and prophets suggests the continuing witness and suffering of these groups until the time of the end.[47] Believers have been tried and executed in the world's courts, but it is the world that is really on trial (cf. John 16:8–11); this passage may reflect the Old Testament laws concerning bloodshed and false witnesses (Gen. 9:6; Deut. 19:16–19).[48]

God commanded Jeremiah to hurl a stone into the middle of the Euphrates to symbolize the permanent fall of Babylon (Jer. 51:63–64). In Revelation this becomes a millstone into the sea (Rev. 18:21), probably recalling Jesus' warning that those who cause any little ones to stumble will be killed in this manner (Mark 9:42; Luke 17:2); the words in each case refer to the huge millstone turned by a mule, not the kind a woman might use by hand.[49] Such drowning was considered a terrible fate, and with such a heavy weight there would be no escape.[50]

When God judged Judah by means of Babylon, Jerusalem became desolate, without lighted lamps, the sounds of millstones, or the joyful sound of newlyweds (Jer. 25:10; cf. 16:9). The angelic announcement now shows that Babylon, oppressor of God's people, reaps what it has sowed against God's people, mentioning also the stilling of mills, newlyweds, and lamps (Rev.

---

45. The shift between second-person address to Babylon (18:22–23) and third-person description of Babylon (18:21, 24) was standard in prophetic literature, including judgment speeches (Aune, *Prophecy in Early Christianity*, 285).

46. Jewish literature included many examples of victors (righteous or unrighteous) rejoicing over their foes (T. Levi 15:3), including over Babylon (2 Bar. 11–12), and the righteous would eternally behold the torment of the wicked (1 Enoch, 27:3–4).

47. Some apply "prophets" here only to Old Testament prophets, but this text probably includes prophets of this era (Bruce, "The Spirit in the Apocalypse," 338). On the continuance of these gifts, see Eph. 4:11–13; Craig S. Keener, *3 Crucial Questions About the Holy Spirit* (Grand Rapids: Baker, 1996), 81–127 (esp. 101–7); Jack Deere, *Surprised by the Power of the Spirit* (Grand Rapids: Zondervan, 1993), 99–115, 229–66 (esp. 241–52).

48. Caird, *Commentary on Revelation*, 229–30; Allison A. Trites, *The New Testament Concept of Witness*, SNTSM 31 (Cambridge: Cambridge Univ. Press, 1977), 172.

49. A millstone around the neck may have become traditional for an encumbrance (*b. Kid.* 29b, bar.), but Jesus means it more harshly (cf. 1 En. 48:9). A donkey could pull about half the weight a mule could, easily over a hundred pounds (cf. Rapske, "Travel," 8); at worst, one would use an old horse (Babrius, 29.1–2).

50. Drowning was typically a Roman punishment (e.g., Livy, 1.51.9—drowning with a crate full of stones; 27.37.5–7; Babrius 27), but it was not unknown among Jews (Josephus, *Ant.* 14.450).

18:22–23).[51] By contrast, new Jerusalem will need no earthly lamp, illumined by the glory of God and the Lamb (21:23; 22:5), and that city herself will be a bride (19:7; 21:2, 9; 22:17). That the harpists will no longer be heard in Babylon (18:22) may contrast with the harpists heard in heaven (14:2). God's people struggled to use their harps in captivity (Ps. 137:2–4), but the new temple city will prove a fitting place for harps (cf. 2 Chron. 9:11; 20:28; 29:25).

The mention of "magic spell[s]" is significant (18:23). Sorcery is linked with prostitution in the description of the biblical Jezebel (2 Kings 9:22), a model for the prostitute in Revelation (2:20). More to the point, Babylon, who thought herself a queen (Isa. 47:5–7; Rev. 18:7) and denied her impending widowhood (Isa. 47:8; Rev. 18:7), vainly thought to protect herself by sorceries (Isa. 47:9, 12). But if the prophecy against Babylon in Isaiah 47 supplies the concept, the oracle against Nineveh the prostitute supplies the language: " . . . a harlot, alluring, the mistress of sorceries, who enslaved nations by her prostitution and peoples by her witchcraft" (Nah. 3:4). Magic was a major practice in Asia, especially Ephesus (Acts 19:13–19).[52] But Revelation warns that anyone who practices it will be judged (21:8; 22:15; cf. 9:21).[53]

But Babylon's greatest sin was "the blood of prophets and of the saints" (18:24), the witnesses of Jesus (11:3, 7; 17:6). The addition of "all who have been killed on the earth" may refer to the prophets and saints, but may also point beyond them to the broader critique of Rome's economic injustice (suggested in 18:5–19). Clearly in this context God is concerned about the crushing of Egypt's peasants, the brutality of slavery, and other methods by which Rome exploited most of the empire.[54] John as a Jew likewise must have shared the pain of his people crushed by the Romans in A.D. 70, a bloody conquest the Romans widely commemorated on coins and by taxing

---

51. The bridal chamber epitomized joy, and its interruption epitomized mourning (e.g., 1 Macc. 1:27; 9:39–41; 3 Macc. 4:6; Josephus, *War* 6.301); hearers' hearts might be moved by the specificity of judgment on those too young to be married or newlyweds (Lam. 1:18; 2:21; Sib. Or. 3.480–82, 525–27). In Jer. 31:13 and 33:11, God promised to reverse Israel's "bridal" sorrow of 16:9 and 25:10.

52. See Floyd V. Filson, "Ephesus and the NT," *BA* 8 (Sept. 1945): 73–80 (p. 80); Clinton E. Arnold, *Ephesians: Power and Magic*, SNTSM 63 (Cambridge: Cambridge Univ. Press, 1989), 14–16; Paul Trebilco, "Asia," 291–362 in *The Book of Acts in Its Graeco-Roman Setting*, ed. D. W. J. Gill and C. Gempf (Grand Rapids: Eerdmans, 1994), 314.

53. Although magic was widely practiced in early Jewish circles (Acts 13:6; Craig S. Keener, *The Spirit in the Gospels and Acts* [Peabody, Mass.: Hendrickson, 1997], 29–30 n. 21), many Jewish circles condemned it (Wisd. Sol. 17:7; 2 Bar. 66:2; m. Sanh. 7:11; Urbach, *Sages*, 1:97–100), maintaining the appropriateness of the biblical capital penalty (p. Hag. 2:2, §5; Sanh. 7:13, §2).

54. See Bauckham, *Climax of Prophecy*, 349.

all Jews throughout the empire.[55] But given the parallel in language with 18:20, the climax of Rome's sin was its martyrdom of God's messengers.

Bridging Contexts

SEARCHING FOR MODERN **equivalents of Babylon.** The lament John hears (18:2) is a fitting literary form for a city's destruction in his day. Although our audiences today tend to be less biblically literate and hence unaware of this literary form's use in oracles of judgment, we may recapture the same basic shock effect for our generation by uttering a mock eulogy over a sinful people. Most people today are aware of eulogies (a rhetorical form performed regularly at funerals), and because they are not accustomed to thinking of the "death" of their nation or others' nations, the image can be jarring.

For John, Babylon's fall seems to end the present world order (18:2–9). But the present world order did not collapse with the fall of Rome. Skeptics may therefore suggest that John is wrong. The reverse, however, is true: History has vindicated John's most extraordinary claim! The mighty Roman empire of John's day collapsed, but the persecuted church it sought to eradicate not only remains but has spread to every inhabited continent. Whereas Rome was the Babylon of John's day, however, it was only one of several actors in Babylon's role. Subsequent history reminds us that just as the false prophetess of Thyatira was a new Jezebel, the false prophet of Pergamum a new Balaam, the evil emperor a new Nero, and Rome a new Babylon, so the empires of history continue to return in successive incarnations that repeat the same basic lies. That the Babylon of John's day has fallen, however, like most Babylons since and all that have preceded it, gives us courage that the final Babylon, too, will perish before the glory of God's invading kingdom.[56]

In applying the passage, we should look for modern equivalents to Babylon's mercantile empire that made Babylon rich while most of the people of the empire, though remaining poor, were seduced by its grandeur. The problem may be not wealth per se but the grave inequity of opportunity in the empire; the luxury items (18:12–13) represent a squandering of resources (acquired for Rome through conquest) or status symbols while

---

55. See Kraybill, *Imperial Cult and Commerce*, 203–4.

56. Early twentieth-century conservative Protestant polarities saw "enemies" such as urban life, Roman Catholicism, or Judaism, and later as communism; early twenty-first century "enemies" may appear as Islam or New Age ideology (Robert Wuthnow, *Christianity in the 21st Century* [New York: Oxford, 1993], 121). But John's perspective does not allow such selective polarities; it is the whole world's values versus the kingdom's (though these overlap in practice even in much of the church).

neglecting others' need (we suggest some contemporary parallels in the Contemporary Significance section). Yet the passage applies not simply to the wealth of participants in a mercantile empire (18:11) but also to the arrogance of fancying one's own people invincible (18:7–8). History testifies to the folly of such a notion, though powerful nations today still maintain such arrogance.

Revelation recycles ancient prophetic images of depopulation (18:2) with which many people today are unfamiliar. To communicate the same sort of image today, we can borrow the aftereffects of the atom bomb in Hiroshima, science-fiction images of the results of neutron bombs, or the end of civilization as we know it, at least in our part of the world. The passage portrays the eternally empty carcass of Babylon's remains to testify to the pretense of its earlier grandeur, especially in contrast with new Jerusalem's eternal glory. This image summons us not to put our hope in this world but to invest our time in what will count forever—in people and their needs and destiny.

Sharing in judgment. As in this passage, those who profit from others' sins (those of ancestors or allies) share their judgment. Some doubt the possibility of intergenerational effects of sin, but they are reading their modern Western individualism into the Bible. When God judges Babylon for centuries of collected sins (18:5), he follows a pattern elsewhere observed in Scripture. He punishes children for the sins of their ancestors, though his mercy is greater and those who leave the ways of their ancestors will be exempted (Ex. 20:5–6; Deut. 5:9–10; 7:9; Ezek. 18:14–20). In 2 Samuel 21:1–9 one generation of Israel suffered a famine because the previous generation had mistreated some pagans with whom they had a nonaggression treaty; the famine was stayed only by the execution of the sons of the perpetrator. This is not to say that we should execute people for their parents' crimes today, but to consider what sorts of sins of our ancestors we may be unconsciously walking in. The sins hardest to see are those where our culture shares the same blind spots we have.

Parallels in injustice. How can the blood of all martyrs be laid at the feet of Babylon (18:24)? Had not Jesus laid it at Jerusalem's feet (Matt. 23:35–37)? But "Babylon is the type of every persecuting empire."[57] The saints may suffer in the short run, but vindication always comes in God's time. In bridging the gap between God's concern for injustice (against his saints and others) in this text and in our world today, we must think of the injustices we know of, both those that make the evening news and the many personal stories that never make the news. We need to share God's passion for justice for the broken, by prayer and (where possible) by action.

---

57. Caird, *Commentary on Revelation*, 232.

VINDICATION OF FAITH. This exiled Jewish Christian prophet had the audacity to write down a funeral dirge over the mightiest empire the world had yet known! Such an act may not seem so reckless from the advantage of hindsight, but in John's day it must have appeared an act of either incredible faith or incredible presumption. After all, the Christians were a persecuted minority sect, their prophet was banished on an island for political prisoners, yet he used against Rome an ironic literary form employed by Old Testament prophets to declare its destruction.

Rome, however, did collapse sixteen centuries ago, and the church of Jesus Christ continues to grow. This provides us, John's heirs, a ready platform for faith: All Rome's successors, all the evil empires of history who repress God's people, will be dust and ashes, but God's kingdom will not fail! Empires rise and fall, and our own earthly lives perish with the passing of generations.[58] We must rest our confidence not in the short-term troubles that we read in the news headlines, but in God's long-range purposes in history; the God who triumphed over Rome is the God whose ultimate triumph will come soon enough. John could stand on the shoulders of earlier prophets, recognizing that God's people have remained even when the empires who conquered them collapsed; he could have confidence that God would do the same with Rome, and history has vindicated his faith.

Coming out of Babylon. God warns his people to "come out" of Babylon (18:4). This is a call to holiness, but we must not misunderstand holiness. Holiness is not simply a matter of avoiding certain kinds of activities, as some traditional churches have emphasized; holiness is separation from the world to God. Thus one can express holiness by immersing oneself in God's Word rather than in the world's values emphasized on television; or by turning down a better-paying job because someone felt God wanted him or her to work in a different place, perhaps among the poor. Such holiness may cost us our place in Babylon and much more. One Christian I have called "Stephen" used to pray two hours a day and began to tell God passionately that he loved God so much that nothing else mattered. Then, in 1987, Stephen lost his wife. Now when he says, "God, I love you more than anything," he understands better what he is saying. Ultimately, if we are truly Jesus' disciples, our very lives are forfeit (Mark 8:34–38).

---

58. Even many Romans, considering the fall of Troy, Assyria, the Medes, Persians, Macedonians, and Carthage, could acknowledge that all empires eventually perish (Appian, *R.H.* 8.19.132).

"Come out of her" (18:4) also reminds us that we Christians may share in the judgments on our society, in spite of forgiveness for individual sins. Nations and institutions as corporate entities can stand under judgment (e.g., 1 Sam. 15:2–3); we who participate in such institutions share in their responsibility before God unless we explicitly repudiate our complicity with them and declare their activities wrong (Deut. 21:7–9; cf. Amos 4:1–3). Most of all, the summons to "come out of her" reminds believers that we belong to a different city (Gal. 4:26; Heb. 11:16), whose true wealth is greater than Babylon's glory for which our neighbors strive (Rev. 3:17).

Michaels suggests that Babylon suffers heavy vengeance (18:6) especially because Christians do not retaliate, "leaving room for God's wrath to accomplish its terrible purpose" (13:10).[59] Such a warning becomes more than theoretical for Christians who have lost close friends or family members to martyrdom in many parts of the world. Even those whose only persecution is experiencing slander, however, must consider the demands of this interpretation; if it is true, it requires us to love in a way utterly foreign to the world's comprehension.

The warning that the righteous must escape Babylon reminds us that those who remain in solidarity with a sinful society share its judgments. The modern dichotomy between personal responsibility and societal corruption was unfamiliar to biblical writers. Judas, Pilate, the chief priests, and the people of Jesus' generation were all guilty for condemning him (Matt. 27:4, 24–25; Mark 14:41; 15:1, 15). Sin brings judgment on a whole society (e.g., Josh. 7:1–26; 22:31); a society that cannot bring individual perpetrators to justice must assume responsibility for restitution (Deut. 21:1–9).

God's people should not simply pity crime victims on the evening news or wait for someone else to do something practical to help them. As best as we can, we should take responsibility to help them. Our faith should inform our public policy, because as participants in a sinful society we will share its judgments. Because we are all affected by sin, we should raise our voice against it (Josh. 22:17–18). But when a society is too corrupt to listen, God may simply warn Christians to withdraw before he destroys it (Gen. 19:12–13); those who look back in longing for the world will share its doom (19:26).

Intergenerational effects of sin and its remedy. If intergenerational effects of sin are possible (1 Sam. 15:2; 2 Sam. 21:1–6; Matt. 23:30–32), what should we consider in our own lives? On the personal level, we could consider sinful patterns we may have adopted from behavior we saw growing up; often abused children become abusive, children of alcoholic parents have relationship problems, children of divorce have a more difficult time trusting

---

59. Michaels, *Revelation*, 204.

commitment, and so forth.[60] In each of these cases, God's grace can enable us to transform the legacy of our past, but we must do so by confronting and overcoming it rather than ignoring it.

The corporate level of intergenerational sin is harder for us to recognize because usually those around us share the same blind spots we have. As noted above, God punished a later generation of Israel for breaking its nonaggression treaty with the pagan Gibeonites; yet how many nonaggression treaties did white Americans (as well as some black soldiers) break with Native Americans? During one massacre of mostly unarmed women and children who had a peace treaty with the U.S. government, Native Americans ran to the U.S. flag to surrender and were shot down, including a chief who trusted that the soldiers would listen to him because the white man was his friend. Thirty or forty squaws sent out a six-year-old girl with a flag of surrender, and the soldiers gunned her down, then methodically killed all the squaws and scalped them; a pregnant one was sliced open. When two U.S. soldiers found a five-year-old girl hiding, they shot her dead. After this the Cheyenne learned to reject their own leaders who had trusted whites; they turned instead to armed resistance.[61] Would any Christian justify such a massacre?

In the same way, we often want to say, "Let bygones be bygones," before justice has been served. In the Bible the Exodus was followed by a settlement in a land flowing with milk and honey, but no such settlement took place after slavery here. Israelite law required slaveholders to provide resources for their former servants so they could build their own lives (Deut. 15:13–14); but freed slaves here have never received the promised "forty acres and a mule." After the North officially ended slavery by force, the freed slaves still lacked land necessary to become self-sufficient in the agrarian South; after Reconstruction ended (and after thousands of black leaders were lynched), many became virtual debt slaves on the very estates they had once worked as chattel slaves.[62]

Thus in the early twentieth century millions of rural southern blacks moved to northern cities, hoping to find there employment and a lack of segregation.

---

60. Concerning children of divorce, see Amy E. Black, "For the Sake of the Children: Reconstructing American Divorce Policy," *Crossroads Monograph Series on Faith and Public Policy* 1 (1995); Douglas E. Adams, *Children, Divorce and the Church* (Nashville: Abingdon, 1992); Joan Guest, "The Biggest Divorce," *CT* (Nov. 17, 1989), 30–32; "Breaking the Divorce Cycle," *NW* (Jan. 13, 1992), 48–53; Kevin Chappell, "Co-Parenting After Divorce," *Ebony* (March 1996), 60–64; David Gushee, "Tears of a Generation," *Prism* 5 (Nov. 1998), 9–14, 23–26.

61. John Dawson, *Healing America's Wounds* (Ventura, Calif.: Regal, 1994), 146–48.

62. On Reconstruction, see most fully Eric Foner, *Reconstruction: America's Unfinished Revolution, 1863–1877* (New York: Harper & Row, 1988); on Jim Crow some years later, see C. Vann Woodward, *The Strange Career of Jim Crow* (New York: Oxford, 1957). For further documentation, see notes in Glenn Usry and Craig Keener, *Black Man's Religion*, 158.

What they met instead was a new kind of segregation created by white flight—a white flight that, accompanied by withdrawal of capital, helped create today's northern urban ghettoes.[63] To be sure, suburban whites are not directly responsible for all the sufferings of the inner city today, though white racism did help create the segregated inner cities. But from birth we have educational and economic opportunities not available to other people because of conscious choices our ancestors made on economic rather than ethical grounds. Who will sacrifice, making conscious choices to challenge this disparity by using our skills and advantages to humbly serve others?[64]

In the 1990s some white Christians harshly (and I believe unfairly) criticized Promise Keepers for asking white Christians to apologize to black Christians for sins of the past.[65] Is it possible that God wanted something more, not less, than a hug and an apology? To be sure, suggestions like race-based reparations may be impractical and perhaps, as African-American evangelical John Perkins suggests, useless: He jokes that many poor people would immediately buy an expensive car and the rich people would have their money back![66] More practical would be an investment of our time and money into working for community development in needy communities, empowering the poor to build their own lives.[67]

The spread of sin, guilt, and judgment reflected in this passage is also noteworthy. When God judged Rome, the provinces also suffered, for they

---

63. On the northern migration and discrimination, see Ida Rousseau Mukenge, *The Black Church in Urban America* (Lanham, Md.: Univ. Press of America, 1983), 51–53; Usry and Keener, *Black Man's Religion*, 50–52.

64. John Perkins compares ignoring the past to a baseball team caught cheating into the ninth inning promising, "We will play fair for the rest of the game." He wonders if playing fair at this point might not require more than simply hoping that the losing team can play so well as to close the twenty-point gap in that final inning (John Perkins, *With Justice For All* [Ventura, Calif.: Regal, 1982], 169). A.M.E. Bishop Henry McNeal Turner long ago suggested that white U.S. churches (which long excluded blacks from participating in their missions enterprises) should support black missions involvement (see Gayraud S. Wilmore, *Black Religion and Black Radicalism*, 2d ed. [Maryknoll, N.Y.: Orbis, 1983], 123–24).

65. By contrast, a panel of conservative evangelical biblical scholars, including representatives from many major evangelical seminaries, unanimously concluded that Scripture teaches both corporate and intergenerational sin in some sense, affirming Promise Keepers' commitment to reconciliation (Promise Keepers Theological Summit on Reconciliation, Denver, Colo., Sept. 6–7, 1996). The panel included myself and many noted conservative scholars, such as Walter Kaiser, Grant Osborne, and Craig Blomberg.

66. John Perkins, "Luncheon Address," Reconcilers Fellowship "College, Ethnicity & Reconciliation" conference (Jackson, Miss., Jan. 24, 1998).

67. See John Perkins, *Beyond Charity: The Call to Christian Community Development* (Grand Rapids: Baker, 1993); Stephen E. Berk, *A Time to Heal* (Grand Rapids: Baker, 1997); see also resources from the Christian Community Development Association (3827 W. Ogden Ave., Chicago, IL 60623).

---

were bound up with Rome's interests and corrupted with Rome's agendas.[68] If the United States has become a major exporter of immoral values (see Contemporary Significance section of Rev. 17), it will not suffer alone. All those who drink the cup of fornication will share the cup of wrath (14:8–10; 16:19; 17:4; 18:6).

Working for economic justice. Christians can change many of the injustices we enumerate here. Indeed, at times in history the very evils John denounces so forcefully here were countered by Christians. At its height, the West Indies slave trade employed "some 5,500 sailors and 160 ships worth 6,000,000 pounds sterling a year."[69] But William Wilberforce and his allies, acting out of Christian conviction, fought in Parliament until slavery was abolished throughout the British Empire.[70] In an earlier period, some priests had raised their voices in protest against Spanish colonialists' exploitation of South America's indigenous peoples.[71]

But we must be ready for opposition to even the smallest steps to care for others' needs. Neighborhood groups got the city to shut down a soup kitchen run by one Presbyterian church in Washington, D.C., saying that it drew the wrong kind of people to the neighborhood. The church protested in court that its religious freedom was at stake, but astonishingly the court initially ruled that feeding the hungry (at least in that neighborhood) cannot be part of a church's mission.

When I went with a pastor friend of mine and his congregation to distribute some food to the homeless on the street in one northern city, he informed me that we risked being ticketed by police.[72] Despite the fact that the shelters were filled to capacity and it was winter, some city officials were working against feeding the homeless outside the shelters. The official reason was to get the homeless off the street, but another reason was to make the downtown more inviting to businesses; while improving the quality of life downtown was a valid civic concern, many of the homeless had nowhere else to go.

Similarly, when I worked with a mission that preached the gospel and fed the homeless, we faced opposition from local bars for attracting the "wrong

---

68. Cf. comments in Richard, *Apocalypse*, 135.

69. Charles Colson, *Kingdoms in Conflict* (Grand Rapids: Zondervan, 1987), 166. On the British slave trade, see also Mark Galli, "A Profitable Little Business," *Christian History* 53 (1997): 20–22.

70. Colson, *Kingdoms in Conflict*, 95–108. See further Christopher D. Hancock, "The 'Shrimp' Who Stopped Slavery," *Christian History* 53 (1997): 12–19.

71. See Justo L. González, "Lights in the Darkness," 32–34; and John Maust, "Champions for the Oppressed," *Christian History* 35 (1992): 35–38.

72. It should be noted, however, that many officers have worked to help the homeless (see Penni Roberts, "Helping the Homeless Is No Walk in Park for Officers," www.phila-tribune.com/72897–4pl.htm, downloaded April 21, 1999).

kind of people" to that section of town; a homosexual bar had opposed our presence at our previous location. Where were these people supposed to go? Many were homeless because of substance abuse; but many were homeless because they were mentally ill and budget cuts had forced them from their institutions and onto the streets; others were homeless because they had lost their jobs and their savings had run out—a situation I have nearly shared a few times in my life.[73] The problem is easier to identify than the solution; but should we not do at least what we can?

Economic exploitation and negligence are also part of Babylon's hideous pattern of sin in this text. Former televangelist Jim Bakker, transformed through his reading of Scripture in prison, suggests that Revelation's prostitute "is materialism. [Some] . . . used to teach that the harlot was the Catholic church. That was escapist—we wanted to blame somebody else and never look at ourselves."[74]

The majority of evangelical Christians now live in poor countries. Although we have much reason to think about economic injustice and the Bible frequently addresses it (e.g., Prov. 13:23; 14:31; 19:17; 21:13; 22:7, 9, 16, 22; Isa. 10:2; 58:7; Jer. 5:28; Ezek. 18:7–17; 22:29; Dan. 4:27; Amos 2:6–8; 4:1–2; 5:11–12; Zech. 7:10; Mal. 3:5; Luke 6:20; 14:13; 16:19–25; 18:22; 19:8; Gal. 2:10; James 2:2–6), most Western Christians do not like to think about it. (This may make us uncomfortable with Prov. 29:7: "The righteous care about justice for the poor, but the wicked have no such concern.")[75] Indeed, social scientists who studied factors shaping U.S. attitudes toward poor nations found "that religion plays no significant role at all!"[76]

Commercial exploitation or neglect of other peoples should give us reason to pause, especially if we uncritically accept our nation as a leader in all aspects of international virtue. To be sure, many nations have done the same throughout history and at the present time, but the United States at the time of this writing retains one of the largest economies in the world and thus is able to

---

73. Cf. similar debates (from various perspectives) in "New Richmond Law Recognizes Churches' Right to Feed the Needy" (Nov. 1997, at www.freedomforum.org); "S. L. Pastor Files Suit Against City: Citations for Aiding Needy Called Unconstitutional," *Salt Lake Tribune* (March 20, 1997); these examples were supplied by Fred Clark at Evangelicals for Social Action. See also comments on homelessness in Contemporary Significance of 6:1–8.

74. "The Re-education of Jim Bakker," *CT* (Dec. 7, 1998), 62–64 (p. 62).

75. For a biblical perspective on possessions and justice, see esp. Craig L. Blomberg, *Neither Poverty Nor Riches* (Grand Rapids: Eerdmans, 1999). For some perspectives on implementation, see *Economic Justice for All: Pastoral Letter on Catholic Social Teaching and the U.S. Economy* (Washington, D.C.: National Conference of Catholic Bishops, 1986).

76. Ronald J. Sider, *Rich Christians in an Age of Hunger*, 3d ed. (Dallas: Word, 1990), 38.

dictate trade patterns in our own interests.[77] "The World Bank reports that protectionist practices by the industrialized countries slim down the income of Third World countries by nearly twice the sum of official aid to them."

Today over one billion people subsist on the equivalent of less than one dollar a day, and matters are only growing worse. The economic gap between rich and poor countries has doubled since 1960: the richest 20 percent of the world's population has gone from absorbing 70 percent of the world's income in 1960 to nearly 83 percent by the 1990s; the poorest 20 percent dropped from 2.3 percent to 1.4 percent in the same period, so that the income ratio of richest to poorest changed "from 30 to 1 in 1960 to 59 to 1 in 1989."[78] Because we have many Christians here and because citizens of our nation and shareholders in our corporations have a voice, one would hope that more Christians would work to make things more equitable on behalf of our brothers and sisters struggling in many other nations.

Lest we be tempted to think that the United States was once a greater moral giant in international relations—known, for example, for welcoming all oppressed immigrants—we should recognize that matters used to be worse. In 1790 our first citizenship law allowed only "free white persons" to become citizens; as late as the 1940s immigrants from Japan and India had to prove they were white. The law was officially repealed only in 1952![79]

Even today serious prejudices remain. A white New Zealander told me of his mistreatment when seeking citizenship here, though he noticed that people of color or those whose first language was not English were treated far worse. The top officials of an African evangelical denomination, traveling without their families, were initially denied visitors' visas even though they had been invited by a large U.S. mission; some of my minister friends from that nation, seeking to attend seminary in the United States, were turned away by the embassy without even looking at their documents, after it pocketed their application fees (the equivalent to four months' salary there). When I visited

---

77. Colonial powers not only raped natural resources of many peoples for their own profit, they also repressed Christian missions in many areas; see Yusufu Turaki, "The British Colonial Legacy in Northern Nigeria" (Ph.D. diss., Boston University, 1982); Elizabeth Isichei, *A History of Christianity in Africa From Antiquity to the Present* (Lawrenceville, N.J.: Africa World Press; Grand Rapids: Eerdmans, 1995), 233.

78. Andrew Sung Park, *Racial Conflict and Healing*, 34, 60. In the U.S., while the wealthiest 5 percent made an annual increase of over $6000 a year, the lowest 20 percent lost over $200 (*Bread for the World Newsletter* [Sept. 1998], 7); for increasing disparity, see also *Economic Justice*, 8, 90–91, citing U.S. Bureau of the Census statistics. American treatment of some individuals abroad may be illustrated by Chuck Colson's haunting memory of his preconversion abuse of an impoverished old man for entering government property in the Caribbean (*Loving God*, 100–101).

79. Ellis Cose, "One Drop of Bloody History," *NW* (Feb. 13, 1995), 70.

their country, by contrast, I was received with more gracious and sacrificial hospitality than I have experienced anywhere else. The United States is different from Babylon and Rome in many respects, but sometimes proves similar in its arrogance. Some judgment may prove helpful for us spiritually.

More to the specific point, we consume luxury goods often at the expense of others' resources (cf. 18:12–13). The lifestyle of the average middle-class American family compared to that of the world's billion poorest people is roughly equivalent to that of a medieval aristocrat compared with his serfs.[80] We are not talking about people merely not wishing to work or dissatisfied with their income, but with some 450 million people who are "malnourished or facing starvation."[81] The infant mortality rate is up to ten times higher in developing nations than in the developed world; over 250,000 children die weekly from malnutrition and easily preventable sicknesses.[82] Over two million deaths a year could be prevented by bags of oral rehydration salts—costing Westerners only 10 cents each.[83]

Eighty percent of brain development occurs by age two, yet 150 million children in the world lack the protein intake necessary for adequate brain development, leading to permanent retardation.[84] Amazingly, one study argues that "it would only cost $30–$40 billion a year to provide all people in developing countries with basic education, health care, and clean water— the amount spent on golf every year."[85] For all their differences, radical Western consumerism and Marxism share the philosophic premise that economics is paramount; both view Mammon rather than God as the controlling force in life.

---

80. See Sider, *Rich Christians*, 19. Inequities within the United States also exceed any scale of pure meritocracy; if one excludes real estate (like houses), two percent of Americans (as of the 1980s earning annually over $125,000) hold 54 percent of the nation's wealth (*Economic Justice*, 91, citing Federal Reserve Board statistics).

81. *Economic Justice*, 3. Although laziness exists and can cause or exacerbate poverty (Prov. 13:4; 19:24; 20:4; 21:25; 24:30–34; 2 Thess. 3:10), work is not available for everyone in all societies, and some jobs pay barely enough to cover rent and food, much less healthcare (cf. *Economic Justice*, 96)—as I know from my own experience for a few years after finishing Bible college, while pastoring and working in a restaurant part-time (how much more for those who could never afford to attend college).

82. Sider, *Rich Christians*, 9. Note that the infant mortality rate per 1000 live births is 7 in Sweden, 9 in the U.K., 10 in the U.S., 58 in Guatemala, 98 in India, and 172 in Mozambique (p. 12). To help us grasp the impact of the infant mortality rate number, some have compared it with eighty Boeing 747 jets full of children crashing each day, or the first atom bomb being dropped again every few days.

83. Ibid., 11.

84. Ibid.

85. Ronald J. Sider, "Evangelicals in the Balance," *Prism* (March 1998), 36–37, 46 [p. 37, citing a U.N. study]).

Which countries should bear the greatest responsibility for international development? Whereas in the late 1980s the U.S. per capita Gross National Product was $18,530, in India it was $300, and in Bangladesh, $160.[86] Given such disparities in wealth, one would think that the United States could afford to provide much help to countries currently limited in economic resources. Remember too that our location of birth is not due to any merit in ourselves, but is a gift from God for which we must one day make account. Yet in assisting developing countries, Norway ranks highest (with development assistance as 1.12 percent of its Gross National Product), Canada seventh (.50 percent), and the United States second from the bottom (.25 percent) among developed countries.[87]

In a given year, the United States may budget twenty times "as much for defense as for foreign assistance, and nearly two-thirds of the latter" for military aid or for nations viewed as strategic to our own interests.[88] Admittedly the difficulties of getting resources to those who need them are complex, but one still wonders about the overall priorities in question.[89] Advertising makes us think that we need more things and makes us forget our love for others—though one could hope to find much greater reward in enduring relationships with international friends than in accumulating possessions.[90]

Because this commentary addresses especially Christians, it is important to note what Jesus demands of his followers. Our ability to change our nation's behavior is often severely limited by the consumer culture's dominance, but we do not confront the same public obstacles in changing our own behavior. Scripture is explicit that disciples of Jesus cannot value possessions (Luke 14:33) and that failure to care for fellow disciples' needs is a sign of a lack of saving faith (James 2:14–17); it also indicates that such concern should cross geographical boundaries (Rom. 15:25–27; 1 Cor. 16:1–4). Paul's central mission was preaching the gospel, but he did not forget the needs of the poor,

---

86. Sider, *Rich Christians*, 19, 21, with statistics from the World Bank.

87. Ibid., 31 (1988 statistics). Australia provided aid at .46 percent; the United Kingdom at .32 percent; Japan at .31 percent; and New Zealand at .27 percent.

88. *Economic Justice*, 141 (citing 1985 statistics); U.S. defense expenditures in the mid–1980s were nearly $300 billion a year (ibid., 9).

89. Christianity is not tied to a particular economic system or to particular solutions, but Christians must evaluate all systems according to their impact on people, esp. those most vulnerable (*Economic Justice*, 66). Thus Milton Friedman, "Good Ends, Bad Means," 99–106 in *The Catholic Challenge to the American Economy*, ed. Thomas M. Gannon (New York: Macmillan, 1987), objects to some of the ideas in *Economic Justice*, though strangely he views its claim that "adequate food" is a basic right as an infringement on the freedom of others (106)—exalting such freedom above others' need to live.

90. For the same basic idea in greater detail, see Tony Campolo, *Wake Up America* (Grand Rapids: Zondervan, 1991), 5–10.

and brought resources from more affluent parts of the church to help others (2 Cor. 8:13–15; Gal. 2:10). One wonders about the nature of stewardship in affluent America when church members give on average less than 2.5 percent of their income, most of which remains within their own congregation.[91]

Revelation 18 reminds us that God does not look the other way in the face of economic injustice; he will bring down every economic empire in time. West Africa and China were far more prosperous than most of Europe during the Middle Ages; British imperialism overturned Spanish and Arab imperialism only a few centuries ago; no nation remains "on top" or in the limelight forever. Many North American Christians squander money on things we do not need, ignoring genuine needs of Christians elsewhere despite the explicit teaching of Scripture (2 Cor. 8:14–15). We sometimes do this by blaming the people of those nations for their poverty or for their bad governments. Instead, we should remind ourselves of God's justice and invest our resources in expanding the gospel and serving people's needs, for Scripture and history assure us that our own resources are ours only for a short season.

We should add here a caveat lest we miscommunicate our point. Possessions are not wrong in themselves; they simply have no value compared with the genuine needs of our brothers and sisters in Christ (cf. Acts 2:44–45; 4:34–35).[92] If fifty cents can supply sufficient food for a child for a day in some famine-stricken areas, I should care enough about that child to be careful what I do with even what seems the least of my resources.

Firsthand exposure to genuine human need can perhaps stir our hearts better than statistics can. Tony Liston, a young pastor from Oklahoma, spent two days in a private hospital room in the Philippines for $47; he had barely noticed a beggar woman outside when he entered. When he was released, he spotted the naked corpse of the beggar woman stuffed into a nearby dumpster; she had died of the same affliction for which he had just been treated. "She had no money," the nurse replied matter-of-factly. Tony was so shaken that his life was never the same again.[93] While one cannot more thoroughly nuance one's point in a few paragraphs, I hope that we will

---

91. See Sider, "Balance," 46.

92. One cannot read these Acts passages as negative models; they use ancient language depicting an ideal community (see academic sources cited in Craig Keener, *The Spirit in the Gospels and Acts* [Peabody, Mass.: Hendrickson, 1997], 198–99).

93. See Stan Guthrie, "Why Tony Spent the Night in a Chicken Coop," *Mission Today* 94 (1994): 148–54. Cf. the fictitious experience of a Colombian pastor confronted with the excess of North American Christianity in Jim Reapsome, "Victor's Reality Check," *Mountain Movers* (April 1995), 30 (reprinted from *Pulse* [Dec. 2, 1994]); also the plea for simplicity as part of witness among missionaries in Roger S. Greenway, "Eighteen Barrels and Two Big Crates," *The 1994 Great Commission Handbook*, 28–29, 36.

embrace the basic point—that we should become more conscientious about using our resources according to what matters most to God's heart.

Shedding of innocent blood. This chapter closes by denouncing the shedding of innocent blood. Rome shed much blood through its brutal system of slavery, but also its slaughter of slaves and criminals for public entertainment. Those of us who affirm that a fetus is a live human being (and it is difficult biologically to guess what it would be if it were not alive and human!) will see abortion as bloodshed.[94] After the U.S. Supreme Court ruled that abortion was legal, the number of abortions to date of this writing has been equivalent to the slaughter of one tenth of the U.S. population—more innocent blood per capita than was necessary to bring God's judgment on Judah (2 Kings 21:16; 24:4).[95] Once so much blood was shed, not even Josiah's brief revival could turn back God's wrath—although it was delayed (2 Kings 22:15–20).

While our passage probably addresses all innocent bloodshed, it focuses on persecution of Christians, a transgression that occurs in many nations today.[96] Although the West, with its tradition of religious tolerance, is currently not high on that list, many people here do not show much interest in religious persecution elsewhere. Shortly before writing this commentary, the House of Representatives passed the Freedom From Religious Persecution Act by 375 to 41. The Senate also passed it, but some corporations lobbied hard against this act because of how it might affect their profits, ultimately depriving the bill of any ability to enact sanctions.

Unocal, for example, "is heavily invested in a $1 billion natural gas pipeline in Burma, a project which requires the company to deal closely with that country's violently oppressive military dictatorship." The current government there jailed the elected president, has used slave labor on various projects, probably including the pipeline, and is known for various human rights offenses.[97] Today, as in John's day, profit margins matter more to some people than justice. God has promised to set those matters straight.

---

94. Cf. George Will, "Life and Death at Princeton," *NW* (Sept. 13, 1999), 80–82. On prenatal development, see, e.g., *Science Digest* (Dec. 1982), 46–53. Doctors can now rescue premature babies small enough to fit in an adult's palm ("Preemies," *NW* (May 16, 1988), 62–70; cf. "The Tiniest Patients," *NW* (June 11, 1990), 56; on programs for premature infants, see Elizabeth Sledden, "When Will Life Be Normal?" (Austin, Tex.: Hogg Foundation for Mental Health, 1989).

95. Abortions in the United States, first legalized in 1974, currently average about one and a half million a year (cf. "On Demand = Less Demand," *NW* [June 27, 1994], 49, despite their application of the data). The recently approved "morning-after" pill may make abortion statistics much more difficult to gather.

96. See International Christian Concern, 2020 Pennsylvania Ave. NW, No. 941, Washington, D.C. 20006.

97. Fred Clark, "USA*Enrage," *Prism* (July 1998), 30–31 (p. 30) ("USA*Engage" is the lobbying group for the largest exporters in the United States, many of whom do business with repressive regimes).

Revelation 19:1–21

A FTER THIS I heard what sounded like the roar of a great multitude in heaven shouting:

"Hallelujah!
Salvation and glory and power belong to our God,
2   for true and just are his judgments.
He has condemned the great prostitute
    who corrupted the earth by her adulteries.
He has avenged on her the blood of his servants."

³And again they shouted:

"Hallelujah!
The smoke from her goes up for ever and ever."

⁴The twenty-four elders and the four living creatures fell down and worshiped God, who was seated on the throne. And they cried:

"Amen, Hallelujah!"

⁵Then a voice came from the throne, saying:

"Praise our God,
    all you his servants,
you who fear him,
    both small and great!"

⁶Then I heard what sounded like a great multitude, like the roar of rushing waters and like loud peals of thunder, shouting:

"Hallelujah!
    For our Lord God Almighty reigns.
⁷Let us rejoice and be glad
    and give him glory!
For the wedding of the Lamb has come,
    and his bride has made herself ready.
⁸Fine linen, bright and clean,
    was given her to wear."

(Fine linen stands for the righteous acts of the saints.)

⁹Then the angel said to me, "Write: 'Blessed are those who are invited to the wedding supper of the Lamb!'" And he added, "These are the true words of God."

¹⁰At this I fell at his feet to worship him. But he said to me, "Do not do it! I am a fellow servant with you and with your brothers who hold to the testimony of Jesus. Worship God! For the testimony of Jesus is the spirit of prophecy."

¹¹I saw heaven standing open and there before me was a white horse, whose rider is called Faithful and True. With justice he judges and makes war. ¹²His eyes are like blazing fire, and on his head are many crowns. He has a name written on him that no one knows but he himself. ¹³He is dressed in a robe dipped in blood, and his name is the Word of God. ¹⁴The armies of heaven were following him, riding on white horses and dressed in fine linen, white and clean. ¹⁵Out of his mouth comes a sharp sword with which to strike down the nations. "He will rule them with an iron scepter." He treads the winepress of the fury of the wrath of God Almighty. ¹⁶On his robe and on his thigh he has this name written:

KING OF KINGS AND LORD OF LORDS.

¹⁷And I saw an angel standing in the sun, who cried in a loud voice to all the birds flying in midair, "Come, gather together for the great supper of God, ¹⁸so that you may eat the flesh of kings, generals, and mighty men, of horses and their riders, and the flesh of all people, free and slave, small and great."

¹⁹Then I saw the beast and the kings of the earth and their armies gathered together to make war against the rider on the horse and his army. ²⁰But the beast was captured, and with him the false prophet who had performed the miraculous signs on his behalf. With these signs he had deluded those who had received the mark of the beast and worshiped his image. The two of them were thrown alive into the fiery lake of burning sulfur. ²¹The rest of them were killed with the sword that came out of the mouth of the rider on the horse, and all the birds gorged themselves on their flesh.

THIS PASSAGE CONTRASTS the fate of Babylon, the prostitute (19:1–5), and the future new Jerusalem, the bride (19:6–9; cf. 21:2). Both events invite the praises of heaven, reflecting the fulfillment of God's perfect purposes (19:1, 3–7); God alone deserves praise for such events and their proclamation (19:10). In God's design, the prostitute will die and be burned by her alienated lovers (17:16–17); by contrast, the Lamb welcomes his bride (19:6–9).

The Prostitute and the Bride (19:1–10)

MOST EARLY JEWISH readers, even those who used only Greek, would know that "Hallelujah!" (19:1, 3, 4, 6) meant "Praise Yahweh!" in a particularly emphatic form. The expression appears untranslated 23 times in the LXX (the Greek version of the Old Testament), always in Psalms (except for two references in the Apocrypha).[1] Jewish traditions elsewhere emphasize end-time joy and report exultation over the destruction of the wicked (see also comment on 18:2).[2] Thus, the mourning over Babylon in 18:2 is purely a literary device; members of the audience that identify with the world and what it values may mourn (18:9, 11), but those who identify with heaven and what it values will rejoice (19:1, 3–5).

In a context of people hailing a conqueror, "salvation" (or "deliverance") (19:1) can refer to triumph (cf. 7:10; 12:10); the prostitute was stained with the blood of murdered saints (18:24), and God had exacted vengeance for them (19:2). Earlier biblical tradition also summoned others to rejoice at the judgment of those who oppress God's people (Deut. 32:43; Jer. 51:48–49).

God's judgment does not simply stop Babylon's oppression; he avenges her incomprehensible injustices. Babylon, the city of the world system, is the new Sodom (11:8). The smoke of her death rises forever (19:3), suggesting eternal torment (14:11; cf. Isa. 34:10).[3] Although "eternal" is applied more broadly in Revelation (Rev. 14:11; 20:10), it is not impossible that such an image of Rome's "*eternal* judgment may be a partial polemic against

---

1. See also Tobit 13:18; 3 Macc. 7:13. Not surprisingly, it also appears in Aramaic texts (Aramaic incantation text 20.12). Shepherd, *Liturgy*, 78, finds parallels with Hallel Psalms (Ps. 113–18), some of which in Greek refer to the Exodus (Ps 114:1; LXX 113:1); but these account for only about one quarter of LXX uses.

2. For eschatological joy, see Isa. 66:10; Tobit 13:10–14; 1QM 17.7; Jub. 23:30; 1 Enoch 5:7; 25:6; 47:4; 103:3; Ps. Sol. 11:3; on exultation over the destruction of the wicked, see 1 Enoch 47:4; 94:10; 97:2; T. Job 43:17.

3. See Sib. Or. 3.504–6; cf. Jer. 17:4. The earliest image was eternal desolation (Deut. 13:16).

the mythical name *Roma aeterna* ('eternal Rome'), which was one of the names for the Roman Empire."[4]

By judging the world system, God has begun to reign (19:6; cf. 11:17).[5] Presumably among those who now join in triumphant praise are the martyrs, especially if the sound of "rushing waters" in 19:6 recalls 14:2. All God's "servants" (cf. 1:1)—that is, those who fear him (cf. 11:18)—offer praise in 19:5; this group is also coextensive, at least in principle, with the martyrs mentioned in 19:2, because all true followers of Christ are potential martyrs (cf. 20:4). This group explicitly cuts across class lines, for like the world (6:15; 13:16; 19:18; 20:12), they include "both small and great" (19:5; cf. 11:18).[6]

Weddings are generally characterized by joy, and ancient sources emphasize the responsibility of wedding guests to promote the newlyweds' joy.[7] The promise of this banquet appears also as a beatitude (19:9), a common literary form ("Blessed [or happy] are those who . . ."); this form appears in Revelation seven times, usually as an encouragement to persevere (1:3; 14:13; 16:15; 19:9; 20:6; 22:7, 14).

The "wedding supper" was a frequent figure for the coming messianic era (e.g., 1 En. 62:14; 3 En. 48A:10).[8] God had promised a splendid banquet (Isa. 25:6), when he would destroy death and wipe away the tears and shame of his people (25:8). Some Jewish teachers even decided that Leviathan, the great many-headed serpent, would be slain (27:1) and served as the food at the messianic banquet. If this idea was pervasive when Revelation was written, it may be relevant that the marriage supper of the Lamb is contrasted with the great supper of God, in which birds feast on the carcasses of the wicked (19:9, 17–18).[9] With judgment coming, a Jewish sage roughly contemporary with Revelation proclaimed that all was prepared for the banquet (R. Akiba in *m. Ab.* 3:17).

---

4. Beale, *Revelation*, 929.

5. The NIV's present tense "reigns" may obscure the Greek aorist tense here, though the aorist's sense may be inceptive.

6. Aune, *Revelation*, 3:1027, cites a Greek parallel to the voice that in 19:5 "acts as a choir director"; but this is common in the Psalms, reflecting the role of the Levite singers who prophesied in giving thanks to God (e.g., 1 Chron. 25:1; Ps. 95:1–2).

7. See S. Safrai, "Home and Family," 728–92 in *JPFC*, 759. As symbols of joy, weddings contrast starkly with mourning (*p. Ket.* 1:1, §6; Jer. 7:34; Matt. 11:17).

8. E.g., *m. Ab.* 4:16; *tos. Ber.* 6:21; Matt. 8:11; abundantly in later sources, e.g., *b. Ber.* 34b; *Sanh.* 99a; *Shab.* 153a; *Gen. Rab.* 51:8; 62:2; *Ex. Rab.* 19:6; 45:6; *Lev. Rab.* 13:3; *Num. Rab.* 13:2; *Koh. Rab.* 9:8, §1; *Pes. Rab.* 41:5; see further Robert M. Johnston, "Parabolic Interpretations Attributed to Tannaim" (Ph.D. diss., Hartford Seminary Foundation, 1977), 593–94. Bridal language could apply to love for wisdom (Wisd. Sol. 8:2–3), but eschatological texts normally apply it to God's relationship with Israel (Isa. 49:18; 61:10; 62:5).

9. For Leviathan as end-time food, see 2 Bar. 29:4; *b. B.B.* 74b–75a; *Pes. Rab Kah.* Sup. 2:4; *Pes. Rab.* 48:3.

What does Revelation mean by the bride being "ready" (19:7; cf. 21:2; Matt. 22:8)? To make herself ready for the wedding a bride would bathe herself and adorn herself in special array.[10] Here the special array is the "righteous acts of the saints," who comprise the bride (Rev. 19:8; perhaps this reflects the bridal array of righteousness in Isa. 61:10). While white linen robes were appropriate for worship (see comment on Rev. 4:4), they appear here also as appropriate for marriage.[11]

The fine linen of the saints (19:8; cf. 19:14) contrasts with the fine linen of the prostitute (18:12, 16). High-class prostitutes were known for their elaborate garb, but the saints are dressed in wedding apparel beautiful to the groom, and this wedding apparel consists of their "righteous acts."[12] In some later Jewish texts, end-time suffering could help prepare the righteous for the coming world as participation in wedding preparations qualify one to participate in the wedding banquet.[13] Presumably the prospective bride is also portrayed as the saints in fine linen coming with Jesus in 19:14; by contrast, Jesus himself is clothed in a bloody robe (19:13), for the task of vengeance will precede the wedding celebration (cf. Matt. 22:7–8).

That John begins to worship the messenger (Rev. 19:10) is not surprising; his message is easily confused with God's (21:5–6). Yet the "fellow servant" here is not a fellow mortal, but is an angel (cf. 22:8–9). Christians and angels have different functions, but both may proclaim God's message.[14] The angel's explicit prohibition of worshiping him may be guarding against certain syncretistic practices among Jews of Asia Minor, in which some worshiped angels.[15] The emphatic demand that God alone is to be worshiped challenges

---

10. E.g., Eph. 5:26; *Ex. Rab.* 23:5; Everett Ferguson, *Backgrounds of Early Christianity* (Grand Rapids: Eerdmans, 1987), 54–55. The array could include white linen, bracelets, and costly ornaments with names inscribed (Jos. & Asen. 3:6/9–11; 4:1/2).

11. They can symbolize joy (*p. R.H.* 1:3, §27); hence the burial clothes of the righteous (Ps-Philo, 64:6; cf. Test. Abr. 20:10A; Life of Adam 48.1; Apoc. Moses 40.1–3; *b. Ber.* 18b).

12. On the garb of high-class prostitutes, see Ps-Melissa, *Letter to Kleareta*; moralists preferred moral adornment (e.g., Isocrates, *Demon.* 15, *Or.* 1; Crates, *Ep.* 9; 1 Tim. 2:10). The term for "righteous acts" appears elsewhere in this book only for God's acts (Rev. 15:4).

13. *Lev. Rab.* 11:2.

14. The idea of an angel being moved by God's Spirit probably would not have appeared problematic to John's audience, for the same revelatory Spirit apparently is associated both with angels (cf. Ezek. 1:12, 20–21; 10:17; 1 En. 68:2) and humans (Ezek. 2:2; 1 En. 71:5). Angels as agents served a somewhat prophetic function (Zech. 1:14; Jub. 2:1).

15. See Col. 2:18; R. A. Kearsley, "Angels in Asia Minor: The Cult of Hosios and Dikaios," 6:206–9 in *New Documents Illustrating Early Christianity*, ed. S. R. Llewelyn with R. A. Kearsley (North Ryde, N.S.W.: Ancient History Documentary Research Centre, Macquarie University, 1992); Kraabel, "Judaism in Western Asia Minor," 143–45. In early Christian material, see Asc. Isa. 9:36. In view of the parallel between Michael and Christ in Rev. 12:7 (cf. 1:15), this passage may implicitly oppose an angel Christology (as is attested later;

all forms of idolatry, including those offered the emperor in the name of loyalty to the state.

Most significant, the angel declares that he is simply acting as God's agent (19:10b). The prophetic Spirit empowers those who speak the message about Christ (19:10; cf. Acts 1:8; 2:17–18; 1 Cor. 12:3); all believers are thus potential prophets, anointed with God's Spirit to speak his message in his place.[16] For many of John's Jewish contemporaries who believed that the Spirit of prophecy had been suppressed and would not be restored in its fullness until the messianic era, the present activity of the Spirit in testifying about Jesus throughout the book of Revelation would attest his identity as the true Lord.[17] For those who too readily believed any prophecies without seeking to evaluate true from false and thus accepted messages from "Balaam" (2:14) and "Jezebel" (2:20), the reminder that true prophecy exalts Jesus (19:10) would also be essential.

Holy War (19:11–21)

IF GOD'S MESSENGER in 19:10 is the wrong one to worship (cf. "worship God"), 19:11–16 abruptly and immediately reveals the proper object of worship. As God's "Word" (19:13), Jesus is "Faithful and True" (19:11), like other words of God (21:5; 22:6); earlier in Revelation this phrase alluded to faithfulness in testifying God's truth regardless of the cost (1:5; 2:10, 13). Jesus "judges and makes war" (19:11). The former attribute belongs to God (6:10; 11:18; 18:8, 20; 19:2; 20:12) and to the Messiah, who will strike the wicked with his mouth (Isa. 11:4; cf. Rev. 19:15).[18] The latter is the image of the end-time holy warrior, a final response to the worshipers of the beast who demanded, "Who can make war against him?" (13:4). All along God has allowed the beast to make war with his people on earth (11:7; 12:17; 13:7); but when the right time comes, they will make war on the Lamb himself and be destroyed (17:14; 19:19; 20:8).

---

see Epiphanius, *Her.* 30.164–65; Jean Daniélou, *The Theology of Jewish Christianity* [Chicago: Henry Regnery, 1964], 67, 117; cf. G. Juncker, "Christ As Angel: The Reclamation of a Primitive Title," *TrinJ* 15 [1994]: 221–250). See further R. Bauckham, "The Worship of Jesus in Apocalyptic Christianity," *NTS* 27 (1981): 322–41.

16. See also David Hill, "Prophecy and Prophets in the Revelation of St. John," *NTS* 18 (July 1972): 401–18 (414); cf. Acts 1:8; 2:17–18; 1 Cor. 14:1, 31.

17. On the belief in the suppression and restoration of the Spirit's prophetic role in some early Jewish circles, see C. S. Keener, *The Spirit in Gospels and Acts* (Peabody, Mass.: Hendrickson, 1997), 13–16. On the attesting function, see also J. M. Ford, "'For the Testimony of Jesus Is the Spirit of Prophecy' (Rev 19:10)," *ITQ* 42 (1975): 284–91.

18. In later Jewish tradition, a Messiah's inability to judge (by smell!) rendered him an impostor (*b. Sanh.* 93b).

God often sent his people to holy war in the Old Testament, and early Jewish sources expected an end-time battle to throw off the yoke of Rome and other pagan oppressors.[19] Such sources even warned of blood among other signs in the heavens (Sib. Or. 3.800–804), and finally a battle of foot-soldiers and cavalry in the heavens (3.805–8). But whereas "the armies of heaven" (either believers [cf. 17:14], as fine linen implies [19:8], or holy angels [cf. Zech. 14:5]) are with Jesus here (19:14), they execute no violence themselves; Jesus is the mighty warrior who strikes the wicked (19:11, 15, 21). Biblical prophets predicted God himself as the ultimate holy warrior (Isa. 42:13; Hab. 3:11–14; Zeph. 3:17; cf. 1QM 18.1–3), cloaked for war (Isa. 59:17), including the blood of the winepress as here (Isa. 63:3); clearly Jesus assumes this divine role here.

Jesus rides on a white horse (19:11), as do his hosts (19:14). White horses were usually considered the best.[20] Such horses were appropriate mounts for rulers, important officials, and conquerors entering Rome in triumph,[21] but the idea of a "King of kings" (cf. 19:16) mounted on a white horse may be drawing on the image of the Parthian king.[22] If Rome fears a Parthian invasion, how much more should they fear the true Lord from heaven!

Jesus' fiery eyes indicate divinity and fury (see comment on 1:14); his "many crowns" indicate that he is Ruler over all the kings of the world (19:12, 16; cf. 1:5). Jesus has a hidden name (19:12), just like the saints (2:17). Perhaps this name is a secret only to the world, already accepted among the saints but revealed to all humanity at Jesus' coming—the "Word of God" (19:13) or "King of kings and Lord of lords" (19:16).[23] His cloak dipped in blood represents a terrifying image to the average ancient reader.[24] But this passage draws the language specifically from Isaiah 63, indicating that the

---

19. On holy war imagery here and in Revelation, see Fiorenza, *Revelation*, 162; Bauckham, *Climax of Prophecy*, 210–37; S. G. F. Brandon, *Zealots*, 320, wrongly finds here an allusion to a Zealot tradition about the earthly Jesus. For holy war imagery, see also Jub. 38; in the end-time, see 1QM passim; 1 Enoch 1:4; for the saints' role, see 1 Enoch 98:12; 4QpNah 4.3; 1QpHab 5.4; 1QM 14.7; 16.1.

20. So Homer, *Il.* 10.436–37. But for a contrary view, see Virgil, *Georg.* 3.82–83.

21. See Suetonius, *Dom.* 2; Jos. & Asen. 5:4/5; Livy, 5.28.1.

22. Some see the horseman as the antithesis of the Antichrist in 6:2 (M. Rissi, "Die Erscheinung Christi nach Off. 19,11–16," TZ 21 [1965]: 81–95).

23. Angels also proved reluctant to reveal their names (Gen. 32:29; Judg. 13:18), perhaps to avoid supporting the pagan view that knowledge of a spirit's name gives one power over it; but this reluctance does not suit the coming king (Mounce, *Revelation*, 345). Aune, *Revelation*, 3:1056, suggests that ancients feared deities with unknown names; this would be true especially of Israel's God, whose name magicians tried to use (cf. Acts 19:13).

24. A horrible Fury is portrayed this way in Ovid, *Metam.* 4.481–84.

world will finally realize at his coming that Jesus himself is God.[25] The blood is from those slain from his winepress, the whole world (19:15; cf. 14:18–20), as in Isaiah 63:2.[26] The heavenly armies could possibly include angels (Zech. 14:5), but certainly include believers (Rev. 17:14; cf. the linen in 19:14 with 19:8). The army that overcame the beast by martyrdom (14:1–5) will now share Christ's final triumph (cf. the "rod" in 19:15; also 2:27).

For many Jewish hearers, the "sharp sword" would recall a popular apocryphal work, the Wisdom of Solomon, in which God's Word leaps from heaven like a mighty warrior (cf. Rev. 19:13), bringing forth God's commandment as a sharp straight sword to kill the disobedient (Wisd. Sol. 18:15–16; cf. Ps. Sol. 17:24–27, 35–36; see comment on Rev. 1:16). Because the sword issues from Jesus' mouth, some interpreters apply it to an eschatological war of ideologies before Jesus' return; while such ideological conflict is likely (6:9; cf. Isa. 49:2; 66:16; Hos. 6:5; Matt. 24:14), the allusion to Isaiah 11:4 and to Psalm 2:9 probably demands more than this in this passage (cf. 2 Thess. 2:8),[27] for it can also signify literal bloodshed (Isa. 34:5; Jer. 12:12; 47:6).

Jesus' title, "KING OF KINGS AND LORD OF LORDS" (19:16), may recall the title of the Parthian ruler, as noted above. Sometimes called merely the "great king," he was also called "king of kings."[28] This was a title for the eastern monarchs also in the Old Testament period (Ezra 7:12; Ezek. 26:7; Dan. 2:37), but it always applied best of all to the true supreme Ruler, God (Deut. 10:17; Ps. 136:3; Dan. 2:47; Zech. 14:9; 1 Tim. 6:15).[29] Ancient Judaism continued to apply the title almost exclusively to God.[30] Revelation applies the

---

25. Though later texts sometimes apply this text to the Messiah (e.g., *Pes. Rab.* 37:2); cf. the midrashic combination with Isa. 63:2 also in the later Palestinian Targum to Gen. 49:10–11 (Martin McNamara, *Targum and Testament* [Grand Rapids: Eerdmans, 1972], 141). On Isa. 63:2–3 here, see Fekkes, *Isaiah*, 197–99.

26. Warriors are sometimes portrayed as wetted with blood (Ps. 58:10; 1QM 14.2–3; cf. murderers in Isa. 1:15). The idea that it is here Jesus' blood at the hands of his enemies (John A. T. Robinson, *Twelve New Testament Studies*, SBT 34 [London: SCM, 1962], 173) violates this context.

27. For the ideological interpretation, see e.g., Bowman, *First Christian Drama*, 129; cf. Job 5:15; Isa. 49:2. Even a noneschatological text associating the sword with Scripture implied literal execution (*Sifre Deut.* 40.7.2); for violent commands "from the mouth," see also Judith 2:2–3.

28. Suetonius, *Calig.* 5; Plutarch, *Pompey* 38.2; on "great king," see Herodian, 6.2.1.

29. The divine title also appears in Dan. 4:37 LXX; see T. B. Slater, "'King of Kings and Lord of Lords' Revisited," NTS 39 (1993): 159–60, developing G. K. Beale's application to 17:14.

30. For God as "King of kings," see 1 Enoch 9:4; 84:2; 3 Macc. 5:35; Philo, *Decal.* 41; *Spec.* 3.18; PGM 13.605; 3 Enoch 22:15; 25:4; *m. Ab.* 3:1; *tos. Sanh.* 8:9; *Sifra Sav Mekhilta De Milium* 98.8.5; ARN, 25A; 1, §1B; Aramaic incantation text 67.2; pagans could apply the title to Zeus (Dio Chrysostom, *Second Discourse on Kingship* 75) or other high deities (PGM, 2.53–54; 4.640–42; *Book of Dead Spells*, 185Eb, part S–1).

title consistently to Jesus (17:14; 19:16), the true Ruler over the earth's other kings (1:5). That the name was written on Jesus' thigh need not have puzzled ancient hearers; thus, commentators observe that the Greeks sometimes branded horses on their thighs and some wrote names on statues in Rome.[31]

Whereas the saints will partake of the promised messianic banquet (19:9), the wicked will be the banquet on which scavengers feed (19:17). Their blood will flow as if from a winepress (19:15), borrowing an earlier biblical image (Isa. 63:2–3; cf. 9:5; 34:3–7; 49:26). The image of carrion birds feasting on the flesh of corpses killed in battle was a familiar one to ancient readers (1 Sam. 17:44–46; Jer. 16:4; Ezek. 29:5).[32] Given common Greek views of one's image enduring in the realm of departed spirits, the only fate worse than death itself was death followed by lack of burial, in which one's remains are devoured by animals. Jewish literature also anticipated the wicked lying unburied in the end time, devoured by vultures and other animals (Sib. Or. 3.643–45). But most of Revelation's first audience would recognize the clear and immediate source of the language of this passage: God invited beasts and birds to devour the flesh of the army that opposed him in Ezekiel 39:17–20.

God then hurls the leaders of Satan's army into "the fiery lake of burning sulfur" (19:20). This burning sulfur may allude to the fate of Sodom (Gen. 19:24), but the punishment in this lake of fire is eternal (Rev. 14:10) and contrasts with the sea of glass in God's presence (4:6).[33]

Bridging Contexts

COMMUNICATING BIBLICAL IMAGES. Some images communicate in most cultures. Although a "messianic banquet" does not evoke the wide range of biblical and ancient Jewish associations for most hearers today that it would have for its first audience, most cultures have wedding celebrations. Our culture can relate to a wedding banquet as a picture of joy and (if our society were not so prone to divorce) a promise of continued blessing.

Sometimes we read our theology into the text. Some suggest that the marriage supper of the Lamb takes place during the Tribulation preceding Jesus' return. The text, however, says that at the end of the age the bride is merely

---

31. Ford, *Revelation*, 323, citing Cicero, *Verr.* 4.43; Justinius, 15.4–5.

32. E.g., Homer, *Il.* 1.4–5; 22.42–43; *Od.* 3.258–60; Livy, 25.12.6; Appian, *R.H.* 11.10.64; Lucan, *C.W.* 7.831–35; on vulures specifically, see Aelian, 2.46; 10.22; Longinus, *Sublime* 3.2. Ancient writers often lapsed into poetic license when recounting battle slaughter (even to a degree in 1QM and 4QpNah 2.2–4).

33. For the fire, see 1 Enoch 54:5–6; 63:10; for the burning sulfur, 1QpHab 10.5; the later Apoc. Zeph. 6:1–2.

ready; the marriage supper in Revelation, as in early Judaism, was a banquet prepared for the righteous in the messianic era or the world to come.[34]

Sometimes we wish we had a text to read our theology into. A friend once insisted to me that her dog would be in heaven. The only text I could think of that might suggest animals in heaven at that time was this passage, but it was probably not a helpful one. Should we think of Jesus and his saints riding on literal horses? That God can create angelic horses of some sort is not impossible, and ancient readers would not have recoiled at the idea. Thus Greek and Roman literature knew of immortal horses, horses that could fly between heaven and earth, and other supernatural, winged horses.[35]

Jewish people could envision as God's hosts armed troops worshiping him in heaven (2 En. 17:1); in this period, Jewish people expected heavenly angels to appear on horseback (2 Macc. 5:1–4; 11:8; 4 Macc. 4:10; contrast T. Abr. 2A). But most likely John's vision adapts the most fierce war imagery of his day. God's heavenly host in the Old Testament was portrayed as mounted on chariots, in keeping with the most dangerous troops of its day (2 Kings 2:11; 6:17; Ps. 68:17; Hab. 3:8). The elite troops of John's day were mounted warriors without chariots. Today perhaps it would not be irreverent to picture them (for purposes of comparison) as coming in space ships and nuking the world.

Revelation probably blends many horrifying images, demanding repentance without attention to chronological sequence. Thus, for example, in Ezekiel 38–39, the birds are invited to devour the slain after the rebellion of Gog and Magog; in Revelation 19–20, the sequence is reversed if one follows the order of the text.[36] The nations are defeated in this battle (19:15; cf. 2 Thess. 1:9), yet some among the nations survive in 20:3, 8. The point here is not exact descriptions but the blending of various end-time details that invite obedience to God's will.

Serious misinterpretations. Serious failures to bridge contexts sometimes occur. Often drawing from biblical images of holy war with less attention to Jesus' teachings on nonretaliation, medieval Christians practiced atrocities no

---

34. Thus even Lindsay, *New World Coming*, 255–56, places the supper during the Millennium, citing Jesus' promise about the Father's kingdom (Mark 14:25).

35. See Homer, *Il.* 5.367–69, 770–72; 17.444; Ovid, *Metam.* 4.214–16, 262–63, 765–86; Apollodorus, 2.3.2; 3.13.5. The chariot of a sorceress might be drawn by winged serpents (Ovid, *Metam.* 7.350); a goddess's chariot might be drawn by winged dragons (8.795). Some ancients also conceived of deceased animals in the netherworld along with deceased people (Homer, *Od.* 11.572–75; *Battle of Frogs and Mice* 236; Aristophanes, *Frogs* 209–20; Virgil, *Culex* 208–384), although there is no reason to believe that these are deceased spirit-horses.

36. This interpretation assumes a typical premillennial reading. On an amillennial reading, Rev. 20 recapitulates the end-time battle already recounted in Rev. 19, so there is no conflict.

less serious than those attributed to the Muslims that they were avenging.[37] Following the medieval custom toward a city that failed to surrender, the Crusaders slaughtered nearly wholesale the Muslim and Jewish civilians they encountered in Jerusalem, including women and children; then they praised God for giving them victory.[38] To be sure, they were invited by repressed Eastern Christians to defend them; Turks were themselves expansionist, and the Seljuk Turks had limited Christian access to holy shrines that many medieval Christians thought vital for their salvation.[39] Yet these warriors somehow failed to recognized that "the sword is never God's way to extend Christ's kingdom."[40] This lesson raises questions for those who prove more committed to their earthly country's national security at any cost than for New Jerusalem's Christian ethics at any cost.

Some fringe interpreters today exploit this text's image of the final battle to support agendas that appear even more troubling than the Crusades. For example, members of the small Aryan supremacist sect Christian Identity expect to participate in the final Armageddon by slaughtering people of other races and racial allegiances. As one of the leaders has declared, "God has ordained that his people be a warring people. . . . Lord of Hosts means Lord of a mass of people organized for war." Some patriots related to this movement are currently stockpiling weapons and engaged in terrorism; to the chagrin of leaders of nonracist militias, these white supremacists have been infiltrating nonracist militias to try to take them over to create a race war in the United States.[41] One of their ministers cites the Old Testament example of holy war, arguing that God advocates slaughtering all the enemies, including babies.[42]

---

37. Muslims had also slaughtered noncombatants, including babies and the elderly, though taking young women as concubines (Ronald C. Finucane, "Women of the Cross," *Christian History* 40 [1993]: 36–37 [p. 36]).

38. Often recorded (cf. Mark Galli, "Bloody Pilgrimage," *Christian History* 40 [1993]: 8–15 [p. 15]).

39. See Bruce L. Shelley, "How Could Christians Do This?" *Christian History* 40 (1993): 16–19; cf. Adriaan H. Bredero, *Christendom and Christianity in the Middle Ages*, tr. R. Bruinsma (Grand Rapids: Eerdmans, 1994), 19; some Crusades also redirected knights' aggressions from each other to external aggressors (ibid., 107) and strengthened the pope's political hand as head of Europe (Geoffrey Barraclough, *The Medieval Papacy* [New York: W. W. Norton, 168], 91). Cf. also the medieval predisposition to think in terms of blood feud, honor, and vengeance (Jonathan Riley-Smith, "Holy Violence Then and Now," *Christian History* 40 [1993]: 42–45 [p. 43]).

40. Shelley, "Christians," 19.

41. "The Patriot Movement," *Southern Poverty Law Center Intelligence Report* (Spring 1998), 6–7.

42. "Identity Crisis," *Southern Poverty Law Center Intelligence Report* (Winter 1988), 7–12 (p. 12).

The present and projected nature of their "war" hardly seems worthy of the name "Christian," yet their behavior is tarnishing the adjective in the eyes of many secularists:

> Followers of a racist version of Christianity were charged last year with interpreting the Bible to justify the murder of an entire Arkansas family, including an 8-year-old girl, in pursuit of the "Aryan" republic they planned. Another white racist group was convicted of bombing and robbing banks in Washington, saying the Bible outlaws charging interest.[43]

Warriors for this "Christian" Identity sect taped "a plastic bag over a terrified eight-year-old girl's head," secured it, suffocated her, and then deposited her body in a swamp. Another such "warrior" shot off a victim's finger's one at a time, had the flesh flayed from his thighs, and then killed him. Feeling that a five-year-old white boy had offended Yahweh, the same leader ordered the boy sexually abused; the boy finally died of a broken neck after several weeks of torture.[44] The group promotes a tract called "Vigilantes of Christendom," and at the time of writing has at least "94 active ... ministries in 34 states." An "explosive concoction of race hate and delusional end-times paranoia," radical Christian Identity members view themselves as instruments of God's final judgment and hence are becoming prone to killing people randomly.[45]

But those who exploit biblical images of the final battle to support their violent agendas teach the opposite of this text's point. Believers suffered and proclaimed Christ nonviolently throughout the rest of the book of Revelation. Here the text cannot be more explicit that Jesus himself (in the Old Testament, God) destroys the enemy armies by his own sword (19:11, 15, 21); his hosts are with him (19:14, 19), but do not participate actively in the slaughter. Further, these hosts come from heaven (19:11, 14); the earthly armies may or may not all be allied with one another, but they are all opposed to Christ (16:12–

---

43. "Religion Stokes the Fires," *Southern Poverty Law Center Intelligence Report* (Winter 1998), 2. In May 1998 three survivalists killed and wounded police officers in Colorado after reportedly preparing desert bunkers for the world's end (*Southern Poverty Law Center Intelligence Report* [Summer 1998], 3); those of us who argue for a consistent prolife ethic will also be disturbed by "antiabortion" terrorism and its developing connections with white supremacist terrorism (see Frederick Clarkson, "Anti-Abortion Extremism," *Southern Poverty Law Center Intelligence Report* [Summer 1998], 8–16).

44. "Identity Crisis," 7.

45. Ibid. Many others are turning to neopagan, Norse religion (like the Aryan supremacists of the leaders of Hitler's Third Reich) for support; see "The New Barbarians," *Southern Poverty Law Center Intelligence Report* (Winter 1998), 15–16.

14; 19:19). Those militant groups on earth committed to genocide are certainly among those doomed to death at Jesus' hand at his return!

JUDGMENTS SENT BY GOD. The opening image of this chapter, exaltation over Babylon's fall, is the heavenly answer to the preceding chapter's lament over the prostitute's demise. "How odd, as it seems to us, that the death of a society—especially, perhaps, the violent disintegration of this most rich and most powerful of all nations: Babylon—should incite jubilation in heaven."[46] It is hard for us to be comfortable in this world and the status it values, yet hear clearly heaven's rejoicing in judgment. It is particularly difficult if one of the societies receiving God's judgment is our own, especially when we think concretely in terms of judgments' effects on people we know and care about. His compassion is one reason God delays judgment and enacts it sparingly, but in the broader scope of history the judgments are necessary for the repentance of some and vindication of others. If our devotion of time and energy is more to what the world offers than to God's purposes, we may be among those needing repentance. God will ultimately judge all nations (Ps. 110:6; Jer. 25:31; Joel 3:12).

God often sends judgment to stop oppression, but he also sends judgment to avenge oppression, vindicating his justice for the oppressed. In this world God does not settle all scores in the short run, but his justice is always satisfied in the end. Even repentance does not allow sins to escape justice—for the scores of the repentant were settled in advance on the cross.

Joy and worship. Verses 1–10 promise that vindication and joy are coming for the righteous (19:1–5), because God reigns sovereignly (19:6). It promises deeper intimacy with God in a permanent union like marriage (19:7). Insofar as Jesus' meals with sinners were a foretaste of the messianic banquet, those who fellowship with him now (cf. 3:20) experience a foretaste of their future blessing. The righteous acts of the saints make up our bridal array, hence may prepare our future intimacy with God (19:8).

This section also teaches that we should not worship anything or anyone other than God, including angels (19:10). (By contrast, this reminds us that Jesus is worshiped in Revelation as fully divine.) This is important in our preaching and teaching, because outside the subculture of the biblically literate, many who possess inadequate understanding of Christian teaching

---

46. William Stringfellow, *An Ethic for Christians and Other Aliens in a Strange Land*, 3d ed. (Waco, Tex.: Word, 1979), 25 (this book was brought to my attention by John Herzog of Bethel College).

appeal to angels—undoubtedly fallen ones—for occult purposes (as in the magical papyri of the ancient Mediterranean world).[47]

Empowered by the Spirit. This passage also reminds us that the Spirit empowers us to speak for God (19:10). That the testimony about Jesus also implies prophetic empowerment by the Spirit (19:10) has important implications for us today.[48] Some Christians rank the anointing of other Christians based on their possession of particular spiritual gifts, but Christ gave all of us his Spirit to testify about him (Acts 1:8). Thus, every Christian who witnesses about Jesus experiences in some measure the empowerment of the Holy Spirit (cf. 1 Cor. 12:3).[49] (Although I have found that prayer in tongues helps me personally to grow in sensitivity to the Spirit, including for evangelism, most of my witnessing partners and other ministry colleagues whose zeal and effectiveness I most respect have never done so.)

This empowerment by the Spirit also means that our effectiveness can far exceed our natural human abilities. One may think of the timid young man who suddenly began preaching to two hundred of his coworkers; he continued preaching from that time on, and today James Robison is widely known as an evangelist.[50] Likewise, I am normally introverted and shy (a mild-mannered professor type), but I find that God regularly provides a supernatural boldness when I testify for Christ; indeed, when I am sick and exhausted God usually provides health and strength during the full duration of my testimony or preaching.

The Spirit's leading in witnessing can be extraordinary or appear more ordinary. I often use the example of one occasion where the Spirit directed me to talk at length about the background of a person with whom I was sharing Christ—whom I had never before met—and who readily accepted Christ, noting that God had revealed the secrets of her heart (1 Cor. 14:25).

---

47. See Timothy Jones, "Rumors of Angels?" *CT* (April 5, 1993), 18–22; Kenneth L. Woodward, "Angels," *NW* (Dec. 27, 1993), 52–57. For one example, see Joyce Keller, "Your Angel Astrology Love Diet: How Your Guardian Angel and Star Sign Can Work Together to Make You Slimmer and Happier" (Lantana, Fla.: MicroMags, 1998). Keller claims to be "clairvoyant since birth," a psychic and hypnotherapist, and warns that "any angelic intercession has to be within our soul's karmic pattern" (p. 4). The booklet advocates invoking angels for weight loss (p. 7) and counsels (in the name of a zodiac angel) to marry hastily, repenting "at leisure" (p. 61).

48. We read "testimony of Jesus" as an objective genitive (Bruce, "The Spirit in the Apocalypse," 338), but the subjective element is not necessarily incompatible here (Boring, *Sayings*, 106).

49. See my discussion of this issue in greater detail in Keener, *3 Questions*, 35–61. On all believers as the prophetic community, see F. F. Bruce, *The Time Is Fulfilled* (Grand Rapids: Eerdmans, 1978), 103; E. Schweizer, "πνεῦμα, πνευματικός," 6:389–51 in *TDNT*, 449.

50. See Deere, *Surprised by the Voice of God*, 33–36.

But on more occasions, I simply feel the Spirit checking me or urging me in what to say and providing boldness to testify uncompromisingly about our Lord Jesus Christ (Eph. 6:19).

Applying holy war. The portrait of holy war in 19:11–21 also commands our attention. It reminds us that Jesus is the all-powerful One, with whom the final vindication of justice lies. Although we must do our best to work for justice and mercy, we cannot realistically fulfill the postmillennial vision of establishing God's kingdom on earth; rather, our omnipotent Lord will settle these matters when he returns. In this world we do not win all the battles, but that is not daunting with a longer range perspective; when our Lord Jesus comes, nothing can stand against him![51] The punishment of the wicked in this passage provides theodicy for those who question God's justice in this world, vindication for the oppressed righteous, and a warning not to become too comfortable with the partial blessings of the present age.

If we have rightly interpreted the sword from Jesus' mouth (19:15), it provides an encouragement as well. Other mouths may slander us (11:10; 12:15; 13:6), but what ultimately matters is the just decree of life or death from Jesus' mouth.

---

51. For comments on nineteenth-century evangelical postmillennialism and the twentieth-century experiences that shattered its excessive optimism, see comments on Revelation 20, below; also see esp. Stanley Grenz, *The Millennial Maze* (Downers Grove, Ill.: InterVarsity, 1992), 65–89.

Revelation 20:1–15

ND I SAW an angel coming down out of heaven, having
the key to the Abyss and holding in his hand a great
chain. ²He seized the dragon, that ancient serpent,
who is the devil, or Satan, and bound him for a thousand
years. ³He threw him into the Abyss, and locked and sealed it
over him, to keep him from deceiving the nations anymore
until the thousand years were ended. After that, he must be
set free for a short time.

⁴I saw thrones on which were seated those who had been
given authority to judge. And I saw the souls of those who
had been beheaded because of their testimony for Jesus and
because of the word of God. They had not worshiped the
beast or his image and had not received his mark on their
foreheads or their hands. They came to life and reigned with
Christ a thousand years. ⁵(The rest of the dead did not come
to life until the thousand years were ended.) This is the first
resurrection. ⁶Blessed and holy are those who have part in the
first resurrection. The second death has no power over them,
but they will be priests of God and of Christ and will reign
with him for a thousand years.

⁷When the thousand years are over, Satan will be released
from his prison ⁸and will go out to deceive the nations in the
four corners of the earth—Gog and Magog—to gather them
for battle. In number they are like the sand on the seashore.
⁹They marched across the breadth of the earth and surrounded the camp of God's people, the city he loves. But fire
came down from heaven and devoured them. ¹⁰And the devil,
who deceived them, was thrown into the lake of burning sulfur, where the beast and the false prophet had been thrown.
They will be tormented day and night for ever and ever.

¹¹Then I saw a great white throne and him who was seated
on it. Earth and sky fled from his presence, and there was no
place for them. ¹²And I saw the dead, great and small, standing
before the throne, and books were opened. Another book was
opened, which is the book of life. The dead were judged
according to what they had done as recorded in the books.
¹³The sea gave up the dead that were in it, and death and

Hades gave up the dead that were in them, and each person was judged according to what he had done. ¹⁴Then death and Hades were thrown into the lake of fire. The lake of fire is the second death. ¹⁵If anyone's name was not found written in the book of life, he was thrown into the lake of fire.

THERE IS LITTLE DOUBT that Revelation 20 is the most debated chapter in this book. It deals with the Millennium (a Latin word meaning "one thousand"), the thousand-year reign of Christ depicted here. In addition to looking at specific verses, we will analyze in broad outline the different positions evangelicals have taken on this issue.

The Thousand Years and First Resurrection (20:1–10)

INTERPRETERS OF THIS chapter are divided into three broad schools of thought: *premillennialists*, who believe Jesus will return to establish a specific thousand-year kingdom; *amillennialists*, who generally believe that the thousand-year kingdom is symbolic for the present age; and postmillennialists, who believe that Christians help establish the thousand-year kingdom on earth prior to Jesus' return. Most evangelicals today are premillennialists or amillennialists.

Although amillennialism as a system has more biblical support than many premillennialists will allow, this commentator believes that the present text reads as if the Millennium follows rather than recapitulates the Tribulation period in history (chs. 6–19).[1] Such an observation does not settle whether the thousand years is literal or figurative—a matter on which premillennialists themselves are divided—nor does it settle whether amillennialism or premillennialism on other grounds is more likely correct[2] (see further discussion on that question under Bridging Contexts, below). But it does affect our approach to the structure of the book of Revelation, which may affect our applications of this passage.

---

1. For various views on the millennium, see Robert G. Clouse, ed., *The Meaning of the Millennium* (Downers Grove, Ill.: InterVarsity, 1977). For a more complete survey of millennial views from the Reformation forward, see Petersen, *Preaching in the Last Days*, 232–47.

2. Many premillennialists are not sure whether the period is literally one thousand years or whether that might be a symbolic number (see Johnson, *Revelation*, 189–90); dispensationalists usually take it literally whereas historic premillennialists more often interpret it as simply a lengthy period (Lewis, *Questions*, 127). For arguments that it is nonliteral, see Beale, *Revelation*, 1017–21.

To be sure, as amillennial scholars note, it is difficult to interpret most of Revelation as a continuous chronological account; the seals, trumpets, and vials appear to be parallel in their inception and completion.[3] Revelation emphasizes future eschatology, but is not without some "realized eschatology" (implying blessings of the future available in the present; see comment on 22:17). Further, many of the expressions about the end in chapter 20 plainly parallel previous descriptions of the end in Revelation.[4] But these parallels may suggest merely that a later end repeats what was unfinished in a former one, if other factors warrant.[5] Indeed, other factors do favor reading this thousand years as following the Tribulation in the narrative plan of the book.

(1) The binding of Satan during the thousand years hardly matches Satan's furious deceptive and murderous activity during the present era (12:12–13; 13:11–15; 20:2–3).

(2) The saints have already been martyred, suggesting that the Tribulation period precedes the Millennium (20:4).

(3) The resurrection of the righteous is parallel to and contrasted with the rest of the dead returning to life after the thousand years (20:4–6), suggesting a bodily rather than symbolic resurrection (the future resurrection rather than our spiritual new birth or natural death or unity with Christ's resurrection).[6] Even by itself, though "come to life" can refer to realized eschatology (e.g., John 11:25; Gal. 2:20), it is also an acceptable euphemism for resurrection (Rev. 2:8; cf. John 5:25; Rom. 6:10; 2 Cor. 13:4; 1 En. 103:4; Sib. Or. 4.187–90); the context here points still more clearly to the latter understanding.

---

3. Joachim of Fiore (c. 1135–1202) thought Revelation predicted in detail the course of history, but did allow recapitulation (Wainwright, *Mysterious Apocalypse*, 49–53), though others saw it as in chronological sequence (pp. 53–55).

4. See R. Fowler White, "Reexamining the Evidence for Recapitulation in Rev 20:1–10," *WTJ* 51 (1989): 319–44; Meredith G. Kline, "*Har Magedon*: The End of the Millennium," *JETS* 39 (June 1996): 207–22.

5. "To John it is not a case of the same story being told twice, but of history repeating itself" (Michaels, *Revelation*, 226).

6. For symbolic views, see Norman Shepherd, "The Resurrections of Revelation 20," *WTJ* 37 (1974): 34–43; James A. Hughes, "Revelation 20:4–6 and the Question of the Millennium," *WTJ* 35 (1973): 281–302; Meredith G. Kline, "The First Resurrection," *WTJ* 37 (1975): 366–75; Philip E. Hughes, "The First Resurrection: Another Interpretation," *WTJ* 39 (Spring 1977): 315–18; Paul A. Rainbow, "Millennium as Metaphor in John's Apocalypse," *WTJ* 58 (Fall 1996): 209–21; for a careful and detailed amillennial interpretation, see especially Beale, *Revelation*, 972–1021. For various premillennial interpretations, cf. George E. Ladd, "Revelation 20 and the Millennium," *RevExp* 57 (1960): 167–75; Jack S. Deere, "Premillennialism in Revelation 20:4–6," *BibSac* 135 (Jan. 1978): 58–73; J. Ramsey Michaels, "The First Resurrection: A Response," *WTJ* 39 (1976): 100–109. Walvoord emphasizes that the new birth occurs during this age, not before (*Prophecy Knowledge Handbook*, 626).

(4) Revelation 20 "presupposes all that has transpired in chapters 12–19."[7] Thus the beast and false prophet are already in the lake of fire before the Millennium (20:10); likewise, the devil cannot deceive "anymore," suggesting a suspension of his deceptive work that transpired from 12:9 on.

(5) In hindsight we recognize that the period between Jesus' first and second comings is longer than one thousand years, but in John's own day such a figure for the intermediate period must have seemed too long (1:3).

The idea of an intermediate, messianic kingdom appears frequently in early Jewish literature, as commentators regularly point out.[8] Estimated durations of the period, however, vary considerably in the sources, such as three generations or four hundred years (see 4 Ezra 7:28–29); the same rabbi might provide four different estimates of the period's duration, based on four different exegeses of Scripture.[9] First Enoch allows so many brief transitional periods that the end appears to come gradually (1 En. 91:8–17).

Although not dominant, some of these portraits of the end time employ schemes that use thousand-year periods, sometimes with the seventh thousand years as a final Sabbath period.[10] (Thus some premillennialists have suggested that the "thousand years" represents not so much the length of the intermediate kingdom as its character: a period of rest.) One ancient oracle predicted Rome's collapse at the end of six thousand years, followed by a thousand-year period of peace.[11] While John probably employs such background, to some degree he may also be interpreting the events according to their sequence in Ezekiel 36–48: resurrection and kingdom (Ezek. 37); Gog from Magog (chs. 38–39); and the new temple and city (chs. 40–48).[12] But the

---

7. Michaels, *Revelation*, 222.

8. Among scholars, see Leon Morris, *Apocalyptic* (Grand Rapids: Eerdmans, 1972), 44–45. For the intermediate messianic kingdom, see 2 Bar. 40:3; Sib. Or. 3.741–59, 767–95; T. Abr. 13A; *Sifre Deut.* 34.4.3; *b. Pes.* 68a.

9. See Bonsirven, *Judaism*, 212–13, on R. Eliezer. For three generations, see *Sifre Deut.* 310.5.1; *Pes. Rab. Kah.* 3:16.

10. See *b. Sanh.* 97ab, although also listing various other schemes; perhaps Ps-Philo, 28:8, variant reading; Life of Adam 51:2 (contrast parallel in Apoc. Mos. 43:3). One thousand years was the longevity of the mythical phoenix (*Gen. Rab.* 19:5); pagans could employ one thousand years for cycles between reincarnations (Plato, *Rep.* 10.621D; cf. less definite period in *Phaedo* 113E–114B) or the longevity of the Sibyl (Ovid, *Metam.* 14.144); see other pagan parallels in Beasley-Murray, *Revelation*, 286. For these views in early Christianity, see Chadwick, *Church*, 78 n. 1. Cf. use of the "millennium" in the Soncino translations of *Gen. Rab.* 20:1; *Ex. Rab.* 25:3, 8, 12; 32:9; 45:6.

11. Aune, *Revelation*, 3:830–31, citing the *Oracles of Hystaspes*.

12. See further Moyise, *The Old Testament in Revelation*, 66–67; Rissi, *Time and History*, 116; Beasley-Murray, *Revelation*, 288–89; Ladd, *Theology*, 557; Boring, *Revelation*, 209. Ryrie, *Revelation*, 115, envisions a different battle because "the time is different (Ezek. 38:16) and the judgment is dissimilar (Ezek. 38:19–22)."

---

correspondence with Ezekiel is not exact or complete by itself; Ezekiel 37 lacks an explicit millennium, and Revelation 21–22 lacks a physical temple.

Interpreters apply the significance of this traditional intermediate period differently accordingly to their different schemas. Premillennialists find in the typical intermediate period of apocalyptic literature confirmation that John likewise sees an intermediate period here; one can also argue for some delay of the final consummation in passages like Isaiah 24:22 and Daniel 7:12. Amillennialists, by contrast, may suggest that John is not predicting true future events based on a Jewish literary device; John is simply using this literary device to communicate Christian truth after he has demythologized it. But as Caird points out, the Millennium was not an indispensable literary device; many Jewish texts included other durations for an intermediate period or none at all.[13] Then again, "one thousand years" could indicate simply great longevity (Jub. 23:26–28; see the Bridging Contexts section, below).

God delegates the "key" to the Abyss to an angel here (20:1), as in 9:1. The idea of "binding" an evil angel (20:2; cf. 9:14) appears regularly in Jewish texts. Thus in one widely read Jewish work, God commands an archangel to bind (and so immobilize) a leader of rebellious angels until he will be cast into the fire on the Day of Judgment (1 En. 10:4–6). Likewise, another Jewish work written some two centuries before Revelation recounts good angels binding evil angels until the final Day of Judgment.[14] Jewish texts also speak of "binding" or immobilizing demons in the present (Tobit 8:1–3), following a frequent magical usage attested also in the magical papyri.[15]

But Revelation draws on the more familiar use in apocalyptic texts, in which a spirit or evil angel is decisively bound until the Day of Judgment. In such texts bound angels can also be thrown into the Abyss (1 En. 88:1). Some early Jewish texts looked forward to end-time deliverance from Satan's activity.[16] Once Satan is bound in the Abyss, the angel "seals" it, preventing any chance of his escape (cf. Dan. 6:17); Satan cannot act during that period as he does in the present.

The martyrs of 20:4 died "because of the word of God" and "because of their testimony for Jesus"; suffering for this cause is such a recurrent motif in Revelation (1:9; 6:9; 12:11) that it constitutes a virtual invitation to John's

---

13. Caird, *Commentary on Revelation*, 250–51.

14. Jub. 5:6; cf. 10:5–7, 11. For further examples of binding evil angels or others who are evil, cf. also 1 Enoch 10:12–14; 13:1; 14:5; 21:3–4; 22:11; 90:23; T. Levi 18:12.

15. See T. Sol. 3:7; ch. 18.

16. See Jub. 23:29; 50:5; Ass. Moses 10:1; T. Levi 18:12. For events within history, Jub. 48:15–18; cf. 40:10; 46:2. Aune, *Revelation*, 3:1081, relates the image (probably rightly) to the binding of Titans in Greek myth.

audience to participate in paying the price. Beheading the saints who refused to worship the beast or his image (20:4) recalls 13:15. Beheading was the primary method of execution for Roman citizens; after being bound to a post, stripped naked, and whipped, they would be forced to kneel and then be decapitated. During the period of the Republic executioners used axes; in this period, provincial executions employed swords.[17]

Because John envisions the whole church needing to resist the world system, he can portray the church as a martyr church, though his wording can allow for others who have withstood the beast but were not specifically martyred.[18] Recent chapters repeated the refrain of the blood of the righteous (16:6; 17:6; 18:24); Jesus' followers "conquer" or "overcome" the way he did, through death (3:21; cf. 5:5–6).[19] But while the present world executes judgment against the saints, the saints rule the future world (5:10)—both the "thousand years" (20:4, 6) and eternally (22:5). The righteous oppressed sought vindication (6:10); now it has finally come.

In contrast to the promise of the "first resurrection" is the "second death" (20:6; see comment on 2:11); the resurrection to damnation is so horrible that its life is called "death" as opposed to the eternal life inherited by believers. Daniel had predicted a resurrection of the damned (Dan. 12:2), which is followed by some Jewish writers (2 Bar. 51:1–2; cf. *tos. Ber.* 6:6) and by all early Christian writers who are explicit on the subject (John 5:29; Acts 24:15; cf. Matt. 5:29–30; 10:28; 25:46).

After the thousand years, Satan will be loosed to rouse Gog and Magog against the camp of the saints (20:8–9); in accordance with his nature (cf. John 8:44), he "gathers" the nations for war again (16:16; 19:19). This army is numerically "like the sand on the seashore" (20:8), a common figure in the Hebrew Bible for saying a group of people are innumerable, although most of these texts are plainly hyperbolic.[20] This is larger than even the earlier armies of the East (two hundred million, 9:16), certainly overwhelming again the (figurative) number of God's servants (7:4, though cf. 7:9).

John draws this image from Ezekiel, but whereas in Ezekiel Gog is ruler of Magog, here Gog and Magog together merely symbolize all the nations,

---

17. E.g., Livy, 2.5.8; Seneca, *Dial.* 3.18.4; *m. Sanh.* 7:3; ARN, 38 A; John E. Stambaugh and David L. Balch, *The New Testament in Its Social Environment*, LEC 2 (Philadelphia: Westminster, 1986), 35. See Aune, *Revelation*, 3:1086, for further details.

18. Cf. Rissi, *Time and History*, 117; Ladd, *Theology*, 628–29; Michaels, *Interpreting Revelation*, 136. Neither interpretation leaves much room for a stage of the resurrection preceding the "first" resurrection (pace Strombeck, *Rapture*, 194).

19. Michaels, *Interpreting Revelation*, 135–36.

20. See Gen. 22:17; 32:12; 41:49; Judg. 7:12; 1 Sam. 13:5; 2 Sam. 17:11; 1 Kings 4:20; Isa. 10:22; 48:19; Jer. 15:8; 33:22; Hos. 1:10; Hab. 1:9.

the nations "in the four corners of the earth."[21] Given other early Jewish commentators' use of Ezekiel, it is not surprising that Gog and Magog had become familiar in Jewish texts about the end time.[22] In many Jewish texts Gog serves a mythical function; in some various evil oppressors fill the role of the final Gog if God intends that as the end time.[23] Jewish writers typically used the invasion of Gog to predict the gathering of all nations against God's people, and Revelation likely employs this image the same way.[24]

Some commentators have suggested that this event represents a mock "parousia" or "second coming" of Satan; if so, in God's providence it becomes merely a stage for Satan's final defeat (20:9–10). "Fire ... from heaven" is a familiar punishment employed by particular prophets (11:5; cf. 2 Kings 1:10, 12; Luke 9:54), but here the fire obliterates the entire enemy host, as in the case of Sodom (Gen. 19:24–25). Revelation may draw on the warning that God will cast fire on Magog in Ezekiel 39:6, and especially draws on the threat of 38:22, that God will cast fire, hailstones, and burning sulfur on this army. This description portrays the fate of end-time Magog like Sodom (or to a lesser degree Egypt; cf. Rev. 11:8). Some other early Jewish texts reflect a similar fate for Israel's final enemies.[25] The point in Ezekiel is that God will be glorified through their destruction (38:16, 23) and will defend his people (38:14–16).[26]

---

21. On the "four corners," cf. comment on 7:1. On Ezekiel's use of Gog and Magog and other terms, see especially Edwin M. Yamauchi, *Foes from the Northern Frontier* (Grand Rapids: Baker, 1982). In this period, some interpreters held "Magog" to refer to the Scythians; see Josephus, *Ant.* 1.123; *Jub.* 9:8 (though *Sib. Or.* 3.319–20 places Magog in the south).

22. E.g., 4QpIs fr.; 1QM 11.15–16; *tos. Ber.* 1:11; *Mekilta Amalek* 2.115–16; *Sifra Behuq. pq.* 8.269.2.15; *Sifre Num.* 76.2.1; *Pes. Rab Kah.* 22:5; *Ex. Rab.* 12:2; *Midr. Ps.* 17.9 on 17:13; note the exaggerated numbers in *b. Sanh.* 95b. These are normally distinguished from messianic times following the Messiah's triumph (*Sifre Deut.* 343.7.1; *b. A.Z.* 3b; *Pes. Rab Kah.* 27:5; *Gen. Rab.* 88:5; though cf. 3 Enoch 45:5). Cf. the end-time "army of Belial" (Satan) in 1QM 11.8; 15.2–3; and the camp of the saints (1QM 3.5).

23. See *b. Sanh.* 94a (although here candidates for end-time Messiah can also shift); 1 Enoch 56:5 substitutes Parthians for Magog.

24. See Beasley-Murray, *Revelation*, 297 (citing 4 Ezra 13:5–11; *Sib. Or.* 3.662–68; cf. *Sib. Or.* 3.319, 512).

25. For such judgments against end-time Magog, see *Sib. Or.* 3.669–74, 685–92; against Rome in 3.52; against the new Nero and other kings in 5.377–79; cf. other divine destruction in 1 Enoch 56:7–8; 1QM 11.16. For fire from heaven to destroy God's enemies, see further Wisd. Sol. 10:6; 2 Bar. 27:10; T. Zeb. 10:3; cf. *Sib. Or.* 1.79; 2.252–53; in pagan texts, cf. Athenaeus, *Deipnosophists* 12.523ab.

26. For God's protection of his people in the end time, like a wall of fire around them, see *Sib. Or.* 3.705–6 (drawing on the image of Zech. 2:5); for later texts, see Ira Chernus, "'A Wall of Fire Round About': The Development of a Theme in Rabbinic Midrash," *JJS* 30 (1979): 68–84.

The holy city will be unwalled; otherwise, the inhabitants would spill out of the walls because there will be so many of them (Zech. 2:4); thus God himself will be a "wall of fire" around her (2:5; cf. 9:8). But the language of a "camp" of the saints (Rev. 20:9) probably suggests more than that the inhabitants spill out beyond city walls; rather, it alludes to Israel's experience in the Exodus or as a unit of war.[27] This reminds John's audience that even during the thousand years God's people must remain vigilant until their final victory, a reminder that invites even greater vigilance for the saints in the present time.

Final Judgment (20:11–15)

THE SCENE OF battle judgment gives way to the Final Judgment before God's throne. Jewish traditions often describe this day; the time for mercy and patience are over (4 Ezra 7:33), and the wicked will be ashamed (1 Enoch 97:6).[28] That there is "no place" for earth and sky (Rev. 20:11; cf. 12:8) reveals how dramatic is God's appearance as Judge, and it paves the way for the new heavens and earth (21:1). No one can see God in his glory and live (Ex. 33:20), and the sight of God will banish creation; but in the new creation, his servants will see his face (Rev. 22:4–5).

The "books" also contribute to this picture of dread for the wicked (20:12). In some Jewish traditions, angels report human misdeeds before God's tribunal immediately after the earth's destruction and before the resurrection of the wicked (cf. Sib. Or. 2.215–16). Commonly Jewish texts depict heavenly books of judgment reporting people's works, ready to be produced in the Day of Judgment.[29] The books here reflect those of Daniel 7:10 (cf. likewise 4 Ezra 6:20).[30]

Here both "death and Hades" are judged. "Hades" (20:13–14) is the realm of the dead, and those remaining in it are those not raised at the first resurrection (20:4–6), hence the damned.[31] The idea that Hades will return what has been entrusted to it fits Jewish pictures of the resurrection of the dead for judgment (1 En. 51:1; 4 Ezra 7:32; Ps-Philo 3:10).[32] That the sea also

---

27. Cf. Heb. 13:11, 13; 1QM 3.5; 4.9; over seventy-five times for the Exodus camp in the LXX.

28. For the Day of Judgment, see also 1 Enoch 90:20; *Pes. Rab Kah. Sup.* 2:2.

29. See Jub. 28:6; 39:6; 1 Enoch 39:2; 81:1–4; 89:70–71; 91:14; 93:1–3; 98:7–8; 104:7; 2 Enoch 19:5; 44:5 A; 3 Enoch 44:9; T. Ab. 10 B; 12 A; Apoc. Zeph. 3:6–9; 7:1–6. In some sources the "book of the living" might be distinct from this (Apoc. Zeph. 9:2), concerning who will die and whom he will raise (3 Enoch 18:24–25; b. R.H.32b).

30. On the book of life, see comment on 3:5; on being judged "according to what [they] had done," see comment on 22:12.

31. Angels could break the gates of Hades to bring the wicked to judgment (Sib. Or. 2.228–30).

32. So also Bauckham, *Climax of Prophecy*, 56–61 (citing also 2 Bar. 21:23; 42:8; 50:2).

must give up its dead answers the concern of many people in antiquity, including some Jews contemplating the resurrection, concerning the fate of the unburied.[33]

The stark picture of the banishment of the wicked to a place of fire is meant to grip the hearer's attention, but it would not surprise an early Jewish-Christian reader.[34] Jewish tradition recognized that God will banish the fallen angels, Gentiles, and disobedient Israelites to the Abyss of fire (1 Enoch 90:24–27), but Revelation prefers a more graphic, oxymoronic picture of a "lake of fire" (Rev. 19:20; 20:10, 14–15; 21:8), over which the saints have come victorious (15:2; the "lake of fire" may reflect the "river of fire" in Dan. 7:10). Although fire can communicate instant annihilation rather than eternal torment, earlier Christian tradition portrayed an unquenchable burning (Matt. 3:12; Mark 9:43; Luke 3:17), and Revelation elsewhere speaks of eternal torment (14:10–11), implied also in this context for the lake of fire (20:10).[35]

VIEWS OF THE MILLENNIUM. Reviewing the history of interpretation helps us understand where our views come from so we can take adequate account of them and try to hear Scripture objectively by reducing (insofar as possible) our bias in interpretation. Revelation 20 has been the subject of considerable debate over the entire span of church history. The earliest church fathers believed in a literal, future, thousand-year reign of Christ.[36] Papias, for example, is said to have reported that the

---

33. See ibid., 68 (citing 1 Enoch 61:5; Sib. Or. 2.233), though Bauckham prefers to see this "sea" as a synonym for the realm of the dead; Aune, *Revelation*, 3:1102. Cf. esp. Achilles, *Tatius* 5.16.1–2

34. For Satan thrown into the eternal fire (20:10), see T. Jud. 25:3; for human rulers, 1 Enoch 54:1–2; for the Wicked Priest (an antichrist figure), 1QpHab 10.4–5; for all the wicked, 1 Enoch 100:9; 108:3; 1QpHab 10.13; 4 Ezra 7:36; Gen. Rab. 20:1. For the ancient "river of fire" see C. S. Keener, *A Commentary on the Gospel of Matthew* (Grand Rapids: Eerdmans, 1999), 129; cf. *Egyptian Book of the Dead*, Spell 17b, part S3.

35. For the annihilationist position, see "John's Stott's Response to Chapter 6," 306–31 in David L. Edwards and John Stott, *Evangelical Essentials: A Liberal-Evangelical Dialogue* (Downers Grove, Ill.: InterVarsity, 1988), 313–20; Marie-Émile Boismard, "Le sort des impies dans l'Apocalypse," *Lumière et Vie* 45 (1996): 69–79; for annihilation after or without a resurrection of the lost, see Ps. Sol. 3:11–12; 13:11; 1QS 4.13–14; most sinners in tos. Sanh. 13:3.

36. See Wainwright, *Mysterious Apocalypse*, 21–30. Larry V. Crutchfield, "The Apostle John and Asia Minor as a Source of Premillennialism in the Early Church Fathers," *JETS* 31 (1988): 411–27, suggests John's influence in Asia Minor spawned the millenarianism of the early Asian fathers. Some argue that the church fathers derived the view from Jewish apocalyptic messianic kingdoms rather than from Revelation (Leonhard Goppelt, *Theology of the New Testament*, 2 vols., tr. J. E. Alsup, ed. J. Roloff [Grand Rapids: Eerdmans, 1981–1982], 2:194).

apostle John promised a material, agricultural paradise to come, in a Millennium after the resurrection of the righteous.[37]

The mid-second-century Christian philosopher Justin Martyr accepted a literal, future, thousand-year reign of Christ in a rebuilt Jerusalem after the resurrection of the righteous, though he admitted that some Christians held other views; he proves his case from Isaiah and Revelation.[38] Irenaeus, a late second-century bishop, tends to interpret many biblical prophecies literally, including those in Revelation, and warns against allegorizing them.[39]

By the time of church historian Eusebius in the fourth century, however, nearly all Christian leaders assumed that the Millennium represented the present era. Thus Eusebius reported that, in contrast to many hard-hearted heretics, some premillennialists proved more teachable; shown their "error," they became amillennial.[40] The Council of Ephesus in 431 condemned belief in a literal Millennium as superstition.[41]

The amillennial viewpoint dominated most of subsequent church history: Augustine, Calvin, Luther, and many prominent church leaders cited by evangelicals on other issues today were amillennial.[42] Perhaps recognizing arguments for more than one position, Wesley reportedly believed in two millenniums, a heavenly and an earthly one.[43] For the first thousand years of church history, amillennialists generally believed in a literal present Millennium; after a thousand years followed the church's deliverance from Rome without Christ's return, amillennialists generally reinterpreted the Millennium as the present period but the thousand-year duration as symbolic.

Some amillennialists interpret this "millennial" period not as the whole course of the present Christian era but as the period after the Roman persecutions; this view allows for a distinction between the "Tribulation" as a time of Roman oppression and the Millennium. A serious problem with this distinction is that the church suffers in many parts of the world today no less

---

37. Frags. 4, 6; in Irenaeus, *Her.* 5.32; Eusebius, *H.E.* 3.39.

38. See his *Dial.* 80 and 81.

39. Irenaeus, *Her.* 5.34–35.

40. Eusebius, *H.E.* 7.24. On early amillennialism, see Wainwright, *Mysterious Apocalypse,* 33–48.

41. Kyle, *The Last Days,* 39.

42. For medieval views, see ibid., 41–54; for the Reformers, 55–76; David Wright, "Millennium Today," 13–15, and John R. Franke, "Salvation Now, Salvation Forever," *Christian History* 61 (1999):20–22.

43. Wesley, *Commentary on the Bible,* 608–9, is largely premillennial, but sees two distinct thousand-year periods, one in which the devil is bound (20:2–3, 7) and a second and subsequent one in which the saints reign (20:4–6; ibid., 610).

seriously than under imperial Rome.[44] Others, probably the dominant amillennial position today, interpret the Millennium as the entire period between the first and second comings of Christ, the way many interpret the "Tribulation" period in Revelation (12:5–6).[45]

In recent centuries premillennialism has gained considerable ground, especially around the beginning of the twentieth century when dispensational premillennialism, originating with John Nelson Darby in the 1830s, began to take hold in evangelical thought.[46] Concerned with the legalism he perceived in the church and associated with its adherence to parts of the Bible addressed specifically to Israel, Darby sought to distinguish which parts of the Bible addressed national Israel and which addressed the church. He argued that God dealt with Israel until the church age and would again deal with Israel during the final Tribulation, after the church's Rapture to heaven; for the most part early dispensationalists accepted only the New Testament letters as directed primarily toward the church. The original form of dispensationalism has changed considerably over the years, however; today's "progressive dispensationalism" is a far cry from (and a more biblical model than) Clarence Larkin's charts, Scofield's original reference Bible, or Darby's teaching in 1830.[47]

Most nineteenth-century American evangelicals held a view that few people today advocate, and their view actually helped motivate them to evangelize the world.[48] They were postmillennial: They believed they would establish the kingdom on earth to prepare the way for Jesus' return. Like premillennialists they embraced a future Millennium; like some amillennialists, they believed in a reign of peace before Jesus' return but following the time of persecutions. This postmillennial view fueled the activist faith of nineteenth-century evangelicals in the United States as they evangelized

---

44. For the latter, see Johann Gottfried Eichhorn (1752–1827), cf. Wainwright, *Mysterious Apocalypse,* 127. More recently, cf. Feuillet, *Apocalypse,* 120–21.

45. See Sydney H. T. Page, "Revelation 20 and Pauline Eschatology," *JETS* 23 (1980): 31–43. Some make the Millennium symbolic of the old economy (Corsini, *Apocalypse,* 369).

46. On the revival of premillennialism, see Wainwright, *Mysterious Apocalypse,* 67–87.

47. For the history of dispensational thought, see Craig A. Blaising, "The Extent and Varieties of Dispensationalism," 9–56 in *Progressive Dispensationalism,* by Craig A. Blaising and Darrell L. Bock (Wheaton, Ill.: Bridgepoint, Victor, 1993); cf. Timothy P. Weber, "How Evangelicals Became Israel's Best Friend," *CT* (Oct. 5, 1998), 38–49; other perspectives in Charles C. Ryrie, *Dispensationalism Today* (Chicago: Moody, 1965), 74–76.

48. See Steven R. Pointer, "Seeing the Glory," *Christian History* 61 (1999): 28–30. For a careful articulation of the postmillennial perspective, see especially Kenneth L. Gentry Jr., "Postmillennialism," 11–57 in *Three Views on the Millennium,* ed. D. Bock (Grand Rapids: Zondervan, 1999). The most defensible form is the view that Rev. 19 depicts Jesus' judgment (symbolically) on Rome and chapter 20 is Jesus final coming.

and worked to abolish slavery. Leading figures of the Great Awakenings like Jonathan Edwards (often noted for his influential theology) and Charles Finney (a prominent voice in a revival in which hundreds of thousands of conversions occurred) were postmillennial. This view provided excellent motivation for mission, but eventually shattered against the hard reefs of reality: Christian devotion, no matter how sincere, cannot fully establish God's kingdom without God's direct intervention.[49]

This survey of views has been so brief as to risk misrepresenting the greater diversity of views that stands behind it, but it should illustrate the point that committed Christians have held many different views about the end-time, yet retained God's blessings. That postmillennialism was the dominant view of nineteenth-century American evangelicals and helped fuel the missions movement should give us pause. Most of us hold views about the Millennium that we "know" are right because we move in circles that share the same views we do. I know many Christians who could not imagine their view being wrong, because every passionate believer they respect in their circles holds that view. But if we had been in Jonathan Edwards' or Charles Finney's circle, we might have taken postmillennialism for granted no less.

Perhaps our spiritual predecessors would have questioned whether we were truly evangelicals had we doubted postmillennialism! To be sure, it is easy for us today to recognize that postmillennialism does not fit enough of the biblical evidence. But because any system of thought looks consistent from within the system (whether the views of Jehovah's Witnesses or our own), we should not rest so easily that our own views fit all the evidence unless they have been tested in dialogue with Christians who can challenge them.

Apart from Billy Graham and perhaps Luis Palau, Bill Bright, and some others like them, few of us today have had the direct impact that John Wesley, Charles Finney, or D. L. Moody had on their generations: yet all three of them held quite different views about the end times. It seems clear, at least to many of us, that God does not dispense his blessings based on our views about the end time, and that we ought to learn from his example a lesson about charity toward those who hold other views on this matter.

Literal or symbolic? The two millennial views most widely held in different sections of Christendom today are premillennialism and amillennialism. Each has more arguments in its favor than advocates of the opposing position generally recognize. In favor of premillennialism is the most natural

---

49. See the views in Stanley J. Grenz, *The Millennial Maze: Sorting Out Evangelical Options* (Downers Grove, Ill.: InterVarsity, 1992); Kyle, *The Last Days*, 79–81. Many medieval chiliasts also expected a golden age of indeterminate length after Antichrist's defeat and before Christ's coming (Kyle, ibid., 53). In secularized and liberal forms, postmillennial optimism could yield America's Manifest Destiny or something like Germany's Thousand-Year Reich.

reading of Revelation 20, outlined above: The thousand years begins with the resurrection of those killed during the Tribulation that preceded it and closes with the devil being hurled into the same place of torment where the beast and false prophet of the Tribulation have been for the duration of the thousand years. In addition, some see clues to the Millennium in other texts, such as 1 Corinthians 15:23–24 (although this passage by itself is not sufficient to argue for an intermediate period between the present and eternal future).[50]

Some premillennialists (especially those who are also dispensationalists) also find abundant references to the Millennium in the Old Testament. If one takes both Ezekiel and Revelation literally, Ezekiel's new temple (Ezek. 40–43) cannot occur after the Millennium (Rev. 21:22), but it is not impossible that it could occur during the Millennium. In the eternal future, God's servants serve him before his face (22:3–4), so it is reasonable that the descriptions of earthly, agricultural blessings (e.g., Amos 9:13–14) take place during an interim period before that eternal future reign (though cf. Rev. 22:2). Such a means to reconcile diverse pictures of the end time in the Prophets would have made sense to John's contemporaries.[51] Dispensationalists who find in Old Testament prophecies promises of the restoration of national Israel and yet find in Revelation 21–22 the eternal hope of the church, can seek to harmonize the two by affirming both: One occurs during the Millennium and the other afterward.[52]

Such views can be challenged. The eternal future in Revelation 21 is no less rooted in the church's heritage in Israel than is Revelation 20: Though the holy city of chapter 21 descends from heaven, it is still a new Jerusalem, founded in the twelve tribes of Israel (21:12) as well as in the twelve apostles of the Lamb (21:14). Further, many of the Old Testament descriptions

---

50. Some do find an intermediate kingdom in that text (cf. Hans Joachim Schoeps, *Paul: The Theology of the Apostle in the Light of Jewish Religious History*, tr. H. Knight [Philadelphia: Westminster, 1961], 105; Rissi, *Time and History*, 126). But the grammar is unclear (W. D. Davies, *Paul and Rabbinic Judaism: Some Rabbinic Elements in Pauline Theology*, 4th ed. [Philadelphia: Fortress, 1980], 292–93; T. Francis Glasson, *The Second Advent: The Origin of the New Testament Doctrine*, 3d rev. ed. [London: Epworth, 1963], 212; Gordon Fee, *The First Epistle to the Corinthians* [Grand Rapids: Eerdmans, 1987], 753).

51. See Talbert, *Apocalypse*, 93–94, who cites various strands and some Jewish writings that include both views; also Aune, *Revelation*, 3:1104–8. Cf. also Morris, *Apocalyptic*, 51; D. S. Russell, *The Method and Message of Jewish Apocalyptic* (Philadelphia: Westminster, 1964), 286–97.

52. Craig Blaising, "Premillennialism," 157–227, in *Three Views on the Millennium*, 160–64, contrasts the "spiritual vision model" (which emphasizes only the heavenly and spiritual) with the "new creation model" (which emphasizes embodied life on earth). But Robert B. Strimple, "An Amillennial Response to Craig A. Blaising," 256–76 in ibid., responds that modern amillennialists do not hold to a purely nonphysical eschatological hope (259).

of the future are clearly symbolic images, meant to graphically convey the future hope in terms that made sense to ancient Israelites. In their day beating swords into plowshares (Mic. 4:3) symbolized peace; today we might prefer the image of melting down guns or disarming missiles.

But if the images are symbolic, they also do not have to be fully harmonized on a literal level—which saves us some embarrassments from which even the most traditional dispensationalism could not rescue us.[53] It is possible that Revelation includes a Millennium to allow us to harmonize some major portraits of the end time in the Old Testament prophets; but we would need more than a single Millennium to harmonize all the different pictures of the end in the Bible! Some texts speak of the ingathering of Gentiles at the end (e.g., Isa. 2:2, 4; 11:9–10; 42:6; 49:6), others of their subjection and bringing of tribute (Isa. 11:14–15; 49:22–23; 54:3; 60:6–14; 66:18–20), and others of their destruction (Isa. 29:5–8; 30:27–28; 34:2–3).

But the function of most of these texts is to promise Israel's restoration and exaltation among the nations that once ridiculed her; thus, to force these poetic images into contradictory molds is to misunderstand them. They do have implications for the salvation of Gentiles who embrace Israel's heritage in Jesus and the lostness of the rest of the world, but these implications become clear only in the light of the rest of biblical theology.

Even in the eternal future, if one takes Revelation 21:24–26 literally, one questions whether the outsiders are non-Christians that do not face eternal punishment, or Gentile Christians kept outside the new Jerusalem as spiritually second-class to Jewish Christians—or is this simply a symbolic way of describing the exaltation of God's people? Neither of the first two alternatives fits the rest of New Testament theology.

Further, one gets the distinct impression from Paul (Rom. 2:5–9; 2 Thess. 1:7–9) and Peter (2 Peter 3:10) that all non-Christians will be destroyed when Jesus comes back, an event that would not leave anyone on earth to enter the Millennium.[54] A premillennialist can argue in response that Paul and Peter are speaking in general terms, whereas Revelation provides a more detailed chronology of events. This response is a legitimate one, but it illustrates our interpretive problem: We simply cannot take all the texts completely "literally," nor are we meant to do so. If one spends much time actually reading Isaiah, Ezekiel, or the other prophets, clearly they use a variety of

---

53. Some popular dispensationalists have tried to settle issues by appealing simply to the "literal" meaning of texts (Lindsey, *New World Coming*, 267), without acknowledging that they themselves cannot take all the texts literally.

54. Some may appeal to Matt. 24:40–41 to allow that some will be "left," but in context those who are "taken" are taken to judgment (24:39), and even if those who "left" are not Christians it is not clear that they will be left very long.

symbolic images to convey the future promise, and these prophets would not have been interested in harmonizing them all on a literal level.

Amillennial interpreters usually point to the preponderance of passages like those in Paul or Peter as against the single, clear assertion of a future thousand years in Revelation. (Many premillennialists counter by appealing here to "progressive revelation.") Since we must interpret some passages symbolically anyway, amillennialists note, and since Revelation is full of symbolic language, does it not make more sense to interpret Paul's letters and the rest of the New Testament literally and Revelation symbolically, rather than the reverse? Thus amillennialists point to various New Testament passages in which Paul or other interpreters appear to apply Old Testament promises about the future kingdom to the present era of faith in Christ (e.g., Acts 2:17; 15:15–18; Rom. 9:24–25). If the apostles interpreted such Old Testament promises spiritually, should we not follow their example?

As to national Israel, many amillennialists today will acknowledge that Paul allows for the return of the final generation of Jewish people as a whole to faith in Jesus (Rom. 11:26); but they contend that ethnic Jewishness does not imply a Jewish nation-state or a spiritual distinction between Jewish and Gentile Christians.[55] Amillennialists from Augustine onward have often suggested that John adapted the traditional intermediate kingdom of Jewish apocalypses but reapplied it in a symbolic way, the way we have elsewhere argued he reapplied the Tribulation image (12:5–6).[56] Less persuasively, many (going outside Revelation) interpret Satan's binding in 20:2 in light of Matthew 12:29. But although Revelation elsewhere draws on the Synoptic Gospel tradition, it may demand too much of John's readers to presume their knowledge of that text as against the widespread Jewish tradition about binding demons, and even if they did know the text, it is not clear that they would have applied it the same way.

Strong arguments are available for both millennial positions and tend to rise or fall on how one reads the rest of the Bible. In general, if one starts with Revelation 20, one will be premillennial; starting from that premise, those so inclined can also apply many promises about national Israel to that period in a literal manner (although Rev. 20 itself does not demand that we attribute those promises to that period). If one starts with most New Testament passages about the end time, one will probably be amillennial and then need to

---

55. For one view affirming both a new Israel (including both Jewish and Gentile Christians) and an eschatological conversion of ethnic Israel, see Thomas R. Schreiner, "The Church As the New Israel and the Future of Ethnic Israel in Paul," *Studia Biblica et Theologica* 13 (April 1983): 17–38.

56. See Ford, *Revelation*, 351.

determine what to do with Revelation 20. Each view makes sense on its own presuppositions, but often sounds like special pleading to one who starts with different presuppositions.[57] Because it would take a survey of all Scripture to test such presuppositions, we cannot engage such a test here. But we can point out the reasons why Bible-believing Christians have come to different convictions on the matter and invite us to greater charity toward others who differ.

Personal perspective. Here I can only summarize the results of my own attempt to pull together my understanding of the larger biblical picture.[58] First of all, we should interpret each text in its context and on its own terms. Note, then, that the Old Testament prophets had a message for their own generations as well as for us. Their generations would have taken little solace in an interpretation of prophecy that claimed: "I am divorcing Israel and replacing her with the church"; they expected a genuine restoration of Israel.[59] At the same time, the early Christians understood these promises in light of Jesus' triumph, and their interpretation provides guidelines for our own. Whatever the literal blessings in the future kingdom, we experience the spiritual benefit of Christ's kingdom in the present (Gal. 3:14; Eph. 1:3).

Further, the Old Testament prophets themselves (e.g., Isa. 19:22–25; 56:3–8), confirmed by the New Testament writers (Rom. 16:25–26), affirmed that the future of the covenant people included more than people genetically descended from Abraham. In the Old Testament Gentiles routinely joined the covenant people (e.g., Josh. 6:25; Ruth 1:16; 2 Sam. 8:18), whereas many Israelites broke covenant with God (e.g., Ex. 32:10; Ps. 95:8–11). In the first century, Judaism still regularly accepted Gentiles as converts into their faith and people.[60]

To be sure, no one expected such a large influx of Gentiles into God's people that they would end up outnumbering the Jewish remnant, but Paul is

---

57. For ways that different presuppositions lead to different conclusions in views of the Millennium, see Darrell L. Bock, "Summary Essay," 279–309 in *Three Views on the Millennium*, 285–90; one major issue is how the Old Testament relates to the New (ibid., 290–93).

58. One readable survey of Old Testament background for eschatology is Lewis, *Questions*, 19–49.

59. To be sure, outside of Rom. 11 the New Testament provides little explicit indication of Israel's restoration (though cf. Matt. 23:39; Acts 3:19–21), but the early Christians had to spend more time defending their inclusion of Gentile Christians in the people of God. This is a matter of emphasis and audience, not a matter of contradiction. Justin's replacement theology (Justin, *Dial.* 11; 119; 123; 135) is far more graphic (see Ben Zion Bokser, "Justin Martyr and the Jews," *JQR* 64 [Oct. 1973]: 97–122 (p. 99); [Jan. 1974]: 204–11 (p. 208); Eric F. Osborn, *Justin Martyr* [Tübingen: J. C. B. Mohr, 1973], 175–78).

60. See Craig S. Keener, *The Spirit in the Gospels and Acts* (Peabody, Mass.: Hendrickson, 1997), 62–64, 146–48.

clear that the final generation of Jewish people as a whole will turn to faith
in Jesus (Rom. 11:26–27; otherwise he is changing the meaning of "Israel"
from 11:25 to 11:26 without warning). Paul was not radical for saying that
Gentiles could become part of the people of God (a view shared by most of
his Jewish contemporaries); he was radical for saying that they could do so
without circumcision—that is, without becoming ethnically or culturally
Jewish. At the same time, it is doubtful that even Paul anticipated the utterly
non-Judaic character of most of today's church, mostly alienated from its
Jewish roots (11:18).

Perhaps the final turning of Jewish people will come only as Gentile Christians rediscover their spiritual heritage in Israel's history (cf. Rom. 11:14).
Then, instead of claiming to be a corporate "replacement" for Israel per se, we
can recognize that Gentile Christians have been grafted into Israel's faith
meant to bless the world. Perhaps today's Jewish Christians (Messianic Jews)
can help Gentile Christians find the way back to this perspective.[61]

On this basis, I am skeptical of a future promise for national Israel that
excludes ethnically Gentile Christians who have been grafted into Israel's heritage and hope (cf. Rom. 2:29; 9:6–13; Gal. 3:29). (Such a scenario may prove
an especially traumatic choice for Jewish Christians: Would they share the destiny of the church or of ethnic Israel?) At the same time, I cannot think that
the Old Testament prophets intended a "replacement" of Israel now unrelated
to her historical heritage. Perhaps the whole biblical picture suggests a future
grounded in the history of the patriarchs, David, and the prophets, but one
in which Gentile Christians share fully as those grafted into the covenant—
and who should recognize (better than most do now) their spiritual heritage.

Nor do I believe that this hope grounded in Israel's history is limited to
the Millennium; the very fact that the eternal city of Revelation 21 is called
the new Jerusalem grounds our future hope in our spiritual history. I recognize that such a solution will appeal neither to some traditional dispensationalists nor to some traditional covenant theologians; I offer it merely as
my own attempt to synthesize the diverse array of biblical portraits of our
future hope. The Bible is a big book, and few of us have mastered it well
enough to think we are beyond learning more.

In the end, some scholars argue that our contemporary millennial debates
miss the point of Revelation entirely. As one evangelical commentator points

---

61. For an important Messianic Jewish perspective, see Daniel Juster, *Jewish Roots: A
Foundation of Biblical Theology* (Shippensburg, Pa.: Destiny Image, 1995); for a history of part
of the movement, see Yohanna Chernoff with Jimi Miller, *Born a Jew ... Die a Jew: The Story
of Martin Chernoff, a Pioneer in Messianic Judaism* (Hagerstown, Md.: EBED, 1996); Robert I.
Winer, *The Calling: The History of the Messianic Jewish Alliance 1915–1990* (Wynnewood, Pa.:
Messianic Jewish Alliance of America, 1990).

out, John's vision occurs within a premillennial framework; yet the real debate among millennial views arises when we ask whether to press his vision as a literal plan for the future.[62] Revelation does have a future Millennium, but the book presents not a chronologically sequenced series of future events, but various images that weave together different threads of end-time expectation. Revelation places complementary visions of the end side-by-side, in a manner analogous to the diverse Old Testament portrayals of creation. These scholars suggest that we have misunderstood the point of Revelation because we have misread its literary genre.[63]

While this approach seems in many ways the most sensitive to the nature of the prophetic genre that Revelation develops, it comes as no surprise that it has eluded many interpreters through history. Many of Revelation's first readers, like many of the earliest church fathers, probably never caught the nuances of this approach; it often seems more natural to us to take everything literally—until confronted by other prophecies that on the literal level contradict the ones we started with, forcing us to at least consider such questions. The complexity of these issues thus calls for much charity toward those with whom we may disagree on millennial details.

Identities in Revelation. We should briefly touch on at least one more issue before leaving this section. The proposed identities of various players in this narrative have shifted according to the headlines of the day, many generations assuming their list of evil empires to be the final one. Luther and many Reformers saw the Pope as the Antichrist and the Turks as Gog, allies of the Antichrist.[64] Somewhat more up to date is one etymologically strained line of interpretation of some modern prophecy teachers that identifies Gog with Russia. In this line of thinking Meshech and Tubal (Ezek. 38:2–3), for example, are Moscow and Tobolsk![65] But Gog and Magog had specific meaning for the first audience of Ezekiel, and for Revelation's audience they connoted the people of the final battle mentioned in Ezekiel.[66]

---

62. Michaels, *Revelation*, 220. With I. T. Beckwith and Robert Mounce, Michaels argues for a future millennium that is not necessarily literal, a buffer between the Roman empire's collapse and the ultimate end of the age, an interim period that in fact happened (cf. also Caird).

63. See Talbert, *Apocalypse*, 96–97 (citing on creation, e.g., Gen. 1:1–2:3; 2:4–24; Ps. 74:12–17; 104); Boring, *Revelation*, 205–6; cf. Mounce, *Revelation*, 359.

64. Kyle, *The Last Days*, 61.

65. Rather, these peoples were Moschi and Tibareni known in ancient Asia Minor (see Mounce, *Revelation*, 362 n. 28). Lindsey's emphasis on Russia as "Gog" became more difficult after the breakup of the Soviet Union (Robert G. Clouse, "Late Great Predictions," *Christian History* 61 [1999]: 40–41).

66. For their original meaning ("Gog" is probably based on a Lydian king in what is today Turkey), see Yamauchi, *Foes*, as noted above.

Some views demonstrably contradict the text. Greg Beale may well be correct, however, that Revelation recycles the image precisely because after Ezekiel the image could simply apply to the end-time enemy, hence to any enemy of God's people (the way we would speak of someone being a "Hitler" today).[67]

Consistency in our interpretive method is important. Working from particular logical constructs, Jehovah's Witnesses expect the resurrection of the righteous to occur in stages, allowing the raised opportunity to get enculturated.[68] But the text itself declares a first resurrection that leaves all "the rest of the dead" only for the raising of the lost for judgment at the end of the Millennium (20:4–6). The view itself is not so surprising as the inconsistent hermeneutic behind it, because on many points Jehovah's Witnesses interpret Revelation quite literally (such as the number 144,000), but here would criticize a literal interpretation as pedantic!

PASTORAL APPLICATION. Those who interpret the Millennium of Revelation 20 as symbolic for the present age will find in it an encouragement that believers in the present have been raised with Christ, share a role in Christ's kingdom in the world, and will be spared from the horror of a final judgment without Christ.

We have argued above that in context the passage most naturally suggests a future Millennium and therefore a future hope. This suggestion does not begin to solve the interpretive problems: One can argue that the Millennium, like many other portraits of end-time hope, is merely symbolic. One can argue that it borrows from a fairly common apocalyptic image of an interim kingdom and does not describe a literal interim between the present and future ages. Thus, not everyone who affirms a future Millennium in Revelation 20 may affirm a literal thousand-year interim reign in practice!

But on the level of pastoral application, such interpretive distinctions between a literal or symbolic future period do not affect the most important points. Whether in a temporary intermediate kingdom or in the new heavens and new earth, we will be with Christ.[69] Revelation 20 is a promise of

---

67. Beale, *Revelation*, 1025.

68. See *Revelation: Grand Climax*, 289, 300.

69. Cf. Arthur D. Katterjohn with Mark Fackler, *The Tribulation People* (Carol Stream, Ill.: Creation House, 1976), 77. Tenney, *Revelation*, 159, warns other premillennialists not to exaggerate the Millennium's importance, since the eternal state is our goal; likewise, Oscar Cullmann, *The Early Church*, ed. A. J. B. Higgins (London: SCM, 1956), 156, emphasizes the essence rather than the details.

future hope, particularly relevant to those who have suffered (like the martyrs of 20:4). Jesus will raise those who have suffered for him, and they will be rewarded by reigning with him (cf. 2 Tim. 2:12).[70]

The devil cannot act without God's permission (Rev. 20:2–3), which in turn encourages us not to be afraid of his present activities, including his persecution (12:12). When God deems the time appropriate, it will take only one angel to imprison the devil (20:1)—as Luther's hymn puts it, "one little word shall fell him." If Satan's return after the Millennium represents a "mock parousia," as some have argued, the passage may remind us that though he sometimes "comes back" after what seems to be the final "knock-out punch," his final defeat is secure, as is the preservation of the church (Matt. 16:18).

Those who do not actively submit to Christ's lordship, even if they have been in settings where they were rarely tested, remain susceptible to the devil's deceptions (20:8) and will be banished to eternal torment at the final judgment (20:14). In the final analysis, the questions of future curiosity we ask about this chapter are often the least important questions for today's church. Without understanding all the details about the future Millennium, one has more than enough preaching material in this passage to encourage believers to persevere and fulfill Christ's purposes in the world!

The Millennium fulfills another important theological function in Revelation. Earlier judgments failed to bring repentance (9:20–21; 16:9, 11, 21), and now the deceiver finds human hearts receptive to rebellion despite his thousand-year absence. "The millennium proves, then, that humans cannot blame their sinfulness on their environment or circumstances." This exposes human evil; even where corporate sin is abolished, individual depravity will remain, frustrating God's corporate redemptive activity until the final end.[71] One may compare C. S. Lewis's parable of human depravity in *The Great Divorce*, where he suggests that most of the damned remain unrepentant. On a literal level, the damned will surely regret their course; but Lewis's primary point seems to be that unregenerate humans prefer sin to God's righteousness.

If the saints must remain vigilant even during the thousand years (see comment on 20:9), on our reading this should summon us to ever greater

---

70. Barbara Wootten Snyder, "How Millennial Is the Millennium? A Study in the Background of the 1000 Years in Revelation 20," *Evangelical Journal* 9 (Fall 1991): 51–74, argues that the "thousand years" communicates theology about Jesus as the Messiah; whether the duration is literal is less urgent.

71. See Talbert, *Apocalypse*, 95. In Jewish texts, see, e.g., *Sifre Deut.* 318.1.10; there would be neither merit nor guilt in the intermediate messianic period when temptation was abolished (*Koh. Rab.* 12:1, §1). Cf. traces of sin, inviting a heroic new war, in the utopian vision of Roman hope for the Augustan era (Virgil, *Ecl.* 4.4–7, 31–36).

vigilance in the present. While I find unusual many practices currently countenanced in the name of "spiritual warfare," they may be less disconcerting than the more prevalent attitudes in much of Christendom that virtually acts as if powers hostile to our mission do not exist!

The triumph of God. God's defense of a city that embodies the heritage of his people from David's time forward (20:8–9) points to his love and faithfulness toward his own people. The passage also reveals that we may be outnumbered (20:8; cf. 7:4), but in the end God's purposes will triumph, and he will keep the church from being ultimately defeated by the world's evil oppressors. We can stand firm against evil even when the battle appears futile; victory belongs to the Lord! As the entire Bible and our Christian experience reminds us, however, we cannot triumph against this world's odds apart from his help.

The presumption of nations gathered against God is immediately revealed when he destroys them (20:9). Through much of history, God allows the suffering of his people; but this is a sign of his merciful restraint and sovereign purposes, not of his impotence. When he wills, he can slay his enemies in a moment. Thus a third-century rabbi understood God's response to Magog in Ezekiel: "O you evil ones, do you rouse yourselves to war against me?"[72] As Joel 3:9–12 notes, such actions of the end-time Gentile forces against God's people will prove futile. Revelation also teaches what some other Jewish traditions declare: God himself will overthrow Gog and Magog, too powerful for Israel to defeat in its own strength (cf. Ezek. 38:11–12, 14).[73]

Some skeptics have charged Christians with a hope that is merely "pie in the sky," that is, with living for an uncertain hope while neglecting issues of pressing concern in the present life. Biblical hope, however, summons us to lives of holiness in the present (Titus 2:12–13; 1 Peter 1:13–16; 1 John 3:3). The heavenly books in this passage (Rev. 20:12) remind us that the deeds we do in this life really do matter in an ultimate sense.

This passage, like most others in Revelation, provides preachers and teachers an adequate transition for what many nineteenth- and twentieth-century evangelicals have called an "altar call." The knowledge of final judgment calls all to repentance in the present, for someday—when it is no longer possible to ignore God and his perfect way—it will be too late to repent.

72. *Pes. Rab Kah.* 9:11.
73. *Pes. Rab.* 31:9.

Revelation 21:1–22:5

❧

THEN I SAW a new heaven and a new earth, for the first heaven and the first earth had passed away, and there was no longer any sea. ²I saw the Holy City, the new Jerusalem, coming down out of heaven from God, prepared as a bride beautifully dressed for her husband. ³And I heard a loud voice from the throne saying, "Now the dwelling of God is with men, and he will live with them. They will be his people, and God himself will be with them and be their God. ⁴He will wipe every tear from their eyes. There will be no more death or mourning or crying or pain, for the old order of things has passed away."

⁵He who was seated on the throne said, "I am making everything new!" Then he said, "Write this down, for these words are trustworthy and true."

⁶He said to me: "It is done. I am the Alpha and the Omega, the Beginning and the End. To him who is thirsty I will give to drink without cost from the spring of the water of life. ⁷He who overcomes will inherit all this, and I will be his God and he will be my son. ⁸But the cowardly, the unbelieving, the vile, the murderers, the sexually immoral, those who practice magic arts, the idolaters and all liars—their place will be in the fiery lake of burning sulfur. This is the second death."

⁹One of the seven angels who had the seven bowls full of the seven last plagues came and said to me, "Come, I will show you the bride, the wife of the Lamb." ¹⁰And he carried me away in the Spirit to a mountain great and high, and showed me the Holy City, Jerusalem, coming down out of heaven from God. ¹¹It shone with the glory of God, and its brilliance was like that of a very precious jewel, like a jasper, clear as crystal. ¹²It had a great, high wall with twelve gates, and with twelve angels at the gates. On the gates were written the names of the twelve tribes of Israel. ¹³There were three gates on the east, three on the north, three on the south and three on the west. ¹⁴The wall of the city had twelve foundations, and on them were the names of the twelve apostles of the Lamb.

¹⁵The angel who talked with me had a measuring rod of gold to measure the city, its gates and its walls. ¹⁶The city was

laid out like a square, as long as it was wide. He measured the city with the rod and found it to be 12,000 stadia in length, and as wide and high as it is long. [17]He measured its wall and it was 144 cubits thick, by man's measurement, which the angel was using. [18]The wall was made of jasper, and the city of pure gold, as pure as glass. [19]The foundations of the city walls were decorated with every kind of precious stone. The first foundation was jasper, the second sapphire, the third chalcedony, the fourth emerald, [20]the fifth sardonyx, the sixth carnelian, the seventh chrysolite, the eighth beryl, the ninth topaz, the tenth chrysoprase, the eleventh jacinth, and the twelfth amethyst. [21]The twelve gates were twelve pearls, each gate made of a single pearl. The great street of the city was of pure gold, like transparent glass.

[22]I did not see a temple in the city, because the Lord God Almighty and the Lamb are its temple. [23]The city does not need the sun or the moon to shine on it, for the glory of God gives it light, and the Lamb is its lamp. [24]The nations will walk by its light, and the kings of the earth will bring their splendor into it. [25]On no day will its gates ever be shut, for there will be no night there. [26]The glory and honor of the nations will be brought into it. [27]Nothing impure will ever enter it, nor will anyone who does what is shameful or deceitful, but only those whose names are written in the Lamb's book of life.

[22:1]Then the angel showed me the river of the water of life, as clear as crystal, flowing from the throne of God and of the Lamb [2]down the middle of the great street of the city. On each side of the river stood the tree of life, bearing twelve crops of fruit, yielding its fruit every month. And the leaves of the tree are for the healing of the nations. [3]No longer will there be any curse. The throne of God and of the Lamb will be in the city, and his servants will serve him. [4]They will see his face, and his name will be on their foreheads. [5]There will be no more night. They will not need the light of a lamp or the light of the sun, for the Lord God will give them light. And they will reign for ever and ever.

Original
Meaning

JOHN'S VISION OF the future utopia now turns to
Isaiah's promise of the new heavens and earth (Isa.
65:17; 66:22); in Isaiah as in Revelation, the context also speaks of a new Jerusalem (Isa. 65:18).[1]
The previous earth and heaven (NIV: "earth and sky") had fled from God's face
(NIV: "presence"; 20:11), and God now replaces the old creation with a new
one able to endure the revelation of his glory (21:23).

A New Creation (21:1–8)

THE NEW EARTH became a familiar topic of Jewish end-time discussion (1
En. 91:16), normally occurring after the resurrection of the dead (Ps-Philo
3:10).[2] At a minimum, the earth had to be purified (cf. 1 Enoch 10:7). But in
many end-time scenarios, the Day of Judgment would transform the heavens and the earth (1 Enoch 45:4–5). Two models of new creation—renewal
and replacement—existed in early Judaism, but given such factors as the
lack of sea, Revelation seems to use at least the image of the latter.[3]

The lack of sea may have been extrapolated from the fact that Isaiah's
promise mentioned only the new heavens and new earth, not any seas, but
the absence of the sea probably also serves some other purpose. Some associate its absence with the defeat of the sea, connected with the destruction
of evil, in Canaanite mythology and Israelite symbolism.[4] Or the sea may be
the place of the dead (20:13) or the realm of the Antichrist (13:1), though
this view is hard-pressed to explain more positive sea images in the book
(5:13; 15:2).[5] One can connect its absence with the lake of fire in Revelation,
in which believers have no part (cf. 15:2).

Some Jewish traditions implied an end-time destruction of the sea (Sib.
Or. 5.157–59).[6] Within Revelation's own context, the drying of the sea may
signify an end to any further need for mercantile trade (Rev. 18:17); God will
supply all the needs of his people (22:2).[7] In the whole context of Revelation

---

1. Also associated in Jub. 1:29. On ancient utopias, see Aune, *Revelation*, 3:1191–94.
2. See the eschatological new creation in Jub. 1:29; 4:26; 1 Enoch 72:1; 2 Bar. 44:9;
2 Peter 3:13.
3. Even a literal "replacement" need not imply a creation from nothing. Cf. Gale Z.
Heide, "What Is New About the New Heaven and the New Earth? A Theology of Creation
from Revelation 21 and 2 Peter 3," *JETS* 40 (1997): 37–56 (transformation of the present
creation rather than recreation from nothing).
4. E.g., Beasley-Murray, *Revelation*, 307.
5. Rissi, *Future of the World*, 55.
6. Such a destruction need not imply that water ceases (cf. 22:1); whereas the sea is dried
up in Sib. Or. 5.447–48, other places for water are formed in 5.449.
7. Virgil also envisioned an era of prosperity in which ships would no longer trade
because all lands would bear sufficient fruits (*Ecl.* 4.37–39).

the disappearance of the sea may well spell an end to the "many waters" of the followers of the beast (17:1, 15) that arose from the sea (13:1).

The new Jerusalem (21:2; see also 21:9–22:5) had become a familiar Jewish expectation. God prepared this city for his people (4 Ezra 8:52). That this city would descend from heaven (21:2, 10) is not surprising (Gal. 4:26; Heb. 11:16; 12:22).[8] Some texts look for a restored and exalted Jerusalem (Tobit 13:7–16; Ps. Sol. 11:2–6); others speak of a currently hidden city that will then be revealed (4 Ezra 7:26; 2 Bar. 4:2–6).[9] The point of its descent from heaven here is that the city comes from God, not by any human abilities (Rev. 3:12).[10]

Jewish people regularly called Jerusalem by the title "the Holy City," as here (21:2, 10; cf. 11:2; 22:19); God renews a holy city once defiled (11:2).[11] Just as Babylon in Revelation represents the people of Rome and not simply its location, and just as "Jerusalem" in the Old Testament usually included the people and not simply the site, "new Jerusalem" undoubtedly includes the people of God.[12] This city is the "bride" (21:2), just as we know the church is (2 Cor. 11:2; Eph. 5:23).[13] Jerusalem's bridal adornment here is appropriate; other texts describe Jerusalem's beautiful adornment (on the analogy of clothing) in the end time (Isa. 52:1; Ps. Sol. 11:7), including bridal array (Isa. 61:10).[14] Probably both Christ (cf. Jn 14:3) and the church play roles in "preparing" her for her marriage; 19:7 uses the active voice for the bride preparing herself whereas 21:2 uses the passive voice.

---

8. Cf. the "heavenly city" (Sib. Or. 2.40), "heavenly Jerusalem" (4 Ezra 10:25–28), "the city above" (4 Bar. 5:35).

9. For restoration, see also b. Ber. 44a; Pes. Rab. 17:2. For a new or hidden Jerusalem. Roloff, *Revelation*, 235, cites also 4 Ezra 8:52; 10:27, 54; 13:36; one might add b. Hag. 12b; the Qumran New Jerusalem text. On analogous heavenly/earthly parallels in apocalyptic texts, see Ford, *Revelation*, 361. Jewish tradition also knew God "descending" to dwell with his people in the future (Jub. 1:26). Something built by a deity was considered much greater than what was built merely by human hands (Apuleius, *Metam.* 5.1).

10. In some Jewish texts, God himself would rebuild Jerusalem (1 Enoch 90:29; Pes. Rab. 26:7; 28:1; 33:1; probably 4 Ezra 8:52; cf. Ps. 147:2); for a full discussion of restoration eschatology, see E. P. Sanders, *Jesus and Judaism* (Philadelphia: Fortress, 1985), 77–90.

11. Neh. 11:1, 18; Ps. 46:4; Isa. 48:2; 52:1; Dan. 9:16, 24; Zech. 8:3; Sir. 36:13; Tob. 13:9; 2 Macc. 3:1; 11QTemple 47:14–15; Matt. 4:5; 27:53.

12. Most commentators recognize New Jerusalem as a people or at least including the people; e.g., Robert H. Gundry, "The New Jerusalem: People As Place, Not Place for People," *NovT* 29 (3, 1987): 254–64; Bruce, *Message*, 87.

13. The Targum to Ps. 48, of uncertain date, also portrays Jerusalem as a bride (Ford, *Revelation*, 361). For early Christian portrayals, see L. Cerfaux, *The Church in the Theology of St. Paul*, tr. G. Webb and A. Walker (New York: Herder & Herder, 1959), 360.

14. See a more detailed description of the adornment in 21:11–21, below. For details about the adornment, see comment on 19:7. Linen (19:8) and pearls (21:21) represent regular adornment for brides from wealthy homes (Fekkes, *Isaiah*, 249, citing Pliny, *Ep.* 5.16).

The promise that God "will live" (*skenoo*) with his people (21:3) was a frequent Jewish hope that ultimately points back to a promise of God's covenant for Israel (Ex. 25:8; 29:45–46; Lev. 26:12; 1 Kings 6:13; Ezek. 37:27; Zech. 2:10–11), including in the future temple (Ezek. 43:7, 9).[15] This promise is spelled out more clearly when the text reveals that new Jerusalem is a temple city (21:22) and is shaped like the Most Holy Place (21:16). The restoration of the temple was a specific hope for restored Jerusalem (Ezek. 37:26–28; 41–48), but in Revelation this hope is transferred to the entire city.[16] This will be the most explicit "tabernacling" of God with humanity since the Incarnation (see John 1:14, which declares that Jesus, the Word, "made his dwelling" [lit., "tabernacled"] among us, the only New Testament use of *skenoo* outside Revelation), though deceased believers in heaven have already experienced it (Rev. 7:15). This promise was expected for end-time Israel, but here all who "overcome" receive it (21:7).

Emphasizing the presence of representatives from all nations, the Greek may even read, "they will be his peoples" (plural) rather than the singular in the NIV.[17] This may fulfill the promise that many nations will become God's people and he will live among them (Zech. 2:11; cf. Isa. 19:25).

John describes the new creation (21:1) not to satisfy our curiosity about the future, but to comfort us about the eventual change in the nature of this world. The passing of "the old order of things" and the making of all things new (21:4–5) include the end of sorrow (see comment on 7:17) and its causes, especially death—the reality of which believers in the present merely

---

15. For the Jewish expectation, see Jub. 25:21; Life of Adam 29:7; *Sifra Behuq. pq.* 3.263.1.5. On the development of the biblical promise here, see especially Walter C. Kaiser Jr., "The Old Promise and the New Covenant: Jeremiah 31:31–34," 106–20 in *The Bible in Its Literary Milieu*, ed. V. L. Tollers and J. R. Maier (Grand Rapids: Eerdmans, 1979), 114; though Fekkes, *Isaiah* 169, sees esp. Ezek. 37:27. Appropriate to the bridal context (21:2), Fekkes, *Isaiah*, 248, thinks that 21:3 recalls a covenant formula ultimately resembling ancient Near Eastern marriage contracts.

16. For a restored temple, see 1 Enoch 90:28–29; Jub. 1:27–28; Tobit 13:10; 14:5; Sib. Or. 3.657–60, 702, 772–74; 2 Bar. 4:3; 32:4; *tos. R.H.* 2:9; *Shab.* 1:13; the fourteenth benediction of the Amida (Oesterley, *Background,* 65); cf. also surrogate temple features in synagogues (e.g., T. Friedman, "Some Unexplained Features of Ancient Synagogues," *Conservative Judaism* 36 [1983]: 35–42). For eschatological "tabernacles," see T. Abr. 20 A; 2 Enoch 65:10, rec. J; b. B.B. 75a.

17. The matter is uncertain: a few earlier manuscripts have the plural, considered the more difficult hence the more probable reading, but a wider geographical distribution favors the singular. For the pros and cons with slight weight favoring the plural, see Bruce M. Metzger, *A Textual Commentary on the New Testament,* 2d ed. (New York: United Bible Societies, 1975), 763; in favor of the plural, see F. F. Bruce, *The Message of the New Testament* (Grand Rapids: Eerdmans, 1981), 87 n. 8.

experience a foretaste (2 Cor. 5:17).[18] The passing of these "first things" (lit. trans. of Rev. 21:4; see also LXX of Isa. 65:16), including suffering, directly echoes the new creation promise of 65:16–17; the deliverance from both tears and death echoes 25:8. This passing of mourning is in stark contrast to the fate of the wicked (Rev. 18:7–8, 15, 19; cf. Matt. 8:12). John is then again commanded to write (Rev. 21:5; cf. 1:11, 19; 14:13) because these words are true (cf. 19:9).

The announcement "It is done!" (21:6) suggests completion, like an analogous saying of Jesus (using a different word) at the conclusion of his work in John 19:30; God's purposes in history have come to their conclusion (cf. Rev. 10:7; 16:17) by creating a people with whom he will live (cf. Eph. 1:10). By declaring that he is "the Alpha and the Omega" (Rev. 21:6), God reminds us that he is able to accomplish what he promises (see comment on 1:8). By offering water from the spring of life, he recalls 7:17 and contrasts the polluted waters of the present era of judgment (8:10; 14:7; 16:4); this promise anticipates the fuller description offered in 22:1, 17. The thirst referred to here may be less an implicit exhortation (as in John 6:35; 7:37) and more an invitation to the weary who have suffered the traumas of this age (Rev. 7:16). Offering this drink "without cost" (21:6; cf. 22:17) probably echoes Isaiah 55:1, an invitation to Israel in the context of its promised restoration.

By itself suffering does not sufficiently qualify one for the kingdom; rather, one must overcome (21:7). In the context of Revelation, overcoming addresses such varied tests as compromise with the world's values (2:14, 20), dependence on our own strength (3:17), and persecution (2:10); but persecution is the test Revelation particularly emphasizes for the end-time witnesses of Jesus (12:11; 13:7). Jewish texts often speak of inheriting the world to come (21:7), a common figure of speech among early Christians as well (e.g., Matt. 25:34; Rom. 8:17; 1 Cor. 6:9).[19] Here the overcomers inherit "all this," that is, the new and sorrowless world God has prepared for them (Rev. 21:1–6).

The promise that God will be his people's God and they will be his people is the most basic component of the ancient covenant formula (Gen. 17:8; Ex. 6:7; 29:45; Lev. 11:45; 22:33; 25:38; 26:12, 45; Num. 15:41; Deut. 29:13). The prophets rehearse the same covenant formula (Jer. 7:23; 11:4; 24:7;

---

18. Some Jewish writers also spoke of present transformation, as when Wisdom makes "all things new" (Wisd. Sol. 7:27); but the usual complete hope was for the future new creation (see comments on 21:1). Much later rabbis also applied this eschatological image to a present new beginning (*Lev. Rab.* 29:12), consonant with their image that one who converted another "created" him (*Sifre Deut.* 32.2.1; ARN 12A; 26, §54B); God would also "create" a new heart for his people (Jub. 1:20–21).

19. For Jewish sources, see Jub. 32:19; 1 Enoch 5:7; 4 Ezra 6:59; 7:96; 2 Bar. 51:3; *Mek. Beshallah* 7.139–40. See esp. Jer. 3:19; Zech. 8:12.

30:22; 31:33; 32:38; Ezek. 11:20; 14:11; 36:28; 37:23, 27; Zech. 8:8).[20] But Revelation slightly adapts it: He will be the overcomer's God, and the overcomer will be his own child (Rev. 21:7). God had earlier declared Israel his children (Ex. 4:22; Deut. 32:19–20; Hos. 1:10; 11:1), but here in the end time he publicly honors individual believers as his own children (21:7; cf. Matt. 5:9; Rom. 8:19; 1 John 3:2).[21]

All these promises culminate, however, in a warning: Those who fail to overcome, who prove disobedient, will be damned (21:8). Traditional cities kept some groups outside their walls, such as foreigners, traders, and prostitutes, though these groups could work inside the city; outside the new Jerusalem, however, is hell.[22] The NIV's "their place will be" is more literally, "they will have their part [or share] in"; this is the language of inheritance, a deliberate contrast with the inheritance of the overcomers in 21:7. The "fiery lake" is the destination for all who will not inherit the new Jerusalem and the new creation of 21:1–6. "The second death" (21:8) contrasts with the abolition of death in new Jerusalem (21:4).[23] Those who begin as believers must "overcome"; apostates, like those who never professed Christ to begin with, will be lost.

The list of those excluded from the new Jerusalem (21:8) appears in related forms in 21:27; 22:15. Vice lists were a common literary form in ancient texts, but Revelation tailors this list to specific issues confronting its audience.[24]

- The "cowardly" may be those who fear persecution (2:10) more than they revere God (11:18; 14:7; 15:4; 19:5).[25]

---

20. In Jewish tradition, see Jub. 2:19; 12:24; 15:32.

21. For the public vindication of God's servants as his children in the end time, cf. Jub. 1:24–25; Ps. Sol. 17:30; Sib. Or. 3.702–4.

22. On groups excluded from inside the city walls, see Richard L. Rohrbaugh, "The Pre-Industrial City in Luke-Acts: Urban Social Relations," 125–49 in *The Social World of Luke-Acts: Models for Interpretation*, ed. J. H. Neyrey (Peabody, Mass.: Hendrickson, 1991), 145. Cf. exclusion from Eden in Gen. 3:24.

23. The exclusion of the wicked from enjoying the new creation was assumed (1 Enoch 45:5); this also applies to new Jerusalem (b. B.B. 75b, at least attributed to a first-century teacher).

24. For vice lists, see Plato, *Laws* 1.649D; Aristotle, *E.E.* 2.3.4, 1220b–21a; *V.V.* 1249a–51b; Epictetus, *Disc.* 2.8.23; Diogenes, *Ep.* 36 (to Timomachus); Maximus of Tyre, *Disc.* 36.4; 1QS 4.9–11; Wisd. Sol. 14:25–26; Philo, *Sac.* 32; *Post.* 52; Sib. Or. 2.255–82; T. Levi 17:11; Rom. 1:28–32; Did. 5.1–2. For end-time vice lists for the judgment, see 1QS 4.9–11; Sib. Or. 2.255–82 (Christian material); b. Sanh. 103a. For contextualizations of this list similar to our own, see Mounce, *Revelation*, 375; Kraybill, *Imperial Cult and Commerce*, 199.

25. Philosophers also condemned cowardice (e.g., Epictetus, *Disc.* 1.9.33; Aune, *Revelation*, 3:1131, cites texts applying it to moral degradation), but Revelation applies it more contextually. Johannine literature also applies "fear" to uncertainty about the Judgment Day (1 John 4:18) and unbelief to failure to overcome (5:4).

- The "unbelieving" are those who prove faithless, unwilling to maintain their faith in the midst of testing (2:13, 19; 13:10; 14:12).
- The Greek word translated as "vile" (*ebdelygmenos*) is related to words that refer to "abominations" (17:4–5; 21:27), that which is disgusting before God (Deut. 14:3; 17:1; Prov. 15:9, 26). Most often in the LXX this word applies to two sins: sexual immorality (Lev. 18:22–29; Deut. 22:5; 23:18; 24:4; 1 Kings 14:24; Jer. 13:27; Mal. 2:11) and—by far most frequently—idolatry (over forty times).[26] Those who compromise with the cult of the emperor or other forms of paganism and worldliness fall into the "abominable" or "vile" category.
- "Murderers" (cf. 9:21; 22:15) is a broad designation but includes those who kill God's saints (2:13; 6:11; 13:10, 15); this may include those who betrayed Christians to the government (2:9; 3:9), who to save oneself refused to love sufficiently to withhold betraying others (cf. 1 John 3:14–16), or who would not meet a fellow Christian's needs (1 John 3:17). Such murderers will justly suffer the second death (20:14).
- The "sexually immoral" (cf. 9:21) in Revelation often point to spiritual immorality (2:14, 20; 17:1–2, 5, 15–16; 18:3, 9; 19:2), but unless readers have this in mind, they would suppose it most naturally refers to the notorious literal physical immorality of paganism. In either case, the sexual unfaithfulness of the world's citizens contrasts sharply with the sexual purity of the bride, the holy city, and her inhabitants (14:4; 19:7–8; 21:2).
- "Those who practice magic arts" (cf. 22:15) translates a word in Revelation that includes the world's seductive signs (13:13–14) and perhaps even its seductive power (18:23); in the broader sense, it includes any deceptive tools of demons (9:20–21; Gal. 5:20).[27]
- "Idolaters" include all who have succumbed to the demands of the imperial cult or who worshiped the idols of the world system (2:14, 20; cf. 1 John 5:21); they worship the image of the beast (Rev. 13:15).

---

26. For idolatry, most clearly Deut. 7:25–26; 12:31; 13:13–14; 17:3–4; 18:9–12; 20:18; 27:15; 29:17; 32:16; 1 Kings 11:5, 33; 21:26; 2 Kings 16:3; 17:32; 21:2, 11; 23:13; 2 Chron. 15:8; 28:3; 33:2; 34:33; 36:14; Isa. 2:8, 20; 17:8; 44:19; 66:3; Jer. 7:30–31; 16:18; 32:35; 44:17–23; Ezek. 5:11; 6:9; 7:20; 8:10; 20:7–8, 30; Hos. 9:10; Zech. 9:7.

27. Many Jews would have accepted the damnation of sorcerers (Sib. Or. 2.283; cf. 1 Enoch 65:5; Asc. Isa. 2:5). Nevertheless, many Jews in following centuries participated in what we would regard as magical practices (e.g., *CIJ*, 2:62–65, §819; b. Sanh. 65b; Judah Goldin, "The Magic of Magic and Superstition," 115–47 in *Aspects of Religious Propaganda in Judaism and Early Christianity*, ed. E. Schüssler Fiorenza, UNDCSJCA 2 [Notre Dame: Univ. of Notre Dame Press, 1976]).

- "Liars" includes not only false prophets (2:2; cf. 1 John 2:22) like Balaam and Jezebel (Rev. 2:14, 20) but also those who falsely claim to follow the truth (3:9; cf. 1 John 2:4; 4:20), in contrast to the saints (Rev. 14:5).[28]

Materials and Dimensions
of the New Jerusalem (21:9–21)

ROMAN RHETORICIANS OFTEN provided stirring descriptions of cities that utilized their best skills at *encomium*, or praising their subject.[29] They tried to give descriptions so vivid that hearers could virtually "see" what they were describing (Theon, *Progymn.* 7.53–55). The Old Testament contained stirring descriptions of Jerusalem, the city of God (Ps. 48), and the end-time city (Isa. 2:2–3). Ezekiel provided a verbal design for the new Jerusalem and especially the temple mount in Ezekiel 40–48. Subsequent Jewish texts developed this picture further,[30] some identifying the new Jerusalem with paradise (4 Ezra 8:52).

Yet such descriptions are often meant to stir appreciation for God's faithfulness rather than emphasize literal details; thus, for example, one description of end-time Jerusalem (Tobit 13:9–17), including streets paved with precious stones, is part of Tobit's praise to God (13:1–18).[31] Isaiah, who predicted crystal gates and walls of precious stones (Isa. 54:11–12), also speaks of walls of salvation and gates of praise (60:18). By contrast, Zechariah predicts Jerusalem will need no walls because God himself will be a wall of fire around her (Zech. 2:4–5). However else one reads the details of this city, this new Jerusalem "shone with the glory of God" (Rev. 21:11), as the rest of the description illustrates (21:23).

The angel invites John to see the bride, Jerusalem, and carries him away "in the Spirit" (12:9–10, presumably in the visionary state)—just as in 17:1–3, where he was taken to view the prostitute Babylon. Babylon was in the desert; Jerusalem descends from heaven. That John views the descent

---

28. Jewish tradition also expected the damnation of liars (cf., Sir. 20:25; ARN 45, §§125–26B). In Revelation liars are those committed "to that fundamental falsity which is the nature of the dragon and his earthly agents," the world's deception (Caird, *Commentary on Revelation*, 267), which includes idolatry (Isa. 44:20).

29. E.g., Isocrates, *Panathenaicus* and *Panegyricus*. For Israel as a "city," cf. *Pes. Rab Kah.* 24:11. For praising cities as if people, cf. David L. Balch, "Two Apologetic *Encomia*: Dionysius on Rome and Josephus on the Jews," *JSJ* 13 (1982): 102–22.

30. See J. Licht, "An Ideal Town Plan From Qumran—The Description of the New Jerusalem," *IEJ* 29 (1979): 45–59.

31. Some end-time visions are predominantly rural (Joel 3:18; Sib. Or. 3.744–49; cf. Virgil, *Ecl.* passim), but for an urban audience this urban future is more appropriate (cf. Sib. Or. 3.750–51).

of the heavenly Jerusalem from a mountain may recall apocalyptic traditions about visionary mountains (e.g., 1 Enoch 17:2), or it may represent an ideal location for viewing this sight (Ezek. 40:2; cf. Matt. 4:8). But the mountain itself may point to the end-time Mount Zion (Rev. 14:1; cf. Isa. 2:2–3), thus contrasting with the seven mountains on which Babylon sits (Rev. 17:9).[32]

John saw a glorious city in his vision. Some sources expected the end-time Zion to shine with glory (4 Ezra 10:25–27). After its destruction, Josephus (*War* 5.208–10) reminisced about the wealth of the first-century Jerusalem temple, whose gates were adorned with gold and silver. But God had promised earlier exiles the glory of a future temple greater than any they had seen (Hag. 2:9). The older Jewish Christians among John's audience, who remembered the splendor of the temple, would be touched by a description of new Jerusalem's glorious future, just as their Jewish contemporaries commented on its glorious future.[33]

That names were written on the gates and foundation stones (21:12–14) would not have struck ancient hearers as unusual; wealthy supporters who funded city building projects often had their names inscribed on them.[34] Yet the benefactors named on the new Jerusalem were not wealthy supporters, but those whose lives provided foundations for God's people. The presence of both the twelve tribes and the twelve apostles emphasizes the link and continuity between ancient Israel and Christ's church.

Some Jewish traditions spoke of twelve gates of heaven (1 En. 33–36, 72–82); the gates here in Revelation represent the twelve tribes of Israel (cf. Ezek. 48:31–34).[35] John's new Jerusalem resembles some other Jews' vision of the new temple (Qumran's Temple Scroll commemorates the twelve tribes' names on twelve gates of the temple), except that earlier in his book he incorporated all believers in Jesus into the heritage of these tribes (Rev. 7:4–9). Many Roman towns apparently had three gates providing entrance on one side, but new Jerusalem provides such access on all sides, implying that it welcomes people from all directions.[36]

---

32. For the seven visionary mountains of paradise, see 1 En. 18:6–8; 24:1–3; 77:4. Jewish depictions of Jerusalem placed it on a mountain (Ep. Arist. 83–84, 105–6; Jub. 4:26), especially in utopian texts (cf. exaggerations in Ep. Arist. 116); the Old Testament regularly calls Zion God's "holy mountain" (e.g., Ps. 2:6; 3:4; 48:1; Ezek. 20:40; Joel 2:1).

33. See across several centuries e.g., Sir. 36:16; *Pes. Rab Kah.* Sup. 6:2.

34. Kraybill, *Imperial Cult and Commerce*, 212.

35. Judaism traditionally linked all twelves with Israel's tribes, e.g., the twelve months (Jub. 25:16); though some twelves evoked the zodiac (e.g., Josephus, *Ant.* 3.186; *War* 5.217), this, too, could represent Israel (cf. *Pes. Rab Kah.* 16:5; *Ex. Rab.* 15:6; *Pes. Rab.* 4:1; 29/30A:6).

36. Kraybill, *Imperial Cult and Commerce*, 211–12.

In biblical tradition twelve stones pointed to the twelve tribes (Josh. 4:3–9); in the high priest's breastplate in Exodus 28:17–21 they are specifically inscribed with the names of the tribes.[37] Here, however, the foundation stones refer to the twelve apostles of the Lamb, in keeping with the Christian image of the new temple's true foundations (Eph. 2:20; Heb. 11:10; 1 Peter 2:5).[38] Although Jesus is our ultimate foundation (1 Cor. 3:11), early Christian tradition already emphasized that the church was built on the foundation of apostles and prophets who revealed Jesus' message.

The measuring rod (21:15) is an important stage device that allows John to recognize the supernatural enormity of the city (21:16).[39] It recalls the measuring of Jerusalem (Zech. 2:1–2) or the temple (Ezek. 40–41) in the Hebrew Bible and reminds John's oppressed audience that the persecuted remnant whose measuring began in Revelation 11:1–2 is the prototype for the glorious future city. Ezekiel's new Jerusalem was 18,000 cubits all around; John's is nearly two thousand times larger.[40] The symbolic numbers portray this city as the dwelling of God's people: 12,000 (stadia) and 144 (cubits; 21:16–17) both recall the number of God's servants (7:4–8). The use of a square number like 144 may also offer a vivid contrast with the triangular number 666 (13:18), like the foundation of a foursquare city versus that of a pyramid.

The square shape of the city (21:16) fits some ancient building plans.[41] Walls in Syria-Palestine were generally irregular because of "the uneven topography," in contrast to more level land in Egypt and Babylonia;[42] the new Jerusalem differs in this way from the old Jerusalem. Ancient Israelite towns usually grew randomly, but Greek and Roman cities were carefully planned around the central agora with public works around it.[43] Ezekiel also reports

---

37. Also noted in later Jewish tradition, e.g., Ep. Arist. 97; Josephus, *War* 5.234; *Ant.* 3.169; *Ex. Rab.* 38:8–9.

38. See Joseph M. Baumgarten, "The Duodecimal Courts of Qumran, Revelation, and the Sanhedrin," *JBL* 95 (March 1976): 59–78 (p. 77). Note also Qumran's application of foundation walls to its leadership council of twelve in 1QS 8.7–8 (Raymond E. Brown, "The Dead Sea Scrolls and the New Testament," 1–8 in *John and Qumran*, ed. J. H. Charlesworth [London: Geoffrey Chapman, 1972], 7).

39. Qumran depictions of new Jerusalem also include an angel who measures (Vermes cites 5Q 15; cf. 1Q32; 2Q24; 5Q15). For indescribable splendor of heavenly dwellings, see 1 Enoch 14:15.

40. By contrast, Babylon and Alexandria's walls had a circumference of only nine miles, and famed Nineveh was even smaller (Aune, *Revelation*, 3:1160).

41. Traditionally including Babylon and Nineveh. 5Q 15 has an orthogonal design as in some ancient cities (Michael Chyutin, "The New Jerusalem: Ideal City," *Dead Sea Discoveries* 1 [1994]: 71–97). The square also symbolizes perfection in some texts (Talbert, *Apocalypse*, 101, cites Plato, *Protagoras* 344A; Aristotle, *Rhet.* 3.11.2).

42. Aune, *Revelation*, 3:1159–60.

43. Kraybill, *Imperial Cult and Commerce*, 211.

that the new Jerusalem will be laid out as a square, with three gates for three tribes of Israel on each of the four sides of the city (Ezek. 48:16, 31–35).[44]

But while this background plays an important part, the new Jerusalem is not merely square; it is cubic, despite the utter incongruity with all human imagination of a city 1,500 miles high! Thus, most of all the shape recalls the Most Holy Place (1 Kings 6:20); not only will God live with his people in Jerusalem (Rev. 21:3), not only will the entire city be like a temple, but it will be like the Most Holy Place. It is thus not surprising that the city does not need a temple other than the Lord himself (21:22). Believers will experience God's presence in its full intensity, as never before! If the church is a temple already (Eph. 2:18–22), our future experience is like the holiest part of the temple, inviting continual worship and enjoyment of God's presence.

The dimensions of the city are supernatural (21:15–16), contrasting starkly with the pretensions of the doomed "great city," Babylon (18:10, 16, 18–21).[45] Technically, a wall seventy-two yards (sixty-five meters) high or even thick (21:16)[46] would prove utterly inadequate to protect a city 1,500 miles high (21:16), but the purpose of the numbers is not literal so much as to emphasize the city's future glory and to suggest that, when history is complete, God's remnant through the ages will not prove as small as it now appears to persecuted churches of John's generation. The height is the most dramatic feature (perhaps even more for modern readers, who recognize that even at less than six miles above sea level, at the top of Mount Everest, it is already difficult to breathe). What humanity could not accomplish in Babel—a city to the heavens (Gen. 11:4)—God grants as an overwhelming gift.

Why does Jerusalem need a wall in the eternal era of peace? Certainly the purpose is not to keep anyone out, since no one will ever close its gates

---

44. The square shape (one dimension short of a cube) is also significant in new temple and new Jerusalem imagery; see Ezek. 40:47; 45:2; 48:20; for the altar, Ex. 27:1; 30:1–2; 37:25; 38:1; Ezek. 43:16; for the ephod, Ex. 28:16; 39:9. Farrer suggests that if the city were 12,000 stadia along each of the 12 boundary lines of the cube, this would yield 144,000 (Mounce, *Revelation*, 380); but probably only the most geometrically proficient would think to count these edges.

45. Later rabbis also expected Jerusalem and the Holy Land to expand and grow in height to heaven (*Sifre Deut.* 1.11.1; *b. B.B.* 75b; *Pes. Rab Kah.* 20:7; *Deut. Rab.* 4:11; *Song Rab.* 7:5, §3. citing Isa. 54:2). A rhetorician could hyperbolically depict Rome as able to fit all people (Lucan, *C.W.* 1.511–13), but John's apocalyptic images are more dramatic. Some opined that the present world could not simultaneously contain all people who have lived (4 Ezra 5:44), so a city even limited to the righteous remnant must be supernaturally large (cf. the hyperbolic language in Sib. Or. 5.249–52). In some traditions the righteous would live in the heights (2 Bar. 51:10), as would the new Jerusalem (*b. B.B.* 75b).

46. Thickness is more likely in view (Ezek. 41:9, 12; see Aune, *Revelation*, 3:1162), though the matter remains debated.

(21:25). Nor is the description of the walls perfectly literal (see comments on 144 cubits, above [21:18]). But ancient cities of substantial size always had walls, so one is needed in the description of the greatest of cities.[47] Further, if there were no walls, there would be no description of the splendid gates! Gates provided cities in Asia Minor and elsewhere the best opportunities to flaunt "imperial triumphal architecture";[48] without these gates, Revelation would miss an opportunity to reapply biblical symbolism in its specifically Christocentric way.

That angelic measurements are also human (21:17) must mean normal angels, not those of extraordinary size as in 10:2.[49] The human measurement here explicitly recalls Ezek. 40:5, but Bauckham argues that it simultaneously offers a vivid contrast to Revelation 13:18: the number of a human who is a beast versus the measurements of a human that are also angelic (21:17). The beast's kingdom debases humanity to a beastly level, whereas the new Jerusalem raises it to an angelic level.[50]

That the walls are of jasper (21:18; cf. 21:11) means that they reflect God's glory (4:3), perhaps the most important feature of the city (21:19, 23; cf. Zech. 2:5); Isaiah had promised walls of precious stones (Isa. 54:12). This jasper was "clear as crystal" (Rev. 21:11), like the heavenly waters (4:6; 22:1), to allow the glory of God to shine through. That the city is of gold may reflect images from the original paradise (Gen. 2:11–12) but more likely reflects the commonness of what is now regarded as wealth (cf. Rev. 3:18), a stark contrast with the mere gold decorations of "wealthy" Babylon (17:4; 18:12, 16). That the gold is like glass matches no refining known to humanity, and in antiquity even glass was rarely fully "clear"; such clarity suggests again God's glory (4:6; 15:2; cf. Ex. 24:10; Ezek. 1:22).[51]

The "precious stones" of the foundations of the city (21:19–20, developing 21:14) recall God's promise in Isaiah 54:11–12, a promise developed in later

---

47. Cf. Ladd, *The Last Things*, 112–13; Rissi, *Future of the World*, 67.

48. Aune, *Revelation*, 3:1154.

49. Angels repeatedly appear as "people" in 2 Enoch, e.g., 20:1–2. In some later Jewish traditions, Moses in heavenly visions could view angels as people (*Pes. Rab.* 20:4); or angels could assume either angelic or human form (*Gen. Rab.* 50:2). Revelation is ambiguous only occasionally (e.g., Rev. 22:8–9).

50. Bauckham, *Climax of Prophecy*, 397–98; also noting that the Greek term for "beast" in Hebrew letters is 666, whereas "angel" in Hebrew letters is 144 (cf. Gideon Bohak, "Greek-Hebrew Gematrias in 3 Baruch and in Revelation," *JSP* 7 [1990]:119–21).

51. The gold's purity in 21:18, 21, although appropriate to a refined metal, appears also in the Greek of 15:6; 19:8, 14; it may contrast with what the Greek calls the impurity of what relates to Babylon in 16:13; 17:4; 18:2. Gold could be compared with glass, but not on grounds of appearance (ARN, 24A).

Jewish traditions (e.g., Tobit 13:16).[52] Some rabbis predicted precious stones and pearls thirty by thirty cubits for Jerusalem's gates (*b. B.B.* 75a). Closer to Revelation's images, a Qumran commentary on Isaiah 54:11–12 applied its statements about precious stones figuratively to the remnant of Israel and its leaders.[53] That John repeats his mention of adornment in Revelation 21:19 (NIV, "decorated") from 21:2 (NIV, "beautifully dressed," the same Greek word) suggests that this is a description of new Jerusalem's bridal garments, a stark contrast with Babylon's prostitution apparel (17:4).

John then lists the stones—derived from the priest's breastplate (Ex. 28:17–20) and from Tyre's wealthy decorations (Ezek. 28:16), omitting some of each to arrive at twelve but including nine stones that appear in both lists. Not only is this a priestly city (suggested by the allusion to the high priest's breastplate, cf. Rev. 1:6), but the city of economic sufficiency and justice contrasts sharply with Tyre, an economic exploiter that provided the model for Babylon in Revelation 18. Jerusalem's true clothing puts to shame the ostentation of Babylon (17:4).[54]

Isaiah had promised gates of crystal (Isa. 54:12); the gates of pearls here (Rev. 21:21) again contrast sharply with the gaudy but inferior pearl decorations of Babylon (17:4; 18:12, 16). Later Jewish tradition emphasized that angels in the sea bottom were fashioning Isaiah's pearls during the present era (*Pes. Rab Kah.* 18:5; *Pes. Rab.* 32:3/4). An expensive pearl might be worth more than other possessions (Matt. 13:45–46).[55]

---

52. See in some detail *Pes. Rab Kah.* 18:4–6, where such gates of literal pearl and precious stone are being fashioned beneath the sea in the present. See further, with much attention to prerabbinic texts, William W. Reader, "The Twelve Jewels of Revelation 21:19–20: Tradition History and Modern Interpretations," *JBL* 100 (Sept. 1981): 433–57; Fekkes, *Isaiah*, 239. Cf. the "costly stones" (NIV: "quality stone") for the temple foundation in 1 Kings 5:17, though it is difficult for interpreters to read these as gems. In view of the "brilliance" of 21:11, it may be relevant that some traditions so spoke of specially luminous stones (Ps. Philo 26:9–14; *b. Sanh.* 108b; *Gen. Rab.* 31:11; *Pes. Rab.* 32:3/4).

53. See J. A. Draper, "The Twelve Apostles As Foundation Stones of the Heavenly Jerusalem and the Foundation of the Qumran Community," *Neot* 22 (1988): 41–63.

54. Cf. comments in Kraybill, *Imperial Cult and Commerce*, 209; Reader, "Jewels," 456; parallels in Ps-Philo show that the literary contrast is not merely accidental. Some later traditions opined that the city's precious stones would supply everyone's economic needs and hence settle all economic disputes (*Pes. Rab Kah.* 18:6; *Pes. Rab.* 32:3/4). Beale, *Revelation*, 1080–88, provides a useful summary of the various backgrounds. Even on the high priest's breastplate, the precious stones stood for the glory of God's people (Wisd. Sol. 18:24). The sequence in which John lists the stone also appears a deliberate echo of Exodus (for explanation, see Caird, *Commentary on Revelation*, 275–77, although he is probably wrong about the antizodiacal connection; see T. Francis Glasson, "The Order of Jewels in Revelation xxi.19–20: A Theory Eliminated," *JTS* [1975]: 95–100).

55. Fekkes, *Isaiah*, 243, explains how pearls represented a natural interpretation of Isa. 54 (they were the kind of precious stone one could drill through).

Revelation's comment on the "great street" (21:21) is also significant. Those who remembered the first Jerusalem (destroyed probably over two decades earlier) might remember its major north-south and east-west streets (from ten to thirteen meters wide); but the vision of the new Jerusalem is far greater.[56] After describing new Jerusalem's adornment with precious stones, Tobit declares that its streets will be paved with beryl (Tobit 13:16; cf. Rev. 21:20) and will offer praise to God (Tobit 13:17). Although new Jerusalem has twelve gates, hence undoubtedly numerous streets, Revelation speaks of a single "street" (Rev. 21:21). Probably this simply refers to the primary thoroughfare (see 11:8; 22:2; Judg. 19:15–20; Est. 6:9–11). [57]

God's Presence and Glory in the New Paradise (21:22–22:5)

THE LACK OF a temple in the new Jerusalem (21:22) contrasts starkly with traditional Jewish expectations of the end time, in which a new temple was the central feature of the city. A prayer in the regularly recited Eighteen Benedictions looked for a renewal of the temple, as did other Jewish sources.[58] This picture of the new Jerusalem would have appeared striking even to a pagan unfamiliar with Jewish expectations; all normal Greek and Roman cities included temples.[59] But this lack of future temple in John's vision is not really a repudiation of Ezekiel's vision of a future temple in a new Jerusalem (Ezek. 41–48); rather, the new city itself is wholly a temple, the dwelling place of God (21:3, 16, 22). God lives among his people and they live in him, a present reality (John 15:4; cf. Isa. 8:14; Ezek. 11:16), taken to a deeper level in the time to come.

Not only will the city have no temple, but it will require neither sun nor moon (21:23), which have been abolished (8:12; cf. 7:16); not only the city but the entire created order will walk in explicit dependence on God. God

---

56. On Herodian Jerusalem's streets, see Aune, *Revelation*, 2:618; compare Rome's *Sacra Via* (620).

57. Roman cities generally had two major streets around which other streets were organized: The *cardo* ran north and south and near the center of the city intersected the *decumanus*, which ran east and west (J. Julius Scott, *Customs and Controversies* [Grand Rapids: Baker, 1995], 240). Beasley-Murray, *Revelation*, 326, suggests the street recalls the heavenly thoroughfare ancients found in the Milky Way.

58. See Jub. 1:27–29; 1 Enoch 90:28–29; Sib. Or. 3.702–6; m. Ab. 5:20; Taan. 4:8; fully Talbert, *Apocalypse*, 102. E. P. Sanders, *Jesus and Judaism* (Philadelphia: Fortress, 1985), 86, suggests a polemic here against traditional Jewish expectations. Some later strands of expectation did dismiss sacrifices (*Pes. Rab Kah.* 9:12).

59. Arrian, *Indica* 7.2; Kraybill, *Imperial Cult and Commerce*, 213. A few people opposed temples (Sib. Or. 4.27–28), but they were a minority.

had promised his people that in the time of their restoration, the time of new Jerusalem, they would need neither sun nor moon; God himself would be their glory and, better than sun and moon, would never set or wane (Isa. 60:19–20; cf. 13:10; 24:23). Even an angel could illumine the earth (Rev. 18:1); how much more God and the Lamb (21:23; 22:5; note that what Isaiah says of God Revelation applies here to the Lamb).[60] Although one might see a torchlit city at night against a darkened horizon, most ancient cities were poorly lit at night. The new Jerusalem, by contrast, is full of continual light.

Whereas some texts warn that God will destroy the nations (at least their armies; Isa. 17:13–14; Jer. 25:31–32; 30:11; Joel 3:2, 10–19; Mic. 4:1–4, 11–13; Zeph. 3:8; Hag. 2:22; Zech. 12:9), other texts indicate the nations will remain in the end time (Isa. 2:4) and will serve Israel (Isa. 45:14; 49:23; Dan. 7:14). Whereas some texts exclude Gentiles from the future Jerusalem (Isa. 52:1; Joel 3:17; cf. Zech. 14:21), in others they will bring their wealth into Jerusalem (Ps. 72:9–11, 16; Isa. 45:14; 60:5–16; 61:6).[61] This is the most positive vision of the future possible: Whereas Gentiles once trampled the temple city (Rev. 11:2), now they honor it, coming to worship God (15:4; cf. Ps. 102:15; Zech. 14:16–19). The nations walk in the light of Jerusalem (Rev. 21:24; cf. Isa. 2:3–5; 60:2–3).

In Revelation the gifts that the nations bring are not simply wealth but "glory" (21:24 [NIV, "splendor"], 26); they offer their glory to God in light of God's greater glory (21:23), forsaking idolatry. The nations once brought their wealth into Babylon (18:12–16); now they bring it to the true city of God. They can enter the city, however, only because their names are in "the Lamb's book of life" (21:27). The nations are finally converted to God's ways (Isa. 19:19–25; Jer. 3:17; Zech. 2:11; 8:22–23)![62]

That the gates of the new Jerusalem are never closed (21:25) suggests unlimited access (borrowing the exaltation image of Gentiles continually bringing tribute, Isa. 60:11). To control access, Roman cities usually pro-

---

60. Other early Jewish writers recognized that God would shine on his people (1 Enoch 1:8; 50:1; 58:2–6; 96:3; 1QH 18.28–29; 4 Ezra 7:39–44; cf. 1QM 1.8; 2 Enoch 65:10; Sib. Or. 2.329; 4.190–92; Pes. Rab Kah. 21:5); see further comment on 22:5.

61. Sanders, *Jesus and Judaism*, 214, cites also Mic. 4:13; Zeph. 2:9. See also Tobit 13:11; 1QM 12.14; Sib. Or. 3.772–74. Like the Bible, Jewish traditions were diverse: The nations would not profit from Israel (*Sifre Deut.* 315.1.1), and only the invited could go to Jerusalem (*b. B.B.* 75b), or God would even trick the nations into coming to Jerusalem, whence he would banish them to Gehenna (*Pes. Rab Kah.* 2:2).

62. Cf. perhaps Ezek. 39:21; T. Jud. 25:5; Sib. Or. 3.716–19. Some traditions allowed the continuance of the nations without their conversion (Mic. 4:5), or that only some will be converted (Zech. 14:16–19).

vided entrance on only one side of the city. For safety reasons, city gates were usually shut at night. But new Jerusalem welcomes all (22:17) and has no enemies to fear. Further, this city never experiences night, for the light of God's glory is unfailing (21:25). The righteous may enter by the gates (3:7; 22:14), and there is no other way to enter (cf. John 10:1). In Jewish tradition, Jerusalem and its temple constituted the center, or navel, of the earth.[63]

But like the earlier promise of 21:1–8, the promised joy of the new Jerusalem serves as a warning as well as a comfort, for not all will inhabit it (21:27). Ancient sanctuaries often served as a refuge for criminals, but the Bible permitted this only in the case of inadvertent sins (Ex. 21:14; Num. 35:22–25). This holy city will not harbor any who practice evil.[64] As in Revelation 21:8, the wicked will be banished (cf. Zech. 5:3–4).[65]

"Then the angel showed me" (22:1) could indicate a subsequent vision to what John is shown in 21:10 (cf. 21:27 with 21:8 and perhaps 22:15), but because this statement lacks other transitional features it probably continues the vision of the new Jerusalem. It may be from a different perspective, but this paragraph continues elements of the previous description (e.g., the street, 22:2). In any case, 22:1–5 climaxes John's vision of a new creation.

That a "river" flows from God's throne may reflect biblical images of water flowing from the future Zion (Ezek. 47:1–12; Joel 3:18; Zech. 14:8). This crystal river directly from God's throne replaces the earlier crystal sea (Rev. 4:6; 15:2; 21:1). Even present Jerusalem had a water supply that some poetically described as a river (Ps. 46:4; 4 Ezra 5:25).[66] All strong cities must have their own water supply (see comment on 3:15–16: Laodicean Christians may have taken special note), and new Jerusalem has an eternal supply.

The river "of the water of life" (22:1) probably evokes the rivers of the first paradise (Gen. 2:10), especially given the conjunction of this image with the tree of life. This is not surprising, because Jewish texts often portrayed

---

63. See Jub. 8:12, 19; Sib. Or. 5:249–50; tos. Kip. 2:14; b. Yoma 54b; cf. Ezek. 5:5; 38:12. This responded to the Greek and Roman claim that Delphi was the center (e.g., Euripides, *Medea* 667–68; *Orestes* 591; Varro, 7.2.17; Livy, 38.48.2; Ovid, *Metam.* 10.168; 15.630–31; Lucan, *C.W.* 5.71).

64. Hemer, *Letters to the Seven Churches*, 48–51; for this function of sanctuaries, see Hesiod, *Works and Days* 327; Euripides, *Madness of Heracles* 48; Diodorus Siculus, 11.89.6–8; Livy, 35.51.1–2; Appian, *R.H.* 12.1.7.

65. A *pomerium*, i.e., a boundary excluding activities illegal within a city, extended for a mile from every side of Roman towns and cities (Kraybill, *Imperial Cult and Commerce*, 212); but 21:17 speaks of the wall itself.

66. Diaspora Jews sometimes exaggerated the temple water system (Ep. Arist. 88–91). "Crystal" in the LXX can relate to ice (Job 6:16; 38:29; cf. Ps. 147:17; 148:8), but the source here is Isa. 54:12; Ezek. 1:22.

the end time in terms of the beginning time.[67] Some writers associated Eden with new Jerusalem (T. Dan 5:12) or viewed it as equivalent to the Most Holy Place (Jub. 8:19; cf. Rev. 21:16). Many expected an end-time paradise.[68]

Visions of the future often included descriptions of supernatural agricultural plenty and diminished or abolished labor (Joel 3:18; Amos 9:13).[69] Some portraits of prosperity alluded to the primeval garden.[70] "Paradise" literally meant a "garden," and paradise-like images regularly included rivers and fruitful trees.[71] This could include the tree of life mentioned in the original paradise (1 Enoch 24:4–25:7; 4 Ezra 8:52; 2 Enoch 8:3; T. Levi 18:11). Revelation's tree comes from the various fruit trees for healing on either side of the temple river in Ezekiel 47:12; unlike trees whose fruits were seasonal (e.g., Mark 11:13), these trees bear fruit every month.[72]

Some Jewish writings developed this image into twelve trees, probably based on the twelve months they will bear fruit (Jub. 21:12; T. Levi 9:12). Revelation, however, prefers to present these as one tree (such as Eden's original tree of life) with twelve fruits—presumably to emphasize that believers have one source of eternal life, namely, Jesus.[73] Whereas shops often lined

---

67. See 4 Ezra 8:52–54; 9:5–6; Ep. Barn. 6:13; perhaps Acts 3:21. See further D. S. Russell, *The Method and Message of Jewish Apocalyptic* (Philadelphia: Westminster, 1964), 280ff.; French L. Arrington, *Paul's Aeon Theology in 1 Corinthians* (Washington, D.C.: Univ. Press of America, 1978), 77–81. Ancients would have understood the image of one river for the world: Greeks thought the river Oceanus surrounded the world, and some thought that the Nile coalesced with Oceanus (Diodorus Siculus, 1.12.6) or the Euphrates (Pausanias, 2.5.3) as the same river. Some Jews thus held the four rivers of Gen. 2 to the Ganges, Euphrates, Tigris, and Nile as four parts of Oceanus (Josephus, *Ant.* 1.38–39).

68. See 4 Ezra 7:123–24; 8:52; 2 Bar. 51:11; T. Levi 18:10; *Sifra Behuq. pq.* 3.263.1.5; on paradise after death see 1 Enoch 60:8; 61:12; T. Abr. 20 A; 10 B. This was often compared with (Isa. 51:3; Ezek. 36:33–35) or called (*m. Ab.* 5:20; 1QH 6.16–17) Eden. Later rabbis regularly contrasted the eschatological Eden with Gehenna (ARN, 25A; b. Ber. 28b; Erub. 19a; Yoma 87a; Ex. Rab. 7:4; Lev. Rab. 32:1; Koh. Rab. 7:14, §3) and spoke of it as the destination of the righteous (b. Temurah 16a; Num. Rab. 13:2).

69. See further 2 Bar. 29:5–7; Sib. Or. 3.744–49; b. Ket. 112b; cf. 1 Enoch 10:18–19; among Romans, Virgil, *Ecl.* 4.18–25, 37–40.

70. E.g., *Sifra Behuq. pq.* 1.261.1.6.

71. 1 Enoch 31:1–3; 32:3–6; 3 Enoch 42:2; Lev. Rab. 22:10. Cf. also the trees of judgment in 1 Enoch 29:2. In Greek *paradeisos* ("paradise," borrowed from Persian) usually signified a garden or park (e.g., Dio Chrysostom, *79th Disc.* 6; Longus, 4.1–2; Philostratus, *V.A.* 1.37; Philo, *Creation* 153).

72. Pagans also recognized as ideal a place where trees bore fruit all year round (Homer, *Od.* 7.114–19). They envisioned a primeval golden era in which Earth provided fruits without human labor (Ovid, *Metam.* 1.101–6; Babrius prologue 12) every month of the year (Ovid, *Metam.* 1.106). Early Judaism assigned each month to an angel (1 Enoch 82:11–20).

73. John's reapplication of Ezekiel's image may presuppose a collective use of "tree" for "trees," as does occur in Greek and Hebrew (Aune, *Revelation*, 3:1177, cites various texts,

the main streets of ancient cities, Revelation presents a different kind of provision. To Ezekiel's "healing" Revelation adds, "of the nations," emphasizing again that God's end-time community includes peoples from all nations grafted into his city (Rev. 7:9).[74]

The specific language of abolishing the curse (22:3) refers to Zechariah 14:11; God's people will become a blessing instead of a curse (Zech. 8:13). But in this context about paradise, abolishing the curse also evokes a reversal of the Fall (Gen. 3:14, 17). Jewish tradition commented on an end-time cursing of the wicked, but blessing for Israel (1 En. 5:5–6; 97:10; Tob. 13:12). The "throne" in the midst of the new Jerusalem might remind ancient hearers of the forum and theater at the center of typical Roman towns.[75]

That his servants will "serve" him (22:3) may imply worship; this is a common Christian meaning of *latreuo*, the Greek word for "serve" used here; the other use of this word in Revelation also locates this worship in the heavenly temple (7:15).

The righteous "will see [God's] face" (22:4)—a statement that takes them beyond the vision granted to Moses, God's servant (Ex. 33:20; cf. John 1:18; 1 John 4:12).[76] Traditional Jewish expectation included seeing God's face in the end time or in heaven after death (4 Ezra 7:98).[77] Whereas seeing God's face banished the old earth and heavens (Rev. 20:11), requiring a new creation (21:1), God's children will live with him (21:3) and see his face and its glory (22:4–5). Such light obliterates the night (21:25; 22:5). The shining of God's face on people, used metaphorically, referred to his favor (Num. 6:25; Ps. 31:16; 67:1; 80:1, 3, 7, 19; 119:135),[78] but when used as an end-time image connotes far more experientially than in the present world. The image of new Jerusalem's future glory is probably related to seeing God's face. When Moses saw God's glory, he reflected it (Ex. 34:30). In a later midrash the righteous will shine like the sun because God's glory will shine on them (*Lev.*

---

including Gen. 1:11–12; 3:8), but it allows him to point to the "tree of life" tradition, which is singular.

74. Other visions of the future era included health (e.g., Isa. 65:20; Jub. 23:29–30; 1QS 4.6; 2 Bar. 29:7; *Gen. Rab.* 20:5; *Pes. Rab.* 29/30B:3).

75. Kraybill, *Imperial Cult and Commerce*, 212.

76. See also Wesley, *Commentary on the Bible*, 612.

77. *CIJ* 1:452, §634; 1:509, §696; 1 En. 90:35; ARN, 1 A; *Sifra Behuq. pq.* 3.263.1.5; *Sifra VDDen. pq.* 2.2.3.2; *Sifre Deut.* 310.6.1; 357.19.1. Cf. further A. Marmorstein, *The Old Rabbinic Doctrine of God: Essays in Anthropomorphism* (New York: KTAV, 1937), 95–99; Kenneth E. Kirk, *The Vision of God: The Christian Doctrine of the Summum Bonum* (New York: Longmans, Green & Co., 1934), 14–15. Jewish people also spoke of a primeval light (2 Enoch 24:4; 3 Enoch 5:3; b. Hag. 12a), which might be restored in the end time.

78. Cf. Aune, *Revelation*, 3:1181, who regards the Old Testament usage as a solar metaphor.

Rab. 30:2). Jewish tradition portrayed the righteous as shining with glory in the future era (Dan. 12:3; Wisd. 3:7–8; 1 En. 39:7; 108:11–15).[79]

Bridging Contexts

TO OVERCOME. The summons to overcome (21:7) remains relevant regardless of how close or distant our trials seem analogous to those of John's first audience. Even those with the most comfortable situations eventually face sickness, death, or bereavement. Each of the seven churches in Revelation had different trials, yet each was called to overcome (2:7, 11, 17, 26; 3:5, 12, 21); each of us today has different trials, but all are called to overcome (21:7).

The new earth and paradise. We return to our primary example of poor interpretive methodology in Revelation: A careful reading of this book reveals that Jehovah's Witnesses are wrong about Jesus' deity, wrong about the identity of the 144,000, and wrong about a number of other matters. But we should grant that they are right in one sense when they speak of life on the new earth. By contrast, many modern Christians have bought into a view of the future that the Bible normally restricts to the deceased in the present: *heavenly* bliss. Yet much of the biblical perspective for the future is earthly and physical, though also of the Spirit (1 Cor. 15:44) and portrayed in symbolic language. Western Christendom has inherited an allegorical view of heaven from the Platonism of some of its early interpreters, but the New Testament emphasizes resurrection for bodily existence, ultimately on the new earth.[80]

The graphic images of future paradise (and exclusion from paradise) would have moved John's original audience, and we may retell images in such a manner as to move our own culturally different audiences. It is said that James McGready, an early leader of camp meetings that profoundly shaped Protestant religion in nineteenth-century North America, "would so describe Heaven, that you would almost see its glories."[81] Such graphic depictions follow John's own method here. But we may struggle to translate Revelation's

---

79. Cf. Qumran's commentary on Isa. 54:11–12; Ps-Philo, 26:13; 4 Ezra 7:97; 2 En. 65:11 A; *Sifre Deut.* 47.2.1–2; *Pes. Rab. Kah.* 27:2; Matt. 13:43.

80. The earth may be purged or recreated, but it remains "the earth, not a transcendent realm beyond it" (Norman Perrin, *The Kingdom of God in the Teaching of Jesus* [Philadelphia: Westminster, 1963], 69). On "spiritual" in 1 Cor. 15, see George Eldon Ladd, *A Theology of the New Testament* (Grand Rapids: Eerdmans, 1974), 370; idem, *The Last Things,* 82–83; Gordon D. Fee, *God's Empowering Presence: The Holy Spirit in the Letters of Paul* (Peabody, Mass.: Hendrickson, 1994), 28–31; idem, *The First Epistle to the Corinthians,* NICNT (Grand Rapids: Eerdmans, 1987), 786.

81. Timothy K. Beougher, "Did You Know?" *Christian History* 45 (1995): 2–3 (p. 2).

images of hope into culturally intelligible images for our time; for many prosperous, nonagricultural Westerners, shopping malls may best epitomize full provision, but that image might evoke instead the consumerism and acquisitiveness more akin to Babylon. We must find other ways to articulate full sufficiency while focusing on the Lamb.

The description of new Jerusalem (21:9–22:5) responds to the deepest longings of the seven churches, especially those most steeped in their biblical heritage. If we were more immersed in the images of the Old Testament prophets, the description would connect more with us; the best way to establish that connection, therefore, is to immerse ourselves in Scripture. On another level, however, the narrative connects with anyone who understands the language; the hope of new Jerusalem includes the fulfillment of all human needs, including hunger, thirst, relationships, and relationship with God. That it is rooted in our biblical heritage in ancient Israel and the apostolic ministry indicates that it was designed specifically for us who embrace that heritage. Those who do not like history may not appreciate this heritage fully, but a taste for biblical history, as for healthy food, can be acquired.

What is more striking than the earthly site of paradise is its urban character. An urban ministries specialist points out that salvation history begins in a garden but ends in a city.[82] This need not be a purely modern reading of the text: Tension between rural and urban communities ran high in the first century, allowing us to suppose that they often may not have appreciated one another positively.[83] This perspective is certainly right in its basic point: God can be at home in the city as well as in the countryside; he is wherever his people are. Although Jesus' following rose mainly from the Galilean countryside and villages, Paul focused his ministry on the cities as cultural centers from which the gospel began to spread (cf. Acts 19:10).

But while this passage reminds us that God can use cities as well as gardens, the differing images of paradise may say more about their different cultural settings than about God's preference for gardens or cities. Whereas most of the earliest period depicted in Genesis was preurban, relevant for the seminomads who transmitted it, Revelation is written to urban churches who used Jewish symbols already circulating in urban contexts.[84] In other words, God inspired

82. Raymond Bakke, *The Urban Christian* (Downers Grove, Ill.: InterVarsity, 1987), 78. For a more recent perspective on biblical groundwork for urban ministry, see idem, *A Theology As Big as the City* (Downers Grove, Ill.: InterVarsity, 1997). Both works are very insightful.

83. See Longus, 2.22; M. I. Finley, *The Ancient Economy*, Sather Classical Lectures 43 (Berkeley: Univ. of California Press, 1973), 123–49; Ramsay MacMullen, *Roman Social Relations: 50 B.C. to A.D. 284* (New Haven, Conn.: Yale Univ. Press, 1974), 15, 30, 32.

84. The conjunction of paradise and tree of life imagery with a city, both in Rev. 21:9–22:5 and in 4 Ezra 8:52 (though distinct in Jub. 4:26), shows that these hopes had become conflated by this period.

biblical writers and provided visions that contextualized their message in images that their audiences could relate to. Perhaps we should do the same, though the power of the original images should be translated, not abandoned.

The relation between the Testaments. These passages in Revelation raise the question of the relation between the Old and New Testaments. How do we explain new Jerusalem's lack of temple in light of Ezekiel's detailed plan for an end-time temple? Some interpreters take both literally by placing Ezekiel's temple in the Millennium of chapter 20, though it is not mentioned there. Others find in Ezekiel's temple a symbolic portrayal of restoration in the second temple, fulfilled in Jesus; the New Testament applies the image to Jesus at least on a symbolic level (John 7:37–39). Some such reapplication of Old Testament imagery seems necessary; clearly the promise of eternal Davidic rule for Christians means not David himself but his line established forever in Jesus (Jer. 30:9; Ezek. 34:23–24; 37:24–25; cf. Hos. 3:5).[85] But given God's consistency in dealing with his people through history, an application in the short run does not necessarily exhaust the sense of the prophecy for the future.

It is, however, also possible that Ezekiel and Revelation both portray the same future in different symbolic ways. The central point of both images is glorious restoration, but Revelation's image of no temple is more glorious than Ezekiel's temple in that it presupposes the entire city (and God's people) as a temple (Rev. 21:3, 16, 22). In the expansive tendency of ancient Jewish and Christian end-time expectation, a greater fulfillment was never an abrogation of less exalted hopes. Rather, it was a yet better way to envision that which was beyond mere words and images to describe. As Paul reminds us, "No eye has seen, no ear has heard" (1 Cor. 2:9; cf. Isa. 64:4), though the Spirit has given us a foretaste of our experience with God (1 Cor. 2:10).

Literal or symbolic? Are the precious stones of the new Jerusalem (21:18–21) literal or symbolic, as likely in the prophetic poetry from which the image is taken (Isa. 54:11–12)? God can, of course, create such precious stones literally; but even if he did so, it would probably be to make the same point as the symbolic interpretation prefers: What is rare and precious now will be abundant then. God's people will experience no lack, and the future glory of the city for which we endure now is greater than the greatest splendor of the world's greatest institutions, including Rome (ch. 17), modern technology, or anything else that entrances our imagination.

In the same way, should we take the numbers 12,000 and 144 (21:16–17) literally? The use of symbols in apocalyptic literature and especially the con-

---

85. The biblical prophets themselves recognized that they meant David's house when they spoke of David's eschatological rule (Ps. 89:3–4; 132:10–11, 17; Isa. 16:5; 55:3; Jer. 33:17, 21–26; Amos 9:11; Zech. 12:7–12; 13:1), a special end-time ruler (Isa. 9:6–7; Jer. 23:5; 33:15).

sistent numerical patterns in Revelation (see 7:4–8) invite us to take these numbers symbolically. Here the numbers are symbolic for God's people, reminding us who will live there (7:4–8).

To what extent is the divinely bestowed light of the end-time Jerusalem (21:23–24; 22:5) intended to be taken literally? Isaiah's declarations of end-time light must be read alongside his statement that celestial lights will increase (Isa. 30:26; cf. also 1 En. 91:16). Some texts also speak of Zion's "light" figuratively (2 Bar. 10:12). In any case, it is a portrait of a future without the sort of hardships imposed by darkness (cf. John 9:4; 11:10).

We should refuse to read any of the images in isolation from the others in the same context. Thus, for example, one can interpret the lack of night (21:25) as a lack of rest for the weary or (for those reading this text during a summer heat wave) the danger of sunburn from intense exposure.[86] But the conjunction of positive images invites us to understand each one positively, as pieces of an entire portrait of a future paradise. Sunburn will be impossible, for there will be no sun (21:23) or heat (7:16), again reading the absence only of what these stood for negatively. According to today's laws of physics, of course, life without the sun is impossible. A literal lack of heat reduces the temperature to absolute zero; but the point again is not a pedantic literalism, but the paradise painted by accumulated positive images.

The nations. The image of the conversion of the nations (21:24) is a problematic one if pressed on a literal level against other images in Revelation.[87] One possibility is that God creates new peoples for his saints to rule, but because this is not stated, commentators have rarely proposed it. The narrative as it stands leaves a major gap. The unconverted appear to be destroyed in 19:15, 18, 21, and their survivors appear to be deceived and destroyed in 20:8–9. But here their survivors are converted, yet appear distinct from God's people who live in the new Jerusalem (also distinct from the wicked in 21:27). The "kings of the whole world" served the powers of the Antichrist (16:14; cf. 17:2, 18; 18:3, 9; 19:19), so some argue that after they die (19:19–21; 20:15), they are raised and reconciled, implying that everyone will ultimately be saved.[88]

---

86. Some later Jewish traditions restrict the rest of the wise in the world to come because they would study continually (*b. Ber.* 64a), but this does not fit the context in Revelation (cf. Eccl. 12:12 for a different view).

87. Jewish end-time literature lacked clear consensus among its end-time images concerning Gentiles; see Terence L. Donaldson, "Proselytes or 'Righteous Gentiles'? The Status of Gentiles in Eschatological Pilgrimage Patterns of Thought," *Journal for the Study of the Pseudepigrapha* 7 (1990): 3–27.

88. Rissi, *Future of the World*, 77–78. One could find this potential in Revelation, yet regard its realization as uncertain (cf. Walter E. Pilgrim, "Universalism in the Apocalypse," *Word & World* 9 [Summer 1989]: 235–43).

But this view "reads far too much theology into incidental references which are more easily explained in another way."[89] The narrative of Revelation simply does not allow these same kings to be reconciled when they are raised; they are instead banished to the second death (20:14–15), to suffer forever (14:11; 19:3). This rules out universalism, but leaves a continuing problem: Where in the text do we find the survivors of the final war? We probably should seek the solution on the level of interpretive principles. As we have pointed out, even Isaiah presents competing images of the end time too complex to be resolved simply by attributing some to the Millennium and others to the eternal future (the nations destroyed, converted, and subjugated). This is problematic to us, however, because most of us remain unfamiliar with the nature of prophetic and apocalyptic images, which can make a graphic point without being pressed literally in ways that contradict other images in the same book. God's future glory resolves his purposes for all peoples without actually implying that every person will be converted.

Do these competing visions suggest divergent potentials for the future, that the nations may be either converted or destroyed, depending on the faithfulness of Christ's church? More likely, they serve the same function as the two forms of the innumerable multitude, some worshiping Christ and some worshiping the beast. Although the peoples of the world join the world system in crushing God's people, many representatives from these peoples will instead join God's people. Note that even in this vision, no one enters the city without being in the Lamb's book of life; the vision does not embrace universalism (21:27). The image of the nations bringing glory into Jerusalem also emphasizes the glory of new Jerusalem: if you persevere, you will be vindicated (e.g., Isa. 61:9; 62:2; Mal. 3:12). In the end, even those who slandered you will bow before you and acknowledge that you were right (Rev. 3:9).

Eden. Jewish teachers circulated various legends about Eden, most of which took it literally. Some traditions, for example, mentioned many trees in Eden, all of which were holy (Jub. 3:12). Many believed that the garden still existed somewhere.[90] Some Jewish visionaries even claimed to have seen the water of life (1 Enoch 17:4) in mythic regions near the river of fire (1 Enoch 17:5, modeled after a Greek mythical river of fire), or the garden of Eden itself (Apoc. Abr. 21:6). Meanwhile, some Diaspora Jews allego-

---

89. Mounce, *Revelation*, 384–85, who follows Beckwith and Glasson in the view that Revelation takes over images from the prophets, but that its significance is different from the concrete images in the prophets.

90. E.g., b. *Tamid* 32b; *Gen. Rab.* 33:6; *Song Rab.* 1:15, §4; 4:1, §2. Among traditions about Eden, it was created before the rest of the world (b. *Ned.* 39b, bar.; *Pes.* 54a, bar.) or on the third day of creation (*Gen. Rab.* 15:3).

rized Eden, for example claiming that it was a garden of heavenly virtues.[91] Even Palestinian Jews occasionally adapted such language figuratively (1 Enoch 39:5); some spoke of rivers of joy and love flowing from God's throne (2 Enoch 22B:7; for figurative uses of tree of life imagery see comment on 2:7). But even when Eden is employed figuratively, it is often by Jewish writers who accepted a literal Eden as well.

Yet if we press literally the image of the tree-bordered river down the middle of the street (22:2), we may envision today a divided highway with a straight river and vegetation down the middle. But most likely this vision should not be pressed literally: Is one tree literally on both sides of the river, extending the entire length of the thoroughfare?[92] God could certainly create a tree whose roots beneath and beside the river network what appears to be fruitful vegetation along the length of the river. But to demand that he do so misses the point of the imagery.

Rivers flowing from the throne probably reflect the same image implied in John 7:37–39, where the water is the Holy Spirit.[93] Jerusalem had no literal river through it (cf. Isa. 7:3); Old Testament passages that speak of such a river (Ps. 46:4; cf. Ezek. 47) may therefore be using the river as "a symbol of God's presence."[94] John reapplies the familiar images of paradise to promise us the fulfillment of our greatest longing, for God's own presence. If we press diverse biblical images of the future paradise too literally, they will end up contradicting one another![95]

Hopes of paradise are shared among various cultures. Many traditional African religions, for example, envision as the happy life God's presence among the people, providing all their earthly needs, though they do not often speak of a future restoration of the primeval paradise.[96] But all cultures' hopes for paradise are not the same, in contrast to one Star Trek film that naively depicted an illusory Eden that was also the yearning of Vulcans and all other civilizations. Even if we dismiss the polygamous fantasies of Mormons and

---

91. Philo, *Creation* 153–54; *Conf.* 60–61. For Philo the river represented the divine Word (*Som.* 2.242–43) or flowed as virtue from Eden, which represented the Word (*L.A.* 1.65).

92. The tree may represent Ezekiel's "trees," but as suggested above, John probably deliberately employs the singular to make a point. Ancients could claim that the tree of life was a five-hundred-years' journey in size (*Gen. Rab.* 15:6), or could envision one "river" watering many fruit trees (Jos. & Asen. 2:11–12/19–20).

93. Cf. John A. T. Robinson, *Twelve New Testament Studies*, SBT 34 (London: SCM, 1962), 174.

94. Cf. "River," 729–31 in *Dictionary of Biblical Imagery*, ed. Leland Ryken et al. (Downers Grove, Ill.: InterVarsity, 1998), 730.

95. Naturally writers, whether urban or rural, emphasized the images dearest to their hopes. Thus some later rabbis portrayed paradise as a wonderful place to study the Bible (e.g., *b. Ber.* 18b; 64a; *Song Rab.* 6:2, §6)!

96. John S. Mbiti, *African Religions and Philosophies* (Garden City, N.Y.: Doubleday, 1970), 127.

Muslims, the annihilation of self in a Buddhist nirvana, or the deification of New Age aspirations, and focus instead on the closest parallels for the Christian vision in Jewish apocalyptic, the Christian paradise exhibits a distinctively Christian angle. Believers will worship God and the Lamb forever; paradise is not paradise without our Redeemer, the Lamb of God (22:3–4).

Our dependence on Christ appears even in the final era, when he remains not only our King but God's Lamb, our Intercessor, the Source with the Father of our living water.[97] Nor was one dose enough; a tree for healing suggests that God's people will continue to depend on Christ through all eternity. The picture of the end is not meant to be comprehensive, but to comprise an invitation: Let the one who wills come and taste God's wondrous paradise, of which this book has afforded a powerful visual sample (22:17). Anyone who chooses to miss out on this promise does so at his or her own loss (22:14–15).

PRINCIPLES FOR TODAY. This passage provides many principles relevant for our lives today. (1) New Jerusalem is God's creation (21:2: "from God"); all we can do is prepare our adornment with righteous acts (19:8; 21:2). Often even our Christian subculture invites competition with other Christians, denominations, ministers, and so forth. I find myself tempted at times to blend into some particular denomination's or movement's values to have a spiritual home; but God demands faithfulness above all, and those of us who achieve the most status in our Christian subcultures may actually have the least in the world to come (Mark 9:37; Luke 9:48). We may adorn ourselves for the new Jerusalem, but it is ours only by the grace of our heavenly Father's love for us.

(2) The time for adorning ourselves with "righteous acts" (19:8) is now. Even though Revelation emphasizes the new Jerusalem as a future city, it is being built in the present. If the character of Babylon is evident in the world around us, the glory of God's presence among us should be revealed at least in the way we live. In John's theology, God's glory is revealed in us through how we treat one another (John 13:34–35; 17:22–23; 1 John 4:12). In New Testament theology, though hope directs our attention toward the future, it also has implications for how we live in the present (Rom. 12:12; Col. 1:4–5; Titus 2:12–13; 1 John 3:3). The most faithful of John's audience (esp. in Smyrna and Philadelphia) would have seen themselves as a persecuted minority; but Revelation also summons them to see themselves as heirs of the

---

97. See the comments of Strong, *Systematic Theology*, 776.

future. If we see ourselves according to the destiny to which God has called us, we will act accordingly.

(3) The promise that sorrows and troubles will pass is helpful in grief counseling, at funerals, but also in facing the obstacles of life; each reader and expositor probably can think of numerous specific applications for his or her own situations.

(4) God's perfect dwelling will be with us; we will enjoy the intimacy of the Most Holy Place with him forever. If that is truly the future we yearn for, then we should enjoy the intimacy now available with him in prayer.[98] That the new Jerusalem itself is a temple city promises us a continual experience of worship; as its citizens, we should begin to enjoy that worship now. Scripture indicates that we are already God's temple and dwelling place (1 Cor. 3:16–17; 2 Cor. 6:16; Eph. 2:21–22); his presence is what sustains us in the face of our trials (Jer. 1:8; Acts 18:10; Heb. 13:5–6). In the future we will continue to be his dwelling for worship, except without the current distractions.

(5) The passage is full of contrasts between Babylon and the new Jerusalem. When I preach from here, I focus on how much greater is God's city than what this world offers, to remind us to live for God's promises and not for present satisfaction.

God's incredible love. John borrows the image of the new Jerusalem as Christ's bride from earlier sources (ultimately Israel as God's bride in the Hebrew Bible). But he probably intends to convey the same image of God's intimacy and love for his people implied in those earlier sources. One time in my life when I felt deeply in love, the force of this passage struck me: No matter how much I might love, my love was only a shadow of Christ's love for us. Perhaps any symbol communicates only imperfectly the depth of Jesus' love for us, but our best approximations of unselfish love, such as a strong marriage, can provide us some beginning sense of it. The ultimate portrait of God's love for us is Jesus' dying for us on the cross while we were yet his enemies (Rom. 5:6–10). Paul tells us that the Spirit comes into our hearts, pointing to that cross, and declaring, "See, I love you! I love you! I love you!" (cf. Rom. 5:5).

To the overworked pastor who feels unappreciated, to the wounded wife abandoned by her husband, to the shy child teased by peers for her weight or his pimples, to any of us in our brokenness, the greatest comfort is God's love. We can afford to be vulnerable with him concerning our pain, because

---

98. On this intimacy with God, from various perspectives, see J. I. Packer, *Knowing God* (Downers Grove, Ill.: InterVarsity, 1973); Craig S. Keener, *3 Crucial Questions About the Holy Spirit* (Grand Rapids: Baker, 1996), 131–80; Jack Deere, *Surprised by the Voice of God* (Grand Rapids: Zondervan, 1996).

we know he shares our pain with us. When the hardships seem too great to bear—as they must have seemed to many of the first Christians who heard Revelation read to them—we must remember that his love gives us a promise of fulfillment ahead. And if the hardships tempt us to doubt his present love and our future hope, we only need look back to the cross, where God in the flesh shared our pain with us and in our stead.

True wealth. We also recognize that the standard of wealth for which people strive in this world will be a common substance by the standards of the coming world (21:18, 21). The truest wealth is the glory of the Lamb (21:11, 23–26; 22:5). For which world's wealth will we devote our own labors (3:17–18)?[99] We need no worldly wealth, no physical temple, not even created lights like sun or moon (21:22–26); God is the direct source of all. Even water flows from his throne (22:1), nourishing also the tree whose fruit brings life (22:2). To practice for the future, we should learn to depend on him now.

Following Christ or the world's values. The vice list (21:8, 27) warns that we cannot truly follow Christ, yet deny him in how we live; fear and unbelief dare not dissuade us from martyrdom, so we need to strengthen Christian faith now before the test comes. We dare not compromise with the world's values or betray or slander fellow Christians before the world or indulge false prophets of compromise in the church.

The lists of sins provide the severest possible warnings against such offenses (21:8, 27). This includes sexual immorality and magic arts. I came home and wept when I first encountered ministers who believed that sexual immorality was irresistible or feared to preach against it lest they offend their congregations. Given the warning here, one wonders how a shepherd can be faithful to the call and not address such matters of spiritual life and death to whatever extent necessary.[100] Many cultures distinguish between "black magic" and "white magic," but Revelation offers no such distinction because all magical activity is rooted in the demonic (9:20–21; 21:8; 22:15). Today this (and related biblical prohibitions of divination) include such sources as the "psychic hotlines"; in at least some church circles where I have ministered, more professing Christians were involved in such practices than one would have guessed.

Communicating eternal judgment and eternal bliss. America's culture of tolerance has made talk of eternal judgment unfashionable, but we must find

---

99. For comments on materialism, see esp. Contemporary Significance on 18:11–19.

100. On abstinence, see Michele Ingrassia, "Virgin Cool," *NW* (Oct. 17, 1994), 58–69; Robert C. Noble, "'There Is No Safe Sex,'" *NW* (Apr. 1, 1991), 8; Katherine Bond, "Abstinence Education: How Parents Are Making It Happen," *Focus on the Family* (Sept. 1998), 12–13; see other sources in Contemporary Significance of 2:14.

relevant ways to communicate that image at the appropriate time.[101] "Four sections in the latter part of John's prophecy end on the same note of stern warning (20:15; 21:8, 27; 22:15)."[102] The only alternative to damnation in this passage is "overcoming" (21:7–8); chapters 2–3 reveal that each church faces different tests, but all are called to overcome.

The use of numbers 12,000 and 144 (21:16–17) emphasize, as we have noted, that the new Jerusalem is a city prepared for God's servants (7:4–8). The magnificent dimensions also emphasize that God's tiny remnant in this age (cf. 7:4; 11:1–2) have a glorious future, higher than the tower of Babel could have been and more splendid than Babylon in this age.

That the tree is for "the healing of the nations" (22:2) does not indicate that all people who have ever lived with be saved, a proposal that blatantly contradicts the theology of Revelation.[103] Rather, it reminds us that representatives of all peoples will follow the Lamb in this age and constitute the nations in their ideal character in the world to come (21:24), bringing the gifts of all cultures to worship Jesus (see comment on 7:9). Indeed, the single tree of life in 22:2 (in contrast to Ezekiel's trees) and single street in 21:21 and 22:2 may point to the fact that God has provided only one source of life and one "way" into the new Jerusalem (cf. John 14:6). To be sure, that street's singleness refers to the main street and is a figure of speech (11:8), as may be the tree; but taken together with Revelation's other Christocentric images, they emphasize the necessity of being in the Lamb's book of life, of being the Lamb's followers (14:4; 21:27).

---

101. I attempted to communicate this in a culturally relevant way in the illustration in Craig Keener and Glenn Usry, *Defending Black Faith* (Downers Grove, Ill.: InterVarsity, 1997), 129–31.

102. Michaels, *Revelation*, 254.

103. Pace Rissi, *Future of the World*, 80.

Revelation 22:6–21

💧

THE ANGEL SAID to me, "These words are trustworthy and true. The Lord, the God of the spirits of the prophets, sent his angel to show his servants the things that must soon take place."

⁷"Behold, I am coming soon! Blessed is he who keeps the words of the prophecy in this book."

⁸I, John, am the one who heard and saw these things. And when I had heard and seen them, I fell down to worship at the feet of the angel who had been showing them to me. ⁹But he said to me, "Do not do it! I am a fellow servant with you and with your brothers the prophets and of all who keep the words of this book. Worship God!"

¹⁰Then he told me, "Do not seal up the words of the prophecy of this book, because the time is near. ¹¹Let him who does wrong continue to do wrong; let him who is vile continue to be vile; let him who does right continue to do right; and let him who is holy continue to be holy."

¹²"Behold, I am coming soon! My reward is with me, and I will give to everyone according to what he has done. ¹³I am the Alpha and the Omega, the First and the Last, the Beginning and the End.

¹⁴"Blessed are those who wash their robes, that they may have the right to the tree of life and may go through the gates into the city. ¹⁵Outside are the dogs, those who practice magic arts, the sexually immoral, the murderers, the idolaters and everyone who loves and practices falsehood.

¹⁶"I, Jesus, have sent my angel to give you this testimony for the churches. I am the Root and the Offspring of David, and the bright Morning Star."

¹⁷The Spirit and the bride say, "Come!" And let him who hears say, "Come!" Whoever is thirsty, let him come; and whoever wishes, let him take the free gift of the water of life.

¹⁸I warn everyone who hears the words of the prophecy of this book: If anyone adds anything to them, God will add to him the plagues described in this book. ¹⁹And if anyone takes words away from this book of prophecy, God will take away

from him his share in the tree of life and in the holy city,
which are described in this book.

²⁰He who testifies to these things says, "Yes, I am coming
soon."

Amen. Come, Lord Jesus.

²¹The grace of the Lord Jesus be with God's people. Amen.

THIS SECTION CONCLUDES the book, offering final
testimonies from God, the Lamb, the Spirit, the
bride, and the prophets who speak to the bride
for the Spirit. It underlines emphatically the message of the rest of God's revelation to John.

"The God of the spirits of the prophets" (22:6) may have been a familiar phrase. The Old Testament calls him the "God of the spirits of all
mankind" (Num. 16:22; 27:16), and early Christians called him the "Father
of our spirits" (Heb. 12:9). This became a familiar description of God in early
Judaism, though not exclusively in prayer.[1] Sometimes "the spirits" refer to
angels assigned to people (1 Enoch 20:3), so some think that it refers here
to spirits associated with prophesying (as some understand 1 Cor. 12:10;
14:32; Rev. 22:9). It can also refer to the Holy Spirit as "the seven spirits"
(cf. Rev. 1:4), who also inspires prophecy (19:10). Most likely, however,
given its usage in the Old Testament, the phrase refers to God as ruler over
human spirits—in this case, specifically those of his prophets (as others
understand 1 Cor. 14:32).

The God of the prophets has spoken once again to "his servants the things
that must soon take place," and "these words are ... true" (22:6).[2] Most of this
verse repeats the announcement in 1:1 that God had sent his message by his
angel, just as the promise of his coming and his blessing on the obedient in
22:7 echo 1:3, and "I, John" in 22:8 echoes the narrative introduction in 1:9.
Because ancient writers often bracketed their writings or portions of their
writings, these echoes are a way of letting the hearers know that the book is
nearly at an end.

Those who heed this true prophecy will be rewarded, for Jesus is "coming soon" (22:7) to reward each according to one's deeds (22:12). The promise

1. E.g., 1QH 10.8; Jub. 10:3; 1 Enoch 37:4; 38:2, 6; 39:2, 8–9, 12; 40:1–2, 4; CIJ, 1:524,
§725; PGM, 62.25–26; 1 Clem. 59.3; b. Ber. 60b; other sources in G. Adolf Deissmann,
Light From the Ancient East (Grand Rapids: Baker, 1978), 424; John Bowman, tr., *Samaritan Documents Relating to Their History, Religion and Life*, POTTS 2 (Pittsburgh: Pickwick, 1977), 328.

2. Beale, *Revelation*, 1124, makes a good argument for an echo here of Dan. 2:45.

of "coming soon" frames 22:7–12 and in a broader way 22:7–20, forming a recurrent theme of the closing section.[3] Jesus' coming recalls 1:7 (see comment there) and the fuller description in 19:11–16; "soon" recalls 1:3; 2:16; 3:11. Now in 22:8, John mentions his own name for the first time since chapter 1 (1:1, 4, 9), and for the same reason: to provide eyewitness testimony, much as the beloved disciple does in the Gospel of John (John 19:35). That the prophetic angel refuses John's worship (Rev. 22:8–9; cf. 19:10) reminds the reader that God and the Lamb alone are worthy of worship. Thus, by way of contrast, John once again underlines the deity of Christ emphasized elsewhere in the book.

God instructed Daniel to seal up his prophecy (Dan. 12:4, 9), because the time of the end was a long time away (8:26; 9:24; 10:14).[4] By contrast, Revelation must remain unsealed (Rev. 22:10), for it addresses events that had already begun in that period (see comment on 12:5–6). The time appears so near that each may as well continue in his or her current behavior (22:11), receiving the reward that is due (22:12). This passage probably also indicates that the end time is at hand, because Daniel had spoken about the wicked continuing in their wickedness (Dan. 12:10); the wicked will fulfill their negative role in God's plan in history.[5]

In practice, however, God is not inviting anyone to continue in rebellion; rather, the language is ironic, serving the rhetorical function of challenging unrepentance, as often in the biblical prophets (Isa. 29:9; Jer. 44:25; Amos 4:4).[6] God invites those who will to hear, and those who choose rebellion to face the consequences of their rebellion (cf. Ezek. 3:27).[7] John would agree with his Jewish contemporaries, however, that once the end comes, the Lord will justly award each person according to what he or she has merited (Rev. 22:12; cf. 20:12).[8]

Where most of John's non-Christian Jewish contemporaries will find his words uncomfortable, however, is his claim that Jesus will be the Judge on the final day (22:12), a role non-Christian Judaism reserved in its most exclu-

---

3. Aune, *The New Testament in Its Literary Environment*, 241, argues that 22:10–21 may function as a closing epistolary postscript, hence summarizing the themes of the book.

4. Pseudo-Enoch claimed his words would be understood only in the end time (1 En. 100:6). Something "sealed" was "shut up," inacessible (Isa. 29:11; *b. Sanh.* 103b).

5. See Beale, *Revelation*, 1131–33.

6. See also Eccl. 11:9; Matt. 23:32; Sib. Or. 3.57–59. The call to repentance is more explicit in Did. 10.6. The term for "filthy" appears in the LXX at Zech. 3:3–4.

7. The punishment for rejecting a good teaching is to remain as one is (Epictetus, *Disc.* 1.12.21–22; *PGM*, 4.749–50).

8. See Ps. 62:12; Prov. 24:12; Jer. 17:10; Sir. 16:12, 14; 4 Ezra 7:35; Matt. 16:27; Rom. 2:6; 2 Cor. 11:15; Rev. 22:12; *Pes. Rab.* 8:2. On rewards, see comment on 11:18.

sive sense for God.[9] Those who catch the allusion to Isaiah will recognize even more plainly that Jesus claims to be divine here, for God promised to come with his reward ("his reward is with him") in Isaiah 40:10; 62:11.[10] Revelation reinforces this implication of Christ's deity in 22:13, where in three different ways the speaker (22:13) is called first and last—hence God (Isa. 41:4; 44:6; 48:12; see comment on 1:8, 17). By emphasizing that he is "the Beginning and the End," Jesus also reminds the recipients of this book that he rules history. Jewish texts about the end-time sometimes reminded readers that as God created the world, it was God who had power to conclude it (4 Ezra 6:6).

The summons to "wash … robes" (22:14) sounds a strong note of warning especially to Sardians, the defilement of whose robes had already been declared to them (3:4).[11] Such robes must be washed in Jesus' blood (7:14) to be ready for his imminent return (16:15), as noted in this context (22:12). Those who are prepared for Jesus' return, dependent on his blood, may partake of "the tree of life" (see comments on 2:7; 22:2) and enter "through the gates into the city" (22:14; see comments on 21:25–26); the allusions back to the gates and the tree suggest that 22:14, along with 22:15 (which alludes to 21:8, 27), summarizes what precedes.

But not everyone will be welcome to enter the city; future paradise for the faithful does not imply universalism. Just as the gates were open only for those in the Lamb's book of life in 21:25–27, so in 22:15 Jesus provides a partial list of those who will be excluded (see comment on 21:8). Those who practice magic arts (9:21; 18:23), the sexually immoral (2:14, 20; 9:21; 14:8), and idolaters (13:14–15) all participate in the system of the beast; those who participate in the killing of Christians count as murderers (2:9–10; 13:15); those who love and live according to "falsehood" presumably include those deceived by the Antichrist's system (3:9; 14:5; cf. John 8:44; 2 Thess. 2:10; 1 John 2:22). "Dogs" may refer to a male homosexual prostitute (Deut. 23:18), developing further the warning against sexual immorality.[12]

---

9. E.g., Sib. Or. 4.183–84; 1 Enoch 9:4; 60:2; 62:2. In more general senses it could apply to Abel (T. Abr. 12–13A; 11B), Enoch (3 Enoch 16:1), or the son of man (1 Enoch 69:27), but Jesus appears in the supreme sense (cf. Matt. 7:23; 25:31–33).

10. Revelation's "what he has done" (22:12) also shares a term with Isa. 40:10; 62:11 LXX, but probably only by way of connecting it with Ps. 62:12, which is what Revelation cites for that line. Jewish interpreters frequently linked texts on the basis of common key words.

11. We regard the summons to wash their robes as the likelier reading, based on more of the textual evidence, but some prefer "those who do his commandments," based on patristic evidence and the rest of Revelation (see Stephen Goranson, "The Text of Revelation 22:14," *NTS* 43 [1997]: 154–57).

12. Dogs were often viewed as sexually immoral (Aelian, *Animals* 7.19); the title became a familiar insult in ancient pagan tradition (Homer, *Il.* 8.527; 9.373; 11.362; 20.449; 22.345;

Not only does John testify (22:8), but so does Jesus, who stands behind this entire revelation (22:16).[13] Jesus is not merely "the Offspring of David," but his "Root" (22:16; cf. 5:5). Whereas the promised Messiah is a branch from David's family line (Isa. 11:1)—and this could be in view here—given the whole context of Revelation's Christology, this passage may present him as much more, as the very root from which David's line grew and on which it ultimately depends.[14] As the "bright Morning Star," Jesus compares his glory with a celestial body often worshiped by John's contemporaries, and also claims to be Messiah (Num. 24:17).[15]

"The Spirit" in 22:17 is probably the Spirit who inspires the prophets to speak (as also in the letters to the seven churches, e.g., 2:7).[16] Perhaps the Spirit speaks through "the bride" here, presenting the bride as a prophetic community; or perhaps the Spirit speaks and is seconded by the bride.[17] It is possible that with the word "Come," the Spirit and the bride are inviting the thirsty to drink, which is later echoed in a cry for Jesus to come (22:20). But though Revelation is not addressed only to first-time readers, it seems noteworthy that one approaching the Spirit's and the bride's invitation will initially do so from the preceding context rather than the line that follows. Thus, it is more likely that in the word "Come," they are crying for Jesus to come, following his promise in 22:7, 12 and anticipating a final prayer of this nature in 22:20. This reality evokes the welcome of the thirsty to come and

---

Od. 17.248; 22.35; cf. Mark 7:27). Marc Philonenko thinks Revelation spiritualizes the sort of ban against dogs in the Jerusalem temple found in 4QMMT ("'Dehors les Chiens' [Apocalypse 22.15 et 4QMMT B 58–62]," *NTS* 43 [1997]: 445–50); but would unclean animals have been allowed in the literal temple in any case?

13. Because "you" (plural; cf. NIV note) here appears to differ from the (seven) churches, Aune thinks it probably applies to the prophets of 22:9 ("The Prophetic Circle of John of Patmos and the Exegesis of Revelation 22.16," *JSNT* 37 [1989]: 103–16; idem, *Revelation*, 3:1225–26).

14. Cf. a similar argument implied by the structure of Matthew's genealogy (Craig S. Keener, *Matthew* [Downers Grove, Ill.: InterVarsity, 1997], 53). For the patriarchs as roots, cf. *Pes. Rab Kah.* 15:5; Rom. 11:16.

15. On the morning star, see comment on 2:28, though many commentators distinguish that star (which need not be Christ himself) from this one. For Balaam's star as messianic, see also 1QM 11.6–7; besides other sources in commentaries, see Richard N. Longenecker, *The Christology of Early Jewish Christianity* (Grand Rapids: Baker, 1981), 112, n. 221.

16. On the Spirit's association with prophecy among John's contemporaries, see Craig S. Keener, *The Spirit in the Gospels and Acts* (Peabody, Mass.: Hendrickson, 1997), 10–12. For the Spirit's responding, see *Sifre Deut.* 355.17.1–6; 356.4.1.

17. See Bruce, "The Spirit in the Apocalypse," 342–43, idem, *Time Is Fulfilled*, 112, and Caird, *Commentary on Revelation*, 287, who favor the bride seconding the Spirit in invoking Jesus' return, the Marana tha prayer; I tentatively favor the Spirit speaking this through the bride.

fits other early Christian teaching on the eagerness of the Spirit and the saints for Jesus' return (Rom. 8:22–23, 26).

This invitation to "the water of life" from God's throne (22:17) probably indicates the present availability of the water as well as an invitation to drink in the future; hence, "let him take the free gift of the water of life." One's "share in the tree of life and in the holy city" (22:19) refers to a future inheritance (21:7), but it is not incompatible with the present foretaste of the kingdom, like the concept of eternal life in John's Gospel (John 3:16).

The final of John's seven letters to the churches indicates that we may dine with Jesus now (3:20) and so receive his spiritual adornment (21:2, 19), wealth (21:18), and healing (22:2) in the present era (3:18). If it is legitimate to read Revelation's description of the new Jerusalem together with John's Gospel, the fruit (22:2) may refer to the life of Jesus in believers (John 15:2), and the water of life flowing from the throne (Rev. 22:1) to the believer's present experience of the Spirit (John 4:14; 7:37–39; the term for "flowing" appears with the Spirit who "goes out" in John 15:26). We are promised future glory, but we can experience a foretaste of that glory in our present relationship with God.

Added to John's testimony in 22:8 and to that of Jesus in 22:16, plus that implied by the confident prayer of the Spirit and the bride (22:17), are a solemn curse against anyone who tries to change the book (22:18–19) and another testimony by the faithful witness Jesus (22:20).[18] This is a standard sort of claim for a book or writing that claims to be inspired; it refers to the individual book of Revelation (though the *principle* applies to the rest of the Bible, too, since its basis is the book's inspiration).

Moses had warned hearers of the law not to add to or subtract from it (Deut. 4:2; 12:32); later Jewish writers claimed that the Septuagint was perfect and not to be revised (Ep. Arist. 310–11); 1 Enoch required careful transmission (1 En. 104:11–13) and threatened with damnation any who altered its prophetic words (108:6).[19] That every curse in the book will be against such a person also fits biblical and Jewish expectations (Deut. 29:19–20, 27).

Revelation closes (immediately before its expected epistolary blessing in 22:21) with what was probably at that time the familiar prayer, "Come, Lord Jesus" (22:20; Did. 10.6). Roughly the same prayer in Aramaic, "*Marana tha*"

---

18. On the curse formula, see Aune, *Prophecy in Early Christianity*, 115–16, 288. That the book is unsealed (albeit figuratively; 22:10) renders it more susceptible to changes.

19. Josephus noted that no one dares add to or change the Scriptures (Josephus, *Apion* 1.42; cf. Prov. 30:6). Later rabbis also agreed that no one could ever alter a single letter of Torah (b. *Sanh.* 107ab; p. *Sanh.* 2:6, §2; *Gen. Rab.* 47:1; cf. Matt. 5:18); the Levites were to ensure this (*Pes. Rab Kah.* Sup. 1:8). Later Gnostics actually freely adapted the New Testament text, the sort of matter Revelation warns against (Beasley-Murray, *Revelation*, 346).

("Come, O Lord"), appears in 1 Corinthians 16:22, which suggests that these words reflect the longing of even the earliest Aramaic-speaking churches, which already recognized Jesus as the coming, divine Lord.[20]

Bridging Contexts

READING PRESUPPOSITIONS INTO a passage. Interpreters too often read their own presuppositions into the biblical text. Cults provide a stark example. Returning to our starkest and least controversial example of poor interpretive method, Jehovah's Witnesses, aware that "the Alpha and the Omega" represents a divine title (1:8), claim that "Jehovah" and not Jesus is speaking in 22:12.[21] Yet this view is astonishing, given Revelation's typical use of language. A Jehovah's Witness who did not know that this violated their teaching admitted to me that 22:12 sounded like Jesus' speaking; after all, elsewhere in the book Jesus is the one who gives to each according to their deeds (2:23), and everywhere else in Revelation the speaker who is "coming soon" is Jesus (2:16; 3:11; 22:20).

Clearly Jesus is speaking in 22:16, as Jehovah's Witnesses must concede.[22] Because speakers do change in this section (22:8–9; cf. Gen. 16:10), it is helpful to remember other compelling details as well.[23] "The First and the Last" (Rev. 22:13) is used everywhere else in Revelation for Jesus (1:17; 2:8), "Beginning" is used once for him (21:6), and "the Alpha and the Omega"— plainly a divine title—is a divine title because it means precisely this (Isa. 44:6; 48:12; see comment on 1:8).

Coming soon. This passage repeatedly emphasizes that Jesus is "coming soon" (22:7, 12, 20). This is a major emphasis in the text, and it has generated many responses (see comment on 1:3). One way to communicate this text today is to reiterate afresh the sense of imminence in the Lord's return. Whatever else the text means, it calls us to be ready for our Lord's coming, watching and looking forward to that day. If the thought of his coming gen-

---

20. For further comments, see Oscar Cullmann, *Early Christian Worship* (Philadelphia: Westminster, 1953), 13–14; idem, *The Christology of the New Testament* (Philadelphia: Westminster, 1959), 210; Otto Betz, *What Do We Know About Jesus?* (Philadelphia: Westminster, 1968), 108; Gordon D. Fee, *The First Epistle to the Corinthians* (Grand Rapids: Eerdmans, 1987), 838–39.

21. *Revelation: Grand Climax,* 316.

22. Ibid., 317–18.

23. The apparent change of speakers may point to an "angel" who prophesies for God, perhaps as in some cases of the Old Testament "angel of the LORD"; on this activity of the Lord's angel, see John H. Walton and Victor H. Matthews, *The IVP Bible Background Commentary: Genesis-Deuteronomy* (Downers Grove, Ill.: InterVarsity, 1997), 43.

erates panic, it is because we have become too attached to this world and what it values. There should be nothing we desire more than to see our Lord at his return.

Warnings. Revelation warns that its fulfillment is so imminent that people may as well continue in their current behavior (22:10–11). Rhetorically, this functions especially as a call to perseverance for the book's primary audience, but it also functions as a warning to shake Sardian and Laodicean Christians from their complacency. Some may complain that the promise that the events were about to take place never materialized, at least not in the sense of Jesus' promised return (22:12). Even Rome's fall tarried several more centuries, although that promise did come to pass. But the rhetorical function of the language is not to give times or seasons (no date is offered), but to summon us to preparedness. The text teaches what many of us mean by imminence: Until he comes, Jesus' return is always potentially near, and we must always remain watchful, for inevitably he will come, catching the morally unprepared.

The warning against adding to this book should not be construed as a cessation of prophecy or other means of God's revealing himself to his people.[24] (1) This is simply the closing of the book of Revelation, and the first audience could not take this verse any other way than not adding to the book of Revelation itself; analogous warnings appear in other texts, as we have noted, and always refer only to the work to which they are attached.

(2) The completed New Testament nowhere leads one to assume that gifts such as prophecy will cease before Christ's return (1 Cor. 13:8–13, especially 13:12); in fact, Revelation expects prophets until the Lord's return (Rev. 11:10; 16:6; 18:20, 24).[25]

(3) We may also distinguish between *revelation* in a more general sense and as canon. The Bible recognizes many legitimate prophets whose prophecies are nowhere recorded (e.g., 1 Kings 18:13; 1 Cor. 14:29–32); God himself spoke many things nowhere recorded in Scripture (implied even in

24. Robert L. Thomas, "The Spiritual Gift of Prophecy in Rev 22:18," *JETS* 32 (June 1989): 201–16, associates (in our view, wrongly) this verse with the cessation of prophecy.

25. On the continuance of gifts, see Gordon D. Fee, *God's Empowering Presence: The Holy Spirit in the Letters of Paul* (Peabody, Mass.: Hendrickson, 1994), 893–94; idem, *Gospel and Spirit: Issues in New Testament Hermeneutics* (Peabody, Mass.: Hendrickson, 1991), 75–77; Jack Deere, *Surprised by the Power of the Spirit* (Grand Rapids: Zondervan, 1993), 99–115, 229–66; Craig Keener, *3 Crucial Questions About the Holy Spirit* (Grand Rapids: Baker, 1996), 79–130. For four views, see Wayne A. Grudem, ed., *Are Miraculous Gifts for Today?* (Grand Rapids: Zondervan, 1996); see also excellent discussion of the gifts by D. A. Carson, *Showing the Spirit* (Grand Rapids: Baker, 1987), and Max Turner, *The Holy Spirit and Spiritual Gifts* (Peabody, Mass.: Hendrickson, 1998).

Revelation; see 10:4). The function of a canon, however, is a measuring stick, a critically agreed minimum of authoritative, accurate revelation by which we can evaluate all other claims to revelation. The Bible itself teaches us that it is not all that God ever spoke, but it remains wholly God's Word and therefore the standard and criterion for measuring other claims.

Although the warning in 22:18–19 does not refer to the cessation of prophecy and hence the close of the Christian canon, there is little dispute among most Christians today that Revelation is the final book in the canon. We do believe, of course, that the canon is now closed (i.e., no more books will ever be added to the Old or New Testament), but a closed canon does not mean that God is no longer able to speak in dramatic ways as he did in Scripture itself and as Scripture itself leads us to expect.[26]

TRUTH AND FULFILLMENT. This passage emphasizes that God's promises are "trustworthy and true" and that he will fulfill them. This principle encourages us concerning the individual promises we feel we are waiting on in our own lives, but the text speaks to something much larger: God's entire purpose in redemptive history. We may not live to see every fulfillment even of what God has called us to do in this life; biblical figures like Jeremiah (Jer. 43:1–7) and Paul (2 Tim. 1:15) did not, but God fulfilled his good words nevertheless (e.g., 2 Chron. 36:21–22; Ezra 1:1; Dan. 9:2).

God summons us to remember the coming era, when all his remaining promises will be fulfilled (Acts 3:21–25; Eph. 3:6; 1 Tim. 4:8; Heb. 6:12). Holding fast such promises empowers us to remain faithful in the present tasks he has given us to accomplish, as we bear in mind their ultimate eternal significance (Eph. 1:17–20; 2 Peter 1:4). The graphic promises of future hope offer a present invitation to taste many of them in advance through the Spirit, who is the foretaste of our future world (1 Cor. 2:9–10; Eph. 1:3, 13–14; cf. Heb. 6:4–5).

Worship. This passage reminds believers that no matter how magnificent any created being's role is, God alone merits our adoration (22:8–9). Even in the church, celebrity cults, anxiety over how others perceive our performance in worship, and other matters can distract us from the purity of our worship before God. Remember that, in the end, God is the One whom

---

26. See esp. the arguments of Deere, *Surprised by the Voice of God*, passim. Scripture does not restrict the word we translate "revelation" (*apocalypsis*) to Scripture (1 Cor. 14:6, 26, 30; Gal. 2:2), so it dishonors and contradicts Scripture to insist that those who claim there is revelation beyond what is in Scripture are "liberal."

we must please above all others (Gal. 1:10; Col. 3:22) and whom we must please in our worship; doing so will help us fix our attention again on him.

Obedience. We also learn that the prophecy is unsealed (22:10), meaning that the message of the entire book should be applicable for God's people throughout this age. Without resolving every detail of prophecy, we can recall all the vital truths this book provides for our obedience and hope. This includes warnings against particular sins (22:15; see comment on 21:8), but especially the sin of identifying with Babylon or the world, which is hostile toward God, and the new Jerusalem to come, which is our true home (3:12; cf. Heb. 11:10, 16; 12:22; 13:14).

We must also keep in mind that we will be judged for our deeds performed in this life (22:12). Too often Christians have used other theologies to justify regularly sinning and then asking forgiveness as if there are no consequences. Revelation reminds us that on some level there are consequences to all the choices we make, that these consequences are just, and that therefore we should bury the excuses. When we sin, we deceive ourselves if we say that we *cannot* stop; we should be honest enough to admit that we do not *choose* to stop. Such honesty is a prerequisite to acknowledging that Christ offers us the grace to live holy if we will appropriate it. The warning to wash our robes (22:14) can apply to church people (3:4). In view of Jesus' coming (22:12), we must "get ready."

The vice list (22:15) reinforces this call to moral preparedness. But despite the strength of this call to holiness for those already in the church, 22:11 does not mean it is too late for those who will repent now to do so (2:5, 16, 21–22; 3:3, 19; 9:20–21; 16:9, 11; see above on the rhetorical force of 22:11). This list of sinful behaviors probably starts with male prostitutes, and many churches today would be nervous embracing someone from such a background. But God desires to reach all people. When a friend from Teen Challenge and I shared Christ with a male prostitute on the streets of Chicago, he quickly opened up and noted how much he wanted out of his current lifestyle.

True, the sinners on the list will be banned from the holy city; but the good news of the gospel is that former prostitutes, liars, idolaters, and others who have now "wash[ed] their robes" (22:14) will be welcome in the city. Revelation warns us about the exclusion perhaps in part to promise that Christians who currently endure the hostility of the world will someday have nice neighbors (22:14), but also to summon those who are living wrongly to be transformed by Christ (cf. 22:17).

Not adding to the book of Revelation (22:18) provides a stern warning. While its focus refers specifically to this book, it illustrates the broader principle that we should never add to God's words (Prov. 30:5–6; perhaps

Gen. 3:3), whether in Revelation or anywhere else. In practice, sometimes our theological extrapolations or the ways we get around the biblical text to make it more convenient can accomplish precisely that! Various Christians may disagree on which particular positions reveal such extrapolations, but we must guard our own hearts to make sure we do our best to hear and obey all of God's Word with integrity.[27]

Come, Lord Jesus. We close with one final observation. Not every Christian today feels comfortable praying, "Come, Lord Jesus" (22:20). Suffering Christians long for Jesus' return, but some people are more comfortable with the world and view the end of the present world order with anxiety (cf. 3:3). Sometimes we love things that are not wrong, but if we yearn for them more than we yearn for Jesus, those priorities are wrong.

Many years ago I was regularly praying anxiously for a marriage partner. But one day I walked into a church and heard my brothers and sisters singing about Jesus' return. It suddenly struck me that I was longing for a wife more than I was longing for Christ's return. I repented and asked the Lord to help me get my heart in order before him. Any other longing we have will be but a shadow of our desire for the greatest and truest love available, the love to which the Lamb's shed blood stands as an eternal testimony.

---

27. See Dietrich Bonhoeffer's challenge to those who try to evade the plain sense of Jesus' teachings on sacrifice (*The Cost of Discipleship*, rev. ed. [New York: Macmillan, 1963], 88–91).

Scripture Index

Scripture Index

Scripture Index

Other Ancient Sources

Note: pseudonymous authors like Ps-Cicero will appear under their alleged author.

Other Ancient Sources

Other Ancient Sources

Subject Index

Subject Index

Subject Index

Author Index

Author Index

Author Index

Author Index

Author Index

Author Index